THE
CONQUEST
OF THE
LAST MAYA
KINGDOM

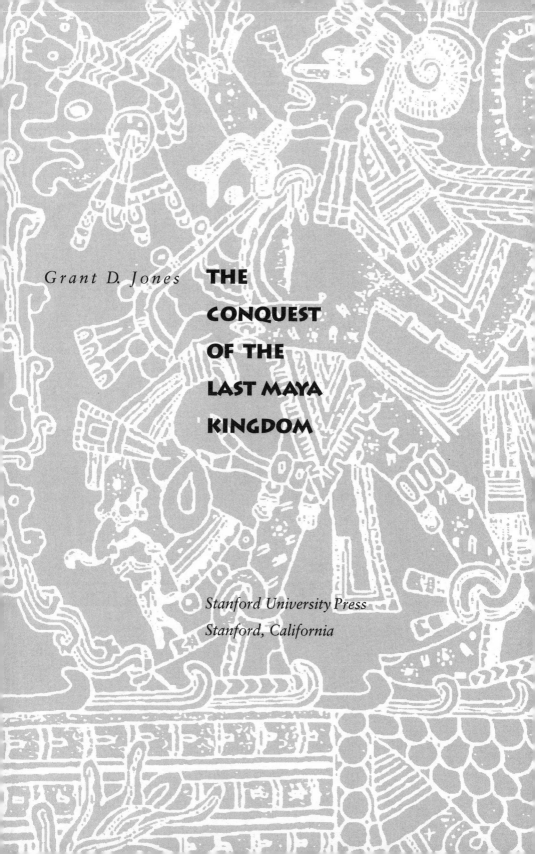

Grant D. Jones

THE CONQUEST OF THE LAST MAYA KINGDOM

Stanford University Press
Stanford, California

Stanford University Press
Stanford, California
© 1998 by the Board of Trustees of the
Leland Stanford Junior University

Printed in the United States of America

CIP data appear at the end of the book

To the memory of the Maya people
whose lives were transformed
or cut short by these events, and
to their living descendants

Acknowledgments

The board of managers and staff of the School of American Research in Santa Fe, New Mexico, provided a stimulating working environment during a fellowship year and two following summers that I spent there writing portions of this book. I wish to thank in particular Douglas W. Schwartz, Cecile Stein, and Jonathan Haas for their efforts in making life at SAR so pleasant and productive.

Charles A. Hofling, the principal authority on the contemporary Itzaj Maya language, spent many hours generously assisting me in questions of orthography and how best to represent and interpret colonial-period Itza place names, personal names, titles, and other terms. My appreciation for his critical acumen and skepticism cannot be overstated, although I recognize that he may well discover that some of my interpretations fall short of his own high standards. I also thank his colleague Fernando Tesucún for assistance in identifying contemporary Itzaj place names.

I thank the administration of Davidson College, especially Vice President for Academic Affairs and Dean of the Faculty Robert C. Williams, for financial assistance and personal support for background research and the actual preparation of this manuscript. Mayanist and Davidson colleague William M. Ringle read major portions of the manuscript of this book and offered valuable criticism. Mary Gilreath, now a Davidson College graduate, as a student research assistant provided extensive and expert assistance in the preparation of the manuscript. Daniel Ruggiero, also now a Davidson College graduate, helped analyze eighteenth-century church records from San Luis, Petén, Guatemala. Charles Houck, a Davidson College graduate and currently a doctoral candidate in anthropology at Tulane University, composed the maps in this book.

The National Endowment for the Humanities provided major support for the research and writing of this book by means of a resident fellowship at the School of American Research, a sabbatical fellowship for college teachers and independent scholars while in residence at Davidson College, and a summer research fellowship for work at the Archivo General de Centro América in Guatemala City. My earlier work at the Archivo General de Indias was supported by a fellowship from the American Council of Learned Societies and assistance from Hamilton College. Without the assistance of the administrations and staff members of these archives, none of this research would have been possible. The National Science Foundation has generously supported the continuing archaeological and ethnohistorical research of Proyecto Maya Colonial.

Numerous other individuals contributed ideas, read portions of the manuscript, and commented on presentations concerning its progress. Although I cannot possibly recognize separately all of these generous persons, none of whom bears any responsibility for what is written here, I wish especially to thank Anthony P. Andrews, Nancy M. Farriss, Lawrence Feldman, Elizabeth Graham, Richard M. Leventhal, Jorge Luján Múñoz, David M. Pendergast, Rómulo Sánchez Polo, Norman Schwartz, George Stuart, and Rosemary Lévy Zumwalt. For his insights in questioning the authenticity of certain manuscripts concerning these events, especially the Canek Manuscript, I recognize the special contribution of Hanns Prem. For the expertise and critical eye that Temis Vayinger-Scheer brought to her reading of the final manuscript, I am most grateful.

In particular I wish to express appreciation for the intense and productive assistance of Don S. Rice and Prudence M. Rice in the interpretation of archaeological and ethnohistorical evidence for the Itzas and their Petén neighbors. To the reviewers of the manuscript, including George Lovell, I owe special thanks for offering helpful suggestions for revision.

I owe a major debt of gratitude to Jane Kepp, whose editorial skills and analytical grasp of such a complex topic improved this book immeasurably. Without her insights and high standards for consistency and clarity this would have been a far less satisfactory work.

My wife, Mary Armistead Jones, has tolerated long periods of concentrated work that have all too frequently interfered with normal life. She has also served as a tireless and critical editor of earlier drafts of the manuscript, and I cannot express the depth of my appreciation for her assistance and affection throughout the years of work that have resulted in this final product.

Contents

Maps and Tables   xi
Spelling and Pronunciation in Mayan Languages   xiii
Introduction   xix

Part One   The Itza World

1   The Itzas and Their Neighbors   3
2   Itza-Spanish Encounters, 1525–1690   29
3   Itza Society and Kingship on the Eve of Conquest   60

Part Two   Road to the Itzas

4   Power Politics   111
5   The Birth of the Camino Real   129
6   Franciscans on the Camino Real   148

Part Three   The Peace Seekers

7   The Itza Emissaries   167
8   Avendaño and Ajaw Kan Ek'   187

Part Four   Prelude to Conquest

9   Itza-Spanish Warfare   223
10   The Costs of the Camino Real   245
11   The Eve of Conquest   265

Part Five   Victims and Survivors of Conquest

12   Occupation and Interrogation   295
13   Prisoners of Conquest   323
14   Reconquest, Epidemic, and Warfare   356

Contents

15 Missions, Rebellion, and Survival   387

Notes   425
Glossary   523
References Cited   527
Index   539

x

Maps and Tables

Maps

1 The Maya lowlands of the sixteenth and seventeenth centuries   xx

2 Lowland Maya language distribution during the sixteenth and seventeenth centuries   4

3 Major Maya political regions in central Petén on the eve of Spanish conquest   6

4 The Itza core region   8

5 The Kowoj region   17

6 The Yalain region   18

7 Street plan of modern Ciudad Flores, Petén   70

8 The route of the camino real   130

9 English translation of sketch map of Lago Petén Itzá and surrounding regions drawn by Fray Andrés de Avendaño y Loyola, 1696   193

10 Early eighteenth-century missions in the vicinity of Lago Petén Itzá   390

Tables

1.1 Distribution of Petén Surnames by Territory and Location   24

3.1 List of Towns Dictated in 1702 by Ajaw Kan Ek' and Others   62

3.2 Itza Men and Women in the Chunuk'um *Matrícula,* Belize River, 1655   76

3.3 Individual Itza Names by Type in the Chunuk'um *Matrícula,* Belize River, 1655   77

3.4 Original and Edited Transcriptions of Avendaño's List of Twenty-two Parcialidades of Nojpeten, 1696   85

3.5 Tentative Breakdown of Titles and Names of Twenty-two Itza Leaders Listed by Avendaño, 1696   86

3.6 Tentative Reconstruction of Equivalent Persons and Positions Among the Highest-Ranking Itza Nobility, 1695–1702, Based on Comparison of Principal Sources   90

3.7 Principal Pairs of Itza Rulers   96

3.8 Proposed Paired Principals of Nojpeten, with Associated Yearbearers, Directions, Quarters, and New Year Days   98

14.1 Comparison of Three Censuses of Guatemalan Settlers Who Went to Petén, Indicating Effects of Epidemic Disease 1699   360

15.1 Numbers of Mission Families at Founding (Late 1702–Early 1703) and of Mission Houses in June 1703   394

15.2 Reconstruction of Mission Population Growth, 1702–3   395

15.3 Population Change in the Mission Settlements, 1703–16   407

15.4 Census of the Maya Population of the Colonial Towns of Petén, 1712   410

15.5 Population of Petén Towns and Cattle Ranches, 1766   416

Spelling and Pronunciation in Mayan Languages

This book uses the orthography for the writing of Mayan languages approved by the Academy of Mayan Languages of Guatemala (AMLG). I decided to employ this orthography in place of the more familiar one developed during the sixteenth century only after consulting extensively with the Mayan linguist Charles A. (Andy) Hofling, whose dictionary of the modern Itzaj language, written with Fernando Tesucún, has recently been published.[1]

A principal advantage of the AMLG orthography is that it has already become a standard in Guatemala for the writing and teaching of Mayan languages. Therefore, both Mayan- and Spanish-speaking readers in that country will find the orthography familiar once this book is available in Spanish translation. The AMLG orthography will probably become the standard in Mexico as well, and it bears close similarities to that employed in the widely consulted Cordemex dictionary of Yucatec Maya.[2] It is also widely used by Mayan epigraphers.

Another advantage of AMLG, in comparison with the colonial orthography, is the greater accuracy with which it reflects the spoken language. This advantage, of course, cannot be fully realized when working with colonial sources in their original orthography. We cannot be certain that seventeenth-century Itzas pronounced all words the same way as their modern Itzaj descendants, whose speech can be recorded in accurate detail. An example is the name of the people who are the subject of this book, which I have written Itza. Hofling writes it Itzaj, whereas in 1697 it may have been Itza'; the final j in the modern language may be borrowed from the Spanish pronunciation of the name. Because Spaniards, however, never recorded glottal stops following vowels and frequently omitted the consonants j and l following vowels, we cannot be certain how the name was pronounced.

For this reason I follow a modified version of AMLG when recording

Consonants in Mayan Languages

	Labial	Dental	Alveolar	Palatal	Velar	Glottal
Stops						
voiceless	p	t			k	'
glottal	p'	t'			k'	
voiced	b'					
Affricates						
voiceless			tz	ch		
glottal			tz'	ch'		
Fricatives						
voiceless			s	x		j
Liquid		1				
Vibrants			r			
Nasals	m	n				
Semivowels	w			y		

colonial-period Maya names, places, and other terms. I omit glottal stops and other consonants that follow vowels unless the consonant is indicated in the original spelling. For similar reasons I do not distinguish long vowels (such as *aa*) from short ones (*a*), nor do I distinguish *ä* from *a* (or *u*, with which it was sometimes confused). In some cases, however, when a colonial-period name has an obvious modern Itzaj counterpart, I indicate this in parentheses using all distinguishing features as written by Hofling.

Those who recorded the Itza language in the seventeenth and early eighteenth centuries were primarily Yucatecan military men and priests. They often made errors as they heard the names of persons and places that were unknown in Yucatán. This led to wide variations in spelling. Deciding how to write such names today has been difficult, and I am indebted to Andy Hofling for his tireless assistance in working them out. Some of these problems have no absolute solution. I have made many decisions myself, and as a nonlinguist I take full responsibility for the errors that remain.

The accompanying tables list the basic phonetic elements of Mayan languages as they are recorded in the AMLG orthography, omitting the sounds *d', f,* and *g* used in Spanish loan words.[3] The only incidence of *g* in the seventeenth-century Itza area was in the toponym Gwakamay, where it was pronounced like *g* in *good* or *gato.*

I have drawn the following pronunciation guide from Hofling and

Vowels in Mayan Languages

	Front	Central	Back
High	i, ii		u, uu
		ä	
Mid	e, ee		o, oo
Low		a, aa	

Tesucún's dictionary, again omitting the Spanish borrowings *d', f, g.* Although the sound *r* occurs infrequently as a native Mayan sound, it is included.

Sounds foreign to many English speakers include the vowel *ä* and the glottalized consonants, indicated by an apostrophe. The vowel *ä* is similar to, but higher than, the schwa in English words, such as the underlined vowels in *the sofa.* The other vowels have values similar to those of Spanish vowels, but vowel length is distinctive. The glottal stop (') is produced by closing and opening the glottis, as in the catch in English *uh-uh.* Other glottalized consonants are produced by closing the glottis and allowing pressure to build before release. In the case of *b',* the air flows inward on release (is imploded). In the cases of the other glottalized consonants (*ch', k', p', t', tz'*) the air flows outward (is ejected).

a   low back vowel, like the English *a* in *father* or Spanish *a* in *gato.*

ä   a mid-high central vowel, somewhat higher than the schwas in *the sofa.*

aa   long low back vowel.

b'   glottalized bilabial stop, like English *b,* but imploded.

ch   palatal affricate, like English *ch* in *church* or Spanish *ch* in *chile.*

ch'   glottalized palatal affricate.

e   mid front vowel, ranges from English *e* in *met* to Spanish *e* in *dedo.*

ee   long mid front vowel.

i   high front vowel, ranges from English *i* as in *pin* to Spanish *i* as in *pino.*

ii   long high front vowel.

j   glottal fricative, like English *h* in *house* or Spanish *g* in *gente.*

k   voiceless velar stop, like English *k* in *keep* or Spanish *c* in *copa.*

k'   glottalized voiceless velar stop.

l   lateral liquid, like English *l* in *look* or Spanish *l* in *libro.*

m   bilabial nasal stop, like English *m* in *many* or Spanish *m* in *mano.*

n   dental nasal stop, like English or Spanish *n* with tip of tongue against upper front teeth.

o   back vowel like English *o* in *bold* or Spanish *o* in *coco*.

oo   long mid back vowel.

p   voiceless bilabial stop, like English *p* in *pen* or Spanish *p* in *poco*.

p'   glottalized voiceless bilabial stop.

r   alveolar vibrant flap, like *tt* in English *kitty* or Spanish *r* in *pero*.

s   alveolar sibilant, like English *s* in *some*, or Spanish *s* in *son*.

t   voiceless dental stop, like English or Spanish *t* with tip of tongue against upper front teeth.

t'   glottalized voiceless dental stop.

tz   voiceless alveolar affricate, like English *ts* in *cats*.

tz'   glottalized voiceless alveolar affricate.

u   high back vowel, like English *oo* in *moon* or Spanish *u* in *nudo*.

uu   long high back vowel.

w   labio-velar glide, like English *w* in *wood* or Spanish *hu* in *huevo*.

x   voiceless palatal fricative, like English *sh* in *shell*, or Spanish *x* in *Uxmal*.

y   palatal glide, like English *y* in *yell*, or Spanish *y* in *yerba*.

'   glottal stop, like the catch in English *uh-uh*.

In this book the colonial orthography is used when a Mayan word appears in a direct quotation from a colonial source. It is also used for most towns with names of Mayan origin in Guatemala that fall outside the Petén region (e.g., Huehuetenango, Comitán). On the other hand, in order to maintain consistency in the writing of Yucatecan Maya (of which Itza is a member), I have converted the names of Maya towns throughout the Yucatán peninsula to AMLG (e.g., Oxkutzcab to Oxk'utzkab'). Because these variations may be confusing, the following may serve as a general equivalency guide to the colonial and AMLG orthographies:

ALMG	Colonial	ALMG	Colonial
ä	a, u	i	i
a	a	ii	i, ii
aa	a, aa	j	j, h
b'	b	k	c
ch	ch	k'	k
ch'	cħ	l	l
e	e	m	m
ee	e, ee	n	n

ALMG	Colonial	ALMG	Colonial
o	o	tz	tz
oo	o, oo	tz'	ɔ, dz
p	p	u	u, v
p'	pp, ꝑ	uu	u, uu
r	r	w	u, v
s	s, ç, z	x	x
t	t	y	y
t'	th, tħ	'	absent

INTRODUCTION

On March 13, 1697, Spanish troops from Yu-
catán attacked and occupied Nojpeten, the small island capital of the
Maya people known as Itzas, the last unconquered native New World
kingdom. The capture of this small island in the tropical forests of northern Guatemala, densely covered with whitewashed temples, royal palaces,
and thatched houses, turned out to be the decisive moment in the final
chapter of Spain's conquest of the Mayas. Climaxing more than two years
of intensive preparations and failed negotiations, the moment only inaug-
urated several more years of struggle between Spaniards and Mayas for
control over the vast tropical forests of what is now the central area of the
Department of Petén, Guatemala (map 1).

The Itzas had dominated much of the lowland tropical forests around
Lago Petén Itzá since at least the mid-fifteenth century, when their ancestors, it was said, migrated there from Chich'en Itza in northern Yucatán.
Their immediate neighbors, known as the Kowojs, were said to have
migrated from Mayapan to Petén at the time of the Spanish conquest of
Yucatán, probably during the 1530s. The remoteness of these groups and
the physical inhospitality of the land had undoubtedly contributed to
Spain's failure to pursue their conquest during the century and a half
following the relatively late final conquest of Yucatán in 1544. No less
significant had been the Spaniards' fear of the Itzas, whose reputation as
fierce warriors who sacrificed their enemies gave pause to military conquerors and missionaries alike.

In this book I examine with a critical eye the events that preceded and
followed the 1697 conquest of the Itza capital of Nojpeten and surrounding regions, focusing on the short time between 1695 and 1704. During
those years the Spanish Basque military man Martín de Ursúa y Arizmendi, commanding an army of Yucatecan soldiers, planned and executed the attack on the Itza capital. Despite protracted resistance from

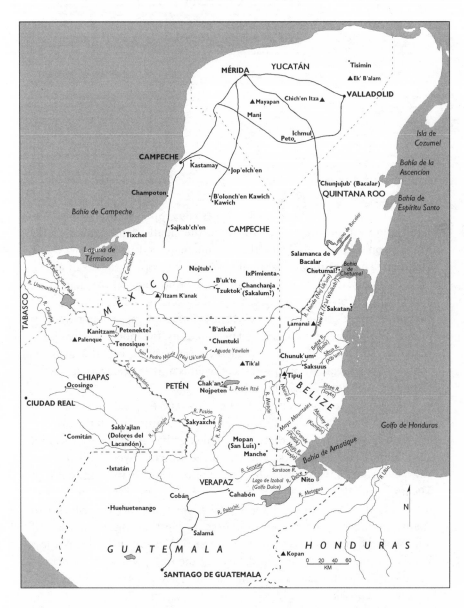

Map 1. The Maya lowlands of the sixteenth and seventeenth centuries.

thousands of native inhabitants, many were eventually forced to move into mission towns. In 1704 these mission inhabitants staged an abortive rebellion that threatened to recapture Nojpeten from its conquerors. Because these events were deeply complex, this account includes details that enable us to grasp some of the layers of political intrigue and action that characterized every aspect of the conquest of the Itzas and its aftermath.

The Spaniards left documentation on the conquest that is staggering in its quantity and challenging to the scholar who tries to make sense of it. My goal in studying this documentation has been to understand these events as a series of unfolding interactions between conquerors and conquered. The major challenge has been to understand the Itzas as independent actors who faced would-be Spanish conquerors with strategies of self-preservation developed over nearly two centuries of European domination of the lands surrounding Itza territory. Far from being naive about Spanish methods of conquest and colonization, the Itzas demonstrated awareness and understanding of their enemy. At the same time they acted in the context of an ancient and highly traditional culture, purposefully retaining political, military, religious, and social institutions that had served them well even before the sixteenth-century conquests that isolated them in a sea of Spanish colonies.

This long familiarity and indirect contact with European colonialism is one of the major features distinguishing the conquest of the Itzas from the sixteenth-century Spanish conquests of the Aztecs, Mayas, Incas, and other complex New World societies. In contrast, the Spaniards had only a feeble understanding of the Itzas and their immediate neighbors in Petén. They held stereotypical images of them as brutal, barbaric, and superstitious people whose conquest was an inevitable and necessary part of the civilizing mission of church and state. These images portrayed Satan at work in the jungles, protecting the last unconquered kingdom of Mayas from the liberation of the gospel and the enlightened administration of the Spanish Crown.

By the late seventeenth century, conquests of this scale were a thing of the past. Unfazed by the anachronism, Ursúa, a descendant of sixteenth-century military conquerors, set about to cast himself in the image of his aristocratic forebears. Despite criticism from his more "modern" enemies in the colonial administration, he designed a program to subjugate the Itza kingdom, first by a brief effort to employ peaceful strategies of diplomacy and then, when these failed, by a costly and ambitious project that resorted to force of arms and violence.

The conquest of the Itzas became Ursúa's obsession, not only because he hoped to enrich himself by collecting tribute from the conquered, a goal he never achieved, but also because he desired fame and promotion within the colonial administrative system. His success and notoriety in Spanish circles earned him titles of nobility and, after the conquest, an appointment as governor of the Philippines. The price paid for his achievements, however, was high, both in monetary terms and in loss of human lives. No viable colony emerged from the conquest, and epidemics soon devastated the native population, leaving little for Spaniards to administer. Ursúa quickly abandoned the project, and Petén was left under the care of military administrators and a handful of missionaries. The conquest of the Itzas was, in retrospect, one of the more poignant tragedies in Latin American history.

This book offers the first detailed account of these events since the publication of Juan de Villagutierre Soto-Mayor's massive *Historia de la conquista de la provincia de el Itza* in 1701.[1] Villagutierre, a lawyer, prolific writer on Spanish-American colonial history, and official *relator* (chronicler) of the Council of the Indies in Madrid, never visited the Americas. Although his book has been widely cited by recent scholars, who have had few other sources to rely on, its contents are often biased and unreliable. Apparently his book was commissioned by the Council of the Indies in order to support Ursúa, whose reputation was under attack by critics who regarded the conquest as a colossal error in judgment, an inhumane application of colonial power, and a waste of scarce colonial funds.

The council made available to Villagutierre all of the documentation it had received on the conquest of the Itzas from Mexico, Yucatán, and Guatemala. He read and utilized this huge quantity of material thoroughly. Because he almost never cited his sources, however, it is impossible to separate his frequent faithful paraphrasing of original letters and other documents from his equally common lengthy personal editorial comments. He often mistranscribed the names of key personages and places, making it difficult for modern readers to make critical connections among people, locations, and events.[2]

As readers of the endnotes and bibliography in this book will discover, numerous other primary and secondary sources provide valuable information on many pieces of the puzzle of this conquest. Until now, however, it has been impossible to connect these pieces satisfactorily, primarily because the massive documentation that Villagutierre consulted had not been intensively restudied from a contemporary perspective. It is this documentation that forms the backbone of this book, although I have tried to consult as many other sources as I could locate.

My research for this book began in earnest in 1982–83 with a search for the extant documentation on the conquest of the Itzas and related events in the Archivo General de Indias in Seville, Spain. Assisted by the results of Nicholas Hellmuth's previous search for such materials,[3] I found virtually all of the documents used by Villagutierre. During the summer of 1988 I found a small number of additional materials in the Archivo General de Centro América in Guatemala City, and during 1988–89 I completed the transcription and computer indexing of microfilmed and photocopied relevant manuscripts. Since then I have identified other sources as well, including sources containing ethnohistorical evidence for Itza social and political organization, which I studied intensively during 1995–96.

I do not pretend to present here a full ethnohistorical reconstruction of the culture and social life of the Itzas and their immediate Petén neighbors. In any case, much of the information we now have about topics such as religion, trade, and material culture must be considered in light of new archaeological studies being carried out in central Petén by Proyecto Maya Colonial, co-directed by Don S. Rice, Prudence M. Rice, Rómulo Sánchez Polo, and myself. Although readers will find much ethnographic detail here, only chapter 3 is devoted entirely to an ethnographic issue — the all-important question of the social and political organization of the Itza kingdom.[4]

Part One of this book provides ethnographic and historical background to the conquest of the Itzas. The first chapter gives an overview of the three principal Yucatec-speaking groups that occupied Petén at the time of the 1697 conquest. Chapter 2 summarizes the history of Spanish contacts with the Itzas and their neighbors, beginning with the journey led by Hernán Cortés across Petén in 1525, during which he met with the dynastic Itza ruler, Ajaw Kan Ek', and traveled south across Itza-controlled territory to the Gulf of Honduras. On that journey Cortés left a lasting symbol of his contact — a horse, which later died and which the Itzas supposedly transformed into an object of veneration.

Chapter 3 describes what can be reconstructed of Itza Maya social and political organization, suggesting that the Itzas possessed a complex lineage system that stressed both maternal and paternal links and the importance of marriage ties between lineages. While patrilineal descent remained the most important organizing principle, a limited form of matrilineal descent may have constituted the critical marker of the nobility's right to rule. The ruling Kan matrilineage controlled, at least symbolically, the governance of the capital and four territorial quarters that were also associated with the four quarters of the capital. Patrilineal affiliation seems to have been called upon primarily to seal alliances between high-ranking noble groups. Intermatrilineage alliance — with the Kans controlling the top levels of governance and other lineages occupying second-level positions — created a system dominated by a single elite group that allowed others to share rule at lower levels.

Chapter 3 also proposes that military chieftains from outlying towns and regions represented their towns on the Itza ruling council. They may have doubled as the principal priests charged with the rituals concerned with calendrical prophecies for twenty-year periods known as *k'atuns*. The incorporation of such nonroyal elites in the organization of the kingdom might be one way the Itzas succeeded in mounting such an effective military resistance to Spanish intrusions on their territorial edges for so many years.

Part Two considers the political, religious, and economic elements involved in decisions to construct a new road — a *camino real* — connecting Guatemala and Yucatán, as well as the road's initial impact on the native populations through whose lands it was routed. Chapter 4 presents the Spanish political background of the 1697 conquest: the elite Basque ancestry of Martín de Ursúa, his political connections to the Royal Council of the Indies in Spain, and his plans, in cooperation with the Guatemalan colonial hierarchy, for constructing the road from Yucatán that would reduce the threat of coastal piracy that had long plagued the coastal trade and mail routes. As interim governor of Yucatán, Ursúa began work on the camino real in 1695. The Council of the Indies specifically ordered that the task not disrupt militarily the lives of natives who might be encountered along its route.

Chapter 5 recounts the failed first attempt by Spanish troops from Yucatán to open the new road, first through the territory of Kejach Mayas (see map 2) whose hostility discouraged them from proceeding further. Meanwhile, Guatemalan troops, coordinating their efforts with those of the Yucatecans, managed to occupy the Chol-speaking "Lacandon" town of Sakb'ajlan in 1695. Subsequent actions by Guatemalans and Yucatecans soon revealed, however, that they both hoped to conquer the Itzas, who lived far from the proposed road. A Guatemalan captain, accompanied by Dominican missionaries, encountered Itzas near Lago Petén Itzá, but he and his officers abandoned any immediate thoughts of attacking Nojpeten when they realized the dangers and the magnitude of the task. With a dramatic race toward the Itzas already under way, the Yucatecans soon rerouted the camino real directly toward Lago Petén Itzá.

Chapter 6 records the effects of Governor Ursúa's decision to send

Franciscan evangelists to accompany the troops and Maya workers from Yucatán as they opened the camino real southward through Kejach Maya territory toward Nojpeten, the Itza capital. These missionaries, excited by prophetic reports that the Itzas were about to submit peacefully, competed among themselves to reach them first. Working with captured Kejach Mayas along the road, they also documented the horrors implemented by Ursúa's military captain, who sent many of his captives to work as laborers in his economic enterprises in Campeche.[5]

In 1695 Spaniards in Yucatán received notice that the Itza ruler, Ajaw Kan Ek', citing Itza prophecies, was willing to consider terms for surrendering his people to Spanish rule and Christian conversion. Reports of Maya prophecies that predicted the coming of a new age in which the Itzas would succumb to Christ and the Spanish king began to circulate in earnest in Spanish circles. They were reinforced by the arrival AjChan, son of the Itza ruler's sister, as his uncle's ambassador in Mérida at the end of the year. These events represented a brief effort by parties on both sides to seek a peaceful solution to the Itza "problem," the subject of Part Three. Chapter 7 details these events and the complex circumstances leading up to the royal nephew's declaration of his uncle's desire to join the Spanish empire and the decision by Ursúa to demand the ruler's immediate surrender on Spanish terms.

While AjChan was committing the Itzas to Spain in Mérida, the Franciscan friar Andrés de Avendaño was traveling to Nojpeten, aware of the Itza ruler's decision to send his nephew as his emissary. Chapter 8 analyzes Avendaño's detailed account of his journey and visit to Nojpeten, his successes in reinforcing the ruler's previous decision to surrender, and his dismay in discovering that most Itzas regarded Ajaw Kan Ek' as a traitor to his own people. Avendaño, a party to this treason, hastily slipped out of Nojpeten with his companions and nearly died trying to find his way back to Spanish-held territory. It soon became clear in both Yucatán and Guatemala that Spanish optimism for the peaceful surrender of the Itzas was premature and misinformed.

The perceived failure of peaceful initiatives led to a series of violent encounters between Itzas and Spaniards. Ursúa became convinced that the only option was military conquest. Part Four records the Spanish transition from a mood of elation at the Itzas' imminent surrender to a fierce determination to meet the enemy in battle. In chapter 9 we learn that following Avendaño's expulsion from Nojpeten, the Itzas attacked, captured, and reportedly murdered Yucatecan and Guatemalan soldiers and missionaries rushing separately to Lago Petén Itzá. Ursúa, infuriated, was now determined to strike a military blow at the Itzas, whom he considered to be renegade subjects of the Spanish empire. Chapter 10 describes the costs of the massive preparations that Ursúa engineered during the second half of 1696 and the first weeks of 1697 — political conflicts, financial debts, and sufferings imposed on the Mayas of Yucatán. His aims, which he pursued against great opposition in Mérida, were not only to complete the camino real to Itza territory but also to move troops and heavy artillery to the lakeshore for a large-scale attack on Nojpeten, the island capital.

Ursúa, surmounting opposition to his project in colonial circles, had achieved nearly all of his goals by the end of February 1697, when he arrived at the western port of Lago Petén Itzá. There he commanded a large number of troops, Maya carriers, and boat builders who completed and launched a sizable oar-driven *galeota* (galliot) for use in the attack on Nojpeten. The twelve days between his arrival and the attack on March 13 are the subject of chapter 11. This was an intense period during which Ursúa received several important Itza visitors, some of whom may have wished to find a way to avoid bloodshed. The failure of Ajaw Kan Ek', who had either lost control over his enemies or was in hiding, to accept Ursúa's invitation to participate in discussions incensed the commander. Ursúa and his officers decided in a vividly recorded meeting that the Itzas would be punished for their failure to live up to the agreement reached with AjChan in Mérida over a year earlier.

Part Five documents the Spanish capture of the Itza capital and explores its tragic consequences. The Spanish occupation of Nojpeten on March 13, detailed in chapter 12, was brief and bloody, causing massive loss of life among the capital's defenders. The attackers raised the Spanish flag over a nearly deserted island and immediately destroyed every "pagan" object they could find. They soon managed to capture and interrogate the ruler and other high-ranking Itzas. Finding themselves isolated, however, on their heavily fortified island presidio, the Spaniards now faced starvation and a sea of enemies. These conditions form the subject of chapter 13, which details the interrogation of the Itza high priest and the execution of the ruler of the Kowojs, the robbing of food from Itza cultivations by Spanish soldiers, the abandonment of many surrounding towns by their inhabitants, and the failure of the first resident missionaries to win converts in the region.

By the end of 1698 the "conquest" appeared to be on the verge of collapse. Morale reached a low ebb among the fifty soldiers stationed at the island presidio, long since abandoned to their own devices by Ursúa. Chapter 14 focuses on a belated and tragic rescue mission, organized in

Guatemala and designed to shore up this dismal situation. Ursúa returned from Campeche to exercise joint command over the new military reinforcements with the aging Guatemalan general Melchor de Mencos y Medrano. From March through May 1699, when the surviving reinforcements abandoned the project, conditions went from bad to worse. The Guatemalans had brought with them a devastating epidemic, probably influenza, that killed many soldiers and a large percentage of the Guatemalan families who had been brought to settle at the presidio. The epidemic also ravaged the native population, already beleaguered by Spanish depredations of their food supplies. When the Guatemalans retreated, they took with them, in shackles, Ajaw Kan Ek', his son, and two of his cousins, one of whom was the high priest. The priest and the other cousin both died on the long journey to Santiago de Guatemala (now Antigua Guatemala). The ruler and his son spent the rest of their lives in the capital under house arrest. With the Itza kingship in a state of collapse, bloody wars broke out among Maya groups, reducing their numbers even further. News of new native rulers living deep in the forest intimated that the conquest was not over yet.

Somehow, despite epidemics, constant food shortages, and threats of native rebellions, the Spanish presidio survived. In the final chapter we see that during 1702 and 1703, secular clergy from Yucatán finally succeeded in establishing several mission towns among the surviving Itzas and Kowojs. In 1704, however, a well-planned rebellion by the mission settlers broke out. The rebels' aims, which they initiated successfully, were to murder the Spanish troops and recapture Nojpeten. The rebellion ultimately failed, and the Spaniards stepped up efforts to concentrate the population in fewer, more compact towns. Despite military forays to capture runaways and unconverted people to place in these towns, smallpox epidemics quickly reduced the native population even further; by the mid-eighteenth century only a small fraction of Petén Mayas had survived. Rivals to the Itza kingship had established refuge followings in isolated areas of the forest. One of these, AjChan, the former ruler's nephew, held out as an independent ruler in southern Belize for some years. Yet he, too, apparently reached the end of his long life in a mission town, symbol of the gradual irrevocability of a conquest by firepower and attrition.

part one **THE ITZA WORLD**

At the time of the 1697 conquest, four Yucatecan Mayan-speaking political and territorial groups occupied what is today the Department of Petén, Guatemala, and portions of adjacent central and southern Belize (map 2). All four groups—the Itzas, Kowojs, Kejaches, and Mopans—spoke dialects of the Yucatecan language family, as did the inhabitants of northern Yucatán. Differences in speech among these four groups appear to have been slight, and Yucatecan speakers from northern Yucatán to southern Petén could be easily understood wherever they traveled.

Given these linguistic continuities, we may infer that some groups of Yucatecan-speaking peoples had deep historical affiliations with southern Petén. Social contact between Yucatán and Petén was likely continuous over many centuries, quite possibly back to the Classic period, with ruling families changing location as a result of political fortunes and warfare. The ruling nobilities of at least two groups, however—the Itzas and the Kowojs—claimed to have been relatively recent arrivals in Petén, having migrated southward from Yucatán during the fifteenth and sixteenth centuries. Little is presently known of the precontact history of the Kejaches. I suspect that the fourth group, the Mopans, represented an older resident population in Petén. Their earlier history, too, is poorly understood.[1]

Besides these groups, during Spanish colonial times Yucatec speakers also occupied towns and villages along the Belize and New Rivers in northern Belize—a native region known as Tz'ul Winikob' ("Foreign People").[2] Other Yucatec speakers occupied the region known as La Pimienta in present-day southern Quintana Roo. Many of these, if not most, had migrated from northern Yucatán following the sixteenth-century conquest, seeking relief from conditions associated with the encomiendas allotted there. Others were probably from the preconquest province of Chetumal in the region of Corozal and Chetumal Bays, which Spaniards

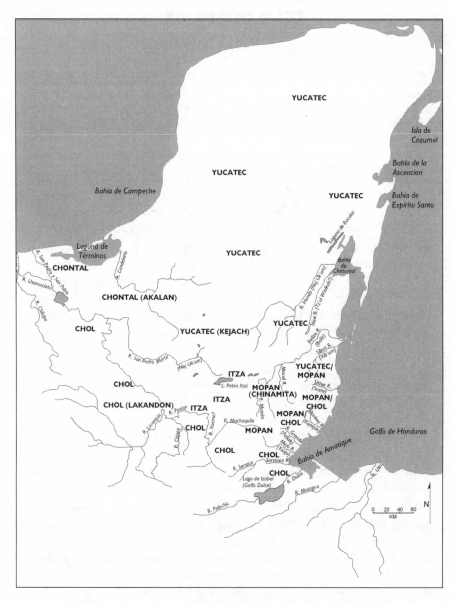

Map 2. Lowland Maya language distribution during the sixteenth and seventeenth centuries.

conquered in 1543 and in which they established the villa of Salamanca de Bacalar (see map 1). The most important colonial-period population center of these people was the town of Tipuj, located on the Macal branch of the Belize River, just east of the present border with Guatemala and almost due east of Lago Petén Itzá. Tipuj, like other Yucatec-speaking Belize towns, became the site of a Spanish mission during the late sixteenth century and paid encomienda tribute to Spaniards living at Bacalar and at Valladolid in Yucatán.

In the late seventeenth century the Itzas were concentrated at the western end of Lago Petén Itzá, with dense populations all the way west to Laguna Sacpuy. The Kowojs occupied primarily the northern shore of the lake and lands to the north and northeast (map 3). The Kejaches lived some distance north of the western end of the lake, occupying lands toward present-day Campeche, Mexico. The Mopans were dispersed over a wide area that included the lands along the present Guatemala-Belize boundary, portions of the Belize River valley in central Belize, and southern Belize. We know from descriptions left by Hernán Cortés and Bernal Díaz del Castillo, who traveled across Petén in 1525, that the Itza heartland was in the same area then as it was in 1697. Over the next 170 years wars among these three groups prompted considerable population movements and political realignments. Had these early explorers been able to see more than a narrow corridor across Petén they would surely have described a distribution of populations and patterns of intergroup relations different from those that existed in 1697.

Along the southern and western frontiers of these groups lived various Maya populations who spoke Cholan languages that were not mutually intelligible with the Yucatecan languages — principally the Manche Chols southeast of the Itzas,[3] the Chols living around Sakb'ajlan to the Itzas' southwest,[4] and the Akalan Chontals to their northwest.[5] The Spaniards had contact with all of these by the end of the sixteenth century, some only fleetingly but others to the extent of forcing them to relocate to other areas under firmer colonial control. Some southern Cholan speakers also spoke Mopan and served as interpreters for Guatemalan Spaniards; native trade between Verapaz and central Petén would have been a major stimulus for such bilingualism.[6] The Chols, however, played only an indirect role in the events that led to the conquest of the Itzas and are considered only in passing in this chapter and elsewhere. 5

The so-called Manche Chols, named for their principal town, Manche, appear more often than the others, because some of them lived nearly adjacent to the southernmost extension of Mopan settlement, which was

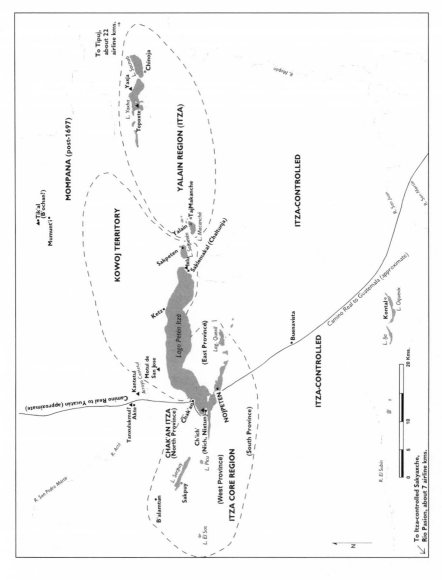

Map 3. Major Maya political regions in central Petén on the eve of Spanish conquest. Hollow dots indicate approximate locations.

at the town of Mopan, later (and still) known as San Luis. Their territory probably originally extended north and northeast from Cahabón in Verapaz, east to the Caribbean Sea, and some distance up the coastal regions of Belize. Dominican missionaries had considerable successes with the dispersed northern Manche Chols in the early seventeenth century. After Itza and Mopan forces attacked the mission settlements in the early 1630s, however, Spanish efforts to work in the region declined until the 1670s, when Dominicans again managed to establish several missions. The Chols soon abandoned these, and despite further Spanish efforts at pacification they rebelled yet again in 1689. Over the next few years the greater part of the Manche Chol population was hunted down and forced to resettle near Rabinal in the Urrán Valley of Guatemala.[7]

The Itzas

The name by which the Itza rulers referred to their territory was Suyuja Peten Itza, possibly meaning "Whirlpool of the Province of the Sacred-Substance Water." A possibly related name, written in Yucatán as "Zuyua," has long been considered by scholars to refer to a mythological origin place of the Mayas associated with the mystical concept of Tollan and claims by Maya ruling elites to their Mexican ancestry.[8] The seventeenth-century Itzas identified their island capital by two names whose meanings are clear: Nojpeten, "Big Island" or "Great Island," and TajItza, "At [the Place of] the Itza."[9] They occupied a central territory stretching over a distance of forty kilometers from Laguneta El Sos on the west to Laguna Quexil on the east, incorporating Laguna Sacpuy and the region northwest of Lago Petén Itza known as Chak'an Itza (map 4). During the late seventeenth century the Itzas also controlled lands east of Lago Petén Itza, the result of wars of territorial expansion carried out earlier in that century (see map 6). I refer to this area as the Yalain region, after the town of Yalain on Laguneta Macanché.

This territory, however, was only the heartland of a people who historically had expanded well beyond these narrow bounds. In 1525, when Cortés traversed their territory, the Itzas had agricultural operations as far south as the Sarstoon River, the present-day boundary between Belize and Guatemala. Even at the end of the seventeenth century Itzas were to be found living as far south as Sayaxché on the Río Pasión and as far east as Laguna Yaxhá.[10] Earlier in that century their eastern sphere of influence

7

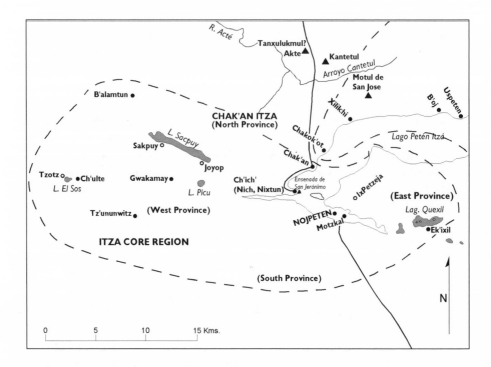

Map 4. The Itza core region. Hollow dots indicate approximate locations.

probably extended into southern Belize even beyond Tipuj. The Itzas were an aggressive, expansionary people, justifiably feared by their neighbors.

ITZA HISTORIES

The Itzas of Petén were the last unconquered representatives of a complex and long-lasting cultural tradition that dominated much of Yucatán from the ninth century A.D. until the sixteenth-century conquest. They survived as an intact society for more than a century and half following the establishment of the Spanish colonial province of Yucatán, owing to circumstances their ancestors could not have been foreseen when they migrated to Petén in the mid-fifteenth century. By seeking refuge in the dense southern forests of Petén from preconquest political disturbances in the north, the southern Itzas unknowingly selected a homeland that would be equally remote from the threat of colonial intervention.

In the native chronicles of Yucatán — texts written in European script in the Maya language during colonial times and known collectively as the

8

Books of Chilam B'alam — the name Itza is applied to the people who founded and ruled Chich'en Itza, which Robert Sharer, echoing others, has called "the dominant political, economic, and religious center of central Yucatan."[11] Many Mayanists, basing their interpretations on a combination of archaeological evidence and readings of these chronicles, have believed that those who founded Chich'en Itza in the ninth century were Maya Chontal-speaking warrior-merchants whose original homeland was in the Gulf coast lowlands of Tabasco. They argue that these Central Mexican–influenced people, whom they label the Putun, engaged in widespread aggressive undertakings beginning in the eighth century that appear to have been intended to control major economic resources and trade routes throughout much of the Maya lowlands. Their expansionary policies may also have been linked to the decline of the great Classic Maya centers of the southern lowlands during the ninth century and to the simultaneous development of a new political order in the northern lowlands, centered at Chich'en Itza.[12]

William Ringle has recently argued that inscriptions at Chich'en Itza indicate that the known elite inhabitants of the city were of local origin and that despite the possibility that Putuns or other Central Mexican–affiliated peoples had been of influence, "these families were able to mediate them and persist in positions of authority until the Spanish conquest."[13] Ringle, Bey, and Peraza have also recently suggested that the Maya chronicles and other ethnohistorical sources exaggerated the power of the Chich'en Itza political system, which they regard less as a militaristic empire than as a "hegemonic tributary system" that had relatively little impact on the lives and cultural expressions of residents in neighboring centers such as Ek' B'alam. In their view, Chich'en Itza was something of an island surrounded by a sea of traditional Yucatecan culture. Although the "iconography of the site would seem to be a new 'world' religion melding the symbols of Classic Maya religion with those of wider Mesoamerica," the northern sites of Yucatán appear to have been little influenced by the Itzas in their architecture and iconography.[14]

Schele, Grube, and Boot have offered a radically different interpretation of the origins of the founders and rulers of Chich'en Itza, based primarily on new decipherments of hieroglyphic texts found there and at other lowland sites and on a rereading of the native chronicles. They maintain, in agreement with other current scholars, that the decline of the southern Classic-period centers was accompanied by intense warfare between many of these centers — that is, by local warfare as opposed to external invasions. Some of these wars, "especially those in which kings

9

were forced into exile or captured and killed, produced a series of refugee elites [who] . . . retreated to allied states."[15] As a result, migrants began moving north to Yucatán as early as A.D. 650–750. There the refugees, accompanied by people fleeing the collapsing city of Teotihuacán in central Mexico, formed a new alliance with resident populations. The eventual result of the alliance, they propose, was the creation of the Itzas as a political entity and the founding of Chich'en Itza as early as A.D. 711.[16]

This last interpretation relies on a rereading of the native chronicles — mytho-historical texts that are often obscure and notoriously subject to alternative understandings — and it contradicts most previous archaeological interpretations. It is not implausible, nonetheless, to assume that the great florescence of architectural innovation, urbanism, and social planning evidenced at Chich'en Itza reflected a synthesis of several sources of influence that could have included local traditions mixed with those of remnant elites from the south as well as Mexican-influenced Chontal speakers from Tabasco. The ruling elites of Chich'en Itza certainly had contact with the Petén heartland: the chronicles state that at one point in their history some of them were forced, as the result of an internal war, to relocate during a K'atun 4 Ajaw (one of the thirteen recurring k'atuns in the cyclical Maya calendar) to a place called Tanxulukmul, in "the heart of the forest." There, in a K'atun 8 Ajaw, they may have founded it as the "cycle seat" of the Petén region.[17] In 1696 Fray Andrés de Avendaño came across a pond of the same name, with an adjacent large ruined pyramid that contained a "noted idol," not far north of the western end of Lago Petén Itzá.[18]

Most scholars have long maintained that Chich'en Itza, despite periodic disruptions, survived as an important center until the early thirteenth century. Recent archaeological studies, however, indicate that the site was already in decline by about A.D. 1000.[19] Nevertheless, it remained a ritual center and pilgrimage site with a small resident population for many years thereafter — even up to the time of the conquest.

Following the decline of Chich'en Itza, a new urban center, Mayapan, inherited its status as the most important political center in Yucatán. Located about one hundred kilometers to the west, Mayapan, a densely populated and walled community, may have been founded as early as the late tenth century. Its principal ruling patrilineage was said to have been that of the Kokoms, a name that also appears in inscriptions at Chich'en Itza, and both its architecture and its governance by a council of territorial rulers appear to have been modeled after those of its predecessor.[20] The rulers of Mayapan were certainly part of the same Itza cultural tradition

10

that had previously dominated Chich'en Itza. Mayapan finally collapsed as a political center in the mid-fifteenth century, only a few decades before the coming of the Spaniards to Yucatán. As a result, a number of smaller provinces emerged from the ruins of Mayapan, although not all of the sixteen Yucatecan conquest-period native provinces that the ethnohistorian Ralph Roys identified would have been part of the original Mayapan polity.[21]

Information that Itza rulers in Petén gave to the Spaniards indicates that they considered themselves to have been the direct descendants of the Itzas of Yucatán. The Ajaw Kan Ek' who ruled Nojpeten at the time of the 1697 conquest stated that his ancestors were from Chich'en Itza and that he still identified with the province of Yucatán.[22] His nephew, AjChan, stated that his deceased mother, the ruler's older sister, had come from Chich'en Itza, suggesting that members of the Itza nobility were still living there in the seventeenth century and successfully avoiding Spanish recognition.[23] The Petén group known as the Kowojs specified that their ancestors had migrated from Tankaj (referring to Mayapan) at the time of the conquest of Yucatán, which would have been about sixty or seventy years after the Itza migration.[24]

The Franciscan historian López de Cogolludo, paraphrasing the account of Fray Bartolomé de Fuensalida, who visited Nojpeten in 1618 and 1619, wrote the most detailed surviving account of the Itza migration to Petén:

> These Itza Indians are of Yucatecan origin, descendants of this land of Yucatán. Thus they speak the same Maya language as [those of Yucatán] do. It is said that they left the territory and jurisdiction that today is [that] of the villa of Valladolid and the town of Chichén Itzá, where today there remain some of the large ancient buildings that are seen in this land and which they admired so much when these kingdoms were discovered. . . . And others from neighboring towns left with them.
>
> Padre Fuensalida says that one hundred years before the Spaniards came to these kingdoms they fled from Chichén Itzá in the age that they call eighth (in their language *Uaxac Ahau*) and settled those lands where they live today. Their flight to an island and such concealed regions was foreseen by the prophecies that they had . . . that people from a nation that would dominate this land would come from regions to the east. Today those whom they call priests preserve the prophecies (written in their ancient characters) in a

11

book like a history which they call *analte*. In it they preserve the memory of how much has happened to them since they settled those lands.

They also say that they went to [those lands] by sea, and in that region that comes out at their lake they have on land a hamlet that they call Zinibacan,[25] which means where they stretched out the sails, because there, having been soaked, they dried them.

They also say that the occasion of the flight was that, while a great king or lord was readying to be married, during the rejoicings and festivities of the wedding another petty king arrived who was enamored with the bride, and falling with armed men upon those of the fiesta, who had been unsuspecting, and causing some harm among them, kidnapped the betrothed woman. This man was less powerful than the first, so seeing that [the latter] would later make war on him, fearful of the harm that would befall him, he had prepared to flee. So, taking the betrothed woman in his company with many of his people, he went to those lands that were so remote and hidden.[26]

Because Fuensalida seems to have been relying primarily on what the Itzas told him while he was at Nojpeten, his abbreviated account is an important one. It places the date of Itza migration from Chich'en Itza to Petén in the mid-fifteenth century, the approximate time of the collapse of Mayapan. The account offers two reasons for the migration: a prophecy that foreigners would come from the east to conquer Yucatán and a specific political event involving conflict over a royal marriage. The Itzas' passage toward the south was by sea, presumably along the eastern coastline of the Yucatán peninsula, probably up the New and Belize Rivers and then overland to Lago Petén Itzá — the same route followed by travelers and traders during the colonial period.

If prophecy did play a role in the Itzas' migration to Petén, it probably did not foretell European conquest. Such a claim was most likely an invention of the Spanish Franciscans, who sought evidence that the conquest was a divinely preordained event to bring Christianity to the New World natives and that even Maya prophecies could be understood as statements of God's will. As for the royal wedding conflict, Roys believed that it was the same event as one mentioned in the Maya chronicles involving a banquet, a love charm, and treachery committed by one Junak Keel during a K'atun 8 Ajaw. The outcome of this event in the chronicles was the expulsion of the Itzas from Chich'en Itza, which Roys believed occurred during the K'atun 8 Ajaw dated at A.D. 1441–61 — the same period during which the Itzas of Petén said they had left Yucatán.[27]

Both Chich'en Itza and Valladolid, the Spanish villa built over the pre-conquest town of Saki or Sakiwal, were located in the southern part of the Kupul province. By the time of the conquest of Yucatán, Chich'en Itza had been in ruins for five centuries, but the surviving town there still housed powerful nobles who exacted tribute from considerable distances in red beads, green stones, maize, produce, and turkey hens. The conquest-period ruler at the town was one NaOb'on Kupul — whose unusual surname, Ob'on, was found among seventeenth-century Itzas. NaOb'on Kupul, identified as an important provincial ruler by early Spanish sources, was killed by the conquerors during the period 1522–33, when Francisco Montejo, son of the conqueror of the same name, briefly established a Spanish villa at Chich'en Itza.[28]

Other names associated with Petén Itza nobility also appear in sources on the Itzas of Yucatán. Kokom, the name of a ruling patrilineage of Mayapan, has been identified not only in the inscriptions of Classic-period Chich'en Itza but also in 1619 as the name of a Nojpeten "captain."[29] Kawil, which also appears in the Chich'en Itza inscriptions, was either a title or, possibly, a surname in Petén, in one case associated with the patronym Itza (Kawil Itza).[30] A Kowoj and his companion, Ek', are named in the chronicles as guardians — presumably territorial rulers — of the "east gate" of Mayapan;[31] the Petén Kowojs were the ruling family of a large territory, and the Kan Ek' dynasty ruled Nojpeten for many generations. More such parallels could be mentioned, although these cannot alone absolutely "prove" the descent of the Itzas and Kowojs of Petén from the Itzas of Yucatán. The sum of the ethnohistorical evidence, however, appears to confirm Itza and Kowoj claims of their descent from the Itza centers of northern Yucatán.

PROPHETIC HISTORY AND THE ITZAS

The theme of "prophetic history" resonates throughout the Maya chronicles of Yucatán, in Spanish interpretations of Maya behavior and in Spanish-Maya interactions. Intensifying during seventeenth-century Spanish encounters with the Itzas of Petén and other peoples of the southern Yucatán frontiers, it reached a climax on the eve of the conquest of the Itzas, when Franciscans in particular were convinced that Itza prophecies had assured their conversion to Christianity at the beginning of a K'atun 8 Ajaw. Because discussions of such prophetic discourse arise throughout this book, a brief explanation is in order.[32]

13

The Maya priests who composed the Books of Chilam B'alam often described events that had occurred in the past in reference to periods of time known as k'atuns. A k'atun was a period of 7,200 days divided into 20 consecutive 360-day periods called *tuns*. A period consisting of 13 k'atuns, or 260 tuns, comprised a larger unit of time, the *may*, which fell just 104 days longer than 256 years of 365.25 days each. At the end of one *may*, the cycle of 13 k'atuns another began, much the way a new century in our own calendar begins upon the completion of ten decades. Until the tenth century A.D. the Mayas had recorded an even larger period of time known as the *b'ak'tun*, which comprised 20 k'atuns, or 400 tuns. Because this "long count" had a fixed beginning point and identified b'ak'tuns and each of their 20 k'atuns in numerical sequence, scholars can correlate long-count dates with the Gregorian and Julian calendars. During most of the Postclassic period, after the mid-tenth century, Maya scribes ceased recording long-count dates, sometimes creating uncertainty as to which cycle of 13 k'atuns writers were referring when they recorded events said to have occurred in a particular k'atun.[33]

During the Spanish colonial period, beginning in 1539, each of the 13 k'atuns within the *may*, or k'atun cycle, was identified both by the name of the day on which it began (always the day called Ajaw, one of the 20 named days of the 260-day calendar known as the *tzol k'in*) and by a numerical coefficient that indicated the 13 sacred day numbers of the tzol k'in.[34] The first k'atun in the cycle was called K'atun 13 Ajaw, the second K'atun 11 Ajaw, the third K'atun 9 Ajaw, and so on in the order 7, 5, 3, 1, 12, 10, 8, 6, 4, 2. During the colonial period considered in this book, the years in the Gregorian calendar that initiated particular k'atuns were as follows: 11 Ajaw (1539), 9 Ajaw (1559), 7 Ajaw (1579), 5 Ajaw (1599), 3 Ajaw (1618), 1 Ajaw (1638), 12 Ajaw (1658), 10 Ajaw (1677), 8 Ajaw (1697), and 6 Ajaw (1717).

The k'atun histories of the Maya chronicles appear at first glance simply to record events that occurred in a given k'atun in the past as a means of organized notekeeping. As many scholars have observed, however, the information pertaining to the same k'atun as it appears in repeated cycles of thirteen often bears striking repetitions in each cycle. The past, that is, occurs again in the future in somewhat predictable forms — with differing details, but with thematic regularities that reoccur. The writing and recitation of k'atun histories, therefore, were acts of prophecy making, because what had occurred once could be expected to occur in some form thirteen k'atuns, or 256 years, later and yet again in future appearances of the same k'atun, ad infinitum.[35] The k'atun historian was a prophet-priest who potentially wielded immense political influence and power, for he could rewrite the past in order to *pre*write the future. What prophets chose to report about previous eras, that is, could be used by political decision makers (who were often priests themselves) to plan and justify their future actions. Prophetic history was a dynamic, ever-changing accounting of time and events that, far from freezing the past as "fact," could always be used to reinterpret and rewrite the past for the convenience of the present. Such practices, minus the formal system of dating one's prophecies, are familiar to modern Western students of history as well.

The most important k'atun in Itza prophetic history was K'atun 8 Ajaw. The "final" occurrence of this era, 1697–1717, represented for Spaniards the time during which the Itzas of Petén would submit to colonial rule and accept Christianity. The Itzas of the time also clearly believed that something of importance would happen, and some of them apparently shared the Spaniards' views. Others, as we shall see in later chapters, embraced different interpretations of what the future would or should bring. The following examples of statements concerning various occurrences of K'atun 8 Ajaw are from the Book of Chilam B'alam of Chumayel:[36]

> 8 Ahau was when Chakanputun was abandoned by the Itza men. Then they came to seek homes again. For thirteen folds of katuns had they dwelt in their houses at Chakanputun. This was always the katun when the Itza went beneath the trees, beneath the bushes, beneath the vines, to their misfortune. [Chronicle I]
>
> 8 Ahau was when the Itza men again abandoned their homes because of the treachery of Hunac Ceel, because of the banquet with the people of Izamal. For thirteen folds of katuns they had dwelt there, when they were driven out by Hunac Ceel because of the giving of the questionnaire of the Itza. [Chronicle I]
>
> 8 Ahau was when there was fighting with stones at Ich-paa Mayapan because of the seizure of the fortress. They broke down the city wall because of the joint government in the city of Mayapan. [Chronicle I]
>
> 8 Ahau was when their town was abandoned and they were scattered throughout the entire district. In the sixth katun after they were dispersed, then they ceased to be called Maya. [Chronicle II]
>
> Katun 8 Ahau is the ninth katun. The katun is established at Izamal. . . . The shield shall descend, the arrow shall descend [upon

Chakanputun][37] together with the rulers of the land. The heads of the foreigners to the land were cemented [into the wall] at Chakanputun. There is an end of greed; there is an end to causing vexation in the world. It is the word of God the Father. Much fighting shall be done by the natives of the land. [Book of Katun Prophecies]

There is confusion over the timing and location of some of the events referred to in descriptions of the recurring K'atun 8 Ajaw. The chronicles for this k'atun apparently refer to events of great antiquity that include the Itzas' expulsion from their early homeland at Chak'an Putun, from Chich'en Itza, and from Mayapan (in about 1461, the first year of the last K'atun 8 Ajaw prior to European conquest). In some cases events are merged or several places are conflated into a single location, making historical reconstructions from the texts exceedingly difficult.

The accounts of K'atun 8 Ajaw consistently refer to misfortunes that befell the Itzas, especially wars and conflicts that forced them from a homeland they had occupied for many years. In addition, some of them provide support for statements by seventeenth-century Itzas that they had migrated from northern Yucatán to Petén a century prior to the conquest of Yucatán. We have seen, however, that the Itzas said that they were from Chich'en Itza, not Mayapan, whose collapse is timed in the chronicles at K'atun 8 Ajaw, in about 1461. The Kowojs of Petén, on the other hand, were said to have migrated from Mayapan at the time of conquest, presumably during the period 1520–43, when military activities in the north were most intense. These contradictions, which cannot yet be resolved, are probably of little significance, because the collapse of Mayapan was associated with disruptions that would also have affected the mid-fifteenth-century population at Chich'en Itza.

The association of war and expulsion with this k'atun must have conformed with the Petén Itzas' perception of the impending initiation (or "turning") of K'atun 8 Ajaw, which was to occur in July 1697. With Spanish troops approaching them from both north and south beginning in 1695, some of their prophet-priests, familiar with versions of these prophecies, probably saw a repeat of earlier events, about which it was written that the "shield shall descend, the arrow shall descend together with the rulers of the land" and "their town was abandoned and they were scattered throughout the entire district." On the other hand, positive visions of the k'atun appear in obviously colonial-period versions of the prophecy: "There is an end of greed; there is an end of causing vexation in the world. It is the word of God the Father." Such Christian-influenced rewritings of the prophecy may have been the sources both for signs of willingness on the part of Ajaw Kan Ek' in 1695 to peacefully accept Spanish rule and Christianity and for the Franciscans' conviction that K'atun 8 Ajaw was the preordained time for this to occur.

The Kowojs

Less well known than the Itzas were their principal political and territorial rivals, the Kowojs, named for their powerful ruling lineage. At the time of the 1697 conquest the Kowojs controlled the northern shore and the eastern port area of Lago Petén Itzá as well as a significant amount of inland territory north and northeast of the lake toward Tik'al (map 5). At about the same time a branch of the Kowojs also had settlements in the area of Lagunas Sacnab and Yaxhá to the east of the main lake (map 6). Although the Kowojs appear to have been culturally similar and linguis-

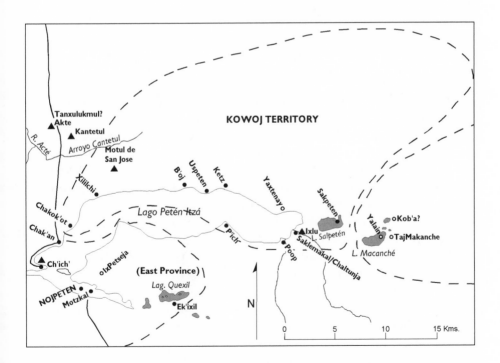

Map 5.   The Kowoj region. Hollow dots indicate approximate locations.

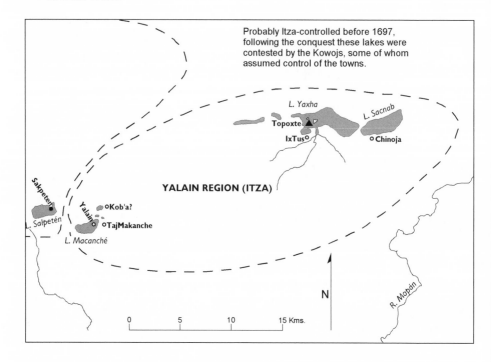

Probably Itza-controlled before 1697, following the conquest these lakes were contested by the Kowojs, some of whom assumed control of the towns.

L. Yaxha

L. Sacnab

Topoxte

IxTus

Chinoja

YALAIN REGION (ITZA)

Salpeten

Yalain

Kob'a?

TajMakanche

L. Macanché

N

R. Mopán

0   5   10   15 Kms.

Map 6. The Yalain region. Hollow dots indicate approximate locations.

tically identical to the Itzas, Spanish sources consistently distinguish between the two as political and territorial groups.[38]

The Kowojs, as we have seen, said that they came from Mayapan at the time of the conquest of Yucatán. The area around Mayapan was then part of the native province of Mani. Mani had been ruled by the Tutul Xiws ever since the mid-fifteenth-century collapse of Mayapan, which various sources attribute to the murder and expulsion of the ruling Kokom family by the Tutul Xiws and their allies at Mayapan. The Kokoms, who may have been descended from a royal family at Chich'en Itza, regarded the Tutul Xiws as Mexicanized foreign intruders to Yucatán. Xiw-Kokom enmity continued for many years after the collapse of Mayapan. It reached a climax when, in 1536, the Kokoms, then in control of the Sotuta province on the eastern boundary of the Mani province, murdered a group of Xiw dignitaries to whom they had promised safe passage across Sotuta for a pilgrimage to Chich'en Itza. Up to that time the Tutul Xiws had been neutral toward the Spanish conquest, which had begun in two unsuccessful phases in 1527–28 and 1531–35. After the 1536 massacre, however, the Xiws actively supported the Spaniards, whereas the Itza-derived people of Sotuta violently opposed them for many years.[39]

Although I have found no confirmation from northern Yucatecan sources that noble Mayas named Kowoj held positions of importance in the Xiw-controlled Mani province, a Kowoj was, as noted earlier, identified at Mayapan in the native chronicles. It is plausible that such a group migrated to Petén following the 1536 massacre of the Tutul Xiws. They might have been caught between the Xiws and the Kokoms as Mani-dwelling sympathizers of the latter who had to escape Xiw retribution by fleeing to safer territory. On the other hand, they might have been Xiw sympathizers or mercenaries who went south to conquer Itza-controlled Nojpeten and later deliver the capital to the Spanish conquerors; if so, they were obviously unsuccessful. Whatever the reasons for their flight from Mayapan, when they first come to light in the documents of the 1690s they are the enemies of a still-ruling Itza king, Ajaw Kan Ek'.

The Mopans

The Mopans, another Yucatecan-speaking group, are one of the least well known, both historically and geographically, of all lowland Maya peoples. Their origins may have been in Yucatán, or they may have been long resident in Petén. Beyond the fact that beginning in the early seventeenth century Spaniards found them living at a town known as Mopan — today San Luis, Petén — and in nearby areas, the extent of their colonial-period distribution has been virtually unknown. What follows is a reassessment of the identity and geographical extent of Mopan populations during the sixteenth century. I believe they were a far larger and more widely spread ethnic group than has formerly been thought.

The earliest Spanish reference to the Mopans of which I am aware is another paraphrase of Fray Bartolomé de Fuensalida's account by López de Cogolludo:

> There are diverse nations in the cordillera which it has been said runs from east to west, because they are the Itzas . . . ; the Chinamitas, their closest neighbors; the [Chol-speaking] Lacandones; the Chakan-Itzas; the Cehaches; the Mopans; and those of a large settlement and city which they say has eight thousand inhabitants. It is called Tulumcí, and they say that there had been some Spanish men and women held captive in it. Father Fuensalida had

19

more certain information that there had been a Spanish woman among them, but not about when or how they arrived there. Tulumcí means agave fortress, because it is completely closed in with henequen plantings, and with only one narrow entrance into it that is closed and surrounded by water. There they are fortified and defended against their antagonists, because these people constantly carry out wars against one another as if they are different nationalities; and sometimes [they fight] those of their own nation, having different caciques. The Chinamitas are so cruel and barbarous that when our religious [priests] told the Itzas when they were with them that they also had to visit them in order to preach the holy gospel to them, [the Itzas] told them not to go there because they were ferocious people and that they would undoubtedly kill them because [they were] *mauinicob,* indicating to them by this word, which means "they are not men," that they were only wild animals and that when [the priests] had to go there they would accompany them so that they would not kill them.[40]

J. Eric S. Thompson concluded that the fortified town of Tulumki (from *tulum ki,* "wall of agave [or henequen]") was actually the principal town of the Chinamitas, because *chinamitl* is the Nahuatl term for "cane hedge" — a rough equivalent of Tulumki.[41] I agree with this assessment, and I also believe that the Chinamitas were a branch of the Mopans living in eastern Petén and Belize.

Fuensalida and another Franciscan, Fray Juan de Orbita, were probably first informed about the location of the Chinamitas by a group of armed Itzas who visited the two Spaniards at Tipuj during their stay there in 1618. The Itza visitors, whose two high-ranking leaders carried stone-tipped lances while the rest carried bows and arrows, told Fuensalida that they always carried these arms when they left their territory in case they encountered "Chinamita Indians," an enemy "nation" with whom they were perennially at war.[42] From this we can conclude that they feared encountering Chinamitas on the route between Nojpeten and Tipuj — territory that in 1698 was identified as Mopan land.[43]

That year the Itza ruler, Ajaw Kan Ek', and his cousin, the high priest AjK'in Kan Ek', told Spanish questioners that Mopans, Chinamitas, and "Tulunquies" were among a number of "nations" located nine days east of Nojpeten who were previously at war with the Itzas. The record of their statement, with spelling variants from a second copy in brackets, reads as follows:

[I]n years past they had four battles with the Aiykales [Aikales] (who are the Mopans), Chinamitas and Tulunquies [Tulumkies] and Taxchinchanob [Tahchinchanob], Zacuanob [Zacabob], Cixchanob [Kicchanob], Ahacob, Chicuyob, Ahchamayob, Tzacalob, Ahkinob, Tezucunob [Tesucunob], Ahchemob, Ahcamalob. They say that they battled four times with all these nations, having been defeated three times, and at the fourth battle they won and up to now have not fought again. They declare that these nations are all living together to the east, and that from this peten the said populations are nine days away by road, and this is how long they spent in going to the said populations.[44]

The first three names in this paragraph, including "Mopans," are political-ethnic designations, whereas the rest, beginning with "Taxchinchanob," are lineage names. My interpretation of this passage is that all of the groups following "the Aiykales (who are the Mopans)" are subsets of the Aikales/Mopans, who should be set off from the rest by a colon. (The term *ayikal*, which in colonial Yucatec meant "rich," was also used by the Itzas as an honorific title for certain local leaders.) The lineage names, all expressed as plurals (with the -*ob* suffix), may be understood to refer to groups of people who constituted the local following of a particular leader with that name. Because all are said to be located in the same area — "all living together to the east" — they clearly constitute an identifiable "people" or larger "nation" living in a contiguous region. Therefore, I hypothesize that they were all, including the Chinamitas or "Tulunquies," part of a larger ethnic population usually identified as Mopans.

Almost all of the lineage names appear to be Mopan. Also found in other sources, they may be rendered as Taxim Chan, Tzakwan, Kixchan (or Kischan), Tzak, Chikuy, Chamay, Tzakal, K'in, Tesukun, Ch'em, and Kamal. In 1695, caciques from the southern Mopan area — all identified as Mopans — bore the names Taximchan, Tesukun, Tzak, and Yajkab'.[45] Early-eighteenth-century baptismal records from the mission town of Santo Toribio, situated along the camino real about halfway between Lago Petén Itzá and San Luis, contain all of these names except Taximchan, Tzakal, and Kamal; the most common name at Santo Toribio was Musul, which is also certainly Mopan.[46] We can conclude that Santo Toribio was populated almost entirely by Mopans, some of whom were probably Chinamitas, because only a handful of people with known Itza names appears there.

The significance of these details is that we can now propose that during

21

the seventeenth century the Mopans, who included the Chinamitas, were distributed far beyond the region around the old town called Mopan (San Luis).[47] Additional evidence allows us to situate the Mopans not only in the area around San Luis but also in areas closer to Lago Petén Itzá, in southern Belize in the vicinity of contemporary Mopan settlements (San Antonio and San Antonio Viejo), inland along the rivers of southeastern Belize, and in the vicinity of the Belize River east of Tipuj (see map 2).[48] Considering the fears of Itza warriors walking to Tipuj in 1618 that they would be attacked by "Chinamitas," this branch of the Mopans was probably also living along the Río Mopan in the region south of Lagunas Yaxhá and Sacnab and in adjacent regions of nearby Belize.[49]

Although most contemporaneous descriptions of Mopans indicated that they lived in small, scattered settlements, Fuensalida's report of a sizable fortified Chinamita town suggests that at least some Mopans lived in larger communities that were "capitals" of politically centralized territories. Spanish descriptions of a scattered Mopan population may reflect Itza and Spanish invasions of Mopan lands during the seventeenth century. That is, only those Mopans who sought refuge in isolated regions where they organized defenses against Itza aggression were able to maintain a degree of political and territorial centralization.

By the time of the 1697 conquest, Mopans living between Nojpeten and the southern town of Mopan were considered to be part of the larger Itza territorial and political domain. In 1696 a Spanish Guatemalan official called them "dependents" of the Itzas.[50] The Guatemalan Dominican Fray Agustín Cano reported learning that the Mopans "had communication with the Ahitzes [*sic*] of the lake. We even understood that they all belonged to one and the same Itza nation, being called Mopan-Itza, Peten-Itza, and that these Mopans were subject to the *reyezuelo* [petty king] of the island of the lake, about whom and about his island or peten and his caciques they gave us much information, although they always refused to show us the road."[51] In calling the Itza "nation" "Mopan-Itza, Peten-Itza," Cano seems to have been designating two principal subgroups, of which the Mopans were the political "dependents" of the Itzas.[52]

The Kejaches

The three Yucatecan-speaking territorial-ethnic groups just discussed — the Itzas, Kowojs, and Mopans — lived in close proximity, intermarried, and waged war among themselves. The fourth Yucatecan-speaking Petén group, the Kejaches, located many leagues to the north of the western end of the main lake, were separated from the central lakes area by a large stretch of nearly uninhabited territory (see map 2). Frequent victims of Itza military attacks, even as late as 1697, the Kejaches seem to have had relatively little recent reciprocal interaction with the Itzas or other Petén groups. Called by the Nahuatl name Mazatlan by Chontal-speaking Akalan neighbors to the north, the Kejach region was distinguished by its heavily fortified settlements at the time of Cortés's expedition, fortifications that protected them from Itza raids.

Despite their physical separation from the Itzas and their vulnerability to Itza hostility, the Kejaches appear to have been closely related to their formidable enemies. Name sharing between the two groups may suggest cultural and historical affinities. In 1696 Franciscan friars produced censuses of two Kejach mission towns, B'atkab' and Pak'ek'em, situated along the camino real. By far the most common names at these two towns — Chan, K'ixaw, and Puk — were also Itza names. Whereas Puk was also common in Yucatán, Chan was less so, and K'ixaw was apparently absent there. Although individuals with common Yucatecan names also appeared in small numbers in the censuses, they may have been refugees from the northern encomiendas or descendants of such immigrants.[53]

These data suggest that the Itzas and Kejaches may have had a common origin, having split at some point prior to the sixteenth century. We cannot know whether such a division occurred before or during Itzá migrations to Petén or as the result of internal warfare in Petén that resulted in Kejach migration northward. Yet another possibility is that the Kejaches represent an indigenous population of great antiquity in this area and that those among the Itzas who shared their names were descendants of Kejaches who had lived around Lago Petén Itzá prior to the Itzas' arrival in the fifteenth century.

Table 1.1 shows the distribution of the presently known surnames of the Yucatecan-speaking peoples of Petén from the sixteenth century through the mid-eighteenth century. For the "core" area of Itza territory, most names were recorded around the time of the 1697 conquest. The column headed "Yalain" includes names from the region east of Lago Petén Itzá. The considerable overlap between the names of this area and those of the core Itza area reflects the seventeenth-century Itza domination of the Yalain region. The third column, "Tipuj Itzas," is based on a listing of people clearly of Itza political affiliation recorded at Tipuj in 1655; some of these names not represented in the core Itza area may reflect intermarriage with the local Yucatec-speaking population of the town.

TABLE I.I
Distribution of Petén Surnames by Territory and Location

Surname[a]	Core Itza	Yalain	Tipuj Itzas	Kowoj	Mopan	San Andrés[b]	Kejach
B'alam	X		X			X	x
B'alamna					X		
B'atab'						X	
B'atun	X						X
Chab'in	X					X	
Chab'le			X			x	
Chan	X	X	X		X	X	X
Chaneb'						x	
Chata	X					X	
Chay						x	
Chayax	X	X				X	
Chen						x	
Chi			X				
Chikuy					X		
Ch'akan					X		
Ch'em					X		
Ek'	X		X			x	
Itza	X	X				X	
Jaw	X		X				
Joil						x	
Jola					X		
Kab'				X			
Kan	X	X	X				
Kanchan	X					X	
Kanche						x	
Kanek'	X					X	
Kante	X		X			X	
Kanul						x	
Kanyokte						x	
Kamal				X		X	
Kawich				X		X	
Kawil (also Kawij)	X		X				
Kech			X			x	
Keliz						X	
Ketz (also K'etz)				X			

TABLE 1.1

(*continued*)

Surname[a]	Core Itza	Yalain	Tipuj Itzas	Kowoj	Mopan	San Andrés[b]	Kejach
Ki			X				
Kib'			X				
Kischan (also Kixchan)					X		
Kitkan	X					x	
Kitis (also K'itis)	X					X	
Kob'			X				
Kokom	X					X	
Kol	X						
Kowoj (also Kob'ow, Kob'ox)	X			X		X	
Kwa	X						
K'in	X				X		
?K'inchil	X						
K'inyokte						x	
K'ixab'on	X					x	
K'ixaw (Kejach: Kixaw)	?					x	X
K'ixchan (also Kixchan, Kischan)						x	
K'u			X				X
K'unil (also K'umil)					X		
Mas			X				
Matab' (also Matub')						x	
May		X	X			x	
Mis						x	
Mo (also Moo)			X			X	X
Muk'ul			X				
Musul					X	x	
Muwan (also Moan)	X				X		
Naa						x	

TABLE I.I

(*continued*)

Surname[a]	Core Itza	Yalain	Tipuj Itzas	Kowoj	Mopan	San Andrés[b]	Kejach
Nojk'ute						x	
Ob'on (also Ab'on)	X				X		
Pana (also Panob', Panub', Punab')	X	X			X	X	
Pix			X				
Poot						x	
Puk	X		X			X	X
P'ol	X		X				
Sab'ak					X		
Sakwan					X		
Sima	X		X				
Tek		X					
Tesukun (also Tesukan (Pipil)	X				X	X	
Tinal			X				
Tun (also Tunich?)	X					X	
Tut	X					X	
Tutz (Tus?)							
Tzak (also Tz'ak)	X				X		
Tzakal					X	x	
Tzakwam					X		
Tzam	X	X					
Tzawi					X		
Tzel						x	
Tzin (Chontal)	X					X	
Tzuk						x	
Tzul (Kejach: Zul)						x	X
Tzuntekum (Pipil)	X				X		
Tz'ib' (also Tzib')	X	X	X		X	x	

TABLE I.I
(*continued*)

Surname[a]	Core Itza	Yalain	Tipuj Itzas	Kowoj	Mopan	San Andrés[b]	Kejach
Us			X				
Xiken (also						X	
Chik'en)		X					
Xok			?				
Xulu (also Sulu)		X	X				

SOURCES: Tipuj names are from Scholes and Thompson, 1977, pp. 63–64. Most of the Mopán patronyms are from AGI, Escribanía de Cámara 339A, Memoria on Peten Itza by Fr. Diego de Rivas, 26 May 1702, ff. 31r–33v, and AAICFP, Santo Toribio, baptismal register, 1709–49. Only the names of "pagan" Mopán parents in the Santo Toribio baptismal register are included here. The register also includes a few cases of clearly non-Mopán names (including Itza, Kowoj, and Chol names), which are not included here. Chontal names are from Scholes and Roys, 1968, pp. 481–90. They consider Tzin to be a Nahuatl-derived honorific suffix, but it seems clear that it served as a surname among the Chontals. Pipil names are from Schumann, 1971, p. 18, 125; Schumann lists some names that existed at San Andrés and San José in recent times but have not appeared in the historical documentation. Other names may well be shared with other groups, and this is not intended to be a complete examination. Not included here are four possible unusual names found in Table 3.1, the statuses of which are not clear. These are Je, K'en, Matza, and Matzin. Other sources are too numerous to list.

[a]Names in italics are not listed by Roys (1940) as surnames found in Yucatán. When these are known to be used by other Maya groups, the name of the groups is indicated in parentheses.

[b]A small x indicates that the name occurred three times or fewer among marriage partners during the years examined.

Only two Kowoj surnames, in the next column, are known with certainty, although there were undoubtedly more than these.

The column labeled "San Andrés" comprises names of marriage partners recorded in church records for the Itza missions San Andrés and San José during the mid-seventeenth century. These people probably included not only some Kowojs but also a few Mopans and perhaps some Kejaches and some recent immigrants brought as workers by the Spaniards from northern Yucatán. The Kejach column, based on the two *matrículas* (censuses) made by Franciscan missionaries in 1696, indicates some overlap with the Itza core area data (in the two known Itza surnames shared by the Kejaches) but much commonality with San Andrés and San José (six names).

27

Mopan surnames represent a highly distinct set, suggesting that this may have been a much older local population. Names on the list that are apparently not also found in Yucatán are indicated by italics. Not surprisingly, this number is quite small for the Itza core area.

Names, therefore, provide confirmation, although hardly exact, of the political and ethnic regions of Petén. They also indicate that boundaries among these groups were not absolute. Names were shared across groups, owing to many years of intermingling and intermarriage resulting from both peaceful and violent encounters. Now, in the early sixteenth century, both kinds of encounters were about to involve people with a new kind of name — Spanish.

T he first Spaniards to visit Itza territory arrived near the shores of Lago Petén Itzá on about Thursday, March 16, 1525. These men, runners sent ahead by Hernán Cortés with a Chontal guide from Akalan, told Cortés that they had seen "a very large lake that looked like an arm of the sea . . . and on a small island in it they saw a town, which that guide told them was the central town of that province of Taiza [Taiça], and that the only way we could reach it would be in canoes."[1]

This was not only the first time Europeans had seen the lake and its island capital but also the first time they described the "province" of TajItza, "At the Place of the Itza."[2] Cortés and his enormous party of Spaniards, Mexicas, and other native peoples moved quickly through Itza territory, although Cortés spent most of a day in the company of Ajaw Kan Ek' on Nojpeten before traveling on to eastern Guatemala. The impact of several thousand foreigners under a powerful leader passing directly through their territory had a lasting and profound effect on the Itza people and their future relationships with the Spanish colonial world.

The Entrada of Hernan Cortés, 1525

The circumstances of this extraordinary journey were reported by both Cortés and his lieutenant, Bernal Díaz del Castillo.[3] Following the conquest of the Aztec capital of Tenochtitlan in 1521, Cortés sent military expeditions to the regions surrounding the Valley of Mexico. One of these, under the command of Gonzalo de Sandoval, defeated the Mixe to the southeast of the valley and then proceeded to the coast of the Gulf of Mexico. There, on the Isthmus of Tehuantepec, a short distance from the coast on Río Coatzacoalcos, Sandoval founded a villa that he named Espíritu Santo. It served as the headquarters for subsequent entradas into western Tabasco and highland Chiapas. Despite initial successes in assigning some indigenous communities in encomienda to citizens of the villa, Spanish control over these regions remained precarious for some years. None of the early expeditions reached far into the eastern interior lowlands until Cortés mounted his own entrada in 1524–25. The journey took him through Nahuatl-speaking areas of Tabasco, the previously uncontacted Chontal-speaking territory of Akalan on Río Candelaria, the Yucatec-speaking region known as Kejach, the province of the Itzas themselves, and finally Chol territory before he reached the Bahía de Amatique in Guatemala (see map 1).

In October 1524, Cortés left Mexico for Espíritu Santo, where he made preparations for his journey. His principal stated purpose for the trip was to find and punish Cristóbal de Olid and others who had defected after Cortés had sent them to Honduras earlier that year. Unbeknownst to Cortés, Olid's companions had already executed him as a rebel before Cortés left Espíritu Santo.[4] Cortés could have chosen a far easier and less dangerous route to the Caribbean coast, going by sea around the Yucatán peninsula. The explorer and conqueror, however, had decided to follow a land route in order to discover "many unknown lands and provinces . . . [and to] pacify many of them, as was later done."[5]

After arriving at Espíritu Santo he learned from several messengers sent to him from Tabasco and Xicalango that certain Spaniards had been causing "much harm" on what he thought to be the east coast of Yucatán.[6] Cortés presumed that these were the Spaniards he was looking for, and the messengers presented him with a painted cloth map showing the route he would have to take in order to reach their location. It later became evident that these depredations had occurred at Bahía de Amatique in the Gulf of Honduras, not in Yucatán.

Cortés wrote that he had brought with him 230 Spanish soldiers, including 93 cavalry, and 3,000 Mexica (Aztec) auxiliaries under the command of important native lords. Most of the massive number of natives undoubtedly served as carriers, cooks, and other service personnel. The famous doña Marina (Malinali) — a native of Tabasco, a speaker of Nahuatl and Chontal Maya who had served as Cortés's interpreter during the conquest of Mexico, now a speaker of Spanish and his mistress — was his principal interpreter for the expedition.[7]

The expedition took a generally eastern route not far from the coastline, eventually crossing Río Grijalva near the present site of Villahermosa. After following the eastern tributary of the Grijalva, the Tacotalpa, upstream to Ciuatan, they went overland to the east until reaching Iztapa on Río Usumacinta. They then followed the Usumacinta upstream to Ciuatecpan, near the junction of Río San Pedro with the Usumacinta. Most of the towns in the heavily settled region through which they passed had been abandoned and burned before the Spaniards' arrival.

Cortés's immediate goal was to reach the Chontal-speaking province of Akalan, known for its wealth and prowess as a trading center. Cortés first met the Akalan ruler, PaxB'olon Acha,[8] at a town on Río San Pedro and, with his entire party, went the short distance to Itzam K'anak on Río Candelaria.[9] PaxB'olon Acha rode one of Cortés's horses. The capital was "very large with many temples," and Cortés apparently considered it more impressive than the Itza capital, Nojpeten.[10] The political structure of the province was similar to that which functioned at Nojpeten at the end of the seventeenth century: a governing council that included the king, four principal leaders representing the four urban quarters of the capital, and representatives of other regional towns.[11]

At Itzam K'anak Cortés learned that Akalan merchants occupied a ward of the town of Nito on Bahía de Amatique, near Lago de Izabal, then known as Golfo Dulce. Because these merchants had seen the Spaniards he was seeking there, he immediately changed the direction of his journey, procuring from them a new, detailed map of the region through which his expedition would have to pass.[12]

The Akalan Chontals provisioned Cortés's party as it headed out on Sunday, March 15, for the journey southeast toward Lago Petén Itzá. On their way to Kejach territory, which was also known by the Nahuatl name Mazatlan,[13] the Spaniards captured two Akalan merchants, forcing them to serve as guides. On the third day his advance party had an armed encounter with several Kejach lookouts, two of whom they captured. These men told him that they were on duty by order of their "lord," patrolling cultivated fields against local enemies. Warfare, it appears, was endemic in the region.

On the next day the expedition arrived at the first of several abandoned Kejach settlements, this one located on a high promontory adjacent to a large lake. The town was highly fortified with a surrounding wall of timbers.[14] The fleeing inhabitants had left behind much recently cooked food and even some small spears and bows and arrows. Cortés sent for the "lord" of the town, promising to assist him in defeating his enemies, and two days later the uncle of the "lord" was brought in, representing the ruler, who was still a boy.[15] The uncle must have been among fifteen leaders, mentioned by Díaz del Castillo, who came begging for Cortés's mercy, pleading that he not burn the town down, because they had only recently built the fortification there as protection from their enemies. Díaz, writing many years later, thought he recalled that the leaders said these enemies were "Lacandones" who had burned and destroyed other towns in the savannahs (*llanos*) through which the Spaniards would subsequently pass.[16] It is more likely that they were Itzas who were forcing the Kejaches to abandon territory and move their upper frontier farther to the north.

The uncle of the lord of the first Kejach town accompanied Cortés to an even larger and more strongly built town called Tiak, seven leagues away. It, too, had been recently abandoned. In addition to external defensive walls, pits, and watchtowers, it had three separately walled wards within. Like the first town, Tiak was ruled by a "lord," who sent food and clothing to Cortés via his representatives but who did not go himself. The messengers, according to Cortés, also represented five or six other towns of the province, each of which was a *cabecera*, a provincial capital.[17]

Cortés's claim that the first town and Tiak were at war with each other seems unlikely; it is far more probable that all the Kejach towns were united in a broad defensive alliance against Itza aggression. Although Díaz did not mention Tiak, he noted that the party passed through several settlements that had been burned and destroyed. The Kejaches, of course, may have burned and abandoned these towns themselves in order to avoid capture by the Spaniards. It is equally plausible that the Itzas did so in hopes of starving out the expedition by preventing the Kejaches from providing food supplies.

After leaving Tiak, the expedition slept at yet another abandoned fortified town, "Yasuncabil," the last town on the southern frontier of Kejach territory. Their guides told them they were now five days from the province of the Itzas. From there Cortés sent his captive Akalan guides home with gifts for themselves and their lord.

ARRIVAL IN ITZA TERRITORY

The region between "Yasuncabil" and Itza territory was unpopulated, extending south across the hilly karst zone north of Lago Petén Itza. On the fifth day, on or about Saturday, March 18, Cortés's scouts saw the lake, and Cortés went on foot to see it for himself, along with a party including Díaz and doña Marina. Once there he learned that his runners had captured an Itza man from Nojpeten who claimed, implausibly, that no one in the area was aware of the expedition. Díaz recalled that they had reached the first Itza town, which they found half abandoned, two days before reaching the lake. If that was the case, then the entire region must soon have been alerted to the approach of the massive expedition.[18]

According to Cortés's account, the captured Itza man had come armed in a small canoe "to examine the road and see whether there were any people." (Díaz recounted that five persons were captured to serve as guides; he mentioned no canoe.) Cortés must have asked how he could pass around the lake and where he could discover canoes, because the Itza told him that he would find some canoes on a "small arm of that lake" where there were "cultivations" (*labranzas*) and inhabited houses. He would, however, have to arrive there without being discovered. Díaz, in his version of the story, recalled that he, presumably along with Cortés and others, first arrived at a town on the shore, where some of the party fished in the lake using old *mantas* (lengths of cloth) and torn nets. This town may have been at or near the present location of San Andrés, known as Chak'an in the seventeenth century and situated on the point of land northeast of Ensenada de San Jerónimo (see map 4). This *ensenada*, or bay, served as the principal port at the western end of the lake, and it was the place where Ursúa would launch his attack on Nojpeten in 1697.

Doña Marina interpreted Cortés's words to the captive or captives: he intended them no harm but was in search of towns further on where there were bearded men with horses. Cortés set off on foot with ten or twelve crossbowmen and issued an order for other armed soldiers to follow behind — by canoe, as we presently learn. On the way they had to walk through a marsh with water that reached above their waists. The road was poor, and the local inhabitants discovered them before they reached the arm of the lake.

According to Díaz, the guides had taken them along a wide road that narrowed at the end, "due to a large river and an estuary that was nearby in which it appears that they [the Itzas] embarked and disembarked in canoes and went to that town where we had to go, called Tayasal, which is on an island surrounded by water; ... and the houses and temples showed their whiteness from more than two leagues from where they were scattered, and it was the cabecera of other nearby small towns."[19] Díaz and Cortés had arrived at the marshy area (the "estuary," crossed by a stream now called Riachuelo Pixoyal) at the western end of the long, narrow arm of the lake that extends for about seven kilometers before opening onto the main body of the lake at Punta Nijtún.[20]

Cortés and his men walked through cultivated areas in the same direction, finding that people were fleeing with their canoes as they approached. They stopped and spent the night in the fields near the hills, taking every precaution possible, for the Kejach guide warned "that there were many of these people and that they were well trained in warfare; all of those neigh-

33

boring provinces feared them."[21] During the night, according to Díaz, four groups of soldiers moved stealthily up the arm of the lake in search of more guides. They captured two canoes loaded with maize and salt along with their occupants—ten Itza men and two women. They brought the prisoners and booty to Cortés, who learned through doña Marina that the captured Itzas were from Nojpeten.

Cortés's account indicates, however, that one of these canoes was the one captured earlier from the Itza spy, who, under cover of darkness that night, piloted the remaining Spaniards to Cortés's encampment.[22] His Kejach guide offered to take this canoe to Nojpeten and deliver a message from Cortés to the "lord," whose name he learned was "Canec"—that is, Ajaw Kan Ek', the proper title and name of the Itza dynastic ruler. The guide, who must have been a trader, claimed to know Ajaw Kan Ek' well and to have been in his house many times. Cortés entrusted the canoe to the guide, promising to reward him if he were successful. The guide left, returning at midnight with two "honored persons" of Nojpeten who said that Ajaw Kan Ek' had sent them to hear Cortés's message for themselves and to learn what he wanted.[23]

AJAW KAN EK' MEETS CORTÉS

Cortés gave these messengers some small gifts, telling them to convey to Ajaw Kan Ek' that the ruler should put aside any fear and visit Cortés where he was, offering to send a Spaniard with them as a hostage. The messengers then went back to Nojpeten with the Spaniard and the Kejach guide. The next morning, at "the hour for mass," the ruler arrived with about thirty Itza men and the relieved Spanish hostage in five or six canoes. Cortés took advantage of the hour, arranging the most spectacular mass that he could manage, sung "with much solemnity" and accompanied by instruments. The ruler, he wrote, paid great attention to the ceremony.

Following the mass, the Franciscan friars preached a sermon for Ajaw Kan Ek' through doña Marina, "in a way that he could understand very well, about matters of our faith, making him understand by many reasons how there was only one God and the error of his own sect." Ajaw Kan Ek' responded, according to Cortés, that he would "later" destroy his "idols" and believe in God, but meanwhile he wished to know how he might follow and honor this God. If Cortés would visit him in his town, he would burn the idols in his presence and invite him to leave a cross there. Cortés thereupon spoke in more detail about the absolute power of the Spanish king, claiming that Ajaw Kan Ek' "and everyone in the world

34

were your [the king's] subjects," including many "in these parts" who had already surrendered to His Majesty's "imperial yoke."

Ajaw Kan Ek' replied that he had never recognized a higher lord or imagined who that might be. However, he recalled, in what must have been a remarkable formal speech, that "five or six years ago those from Tabasco, coming there from their land, had told him that a captain with certain people of our nation had passed through there and that they [the foreigners] had defeated them three times in battle, and that later they had told them that they had to be vassals of a great lord, and all that which I had now told him; that I should tell him if it was the same lord."[24]

Cortés, perhaps stunned by this revelation, responded

> that I was the captain that those of Tabasco had told him had passed through their land and with whom they had fought. So that he would believe this to be true, he should be informed by that interpreter with whom he was speaking, who is Marina, whom I always have taken with me, because there they had given her to me along with twenty women. She spoke to him and verified it, also how I had taken Mexico, and she told him of all the lands that I hold subject and placed under the dominion of Your Majesty. He appeared to be very pleased in knowing it and said that he wished to be Your Majesty's subject and vassal and that he would consider himself fortunate to be [the subject and vassal] of such a great lord as I had told him Your Highness is.[25]

The ruler's agreeable response, if this is what he said, was probably a stalling action designed to please this dangerous enemy and convince him to continue his journey as quickly as possible. Or, as some in Cortés's party suspected, he may have been attempting with sweet words to lure Cortés to Nojpeten so that the Itzas could murder him and his bodyguards, leaving the expedition leaderless and vulnerable to attack.

Once these posturing speeches had ended, Ajaw Kan Ek' ordered his attendants to bring him birds, honey, "a little gold," and red spondylus shell necklaces,[26] which he presented to Cortés, who then reciprocated with unspecified objects. Over a meal hosted by the Spaniards they discussed the purpose and route of Cortés's expedition. Ajaw Kan Ek' was aware of the Spaniards on the seacoast, for he had received news about them from "vassals" working in cacao orchards located near where they were said to be and from merchants who traveled daily between Nojpeten and the coast. He offered to provide a guide for Cortés but warned that the road ahead was rough and mountainous, suggesting that Cortés instead take a shorter route to the sea and then proceed in ships. By now the rest of the huge party must have begun arriving at the western arm of the lake, because Cortés responded that Ajaw Kan Ek' "had already seen that due to the large number of people I had with me and due to the equipment and horses, ships would not suffice and I was forced to go by land." Cortés "entreated" him to allow him to move the expedition across the lake, to which Ajaw Kan Ek' agreed, saying that three leagues farther along the lake the road became drier and that the road leading south began at a point opposite the main island.

Ajaw Kan Ek' then "entreated me much that now that my people had to go to the other side [of the arm of the lake], I should go with him in the canoes to see his town and his house, and that he wished me to see the idols burned and that I make a cross for him." Cortés's officers objected strongly to the proposal, but "in order to please him," Cortés agreed, taking a bodyguard of twenty men, most of them crossbowmen.[27] Although the Spaniards spent the rest of the day on Nojpeten, Cortés unfortunately left no description of what he saw and learned there. Díaz recalled only that the Itzas fed them and gave them some "low-grade gold of little value." The Spaniards left Nojpeten near nightfall with the guide provided by Ajaw Kan Ek', spending the night on the mainland just south of Nojpeten. By now most of the rest of the weary expedition had crossed the lake and reached the area where Cortés slept.

CORTÉS'S LAME HORSE

It was at this camping place that Cortés performed a simple act that would grow into one of the most enduring legends about the first Itza-Spanish encounter, a legend that deeply affected later colonial encounters between Itzas and Spaniards and survives to this day among the Itzas and ladinos of the region. Cortés wrote, "In this town, that is, in those cultivations, there stayed behind a horse whose hoof had been pierced by a stick and who could not walk. The lord promised to cure it. I do not know what he will do." Díaz's version differed somewhat. After Cortés returned from his day at Nojpeten, "he ordered us to leave in that town a reddish-black horse that had taken sick as a result of the deer hunt [earlier in Kejach territory] and whose body fat had been wasted and could not be kept."[28]

According to some Spanish versions of the legend, this horse, the first possessed by the Itzas, soon died and was elevated to the status of an "idol" made of wood or of lime and stone in the animal's shape.[29] One version of this "idol" was finally destroyed by an impetuous Franciscan friar in 1618, setting off a string of violent acts against Spaniards by the angered Itzas. According to Spaniards who occupied Nojpeten in 1697, a leg bone of the horse occupied a position over an altar. Modern versions of the legend make no mention of an "idol" or remains of the horse having been installed at Nojpeten but instead recount that a stone statue of the horse was made on the mainland and fell into the water when the canoe carrying it capsized in a sudden wind.[30] All versions, however, suggest that the horse endured as a significant historical referent.

Six members of the expedition stayed behind at Nojpeten. A black man and two natives, possibly Mexicas from Tenochtitlan–Mexico City, deserted the Spaniards. The other three were Spaniards, exhausted from three days without rest, who "preferred to remain among enemies than to come with us, given so much hardship."[31] The fate of these six is unknown, but the Itzas would have found them to be invaluable sources of information about the newcomers.

THE EXPEDITION DEPARTS

The expedition began to move the next day, without additional food supplies from the Itzas. As they began the journey, Díaz and probably many others were suffering from fevers and heat exhaustion. Their precipitous departure, according to Díaz, was caused by shortages of maize so severe that they marched night and day for three days in constant heavy rain before stopping. The rainy season had begun, and torrential downpours plagued them for the rest of the trip. They had procured their last food supplies from maize fields near the first Itza town, two days north of the main lake; by now these were nearly exhausted. Although both chroniclers frequently mention "cultivations" around the lake, these were apparently of no use as food; they may have been cotton or food crops only recently planted.[32] Cortés presumably requested food supplies from Ajaw Kan Ek', who likely refused in hope that the expedition would starve.

Cortés, who wrote in detail about the party's subsequent experiences, reported that after traveling for two leagues they came upon a savannah with many deer. They speared eight or ten of them from horseback, but the horses were by now so fatigued that two died from the exertion, and others became gravely ill. Eight "long" leagues further they reached the first major town, Chekan, in the vicinity of present-day Santa Ana Vieja. The "señor" of the town was named AjMojan.[33]

Although AjMojan refused to visit the Spaniards, the expedition somehow obtained enough food at Chekan to sustain itself for six days of travel through what the guides said would be uninhabited territory. After passing six leagues beyond Chekan the party found on a river a small settlement also said to belong to AjMojan—a place where traders stopped off to sell goods, presumably intended for transshipment to Nojpeten.[34] Within another twenty leagues or so they passed two additional hamlets, again said to belong to AjMojan. Cortés learned from his guides and the chief leader of the second hamlet, who later escaped with his wife and a son, that at this point the expedition would have to cross an unpopulated stretch of steep hills—the southern section of the Maya Mountains. On the other side they would find a settlement belonging to Ajaw Kan Ek', called Tenkis by Cortés.

By now it was clear that the entire region between Lago Petén Itzá and the far side of the Maya Mountains was controlled by the principal Itza ruler, Ajaw Kan Ek', and the Itza territorial ruler AjMojan. Cortés and Díaz reported no signs of political or territorial competition here, unlike the case in the highly fortified Kejach region north of the Itzas. On the other hand, the territory through which they traveled was only lightly populated, a circumstance that made their search for food almost fruitless.

The journey across the eight-league pass of the southern Maya Mountains took twelve days in constant rain; sixty-eight horses died and many others were injured. If there were human deaths from exposure and starvation, neither Cortés nor Díaz recorded them. Finally they reached the Sarstoon River, where they had to construct a log ford to cross the swollen waters upstream from Gracias a Dios Falls. They found Tenkis one league beyond the river on the day before Easter, April 15, 1525. Díaz led an expedition not far up the Sarstoon to a much larger settlement with ample food supplies. He called this place TajItza (Taiça), indicating that it was inhabited or controlled by the Itzas.[35] Now in Chol-speaking territory dominated by the Itzas, they eventually reached the shores of Lago de Izabal, where they found one group of the Spaniards for whom they were searching.

The Spaniards encountered Chols who were part of a province with their own "ruler" for some distance south of the Sarstoon River, and other Chols occupied the region all the way to Río Dulce and Bahía de Amatique.[36] He also found a number of Akalan traders in the vicinity who had been attacked and robbed by the Spaniards who occupied Nito, where they had their own residential ward; one of these Akalans was a brother of PaxB'olon Acha, the ruler of Itzam K'anak.

The rest of Cortés's tale need not detain us. The indefatigable explorer managed to found two new villas on the coast (Trujillo and La Natividad de Nuestra Señora) and draw up civic codes to govern them. He returned to Mexico City via Cuba in April 1526, and in September the remnants of the original expedition also appeared there — only eighty Spanish soldiers and probably not more than about two hundred of the approximately three thousand Mexicas and other indigenous people who had been forced to leave their homelands two years earlier.[37]

Subsequent Sixteenth-Century Reports on the Itzas

For nearly a century following Cortés's *entrada*, little is heard about the Itzas from Spanish sources. By the mid-sixteenth century, missionary and military efforts from Guatemala and Yucatán began increasingly to affect surrounding groups, but the Itzas were protected by distance, the density of the lowland tropical forests, and a reputation for ferocity that became legendary. The earliest conquest and pacification efforts indirectly affecting the Itzas focused primarily on the Caribbean coast and along the rivers flowing from Petén through Belize. The first of these efforts took place in 1528, when the *adelantado* Francisco de Montejo and his lieutenant, Alonso Dávila, set off by sea and land down the east coast of Yucatán in search of a location for a permanent Spanish settlement in the area. They reached the coastal town of Chetumal, whose inhabitants they confronted in a battle supposedly led on the Maya side by Gonzalo Guerrero, the shipwrecked mariner who had joined forces with the Mayas.[38] Plans to establish a Spanish settlement in the Chetumal area were postponed until 1531, when Dávila and his troops attempted to pacify the Waymil and Chetumal provinces and to establish a villa at Chetumal itself. His attempts were ultimately unsuccessful, and after about a year he was forced by Maya opposition to abandon his new town of Villa Real.[39]

Eleven years later, in late 1543 or early 1544, after the establishment of the city of Mérida and the northern villas of Campeche and Valladolid, Melchor and Alonso Pacheco set out to conquer regions to the south. Theirs was the most notoriously cruel and vicious conquest in the history of Yucatán, far more ambitious in scope than once supposed. Near the mouth of Río Hondo they established the new villa of Salamanca de Bacalar.[40] The Pachecos reached all the way to southernmost Belize, and it is likely that they conquered and "reduced" (that is, congregated into missions) people in the area around Tipuj. Although probably always a **39** relatively small settlement, Tipuj was the center of the native province known as Tz'ul Winikob', which incorporated the larger region drained by the Belize and New Rivers.

The Pachecos established a small number of cacao-producing encomiendas along the rivers of northern Belize, around Salamanca de Bacalar, and on the Belize River as far inland as Tipuj. These encomiendas were never easy to administer, and rebellions broke out in the region as early as 1547. In 1567 and 1568 Salamanca de Bacalar was said to be virtually under siege by hostile Mayas who carried away Maya men and women living around the villa, and several pacification entradas were carried out during those years by Lieutenant Governor Juan Garzón. One of these entradas resulted in the reconquest of Tipuj, which was in the center of a particularly rebellious, apostate territory.[41]

The conquest of Tz'ul Winikob', Waymil, and Chetumal destroyed and displaced centers of Maya leadership. It also dispersed the indigenous population, initiating a pattern of flight to less controlled areas and to neighboring regions controlled by unconquered Maya groups. The conquest enabled the establishment of encomiendas for the purpose of tribute collection and the formation of missions (*visitas*) visited only occasionally by priests from Bacalar. And the establishment of the colonial outpost at Bacalar resulted in the occasional forced resettlement of hostile and runaway groups nearer the villa itself. The Mayas responded not only by fleeing to more remote regions (and welcoming in their midst runaways from northern Yucatán) but also by organizing periodic rebellions.

By the end of the sixteenth century the vast southeastern frontier was administered from a villa, Bacalar, that was nothing more than a poor outpost probably earning more in contraband coastal trading than in rents from the Maya population. The Maya towns in Belize had no permanent Spanish residents, but they were a major attraction for native refugees fleeing the north. The townspeople engaged in a lively underground trade in cacao, forest products, metal tools, and cotton cloth that bypassed Spanish controls but required contact with the Itzas and other regional groups. There was also trade in pottery "idols" and a continuously active non-Christian ritual system that drew together the various frontier Mayas and their brethren from the north.[42]

Efforts to put a stop to such pagan activities in remote quarters were all but ineffective throughout the sixteenth century. By the seventeenth century conditions on the encomiendas of northern Yucatán had worsened, owing to the increasing burden of extortion by illegal *repartimientos* (forced labor contracts for the production of goods), which sent even more Mayas fleeing into the southern forests. These people joined not only established encomienda towns such as Tipuj but also numerous independent frontier Maya polities under the control of charismatic priests and other Maya leaders. Incessant Spanish incursions into these regions to recapture runaways were only temporary plugs in the leaking dam, and encomenderos grew alarmed by significant losses of population. Bureaucrats and military men saw only one solution: the ultimate destruction of Nojpeten and the conquest of the Itzas, whom they viewed as the ideological inspiration and political-military instigators of the entire frontier crisis. So long as the Itzas remained free from Spanish control, the drain on Yucatán's labor resources would continue unabated.[43]

Between 1573 and 1580 several expeditions from Yucatán set off from southeastern Tabasco for Itza territory itself, but none managed to reach Nojpeten. The principal players in these entradas were Feliciano Bravo, the chief government clerk of Yucatán, and Fray Pedro Lorenzo, a Dominican stationed at the Chontal-speaking mission town of Palenque, west of Río Usumacinta. Upon Lorenzo's urging, the governor of Yucatán, Diego de Santillán, named Bravo to head a force accompanying Lorenzo into the eastern interior forests in order to "reduce" pagan populations that had been terrorizing the Tabasco frontier missions. These people were said to live eight days from Palenque, "in the district of Tayça and Tachis."[44]

The 1573 entrada by Bravo and Lorenzo began at Tenosique on Río Usumacinta and then traveled overland to "Río de Tachis," identified as Río San Pedro Mártir, which they followed upstream by canoe for five days. At a "bay where the river widened out" they saw smoke from a nearby settlement, but they failed to find any native inhabitants and turned back to Tenosique. It appears that they had reached a point quite close to Itza territory.[45] It was said that certain pagan natives who lived on an island in a lake "a short distance further in" regularly visited the river, where they had a small temple of "idols." They had recently massacred nearly twenty natives from Pochutla and Lakandon territory who had entered their lands armed but apparently intending no aggression.[46]

In 1579 Governor Guillén de las Casas ordered a second expedition into the same area, renewing Bravo's original commission to head the entrada. Testimony taken a few months earlier from a Maya from Jokab'a, one Pedro Uk, indicated that Uk had gone to Nojpeten when he was a boy. Uk reported that the town had "a population of about two thousand Indians who dwell in houses of the said place. Each Indian does not have his own house, but many live together in each one of the said houses; and they do not have any stronghold or fortress. . . . The said Indians were agreed that they would receive them [the Spaniards] in peace if they wished

41

to have it, and if they saw and understood that they were not going to do them harm; but if they perceived the contrary, and that they wished to make war upon them, they had decided to wage it with them."[47]

The second expedition, which Fray Pedro Lorenzo also accompanied, left Tenosique in 1580, following the same route as the earlier one. Far up Río San Pedro Mártir they encountered blockades preventing further passage and signs of habitation and cultivation. Scouts who traveled onward by foot reported seeing the Itzas' island from a hill about four leagues away (one league equals about four kilometers), describing it as "a peñol [a rocky hill] in a lake at the foot of three sierras which surround it."[48] Their vantage point had to have been somewhere above the main port at Ensenada de San Jerónimo, where the hills are almost precisely four leagues from Nojpeten. This expedition, too, turned back to Tenosique without contacting the Itzas, fearing attack if they were not better armed. Bravo made plans for one last entrada in 1582, which he intended to pursue through Kejach territory in southwestern Yucatán. Apparently he never carried out his intentions.

In 1591 the *alcalde mayor* of Tabasco, Nuño de Chávez Figueroa, informed the Council of the Indies that a secular priest from the *partido,* or district, of Usumacinta — presumably Tenosique — had recently made contact with unconverted Indians "whose residence is called Tayza, which is bounded by this province and those of Verapaz and Chiapa." Figueroa claimed that he had subsequently captured eight hundred persons from a location ten days away from Tenosique, but whether these were Itzas is not clear. Royal cédulas issued the next year approved the peaceful reduction of the region, but the outcome was never reported.[49]

Although none of these later sixteenth-century expeditions had any military impact on the Itzas, such periodic activities along the edges of Itza territory could not have gone unnoticed or been ignored by the inhabitants of central Petén. In the years immediately following, between 1604 and 1606, Franciscan missionaries carried out several *reducciones* among fugitive Yucatec Mayas living in southwestern Yucatán (today southern Campeche), and even in Kejach territory. One Franciscan established a mission as far south as Tzuktok', and another established a particularly remote mission at Sakalum, southwest of Bacalar. Royal decrees issued in 1599 and 1601, however, had banned military and religious entradas farther into the native interior. None of the missions established during this period lasted long, and the inhabitants of the Campeche missions were ultimately moved to Sajkab'ch'en, south of the villa of Campeche, where they served as laborers in logwood enterprises.[50]

42

Seventeeth-Century Itza-Spanish Relations

In 1616 or 1617 a remarkable event occurred on the eve of K'atun 3 Ajaw, which was to begin in 1618. A Franciscan, Fray Juan de Orbita, who had arrived in Yucatán in 1615, set out with a companion for Nojpeten with the apparent intention of convincing the Itza ruler, Ajaw Kan Ek', that the time was at hand to succumb to Spanish rule. His success was such that the two priests took back to Mérida some 150 Itzas from Nojpeten. These people reportedly offered their submission to the Crown, and some of them were appointed as native town council officials by the governor, who gave alcaldes' staffs to the principals.[51] One of these Itzas, probably the leader of the group, was identified as Ajaw Puk, who by his title, Ajaw, must have been one of the four principal territorial rulers of the Itzas.[52] This was clearly a high-ranking delegation on a diplomatic mission of great importance.

The Itza delegation soon returned to Nojpeten, and Orbita initiated plans to return there as well, in order to follow up on their promises. In 1618 he set out from Mérida on his second journey, with another companion, Fray Bartolomé de Fuensalida, who served as the mission's commissary.[53] This time they went through Tipuj, the last nominally Christian Maya town on the way from Bacalar to Nojpeten. Tipuj's 340 souls were by now predominantly Yucatec-speaking Mayas, largely immigrants seeking relief from encomienda conditions in northern Yucatán.[54] An important town leader named Francisco Kumux, who claimed to be a descendant of the lord of Cozumel, offered to go to Nojpeten with a delegation of Tipujans in order to carry a letter to Ajaw Kan Ek' from Fuensalida, in which Fuensalida announced his desire to visit the Itza capital. Kumux returned with two Itza "captains" and more than twenty other Itza soldiers carrying lances and bows and arrows. One of the captains was none other than Ajaw Puk, who had visited Mérida with Orbita a year or two earlier; the other was one AjChata P'ol.

The Itza visitors explained that they were heavily armed against attack by the people called Chinamitas, with whom they were at war. After some delays, the Itzas accompanied Fuensalida and Orbita all the way to a port town known as Chaltunja at the eastern end of Lago Petén Itza.[55] One of the Tipujans, don Diego K'etzal, agreed to go to Nojpeten by canoe in order to announce their arrival. After eight anxious days he returned with the same two Itza "captains" — Ajaw Puk and AjChata P'ol — who had visited the priests at Tipuj. They brought with them four large canoes to ferry the entire party to Nojpeten.

43

Shortly after arriving at the Itza capital, Fuensalida delivered an impassioned sermon to Ajaw Kan Ek' and other Itza "principales" on the power of the gospel, to which they responded to the effect "that it was not time to be Christians (they had their own beliefs as to what should be) and that they should go back where they had come from; they could come back another time, but right then they did not want to be Christians."[56] At this point, according to the account, the priests were taken on a tour of the island town, during which Orbita became enraged upon seeing in a temple a statue representing the horse left by Cortés. Orbita climbed onto the statue — which Fuensalida said they called Tzimin Chak ("Horse of Thunder") — and broke it to pieces with a stone.[57]

This action, understandably, enraged some of the Itza hosts, who cried out with threats to kill the priests. Fuensalida claimed to have calmed them with another sermon, and the next day Ajaw Kan Ek' treated them courteously even while they continued to argue that the Itzas should accept Christianity. They reminded him of the supposed promise made to Cortés by a former Ajaw Kan Ek', who Fuensalida said was the present ruler's father, that he would honor the Spanish king and become a Christian.[58] Ajaw Kan Ek' repeated that "the time had not arrived in which their ancient priests had prophesied that they would have to give up the worship of their gods, for the age in which they were at the present time was that which they call *oxahau* (which means third age) and the one that had been indicated to them was not approaching so soon."[59] The reference to "the present time" was, of course, to K'atun 3 Ajaw; the future k'atun may have been K'atun 8 Ajaw, which would not begin until 1697.

The remaining several days of the priests' visit were uneventful, and when they left, certain Itzas presented them with gifts of elaborate, multicolored cloth, "statues of idols," and "many stones." Their departure across the lake, however, was marred by threats from armed and blackened warriors in canoes who warned them never to return.

Undaunted by these warnings or by the subsequent discovery of widespread "idolatry" at Tipuj, Fuensalida and Orbita returned to Nojpeten in 1619 and found Ajaw Kan Ek' receptive to new overtures. He even agreed to accept a remarkable set of terms offered by Governor Antonio de Figueroa in which the Itza ruler would retain his governing powers, but over a council that would be like the native town councils (*repúblicas de indios*) of Yucatán. His descendants could inherit the *cacicazgo,* as the agreement called the rule that he would exercise, and one of them would serve as his lieutenant. The Itzas would pay no tribute for a period of ten years, after which the amount would be moderate. Ajaw Kan Ek' even ordered that a cross be set up next to his house, agreed to order the abandonment of "idolatry" in favor of Christian practices, and named officials to assist the priests with religious matters.[60]

In short order, however, factions opposed to Ajaw Kan Ek' spoke out against such activities. Fuensalida blamed the ruler's wife for listening to certain "wicked priests" who wanted the friars expelled from the island and for then convincing her husband to agree to their demands. If he did not do so, his enemies — presumably relatives of his wife — would force him "to flee with his family, going with one of his captains named Nakom P'ol, because they did not wish to be Christians." (Nakom P'ol was the same person earlier called AjChata P'ol, who had visited the priests at Tipuj.) The ruler did not oppose their demands, and armed Itzas used harsh force in making the priests leave. After returning to Tipuj they decided that their efforts had been in vain and returned to Yucatán.[61]

As early as Orbita's first visit to Nojpeten in 1616 or 1617 Ajaw Kan Ek' himself had apparently agreed to spearhead a Christianization movement and to accept nominal Spanish rule with himself as cacique of a bitterly divided Itza kingdom. On the second Franciscan visit in 1618 he seemed to have reconsidered the matter, now claiming that the k'atun prophecies did not favor such a radical shift in Itza history. Why he changed his mind yet again in 1619, agreeing to a detailed set of agreements with the colonial government, cannot be ascertained. Whatever his reasons may have been, the friars soon learned that Ajaw Kan Ek' did not speak for all ruling officials, among whom opposition to colonial treaties and Christian priests was violent and insistent.

Parallels between this situation and that described in later chapters — that is, the political factionalism that characterized Itza society just before the 1697 conquest — are strong. During the later period the factionalism was over intrafamilial succession to the Itza rulership that turned brother against brother in a struggle against the ruler's acceding to Spanish demands. Although we cannot confirm that such struggles characterized the early years of K'atun 3 Ajaw as they did the eve of K'atun 8 Ajaw, these remarkable historical parallels suggest that they did.

THE 1624 MASSACRE AT SAKALUM

At the end of January 1624, only five years after Orbita and Fuensalida's second unsuccessful mission to Nojpeten, rebel Mayas at the frontier town of Sakalum, a short distance west of Bacalar, murdered ten or eleven Spaniards and an unrecorded number of accompanying Mayas under the command of Captain Francisco de Mirones y Lezcano. Mirones's party was part of a beleaguered group of soldiers and fellow travelers on an overambitious mission to conquer Nojpeten and pacify the entire region between there and the towns of the partido of Sierra—a region peppered with localized charismatic religious movements under Maya leaders.

These events began in 1621 when Fray Diego Delgado entered the forest as far south as Jop'elch'en, on the road to an infamous region of rebels and runaways known as La Pimienta, west of Salamanca de Bacalar.[62] At Jop'elch'en he created a full reduction town, returning to Mérida by early 1622. By March 19 he was named to accompany a military entrada with aims to conquer the Itzas. It was to be led by the same Mirones y Lezcano who for several years had been a military officer defending the northern coast of Yucatán, where he also held the notorious title of *juez de grana,* or overseer of cochineal production. Governor Diego de Cárdenas had approached Mirones in 1621 with a plan for the armed conquest of the Itzas, apparently from a base at Jop'elch'en, or possibly from one at Sakalum, a mission in the Pimienta region. Mirones agreed to the plan, which was promptly submitted to the Council of the Indies.

Mirones wrote that he had learned of the existence of non-Christian native provinces to which fugitive Mayas and "wrongdoers" from the settled provinces had fled. The inhabitants of these remote provinces, he understood, included not only the Itza "barbarians" but also various "baptized runaways" from Yucatán and their descendants. These peoples collectively exerted a negative influence on the "natives of these provinces," owing to their proximity to them. He noted the recent visits by Fuensalida and Orbita to Nojpeten, claiming that their successes included saying mass, preaching, destroying and burning idols, and convincing various Itzas to convert to Christianity (this last claim was not made by Fuensalida himself). Once such conversion was sworn to, Mirones argued, the Itzas became rebels against the Crown, which then had the right to conquer or pacify them by any means necessary.

Mirones's venture, which also promised to open a road through Itza territory all the way to Guatemala, began in March 1622 with twenty Spanish soldiers and eighty Mayas recruited from the Sierra towns. More Mayas were recruited by his agents, but desertions left him with only a handful by the time he reached his destination. He took sworn testimonies all along the way, especially at Jop'elch'en, seeking to learn what he could expect to find at a place called IxPimienta, where he apparently intended to establish a base from which he would prepare for the final attack on Nojpeten. From this testimony he learned that Jop'elch'en had been founded by fugitives some sixty years earlier. Fugitives continued to arrive there, primarily in small family groups from the region around Jekelchak'an, north of Campeche. Contact between IxPimienta and towns in northern Yucatán was active, mediated by trade in wax and copal from the inner forests in exchange for knives, machetes, and salt. Marriages between the frontier and encomienda towns such as Jekelchak'an were frequent.

Mirones and Delgado entered IxPimienta with a small number of troops on Friday, May 6, and were "received surrounded by Indian men and women carrying palms in their hands and [having placed] a cross at the entrance of the town, before which we all knelt and gave thanks." Baptisms of children began immediately, and the church and the priest's house were completed in three days. Over the next several weeks the Spaniards forced inhabitants of neighboring settlements to move to IxPimienta. This town was an important center of Maya religious activity, administered by four priests designated as AjK'in ("priest") or B'ob'at ("prophet"). These men wore Spanish-style priestly vestments and were apparently in control of the receipt and distribution of trade goods. Emissaries from the town wore long hair and traveled all the way to Jekelchak'an, near Campeche, to visit their wives there.

Sometime over the next months Mirones decided to move headquarters to a place called Sakalum, a short distance farther along the proposed road to Nojpeten. While awaiting the arrival of military reinforcements at Sakalum for the rest of the year, he carried out illegal forced trade with local inhabitants, behavior that was challenged by Fray Delgado. Later that year Delgado left for Tipuj, taking his Yucatec Maya assistants with him. Learning of this, Mirones sent twelve soldiers to accompany him to Tipuj, where Delgado sent a message to the Itzas via don Cristóbal Na, the cacique of Tipuj, who had accompanied Fuensalida and Orbita to Nojpeten in 1618. The Itzas granted Delgado permission to visit them with the twelve soldiers, and Na recruited eighty Tipujans to accompany the party.

The Itzas fell on their Spanish and Maya visitors as soon as they arrived at Nojpeten. First they killed all of the party except Delgado, reportedly offering the victims' hearts to their "idols" and nailing their heads to stakes on a hill in view of the town. The unidentified source for the account of these events claimed that they then told Delgado that he was being killed in retribution for Fuensalida's having taken Itza "idols" back to Mérida with him on his first visit. Delgado's heart was removed and

47

offered to the idols, even as he continued preaching to them. They cut his body into pieces and put his head on a stake with the others. Don Cristóbal Na of Tipuj was among those killed.

Mirones had meanwhile sent a party of two Spaniards, his servant, Bernardino Ek', and other Mayas to check on Delgado and his party. These men learned of the massacre but went on to Nojpeten anyway, where they were manacled and locked in a palisaded corral or stockade. Ek' alone managed to escape, returning to Tipuj and then to Bacalar, where he told his story. The others were presumably killed. Alarmed by the news, Governor Cárdenas ordered that Ek' be sent to warn Mirones and that Captain Juan Bernardo Casanova march quickly to Sakalum with reinforcements from Mani in the Sierra district. Ek' arrived at Sakalum before Casanova, but Mirones did not believe him and had him tortured.

On about January 27, 1624, before Casanova's reinforcements arrived, a group of Mayas attacked the Spaniards while they were defenseless in church and proceeded to kill all of the Mayas who were loyal to them. The leader of the massacre was said to be one AjK'in P'ol. Testimony describing what Casanova's party discovered shortly after the massacre paints a grisly picture, but it appears to be genuine. Ten or eleven Spaniards, including Mirones, had been hanged and beheaded, and their bodies were burned. Mirones's chest had been opened and his heart removed. An unspecified number of Maya men and women had also been murdered but not beheaded. They found signs of ritual sacrifice, and the entire town was destroyed by fire. A letter in Maya, which has been preserved in Spanish translation, was found intact; it may be interpreted as a communication between leaders of the insurrection.

Rumors subsequently abounded that the perpetrators of the Sakalum massacre, together with inhabitants of the towns of the Sierra district, were plotting another attack against Spaniards on Holy Thursday. Over the next two months Casanova and another captain, Antonio Méndez de Canzo, stationed Spanish troops in Oxk'utzkab', Mani, and Tek'ax. Rewards were offered for anyone who could capture AjK'in P'ol, who was reputed to have been the principal leader behind the massacre and to have had a wide following throughout the Sierra towns.

Méndez de Canzo commissioned the Maya governor of Oxk'utzkab', don Fernando Kamal, and 150 Maya archers to track down AjK'in P'ol and his followers in the forests. Kamal's troops found P'ol and his followers with chalices and other silver from the Sakalum church as well as a silver-plated dagger and some clothing belonging to Mirones. The prisoners were dragged back to Méndez, who claimed to have tried them.

They testified to the events of the massacre, presumably under torture, but their account has survived only in summary form. They were then hanged, dragged through the streets, and drawn and quartered. Their heads were cut off and displayed in the plazas of the towns of the Sierra district.

Could AjK'in P'ol have been the Itza territorial ruler, priest, and military leader known as AjChata P'ol and Nakom P'ol, who had treated Fuensalida and Orbita with such courtesy in 1618 and 1619? Without the records of his trial, we cannot be certain. But because the Itzas had massacred two Spanish-Maya parties from Sakalum and Tipuj only a short time before the Sakalum massacre, it is plausible to suggest that the Itza political leadership had put up a massive armed effort to stop Mirones's entrada. This effort, if Spanish accounts are to be believed, included stirring up anti-Spanish sentiment not only in the Pimienta region but also in the encomienda towns of Sierra. Reports of underground Maya trade routes and the free movement of encomienda Mayas back and forth between the southern frontier and the northern towns suggest that Itza and Itza-allied spies could have easily penetrated regions under Spanish control. Such use of underground intelligence was reportedly the method by which Itzas effected a widespread rebellion in the Tz'ul Winikob' region only a few years after the Sakalum massacre, a subject to be taken up shortly.

ITZA-MOPAN ATTACKS ON MANCHE CHOL MISSIONS,
1631–32

Chols from "the province of the Manche" had first visited Dominican missionaries at Cobán in Verapaz as early as 1564, but not until 1604 did Fray Juan de Esguerra and Fray Salvador Cipriano manage to establish a mission at the town of Manche, not far from the town of Mopan on the southeastern fringes of Itza territory.[63] These missionaries had "reduced," or consolidated, six thousand people into nine new towns by 1606. By 1628 another Dominican, Fray Francisco Morán, had penetrated Mopan territory. According to him, the Itzas opposed these Dominican intrusions because Morán was working so close to their own territory. In response they began to harass the Chols, who proceeded to run away from the missions.[64]

In early 1631 the recently appointed alcalde mayor of Verapaz, Captain Martín Alfonso Tovilla, sought permission from the president of the Audiencia of Guatemala to send settlers from Santiago de Guatemala to establish a town in Manche Chol territory.[65] Its purpose was to stabilize the threatened "reduction" towns. On Easter Sunday in April the new settlers arrived at the Chol town called Yol, accompanied by Spanish troops, a battalion of native auxiliaries, and missionaries, including Morán. Finding that the inhabitants had fled, the troops burned the houses and destroyed the milpas — but only after rescuing as much maize as the native auxiliaries could carry. From Yol they moved on to Manche, where Tovilla formally established the new town on May 13, naming it Toro de Acuña in honor of the governor of his birthplace in Spain.

Tovilla extracted confessions under torture from some Yol prisoners, who admitted knowing where the runaways had gone to hide. Tovilla sent two of the prisoners to take the fugitives a message of amnesty, and on May 17 the Spaniards celebrated a fiesta and mass in honor of the town's new patroness, the Holy Virgin Mary of Cortés (a miraculous image in Alcaraz de la Mancha in Spain). That night, according to Tovilla, "we were surrounded by a thousand Indians from Ahiça [AjItza]." They were thwarted from attacking thanks to the divine intervention of the Virgin of Cortés and Tovilla's prior decision to set off a false alarm so that his sleepy guards would remain alert.

On the next day an "Indian," presumably Chol, arrived in town carrying bows, arrows, and other objects that he claimed had been dropped by the Itzas the night before. Placing the women, children, and older people under guard in the church, Tovilla set off with soldiers and native archers in search of signs of the would-be attackers. Only a short distance from the town they found bows, arrows, and quivers. Further into the forest they discovered the Itzas' deserted encampment, where they found "mats made of the bark of trees that they carried in order to cover themselves, bows, arrows, maize, toasted maize meal [*pinol*], tortillas, tamales, cords for tying up the Indians, squashes *de piciete,* deerskins, wood ear plugs — they had left everything."[66] They also discovered "an altar placed under an arbor and the clothing of their priest and three large idols, one the head of a pig [peccary?], the other of an alligator, and another a bear [anteater?] covered with copal, and many incense burners which they were using to cense them. And there were many other little idols made of wood. In addition there were left behind two lances topped with some knives and with many feathers of different colors in place of tassels, and a strong and well-made shield for [protection against] arrows."[67] They followed the Itzas' path all day before spying their encampment, which Tovilla estimated to hold eight hundred persons. Fearing attack, he ordered a retreat back to Manche without confronting the enemy.

The local Chols claimed that some of them had run away earlier out of fear of the Itzas, who attacked them frequently — most recently in 1630, when the attackers kidnapped more than one hundred of them.[68] Another source claims that in that year the Itzas captured more than three hundred Chols, raping the women, killing the leaders, and cannibalizing the body of the principal Chol cacique, don Martín Kuk. Itzas also killed the missionary Fray Jacinto de San Ildefonso. The result, according to this source, was a general uprising throughout Manche Chol territory—the precipitating factor behind Tovilla's effort to repacify Chol territory in 1631.[69]

Tovilla likened the thwarted attack on Manche to what had happened to Mirones at Sakalum seven years earlier.[70] His knowledge of the Sakalum massacre suggests that he already feared Itza attacks in Chol territory and that he *assumed* that the potential attackers were Itzas in the absence of confirming evidence. Part of a later description he wrote of Manche Chol ritual paraphernalia is almost identical to that just quoted describing the abandoned "Itza" objects. This similarity led France V. Scholes and Eleanor Adams to suspect that Tovilla's descriptions were manufactured.[71] Although they may have been in part fabricated, it seems likely that the main events actually occurred.

Rumors of possible Itza attacks continued to circulate in Guatemala. Most of the settlers soon abandoned Toro de Acuña. Recent captives of the Itzas reported that the Itzas were planning an attack on the Manche Chol town. Later reports indicated that they had also attacked other Chol towns, with the assistance of "apostates" from Mopan.[72] In October Tovilla announced that he planned to enlist a large number of native archers and carriers in order to conquer the Itzas, but the project was suspended pending royal approval and was never revived.[73]

Toward the end of 1631 the missionary Morán led twelve Spaniards to the now apostate town of Mopan, where they found only the cacique and some women. The Spaniards killed the cacique and captured forty women, whom they took to Toro de Acuña. Three nights later the Spanish kidnappers were attacked there by Mopans, who freed twenty of the women. The Spaniards' native auxiliaries fled in fear, as did the inhabitants of several nearby Chol towns. Morán and the remaining settlers abandoned Toro de Acuña in fear of further attacks.[74]

In 1632, then president Diego de Acuña sent Tovilla back to Chol territory with a squadron of twenty soldiers in order to assist Morán in renewed efforts to entice the Chols back to the mission. According to Ximénez, Morán succeeded in bringing back, apparently to Toro de Acuña, not only those who had fled the Mopan attacks the previous year but also a number of others. At some point in 1632, however, "the enemy" (by implication the Itzas) recruited more than one thousand natives, presumably Mopans, who attacked the town, killing two Spaniards and a

51

number of Chols and carrying off other Chols as prisoners. Now emboldened, these "godless gentiles" organized yet another attack on the town at
dawn during Lent in 1633. The number of attackers, reported as more
than three thousand, may have been exaggerated. In any case, Morán and
his troops managed to escape with their lives, abandoning their weapons
and hiding in trees. Although details are sketchy, we are told that the Itzas
and their allies set fire to the town, carrying off what was in the church and
the convent and as many Chols as they could capture.[75] When Fray Gabriel de Salazar returned to the area in 1637 he found no sign whatsoever
of any surviving Chols; they had evaporated into the forests.[76]

The events surrounding the Toro de Acuña affair are consistent with
previous accounts of Itza military behavior along their far-flung frontiers.
As early as 1525 Itzas had attacked Kejach towns to their north, apparently
in order to prevent the Kejaches from supporting Cortés's expedition. The
1624 Sakalum massacre was apparently an Itza-sponsored effort to eliminate reduction activities on the northeastern frontier of Itza influence. In
the case of the 1631–33 events in Manche Chol territory, Itzas forced
Spanish withdrawal from reduction communities by terrorizing the local
indigenous populations and, in the end, using Mopan auxiliaries to assist
them. As we shall see in later chapters, the Itzas at the end of the century
would use similar techniques, attacking and kidnapping residents of mission reduction towns along the camino real, in their defense of Nojpeten.

ITZA-SUPPORTED REBELLION IN TZ'UL WINIKOB',
1630–41

Signs of disturbance in Tz'ul Winikob' appeared in 1630, when the Mayas
of two Belize towns deserted their homes and fled to the forest with the
bells and ornaments of their churches. In mid-1638 there were reports of
mass desertions from the interior towns, particularly at Tipuj. By September the inhabitants of several coastal villages had also fled to the forests,
claiming that the Tipujans had sent prophetic messages to them: "[T]hey
were to give obedience to their king and wished them to abandon their
town, saying that if they did not do so all would die and be finished,
because at such a time the Itzas would come to kill them and there would
be great mortalities and hurricanes that would flood the land."[77]

A few runaways were captured and resettled around Bacalar, but most
of them were eventually resettled around Tipuj. One contemporaneous
writer claimed that they had been "encouraged and deceived by those
barbarous infidels of the Tah Itzas, becoming one with them, as a result of
which Bacalar will become more deserted and short of people."[78] Writing

later of these events, López de Cogolludo claimed that the rebels had "completely refused to obey God and the king, horribly rejecting our holy faith. . . . They desecrated the images and burned the temples consecrated to the Divine Majesty and then their towns, and then they fled to the forests."[79] A recent confirmation of this claim was the archaeological discovery of a non-Christian offering within the walls of the nave of the church at Tipuj. The offering was stylistically similar to one of the offerings discovered in a Maya ceremonial complex only a stone's throw from this church.[80]

In 1641 Fuensalida was sent to Bacalar, accompanied by three other Franciscans, to attempt to reconvert the rebels.[81] The centerpiece of their effort was a futile attempt by Fuensalida and two of his companions to recontact Tipuj, to which they sent messengers ahead with a letter. Along the way, the religious found towns burned and deserted from Lamanay to the Belize River.[82] They sent messengers ahead with a letter to be delivered at Tipuj, which they hoped to visit. As they neared the Belize River they saw "some busts like statues of men dressed like Spaniards at points on the road. Those [messengers] who had carried the letter had removed some idols that were next to the statues and had tossed them into the forest undergrowth. . . . The Indians who accompanied the religious said that from this they understood that the rebels had closed the road so that Spaniards would not pass and that their idols guarded the way and would stop and enchant those Spaniards who wished to pass there."[83] The rebels whom they saw were armed and had painted their bodies, and their hair was long in the style of non-Christian Indians.

In a town on the Belize River the friars witnessed what they considered idolatry and were humiliated by the destruction of their own saints' images and crucifix. At this town, far downstream from Tipuj, the friars were tied up, subjected to humiliating insults, and blamed for Orbita's destruction of the "idol" representing Cortés's horse. "They said, 'Let the governor come, let the king come, let the Spaniards come — we are here to fight them. Now go and let it be said. . . . ' Others threatened to kill him [Fuensalida] because among the Itzas he and Father Orbita had broken the idol Tzimin Chac . . . thereby, they said, killing their god — upon which it was understood that Itza Indians were mixed in among them."[84]

Earlier indications of Itza inspirations for this movement were thus fully confirmed. Although willingly awaiting martyrdom, the religious and their Maya companions from Bacalar were not harmed but were sent running for their lives back to Bacalar, their ignominious departure accompanied by screams, whistles, and obscene gestures.[85]

53

Seventeenth-Century Itza Colonial Expansion

The foregoing events indicate that following the Franciscan friars' expulsion from Nojpeten in 1619 the Itzas pursued territorial expansion toward the northeast, east, and south of Lago Petén Itzá — the directions of principal Spanish threats to their territory. Their aim was to protect themselves by securing boundaries inhabited by indigenous groups who were already colonized by Spaniards or who were vulnerable to reduction. The following evidence, some of it circumstantial, provides further details of the methods by which the Itzas incorporated new territories along their expanding frontiers.

ITZA ROYAL FAMILIES AT TIPUJ

So far as we know, following Fuensalida's harrowing experiences in 1641 no Spaniards visited the former mission towns on the Belize River again until 1655. In that year the alcalde of Bacalar, Francisco Pérez, visited the village of Chunuk'um, where he compiled a *matrícula* (census) of people from Tipuj. Pérez had failed to reach Tipuj, claiming that passage beyond Chunuk'um, which was far downstream, was impossible. His failure to progress further was obviously due to fear of attack, for the Tipujans who visited him at Chunuk'um quickly answered his call for them to appear and presumably returned home without difficulty.

Of the 411 persons counted by Pérez, all but 30 bore Christian baptismal names. Three hundred fourteen were indicated to be residents of Tipuj, while the remaining 97 were identified by the names of nine other towns. These other towns had been widely distributed across Tz'ul Winikob' prior to the 1637 rebellion, and their inhabitants had obviously moved to Tipuj — or been taken there forcibly by rebel leaders — as part of a strategy to isolate the Mayas of Belize from Spanish control. These 411 people, who included 103 children, bore Yucatec patronyms identifying them as descendants of Mayas who had migrated from Yucatán to Tz'ul Winikob' over the past century. Even though priests had not visited Tipuj for many years, these people considered themselves sufficiently "Christian" to give their children Christian names.[86]

The thirty non-Christians, all said to be from Tipuj, were identified as "indios del monte," or "forest Indians." Their compound names indicate that they were Itzas, some of whom had intermarried with long-term Tipuj residents who bore Yucatec names (see Table 3.2). Furthermore, we can identify several of them as members of the royal Itza Kan lineage. One of the couples represented a marriage between an AjKan Chi and an IxEk'

Mas, each representing a royal name, Kan and Ek', whose combination in certain types of marriages (but not this one) produced the dynasty of Itza kings known by the double name Kan Ek'.

I had previously thought that these *indios del monte,* almost all of whom were women, had been "rounded up" by Christian Tipujans and were "an 'unconquered' population whose settlements had been raided by Tipujans for their women in response to a general surplus of males."[87] I now believe that they were elite Itza residents of Tipuj. Rather than having been taken to Chunuk'um by the "Christian" Tipujans, these Itzas were representatives of Nojpeten who had themselves taken the Itza-colonized population from Tipuj to Chunuk'um, allowing them to be counted there by the Spaniards. By doing so, they kept Pérez at bay, preventing him from nearing Tipuj while satisfying his desire to demonstrate to his superiors that Tipuj still bore some resemblance to a mission.[88]

As an epilogue to this phase of Tipuj's history, I should note that Tipujans and Spaniards reestablished contact in 1678, when Governor Antonio de Layseca Alvarado sent Sergeant Major Antonio de Porras on an entrada through the Bacalar region toward Tipuj. Nine leaders of the town visited Porras at Chaklol, a center of fugitive Mayas some ninety leagues beyond Jop'elch'en, offering their "obedience" and requesting missionaries. The outcome of this renewed contact, according to one source, was a new voluntary reduction of Tipuj and the baptism of six hundred persons there.[89] Robert Patch, however, has studied documents indicating that the entrada to Tipuj was a violent one in which more Mayas "were killed than were captured. Tipu was forced to sue for peace, and the expedition then withdrew."[90]

ITZA WARS TO THE EAST AND WEST

Although less well known, other accounts of Itza wars on their eastern and western frontiers have survived. They reinforce the conclusion that the Itzas used their military might to control neighboring native territories and thereby maintain buffers against potential Spanish attack. Two cases, one in the vicinity of Yalain on the Itzas' east and the other at Kanitzam on their west, demonstrate this continuing pattern of defensive militarism.

Yalain, the principal Itza town near the eastern end of Lago Petén Itza, was said to be the center of a region that produced foodstuffs for the inhabitants of Nojpeten.[91] AjChan, the sister's son of Ajaw Kan Ek' who in 1695 would serve as his uncle's emissary to Mérida, stated in 1698 that the people of Yalain were originally from Nojpeten "and that his parents had moved to the said settlement, where they have remained until now, in order to make milpa. It is a single and unique population that his father had subdued, and upon his death he [AjChan] succeeded him."[92] (Actually, AjChan's father, from whom he inherited his position as a local ruler, was originally from Tipuj, not Nojpeten; the elder Chan must have moved to NojPeten upon his marriage to the sister of Ajaw Kan Ek'.)[93] After the father's conquest of Yalain, the Chan family probably divided its time between Yalain and Nojpeten. AjChan's extremely close relations with Tipuj in 1695 indicate that his father probably had administrative authority of some sort far beyond the limits of Yalain on Laguneta Macanché. This authority, I suggest, had been legitimated by one or more wars, beginning in the 1630s, that resulted in the incorporation of the entire region from Yalain to Tipuj into the larger Itza political sphere.

In 1697 AjChan was only about thirty, and his father had apparently died only recently from a snakebite.[94] If the son had been born in Yalain, as he implies, then his father must have conquered that town sometime before 1667 but certainly not as early as the Itza-sponsored Tz'ul Winikob' rebellion of the 1630s. The elder AjChan may have been the son of Itza elites residing at Tipuj, perhaps of individuals involved in the Tz'ul Winikob' rebellion.[95]

AjChan did not identify the people whom his father had "subdued" at Yalain. They could have been renegade Itzas opposed to the royal family, or they could have been Kowojs or Mopans. Of these three possibilities, Kowojs would have been the most plausible objects of an Itza attack this close to the main lake. Hostilities between Kowojs and the allies of the Itza ruler were intense at this time and were probably rooted in much older enmities. AjChan later married the daughter of the principal Kowoj leader in what turned out to be only a brief symbol of Kowoj submission to Itza control over this territory. Kowojs attacked Itzas around Yalain on the eve of the 1697 conquest in what I believe was an effort on their part to regain territory lost in the earlier conflict.

It seems probable, if admittedly speculative, that the earlier Itza war over Yalain was fought in order to expel the Kowoj leadership from the area centered politically at Laguneta Macanché, a region perhaps encompassing most of the territory between the eastern end of the main lake and Lagunas Yaxhá and Sacnab. The result would have been the migration of large numbers of Kowoj followers from this region to the northern shore of Lago Petén Itzá, where most were residing in 1697. If this scenario is correct, the goal of such hostility on the part of the Itzas would have been to secure this important corridor to Tipuj and the Belize River from enemies who might have collaborated with Spaniards hoping to recapture

Tipuj and attack Nojpeten itself. The little-known Itza wars with Mopans during the period preceding the 1697 conquest, discussed in the previous chapter, must have been part of an even larger effort to reconsolidate Itza control over the Belize River valley itself.

Itza militarism on the kingdom's western frontier is less well documented than elsewhere, but one reported late incident deserves attention. It was the Crown chronicler Villagutierre, whose writings echoed Ursúa's claims that the bloodthirsty Itzas had to be conquered at any cost, who first published this account as one justification for the 1697 conquest. According to Villagutierre, as Alonso García de Paredes, Ursúa's captain general, was preparing to set out in 1695 on his first entrada into Kejach territory, reports arrived in Yucatán that "a large number of pagan Indians of the Itza nation, and Petenes" had earlier descended Río Usumacinta to Tabasco in a "large fleet of canoes," attacking and robbing towns. Villagutierre wrote that during a battle near the village of Kan Itzam, local defenders killed the leader of the Itza forces and some of the other attackers and put the rest to flight.[96]

Such "barbarian" atrocities, Villagutierre argued, served as a major stimulus to President Barrios of Guatemala to begin an entrada into Chol Lakandon territory. In fact, reports of the rumored Itza attack did not surface until after the occupation of Nojpeten in March 1697; only after that date were they utilized to defend Ursúa's actions at Lago Petén Itzá.

A largely Yucatec- or Itza-speaking town with a few Chontal speakers, Kanitzam had been founded by Franciscan missionaries in 1671, apparently as part of an unreported reduction in the Tenosique area.[97] Ursúa, probably the source for Villagutierre's description of the Itza attack, had written in 1698 simply that "four years ago [1694] a son-in-law of Canek went downstream to the Tabasco towns in canoes with a number of Itzas; they killed him in the district of the town of Anitzam, and that partido was terrorized."[98]

Later sources, probably fueled by legends reinforced in intensity during the intervening years, had turned the purported Itza attack on Kan Itzam into a ritual sacrifice replete with acts of cannibalism. Blas Felipe de Ripalda Ongay testified in July 1697 that "[despite] being so far from the towns of Tabasco all of the people on the peten [Nojpeten] knew the name of Andrés Tzib, cacique of Canizan, on account of [the fact that] three years ago the Itzas went there to capture Indians in order to sacrifice and eat them and that they had pillaged the entire forest."[99] The well-informed Guatemalan captain Marcos de Abalos y Fuentes wrote in 1704 that a Tabascan priest, Bachiller Francisco de Escobar, had written to him in

57

1702 that Kan Itzam had been settled by apostate Kejaches "and that all of them had been baptized and married in the towns of Sahcabchen, Chicbul, and Machich of this province [Yucatán], and that they had no fixed location in the forest, avoiding the Itzas who assaulted them at night, carrying off some of them and tearing out the still living hearts of others to offer to their gods."[100]

The 1694 Itza attack on Kan Itzam probably played little role in either the subsequent Guatemalan decision to open the road to the Chol Lakandons or Ursúa's concomitant road-opening project through Kejach territory. Nor can the claims that the Itzas were in search of sacrificial victims necessarily be taken at face value. It is more likely that they were seeking to maintain some degree of political and military control over their westernmost frontiers and that they were determined to undermine efforts to form reduction communities of runaway Mayas in the area.

Seventeenth-Century Itza Military
Aggression in Perspective

In the events that followed Orbita's 1618 destruction of Tzimin Chak, the "idol" dedicated to Cortés's horse, we see a consistent pattern of Itza behavior. The Itzas clearly sought to destroy any local indigenous support for Spanish activities, particularly reductions and conversions, that threatened the integrity of distant Itza boundaries. As we saw in the case of the Tz'ul Winikob' rebellion in Belize in the 1630s, the Itzas pursued reductions of their own, forcing the relocation of the scattered Belize mission settlements into a single town, Tipuj, which became in essence an Itza colony. The case of the town of Mopan, which in 1631 supported Itza aggression against the Manche Chol missions, may have had parallels with the strategy applied to Tipuj: Mopan, briefly a mission town itself, was probably attacked by the Itzas and subsequently incorporated into the Itza political system as an outlying colony whose duty was to monitor the frontier with Verapaz.[101]

Even as early as their first encounter with Europeans in 1525, the Itza rulers at Nojpeten pursued aggressive political and military strategies that protected them against the colonial conquest methods that had been so successful throughout most of the rest of the Americas. Their principal strategy was to create a wide buffer zone, which they accomplished by punishing those native peoples living along their frontiers who accepted Spaniards in their midst and sometimes by incorporating such groups into a wider alliance by engaging them as rebels against the colonies. Additionally, they gathered information about circumstances in the colonial world beyond their borders — in Belize, Verapaz, IxPimienta, Campeche, and elsewhere. Such knowledge must have required an intelligence network that penetrated all of these regions and, although it cannot be documented, perhaps extended all the way to the colonial capitals.

The Itzas were not, therefore, naive, "untouched" native peoples. Their historical experience with Europeans emerges instead as a series of encounters, often violent, that demonstrated a sophistication achievable only through long-term, intensive study of the European enemy. Although we would wish that the voices of these remarkable native defenders played a larger part in our knowledge of this history, their actions spoke loudly and clearly.

During the months and years preceding the conquest of 1697, politics — the struggle for control over followers, territory, and internal and external policies — were central to the troubled and complex relationships among the Itza ruling nobility, between Itzas and their indigenous neighbors, and, of course, between Itzas and Spaniards. Beneath the volatility, however, certain structural principles that had long sustained the Itzas as a powerful political system continued to operate, even when Itza society faced certain collapse at the hands of its future conquerors.

Itza governance was a complex system grounded in principles of dual rulership, a quadripartite division of elite governance over territories, and a crosscutting system of representation on a ruling council from outlying towns and regions. At least some of these principles reflect ancient cultural features long recognized to have characterized the civilizations of Mesoamerica, in particular the Mayas.[1] More specifically, I suggest that Itza territory was divided into four cardinally arranged provinces that mirrored or were mirrored by the four quarters of the capital of Nojpeten, which was, in essence, a fifth province. Each province, including Nojpeten itself, was governed by a pair of rulers. Four of these pairs represented and resided in their respective quarters of the capital, and the members of each pair stood in a senior-junior relationship to one another. The fifth pair comprised the supreme rulership itself and was shared by the "king," Ajaw Kan Ek', and the high priest, his father's brother's son, known as AjK'in Kan Ek'. These two men ruled, at least symbolically, as a single political persona, embodying dynastic rule over all of Itza territory and over Nojpeten, the political and cosmological center of that territory. All ten of these rulers seem to have had priestly functions as well, and at least some of them served as military leaders.[2]

Duality at another level contrasted these five pairs with a group of thirteen officials known by the title Ach Kat. Their duties are not well understood but may have included military and religious activities. Their number, thirteen, suggests a possible association with rituals for the seating of the thirteen twenty-year k'atuns and for the prophetic interpretations associated with these time periods. Unlike the ten principal rulers, these men apparently did not govern provinces. They may have represented towns, both within and beyond core Itza territory, that had been important places in Itza history.

In this chapter I explore the fascinating Itza system of governance and political geography — topics of great interest to Maya scholars — in order to make sense of Itza strategies and actions in the years before and after the conquest. Much of the chapter is based on previously unreported research and analysis and is therefore necessarily complex and detailed. Before turning to governance, however, let us look at the types of communities in which the Itzas lived, at the demography of the Itzas and Kowojs, at the capital, Nojpeten, and at lineage and descent among the Itza nobility.

The Capital, Towns, and Hamlets

On the eve of the 1697 conquest the Itzas lived in three principal types of communities: the Itza capital itself, towns, and hamlets.[3] Nojpeten, probably the largest of the communities, held symbolic and pragmatic supremacy as a unique locus of political and ritual power and social prestige. Most Itzas, however, lived in forty or more towns distributed across the Itza core region (see map 4). Although few population figures exist, we can say that the towns varied considerably in size, from several hundred persons to more than two thousand.[4] Towns, although relatively small, had qualities that were more "urban" than those of hamlets. In contrast to hamlets, towns contained a relatively large number of houses clustered near one another, were not necessarily adjacent to large horticultural tracts, and were associated with a resident elite whose lineage names were often used, in addition to descriptive names, to identify the community.[5] An extensive list of Itza towns appears in Table 3.1, information dictated in 1702 by Ajaw Kan Ek', his son, and others living under house arrest in Santiago de Guatemala.

61

The Itzas were primarily town-dwelling people, choosing to concentrate themselves in settlements situated in convenient and often defensible locations with relatively easy access to one another and to the main lake. Many of these were surrounded by extensive cultivations in which lay

TABLE 3.1
List of Towns Dictated in 1702 by Ajaw Kan Ek' and Others

Settlement	Population	Principal Lineages and Leaders (Retranscribed)	Principal Lineages and Leaders (Original version)
Towns probably in Itza core area:			
Polol (Polol)	Many	Tut	Tut
Kontal (Contal)	Many	Tut	Tut
Yalkaj (Yalca)	Many	Kanek'	Canec
Sub'elnaj (Subelna)	Many	Kanchan	Canchan
IxMutnaj (Ixmutra)	Many	Tesak Kit Kan	Tesac quit cam
Ajaw Che (Ahache)	Many	Kanek'	Canec
Jolpat (Holpat)	Many	Tzin	Tzin
Chachach'ulte (Chachachulte)	Medium	Kanek'	Canec
Ichek (Ychec)	Few	K'ixab'on	Quixabon
Chenak (Chenac)	Many	K'ix Kan and Kitis	Quix cam y Quitis
Joyop (Hoyop)[a]	Many	B'atab'(?) Puk	Bata puc
Itzunte (Itzunte)	Many	AjMatzin[b]	Ahmatzim
Yaxb'ete (Yaxbete)	Few	B'ak Tun	Bactum
Tz'ununwitz (Sonouitz)[c]	Few	Chab'in	Chauin
Tikul (Ticul)	Many	AjMatzin	Amatzin
Akjok (Acjoc)	Few	AjNoj Chab'in	Anoh Chabin
Chaktis (Chactiz)	Few	AjJe Matza	Ahematza
Jesmoj (Hesmo)	Medium	Koti Kanchan	Coticanchan
Yaxche (Yaxche)	Medium	Tut	Tut
IxKojech (Yxcohech)	Few	AjChak Tut	Achactut
Chacha (Chacha)	Very Few	AjSoy Tun	Azoitum
Gwakamay(?) (Buacamay)	Few	Kanchan	Canchan
IxPetzeja (Ixpetzeha)	Few	AjMuan (Moan) Panaj	Ahmuan pana
Tzotz (Tzotz)	Medium	AjKan Kanek'	Ahcan canec
IxKotyol (Ixcotyol)	Medium	AjB'en Chab'in	Ahuen chabin
Yalak (Yalac)	Many	AjChikan K'itis	Achican quitis
Chulul (Chulul)	Medium	AjUz Kit Kan	Ahus quit can
Towns apparently in Chak'an Itza area:[d]			
Saksel (Zacsel)	Medium	AjTzuntekum	Azuntecum
Saxkumil (Saxcumil)	Few	AjKawil Itza	Ah cauil Ytza
Jolkaj (Holca)	Few	Tesukun	Tesucum
IxPapaktun (Yxpapaktum)	Many	Chata	Chatta
Jolalil (Holalil)	Many	Kowoj, Tzuntekum, and K'ix	Coboctzuntecum y quix

TABLE 3.1

(continued)

Settlement	Population	Principal Lineages and Leaders (Retranscribed)	Principal Lineages and Leaders (Original version)
Yaxche (Yaxche)	Medium	Kowoj	Coboj
Yaxle (Yaxle)	Many	AjKali, B'e Ob'on	Ahcolibeobon
Tilaj (Tilah)[e]	Many	Matz Ob'on	Matzobon
IxTus (Yxtus)	Few	Chuen Ob'on	Chuen abon
Saklemakal (Saclemacal)[f]	Many	AjB'ak Kanek'	Ahbac canec
Timul(Timul)	Few	AjTzazko Kanek'	Ahtzazcocanec
Towns on or near Lake Yaxhá:[g]			
Yaxja (Yaxha)[h]	Many	Kowoj(?)	Cobohe
B'akpeten Laguna (Bacpeten)	Many	Kowoj	Coboj
Chesik'in (Chesiquin)	Few	Chamach and Ken[i]	Chamach y quen
Kanch'ulte (Canchute)	Many	AjK'itan Kowoj	Ahquitan coboj
Nek'nojche (Necnoche)	Few	Kowoj	Coboj
Kets (Quetz)[j]	Many	Kowoj	Coboj
Towns in the so-called Mompana region:[k]			
Sumpan (Zumpan)	Many	Panaj, AjTzam	Panajatzan
Mumunt'i (Mumuntti)	Many	Tut	Tut
Towns in the Yalain region:			
Tajmakanche (Tahma canche)[l]	Few	Tzib'	Tzib
Another IxTus (Ixtuz)	Medium	Chayax	Chayax
Chinoja (Chinotia)[m]	Few	Chamach Sulu (Xulu)	Ch amachsulu
Towns in the Lake Sacpuy region (also in the core area):			
B'alamtun (Balamtun)[n]	Many	Chab'in Idol	Chavin Ydolo
AjLalaich (Ah Lalaich)[o]	Many	Puk	Puc
Petmas (Petmas)	Many	AjUs Puk	Auz puc
Xewlila (Xeulila)	Many	Jaw, Mas K'in	Hau mazquin

SOURCE: AGI, EC 339A, Memoria by Fray Diego de Rivas, 26 May 1702.

NOTE: All names in this table are listed in the order in which they were recorded. They clearly fall into several sets. Settlement names in parentheses are original spellings.

[a]Joyop was probably on Laguneta Picú, just south of the eastern end of Lake Sacpuy.

[b]This name and the AjMatzin that appears three names below are probably the same.

[c]This may be the same town written elsewhere as "Sununbiz," thus accounting in part for the orthographic departure here (AGI, Escribanía de Cámara 339B, no. 18, Capitán José de Aguilar to bishop of Yucatán, 8 Feb. 1704, ff. 23r–25r). The name seems to appear on the to-

Notes continue overleaf

scattered hamlets occupied by those working in the fields. Nearly all towns were located on bodies of water, including the shores of Lago Petén Itzá, Laguneta Macanché, Lagunas Oquevix and Ijá to the south, and smaller lakes and *aguadas* that dot the region. Paths connected these settlements, and people traveled regularly between them. They used canoes to travel between towns along the shore of the main lake and to carry produce and other goods to Nojpeten.

Some towns were much larger and more important than others, especially those that appear to have been the provincial "headquarters" of often absentee elites who served on a core ruling council of eight men (not including the two supreme rulers) that met frequently at Nojpeten.[6] These eight appear to have resided primarily at Nojpeten, having only formal identification with their "home" towns. Although the data are incomplete on this crucial point, I believe that the "home" towns (of which there were certainly four and possibly eight) of the four ruling pairs served as governing centers for the regions that surrounded them. If so, they served as regional capitals, secondary in importance to Nojpeten.

Table 3.1 notes continued

pographic map (La Esperanza sheet) as Tzununhuitz and nearby Sabana Tzununhuitz south. Tzununhuitz is adjacent to the modern settlement of Cobanerita, south of Laguna Sacpuy.

[d]A marginal notation, "region toward Campeche," refers to the following set, all of which were apparently located on or north of the northernwestern shore of the main lake, comprising the Chak'an Itza area (the northern quadrant of the Itza core area).

[e]One colonial translation of *laj* is *cabo,* a cape or promontory in the geographical sense. This set of names seems to be along the north shore of the main lake, moving from west to east. Tilaj ("At the Cape") may have been at Punta Cahuí.

[f]Avendaño (Relación, f. 25v; 1987, p. 28) identified a river that he called "Çaclemacal" as the northern boundary of Chak'an Itza territory. This was not the Saklemakal at the eastern end of Lago Petén Itzá.

[g]Many Kowoj people had resettled in this area after the conquest, joining others already there.

[h]The full passage here reads "Yaxa, another lake with three islands. Many. All people of the Cobohe" ("Yaxa otra laguna con tres islas. Muchos. Toda gente de el Cobohe").

[i]This transcription is uncertain. Chamach is an honorific, and Ken, a Yucatán surname, is not seen elsewhere in the area. K'en is not a known name. This name might be Chamay Xiken.

[j]This town may be recorded out of place, since the only known K'etz was on the northern shore of the main lake. On the other hand, it may be a relocated settlement of that name.

[k]This region, northeast of the main lake, was a refuge area for Itzas during the years following the 1697 conquest.

[l]This is the present-day name of Laguneta Macanche.

[m]Given its adjacency to Ixtus, this is almost certainly the town consistently recorded elsewhere as Chinoja ("Chinoha") or Nojchija ("Nochiha"), probably located on Laguna Sacnab. The discrepancy is probably a copyist's error.

[n]The unexcavated archaeological site that bears this name today, north of Laguna Sacpuy, is still visited by local inhabitants.

[o]In contemporary Itzaj, *lä'lä' ich* is "very old face," suggesting that the town may have been named for a weathered stela (Hofling and Tesucún, 1996).

Little is understood of local, town-level governance. There is over-whelming evidence, however, that individual towns had their own leaders, who in many if not all cases were heads of principal local lineages. Span-iards usually called them caciques. Te B'alam, for example, was the "ca-cique" of Joyop on Laguneta Picú. Chamach Xulu was the "cacique" of Yalain on Laguneta Macanché.[7] This title was apparently equivalent to the Itza title B'atab': B'atab' Puk had become the head of Joyop by 1702 (Table 3.1), and we are told of towns called B'atab' Sima and B'atab' K'u.[8] I suggest later that some towns were represented on the core ruling council of Nojpeten as a result of the high status of their elite leaders.

Although towns sometimes bore the names of their principal leaders, who apparently represented a principal lineage situated there, they were more frequently given geographically descriptive names. These were often names associated with bodies of water on which the towns were situated, such as Chaltunja (White-Earth Water), Chinoja (Shore of the Lake), and Petenja (Island Lake). Others were associated with vegetation, such as Nab'a (Incense Tree), Nek'nojche (Seed of Great Tree), Saklemakal (White Leaf Cassava), and, to the east of Itza territory, Tipuj (At the Reeds). Still others had animal associations, some possibly mythological or ritual in nature: Polain (Head of the Alligator/Crocodile), Tz'ununwitz (Hummingbird Hill), and Job'onmo (Hollow Macaw). And some suggest the presence of ancient ruins, such as B'alamtun (Jaguar Stone), Ichtun (Among Stones), and AjLalaich (Very Old Face).[9]

Itza hamlets — small settlements comprising several extended fami-lies — were usually called *rancherías* or *milperías* by Spanish observers, by which they meant small settlements, often seasonally occupied, associated with swidden cultivations — plots of maize and other cultigens. Occasion-ally they used the term *rancho* in describing Itza or Kowoj hamlets, but they more often used it to describe communities of Mopans and Manche Chols, among whom larger "towns" seem to have been absent. I believe that all three terms — rancho, ranchería, and milpería — refer to a cluster of houses intimately associated with a horticultural plot. Those who lived in these houses, we may presume, were engaged in full-time food production and some hunting of wild game for those who lived in the towns, including elites who did not work as horticulturalists, the elderly, and families en-gaged in other undertakings. Some of the produce from Itza-controlled areas was taken to Nojpeten, presumably as a tribute obligation. The documents, unfortunately, are silent on the issue of such obligations.[10]

Because the area between Lagunetas Salpetén and Macanché and La-guna Sacnab (see map 3) was much less densely populated than the Itza core area, larger towns there may have been outnumbered by hamlets. The town of Yalain on Laguneta Macanché served as the principal Itza administrative center of the region and was surrounded by small, extended-family hamlets distributed among extensive cultivations of maize and other crops. This pattern seems to have been repeated for other rather small towns to the east of Yalain, such as Chinoja and IxTus.[11]

Although the Kowojs also had towns and hamlets (see map 5), whether or not they had a central capital that functioned as Nojpeten did for the Itzas is, surprisingly, uncertain. Nor do Spanish sources inform us of the presence or absence of a central governing council similar to that of the Itzas. In 1697 both the highest-ranking Kowoj ruler, "Capitán" Kowoj to the Spaniards, and his junior ruler, Kulut Kowoj, probably made their residences at Ketz on the northern shore of the main lake. Little is known about this town, and archaeological surveys in the area where it was located have not revealed architecture on the scale of Nojpeten's.[12] The most likely candidate for a central Kowoj capital may be in the eastern port region in the vicinity of the archaeological site of Ixlú and the nearby site of Zacpetén on Laguneta Salpetén.[13] The major town in this area at the time of the 1697 conquest was apparently Saklemakal, probably controlled by Kulut Kowoj.[14] Neither it nor Ketz was then subject to Itza rule.

Extensive cultivable land along the northern shore of Lago Petén Itzá had to be reached by climbing to the flatter areas above the escarpment that reaches to the lakeshore in this area. Kowoj towns there were apparently supported agriculturally by numerous extended-family hamlets in these higher areas, although there were also extensive cultivations in the Ixlú region.[15] Kowoj populations also occupied interior regions well north and northeast of the lake, possibly having established towns of some size away from the lakeshore. Little is known of these, but at least one, which may have been constructed during internecine Maya warfare following the conquest, contained a large wooden stockade. Kowojs also occupied several towns and hamlets around Laguna Yaxhá, in proximity to Itza-controlled communities on and around Laguna Sacnab. This cluster of eastern settlements, however, probably grew considerably after the 1697 conquest as a result of flight from the northern shore of Lago Petén Itzá.

66

Itza and Kowoj Demography

Spaniards found it difficult to estimate the total number of people in any of the major groups occupying central Petén before or in the years immediately after the 1697 conquest. This is not surprising, because prior to the conquest no Spaniard had seen more than a tiny portion of the region. After the conquest they found many towns abandoned, their inhabitants having fled to more remote areas. They left behind cultivations and other signs of habitation so extensive that Spaniards concluded that the total population must have been extremely large.[16] They were unable, however, to say how large it might have been.

Fray Andrés de Avendaño, who visited Nojpetén in 1696, was the only Spaniard to venture a guess: 24,000 or 25,000 souls, plus or minus 1,000. In this number he included Nojpetén, four other "petenes," Chak'an Itza territory, various unidentified towns around the lake, and the people known as Tulumkis, Mopans whom Avendaño had not seen. That he was actually trying to provide an estimate of the people in the general vicinity of Lago Petén Itzá, however, is apparent from his statement that he calculated his total on the basis of the population of Nojpetén multiplied by five: "I make this computation from the peten on which the king lives, because he told me all the petens were equal in people, with little difference [among them]."[17] He therefore must have estimated the population of Nojpetén at 5,000 people (25,000 divided by 5). Although there might be as many as eight islands in the southern arm of the lake, depending on the variable water level, none of these could have supported a population nearly as large as that of Nojpetén. Avendaño clearly misinterpreted the meaning of "peten" to be "island," whereas in this context it referred to an entire province, of which there were five, including Nojpetén.

Referring again to Table 3.1, we see that in 1702 Ajaw Kan Ek' and others distinguished fifty-one communities within the Itza and Kowoj sphere of influence, comparing their sizes to those of towns in the vicinity of Santiago de Guatemala and indicating the names of people associated with each settlement. The comparison towns—all within a five-kilometer radius of Santiago—were Jocotenango and Ciudad Vieja ("many"), San Juan del Obispo and San Pedro de las Huertas ("medium"), and a generic "small town" ("few"). Of the fifty-three Petén towns, they estimated the populations of twenty-seven to be "many," nine to be "medium," sixteen to be "few," and one to be "very few" (Table 3.1).

Their estimates must have been based on preconquest populations, because they appear to be extremely high. In 1684 Jocotenango had a population of 1,104 native tributaries, suggesting a total population of about 4,400; population figures for Ciudad Vieja are not available.[18] In 1638 the tributary population of San Pedro de las Huertas was 153 (perhaps about 600 persons altogether), and in 1755 the total population of

67

San Juan del Obispo was 485.[19] It seems implausible that there had been twenty-one Itza-area communities with populations as large as four thousand, a figure about eight times greater than the size of a comparable "medium" town, which appears to have been about five hundred persons. Allowing for the likelihood of exaggeration, I suggest a figure one-quarter as large, or about one thousand, for towns with "many" persons. Settlements with "few" persons, which presumably included what I have called hamlets, might be estimated at one hundred persons, and the one with "very few" at fifty persons.

Based on these figures, the total population of large Itza-Kowoj towns would have been 51,000, that of medium-sized towns 4,000, and that of small and very small ones 1,650, for a total of 56,650. The Kan Ek' list of towns, however, is not complete; it omits much of the northern Kowoj region and probably various Itza settlements at some distance south of the main lake and west of Laguna Sacpuy. A total preconquest population of sixty thousand seems a conservative estimate.[20]

Following the establishment of the first Itza-area missions, the mission population reached its peak in 1708, with a total of some six thousand (see Table 15.3). Probably not more than a thousand Itzas and Kowojs lived independent of colonial control at that time, suggesting a total surviving population of about seven thousand. This would represent a loss on the order of 88 percent during the first decade of colonial rule, owing primarily to epidemic disease. Both internecine warfare following the conquest and casualties resulting from Spanish roundups of the population would also have contributed to this dramatic decline (see chapter 15).

Nojpeten, The Island Capital

Several years after the conquest the Mercederian friar Diego de Rivas described Nojpeten in these words:

> The Peten of the Itza is an island that is on the arm of a lake, the crossing distance from whose shore to the mainland is a distance such that a loud shout can be heard, although the length of this [lake, along with] another two arms, extends for leagues. The island is four blocks in diameter and sixteen in circumference. The Indians, its native inhabitants, call it Noh Peten, which means large island, not because of its material grandeur (as it is small) but rather because on it its ruler always lived and on it they also had the prin-

cipal temples of their idols and carried out the most solemn functions of their idolatry.[21]

Rivas's measurements precisely describe the modern, roughly circular island of Flores. The contemporary street plan of Flores (map 7) divides the island into four quarters separated by a nearly precise north-south, east-west grid. At the juncture of these quarters today, at the high point of the island, is the central plaza with the Roman Catholic church on its eastern side. The streets that connect the cardinal points may be survivals of the original Itza street plan, which also connected each of the cardinal points to a central plaza. The Itza streets, which intersected each of the four cardinally oriented quarters of the island, were likely the routes along which the annual Wayeb' ceremonies took place (on which more later) and may have been equivalent to the causeways, or *sakb'e*s, of sites such as Ek' B'alam in Yucatán.[22] Map 7 also shows diagonal streets in the northwestern and northeastern quadrants, suggesting the remnants of dividing streets that separated the quarters.

Descriptions of Nojpeten's appearance before it was stormed by the Spaniards are few but tantalizing in their sparse but sometimes vivid details. Bernal Díaz de Castillo, seeing the island in 1525, said that "the houses and temples showed their whiteness" even to viewers standing two leagues away.[23] In 1695 Guatemalans observing from a closer vantage point on the southern shore of the lake described it as "a large, very steep island, shaped almost like a sugar loaf, completely covered with houses, and on the highest point a very large one," near which were two smaller buildings and a "promontory like a tower."[24] They were describing what those who visited the island on various occasions later confirmed: that the town was densely packed with buildings, with temples at the higher central area — one much higher than the rest — and houses surrounding the temples all the way to the shoreline.

The buildings most fully described by Spanish sources include the palace and meeting hall of the principal ruler, adjacent to the eastern landing place of the island, and the temples at the center. A first brief description comes from Fray Bartolomé de Fuensalida, who, according to López de Cogolludo, reported that in 1618 the house of Ajaw Kan Ek' was located about forty paces from the shore, facing a small plaza on which a house had been built for the visiting friars. They were pleased with a location so close to the ruler's dwelling, for they were able to exchange visits with him frequently.[25] Unfortunately, this account offers no further details.

On Avendaño's 1696 visit to Nojpeten the friar found the house of

69

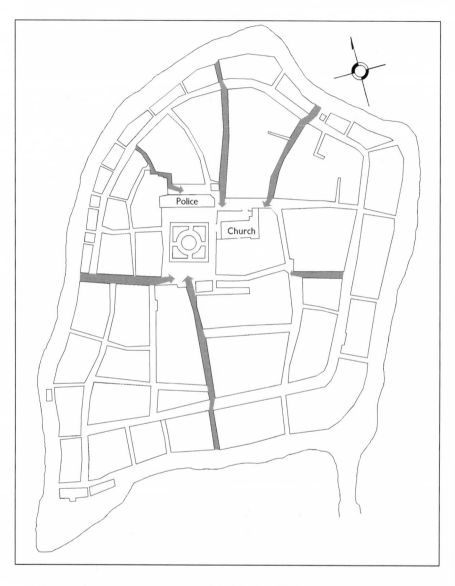

Map 7.   Street plan of modern Ciudad Flores, Petén. By Foundation for Latin American Anthropological Research, Brevard Community College; courtesy Nicholas Hellmuth. Copyright FLAAR 1978.

Ajaw Kan Ek' "half a block's distance" (which would be fifty varas, or about forty-two meters) from the landing place—presumably the same forty paces from the shore described earlier by Fuensalida. In front of it, presumably on a small plaza, was a stone representation of Yaxcheel Kab', the cosmic or world tree, associated with a mask of the deity AjKokaj Mut on its west side.[26] The hall (*salón*) where the ruler received guests was an "anteroom" (*antesala*) to his house. Its walls were of mortared and plastered masonry only about one vara (84 cm) in height; the structure supported a beamed roof covered with palm thatch. Unlike the temples that I describe later, the anteroom had a plastered stone floor.[27]

Inside the entrance to this hall was a "large stone table more than two varas long and proportionally wide, placed on stone pilasters, with twelve seats of the same [material] around it for the priests."[28] Avendaño believed that on this table, called simply "stone table" (*mayaktun*), the Itzas practiced human sacrifice, although he recognized that the room functioned as a public meeting hall. It is most likely that the stone table was a meeting table; the hall was a *popolna* ("mat house"), clearly a center for governance, not a temple dedicated to sacrifices.[29]

The physical size of Nojpeten in 1696 was the same as it was in the midtwentieth century, before the lake rose high enough during the 1980s to force the abandonment of the first row of buildings around the island's perimeter. The landing place for the royal palace and its connected meeting hall was almost certainly at the island's centerpoint on the west side, where today a straight street rises directly from the shore to the south side of the plaza. These two buildings, based on the measurements provided by Fuensalida and Avendaño, would have been located about where today's second, interior blocks begin, about one-fourth the distance between the shore and the central plaza.

Although we are not told where the high priest, the other eight rulers, and the thirteen individuals who bore the title Ach Kat lived, it is reasonable to assume that their dwellings were divided among the four quarters at about the same distance from the shore as the royal palace of Ajaw Kan Ek'. The house plots of the elite dwellings would have been large and undoubtedly cluttered with small outbuildings such as kitchens, oratories, and storage houses. Most of the "commoner" houses would have been situated near the shoreline. During their tour of the island Fuensalida and Orbita saw what they estimated to be about two hundred houses densely clustered along the shore, each housing "parents and children with their families."[30] This density would have allowed an average of less than seven meters of shoreline for each house, suggesting that they were arranged as two roughly concentric circles outside the circle of elite dwellings.

Inside the domestic circle of the principal elites were the temples, of which Fuensalida was the first Spaniard to leave a record. He described them as places "where they keep the idols and are brought together for their dances and inebrieties, which take place whenever they have to idolatrize or make some sacrifice."[31] In contrast to his description of the tightly packed domestic space along the island's edge, Fuensalida reported that "[o]n the high ground and center of the island are the *cues y adoratorios* where they have their idols. [His party] went to see them, and there were twelve or more temples, in grandness and capacity like the larger churches found in the Indian towns of this province of Yucatán, each of which, according to the account, had room for a gathering of more than one thousand persons."[32] It was in one of these commodious buildings that the friars saw the statue of Cortés's horse.

In 1696 Avendaño provided a written description of the temples that conforms closely to Fuensalida's:

> For the worship of the said idols there are nine very large houses constructed in the form of the churches of this province [Yucatán] — all new, with traces of others which have been burned, although they built them again, as I saw in the case of two which had been reconstructed.[33] These "houses" have about a vara and a half of wall, six-fourths [of a vara] in thickness.[34] In three of them the railing or bench will be arranged all around, situated halfway toward the inside; and in the other three [*sic*] — the remainder, which are higher up [on the island] — [the bench will be arranged] such that two of them create two rows of benches all around the said churches, all plastered and smoothed.[35]

Six days after signing his written report, Avendaño provided oral testimony before colonial authorities in which he admitted that he had not seen all nine temples: "He also saw on the said island three or four churches, oratories of the said Indians — although the said reyezuelo told the father commissary that there were nine — all of them large houses with about two varas high of wall, in the center of which rises a railing [*pretil*] of plastered and smoothed mortared masonry that serves as a bench for the Indians, covered with palm thatch on the model of this province."[36]

We can conclude from these accounts that the temples were large structures with plastered exterior masonry walls not more than 1.25 to 1.75 meters in height. They were roofed with a massive structure of beams covered with palm thatch — similar, as Avendaño pointed out, to the village churches of Yucatán that still exist in Quintana Roo. The dark interiors, which created their own mysterious mood, were ideal for large gatherings for ceremonial dances and other rituals.[37] A continuous bench was arranged at some distance from the outer wall in the smaller temples so that the bench surrounded the inner ritual space. In larger temples — those clustered at the top of the island — there were double rows of masonry benches for participants and observers alike.

These large buildings were defined architectural spaces where public ceremony could be carried out for specific purposes. Because Nojpeten was far too small to provide multiple open plazas with associated pyramidal temples, the open halls were an alternative to the mixing of open public spaces and closed priestly rooms atop stepped pyramids. Later descriptions indicate that within the public temples were private rooms for priests and their ritual objects and paraphernalia, confirming that these large buildings had assumed the primary functions of the more typical Maya plaza-temple complex.

The actual number of temples on Nojpeten is of special interest. Fuensalida reported that there were "twelve or more," whereas Avendaño said that the ruler had told him there were nine. The latter number suggests that there was a temple for each of eight provincial ruler-priests plus a single temple for Ajaw Kan Ek' and AjK'in Kan Ek', the high priest. Following their occupation of Nojpeten, Spanish officers counted a total of twenty-one "houses" in which they found "idols" that to them seemed "innumerable." They called nine of these buildings, which they specified as "the tall ones," *adoratorios,* or temples. One of these, said to be the temple of AjK'in Kan Ek,' they described as built in the form of a castle.[38] The ten principal ruler-priests probably controlled the nine largest temples. Perhaps the thirteen Ach Kats presided over the remainder, although Spaniards counted only twelve of these.

Villagutierre, writing in 1701, described what he regarded to be the principal temple of Nojpeten, a structure that differed considerably from those described by Avendaño. It was certainly the same building described as a "castle" (*castillo*) by the Spanish officers. I have been unable to locate a documentary source for the following passage, leading me to conclude that he received the information from a private source:

> Of the twenty-one *cues* or temples that General Ursúa and his men found on the island, the principal and largest one was that of the false high priest Quincanek, father's brother's son of King Canek.

73

This was square in shape with its beautiful wall [*hermosa pretil*] and nine levels [*gradas*], all made of beautiful stone, and each face [*lienzo*] — or façade — about twenty varas in width and very tall.

And on the last step [*escalón*], or level [*grada*], upon entering there was an idol in a crouching position, human in form, with an evil face. And inside the temple, on the front wall [*frontis*], there was another idol of rough emerald which those infidels called the god of battles. It was as long as the extended span between the thumb and forefinger, and General Ursúa attained possession of it. Above this one was another, of plaster, its faced shaped like the sun, with lines [*rayos*] of mother-of-pearl all around it, and outlined by the same, and in its mouth inlaid teeth that they had removed from the Spaniards they had killed.[39]

This building seems to have been a four-sided pyramid with nine "tall" *escalones* or *gradas* — apparently terraces — estimated to be twenty varas (about 16.5 meters) wide, presumably at the base. The term *hermosa pretil*, I believe, referred to a low wall in front of or surrounding the building and almost certainly not to a parapet, as other authors have claimed.[40] The author goes on to say that the temple building itself, which clearly sat atop the stepped pyramid, was "in the shape of a castle," thus identifying it with one of the temples so described by the Spanish officers. By castlelike in form the observers clearly meant a building with relatively high masonry external walls and a flat roof — a completely different type of construction from the large, pitched-roof, thatched temples with low walls described earlier, but one that would describe equally well the temples and oratories of Mayapan.

It is tempting to conclude that this temple was modeled after the principal pyramidal temple, the Castillo, at Chich'en Itza — the Petén Itzas' origin place — or the smaller but similar Temple of K'uk'ulkan, or Castillo, at Mayapan. Both of these pyramids were square, had nine terraces and stairways on all four sides, and were capped by temples that, from their names, were regarded by Spaniards as castlelike in form. At its base the maximum dimensions of the Mayapan Castillo were about 33 by 35 meters; it was about 15.5 meters from the plaza to the top of its steps. The Nojpeten pyramid appears to have been about half this size, a scaled-down model with perhaps only one stairway and with terraces less than a meter high. Even at this size it would have been an impressive building. We are left to wonder why there is no other known description of it or any record of its dismantlement, which must have been a major undertaking.

Itza Social Organization

Although the documentary sources tell us little directly about how either the Itza nobility or commoners were organized, what evidence they provide suggests that the Itza social system placed much importance on kinship relations and marriage. A key to this system, although we can grasp it only at the most basic level, is the Itza system of identifying persons through surnames. As Avendaño pointed out, all Itzas had two such surnames, one inherited from the mother (a matronym) and one from the father (a patronym).[41] Indeed, we can say with some certainty that all Itzas had a "given" name, a day name, and one or both kinds of surnames; of the surnames the matronym always preceded the patronym. In the cases known to us, only the day name or the given name is recorded, never both. Members of the nobility also had one or more titles, which usually preceded their surnames; their given names and day names are omitted in the examples that we have. The common gender-marking prefixes *aj-* (male) and *ix-* (female) frequently precede the entire string of names for all persons and sometimes precede a noble title. It is often difficult to distinguish titles, given names, and surnames, both because there was some overlap or similarity among them and because Spanish recorders often did not write names accurately and consistently.[42]

Tables 3.2 and 3.3 demonstrate how Itzas—in this case the "forest Indians" who visited officials from Bacalar at the Belize River town of Chunuk'um (see chapter 2)—identified themselves by name to Spaniards. Of the four men and twenty-six women listed, sixteen or seventeen have day names. Only two given names can be identified with some certainty.[43] All of them have surnames, and as many as fourteen bear both a matronym and a patronym.

Of special interest is the high frequency of the surname Kan ("Serpent"), which is held by five people. In the case of the first-listed married couple, both bear what I take to be a special variant of this name, spelled "Caan" in the document and probably signifying *ka'an,* "sky." The marriage between two individuals of the same surname was unusual, suggesting, along with the Kaan name itself, that these two were members of the high nobility. As I explain later, I believe that Kan was not only the surname of the principal royal family but was also inherited through a line of females.

Of all of these kinds of names, surnames provide the most important clues about Itza social organization. Recognizing the importance of patrilineally inherited surnames and other indicators of patrilineal descent,

TABLE 3.2

Itza Men and Women in the Chunuk'um Matrícula, Belize River, 1655

Husband	Wife	"Single" Male	"Single" Females
Chuen Kaan (Chuen Caan)	IxMen Kaan (Ixmen Caan)	Ik Kib' (Ic Kib)	Xok K'u (Xoc Ku)
Chuen Kan (Chuen Can)	IxEtz'nab' Kawij (Ixetznab ca Vih)		IxKan Jaw (Ixcan Hau)
AjKan Chi (Ah Canchi)	Ek' Mas (Ekmaz)		Xok K'u (Xoc Ku)
			Sal Puk (Çalpuc)
			IxKi May (Ixci May)
			IxKab'an P'ol (Ixcaban Ppol)
			IxKib' Chab'le (Ixcib Chable)
			IxEtz Pix (Ixetzpix)
			IxKawak Kawij (Ixca Vac Cavih)
			IxB'en Kan (Ixben Can)
			IxKab'an Mo (Ixcaban Mo)
			IxMen Kante (Ixmen Kante)
			IxKan B'alam (Ixcam Balam)
			IxMen Kan (Ixmen Can)
			IxMen Sima (Ixmen Çima)
			IxMuluk Chan (Ixmuluc Chan)
			IxKaw Kech (Ixcau Cech)
			IxTutz Pix (Ixtutzpix)
			IxTinal (Ixtinal)
			IxMuluk Muk'ul (Ixmuluc Mukul)
			IxKab' Us (Ixcab Us)
			IxKan Chan (Ixcan Chan)
			IxMen Kob' (Ixmen Cob)

SOURCES: Scholes and Thompson, 1977, pp. 63–64.
NOTE: The two names recorded as "Kib" and "Cib" are probably the same; I have transcribed both as Kib' (Ik Kib' and IxKib' Chab'le).

TABLE 3.3

Individual Itza Names by Type in the Chunuk'um Matrícula, *Belize River, 1655*

Order	Sex	Male Prefix	Female Prefix	Day Name	Given Name	Matronym or Patronym	Patronym
1	M			*Chuen*		*Kaan*	
2	F		*Ix-*	*Men*		*Kaan*	
3	F				(Xok)	Xok	K'u
4	F		Ix-			Kan	Jaw
5	F				(Xok)	Xok	K'u
6	M			Ik			K'ib'
7	F				Sal		Puk
8	M	*Aj-*				*Kan*	*Chi*
9	F					*Ek'*	*Mas*
10	F		Ix-			Ki	May
11	F		Ix-	Kab'an			P'ol
12	F		Ix-			Kib'	Chab'le
13	F		Ix-	*Etz'[nab']*	*(Etz')*		Pix
14	F		Ix-	Kawak			Kawij
15	F		Ix-	B'en		Kan	(Kan)
16	F		Ix	Kab'an			Mo
17	M			*Chuen*		*Kan*	*(Kan)*
18	F		Ix-	*Etz'nab*			*Kawij*
19	F		Ix-	Men			Kante
20	F		Ix-			Kan	B'alam
21	F		Ix-	Men		Kan	(Kan)
22	F		Ix-	Men			Sima
23	F		Ix-	Muluk			Chan
24	F		Ix-		Kaw		Kech
25	F		Ix-		(Tutz)	Tutz	Pix
26	F		Ix-				Tinal
27	F		Ix-	Muluk			Muk'ul
28	F		Ix-			Kab'	Us
29	F		Ix-			Kan	Chan
30	F		Ix-	Men			Kob'

SOURCE: Scholes and Thompson, 1977, pp. 63–64.

NOTES: Married couples (see Table 3.2) are indicated by italics. Alternative assignments are indicated by parentheses.

My assumptions in parsing these names were as follows: (1) any name known to be a surname in Yucatán (Roys, 1940) and/or among the Itzas can be an Itza matronym or patronym; (2) any such surname that precedes another may be a matronym; (3) any such surname that is not preceded by another is probably a patronym, although Kan appears to be an exception in the case of Itza names, where it may be exclusively a matronym.

The only such presumed surnames among this group that are not found among the 411 Christianized inhabitants of Tipuj in this *matrícula* are Kech, Ki, K'ib', Tinal, Us, and Xok (Roys, 1940, pp. 58–63). Tutz may be the surname recorded as Tus in Yucatán, which appears once among Christianized Tipujans (ibid., p. 43). Kawij is a variant spelling of the name usually recorded as Kawil.

most Maya scholars have long assumed that among the Mayas descent in the male line, from father to son, was the preferred method of transferring power and authority, as well as property, from one generation to the next. This was the pattern seemingly most often recorded for the descent of kings in the Classic-period inscriptions, although the "rules" were flexible enough to allow brothers and other close patrilineal male kin, and even on rare occasions a daughter, to inherit office. Some recent research, however, suggests that matrilineal principles may also have been at work in succession to office in the Maya lowlands from Classic through colonial times.[44]

The Itzas certainly recognized descent in the male line. They, like the Mayas of northern Yucatán, had patronyms that were always inherited by a father's children, whether male or female. With few recorded exceptions, persons with the same surname did not marry each other, indicating the existence of exogamous (out-marrying) groups identified by the name of a line of males. Such partners avoided marriage no matter how distant the relationship between the couple — a pattern well documented in eighteenth-century Itza mission records and early colonial northern Yucatán as well.[45]

The seventeenth-century Franciscan historian Fray Diego López de Cogolludo, in his paraphrasing of Fray Bartolomé de Fuensalida's account of the 1618–19 Franciscan visits to Nojpeten, was the first to hint at the presence of the Kan matrilineage among the Itzas:

> [The Itzas] preserve the same surnames that they had [before they left Yucatán] (and those of Yucatán use them even today). These differ in that they are named with that of the mother first, joined immediately following with that of the father. Thus, the cacique who it was said was called Canek signifies "He who is or is called Can from the mother's side and Ek from that of his father." These of Yucatán now . . . [give their] sons and daughters [only the name] of their father, as is common among Spaniards.[46]

López de Cogolludo clearly meant that "Canek" was two names, Kan and Ek', the first passing from mother to child, and the second, from father to child. He apparently presumed that the first name was the mother's patronym and the second the father's patronym. Avendaño almost always wrote the ruler's name as "Can Ek," indicating that he understood it to be a two-part name, although he did not comment on how the king had inherited his name.[47]

Bishop Diego de Landa, writing in 1560, had described a similar compound naming system in Yucatán:

> They place much emphasis on knowing the origin of their lineages [*linajes*], especially if they come from some house of *Mayapán;* and they seek to find that out from the priests, [since] it is one of their sciences; and they boast much about the men who have been famous in their lineages. The names of the fathers always endure in the sons; in the daughters no. They always call their sons and daughters by the name of the father and of the mother — that of the father as proper [*propio*], and that of the mother as appellative [*apelativo*], so that they call the son of *Chel* and *Chan, Nachanchel,* which means sons [*sic*] of so-and-so people. This is why the Indians say that those of one name are relatives and are treated as such. As a result, when they arrive at an unknown place in need, they immediately produce the name, and if there is anyone [with that name], they are immediately received and treated with every kindness.[48]

The son of a father named Ch'el and a mother named Chan was therefore called NaChan Ch'el, in which the prefix *na-* indicated "from the mother."[49]

Both Landa and López de Cogolludo seem to have considered both names to be patrilineally inherited patronyms, just as double surnames (the mother's and father's *appellidos*) were for Spaniards. The Maya ethnohistorian Ralph L. Roys concluded, however, from his study of names inherited from the mother in the colonial Yucatecan sources (which he called *naal* names), that a man's *naal* name "was derived not from his mother's patronymic [*sic*] . . . but from her matronymic, which she could have inherited only from a female line of maternal ancestors."[50] As in the case described by Landa, such names were sometimes marked by the prefix *na-*, the Maya term for mother. In a convincing example Roys demonstrated that a woman named IxChan Pan, who was married to NaMay Kanche, had a son named NaChan Kanche. Because he inherited the name NaChan from the mother's "first" surname, Chan must in this case have been a matrilineally inherited name. IxChan Pan's mother's "first" surname, in other words, presumably was the same as *her* mother's first surname, just as IxChan Pan's son shared her own first surname. Such a pattern of succession is possible only if the name is inherited through a direct line of females. Had the son inherited his mother's patronym, as other sources have apparently assumed, his name would have been NaPan Kan.

Roys also proposed that the Mayas of Yucatán may have had matrilineal descent groups as well as patrilineal ones. The former type was called *tz'akab'*, and the latter, *ch'ib'al*, which colonial dictionaries seem to have distinguished as descent in the female and the male line, respectively.[51] Although he found no direct evidence of such social forms, he did discover that "while nearly all the *naal* names . . . also occur as patronymics, there were a large number of other patronymics which have not been found employed as *naal* names; and among these are included nine of the eleven principal ruling families of Yucatan at the time of the conquest."[52] In other words, matronyms and patronyms appeared to Roys to be somewhat independent entities, possibly representing different types of social groups, that differed in their geographical distribution and their relative frequency of usage among the elites of Yucatán.[53]

Because there are no other published examples of the NaChan Kanche sort, in which matrilineal descent is strongly implied, the possibility of matrilineal descent remains unconfirmed. Nonetheless, if males and females in early colonial Yucatán had a double naming system, it is no surprise to find that the same or a similar system operated in Petén among people of relatively recent Yucatecan cultural origin. The Itzas, however, never included (at least in the cases known to us) the *na-* prefix with their surnames, making it much more difficult to determine whether a surname was a matronym or a patronym. Only in cases where an individual bore two surnames can we be certain that the first was a matronym.

The Itzas claimed that from before the time of Cortés to that of the last known Kan Ek' ruler, the dynasty reproduced itself with a series of kings named Kan Ek' — with the primary meaning "Serpent Star" and perhaps a secondary meaning of "Sky Star" (*ka'an ek'*).[54] Although it is nowhere explicitly stated by an Itzá source, Spaniards believed that the dynasty passed from father to son, as the continuity of the name Ek' would suggest. They apparently reasoned that if mothers and fathers of kings always belonged to the Kan and Ek' patrilineages, respectively, their children, whether male or female, would always bear the double name Kan Ek'.

The same would have been true, however, if Kan had been a matronym passed on through females, in which case the rulership was reproduced through the successive intermarriage of men with the patronym Ek' and women with the matronym Kan. In the Itza core area the name Kan never appears "in last place" as a patronym (that is, following another surname). It does appear, however, as the first of another double name, Kan Chan, assigned to members of the nobility.[55] This evidence suggests that Kan was only a matronym among the Itzas, never a patronym. This suggests, in turn, that the name Kan was matrilineally inherited in the same way that NaChan Kanche inherited his matronym, Chan, from his mother.

Of equal significance is the fact that Kan is absent as an independent surname in the eighteenth-century Itza-area church marriage registers, although the name appears as part of the compound surnames Kanchan and Kanek'.[56] Ek', on the other hand, does appear in these records, although less frequently than Kanek'. Such compound surnames were treated by the Catholic priests as single patronyms, presumably correctly. Because Kan Ek' represented both a matronym and a patronym when used by Itza royalty, however, the patronymic name Kanek' was a nonroyal name, obviously modeled on the royal one. According to Avendaño, it was taken by the followers or more distant kin of the king, or Ajaw.[57]

From this discussion we may tentatively conclude that Kan was the royal Itza matronym — either the only Itza matronym or the most important one, reserved for high-ranking nobility. If this is correct, Kan was also the royal Itza matrilineage, just as Ek' was the royal Itza patrilineage. Kans also apparently married into other high-ranking patrilineages, as indicated by the name Kan Chan.[58]

Whether or not there were other matronyms and matrilineages in Itza society is not yet fully clear. One possibility is Kawil, of which only two instances are known: Kab'an (day name) Kawil and Kawil Itza, both of whom were heads of Itza towns.[59] Kawil was not a patronymic surname at San Andrés or San José, just as Kan was not, but it may have been a given name.[60] Another candidate is Moan, also represented by two persons, both named Moan Pana and both heads of towns (Table 3.1). Although Moan is a Yucatec patronym, it does not appear later at the postconquest mission towns San Andrés or San José.

Besides giving us glimpses of kinship groups identified by names, the colonial documents tell us something about the more domestic aspects of Itza social life.

Polygyny, the marriage between a husband and multiple wives, was common among the Itza elites but probably not among those of lower status. In at least some cases a man's wives were sisters, an arrangement known as sororal polygyny. The number of wives married to one man is reported to have varied from three to seven.[61] Rural households after the 1697 conquest were sometimes large, with as many as twenty-five persons living in one house at Ixtus in the Yalain area.[62] Such numbers, however, may have partly reflected what amounted to refugee conditions at the time. As we learned earlier, Fuensalida estimated that there were two hundred houses along the shore of Nojpeten in 1618, with royal palaces and temples presumably occupying the rest of the small island. In 1696, when, because of increasing defense needs and migration from rural areas, the population of the island was probably larger than it had been seventy-eight years earlier, Avendaño estimated it at about five thousand people. If at that time there had been 250 houses, the average household size would have been about twenty persons — a rough but not unreasonable estimate.[63]

The Itza Kingdom

The Spanish friars, soldiers, and bureaucrats who knew the Itzas regarded their political system as a small kingdom over which Ajaw Kan Ek' ruled as a despot. The Spaniards called him both king (*rey*) and "petty king" (*reyezuelo*), the latter term emphasizing that in the order of things he stood well beneath the king of Spain. They also knew from statements by Itza royal family members and nobles that under the king was a ranked hierarchy of positions whose incumbents both advised the king and governed the various sections of Itza territory. Such recorded Itza statements, however, are few and lacking in detail. If any Spanish observers fully grasped the nature and structure of the Itza kingdom, they left a sparse record of their knowledge.[64]

Fortunately, careful readings of Spanish documents that incorporate Itza testimony enable us tentatively to reconstruct the main features of the Itza political system. One issue over which there has been much debate is the degree to which Maya political systems were centralized and hierarchical. Most recently Joyce Marcus has argued that since

> at least A.D. 534 onward, the Maya displayed the archaeological manifestations of what anthropologists have called an "archaic state": a stratified, highly centralized, internally specialized society with a professional ruling class. As a political system, the archaic state is seen as having more institutionalized power than the ranked but unstratified societies that preceded it, particularly in the areas of waging war and exacting tribute.[65]

Marcus attempts to resolve conflicting evidence that depicts Maya political systems as sometimes relatively egalitarian (made up of several small components of roughly equal status) and at other times highly stratified (composed of units under a single, powerful rulership). She proposes a "dynamic" model characterized by oscillations between periods of high conflict among smaller, less hierarchical centers and periods of relative peace in which single centers, such as Chich'en Itza, became powerful regional ruling capital centers.[66]

I agree with Marcus that the Itzas represented a more "centralized" pole of this oscillating historical pattern—a quadripartite system ruled by a central kingship that controlled a significant territorial hinterland.[67] In chapter 2 I presented evidence that Itza military and political strategies between 1525 and 1697 resulted in the increased military effectiveness of their political system, to the point that they had created an "empire" of sorts encompassing the native populations along their frontiers. That Spanish observers saw these populations—particularly Chols and Mopans—as disorganized or decentralized reflected less the inherent organizational weakness of these borderland groups than the success of the Itzas in incorporating them into a larger, highly centralized system that could offer effective defense against Spanish intrusion or attack.

As I have studied the evidence concerning the Itza political system over the past years I have gradually shifted from regarding the "Itzas" as a confederacy of political or kinship groups of relatively equal status to seeing them as strongly hierarchical, "ruled" by a small, exclusive set of closely related kin who shared power with other groups only at their convenience or as a matter of political strategy. Although the Itzas did integrate other groups by recognizing their leaders as weaker, subsidiary representatives on the ruling council, the royal family managed to control the joint kingship and all senior territorial rulership positions. I have suggested that Itza history hints at the possibility that this system coalesced through a policy of integration by conquest, in which the Itzas incorporated newly dominated groups by marrying them to existing elites and granting them positions on the ruling council as Ach Kat military-religious leaders.[68]

THE RULERSHIP AND GOVERNING COUNCIL OF NOJPETEN

In April 1695 a Mopan interpreter named "Cacique" Yajkab' provided one of the earliest and most intriguing descriptions of the Itza political order. He gave his brief testimony to the Guatemalan captain Juan Díaz de Velasco, who was escorting Dominican friars hoping to meet Ajaw Kan Ek' at Nojpeten. Yajkab' outlined features of Itza rulership and the physical design of Nojpeten that helps make sense of other, contemporaneous accounts.[69] He testified that the previous "lord and principal cacique" of the Itzas "left three of his sons as governors of the island." He meant, we can assume, that the previous Ajaw Kan Ek' was succeeded by his three sons, all of whom, he said, were named Kan Ek' ("Canec"). Yajkab' also told Díaz de Velasco that the island contained four towns or wards (*pueblos o barrios*). The spellings in the original sources are questionable and inconsistent in two editions of Fray Francisco Ximénez's historical work, but I have interpreted the names of the wards to have been Kan Ek', Kaj Jol ("Town of the Port"), Makocheb' ("Narrow Stairway"), and Noj-peten ("Big District [or Island]").[70]

Yajkab' seems to have made a clear distinction between the title translated as "lord and principal cacique" (*señor y cacique principal*), which is applied to the deceased ruler, and that given to his three sons, who were "governors of the island." By implication, his successor, the new Ajaw Kan Ek', may not have been his son but rather another close relative, possibly his brother's son.

Avendaño's List of Rulers and Elites

When Fray Andrés de Avendaño visited Nojpeten in January 1696, he sought to ascertain something about the organization of people and space on the island capital. He asked various Itza leaders "how many districts [*parcialidades*] that peten [island, in this case] on which we were had, and . . . they told me there were twenty-two," which they went on to describe by their names.[71] The resulting list provides names and titles of persons who apparently made up the Itza governing council, including Ajaw Kan Ek' and other major noble leaders. Avendaño offered almost no interpretation of the list: neither the identities of the individuals nor the significance of their titles is explained. Although the list is difficult to interpret, it is nonetheless an exceedingly important document — a critical key to grasping the nature of the Itza kingdom from the perspective of its own rulers.

Table 3.4 lists Avendaño's original spellings of the names and titles in the first column and my edited transcriptions of them in the second column.[72] Table 3.5 offers a tentative breakdown of these names and titles. I have reordered three of the individuals in this table (numbers 7, 8, and 9) for reasons to be explained shortly.

The first ruler on the list is "Rey AjKan Ek'," whose proper Itza title would have been Ajaw AjKan Ek', in which Ajaw was equivalent to the Spanish *rey,* or king. I believe it highly likely that his name had the dual significance of either Kan Ek' (*kan ek'*, "Serpent Star") or Kaan Ek' (*ka'an ek'*, "Sky Star), and indeed we see the spelling Kaan in the names of the first two individuals listed among the Tipujan Itzas who went to Chunuk'um in Belize in 1655 (Table 3.2).

TABLE 3.4
Original and Edited Transcriptions of Avendaño's List of Twenty-two Parcialidades of Nojpeten, 1696

Literal transcription	Edited transcription
La del Rey Ah Can Ek	La del Rey AjKan Ek'
La de noh ah chata	La de Noj AjCh'ata[a]
La de ah ɔic ɔin batab	La de AjTz'ik Tz'in[b] B'atab'
La de el Casique noh che	La del Cacique Noj Che
La de Ah chatan ek	La de AjCh'atan Ek'
La de Ach cat Cixbon	La de Ach Kat K'ixab'on[c]
La de noh ɔo can Punab	La de Noj Tz'o Kan Punab'
La de noh ɔo can noh	La de Noj Tz'o Kan Noj
La de ɔo can ɔic	La de Tz'o Kan Tz'ik
La de Ach Cat Matan cua	La de Ach Kat Matan Kwa
La de Ach Cat Batun	La de Ach Kat B'atun
La de Ach Cat Baca	La de Ach Kat B'aka
La de Ach Cat, halach vinic	La de Ach Kat, Jalach Winik
La de Ach Cat Mul Çah	La de Ach Kat Mul Saj[d]
La de Ach Cat Kin chil	La de Ach Kat K'in Chil
La de Ach Cat Kin chan	La de Ach Kat K'in Chan
La de Ach Cat Kayan	La de Ach Kat K'ayan
La de Ach cat, Cit Can	La de Ach Kat, Kit Kan
La de Ach Cat Ytza	La de Ach Kat Itza
La de Ach Cat Pop	La de Ach Kat Pop
La de Ach Cat Camal	La de Ach Kat Kamal
La de Ach Catt Mas Kin	La de Ach Kat Mas K'in

SOURCE: Avendaño, 1987, p. 43; Relación, 1696, f. 38r–v. This transcription is based on a new reading of the original text in Avendaño's Relación.

[a]Although recorded as Ch'ata, this is likely the same name recorded frequently as Chata. I assume, perhaps incorrectly, that it is a different name from Ch'atan (three lines below), which I have left as recorded.

[b]Although recorded as Tz'in, this is almost surely the name recorded elsewhere as Tzin.

[c]Although written Cixbon (i.e., Kixb'on), this is almost certainly the name usually written Kixabon (K'ixab'on) and sometimes Cixabon (Kixab'on).

[d]The first letter of this name in the original manuscript appears to be Ç (a "soft" c with cedilla), but this may be a copyist's error. The copyist might have mistaken a dot over the i in Kin below it for the cedilla. The alternative transcription to Saj ("fear") would therefore be Kaj ("town"), making it "Mound Town" (mul kaj). I interpret it as the latter in the text.

TABLE 3.5

Tentative Breakdown of Titles and Names of Twenty-two Itza Leaders Listed by Avendaño, 1696

Order	Masc. prefix	Title	Masc. prefix	Matronym or Patronym	Patronym	Title	Toponym
1		Rey	Aj-	Kan	Ek'		
7		Noj Tz'o		Kan	Punab'		
8		Noj Tz'o		Kan	(Noj)	(Noj)	
9		Tz'o		Kan	(Tz'ik)	(Tz'ik)	
2		Noj	Aj-		Chata		
3	(Aj-)	(Tz 'ik)	(Aj-)	(Tz'ik)	Tzin	B'atab'	
4		Cacique (Noj) (Che)		(Noj)	(Che)		
5	(Aj-)	(Ch'atan)	(Aj-)	(Chata)	Ek'		
6		Ach Kat			K'ixab'on		
10		Ach Kat (Matan)		(Matan)	Kwa		
11		Ach Kat			B'atun		
12		Ach Kat					B'aka
13		Ach Kat, Jalach Winik					
14		Ach Kat					Mul Saj
15		Ach Kat K'in Chil					
16		Ach Kat (K'in)		(K'in)	Chan		
17		Ach Kat K'ayan					
18		Ach Kat (Kit Kan)			(Kitkan)		
19		Ach Kat			Itza		
20		Ach Kat (Pop)					(Pop)
21		Ach Kat			Kamal		
22		Ach Kat		Mas	K'in		

SOURCE: Avendaño, 1987, p. 43; Relación, 1696, f. 38r–v.

NOTE:The procedural assumptions used here are similar to those followed in Table 3.3., but the task is complicated by the presence of poorly understood titles. Alternative parsings are certainly possible in several cases, some of which I have indicated in parentheses.

In the list as ordered in Table 3.5, the three individuals following Rey AjKan Ek' (numbers 7–9) all bear a title string or a title-name string with the common element Tz'o Kan: Noj Tz'o Kan Punab', Noj Tz'o Kan Noj, and Tz'o Kan Tz'ik. Noj is an honorific suggesting "great." I suspect that these three are the sons of the former Ajaw Kan Ek' to whom Cacique Yajkab' referred. There are several possible interpretations of these epithets, none of which can be considered certain. (1) Tz'o refers to the turkey cock, treated here as a sacred "adult male bird" concept, and Kan could be the royal matronym shared by the three brothers. (2) Tz'o Kan may be a misrecording of *tz'akan,* referring to a close companion, particularly a close relative.[73] This would be an appropriate title in light of these three rulers' probable status as sons of the former Ajaw and, therefore, his potential successors. (3) Tz'o Kan may be a misrecording of *tz'u-ka'an,* which could mean "center of sky" or "heart of sky," the name of the creator in the Popol Vuj of the K'iche Mayas of Guatemala and recently proposed (although with different terminology) as a central cosmological referent to the north celestial pole in ancient Maya thought.[74]

Each of these three titles ends with a different word: Punab' ("Mahogany Tree"), Noj ("Great"), and Tz'ik (perhaps "Fierce"). The nature of these final terms is not clear, but perhaps they in some way described the strength and prowess of the individual. I suspect, however, that these were given names or surnames.

The next individual (number 2), Noj AjChata (AjCh'ata in the original text), "Great AjChata," is a man whose lineage patronym was probably Chata. Following him is AjTz'ik Tzin, B'atab': "Fierce Tzin [another lineage name], B'atab'." The next person, Cacique Noj Che, may bear only a title, "Great/Big Tree," or the double surname Naj Che, which appears in Yucatán but has not been recorded elsewhere in the Itza area. AjCh'atan Ek' (number 5) has the patronym Ek' and a title, Ch'atan, that could be Ch'at'an (*aj-ch'a t'an,* possibly "Receiver of Words" or "Receiver, Bearer of Strength, Power"). Ch'atan, however, could be the patronym Chata.

The last fourteen persons all bear the same initial title, Ach Kat. The meaning and significance of this title in terms of the Maya language have eluded all attempts at understanding, because literally it would mean something like "Penis of the Vessel" or perhaps "Head Man of the Vessel," neither a satisfactory or revealing solution. It appears most likely that Ach Kat was a Mayanized form of the Nahuatl title Achcauhtli (plural Achcacauhtin), which literally means "elder brothers."[75] Rudolph van Zantwijk has described the Achcacauhtin of central Mexico as "military chiefs or commanders of medium- to large-sized calpollis," localized communities

87

with common lands and ceremonial center.[76] According to Sahagún, there were six of these on the ruling council of Tenochtitlan.[77]

It would not be surprising to find such institutions among the Itzas, whose ancestors could have been introduced to them through contacts with Nahuatl speakers from Tabasco or perhaps elsewhere. The linguist Otto Schumann observed several aspects of contemporary Itza culture that suggested historical contact with the Nahuatl-speaking Pipils who lived along a stretch of the Pacific coast of El Salvador and Guatemala. These similarities include certain Nahuatl words, surnames, beliefs, and linguistic practices.[78]

In his study of Aztec warfare, Ross Hassig described the Achcacauhtin as "executioners, keepers of the arms, and military trainers" and considered it likely that they were members of the *cuauhpipiltin,* "commoners who had achieved noble status by virtue of their deeds in war."[79] Elsewhere he writes, "The achcacauhtin were warriors in charge of declaring war or subduing rebelling provinces. The achcauhtli position was usually held by a valiant warrior, but rather than being warriors per se the achcacauhtin were a type of judicial officer and oversaw arms, doctrine, and training."[80]

We have no direct information that would enable us to determine whether the position of Ach Kat had military and other functions similar to that of the Aztec Achcauhtli. If the Itzas adopted some aspects of Aztec or possibly Pipil military organization, and not just the title, the Ach Kat positions recorded by Avendaño may have been military in nature. The possible presence of three or four toponyms following the title, as indicated in Table 3.5, suggests that these individuals were associated with certain named places: B'aka (possibly from *b'ak ja',* "bone lake"), Mul Kaj ("Mound Town"), and Pop (*poop,* "mat"). Places named B'aka and Pop are recorded in the documents.[81] K'in Chil may well have an association with the Itza deity K'in Chil Kob'a, which Avendaño described as a "statue" of a man made of stone and lime, situated "in a crevice in a pile of stones."[82] There was a town named K'inchil in the AjKanul province of Yucatán, also associated with an image of K'in Chil Kob'a, who had a vaulted temple.[83]

The holders of the Ach Kat position may have been responsible for the
military recruiting, training, and directing of youths from specific towns or regions of which they were themselves residents. If so, the Itzas would have had a locale-based standing (or easily assembled) army, a likelihood in light of their reputed military prowess. The presence of the additional

title Jalach Winik (often translated "Real Man") appended to one of the Ach Kats (number 13) is particularly intriguing, because in Yucatán this title described a territorial ruler.[84] This man may instead have been the principal military commander among this Itza group. All of the probable surnames among this group differ, suggesting that each represented a different lineage associated with one of the principal towns.[85]

Comparative Accounts of the Principal Rulers of Itza Territory

I return now to the identities of the first set of titled individuals of Avendaño's list, those immediately following Rey AjKan Ek' in Table 3.5. This set, for reasons that will become clear, probably included not just the first seven but the first eight persons following the Ajaw's name, thus including the first Ach Kat (K'ixab'on), whose name was seventh on Avendaño's list. Fortunately, in addition to Avendaño's list, we can call on other sources to explore further the structure of Itza rulership and administration. Table 3.6 presents such information in the form of a tentative cross-tabulation of the rulers described in these several sources (with the order of the original listing indicated in parentheses).

Column I, combining information from two Itza noble prisoners captured by Guatemalans in 1695, lists Ajaw Kan Ek' and Kuch Pop Kit Kan. The first part of the second title-name string, Kuch Pop, identifies this position as probably equivalent to the Yucatecan position Jol Pop ("Head of the Mat"). This part of the title, meaning something like "Bearer of the Mat," referred to the person's responsibility for matters of governance, because *pop* (mat) referred not only to the mat on which the king sat but also to the very principle of governance by council.[86] In May 1695 a noble prisoner named AjK'ixaw told his Guatemalan captors that "the principal cacique or reyezuelo" was named Kit Kan and that he was "very tall and fat" and never left the island capital. I believe that he was referring to Kuch Pop Kit Kan, who was in essence the head of government affairs on Nojpeten. The rest of his title, Kit Kan, is frequently found in association with the highest level of Nojpeten rulership.

Column II lists the titled individuals named by AjChan while he was in Mérida to declare his uncle's readiness to surrender to Spanish rule (chapter 7). Asked whether "the caciques and principal lords of his provinces" had been in agreement with Ajaw Kan Ek' before the declarant left for Mérida, AjChan said that the ruler had communicated with the four listed reyezuelos (petty kings) in addition to Ajaw Tzin, "who is one of the

TABLE 3.6

Tentative Reconstruction of Equivalent Persons and Positions Among the Highest-Ranking Itza Nobility, 1695–1702, Based on Comparison of Principal Sources

I 1695	II 1695	III 1696	IV 1698	V *Other Sources*
(1) Ajaw Kan Ek'	Rey Kan Ek' (1)	Rey AjKan Ek' (1)	Rey Kan Ek' (1)	Rey AjKan Ek' (common)
(2) Kuch Pop Kit Kan	Reyezuelo Kit Kan (2)	Noj Tz'o Kan Punab' (7)	Reyezuelo Kit Kan (2)	
(3)	Reyezuelo Ajaw Matan (3)	Noj Tz'o Kan Noj (8)	Reyezuelo Kit Kan (4)	
(4)	Reyezuelo AjKit Kan (5)	Tz'o Kan Tz'ik (9)	Reyezuelo Kit Kan (5)	
(5)	Reyezuelo AjK'in (4)	*Noj AjChata* (2)	Reyezuelo Tesukan (3)	Reyezuelo K'in Kante (1696) Cacique AjKan (1696)
(6)	Ajaw Tzin, Principal (6)	AjTz'ik Tzin B'atab' (3)	Cacique Tzin (6)	
(7)		Cacique Noj Che (4)	Cacique Tut (7)	Capitán Tut
(8)		AjCh'atan Ek' (5)	Cacique Kan Ek' (8)	
(9)		Ach Kat K'ixab'on (6)	Cacique Kitkan (9)	

SOURCES: Column I: Ximénez, 1971–77, vol. 29, bk. 5, Ch. 65, pp. 356–57. Column II: AGI, P 237, ramo 3, Declaración de un indio que dijo llamarse Ah Chan . . . , 29 Dec. 1695, ff. 191v–196v. Column III: Avendaño, Relación, 1696, f. 38r–v. Column IV: G 345, no. 20, ff. 121v–129v; P 237, ramo 1, Razón individual y general de los pueblos, poblaciones, y rancherías de esta provincia de Zuyuha Peten Itza . . . , 6 Jan. 1698, ff. 80r–84v. Column V: for Reyezuelo K'in Kante, G 151A, pieza 3, Declaration of four Indians from Peten, 20 Sept. 1696, ff. 237v–240r; for Cacique AjKan, Avendaño, Relación, 1996, ff. 25v, 46r, 48r, and Avendaño, 1987, pp. 28, 50, 52.

NOTE: The numbers in the left-hand column indicate the order of the listing given by the sources for columns II and IV, to which those listed in column III have been tentatively reordered to conform (see text). The numbers in parentheses for columns I–III indicate the order in which the individual was listed in the source. The italicized name, Noj AjChata, is probably not the same person as the others in row 5.

indios principales." What is of particular interest here is the quadripartite structure indicated by the four reyezuelos and their apparent seniority over Ajaw Tzin.

Column III reorders the first nine titles on Avendaño's list of heads of parcialidades. The first four positions are apparently equivalent to the four reyezuelos in column III. The three titles containing Tz'o Kan were likely the three sons of the former ruler said by Cacique Yajkab' to have been assigned, upon their father's death, positions as "governors." Their common title was apparently equivalent to the title Kit Kan as seen in columns II and IV. The fourth person, Noj AjChata, identified by his surname, held the same position but was probably not the same person as Reyezuelo AjK'in in column II or Reyezuelo Tesukan in column IV. These last two, I believe, were titles held by one individual, identified elsewhere as Reyezuelo K'in Kante and Cacique AjKan (column V). In 1695 and 1696 this man, also identified as the "uncle" of Ajaw Kan Ek', was at war with the ruler and had apparently been replaced by Noj AjChata before Avendaño arrived at Nojpeten.[87]

The title Kit Kan is of special interest in that it, like Tz'o Kan, apparently refers to the former ruler's three sons. Like Ach Kat, the title may have a rough Nahuatl parallel, in this case to the Aztec title Cihuacoatl borne by the internal heads of the three states of the Triple Alliance, who held positions in a complementary relationship to the supreme ruler. Kit Kan could, in colonial Yucatec, mean "father's sister serpent," paralleling three possible meanings of Cihuacoatl — "female consort," "female companion," or "female snake" — in which femaleness probably referred to junior status in comparison with the ruler himself.[88] This is not to suggest that the Itzas attempted to replicate the position exactly. If that had been the case, then AjK'in Kan Ek', the high priest and ruling partner of Ajaw Kan Ek', would have been the one and only Kit Kan, when in fact he did not bear this title. The three who did were in effect co-rulers in a junior sense with the principal ruling pair.

The next four positions in Avendaño's list (column III) are apparently equivalent to the four caciques in column IV. These are quite clearly junior to the first four, with only one bearing a title without a name (Cacique Noj Che). AjTz'ik Tzin's closing title, B'atab', is almost certainly the Itza equivalent of cacique, suggesting that all four of these personages were known as B'atab'. AjTz'ik Tzin is the same person as Ajaw Tzin in column II and Cacique Tzin in column IV, and AjCh'atan Ek' is the same person as Cacique Kan Ek' in column IV. It is less clear that Ach Kat K'ixab'on is the same person as Cacique Kitkan in column IV. If he was, then his name would have been either K'ixab'on Kitkan or Kitkan K'ixab'on. I do not believe that he bore the title Kit Kan but rather that this was a surname adopted from the high-ranking title shared by the three ruling brothers.

Column IV was dictated by Ajaw Kan Ek' and his co-ruling cousin (not included here), the high priest AjK'in Kan Ek', more than a year following the conquest, while they were held prisoners at Nojpeten. The Spanish description that introduces the list makes it clear that it comprised the membership of the core ruling council at the time of the 1697 conquest: "They declare that always and until [the time of] the entrada of don Martín de Ursúa y Arizmendi [the province of Suyuja Peten Itza] was governed by four kings and four caciques who had their own provinces [*parcialidades*], separate and richly populated, and they are as follows."[89] Again, the three identified as Reyezuelo Kit Kan appear to be the same persons as those with the Tz'o Kan title in column III.[90]

One person remains to be mentioned: Cacique Tut, alias Cacique Noj Che and Captain Tut. He was the war leader usually called simply AjTut, described by Avendaño as the head of the port town of Nich in Chak'an Itza territory.[91] He may also have borne a title such as Nakom, "war captain," for the Spaniards frequently gave him the title *capitán,* the probable Spanish equivalent of the Maya term. Although the other B'atab's did not receive this title, the two principal Kowoj leaders were known as Cacique Kowoj and Captain Kowoj, respectively, indicating a type of political-military dual partnership that is known to have existed in Yucatán.[92]

B'atab' and Ajaw B'atab'

Other sources confirm that, as in column I, the Itza equivalent of *rey* was Ajaw.[93] The four men called reyezuelos by the Spaniards (numbers 2–5, columns II and IV) may have had a single title equivalent to the Spanish *reyezuelo,* or "petty king," but it is nowhere explicitly recorded. Two titles by which three of them were known were obviously Noj Tz'o Kan (or simply Tz'o Kan) and Kit Kan. It is possible that the common title was Ajaw, as applied to Ajaw Matan in column II. The four designated as "caciques" in column IV may well have borne the shorter title B'atab', as applied to AjTz'ik Tzin in column III. This individual, however, was also called Ajaw (column II), leaving open the possibility that all eight rulers under Ajaw Kan Ek' could bear the title Ajaw.

To further complicate the matter, the Spanish commentary on the province administered by Ajaw Kan Ek' (column IV) states, "This king was like an emperor among them, as he ruled over all of the other kings [i.e., reyezuelos] and caciques, who in their language they call batabob; and they testify that this [Nojpeten] is the largest province."[94] By distinguishing kings from caciques, this statement supports the hypothesis that although all eight could bear the title B'atab', one category was higher in rank than the other, marked by the additional title Ajaw. The three titles—Ajaw (one holder), Ajaw B'atab' (reyezuelo, four holders), and B'atab' (cacique, four holders)—appear, therefore, to represent a three-level governing hierarchy.

The Number of Itza Provinces

The commentary for column IV specifies that each of these nine rulers represented a particular province or district (*parcialidad*), suggesting a total of nine Itza provinces. AjChan, however, stated in his testimony (column II) that there were ten Itza provinces, "and each one with many towns . . . the largest of which is that of the great *cayo* [island] of the Itza, which is on an island in a large lake, and on its shores many towns rich in people."[95] AjChan's tenth province might have been his own home region centered at Yalain, east of the main lake. As a "colonized" region, the principal rulers may have considered it to be, in a formal sense, "outside" core Itza territory. It is more likely, however, that he considered Nojpeten to be two "provinces" because, like all the others, it had a dual rulership.

Although these sources indicate that there were nine or ten Itza "provinces," I believe there were actually five: the island capital and four surrounding political territories with paired, hierarchically ranked rulers. The confusion, it seems, was generated by miscommunication between Spanish questioners and Itza informants over the distinction between a "province" and the person or persons who governed it. That is, when asked how many provinces there were, the Itzas responded by listing rulers, not specifying that the provinces were governed jointly by two rulers.

In Yucatán, political territories or provinces such as these were called *b'atab'il*—the territory and town governed by a B'atab'—and the term was defined in the colonial dictionaries as *cacicazgo*. The Itzas, however, used the term *peten* to designate a province.[96] Because *peten* also meant "island" or even "peninsula" (features which, like territories, are surrounded by something "different" from themselves), Spanish writers were often confounded by the term.

We do not know the term used to describe Itza territory as a whole, but it might have been *kuch kab'al*, which, according to the colonial dictionaries of Yucatán, referred to the entire territory administered from a central town—a *cabecera*, in the Spanish. Nojpeten, of course, would have been the administrative center. In Yucatán the B'atab' was the representa-

tive of the "ruler" of the *kuch kab'al,* who was known generically as the
Jalach Winik, a term apparently reserved by the Itzas for the principal
person among those with the title Ach Kat.[97] Ajaw Kan Ek' would have
been the Itza equivalent of the Yucatecan Jalach Winik. In Yucatán the
B'atab' is usually understood to have been only the administrator or governor of a town, whereas the Itza title B'atab' and the possible title Ajaw
B'atab' refer to territorial administrators who also served, I propose, as
heads of the quarters of the island capital. That is, they were both local
and regional governors.

QUADRIPARTITE DIVISION AND DUAL RULE

The division of the Itza polity into four sections, ruled from a center,
reflected an association of territory with a quadripartite cosmos and the
four associated cardinal directions, the year-ending and year-beginning
rituals associated with the cardinal directions, and a host of other cosmological and ritual meanings.[98] Dual rulership in this system was important
not only at the provincial level but also at the highest level of the ruling
hierarchy. The name AjK'in Kan Ek', the Itza high priest and father's
brother's son to Ajaw Kan Ek', appears on none of the lists of ruling
nobility. All sources, however, agree that he shared power equally with his
cousin. In the commentary for the list in column IV of Table 3.6, AjK'in
Kan Ek' is cited as stating that "he testified having ruled over all [of the
other rulers] as the principal priest of them all."[99] On the eve of the conquest AjChan told Ursúa that AjK'in Kan Ek' "is equal in power to the
reyezuelo [Ajaw Kan Ek'] for all things that are ordered."[100] Shortly after
his capture in 1697 the high priest himself answered a question on this
topic posed by Ursúa: "Asked how, being priest, he says he is king, he said:
He is priest and wise man for all of them. For that reason he is called king
of these lands, and because he is father's brother's son to Ah Canek, who is
the legitimate king of these lands." The high priest meant that he and his
cousin shared a single political persona by virtue of the fact that their
fathers were brothers. That is, these two men ruled jointly as a single
person: one primarily in the realm of political affairs and the other in the
complementary but by no means separate realm of the supernatural.[101]

His claim that he was the "legitimate king" may also have referred to
issues of succession. It is possible that his uncle had been the previous ruler
and had inherited the rulership from his own brother, the father of the
present ruler. In this scenario the present Ajaw Kan Ek' would have succeeded to the position as the next in line after his uncle, to be followed
next in line by AjK'in Kan Ek'. If this speculative genealogy is correct,

AjK'in Kan Ek' would have been the brother of the three sons of the former ruler who served as territorial governors with the title Kit Kan.

Such a "joint rulership" model applied at the provincial level would result in four senior-junior "principal pairs," each comprising an Ajaw B'atab' and a B'atab' — or, in colonial terminology, a reyezuelo and a cacique. The difficulty in identifying the membership of these pairs stems from the several slightly varying orderings of rulers provided in Table 3.6 and the consequent uncertainty of the "correct" order that would result in proper pairings.

Fortunately, we can establish with some certainty one of these pairs, that of Ajaw B'atab' K'in Kante and B'atab' Tut. The person who in normal times had held position 5 (Table 3.6, left margin) was almost certainly the individual identified by Avendaño in January 1696 as a "close relative" of Ajaw Kan Ek' and as the principal ruler of the northern Chak'an Itza province, including the port of "Nich" or Nixtun on the western end of the main lake. Avendaño called him Cacique Kan, not Reyezuelo as might have been expected for a person of such importance. His full name might have been AjKan Kante. According to Avendaño, he was at that time in alliance with "Cacique" or "Captain" Kowoj in a rebellion against Ajaw Kan Ek'; both rebels identified themselves with the Chak'an Itza province.[102]

He almost certainly was also the man called Reyezuelo K'in Kante and identified as the ruler of the Yalain region by a group of men from that area who testified in Bacalar in the same year. These men stated that he was at war with Ajaw Kan Ek', whom they no longer considered to be their own ruler. That Ajaw B'atab' K'in Kante, as I shall call him, did in fact claim rulership over both Chak'an Itza and the eastern province is confirmed by the men's offer to provide canoes at the port of Ch'ich' — the same place as Nich or Nixtun — from where the Spaniards could attack Nojpeten.[103] Following the forced exile of Ajaw Kan Ek' to Santiago de Guatemala in 1699, he may have been the person who was installed as the new Itza ruler in the vicinity of B'alam Tun and Laguna Sacpuy (see chapter 14).

When Avendaño reached Nich he identified it as the principal settlement of Chak'an Itza. Its "cacique" was none other than one identity given for the junior half of the pair headed by Ajaw B'atab' K'in Kante: **95** AjTut,[104] who had a reputation as a powerful military leader and long-distance trader. In the years following the conquest he pursued a relentless war against the Kowojs and established a refuge against Spanish encroachment in the region known as Mompana.

TABLE 3.7
Principal Pairs of Itza Rulers

Ajaw B'atab'	B'atab'	Direction Represented
K'in Kan Kante (also held by Noj AjChata, alias Reyezuelo Tesukan)	Tut (Noj Che)	North
Kit Kan (Noj Tz'o Kan Noj)	Kan Ek' (AjCh'atan Ek')	West
Kit Kan (Tz'o Kan Tz'ik)	Kitkan (Ach Kat K'ixab'on)	South
Kit Kan (Noj Tz'o Kan Punab')	Tzin (Ajaw Tzin, AjTz'ik Tzin)	East

That one Noj AjChata (Table 3.6, column III) occupied the position of Ajaw B'atab' K'in Kante in January 1696 is not surprising, given the breach between the latter and the principal ruler. Whether Reyezuelo Tesukan (Table 3.6, column IV) was Noj AjChata or Ajaw B'atab' K'in Kante (column V) cannot be known with certainty. I suspect that the enmity between Ajaw Kan Ek' and his uncle, the ruler of Chak'an Itza, had lasted until the eve of the conquest and that Tesukan, therefore, was a title given to Noj AjChata.

This information establishes quite firmly that this senior-junior principal pair, notwithstanding the political ruptures that characterized this period, controlled both the northern quarter of Nojpeten and that region to the north of Nojpeten known as Chak'an Itza. Ajaw B'atab' K'in Kante had established an alliance with the Kowojs against his own close matrilineal kinsman, Ajaw Kan Ek', as part of a strategy to depose the ruler.

I believe that we can accept the original order of the list recorded as column IV as the most dependable guide to establishing all four of the principal pairs. Returning Reyezuelo Tesukan (3), who probably held Ajaw B'atab' Kit Kan's position by the end of 1695, to his original place (between 2 and 4) would result in the four pairings shown in Table 3.7.

THE POLITICAL GEOGRAPHY OF THE FOUR JOINTLY
RULED TERRITORIES

96 Michael Coe proposed that in preconquest Yucatán, Maya political geography at the territorial level was founded on a cosmological model constructed at the capital town, which served as a centerpoint from which territorial boundaries extended. Coe constructed this model primarily on the basis of evidence concerning the annual counterclockwise ritual rotation of offices on the town governing council, an event that unfolded during the five "unlucky" Wayeb' days that constitute the final, nineteenth month of the 365-day vague year and during the New Year rituals that followed.[105] The Wayeb' days were the "leftover" month of five days that remained after eighteen twenty-day named months had been completed. The first day of the new year that followed in the fifty-two-year Mayapan calendar round used by the Itzas always began on 1 Pop, the first day of the twenty-day month called Pop. Only four named days, known as year-bearers, could logically initiate the new year; these cycled over a four-year period in the following order: K'an (east), Muluk (north), Ix (west), and Kawak (south).

The annual Wayeb' rituals, described in detail by Landa, were marked by a complex circuiting of "idols" within quarters and by ritual dancing and animal sacrifice. The rituals also served as a mechanism whereby important men on the council shifted certain responsibilities and privileges to others for the coming year. This was accomplished by making the new dominant ritual quarter the one that was located adjacent to the old one, moving by one quarter in a counterclockwise direction each year. That is, following a year in which west was dominant (an Ix year), south would become dominant (a Kawak year), then east (a K'an year), and finally north (a Muluk year). This rotation of ritually dominant quarters was essentially a spatiotemporal "walking out" of the cosmological model that structured both town and kingdom.[106]

It would not be surprising if at Nojpeten these important men were the eight paired individuals just discussed: one Ajaw B'atab' and one B'atab' for each of the four quarters or wards of the island çapital, which corresponded in turn with a wider geographical division of Itza territory into four directional quadrants. As a group these men were equivalent to the town councilors known in Yucatán who bore the title of AjKuch Kab' ("bearer of the town"). The person who served as the head of the council at Nojpeten was known as Kuch Pop Kit Kan ("bearer of the mat"), probably equivalent to the Yucatecan Jol Pop.

I have already proposed that the principal pair who ruled the northern Itza territory known as Chak'an Itza were B'atab' Ajaw K'in Kante and B'atab' Tut. With these two in place as rulers of the north, and assuming that the principle of Wayeb' counterclockwise rotation influenced the dic- **97** tation of the list of rulers in column IV of Table 3.6, the four pairs listed in Table 3.7 would represent north, west, south, and east in the order shown there. Table 3.8 further clarifies the proposed associations among senior-junior title holders, yearbearers, territorial directionality, the four direc-

TABLE 3.8
Proposed Paired Principals of Noipeten, with Associated Yearbearers, Directions, Quarters, and New Year Days

Principal Title	Paired Principals (Usual Designation)	Year-bearer	Direction	Name of Quarter of Noipeten	Associated Conquest-Period New Year Days
Ajaw	Kan Ek'		Center	(All of Itza territory)	
K'in	Kan Ek'				
Ajaw B'atab'	Kit Kan				
B'atab'	Tzin	K'an	East	Noipeten	June 21, 1697
Ajaw B'atab'	K'in Kante' (Aj Kan)		North	Makocheb'	June 22, 1694
B'atab'	Tut	Muluk			June 21, 1698
Ajaw B'atab'	Kit Kan				
B'atab'	Kan Ek'	Ix	West	Kan Ek'	June 22, 1695
Ajaw B'atab'	Kit Kan				
B'atab'	Kit Kan	Kawak	South	Kaj Jol	June 21, 1696

tion quarters of Nojpeten, and the late-seventeenth-century dates on which a particular quarter's new year day actually fell.

The north, as we have seen, constituted the Chak'an Itza province (see map 3), which, just before the 1697 conquest, was expanding its influence over Kowoj territory and the Yalain region. It may have been identified with the principal temple of Nojpeten, the pyramidal structure whose principal stairway and principal temple entrance faced north. This may have been the Nojpeten quarter that Cacique Yajkab' called Makocheb', "Narrow Stairway," referring to the temple itself. The port area of En-senada de San Jerónimo was controlled by the rulers of the north, provid-ing access to trade and movement along the main path that led north through Kejach territory and on to Yucatán. Itza military activities against the Kejach region, known since the time of Cortés, would have been administered by the rulers of the north.

The west constituted the heartland of the Itza kingdom in that it was the most populous Itza region and was probably the homeland of the principal ruler and his descendants. As we learned earlier, the principal entrance to the palace of Ajaw Kan Ek' was on the western shore of Nojpeten. This quadrant of Nojpeten was surely that called Kan Ek' by Cacique Yajkab'. Although the western region did not include the port on Ensenada de San Jerónimo, which was controlled by the northern quarter, its lands cut a wide swath all the way from western arm of the main lake to Laguna Sacpuy and possibly beyond. The trade routes southwest toward Río Pasión and on to Guatemala may well have been under its jurisdic-tion, although at the time of the conquest these seem to have been con-trolled by B'atab' Tut of the north. The total population of the western quarter was probably more than the populations of the other three quar-ters combined. I suspect, but cannot confirm, that its principal town (still unidentified) was on or around Laguna Sacpuy.

Little is known of the south, although it is likely significant that the trade and communication route leading directly to Verapaz was under its jurisdiction. Those Mopans who were under the immediate influence of the Itzas at the time of the conquest lived along the southern area of this route, and we know that since the early part of the century Itzas and Mopans had together fought against Spanish penetration into adjacent Chol communities (see chapter 2). It must have been the rulers of the south **99** who administered policies regarding such military activity. I suspect that in Nojpeten itself, the southern quadrant was the one that the Mopan cacique Yajkab' called Kaj Jol, "Town of the Port." The name may have referred to a public port on the south side of the island, where the present-day causeway enters the island from the mainland. This may have been his own designation for the quarter, because this would have been the entrance used by traders plying the region between Verapaz and Nojpeten. The principal town of the south may well have been on the shore immediately south of Nojpeten.

The east would have been the quarter called Nojpeten by Cacique Yajkab'. In terms of immediate territory, it may have been relatively small, incorporating mainly towns along the northern shore of the lower arm of the main lake east of Nojpeten and further east to the nearby Lakes Petenxil and Quexil and other small bodies of water in this vicinity. But the east was, at least symbolically, the gateway to Lagunetas Salpetén and Macanché, the Yaxhá-Sacnab basin, and even the Tipuj region beyond. It is not known whether the paired principals of the east governed, or attempted to govern, these eastern regions, but it is possible that they did so. This area was abandoned immediately after the conquest, and its principal town has not been identified. Although little is known of the junior ruler, B'atab' Tzin, it was said that he died shortly before the 1697 conquest, perhaps as a result of internecine warfare.[107]

The quadripartite territorial model with a central fifth "province," the island capital, simple and symmetrical in design, implies a high degree of physical symmetry on the ground. That is, we would expect each territorial quarter to be essentially a mirror of the others, dividing land and population more or less equally under the governance of more or less equal territorial rulers. We have already seen that by far the largest and most densely populated territory of "ethnic" Itzas was that of the west, with a heavy concentration of nearly contiguous food-producing towns along the western end of the main lake all the way to Laguna Sacpuy, and with other communities possibly as far west as Laguna Perdida. The other three provinces differed from the dominant west in that each had a few towns near the main lake and a vast hinterland that stretched far beyond the immediate region of Nojpeten. Whereas the west was self-contained and thoroughly Itza in population, the other three regions incorporated, or attempted to incorporate, more distant regions that had to be won and colonized through warfare.

For example, the Chak'an Itza province of the north, with its important port town on Ensenada de San Jerónimo, seems to have been small at the end of the seventeenth century. Had its ruler's efforts to ally himself with the Kowoj leaders not been interrupted by the conquest, he might have been able to expand the territory to incorporate most of the Kowoj-controlled region. The north was also a gateway to the Kejach region further north, where the Itzas carried out periodic raids but apparently achieved little effective colonization; it also linked all of Itza territory with the most direct trade route to northern Yucatán.

The east, in addition to its population on or near the main lake, extended outward for a great distance to incorporate the vast, periodically contested region from Laguneta Macanché (and possibly Laguneta Salpetén) east to Tipuj and beyond—including even the eastern Mopans known as Chinamitas. And finally, the south, also a product of long struggles for control over distant populations, could have extended far to the southeast to incorporate as many Mopans as the Itzas could pacify. These alliances, however, were frayed by periodic territorial wars, and the Itzas had recaptured the corridor to Tipuj from the renegade Mopan "Chinamitas"—as well as Kowojs who had occupied Mopan territory—only during the seventeenth century.

ACH KAT REVISITED

I suggested earlier that the fourteen persons on Avendaño's list of Nojpeten leaders with the title Ach Kat (Table 3.5) bore a title derived from the Nahuatl Achcauhtli, a term designating a military chief representing a localized social group. Some of those with the title Ach Kat seem to have been associated with particular places, just as the Achcacauhtin were. In this section I explore the possibility that these people were not only military commanders who represented towns or regions throughout Itza territory but also priests associated with the thirteen approximately twenty-year periods known as k'atuns.

Avendaño, however, listed fourteen, not thirteen, Ach Kats. One of these, Ach Kat K'ixab'on, is clearly a B'atab', a junior territorial ruler. The title designation, therefore, may be incorrect, leaving only thirteen if he is omitted. One Ach Kat bears the additional title Jalach Winik, which in Yucatán signified a territorial ruler who also exercised military and religious authority. Sometimes described as a "bishop," he could also declare war and exact military service from towns under his jurisdiction.[108] Although in Yucatán the Jalach Winik seems to have been equivalent to the Itza supreme ruler, this is obviously not the case for the Itza Ach Kat Jalach Winik, who may have been the principal military commander and priest of the Ach Kats. Therefore, we might speculate that he was the most **101** important member of a group of thirteen Ach Kats, each of whom represented an outlying town or territory.

Avendaño provided important remarks on the significance of the k'atun cycle in the context of his encounters with the Itzas. Following a brief description of Itza painted books, Avendaño added the following carefully phrased explanation:

> These [books] are painted all over with a variety of figures and characters (which the Mexican Indians also used in their ancient customs) that indicate not only the count of the said days, months, and years, but also the ages and prophecies that their idols and simulacrums announced to them — or, better said, the Demon, through the veneration they grant to him in some stones. The ages are thirteen in number. Each age has its own particular idol and its own priest, with a particular prophecy of events. These thirteen ages are distributed among thirteen provinces which divide up this kingdom of Yucatán, and each age — with its own idol, priest, and prophecy — reigns in one of these thirteen parts of this land according to how they have it distributed.[109]

As Munro Edmonson has emphasized, the historical cycling of k'atuns among different places in Yucatán is well documented in a variety of ethnohistorical sources.[110] Avendaño explicitly notes that the k'atun prophecies were "announced" by their "idols and simulacrums" as well as by "some stones" that he considered to be dedicated to the worship of Satan. Each k'atun was therefore associated with an "idol," a stone, and a place where the k'atun was seated. Although we do not know the specifics of Itza k'atun ritual geography, I suggest that those with the title Ach Kat also served as priests in the ritual observances associated with each of the thirteen k'atuns and that they represented each of the seating places of these k'atuns across Itza territory.

The Itzas are known to have consulted their "idols" for advice on various matters, including royal policies and the practice of warfare.[111] López de Cogolludo, in his interpretation of Fuensalida's account, wrote regarding communication with "idols" of warfare:

> They have idols of battles, one called Pakoc and the other Hoxchuncham. They carry these when they go off to fight with the Chinamitas, their mortal enemies along their borders. When they commence the battle, and when they conclude a valiant battle, they burn copal, which is like incense, to them. Their idols customarily give them an answer when they consult them, and they [the Itzas] customarily talk to them and dance with them in their dances. This is why the Indians paint themselves when they dance the aforementioned dance of sacrifice.[112]

It thus comes as no surprise that in colonial Yucatec the word *k'atun* referred not only to the prophecy-associated period of 7,200 days (or twenty 360-day tuns) but also to a soldier, a battalion or army, and warfare and fighting. The Ach Kat may, therefore, have been one kind of soldier-priest who appears to have had responsibility for seeking, receiving, and transmitting supernatural messages regarding prophecy, particularly prophecies concerned with warfare.[113]

I suggested earlier that four of the Ach Kat titleholders may have been associated with place names: B'aka, Mul Kaj, Pop, and possibly K'inchil Kob'a. These places — and there were presumably others associated with other holders of the title — may have been towns not only where soldiers were recruited but also where associated k'atuns were ritually seated. At any one time there could presumably have been only thirteen towns in the Itza sphere of influence where a k'atun could be seated. These locations, however, might well have changed over time as part of the Itza program of warfare and expansion, most recently toward the east during the seventeenth century.

Perhaps the explicit associations among the k'atun calendrical series, governance, prophecy, and warfare came together most dramatically when successes and failures in warfare figured prominently in Itza political life. For example, Itza success in establishing military and political control over Tipuj by the beginning of K'atun 1 Ajaw (1638) might have resulted either in seating the new k'atun at Tipuj or in designating Tipuj as the site for a specifically designated k'atun seating sometime in the future. In this way newly conquered population centers could have been incorporated directly into the central ruling council at Nojpeten by adopting them not only as symbolic elements of the Itza historical and ritual record but also as part of the military structure.

THE RULING COUNCIL IN PERSPECTIVE

To sum up, I believe that the Itza core ruling council comprised Ajaw Kan Ek' and his cousin, the high priest, and eight high-ranking rulers in senior-junior pairs. In addition, thirteen other men (one of whom was a junior ruler) who represented outlying towns or territories as military chiefs and possibly as k'atun priests, joined these ten men as part of an extended governing council of twenty-three members. Ajaw Kan Ek' may have inherited the kingship from his father's brother, to whom it may have passed upon his father's death. All of the eight senior-junior rulers probably resided primarily at Nojpeten, although they represented various territorial provinces and outlying towns. The four highest-ranking ruler-priests apparently bore the title Ajaw B'atab' and normally belonged to the royal Kan lineage. Three were brothers, the son of the former ruler. The fourth was an uncle of Ajaw Kan Ek'. The four junior rulers bore the title B'atab'; only one of these is known to have borne the royal name Kan, whereas the other three represented other elite patrilineages. The thirteen additional members of the council each bore the title Ach Kat. One of these, also known as Jalach Winik, appears to have been in charge of this group.

Ajaw Kan Ek' governed as principal ruler jointly with his father's brother's son, the high priest AjK'in Kan Ek'; together they were considered a dual social persona with contrasting but complementary qualities, duties, and privileges. The "province" that they represented most directly was the island capital of Nojpeten, but they were also associated with the territorial region of the west. In addition, they were the nominal overlords of all of Itza territory, including its colonized populations. The principle of joint rulership probably also applied to the eight senior-junior rulers, with a pair of them representing each of four principal territories. These four provinces were confined to the Itza core area and may have been metaphorical extensions of the four wards that divided the island capital, among which ritual power transfers shifted annually in a counterclockwise cycle.

In contrast to the formal, almost static principles that enabled the Kan matrilineage to dominate this quadripartite structure and its capital center, the group of thirteen Ach Kats may have represented a more dynamic aspect of the political system. An individual Ach Kat may have represented the military, religious, and practical interests of his home communities, whereas the ten principal ruler-priests operated in a more abstract, formalized sphere of central governance, perhaps legitimated by their role as high priests of deity cults. The Ach Kats apparently crosscut the rigid quadripartite territorial structure of the principal rulers, incorporating other lineage groups and perhaps a wider territorial sphere.

WERE THE ITZAS GOVERNED BY "MULTEPAL"?

Ralph Roys concluded some time ago that "a large part of the Yucatan Peninsula had been subject to centralized administration, called a joint government (*multepal*), with its capital at Mayapan."[114] The term *multepal* was based on his reading of passages in the Books of Chilam B'alam of Chumayel, Mani, and Tisimin referring to a decisive battle at Mayapan during a K'atun 8 Ajaw (presumably 1441–61). The passages, which are nearly identical, all contain the compound term *mul tepal*, which Roys translated as "joint government." For example, his translation of the Chilam B'alam of Chumayel text reads, "8 Ahau was when there was fighting with stones at Ich-paa Mayapan because of the seizure of the fortress. They broke down the city wall because of the joint government [*multepal*] in the city of Mayapan."[115] Although he offered no precise description of what form such an institution might have taken, Roys apparently had in mind a confederation of territorial lords who ruled jointly with a single primary ruler or with a trio of ruling brothers. Landa summarily described such a system, said by Maya informants to have existed at both Chich'en Itza and Mayapan.[116]

More recently, Schele and Freidel have argued that a Mayapan-type multepal was also the form of government at Chich'en Itza, where epigraphic evidence suggests that at one point in the city's history a set of five brothers, "a brotherhood of princes," ruled together as apparent equals. Their relationships are indicated by their common relationships to "two, perhaps three generations, of women who were mother, grandmother, and possibly great-grandmother" to them.[117] This, they conclude, constituted the multepal, although they apply the term in a completely different sense to the large "assemblies" of nobles and warriors, respectively, at the Temple of the Chak Mool and the Temple of the Warriors at Chich'en Itza.[118] Although they note "precedents for the sharing of power between a Maya king and his key relatives" at the Classic-period sites of Tik'al, Kopan, and Yaxchilan, they conclude that the "dissolution of the kingship into a council of nobles" evidenced at Chich'en Itza was a "fundamentally new and revolutionary definition of power and government for a people who had acknowledged sacred kings for a thousand years."[119] Indeed, such a system of jointly ruling brothers appears strikingly similar to the kingdom established by the Itzas in Petén.

The time-honored use of the term *multepal* for joint government at Mayapan is, I believe, based on rather thin evidence. The concept of a joint ruling council that governed Maya territories, however, appears to be strong at Chich'en Itza, Mayapan, and Nojpeten. Evidence of a group of titled siblings and titled individuals from other lineages at Chich'en Itza is mirrored, as we have seen, among the Petén Itzas. The historical traditions recounted by Landa indicate that rulership at Mayapan was shared between a principal ruler and subsidiary rulers representing various towns and elite lineages. I suspect that in all of these kingdoms, as I prefer to think of them, such "shared rule" was tempered by a strong principle of lineage domination by a single group of closely related males, two of

105

whom "ruled" as a dual persona. The Itza model proposed here may require a broad reexamination of Postclassic Maya political organization.

Conclusion

At one level the Itza kingdom appears to have been centrally controlled by a single royal matrilineage whose members solidified their power through strategic marriage alliances with other elite kinship groups who played major roles in governance. Territorial control was highly coordinated by the dominant Kans and other high-ranking elites through a system of geographical quarters that almost precisely reflected the social-religious hierarchical structure of the central capital. This was a tightly constructed kingdom that had successfully expanded its influence and solidified its power in the face of nearly two centuries of European domination around its borders.

At another level, however, the Itza political system reflected principles that might be seen as destabilizing and decentralizing. If I have correctly identified the council members called Ach Kat as both military chieftains who represented their towns and regions and priests who represented their towns as places where k'atuns were seated throughout the territorial sphere of Itza influence, then such a group would have symbolized the essence of the instability inherent in both warfare and the cycling k'atun calendar. As war captains, their fortunes would have depended on success in the battlefield, and their loyalty to the central rulership would have been subject to the changing winds of such fortune. The rulers, that is, were always at risk of rebellion by war captains.

As Spanish soldiers and bureaucrats prepared to conquer the Itzas they became increasingly convinced that this was a kingdom with a ruler and high priest who exercised considerable control over their local and territorial leaders. They were correct, but they remained unaware of the constraints under which Ajaw Kan Ek' exercised his secular power. The ruler had to answer to his "court" — his close relatives who were the everyday administrators of the kingdom, elites from other lineages, and representatives from outlying regions. At least one of his closest relatives, an uncle, appeared to be hoping to "dethrone" Ajaw Kan Ek' with the assistance of the long-time enemies of the Itzas, the Kowojs. Others at lower levels were encouraging or allowing the abandonment of towns or were shifting their support to the ruler's enemies. Yet whether they supported Ajaw Kan Ek' or his renegade relative Ajaw B'atab' K'in Kante, the Itzas understood that the Spaniards sought religious conversions and political control that would change their lives forever. And the Spaniards were convinced, after a brief effort to reach a "peaceful" conquest, that the Itzas, regardless of their internal political differences, would ultimately refuse to submit without a fight.

Part Two **ROAD TO THE
ITZAS**

The conquest of the Itzas began with a seemingly straightforward plan proposed to the king in 1692 by the young Basque aristocrat Martín de Ursúa y Arizmendi.[1] Ursúa, who had already been granted the future governorship of Yucatán, proposed to construct a north-south road that would connect Mérida directly with Guatemalan territory. In the process, he would congregate and bring under Spanish political and religious domination any unconquered native populations he might find along the route (that is, "reduce" them). His original proposal made no mention of the Mayas who lived around Lago Petén Itzá, nor did it even hint of his intention to conquer them militarily. Rather, Ursúa offered his plan in response to another set of proposed reduction activities being widely discussed both in Guatemala and at the Council of the Indies. Those activities were designed to construct part of a Guatemala-Yucatán road and at last to bring under Spanish control the unconverted Manche Chols of southeastern Petén and the Chol-speaking Lakandons of the upper Río Usumacinta.

Over time, Ursúa's original plan—to build the northern half of the road, meeting up in Chol Lakandon territory with Guatemalans pursuing their share of the task—became dramatically transformed. In this chapter I tell part of the story: how Ursúa's proposal came into focus and how it was related to the plans under discussion in Guatemalan circles. Circumstantial evidence suggests that Ursúa's support on the Council of the Indies was so strong that he was personally handed the patent to begin constructing the road from Yucatán, notwithstanding that the scope of his project and his administrative control over it would threaten the authority of the resident governor, Roque de Soberanis y Centeno. Ursúa's supporters, it appears, were working behind the scenes to remove Soberanis from office in order to allow Ursúa to assume full control over the governorship well ahead of schedule. Their efforts resulted in Soberanis's excommunication and temporary removal from office. Ursúa thereupon stepped in as interim governor, a move that enabled him to establish momentum in planning, organizing, and initiating his project without opposition.

Because this book focuses on the Yucatecan side of the conquest, I take pains to provide a portrait of Ursúa himself. This chief architect and commanding officer of the enterprise was a man of great stamina and ruthless determination, and he emerges as the central Spanish character in this drama. Although initially beholden to his patrons in Madrid, he quickly assumed near-absolute powers at the local level and, once in power, used his patrons as sources of political protection.

Guatemalan Proposals for New Conquests

On December 6, 1688, the Guatemalan captain Juan de Mendoza petitioned the Crown requesting license to pursue an ambitious reduction of the Chol Lakandons.[2] Mendoza had participated with the president of the Guatemalan audiencia, Enrique Enríquez de Guzmán, in the reduction of indigenous populations in Honduras. The project had been small in scale but successful, resulting in the formation of five towns with a total population of 810. Mendoza now requested a patent from the king to do the same to the Lakandons. He requested fifty armed men, funds for their salaries, and an advancement in his status to the rank of sergeant major, with the title of commander and governor.

Mendoza's petition languished in the Council of the Indies until 1692, when Enríquez de Guzmán, no longer in office but now serving in the royal court in Madrid, represented Mendoza's request before that council. The result was the issuance of a cédula ordering all that Mendoza had requested.[3] The reduction was to take a three-pronged approach through territory with a large native population, and it was to have a strong missionary presence.

The first prong of the Spanish forces would leave from Verapaz, presently in the hands of the Dominicans.[4] The second was to start from Huehuetenango, territory of the Mercederian order, and the third would depart from Chiapas, another Dominican territory. Although the ostensible purpose of the entradas was to pacify the Chol-speaking Lakandons living along the tributaries of the upper Río Usumacinta, they would also move through Manche Chol territory from Verapaz. By implication, all three prongs were intended to penetrate as far as Itza territory in central Petén. Mendoza was to enlist the support of the Dominican and Mercederian provincials, seeking out the experienced Dominican Fray Agustín Cano and the Mercederian Fray Diego de Rivas as the principal missionaries for the project. Mendoza's role as "captain of this conquest" was to be limited to serving as a military escort for the missionaries; he was "not to make war on the Indians, because reducing them is my [the king's] determination, [and] it is accomplished by means of the evangelical word."

Finally, the cédula noted, briefly and almost in passing, that the Guatemalan reduction would be coordinated with another entrada from Yucatán, to take place at the same time. It offered no explanation of the purpose of the Yucatecan entrada or who would direct it, but Governor Roque Soberanis y Centeno was to receive a copy of the cédula. The president of Guatemala, Jacinto de Barrios Leal, and Governor Soberanis were to work out methods for cooperating in the venture.

This brief note was the first indication that plans were under way to grant Ursúa, who was presently in Mexico City, extensive powers to carry out a road-building and reduction project that would open communication routes between Mérida and Guatemala. The details had not yet been worked out, but Ursúa, who must have received a personal copy of the cédula, now had the green light to plan accordingly.

Martín de Ursúa y Arizmendi

Ursúa, a Basque of noble ancestry, was born in the village of Olóriz in the Basque province of Navarra, in the foothills of the Pyrenees. Almost nothing is presently known of his life before his arrival in Mexico in about 1680, but the Pamplonan abbot of Barajoan, Francisco de Elorza y Rada, wrote a few paragraphs about his noble genealogy in 1714.[5] In addition, we benefit from remarks about his career in Mexico made by the famous nineteenth-century Yucatecan historian Bishop Crescencio Carrillo y Ancona.[6]

When he arrived in Mexico, Ursúa held the modest title of sergeant major, serving in the viceroy's militia. He quickly progressed through a series of military and political promotions. His powerful contacts in the royal court and the Council of the Indies engineered his appointment in 1690 as future governor of Yucatán, to succeed Roque de Soberanis y **113** Centeno.[7] Before he left Yucatán in 1708 to become president of the Philippines, Ursúa was named Caballero of the Order of Santiago (a noble privilege of some of his ancestors, including his paternal grandfather) in 1700, and he received the titles of Conde de Lizárraga (which he purchased) and Castillo in 1705 after petitions to the Crown. He died in Manila while in office in 1715.

Ursúa had inherited a strong family tradition of prestigious and valorous service that he was determined to follow. The best known of his namesakes was Pedro de Ursúa, who was born in Pamplona in 1527 and killed by Spanish bandits in the Peruvian Amazon in 1560.[8] Pedro had arrived in Cartagena at eighteen with his Basque uncle, Miguel Díez de Armendáriz, who had been sent from Spain as the city's first *visitador* (official investigator) and judge. During the rest of his short life Pedro de Ursúa conquered and resettled interior native peoples, founded the cities of Pamplona and Ocaña in Nueva Granada (now in the Department of Santander, Colombia), served as military governor of various territories, and put down a rebellion of black slaves in Panamá. We might suppose that the young Martín was deeply influenced by Pedro's career and that he studied Toribio de Ortiguera's account of his ancestor's last years, as well as any family-owned papers about him that still remained in the Ursúa palace.[9]

Martín's grandfather, General Pedro de Ursúa y Arizmendi, was a military man "who, setting off from his fatherland Bastan, served gloriously on land and sea the lords and kings don Felipe the third and don Felipe the fourth, and this [latter] great monarch promoted him to Count of Jerena, a title of Castile."[10] His oldest son, Pedro de Ursúa y Arizmendi de Egües y Beaumont, who inherited the title of Count of Jerena, was probably Martín's father. He attended university in Salamanca, worked as a young man for the Royal Council of Castile, was later promoted to the New Chancery of Zaragoza, and late in life received an appointment on the Council and Chamber of Castile. In 1661 he traveled to South America with his mother's brother, Diego Egües y Beaumont, who was then governor and captain general of the viceroyalty of Nueva Granada.[11]

Martín's older brother, yet another Pedro de Ursúa, was an abbot in Pamplona, and he counted among his other contemporary male relatives the Count of Fresno de la Fuente, who lived in New Spain, and two or more archdeacons of the Pamplona cathedral. These were all highly successful men whose ancestry granted them not only titles of nobility but also positions of power in the royal court, the church, and the military. Moreover, they married women from powerful noble families, creating extensive networks of kinship and marriage that bridged Europe and the Americas.[12]

Elorza y Rada wrote with great admiration about the noble heritage of the Ursúas and the Arizmendis. The Ursúa homestead in the Valle de Bastan, in 1714 the residence of the younger Pedro, then lord of the house of

Ursúa, was "an ancient fortress constructed with embrasures and defense towers, with walls at a distance from the palace, and with a moat and drawbridge that defend its enclosures."[13] The Arizmendis occupied two palaces, named Utalcua and Nas, respectively, in the nearby villa of Osses. Nas had in earlier times been the local royal seat for the court that elected the knights of Navarra, who included members of the Ursúa family.

Elorza y Rada had seen a full-length portrait of don Martín, obviously painted following the conquest of the Itzas and his subsequent purchase of the title of Conde de Lizárraga. He held his general's baton and, in a style reminiscent of the earliest Spanish conquerors, towered over subjugated natives prostrated at his feet. Next to his right shoulder was a frame with a coat of arms symbolizing three of his ancestral lines. Three magpies on a field of gold represented the Ursúas. The two palaces of Arizmendi were represented by two panels: a wild boar at the foot of a tree, over a silver background, and a gold lion bordered with twelve gold crossed bars on a red field. A black and silver chessboard represented the Valle de Bastan, and a gold crown over the four panels portrayed the royal patronage enjoyed by every branch of Ursúa's ancestral family.

Ursúa's own writing and reported behavior invoke a single, consistent, and compelling personal portrait — that of an arrogant, self-aggrandizing, elitist autocrat. Gaining royal patronage to construct a road from Yucatán to Guatemala, he soon ignored the niceties of his contract with the Crown and determined to replicate and even outdo the feats of the early New World conquerors by adding the conquest of the Itzas to his road project. Even in the shambles of the aftermath of his conquest, his reputation marred by scandal and corruption, he pursued a campaign of self-promotion with the royal court and the public alike. Eventually he won the prize that he may have coveted all along: the wealth-generating governorship of the Philippines.

Bishop Carrillo y Ancona, writing in the late nineteenth century, penned a description of Ursúa that must have reflected the folklore of his time. History was not kind to the memory of this ambitious man. Ursúa, he wrote,

> succeeded in establishing such an extraordinarily notable career, by virtue of great and powerful influences, that he came to enjoy extraordinary prestige, even more so at the court of Madrid than at that of Mexico — distinguishing himself by his resolute, bold, and enterprising character. When don Roque de Soberanis y Centeno was governing here in Yucatán, señor Ursúa . . . rewarded himself in a grand manner, augmenting his influences and privileged sup-

115

port at the court by the famous exploit of the pacification and conquest of Petén Itzá, as well as by opening the camino real between
Yucatán and Guatemala. He proceeded to enrich himself greatly,
and he relied as well on the powerful support of don Bernardino de
Zubiaur, a Spaniard like him, a merchant of Campeche who was
the possessor of great wealth and who had a brother on the Supreme Council of the Indies.[14]

Carrillo y Ancona added sarcastically "Lord of Gallows and Knife" to the
official titles that Ursúa had accrued, characterizing him in his role as
governor and captain general of Yucatán as "a great potentate here whom
nothing or no one could oppose or contradict even slightly, as everyone
knew and realized how much influence and power he had at the court."[15]

The existing accounts of the conquest of the Itzas — from events in local
Maya villages to negotiations with Madrid — are so colored by Ursúa's
powerful hand that interpreting events and relationships is often difficult.
In some cases he excised from the document record items that did not support his own objectives and interests, and in others he constructed texts
that he attributed to other voices. He produced his own official reports and
interpretations of events — letters, memoranda, dispatches, and decrees —
in a style that was verbose and self-serving. These he supported with
"officially" produced oral testimonies and reports by his chief military
officers and other clients. The testimonies or depositions, although taken
under oath and with the trappings of legal procedure, are often suspect,
because the interrogators asked leading questions to which the respon-
dents had obviously been coached to provide rehearsed answers.

Despite Ursúa's heavy editorial hand and his proclivity for influencing
and censoring the historical record, his detractors and various independent commentators also managed to contribute substantially to the account of the conquest. Some of these wrote independently to the Crown,
and others were included in official files by Ursúa himself despite their contradictory views of events. Many questions remain, however, especially
regarding certain events such as the days surrounding the storming of
Nojpeten, over which Ursúa maintained strict censorship of information.

So strong were Ursúa's personal connections in the Council of the Indies and the Spanish court that his superiors apparently never challenged
his version of events. The council's official chronicler, Juan de Villagutierre Soto-Mayor, was clearly instructed by council members to produce
a book for public consumption that would reflect Ursúa's version of the
conquest without offering alternative or uncomplimentary interpretations

of the general's role.[16] So successful was this ploy that Villagutierre's report survives to the present day with no challenge to its relentlessly positive portrayal of Ursúa's part in the conquest.

Ursúa was a good military strategist, a stubborn and determined politician, and a strong field commander. He was, however, less interested in governing what he had conquered than in his political and entrepreneurial activities in Yucatán. Following his capture of Nojpeten he all but abandoned the project to weak military delegates who received little moral, military, or financial support from him. He had little interest in details of local governance and no desire to develop a strategy of provincial colonial administration in Petén that responded to local cultural and economic conditions. He expected that once the inhabitants of Itza territory were captured and placed under colonial administration, they would pay tribute to him in the manner of the early conquerors' long-outmoded encomiendas.[17] Ursúa saw himself, in effect, as a latter-day conquistador in an era when conquistadors were out of fashion.

Robert W. Patch has revealed that as governor, Ursúa operated a vast entrepreneurial system that netted him a large income at the expense of the native Mayas of colonial Yucatán.[18] This system, with origins in the sixteenth century, was known as the repartimiento. In Yucatán, Spaniards made advance payments of money or credit, usually through local Maya officials, for distribution to community members. In return they demanded by a certain deadline the delivery of a specific local product, such as raw cotton, cotton thread or cloth, or beeswax. These products were exported to Mexico City from the busy port of Campeche, where Ursúa had made his principal home and had established numerous business ties. During the seventeenth century the governors of Yucatán became the principal monopolists and organizers of repartimientos, assisted by district war captains whom they appointed in major Maya towns. While these war captains were ostensibly charged with defending the peninsula militarily, they in fact carried out both the governor's and their own repartimientos. In addition to the governor and his war captains, the encomenderos (those who held rights to collect tribute from native villages) had been repartimiento operators since the sixteenth century.[19]

Patch has given Ursúa credit for taking the repartimiento system to new levels of profitability:

> The most important of all the entrepreneurs involved in this business with the Indians was the governor, Martín de Urzúa y Arizmendi. Urzúa controlled about 57 percent of all the textiles

contracted, 6.5 percent of the thread, and 80.5 percent of the wax. Of the total value, the governor's share, then, was almost an even 60 percent. Urzúa did not pocket all the profits, for he had to work through middlemen who of course received their share of the revenues. Nevertheless, his income from business with the Indians was considerable, and helps explain why politics in Yucatan in the late seventeenth and early eighteenth centuries revolved around the governor's role in the repartimiento system.[20]

Next to the governor, the second most successful repartimiento operator was a church institution known as the Santa Cruzada (Holy Crusade), originally established in the fourteenth century to raise money for the war against the Moors by selling indulgences. Although the Crown had prohibited such sales in native communities, in Yucatán this changed in about 1675, when another Basque immigrant, Pedro de Garrástegui y Oleado, purchased the post of treasurer of the Santa Cruzada for fourteen thousand pesos and proceeded to sell indulgences at considerable profit to Mayas in exchange for cotton cloth and beeswax. Garrástegui not only negotiated the right to pass his position on to his heirs but also purchased the title of Count of Miraflores, "thereby making himself and his heirs the only family of titled nobility in Yucatan."[21] There can be little doubt that the church's role in the repartimiento system, which also fed the export shipping industry in Campeche, was a major factor in the close alliances that we see in later chapters between Ursúa and the secular clergy of Yucatán.

Ursúa and the Origins of the Camino Real

Martín de Ursúa y Arizmendi arrived in Mexico in about 1680 and in 1692 claimed that he had served the Crown in Yucatán during the intervening years. By this he apparently referred to his role as a practicing lawyer in Mexico City, where, according to Patch, "he had handled lawsuits and business affairs for many people from Yucatan. . . . In fact, the few extant records show that the future governor had dealings with people who served either as alcaldes [chief city council members] or Procurators of Mérida in 1682, 1683, 1685, 1689, and 1690. Contacts like these undoubtedly smoothed the way for a working relationship between the local elite and Martín de Ursúa."[22]

In 1694 Ursúa had risen to the position of *alcalde ordinario* of Mexico City. By 1692, however, he had already gained appointment from the

Crown as proprietary governor of Yucatán and was named to replace Roque de Soberanis y Centeno at the scheduled end of Soberanis's term in 1698.[23] At some point Ursúa married a wealthy Yucatecan, doña Juana Bolio y Ojeda, born and reared in Mérida, and they had several children.[24] Her brother was Maestre de Campo Manuel Bolio, himself a successful repartimiento entrepreneur.[25] Ursúa had brought with him to New Spain and later to Yucatán brothers, sisters, and other relatives and managed to establish a tight network in Yucatecan circles by marrying them off to local residents.[26] He always kept his principal family residence in Campeche, suggesting that his early contacts with Yucatán involved not only legal representation but also his acting as an agent and broker for the city's wealthy merchants and exporters. By the time he assumed the office of acting governor on December 17, 1694, well before Soberanis's scheduled departure from office, he had developed such strong relationships with the leading merchants and other citizens of Campeche that he appointed them to military command positions as part of his scheme to open the road to Guatemala and conquer the native people along the proposed route.

During his early years in Mexico City Ursúa formulated the plan that would eventually result in the conquest of the Itzas. His ambitious ideas probably grew out of suggestions made by his Campeche friends in combination with inside knowledge of the Chol Lakandon reductions proposed by Mendoza. On June 30, 1692, he made a formal request to the king to carry out his plans as soon as he took office as governor of Yucatán.[27] In this letter he claimed in expansive language that

> the most glorious undertaking for the service of God and of Your Majesty in which I can employ myself during the period of my government is the conversion and reduction of innumerable Indians, infidels, and apostates, who are located between the said provinces of Yucatán and those of Guatemala, and the opening of a road from the one set of provinces to the other — not only to facilitate trade, which will be of general utility and in Your Majesty's service, but also for the reduction of so many Indians — toward which end Your Majesty has so ordered the governors of the said province, as well as the president and oidores of the Royal Audiencia of Guatemala, and the prelates of both jurisdictions.[28]

119

Ursúa knew that the Council of the Indies had already acted positively on Mendoza's 1689 proposal for the three-pronged entrada from Guatemala, whereas the cédula enabling it would not be issued for another four months.

ANOTHER GUATEMALAN RIVAL

Ursúa's mention of orders given to the governors of Yucatán certainly referred to a cédula issued to Governor Bruno Tello y Guzmán in 1685 or 1686, granting the Yucatecan encomendero Captain Juan del Castillo y Toledo a patent to carry out an entrada to the native towns of southern Belize.[29] Although the official purpose of the new entrada was to punish the Chols who had murdered three Franciscan missionaries in 1684, Castillo, with the governor's blessing, pursued a different agenda altogether. He instead went armed in 1687 into the Yucatec-speaking independent rebellious zone of La Pimienta, constructing a fortified reduction town there, Santa Clara de Chanchanja, as the intended jumping-off point for his own miliary conquest of the Itzas. On this last part of the plan, he soon found himself thwarted by Ursúa.

Just as Castillo y Toledo and Governor Tello y Guzmán had reasoned several years earlier, Ursúa now argued that improved land communications should be opened between Yucatán and Guatemala and that native populations along its route should be brought together and converted to the Christian faith. Instead of following the by now well-traveled road to Castillo's Chanchanja mission on the southeastern frontiers of the peninsula, Ursúa — although he did not specify this in his 1692 letter — would follow the old road, established earlier in the century, south from Mérida and Campeche through the now-defunct Kejach missions.

Ursúa was well aware of Castillo's desire to be the conqueror of the Itzas, and in his petition to the king he may have hoped to stifle Castillo's plans by tying his own enterprise to the pending conquest of Chol Lakandon territory by the Audiencia of Guatemala. Although Ursúa tried to avoid referring to his desire to pursue a conquest of the Itzas, that he intended to do so was public knowledge in Yucatán. There is every reason to believe that from the outset Ursúa planned to conquer the Itzas — if not through peaceful negotiation, then by military action. Not until late 1696, however, did he openly reveal this plan.

Meanwhile, Castillo y Toledo attempted to convince the Council of the Indies that he be authorized to carry out an entrada to the Itzas via Tipuj, complaining that his efforts to begin a road in that direction had been ignored. In response to Castillo's complaints, the Council of the Indies sent a cédula to the Audiencia of Guatemala on June 22, 1695, requiring that President Jacinto Barrios Leal support and communicate with Castillo while at the same time discussing the matter with by then interim Governor Ursúa — in the hope that through such communication the issue of the route could be resolved.[30] Slow communications between Guatemala and Yucatán made such discussion impossible, and in any case both the route and the key players in the road project had already been determined. Ultimately, Castillo was sidelined by the ambitious Ursúa, whose connections in Madrid were far more significant than his.[31]

THE TERMS AND CONDITIONS OF URSÚA'S OFFER

In his June 1692 letter to the king, Ursúa proposed to carry out his expensive road engineering project and barely disguised military undertaking at his own cost, with no expense to be incurred by the royal treasury.[32] He later claimed that the cost of the project had been borne not only by his personal fortune but also by that of his wife, doña Juana Bolio.[33] The ultimate monetary cost was paid by the native inhabitants of Yucatán in the form of illegal repartimientos demanded by Governor Ursúa.

What turned out in later years to be the most important — and the most hotly debated — section of his proposal was that pertaining to the peaceful evangelism that would accompany the reduction of the native people. As soon as Ursúa took office he wrote,

> I shall put into execution the opening of the camino real from the provinces of Yucatán to those of Guatemala, at the same time *reducing peacefully and gently,* by means of evangelical preaching, all of the Indians who will be encountered in those regions, without allowing the conversion to hinder the goal of opening the road, which is what will best facilitate reducing all of those who live in those regions later on, with continual Spanish passage and trade between the provinces, for which enterprise and attainment it is most essential to move up the time remaining to me before my possession of the said executive power, on account of the preparations that are required.[34]

The phrase "reducing peacefully and gently" (*reduciendo de paz y de paso*) was repeated in all of the Crown's later cédulas approving Ursúa's plan. Ursúa frequently quoted it himself as he cited "proof" that he was following the Crown's orders, but his critics in turn cited his troops' harsh, often violent treatment of the Mayas. The most vociferous of these critics were, not surprisingly, the Franciscan missionaries. Unbeholden to his base of power, they had little faith in Ursúa's good intentions when it came to matters of native spiritual and personal welfare.

The memorial that Ursúa included with this letter, carried by his agents to Madrid, laid out specific requests for supporting royal cédulas. These cédulas included several to Yucatán ordering the bishop and the Franciscan provincial to provide Ursúa with missionaries for the conversion effort; others to the president and *oidores* of the Audiencia of Guatemala, as well as the local governors, ordering that they assist Ursúa and not hinder him in any way; and finally, one to the viceroy of New Spain ordering that he support Ursúa and provide him with food supplies and munitions at fair prices, given their scarcity in Yucatán. In addition, Ursúa requested the power to appoint a military commander or commanders of his own choosing, to recruit soldiers, to make all necessary preparations for his project, and to pay for all supplies at a fair going rate.

His final "request" — a sharply honed abstract of the irony and moral contradiction that was to plague the enterprise from start to finish — was that, once the road had been completed "at his own cost and expense," the king should reward Ursúa and his commanders with an appropriate "prize or remuneration," because "the principal end" that Ursúa sought was nothing less than "the service of God Our Lord and of Your Majesty."

URSÚA'S EMPOWERMENT MADE OFFICIAL

There can be little doubt that while he was in Mexico City Ursúa had been kept well informed of discussions at the Council of the Indies about the Guatemalan captain Juan de Mendoza's proposal to pursue a three-pronged entrada into Chol Lakandon and Manche Chol territory. Mendoza, however, was no longer a player in whatever Guatemalan schemes were operating to put this plan into action; his name never appears in later information about these entradas. At this point, either Enrique Enríquez de Guzmán, now on the Spanish court, or another of Ursúa's Madrid contacts must have engineered his appointment as the next governor of Yucatán on the understanding that the Council of the Indies would support a bid from Ursúa to complement the Guatemalan's reduction plans by proposing to construct the road that would connect the two provinces. The council delayed three years after receiving Mendoza's 1688 petition — until November 24, 1692 — before granting permission to the president of Guatemala to pursue the reductions from Guatemala. Their permission came slightly less than four months after the posting of Ursúa's letter and memorial to the Crown. The timing could hardly have been serendipitous: it would have just allowed Ursúa's correspondence to reach Madrid and the council to hurriedly draft a response to Mendoza's outstanding petition.

The new cédula, however, included one highly significant item missing in the original request: that an entrada, unspecified in nature, would originate from Yucatán at the same time as the departure of the three Guatemalan entradas. Governor Soberanis received a copy of this cédula, as did, presumably, the viceroy of New Spain.[35]

On October 26, 1693, sixteen months after Ursúa had written from Mexico, the Council of the Indies issued a flurry of cédulas granting all that he had asked. His personal role in the road-building project was now official. The cédula to Ursúa, whom Carlos II addressed as sergeant major, was written in warm, appreciative, even personal language, thanking him "for the kindness and love that you demonstrate for the service of God and me, undertaking an enterprise so useful to both, and assuring you of my gratitude and remembrance." The king noted that on November 24, 1692, he had sent orders to the Audiencia of Guatemala and the governor of Yucatán "that they maintain contact and assist in this reduction." The emphasis was on reduction, not road opening. Guatemala and Yucatán must establish a direct route to ensure that they would meet at the same time and place. Local officials must provide any assistance that Ursúa might require of them.[36]

The rest of the king's orders, except for the pointed repetition of Ursúa's promise that the reduction would be pursued "gently and peacefully," pertained to the sorts of particulars that a seasoned commander such as Ursúa would have considered beforehand. Ursúa should make certain that his chosen route would pass along streams providing sufficient water from day to day. If he encountered large rivers, he should look for the best places to build bridges across them. Settlements were to be established every four to eight leagues along the road to ensure that the reduced populations would stay put. If at first this proved difficult, roadside inns should be constructed as rest houses for travelers. In either case, the king reasoned that the trade the road would encourage would attract settlers along the route.[37]

Neither the impending Guatemalan entradas to Chol Lakandon territory nor the likelihood that both Castillo y Toledo and Governor Soberanis would oppose his plans appears to have caused Ursúa much concern, and in all but the case of Soberanis he eventually compromised with rival parties and sought cooperation with them. As he later learned, pursuing the camino real all the way to Guatemala would have been financially and militarily impossible, especially after he shifted his attention **123** from the road itself to the conquest of the Itzas. The Chol Lakandon conquest turned out to be a small affair, pale in comparison with the drama and scale of the Itza enterprise. Ursúa scrapped his original plan to construct a western road through Chol Lakandon territory and routed the road to Guatemala to the east, passing by Lago Petén Itzá on the way to Verapaz.

Other cédulas were shipped out along with the one directed to Ursúa, all dated October 26, 1693. As Ursúa had requested, these were addressed to President Jacinto Barrios y Leal and the oidores of the Audiencia of Guatemala; the viceroy of Mexico, the Conde de Galve; the bishop of Yucatán, Juan Cano y Sandoval; and the Franciscan provincial, Fray Juan Antonio Silva.[38] They were brief and to the point, notifying the recipients of Ursúa's intention and ordering their cooperation and assistance. No cédula was addressed to Governor Soberanis, who was not formally notified of the project until 1694.[39]

The Displacement of Soberanis y Centeno

Roque de Soberanis y Centeno had assumed the governorship of Yucatán on August 20, 1693, replacing Juan José de Bárcena.[40] Like Ursúa, he was a knight of the Order of Santiago. Also like his successor he came from a wealthy and influential family. According to the nineteenth-century Yucatecan historian Eligio Ancona, who did not identify his source,

> [i]t is said that he was still too young for the high position to which he had been elevated and that he would never have achieved it without the influences that his family, one of the richest and most powerful of Cádiz, enjoyed at the court. Don Roque . . . enjoyed pleasures, ardently loved the poor, and the sight of a rich or powerful man upset him. This may have been the secret of the opposition that he encountered from the high clergy and the encomenderos, because shortly after he took charge of the government they drew up many charges against him and sent them to the Royal Audiencia of Mexico. Don Juan Cano y Sandoval, the bishop of the province . . . distinguished himself among his opposers.[41]

Bishop Cano, a man of sixty-five years, accused Governor Soberanis of "short-cutting the maize measures, threatening a conflagration in the Peninsula."[42] Ancona found the accusation implausible, because a man devoted to helping the poor would certainly have protected the food intended for the "destitute and needy classes." The accusation nonetheless justified Bishop Cano's decision to excommunicate Soberanis, who refused to give up his duties as governor. When the matter came to the audiencia's attention, he was suspended temporarily and called to Mexico City in late 1694 to answer the charges.[43]

Ursúa was not scheduled to assume his powers until Soberanis's five-year term had ended in 1698. Ancona claimed that the viceroy was so convinced of the importance of Yucatán in the proposed road-building and reduction project that he decided to appoint Ursúa as interim governor and captain general without delay. Ursúa, after all, had already received the Crown's patent to carry out the expedition. Yucatán was more critical to the project than Guatemala, because "Petén and nearly all the rest of the surrounding tribes spoke the same idiom and possessed the same modes and customs as the natives of the peninsula."[44]

The transitional politics leading up to Soberanis's displacement take us back to September 16, 1693, nearly a year before his misfortunes transpired, and prior to receipt in Yucatán of the cédulas of patent to Ursúa. On that date Soberanis had written to Barrios Leal requesting details of the Guatemalan president's plans to carry out the terms of the cédula of November 24, 1692. Barrios, unaware of Soberanis's subsequent suspension from office but by now informed of Ursúa's appointment as the future leader of the road-opening project, wrote to Soberanis on August 13, 1694, outlining his plan to carry out the Crown's instructions for a dual entrada from Guatemala and Yucatán—without, perhaps for reasons of political delicacy, mentioning Ursúa by name.[45]

The Guatemalans hoped to set out, as originally planned, from Huehuetenango, Chiapas, and Verapaz at the beginning of 1695 and were already recruiting volunteer soldiers. Barrios emphasized how much Guatemala needed cooperation from Soberanis, including pressure on the bishop and the Franciscan *predicador* to recruit missionaries. Believing that the Yucatecans were more familiar with the forests than were the Guatemalans, he asked Soberanis to have a map of the region prepared. So certain was he that the two parties would eventually approach one another from north and south that he suggested they should communicate with smoke signals in order to distinguish their fires from those of the local populations.

Soberanis replied on September 12, reporting that he had already abandoned the capital and was in Campeche. His political situation prevented Yucatán's participation for the time being, but he would have the Campechano captain Alonso García de Paredes, already one of Ursúa's closest associates, prepare the map for Barrios. Barrios quickly responded with stated regret, still emphasizing that preparations for Guatemala's entrada were well under way.[46] He now hoped to initiate the expedition in February and had decided to join the Chiapas party himself, leaving the capital on December 15.[47] He needed the map as soon as possible and requested, in addition, that Soberanis send him two men familiar with the territory. He demanded formal assurances, as implied by the various cédulas, that runaways from any native communities who had been frightened by the Guatemalan entrada would not be treated with hostility by Yucatecan forces.

In November Barrios wrote a biting letter to Bishop Cano concerning his excommunication of Soberanis, accusing him of having acted out of jealousy.[48] His implication was transparent: that the bishop had carried out the excommunication in order to force Soberanis to leave Yucatán. By going on to press the point that whoever might serve as interim governor would override the bishop's apparent objections to the reduction, Barrios may have shown his awareness that Ursúa was about to step in and put the bishop in his place.

Barrios learned of Ursúa's appointment as interim governor on November 23, 1694, in a letter from Licenciado Francisco de Saraza, an oidor on the Audiencia of Mexico. Saraza, who was also to be the judge in the investigation of the charges against Soberanis, had written the letter on October 30, suggesting that Ursúa's appointment may have been arranged before Soberanis was ordered to appear in Mexico City and reinforcing the possibility that his excommunication was part of a plan to remove him from office as soon as possible.[49]

Saraza apparently traveled with Ursúa to Campeche, arriving on December 27, 1694, when the latter took up his duties as interim governor. Saraza's presence there was officially to carry out a *residencia,* or investigation of the charges against Soberanis, and his work was tainted by conflicts of interest. He was a strong supporter of Ursúa's and in late 1695, on the recommendation of Ursúa's agent and relative, Francisco de Ursúa, wrote a glowing report to the Audiencia of Mexico concerning Ursúa's accomplishments on the camino real project. Francisco de Ursúa was attempting to forestall Soberanis's reinstatement as governor, and Saraza was obviously eager for Ursúa to remain in that post.[50] Fray Andrés de Avendaño claimed in mid-1695 that Saraza was a staunch backer of Ursúa's project.[51] In the end, however, Soberanis was exonerated by the audiencia and absolved by the church of all charges in February 1696. In the months following his return to office in early 1696 he pursued a relentless campaign to sabotage Ursúa's plans, nearly forcing Ursúa to leave Yucatán and abandon his project.[52]

Preparation for the First Entrada

Immediately upon taking up the post of interim governor in the waning days of 1694, Ursúa began to implement his ambitious plans.[53] By January 21, 1695, he had already named his old friend and fellow Campechano, Alonso García de Paredes, to take troops southward, ostensibly to meet up with those of President Barrios. The second in command was to be Francisco González Ricardo, another Campechano, although González never served.[54]

García de Paredes was a wealthy man, an encomendero and town councilman with years of experience in matters of "reducing" Mayas in his capacity as war captain of the frontier partido of Sajkab'ch'en. Most of his income apparently came from cutting timber destined for the shipyards at Campeche.[55] He also owned an estancia (ranch) at Sajkab'ch'en and drew additional income from a small encomienda near the border with Tabasco, both areas rich in valuable logwood.[56] His encomienda was situated, to his probable commercial benefit, along the major trade and communications route that ran all the way from Mérida, eventually following the Río Usumacinta to Ciudad Real in Chiapas and continuing to highland Guatemala.[57] García had purchased the post of "permanent regidor" of Campeche, a position that gave him personal and financial influence in ensuring the success of Ursúa's venture.[58] He had also agreed to pay an annual fee for the privilege of serving as Ursúa's lieutenant captain general and supreme magistrate for the opening of the camino real and the reduction of "infidels" along its way.[59]

Ursúa's first instructions to García were vague. He emphasized that the primary purpose of the project was to open a secure land route to Guatemala, and he only implied that any "infidels" discovered along the way were to be reduced and converted. He recognized that conversion was the aim of the Barrios undertaking and that earlier governors of Yucatán had tried and failed to pacify and Christianize these provinces. Of García, however, he required only that "he head out for the said provinces with all the people who are assigned to him in order to meet up with the said lord president [Barrios], opening road up to the said jurisdiction, whom he will notify about everything that he deems appropriate; and he will be under the said lord president's orders. For which his lordship [Governor Ursúa] **127** will assist him at his own cost with the powder, ammunition, and supplies that he needs for the said journey."[60]

García de Paredes received no instructions about how to treat the native people he would encounter. Forgotten were the pious language of

Ursúa's original memorial and the Crown's repetition of his intention to reduce the natives "gently and peacefully." Subsequent actions demonstrated that García understood his job as that of a soldier who was to open a road and confront any resistance militarily. Ursúa's own subsequent support of García indicates that he shared this interpretation. Only one priest, a member of the secular clergy, accompanied García. Ursúa should have appointed missionaries from the regular clergy to accompany the troops, but he did not do so until May. In the meantime, García made a first, short-lived entrada during March and April, which he used primarily in order to capture a number of resistant forest Mayas.

Although Ursúa's official instructions to García de Paredes were to open the road to the point at which he would meet President Barrios and his troops, we will see later that this was never Ursúa's true intention. García struck a path for Lago Petén Itzá and never wavered from it.

chapter five

THE BIRTH OF THE CAMINO REAL

In early March 1695, Captain Alonso García de Paredes set out from Campeche under orders from Governor Ursúa, who had taken office only a few months before. On this, the first of several military entradas destined for Lago Petén Itzá, García took with him a modest retinue of fifty Spanish troops and an additional number of Maya guides, muleteers, road openers, and retainers. The sole churchman accompanying the expedition was the secular priest of Sajkab'ch'en, Bachiller Estévan de Saraus.[1]

The Spaniards were García de Paredes's familiars, chosen from those employed "in his haciendas." No surveyor accompanied the small band, but García had considerable knowledge of the lands to the south, having traveled the existing forest road over the past eighteen years in his capacity as war captain of the district of Sajkab'ch'en (map 8). His occasional forays had taken him at least as far south as Tzuktok', which had been from time to time a settled mission station. Their purpose had been to raid villages and hamlets settled by runaways from encomienda towns — or to capture anyone else he could find in the forests. He would round up the inhabitants and march them off to his and others' Campeche-area encomiendas and ranches, where they would enlarge the population that was forced to participate in repartimientos, to pay tribute, and to perform required labor (*servicio personal*). The distance from Kawich, at the head of this road, to Tzuktok' was some forty-three leagues.[2]

The Failure of the First Entrada

On this occasion García de Paredes took guides from Sajkab'ch'en who could lead the way through the same territory from which many of them at been forcibly removed in earlier years. He made Sajkab'ch'en his military

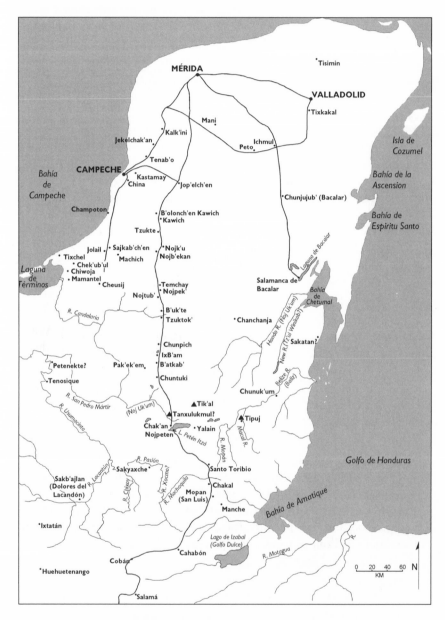

Map 8. The route of the camino real.

headquarters, striking out southward from there through hostile terrain. By mid-April he and his men had turned back, having met armed resistance from the native population. He reported to Ursúa from Sajkab'ch'en on April 21, according to the governor's summary of his letter, "that having come upon a hamlet of Cehach Indians, and having imprisoned some of them as they had not wanted to submit peacefully, because there are many who inhabit those forests, and recognizing that his men had been intimidated, and with resolve not to go further, he decided to retreat to this province and to inform his lordship of the aforementioned."[3]

According to Villagutierre, who saw García's report to Ursúa, at some point the captain led a group of armed scouts to explore the area beyond where workers were clearing the road.

> After walking some distance through the bush they came upon some hamlets of many Indians — pagans and apostates of the Cehach nation — who, upon seeing the Spaniards, defended themselves, starting to shoot arrows.
>
> And despite exhortations that they lay down their arms, listen to [the Spaniards] and submit peacefully, and [understand] that no harm would be done to them, it was impossible to get anywhere with them. To the contrary, it was necessary to begin fighting. As a result, forced to retreat, the pagans (although for a good while they resisted the combat tenaciously) were imprisoned. Some of them said and declared through the interpreters that they were of the Cehach nation, and that there were a great many of that or of other nations who inhabited those forests.[4]

Ursúa reported several months later that the Spaniards had killed eight Kejaches on this expedition.[5] García must have penetrated the forest beyond Tzuktok', because the Franciscan friars identified Kejach territory as beginning at Chunpich, eight leagues south of Tzuktok'.[6]

The resistance his men encountered could hardly have surprised García, considering his reputation in these forests. Villagutierre claimed that he decided to sound the retreat because his own men were so few, "and even the fewest for such barbarism."[7] A more plausible motive is that he needed his available troops to escort the Kejach captives back to Sajkab'ch'en. The troops had already violated the spirit of a reduction that was to be pursued "peacefully and gently," attacking native people along the route, imprisoning them, subjecting them to interrogation, and carrying them off. Their precise fate, of course, is unrecorded, but they may well have been taken to García's encomienda, as were forest Mayas captured near Tzuktok' later in the year. The camino real project had begun as a sequel to many decades of armed intrusions and reductions in this frontier area.

The first entrada lasted a few short weeks, made little progress into the southern forests, and was scarcely noted in further reports on the road opening. Indeed, most of Ursúa's official reports ignored the event altogether, perhaps less because of his embarrassment that García had been so poorly supplied with troops than because of his desire to conceal the fact that he had captured natives by force of arms. Villagutierre's claim that Ursúa received news of the retreat with "great disgust" and "no little disquietude" may have been true, but Ursúa himself revealed no such judgments in writing.[8] Nor is there any indication that Ursúa chastised his captain for his treatment of the Kejaches. Rather, he quickly concluded that better armed preparation was called for next time. García, who returned to Campeche in early May, set out again along the camino real in early June, this time with a veritable army, an extensive supply train, and a military engineer who would survey the road. We shall return to this second entrada later in the chapter, but first let us look at developments on the Guatemalan side of the project.

Itza-Guatemalan Encounters

Guatemalan president Barrios Leal, although in ill health, had departed at the head of his own small army from Santiago de Guatemala on January 15, 1695, reaching Comitán via Huehuetenango three weeks later. Joining other troops sent on before him, he was advised to travel ahead to Ocosingo before entering the Chol Lakandon forests.[9] At Ocosingo the plan of attack was finalized: Barrios would lead three companies of Spaniards and two of Mayas departing from Ocosingo. Captain Melchor Rodríguez would take a Spanish company and a number of Mayas from San Mateo Ixtatán through Huehuetenango. The third party — troops, native path cutters, and muleteers under Captain Juan Díaz de Velasco — would travel southeast from Comitán to Cahabón in Alta Verapaz. Each party was to depart from its station on the last day of February to begin the final Lakandon campaign.[10]

It was Rodríguez's party, with the tracking assistance of the Mercederian Fray Pedro de la Concepción, that discovered the Lakandon town of Sakb'ajlan on April 6 and occupied the deserted settlement on the ninth. The Mercederian provincial, Fray Diego de Rivas, promptly named the town Nuestra Señora de los Dolores, because the first signs of it were found on Good Friday; it was often called Dolores del Lacandón. President Barrios and his men finally found the now-occupied Dolores on April 19. The inhabitants soon started to return, and the process of catechizing and baptizing them began. After constructing a fort, Barrios and his officers decided to begin withdrawing on May 20, leaving behind all but fifty troops, in addition to the priests and a body of native servants. Barrios returned to Santiago de Guatemala on July 4.[11]

With the rainy season now under way, Barrios decided to postpone further action until the following year. This was to be his last entrada, however — he died early the next year. From this point onward, reduction activities in the vicinity of Dolores del Lacandón were small in scale, and any thoughts of extending the muddy path beyond there toward Yucatán were soon abandoned.

A Guatemalan messenger, Diego Bernardo del Río, arrived in Mérida on June 23 with news of the occupation of Dolores del Lacandón and President Barrios's pending return to Santiago de Guatemala with the bulk of his troops. The record of his report, in the form of a brief sworn testimony taken by Ursúa, says nothing about what had become of Juan Díaz de Velasco, whom the president had ordered to set out from his temporary post at Cahabón at the end of February for an undisclosed destination. From this omission we might conclude that del Río had been carefully instructed to keep secret the fact that the final goal of the 1695 Guatemalan campaign was not to reduce the Chol Lakandons but to discover the precise location of the Itzas and to consider how best to pursue their conquest and reduction. Ursúa's record of del Río's intelligence report reveals nothing about the strategy by which, as we will soon see, this initial exploratory mission would be carried out — that is, for Díaz's forces to proceed northward from Verapaz through Manche Chol and Mopan territory all the way to Lago Petén Itzá. There, if the plan had worked, they would have joined President Barrios and his troops, who were to have proceeded eastward from Chol Lakandon territory as soon as their reduction project there had been accomplished.[12]

The Guatemalans, who were aware of Ursúa's designs on the Itzas, were determined to reach them before Ursúa did. It is inconceivable that del Río was unaware of the fighting that occurred between the Itzas and Díaz de Velasco's party during April, described in the pages that follow. Yet Ursúa reported that del Río spoke of the Itzas only vaguely in terms of their legendary ferocity as "warlike and bloodthirsty Indians who eat human flesh."[13]

Indeed, by the time del Río reached Mérida, Díaz de Velasco had already engaged his first Itzas. The Guatemalan captain commanded seventy armed Spaniards, "many" Maya archers from Verapaz, and a host of native muleteers.[14] President Barrios, who was more concerned with reducing the native population than with opening a road, had been careful to appoint missionaries to each of the military branches of his enterprise. Díaz therefore had with him four Dominican friars, the vicar general of whom was Fray Agustín Cano.[15] Guatemalan-born Cano had strong credentials as a well-respected theologian, missionary, and administrator of his order. He was an excellent choice to lead reductions in this area, having participated in reduction missions, without military escort, in the Manche Chol region during 1685 and 1686. He was well educated, opposed to violence against the native people, and able to hold his ground in the company of military officers. One of his companions in the entrada to the Itzas, José Delgado, had participated in the Manche Chol reductions with him.[16] Díaz himself was also familiar with the region, having provided a military escort for the Dominican Fray Francisco Gallegos on a reduction mission to the Manche Chol region in 1676.[17]

This was the first direct encounter between Spaniards and Itzas on their home territory in many years — probably since the murder of Fray Diego Delgado and his Tipujan and Spanish escorts in 1623. By now the Itzas were aware of rapidly accelerating Spanish activities all along their frontiers, and they were not about to be fooled into thinking that these visitors were traders on a peaceful mission of exchange and evangelism. García was advancing south toward Kejach territory. Guatemalan troops and missionaries were exploring in southwestern Petén, and now troops were advancing toward the lake from the south. Defense strategies against the Spaniards were surely being discussed at Nojpeten, and political stresses were bringing the Itza confederacy nearly to the breaking point. It was no wonder, then, that a group of nervous Itza hunters reacted to Díaz's armed military explorers with a volley of arrows.

During March, Díaz's expedition passed without apparent incident through Chol territory, collecting a number of natives whom they impressed as supply carriers.[18] By April 2 the main party had advanced well into Mopan lands and camped at a place known as Mopan, whose principal "cacique" was Taxim Chan; this town was probably at or near the location of present-day San Luis. Cano wrote from there to the Guatemalan oidor José de Escals, who had assumed the president's authority while Barrios was on his expedition, reporting that the Chol and Mopan guides denied any knowledge of the path to the lake, owing to their fear of the Itzas. Delays in the arrival of supplies, as well as the desertion of their carriers, had forced the party to stay there for several days, which Cano welcomed for the opportunity it gave to have "pacified many Mopans, among them four caciques."[19] Nonetheless, most of the local Mopans had fled the area with Taxim Chan. He estimated that they were only three or four days from the lake and presumed that he would meet up with President Barrios's party there, unaware that the president had not even neared the area.[20] Cano emphasized that the large number of abandoned houses and maize fields indicated a large population of Mopans, who he understood were political subjects of the Itza ruler.

On April 6 about fifty musketeers and some native archers left the camp at Taxim Chan's town and within two days found signs of camps made by Itzas who a month earlier had visited this part of Mopan territory.[21] Further along the way, now following a clear road to Itza territory, Díaz de Velasco sent ahead two of his soldiers, two archers from Salamá in Verapaz, two muleteers from Cahabón, the Mopan guide Cacique Yajkab' who also spoke Chol, and another Chol-speaking interpreter from Cahabón. This group was assigned to explore the road beyond Taxim Chan's town.[22] The rest of the force moved ahead to a place called "Río de los Ah Itzáes," ten or twelve leagues south of the lake.[23]

On the savannah just south of the lake—about thirty-two leagues from Taxim Chan's town—the advance party of explorers encountered a group of thirty Itza deer hunters armed with shields, spears, and bows and arrows and accompanied by hunting dogs. Seeing the strangers, the Itzas put down their loads, pulled out their weapons, and drew their bows. The Mopan guide told them what he had been instructed to say—or at least the Spaniards thought he did—"He told the Petenes [i.e., Itzas] that they should be peaceable and not fight, because those were merchants who sold axes and machetes, and that with them had come some padres in order to preach to them and teach them the law of God."[24] With this misinformation communicated, the following events transpired—according to Fray Agustín Cano's reconstruction, which concurs precisely with Captain Díaz de Velasco's field diary:

> While the Mopan Indian said this, [the Spaniards] were encircling the Petenes, and their leader nailed his spear into the ground and went to up to receive the Mopan, giving him his hand with much courtesy. And especially when the Petenes heard him say that padres went along, they started to murmur and began to be agitated. And seeing this, Machuca [one of the Spanish soldiers] told

135

an archer from Salama to grab the Mopan because he had intimated himself with the Petenes, and it appears that he had sold out
our own people. And the Salama Indian, throwing himself into the
midst of the Petenes, caught the Mopan and dragged him out from
amidst all the rest. Then the Petenes became excited, [and] grabbed
their arrows in order to shoot at our men, who, quickly taking up
their muskets, fired two of them, wounding some of the Petenes.
Most of them fled, and three or four Petenes remained where they
were, as though stunned, with their arrows in their hands, without
shooting them at our men. A Cahabon Indian then rushed at them
with his machete, and they too turned to run away, leaving in the
hands of our Indian a good roll of arrows. All of the Indians having
disappeared, they went up to the packs that the Indians had left behind in the camp, and they found them filled with tamales, plantains, and other supplies with which they remedied their need, and
they were able to return to let us know what had happened and all
about the road to the lake.[25]

Prisoners taken subsequent to this encounter reported that the wounded
Itzas had later died.[26]

INTELLIGENCE ON NOJPETEN

Five days later Díaz questioned Yajkab', the Mopan interpreter, concerning the names of the "caciques" of the "Ahitza" and received from him
valuable testimony. The interpreter, who obviously knew Nojpeten first-
hand, stated that the previous "lord and principal cacique" had died and
had left three of his sons, all of whom were named Kan Ek', to govern the
island. These three brothers united whenever they made war on the Lakandons. These brothers, he said, attacked not only the Lakandons but
also the Mopans, taking prisoners to Nojpeten and sacrificing them there.
These were the men whom I identified in chapter 3 as bearing the titles Kit
Kan and Tz'o Kan.

Nojpeten, according to Yajkab', was divided among four "towns or
barrios," which he named.[27] When asked how many Itzas there were, he
replied "that they were not so many, that they are 400 each *zontle,* if not
six or seven *xiquipiles,* which are 8,000 apiece. This is what he declared,
and in order to declare it better he joined his fingers, eyelashes, eyebrows,
and the hair on his head, signifying the multitude of Indians that there are
and that the island is very large and each town like the savanna of the River
of the Toads, which is more than four leagues long and in width much

more."[28] His references to zontles and xiquipiles were measures of cacao beans, four hundred and eight thousand, respectively, expressed in the common Nahuatl terminology. Although the number of zontles is unspecified, and even though Díaz seems to have added the translation into quantities himself, the Mopan seemed to be saying that there were "zontles and zontles" of people, perhaps as many as six or seven xiquipiles of them. Six xiquipiles would have been forty-eight thousand persons, a reasonable estimate of the Lago Petén Itzá area population. It seems less likely that he was exaggerating in order to frighten the Spaniards, as Ximénez claimed, than expressing his best estimate of a sizable population.

Yajkab' probably surprised the Spaniards somewhat by claiming that the Mopans and Itzas spoke the same language, but this was certainly good news for them. On the same day that this testimony was taken, Antonio Machuca set out with twelve musketeers and twenty-five archers, accompanied by thirteen muleteers, to search for President Barrios, to discover whether the Itzas were planning an attack, and to try to capture another guide and interpreter, "because we were disconsolate in not having an interpreter or anyone who knows the language, which is Yucatec." No longer able to trust their Mopan informant, they apparently needed someone else who could speak the Itza language.

The exploratory party had hoped to find a river route to the main lake. Despite the fact that all rivers along the route (the San Juan, San Martín, and Sanicte) flow southwestward, not northward toward the lake, they had at first believed they would be able to take canoes or small boats from the Chakal to a river called "Cancuen" and from there to another river called Xokmo, which Yajkab' had told them flowed directly into the lake of the Itzas. All rivers, he said, flowed to the lake, and none flowed out of it. Soon the Spaniards discovered, however, that rivers flowed neither into nor out of the lake. The rest of the journey would be on foot.[29]

On April 22 the main party, unaware of existing Itza paths, managed to open a trail to the edge of the savannah near the main lake. On the night of the twenty-third a soldier named Beltrán arrived at the camp with an Itza prisoner named Chan, who had been captured in the savannah by the exploratory party. Díaz wrote in his journal a vivid description of this man's capture and his appearance: "Beltrán says that he fired two arrow shots at a soldier. One pierced the man, and the other went into the air. Our men went near him, and when they reached him in order to capture him he defended himself so courageously that all of them combined were not able to subdue him. They wounded him in the head, thereby stunning him, and they tied him up. He arrived in this condition at the headquarters, nude, with his entire chest, stomach, and thighs all worked with designs. The man was a monstrosity, with very large handcrafted earplugs or horns,[30] surely a disgusting thing."[31]

Clearly they had unwittingly taken prisoner a man of considerable importance. Not only was he covered with tattoos and wearing earplugs, but his high social status was further reinforced by his answers to questions put to him:

> [H]e said that he was called Chan and his father Kin Chan, and his mother Ix Puc, and his town Tixbol Pululha, which is of the island, and that his cacique is he of Noh Peten called Kitcan, and he has another name and is called Cuxpop Kitcan. That around the lake there are many people subject to the cacique of the island; that on the island there are many people, that it is large and with large houses, both in the interior and around it. That there are other towns around the lake. That many rivers flow into the lake. That those who sallied forth yesterday when Machuca fired were Ah Itzas, that those of the island are called Petenes and those from around it Ah Itza, and that it is all one nation, and that he was one of them. That one or two died from the shots of Machuca. That they and those of the island eat people and that he was a spy with six others who were later separated. That he had gone to look for merchants to buy axes and machetes and they had not found any, only arrows. He said that the caciques were Cuxpop Kitcan, Aical Chan and Aical Puc. And this is what was understood of him, although he contradicts himself and lies much and on other occasions denies it all.[32]

The prisoner Chan and others of that patronym were members of the high-ranking Chan patrilineage associated with Tipuj and the Yalain province. They had close kinship, marriage, and political ties to the Kan Ek' royal family; one of them, the famous AjChan, visited Mérida later in the year as the envoy of his mother's brother, Ajaw Kan Ek'. The prisoner's father, K'in Chan, was likely Ach Kat K'in Chan. His mother's patrilineage, the Puks, later included the "cacique" of Laguna Oquevix south of the main lake. Kuch Pop Kit Kan was Ajaw B'atab' Kit Kan, the administrative "Head of the Mat" of the ruling council (see chapter 3). The other two "caciques," Ayikal Chan and Ayikal Puk, bore the noble title "Rich Man" but have not been identified individually.

Although Chan provided excellent political intelligence for Díaz de Velasco, he was careful—in contrast to Yajkab', the Mopan interpreter—

to avoid revealing the names of all of the highest-ranking Nojpeten leaders. Díaz would have had no context in which to interpret the positions of the three "caciques" in the larger hierarchy. He probably regarded his success in extracting—by unspecified methods of questioning—yet another confession that the Itzas were cannibals as clear proof of their barbarism. For Chan, however, providing such information may well have been a strategy to keep the Spaniards at arm's length. Chan's statement that he was both a spy and in search of metal axes and machetes is perfectly believable, because the approaching Spaniards must have been seen as either bearing goods or preparing to wage war.

ITZA-SPANISH VIOLENCE

That afternoon the rest of Machuca's scouts returned to the camp, saying that they had intended to go to the lake to discover the best route there and to "record what houses or towns there were on its shores." They camped on a hill about four leagues from the lake and saw that there were also Itzas camped about "a block" away. The next morning they approached these eleven or twelve Itzas, who were roasting a deer they had killed. The Spaniards later claimed that they went up to them with their interpreter to try to talk with them, but the Itzas picked up their weapons, came closer to the Spaniards, and shot arrows at them. The Itzas quickly used up their supply of arrows, but the soldiers found that their powder was too wet for the muskets to fire efficiently. The Itzas thereupon rushed them with their axes, spears, and machetes. After an hour of hand-to-hand combat, six Itzas lay dead from gunshot, knife, and spear wounds. One Itza, even though he was wounded by four balls, kept on fighting until he and his companions began to retreat. Not a single member of the Spanish party, it was said, was wounded, thanks to the mail or cotton padding they were wearing.[33]

The troops chased the fleeing Itzas but at first were unable to capture even one of them. A battle ensued when one Spaniard, struck by a spear, hit his attacker in the head with a machete and then killed him. Another soldier fell to the ground in hand-to-hand combat with an attacker, whom he slashed with his machete; the Itza was wounded and seemed likely to die. During the battle, which lasted for an hour, five or six Itzas were killed. They were so fierce, Machuca reported, that "four good men are insufficient [to fight off] each of these Ahitza Indians." The outcome of this battle, wrote Ximénez, was that "[t]hree Itzas escaped, and one was taken prisoner with three head wounds. This man was cured and recovered and was very content, and he says that he is a cacique of those of

139

Canek and that his name is Kixan. (I saw and knew him in San Reymundo when they took him to Guatemala, and he was a strapping young person about 35 years of age, very robust and stout, striped all over.) He said that they had come as spies and that the entire land, island, and the towns are in arms, as they wish neither to receive us nor to hear the evangelical word."[34]

On the twenty-fourth the prisoner named Chan escaped from the guardroom by chewing through the ropes that had bound him. The sentinel chased him, but Chan threw himself into the river and swam away. The new prisoner, however, proved to be a man of even greater importance than Chan. Soon subjected to questioning, he said that his name was K'ixan (usually recorded as AjK'ixaw by Spanish observers) and that he was from a town called Tib'ayal, on the lakeshore on a small hill. He also listed six other towns named for their "caciques" or, in one case, for a B'atab'. He gave the title and name of Ajaw Kan Ek' and personal names of two "caciques" who bore the honorific Chontal male prefix *pak*- (Pak-Lan and PakNek).[35] Most of the names he mentioned (Chan, Kan Ek', Kawil, K'ixan or K'ixaw, K'u, Sima, and Tun) were represented among the nobility and political leadership of the region.

Captain Díaz de Velasco clearly appreciated the value of his noble prisoner, for he promised the acting president, José de Escals, that he would take AjK'ixaw to Guatemala:

> He is the cacique, according to his declaration, of one of the towns that are on the lakeshore. It would be fitting for your lordship to see him, so that you could see his person and agility and could know his valor. Upon your lordship's order I shall send him later. And I judge that this one will be the means by which the rest might be reduced. By his declaration your lordship can consider the multitude of people that there are on the shores of the lake [and] on the island that is in the middle of it, and that without at least four hundred men all of this land — which is immense — can neither be conquered nor explored.[36]

AjK'ixaw was indeed later taken to Santiago de Guatemala, where he learned Spanish and was questioned at length by the Dominican friars. Other reports in 1695 claimed that AjK'ixaw was actually the *son* of a cacique.[37] His brother, B'atab' Tut, ruled the north with Ajaw B'atab' K'in Kante and controlled the port at Ensenada de San Jerónimo.[38] As we shall see in chapter 9, AjK'ixaw was returned from Guatemala in 1696 as guide and interpreter for another expedition, but he escaped and assisted his Itza allies in capturing and murdering a large party of Spaniards. (He had been baptized just before his escape by one of the Dominicans on that entrada, and Díaz de Velasco had served as his godfather.) Knowledgeable in the Spanish language and familiar with Spanish culture and military tactics, AjK'ixaw became a formidable enemy to the people who had captured him.[39] He was finally recaptured in 1702.[40]

Although just after his first capture AjK'ixaw divulged accurate details that could have been useful had the Guatemalans decided to make contact with the Itza leaders, his information was selective and incomplete.[41] It was sufficient only to make the Spaniards aware that Itza political organization was complex, that the nobility possessed a hierarchy of titles, and that there were many towns with their own leaders. AjK'ixaw's strategy, I believe, was to convince his captors that, considering the small size of the potential attack force, taking on the Itzas militarily would be foolhardy. Their only alternative, he may have reasoned, would be to make a diplomatic-missionary approach, a possibility that he tried to avert by warning that the entire region was readying for attack and had no intention of receiving missionaries.

Although Machuca and his scouts had reached the shore of the lake in sight of Nojpeten, they were terrified of attack and narrowly escaped an encounter with "such a multitude of Indians that we consider it a miracle." On April 24, the day following AjK'ixaw's arrival at the encampment, Cano met with his fellow Dominicans to consider their next move. All of their encounters with the Itzas so far had been hostile, at least eight Itzas had been killed in the field by Spanish gunfire, and others were dying at home from their wounds. Cano, whose mind had obviously been made up beforehand, prepared an advisory memorandum on behalf of the four missionaries that blisteringly criticized the readiness of Díaz's troops to open fire against Itzas who were armed only with spears and bows and arrows.[42]

Cano argued that the sole purpose of the troops was to defend the missionaries, but he recognized that the Itzas were uninterested in hearing the gospel at this point and under these conditions. Rather than risk killing more of them in the name of the faith, the entrada should be abandoned and a retreat begun. The friars suspected that President Barrios had not reached "this tremendous lake," but even if his party was on the other side it would be impossible for Díaz's men to build boats in order to see if they were there. Illness, Cano pointed out, was invading the camp, and the

Verapaz natives who had been recruited for the entrada were abandoning the project daily. The rains were beginning in earnest, and soon the roads would be impassable.[43]

Although Díaz was ready to march ahead and was convinced that his troops, combined with those of Barrios, would have "concluded the reduction of these islanders," he agreed that the president was almost certainly not in the area.[44] He rationalized that illness had become a serious issue, noting that two muleteers had already died. His justification for retreat, however, rested primarily on the inadequacy of military personnel — implying that the missionaries would need a considerably larger backup force in light of probable Itza hostility. The line between spiritual and military conquest was a thin one indeed.

The retreat to Cahabón began almost immediately, and the Itzas were left to contemplate the significance of their new armed conflict with Spaniards. Díaz was later roundly condemned and chastised by the Guatemalan audiencia for his decision to cancel the entrada, and he was ordered to turn back to the lake.[45] The Guatemalans, however, were not to attempt to reach Lago Petén Itzá for another year. The resulting disaster forms the subject of chapter 9.

The Second Yucatecan Entrada

When Captain Alonso García de Paredes returned to Campeche in early May 1695 after his unsuccessful first entrada, Governor Ursúa had not yet learned of the Guatemalans' battles with Itzas during April or of the occupation of the Chol Lakandon town, Sakb'ajlan, renamed Nuestra Señora de los Dolores. On May 2, before García's return to Campeche, Ursúa had already authorized the recruitment of reinforcements for his captain's next entrada. Fifty armed soldiers were to be hired at a salary of eight pesos monthly, providing their own arms and ammunition. Fifty Mayas were also to be engaged, half of whom would carry arms. The other half would serve as muleteers and road workers. On his next journey, García should take with him Captain Manuel Jorge Sesere of Campeche, a "pilot and military engineer."[46] Shortly after Ursúa issued these orders, García returned to Campeche and on May 7 received a promise from the town's cabildo of an additional twenty-five Spanish soldiers, their salaries of eight pesos per month to be paid equally by the six cabildo members.[47]

One council member, Bernardino de Zubiaur Isasi, was the father of

142

Pedro de Zubiaur Isasi, who served as a captain on the second entrada at the tender age of about twenty.[48] The elder Zubiaur, it will be recalled from chapter 4, was Ursúa's friend and contact with the Council of the Indies, where Zubiaur's brother served. He and the other merchant councilmen of Campeche welcomed the opportunity to help subsidize the camino real, not only because of the potential it offered to increase trade with Guatemala but also for the profits they would earn by selling military and food supplies for the forthcoming entradas.

Ursúa, moving quickly, issued an order on May 11 for García to begin his second entrada as soon as possible and for one hundred Mayas to be recruited, twice as many as he had authorized a little over a week earlier. Fifty of these were to be recruited from Sajkab'ch'en at three pesos monthly and suspension of *servicio personal* (probably mostly logging) and encomienda tribute.[49] The other fifty were to be recruited on the same terms from the towns of Tek'ax and Oxk'utzkab', in the partido of Sierra, by Juan del Castillo y Arrúe, the son of Juan del Castillo y Toledo, whose own designs to lead a conquest of the Itza region were described in chapter 4.[50] Both men were well experienced in recruiting Maya road workers and muleteers and, despite their own long-term conquest interests, were perfectly willing to take on a job for Ursúa that would net them, presumably, both influence and a reward for their services. The Castillos had recruited Sierra Mayas for similar purposes during the 1687 entrada to La Pimienta, an advantage that for Ursúa probably outweighed any adversarial reservations he might have harbored toward them. He observed, accurately, that two Maya companies had long existed at Tek'ax and Oxk'utzkab' for the sole purpose of assisting in reductions.[51]

On May 12, García de Paredes and another Campechano, José Fernández de Estenos, offered to assist the new entrada with twenty-five additional non-Maya soldiers to be paid, fed, and supplied ammunition at their own cost. By now the total had reached one hundred armed non-Maya soldiers and one hundred Mayas, about half of them armed. According to Fray Andrés de Avendaño, even more men were later added to this force; he reported that supplies and wages were provided for 115 Spaniards and 150 Maya musketeers.[52] With Maya muleteers and other workers, the final force, he claimed, totaled more than four hundred people.[53] For poverty-stricken seventeenth-century Yucatán, this was a considerable army. **143**

Ursúa lost no time in naming García de Paredes field commander of the camino real project, granting him the impressive title "lieutenant captain general and supreme magistrate of the forests" — the latter implying that he had the power to determine the fate of any Mayas encountered along the way.[54] Fernández de Estenos was to serve as second-in-command.

Ursúa had already instructed Juan Castillo y Arrúe, the Mani encomendero, to activate the two Maya companies from Tek'ax and Oxk'utzkab' and to march them with their muskets, axes, and machetes to B'olonch'en Kawich, where they would be placed under the orders of García de Paredes.[55] At the Tek'ax plaza, Castillo y Toledo ordered Captain don Pascual Itza, "cacique governor of this said town . . . to assemble the officers and soldiers of his company in order to execute that which was ordered by the said lord governor and captain general." Once these men and the town cabildo were assembled and the orders had been read to them by the official "interpreter general of the natives," Nicolás Cardenia, Captain Itza and his officers dutifully replied — according to Castillo's report to Ursúa — that they would comply.[56]

Castillo appointed Bonifacio Us captain of the Tek'ax company, and twenty-four other men were chosen, presumably by the officers, to serve on the entrada. These recruits lined up, gave their names to the interpreter, and received their first monthly payment of three pesos; Us, as their captain, received a two-month advance of six pesos.[57] At Oxk'utzkab' the same procedures were followed, with don Marcos Pot named the "cacique capitán," signing his name B'atab', or town head. Diego Uk was named company captain.[58]

Troops, support personnel, arms, powder, and supplies were all rapidly collected at Kawich, where Castillo y Arrúe was left in charge as supply master. On June 4, 1695, the bulk of this army left under the command García de Paredes.[59] The non-Maya troops were a mix of Spaniards and *castas* — mestizos and mulattos — drawn from the poorer classes of Yucatecan society. The Maya company from Sajkab'ch'en, later documents show, were the elite musketeers of this small army.[60] They seem to have enjoyed, even relished, the responsibility of forcibly rounding up the forest Mayas into reduction towns. As an elite company armed with muskets, they were not required to toil at opening the road or to carry heavy loads — tasks left to other, nameless Maya recruits.

The Direction of the Camino Real

144

Ursúa, as we learned earlier, heard of the Guatemalan occupation of Sakb'ajlan on June 23, when the messenger del Río arrived in Mérida after the long overland trip from Santiago de Guatemala. García had begun his

second entrada only nineteen days earlier and was by now at Tzuktok',
near the boundary with the Kejaches.

This opportunity — the reduction or conquest of the Itzas — now had to
be met quickly, for the Guatemalans had already been to the shores of
Lago Petén Itzá and would soon be returning on a more serious mission.
Although a road had to be constructed to Guatemala, there would be no
reward in opening it directly to Dolores del Lancandón through virtually
uninhabited territory. A road to Lago Petén Itzá could connect with the
southern route from the lake to Cahabón, leaving the Chol Lakandon
territory isolated to the west. Every step of the road construction from
now on confirmed that Ursúa, despite his statements to the contrary, had
planned all along for the camino real to head directly to Lago Petén Itzá.
The urgency of completing the road became even clearer when he learned
of Barrios's return to Guatemala from Dolores.

From the road's starting point at Kawich the surveyor pointed his compass straight south, following as close as the terrain permitted a line along
longitude 90° 5' W. So accurate was this projection that, had it been
followed exactly, the troops would have passed two kilometers west of Laguna Sacpuy and would have had to traverse only about eleven kilometers
to the western end of Lago Petén Itzá. This was superb surveying that indicates prior knowledge of the precise location of the main lake. The surveyor reported that after the road had reached Chuntuki, almost within
sight of Itza territory, he had tried to keep it on a straight line, deviating
only on account of rivers, swamps, and other features.[61]

Ursúa issued new instructions to García on the same day, June 23, on
which del Río made his report about the Guatemalan entradas. At this
point García was within a few leagues of Chuntuki, the first Kejach settlement. There is no doubt whatsoever that his intention was to head as
directly as possible to the main lake of the Itzas. Ursúa, however, writing
in the customary third person, ostensibly now ordered him to head directly to Dolores, claiming that "the goal with which he executed his
departure was only to search for the lord president of Guatemala and to be
under his orders whenever he encountered his lordship or those of another
superior commander." García was to go from Tzuktok', "clearing and
following his road, endeavoring to bend a little toward the left hand and
the eastern side until he succeeds in reaching within sight of the town of
Lacandons, which I know the said lord president discovered and gave the
name of the Villa of Nuestra Señora de los Dolores."[62]

This was pure dissimulation. Bending "a little toward the left hand and
the eastern side" would have taken García even farther from Dolores,

which lay far to the southwest, but it described a perfect route to Lago Petén Itzá. Moreover, Ursúa knew that President Barrios had already departed from Sakb'ajlan.

His further instructions were most specific:

> Before entering it [Dolores], at a distance of about 5 leagues, or at that which appears most suitable to him, he will halt with the people and establish his headquarters, proceeding immediately to lay out a stockaded fort where he finds it most convenient for the best defense and his fortification, with notice that he is to name it Nuestra Señora de los Remedios, who is the protectress of this enterprise and through whose assistance I anticipate that its attainment will be achieved. He is not by any means to go to or interfere in any of the settlements and populations that the lord president of Guatemala might have discovered, because he must abide by the terms that were permitted him.[63]

Along his path García was to survey the location of every hamlet and town that he encountered, without taking detours, recording the distances between them and the size of the native population of each. He was then to go about "reducing them to the pale of Our Holy Mother Church by the gentle methods that His Majesty has determined, which are those of good example and the preaching of the religious missionaries who for this purpose he takes in his company." Once at Dolores he was, according to the official instructions, to contact President Barrios and hand him letters and papers that Ursúa was sending, including García's instructions themselves. The instructions were intended to demonstrate to Barrios that "the goal of having carried out this departure was only for the purpose of aiding that of his lordship."[64]

At this point, however, Ursua's instructions, as though written almost as an afterthought, took a new twist: "Because it is fitting that not one hour should be lost in a matter of such importance, as that which goes forth with the conversion of souls is the principal motivation of this glorious enterprise, the said captain don Alonso García de Paredes will make his way, with the information that he would have acquired about the populations of the Itzaes and Taitzaes, going with the said religious to catechize and reduce their barbarous Indians with the armed escort that seems most appropriate to him for his protection, leaving at the fort that which would be necessary as its garrison." The rest of the instructions assured the captain that he could place missionaries in whatever towns he wished and that Ursúa would request more, if they were needed, from

146

the Franciscan provincial. He himself would supply whatever additional men, munitions, or supplies García requested. Such requests should be forwarded through Juan del Castillo y Arrúe at B'olonch'en Kawich — although the northern headquarters were ultimately established at nearby Kawich. Finally, he was to offer his services to the Guatemalan soldiers or missionaries in case of any uprising among the Lakandons at Dolores.[65]

What can one make of such a set of orders, ostensibly telling Ursúa's field commander to meet up with the Guatemalans at Dolores, to build a fort there, to reduce native populations along the way, and then — and only then — to reduce the Itzas? Ursúa continued to include language in decrees later that year that reiterated the goal of opening the road to establish communication with Guatemala, although he appears never again to have mentioned that the road should proceed to Dolores. Every action taken by García in the months ahead was to proceed along a road leading directly to Lago Petén Itzá. He never once wavered from that course.

Ursúa's intention in writing these instructions as he did must have been to satisfy the Council of the Indies that he was carrying out the terms of his patent by instructing his field commander to route the road to wherever Barrios's men might be found. These had been his original instructions, and he was obviously deviating from them. Should any future criticism be directed at him for not having carried out the Crown's orders or not having cooperated with the Guatemalan enterprise, he would have on record proof that those had been his orders. García did construct a fort shortly after receiving these instructions, but it was at Chuntuki, about twenty-five leagues north of the main lake. This fort served as the military base for the camino real until, in February 1697, preparations for a final assault on Nojpeten were begun and the military headquarters were moved temporarily to within two leagues of the lake.[66]

Fray Antonio de Silva, the provincial of the Franciscan order in Yucatán, responded quickly to Ursúa's request of May 18, 1695, that he provide three missionaries to work with García de Paredes as the road passed south from Kawich. He felt pressure to fulfill the terms of the 1693 cédula that had ordered cooperation with Ursúa, but, more significantly, he was also eager to expand the long-waning influence of his order into new zones now ripe for evangelization. The Franciscans must have been ecstatic over the potential the project offered and delighted that the secular clergy, despite its prior involvement in the area, had not been asked to supply missionaries. Ursúa's request to Silva for Franciscans on the camino real went to the heart of their mission: they would "go on the said entrada and reduction . . . in order to catechize the infidel Indians that are in the said forests and to reduce them to the pale of our holy mother church."[1]

Silva wrote to Ursúa on the thirtieth that he had sent out announcements to his friars across the peninsula, seeking volunteers. Three men were ready to depart: Fray Juan de San Buenaventura Chávez (the mission's commissary), Fray Joseph de Jesús María, and a lay brother who had taken his vows, Fray Tomás de Alcoser. They were to be accompanied by another lay brother, known only as Lucas de San Francisco, who had not taken his vows. Their expenses, including vestments, ornaments, and other ritual items, were to be met from general provincial donations.[2]

In addition, Silva appointed another group, again to be supported by provincial donations. It comprised Fray Antonio Pérez de San Román, the lay brother Alonso de Vargas, and a third person who, for a while, would figure large in the drama ahead — Fray Andrés de Avendaño.[3] As "commissary apostolic missionary," Avendaño led the group.[4] Whereas the first group, as required by Ursúa, would accompany García while the road was being opened, Avendaño and his two companions would not participate with the others, "because," in Silva's words, "we desire the salvation of souls and to serve his majesty along *all roads.*" Instead, "arriving at a convenient spot they should take leave of the said captain and by themselves enter into some of those said infidel provinces."[5] Silva added no details to this vague itinerary, but both Ursúa and García de Paredes surely knew of the Franciscans' intentions to visit Nojpeten. That Ursúa was aware of these plans is indicated by his ready acceptance of Silva's proposal.

Avendaño's First Entrada

Avendaño, Pérez de San Román, and Vargas responded quickly to "the sound of this sonorous trumpet" and had packed their belongings by the time Silva notified Ursúa of their appointment on May 30.[6] They left Mérida on June 2, whereas the mission directed by San Buenaventura did not leave for at least another week.[7]

Avendaño later wrote a detailed report of the missionaries' experiences on both this entrada, which failed to reach Nojpeten, and his second trip in 1696, when he succeeded in meeting with Ajaw Kan Ek' and other Itza leaders.[8] This report, along with shorter versions in the form of sworn testimony,[9] contain valuable details, often couched in florid, biblical language. These details, clearly drawn from a daily journal, concern topics such as local geography, reduction activities along the camino real, cultural information about the Maya inhabitants of the forests, and, not least, insights into the mind and times of an intelligent and fanatically dedicated seventeenth-century Franciscan missionary.

Avendaño's full report is also a political statement in support of Ursúa, who in mid-1695 supported the Franciscans as missionaries of choice on the camino real project. Avendaño completed the report on April 29, 1696, shortly after returning from his second entrada and learning that Ursúa had shifted his support to the secular clergy. His report may be read as a petition for Ursúa to reconsider his withdrawal of commitment to the Franciscans—a petition that attempted to persuade by demonstrating loyal support for Ursúa and personal knowledge of the forest Mayas and the Itzas. His critical blunder may have been in harshly criticizing the **149** violent reduction methods of García de Paredes and his officers. Avendaño, who evaporated as a major figure following his return to Mérida and the completion of his report, erred in assuming that moral and ethical criticism would influence Ursúa's agenda.

TO KEJACH TERRITORY

Avendaño and his companions departed Mérida on June 2, 1695, with a "very broad mandate" from Ursúa — presumably to try to reach Nojpeten. As he traveled south along the road to Campeche he stopped at the Maya towns along the way not only to rest but also to recruit native religious assistants. Before leaving Mérida he had already enlisted three or four of the total of ten men who made up this group: Diego Ken, a regidor of the cabildo of San Cristóbal Extramuros, a native barrio of Mérida; Lorenzo Yaj, a servant of one Captain Velasco; and a "boy" named Francisco K'u, son of María Chuk, Avendaño's personal servant. He might also have recruited Diego P'ol in Mérida; he was a singer (*cantor*) from Telchak, located a considerable distance northeast of the city.[10] At Maxkanu he recruited Nicolás Maz, another singer, and Diego Mo, a sacristan. Luís Ki, a sacristan, joined him at Tepakam. At Kalk'ini he enlisted Marcos Kanul, the town's chapel (or choir) master (*maestro de capilla*).[11] Skirting Campeche along the road toward the southeast, he recruited his last Maya assistants, Nicolás May and Manuel Piste, both cantores at B'olonch'en Kawich.[12]

Avendaño's route had taken him south to the frontier settlement of Kawich, just past B'olonch'en Kawich, where he found a military headquarters of sorts under the command of Juan del Castillo y Arrúe.[13] From there he and his companions would traverse not a new route but rather the old road toward Kejach territory, which the troops and workers who had already gone ahead were clearing and repairing. He found some troops still waiting there, as well as stores of arms, ammunition, and food supplies. While there he met a trader named Juan Ak'e from Jop'elch'en who regularly bought and sold products in the southern forests and who served as a guide for the Spanish troops. "With some finesse and gentle persuasions" the friars extracted some details from him about three native towns that lay some fifty leagues beyond.[14]

The other group of Franciscan friars, who followed the same route a short distance behind Avendaño's group, left Kawich on June 12. Fray Joseph de Jesús María kept a careful daily record of their progress, which I have used to clarify omissions and expand on Avendaño's descriptions of their journey.[15] This group, unlike Avendaño's, was accompanied by Spanish troops as well as Maya guides and carriers.

Avendaño's group left Kawich on the afternoon of June 24 and traveled, for the "retribution of our sins," for several days across uninhabited territory. As they passed landmarks and interesting natural features — aguadas, cinnamon-smelling trees, *chultuns* (underground cisterns), a hollowed stone, an old Christian altar, abandoned fruit orchards, swamps, and savannahs—Avendaño made careful note of them. Although he was an undependable judge of distance, he kept a record of the distances between places in addition to their Maya names.[16]

On June 29 they reached a place called Nojku ("Big Temple"), where they had heard there was an ancient "house of idols." The Franciscans experienced "a Christian curiosity to see the said place in order to exorcise the devil on account of his frauds and to glorify and praise him who is powerful everywhere." Once they climbed the temple they discovered that Spaniards who had passed that way before had already broken many of the "idols." They managed nonetheless to find more than fifty additional ones to break themselves and placed a cross in the temple.[17]

Avendaño was afraid that his Maya companions would be spiritually corrupted upon seeing such influences, and he and the other Franciscans had "continual conversations with them about their familiarity with idolatry and other habitual vices." His greatest fear was that they would abandon him, which apparently they had already threatened to do. He was relieved that they continued to follow along, albeit with "resignation," promising that they would not desert him despite the "risks and dangers" to which they might be submitted.[18]

The second party of Franciscans, arriving at the ruins of Nojku several days after Avendaño had left, found that people had made offerings there during the days since Avendaño had passed by. Jesús María wrote that there were "many buildings in ruins. . . . We found here many different idols, some with faces [*figuras*] and others with none, signs of cacao offerings, two silver reales, bits of cacao, and a small hutia [*conga*]. We broke the idols and praised our true God and lord in that place and set up a cross, which was the third one, and named it Santa María de Nohku."[19] As they traveled south, the number of streams and rivers increased, the water in them became deeper, and flooded areas—*ak'alches*—became wider and longer.

Now Avendaño's party began to see further evidence of local habitation. Around Temchay, "an old deserted town" in the midst of a hilly region, they saw footprints of "forest Indians."[20] Three leagues farther along, at a place called Nojpek, they found a *sarteneja* (a large natural stone basin) filled with water and a milpa with maize and chiles.[21]

Two leagues south of Temchay they encountered the first sign of Spanish troops, who turned out to be part of a company under the command of

151

Captain José Fernández de Estenos. Their camp was two leagues farther at an "old deserted place" called Nojt'ub', which Avendaño described as "a pleasant place with orange and lime trees. In it we saw a large stockade [*cercado*] that the Indians made in order to defend themselves from the Spaniards when they went to remove them fifteen years ago."[22] Jesús María described this still-standing stockade as "a defensive stone wall which the Indians used to fortify themselves sixteen years ago [in 1679] when Captain Alonso García penetrated [this area]."[23]

Nojt'ub' ("Big Deep") was well situated next to a large seasonal aguada and a sarteneja, with a permanent aguada two kilometers to the east.[24] Had the vicinity of Temchay been abandoned for fifteen years, the forest would long since have reclaimed the citrus grove and the stockade. It is more likely that the local population had only recently fled and that García had left Fernández and his soldiers behind with instructions to bring them back.[25]

García had already moved on with his troops and road openers, trying to find the now-obscured path ahead. The two parties of Franciscans waited for a few days, the second group leaving on July 8 and Avendaño probably a few days earlier.[26] Their immediate goal was Tzuktok', about thirteen leagues (fifty-two kilometers) farther south; this town had also been one of those attacked in 1679 by García de Paredes. At a place called B'uk'te, three leagues (twelve kilometers) before Tzuktok', Avendaño's group found a cluster of twelve or thirteen houses whose inhabitants "had just surrendered to the Indian soldiers of Sahcabchen" without offering resistance. García's troops and Maya workers were all there, being fed with produce raised by the people of B'uk'te, who were now held captive; the army had raided maize, beans, and other foodstuffs from their milpas and orchards. Obviously disturbed by this, Avendaño excused the theft of food by rationalizing that the troops had "no other recourse, after the hunger that they had endured for the past three days."[27] Avendaño later learned sordid details about the recent abuse of the inhabitants of B'uk'te and recounted them in detail.[28]

Ursúa received a request for military reinforcements from García de Paredes and announced on July 27 the formation of three new militia companies, or seventy-five additional men. Two companies were to consist of Spaniards, commanded by Captains Fernández de Estenos and Zubiaur Isasi. The third was a company of pardos and mestizos under Alférez José Laines of Campeche. Far from being discouraged from supporting the use of force, Ursúa was willing to supply whatever manpower García de Paredes requested.[29]

Although Ursúa later may have privately cautioned García against using excessive violence, evidence of the continued application of military force later in the year suggests that he gave his Campechano captains a free hand in pursuing the entrada as they saw fit. In any event, committed to proving to the Council of the Indies that he had obeyed the requirement that the entrada be pursued "peacefully and gently," in August 1696 he engineered official depositions from several of the military officers who had been at B'uk'te when the abuses that Avendaño described took place. This testimony, not suprisingly, downplayed Avendaño's accusations of violent treatment.[30]

Tzuktok' was located on a stream called the Concepción, a tributary of Río Caribe, which in turn is a branch of Río Candelaria. Avendaño and his group had arrived there by July 10. They left on July 24, and the second group of Franciscans remained there until August 3. Shortly before Avendaño's departure the troops advanced to Tzuktok', bringing with them the B'uk'te captives, whom they used as forced laborers, and what remained of the pillaged produce. Avendaño described the encampment as consisting of more than four hundred persons, including the Maya carriers. Following Avendaño's departure, the remaining Franciscans continued baptizing and teaching the captives from B'uk'te and offering mass in the ruins of the church built there in 1670 by the Franciscan missionary Fray Cristóbal Sánchez.[31]

Before Avendaño left Tzuktok', he and the other friars met with García de Paredes and Captain Fernández de Estenos to propose a specific policy to be used whenever the troops discovered a native town — citing in their support biblical passages, existing Spanish law, and the Crown's recent "de paz y de paso" clause. The policy was twofold: if any items were taken from the inhabitants, they must be restored to them; and arms could be used only if the inhabitants did not submit peacefully and in a friendly manner. The captains, by now willing to say anything in order to quiet the meddlesome friars, promised to require that before entering a native town a proclamation to this effect would be read and that the death penalty would be applied to anyone who disobeyed it. Surely Avendaño was not naive enough to believe the captains' sincerity in promising the death penalty under dreadful working conditions that were already creating poor morale. Nonetheless, to reinforce the friars' concerns, Fray San Buenaventura delivered a sermon on the issue the very next day.[32]

The officers' lack of ability — if not will — to exert control over their men soon manifested itself. While these discussions were going on, the Sajkab'ch'en company, "who," Avendaño lamented, "never did anything well," had left Tzuktok' to serve as a guard unit for Maya laborers who were clearing the road. Eight leagues south of Tzuktok' they found the first town of Kejaches, called Chunpich, which had been abandoned — with twenty-five *cargas* of maize left behind — on account of rumors of the advancing troops. Fearing attack, the Sajkab'ch'en officers sent back a request to García for reinforcements. Before these arrived, some twenty-five local inhabitants turned up with baskets to retrieve their maize, but the six posted sentinels, perceiving them in their fear to be "thousands," shot at them. The locals retreated unharmed, and the sentinels ran to join the military reinforcement, which was at that moment approaching the town.

Even the normally glum Avendaño perceived the resulting encounter as a comedy of errors:

> When all were together they rushed into battle which our opponents, like brave men, won finely, wounding three of our men without any of them being wounded. The remainder of our men fled, and our opponents, laughing, left them and with cries went their way to those forests by the path on which they all lived. Our men returned to follow that path about four leagues; in that district they found two uninhabited towns, though they were all well supplied by the maize fields and all their produce. These they ate and carried off as a token of their valor, giving as an excuse of their unfortunate engagement that their opponents were not men but demons, not endowed with reason, but brutes, since fearless of death they had flung themselves barbarously on the muskets.[33]

Chunpich was, like B'uk'te, a dispersed community of at least three hamlets. It is clear that the Sajkab'ch'en company had occupied only one of these and that the larger population had prepared its attack well. Contrary to the perceptions of those who could not grasp the natives' willingness to face gunfire, they had not only defended themselves well but had also mounted an effective, well-orchestrated assault with bows and arrows. Not one of them was captured.[34]

On about August 3 García de Paredes moved his entire army to Chunpich with the second group of friars, but not before convincing Avendaño and his group to stay behind at Tzuktok' to look after the B'uk'te captives. Some of these were by now suffering illnesses that they must have contracted from the Yucatecans. Avendaño soon slipped away, however, accompanied only by four of the Mayas who had come with him from Yucatán. He hoped to find the Kejach Mayas who had attacked the Spaniards at Chunpich in order "to bring them to the pale of our holy mother Church." But search as he might, he encountered no one.[35]

He must have met someone during his explorations, however, because he received a vague report about an "obscure path" beyond Chunpich that led to the "nation of the Itzás, for whom and on behalf of whom I have been preparing for years by having studied their language." He found the path to Itza territory, followed it for a while, and met four Sajkab'ch'en musketeers who were returning "exhausted" to rest in the Chunpich house now occupied by their captain. These men handed him a letter addressed to him by Captain Fernández de Estenos, reporting that farther south the troops had found more abandoned towns with only rotten corn left behind.[36] At this point Avendaño decided to turn back to Chunpich to contemplate his next step, without further exploring the road to the Itzas.

AVENDAÑO'S RETREAT

Avendaño thereupon returned to Tzuktok', where he convinced his companions that they should give up the mission entirely and return to Mérida. His list of complaints was growing: Their Maya charges at Tzuktok' were running away daily. Supplies were short. The rains were increasing in intensity. The captains paid no attention to the friars. García de Paredes approached the uncontacted Kejach towns with so little caution that the inhabitants abandoned their homes, taking their goods with them. As a result, the captain, frustrated in his "greed" for booty, sent orders to the Spanish corporal in charge of the small military guard at Tzuktok' that, according to Avendaño, "all of the Indian women and their children who were at the said town of Tzuctok be provided with food supplies so that an Indian from the town of Sahcabchen, alcalde ordinario of the said town and war captain, might take them away to the encomienda of the said Captain Alonso García de Paredes, without letting me know anything."[37]

This action was, as Avendaño realized, old-style reduction for the sole purpose of personal enrichment. García possessed only a small encomienda, and it was now evident that yet another reason for his participation in the camino real project was to continue enlarging his tribute-paying population and his labor supply. The latter would have been the more important, because his much more profitable timber and logwood operations were clearly shorthanded, especially around Río Mamantel, the site of his encomienda.[38]

Avendaño claimed that while they were waiting to decide what to do next at Tzuktok', he and his friar colleagues arrived at a scheme to retrace their steps to Jop'elch'en, north of Kawich, "and from there take the road that I knew along a different route in order to travel without the clatter of arms to the nation of the pagan Itzas, going through the Indian nation of Tipu, which is the opposite route to that which the Spaniards were taking."[39]

Avendaño and his Spanish and Maya companions departed Tzuktok', notifying García of their intentions. When they reached Jop'elch'en they rested for a few days, waiting for an answer from Provincial Silva to a request for authorization for Avendaño to lead an entrada to Nojpeten through Tipuj. The provincial quickly replied that they were to return to Mérida without delay by the way they had gone. They did so, arriving in the capital on September 17.[40]

García, according to Avendaño, was so worried that the friars would report to the governor about his behavior that he revoked the order that the B'uk'te women and children be sent to his own encomienda, which Avendaño mistakenly thought was Sajkab'ch'en.[41] Instead, they were to be returned "to their towns from which they were captured." García blamed Avendaño's failure to do his duty for the loss of their souls and their return to the forests. None of this correspondence, nor that which would confirm or deny Avendaño's claim that Ursúa was angry with both him and his captains, has yet surfaced. Nor did any of it matter in the long run, because Avendaño was already formulating new plans while García and his men went on terrorizing the Kejach people on the road beyond Tzuktok'.[42]

The second party of Franciscans remained behind on the camino real after Avendaño returned to Mérida. While Avendaño was trying to convince Ursúa to grant him the sole responsibility of taking the gospel to the Itzas, San Buenaventura and his companions followed the troops and road openers as far south as Chuntuki, less than forty leagues from Lago Petén Itzá. Convinced from reports of Itza beliefs in an imminent millennium that would lead to their welcoming the Spaniards, these Franciscans, with the blessing of their provincial, nearly beat Avendaño in the race to Nojpeten. In the meantime, however, dramatic events were taking place at Nojpeten and Tipuj that would radically alter the strategy Ursúa ultimately pursued.

156   *The Hour of the Millennium*

Avendaño's hostility to the military's practices had soured his relationship with García de Paredes, who complained to Ursúa that the commissary had abandoned his duties.[43] Convinced that the Franciscans, preferably under his own leadership, must reach Nojpeten before the troops in order to avert violence, Avendaño unsuccessfully petitioned Silva, the provincial, that he be allowed take an alternative route to the Itzas. Although Silva would have been delighted to upstage the secular clergy by accepting this proposal and sending Avendaño to Nojpeten via Tipuj, we shall see from events described in chapter 7 that the secular clergy had already sealed off that route from the Franciscans.

Fray Andrés's only choice was to return to Kejach territory on the camino real, and this time he succeeded in reaching Nojpeten (see chapter 8). Fray Juan de San Buenaventura's group, however, attempted to reach Nojpeten before Avendaño. Millennial thoughts deeply reinforced their enthusiasm for the undertaking.

The second group of Franciscans, led by San Buenaventura, had left Chunpich on August 10 and followed the now-opened road to the abandoned town of IxB'am. On the eighteenth they followed the road openers, who had already moved a considerable distance along what was believed to be the path to the main lake, to the Kejach town of B'atkab'. There a company of thirty musketeers fired at six Kejaches who ran away. They later captured fifteen persons: four women and four children and later a man with six small children. The Franciscans, put in charge of converting them, decided that the patron of B'atkab' would be "the sweetest name of Jesus."[44]

Held up by rain, they waited at B'atkab' for twelve days. On the thirtieth they walked another six leagues to Chuntuki, "another abandoned place with many hamlets." On the way they crossed a river called Uk'um (meaning simply "river"), where fifty-five adults and children "sallied forth." These were taken to Chuntuki and "Christianized." Jesús María wrote that the captives wanted to live in B'atkab' but that "we are keeping them in our company until, with the Lord's blessing, the flooding allows us to go on to the Itzas."[45] While Avendaño was plotting his return to Nojpeten at Tzuktok', San Buenaventura's friars were already waiting to traverse the remaining forty or so leagues to the main lake.

The army and road openers, accompanied by Jesús María, had already pushed the road another seventeen leagues toward the south with the intention of reaching the lake, but they had been forced by the rains to return to Chuntuki, where they waited for dry weather. At the terminus of the road they had discovered "highlands that are presumed to be those that divide this province from that of Guatemala."[46] The land and vegetation beyond these high hills appeared to different, "and it is said that the said hills have as valleys the great savannah of the Chacan Itzas."[47]

Captain Manuel Jorge Sesere, the engineer, reported in late November that the road by that time had reached as far as Chuntuki, which he placed at a latitude of 19° 32' N, almost the precise position of Chuntuki on modern maps. This, he wrote, was the last town of the Kejaches and that the "great Itza" lay five days beyond. The president of Guatemala would now be able "to come in search of this nation by turning east and following the road that I shall now cut. I also state that we have seen the hills of Guatemala, which are very high and flat on top like a meadow."[48] Along the route between Tzuktok' and the end of the new road they had passed by more than twelve abandoned Kejach settlements. Only about fifteen men, women, and children had been "found," and these were sent back to Tzuktok'.[49]

Following Avendaño's return to Mérida, Provincial Silva wrote to San Buenaventura at Chuntuki with important news. He had replaced Avendaño's mission with two new Franciscans, Fray Diego de Echevarría and Fray Diego de Salas. One of them was to work at Tzuktok' and the other was to go to Chuntuki to instruct the Kejaches there. Upon their arrival the four Franciscans already at Chuntuki were to follow the path that supposedly led from Chuntuki to the main lake. García had denied them permission in September to take this path, but by late October, when they received Silva's instructions, his objections to the plan had apparently evaporated. At this point, the friars replied, only the rains were keeping them from going. Fray Joseph de Jesús María was busy learning the language of the Kejach Mayas at Chuntuki in preparation for the mission to Nojpeten, while swatting the mosquitoes that devoured them daily.[50]

San Buenaventura had obviously not packed his bags for this trip with a visit to the Itzas in mind, for he found himself without appropriate religious paraphernalia. Since the two new missionaries were to come soon, he wrote to Silva requesting the items he would need. His list was impressive: communion tables, chalices, chrismatories (vessels for holy oils), surplices, images of saints and the pope, and bells.[51]

Silva's instructions that they were to visit the Itzas as soon as possible raised great excitement among the missionaries. San Buenaventura replied to his letter on October 24 in words of millennial, prophetic proportions:

> There is no doubt that very soon it will be necessary, God willing—being essential, not trifling—to believe that the hour of the Lord has already arrived, that the time [has arrived] when the evangelical light might shine upon the darkness of these blind pagans, seeing that this nation of Cehaches, being so warlike (since it has carried

out so many attacks on the Catholic towns of the borders of the province . . .) is now so docile and tractable that they themselves come forth to look for us, and they promise to look for and call to the rest who wander nomadically in the forests. They also say that for the past six months the Itzas who came to look for iron tools among these Cehaches told them not to run away from the Spaniards when they came, because they knew that the time to establish friendship with them had arrived and that the said Itzas were awaiting the Spaniards' arrival in their lands in order to establish trade and friendship with them.[52]

This passage, filled with allusions to prophecy, is perhaps the first recorded Franciscan pronouncement that the Itzas were agreed among themselves that "the time had arrived" when they should deal peacefully with the Spaniards.

Theirs was not, however, a message of submission or, as the Franciscans seem to have concluded, a request for Christian instruction. All that the Itzas professed was a desire for friendship and trade. These claims nonetheless ring with a certain plausibility because, as we will see in the next chapter, at almost the same time, unbeknownst to the friars, Ajaw Kan Ek' reportedly was issuing even stronger prophetic pronouncements to an emissary from Tipuj. The new k'atun, in Avendaño's vision of history, was about to emerge, and the Franciscans were convinced that its meaning was the voluntary Christianization of the Itzas as well as the Kejaches. The convergence of news of Itza millennial thought with their foreknowledge of Avendaño's views must have had a powerful effect on the friars.

On October 24, sixty-two Kejach men appeared at Chuntuki, apparently voluntarily. They lived fourteen leagues away and said that their settlement, called Pak'ek'em, comprised more than three hundred people besides themselves. San Buenaventura sent the lay brother Lucas de San Francisco with three recently baptized Kejach men to convince the rest of the group to join the small mission at Chuntuki. When he arrived at their town, Brother Lucas, "heated with the zeal of God's honor, abominated their idolatry to them and broke the idols that he found." Despite his rash behavior, they did not attack him but rather repeated the by now familiar statement that the Itzas had advised them that the time had come and they should not run away.

The friars, however, soon abandoned the idea of bringing these people to Chuntuki. San Buenaventura was worried about the arrival of additional refugees because "here they only have some milpas with only maize. They have no beans, or chile, or fowls, because they sustain themselves only on what they hunt."[53] Instead, the friars decided to instruct these new Kejach subjects in their own territory. To reach Pak'ek'em took a full day's walk on a path from B'atkab', six leagues north of Chuntuki. The lay friars Tomás de Alcoser and Brother Lucas returned to Pak'ek'em in early November, finding the inhabitants "so pleased and eager about our arrival that they had already built a special guest house for us. Immediately the cacique and three other people came to see us, among them he who was their sacrilegious minister and priest of their idols, whom we have discovered to be very affable and benevolent — all reasons for which we offer praise and blessings to the great God of mercies for his having transformed these bloodthirsty people into benevolent lambs."[54]

Alcoser and Lucas stayed on at Pak'ek'em to begin constructing a church. The population of the town made it the largest Kejach mission settlement — about 350 people — and the only one not composed of refugees. San Buenaventura was especially proud that there were no soldiers there. The other Franciscans had managed to do what Avendaño had failed to accomplish: to establish their presence in a town at some distance from the road, free of military intervention. As we will see, over the next few months and years the people of Pak'ek'em would pay dearly for their willingness to receive the missionaries.

While waiting for better weather the friars also planned to build a church at B'atkab' "for the seventy first ones and to cultivate them like new plants with the waters of the word so that they may be rooted in the faith." Although unwilling to speak out in direct criticism of García de Paredes, they complained to Silva that the mission inhabitants were terrified by the noise of the arms and artillery. This, combined with heavy daily traffic along the road, sometimes made them wonder whether "the health of these souls" was being well served. "But the principle," wrote San Buenaventura, "is what moves us; that is, confidence in divine power."[55]

The two new friars arrived in mid-November, freeing San Buenaventura and his companions to consider once more preparations for their trip to Itza territory. Two new churches had been completed, one at B'atkab' and one at Pak'ek'em, also known as the "town of the Chans." Thirty-five more Kejaches had come out of the forests and were added to the seventy others already at B'atkab', where Fray Diego de Echevarría was now working. Fray Diego de Salas was at Tzuktok'. Once the Pak'ek'em church was finished, San Buenaventura planned to send Fray Tomás de

Alcoser, presumably along with Brother Lucas, "as ambassador to the Itzas in order to learn whether they are pleased by our going, and with that answer [we would] leave for there." If this were accomplished they would send news of the event to the secular priests in Tipuj, who would in turn send messengers to Chanchanja.[56] From Chanchanja the road went to Jop'elch'en, which was connected directly by road to Mérida, where Silva would at last receive the news. This route was at least double the distance from Mérida as that of the new camino real.

Rather than assume that these friars did not know their geography, we can conclude that they had very specific reasons for proposing this round-about route for sending news of their hoped-for success. Although Silva's letters to the friars have not been located, their replies to him indicate that they had received no news of the provincial's ruling that Avendaño could not make a second attempt to reach Nojpeten via the alternative route through Jop'elch'en, Chanchanja, and Tipuj. These friars were aware of Avendaño's plans before he left Tzuktok' and would have believed that he would receive their message as he passed along this route—if, in fact, he had not already arrived at Nojpeten. Passing such a message through Tipuj would have had the added attraction of informing any secular priests who might be there that Itza territory was now firmly in Franciscan hands. Their hope was the same as Avendaño's: that nearly all of the southern pagan region, excluding only Tipuj and the areas under Domini-can control to the south of the main lake, would be part of a Franciscan monopoly.

Although the friars at B'atkab' may have received most of the religious items they had requested for their trip to Nojpeten, they still needed bells—heavy objects that would have required a team of pack animals. In his letter of November 20 San Buenaventura begged Silva again for bells, in metaphorical prose: "It already appears to me that in the pious ears of your very reverend paternity resound the voices, although mute, of the three aforementioned churches of Tzuctok, Batcab, and Pakekem, which is that of the Chans, crying for bells in order to bring together their chil-dren and the faithful at the attendance of the divine worship and service, so that *in cimbalis bene sonantibus*. Although material, the echoes of the inspired sound would be wafted across these wastelands."[57] There is no record of the outcome of Alcoser's planned trip as the Franciscans' ad-vance emissary to Nojpeten, or of San Buenaventura's intentions to follow him there. By mid-December Provincial Silva had yet to hear further news from the friars stationed at B'atkab', but he assumed that Alcoser had carried out his mission and that the work of conversion at Nojpeten had already begun.[58]

Avendaño himself departed again for Nojpeten on December 13, but his reports of that trip avoid any mention of San Buenaventura's mission at B'atkab' or of Alcoser's efforts to reach Nojpeten. There is no reason to believe that they ever fulfilled these plans as originally described. As I recount in chapter 9, however, the Itzas captured San Buenaventura and Alcoser on the shores of Lago Petén Itzá on February 2, 1696, during a heated battle between the Itzas and Spanish troops whom the friars had accompanied. Taken by their captors to Nojpeten, they were later killed. That tragic event came only a few days after Avendaño had been forced to escape Nojpeten under cover of darkness, accompanied by Ajaw Kan Ek' and members of his family.

Military Reinforcements on the Camino Real

Pressures on Ursúa for a rapid closure to the Itza question were growing at the end of 1695. As early as October Ajaw Kan Ek' had reportedly declared his willingness to accept Spanish rule and Christianity, and the stage was being set for AjChan's arrival in Mérida. Ursúa knew by November that President Barrios would be sending another entrada to the Itzas at the earliest possible moment, following up on Díaz de Velasco's embarrassing retreat from the main lake in April.[59] The troops and missionaries on the southern camino real were ready to make their move on Nojpeten. To all appearances, the entire enterprise was about to reach its climax.

When he departed the camino real for Campeche in November, García de Paredes had left eighty-six men garrisoned at Tzuktok' and an unspecified number at Chuntuki. His officers later claimed, with some exaggeration, that the friars had been left in charge of between four hundred and six hundred Kejaches at B'atkab' and Tzuktok'.[60]

In December Ursúa approved the recruitment of yet another 150 non-Maya troops, an additional 100 Maya troops, and an additional contingent of Maya road workers and muleteers.[61] Five more Franciscans would be appointed to accompany them.[62] Fifty of the new Spanish and pardo troops, from Mérida, were commanded by Captain Mateo Hidalgo, and the other one hundred, most of them recruited in Campeche, were under Captain Bartolomé de la Garma.[63] On December 8, the one hundred Maya troops and the fifty non-Mayas under Hidalgo left Campeche with García de Paredes and Manuel Jorge Sesere, the road engineer, their ultimate destination the headwaters of Río San Pedro south of Chuntuki, which Avendaño had called Nojuk'um and which the original troops had reached in October. Garma's troops were not recruited until February 1696 and did not leave until sometime in March.[64]

Disputes Between the Secular Clergy and the Franciscans

During December and January the secular clergy and the Franciscans engaged in a dispute about jurisdiction over the camino real and the Itzas. This dispute, exacerbated by Bishop Cano's recent death, began with claims filed on December 4 by the secular clergy.[65] It continued for months, growing ever more petty and particularistic. Ursúa found himself in trouble for having played the two religious groups off each other, promising each that it had the authority to introduce Christianity to the Itzas — the Franciscans along the camino real and the secular clergy through Tipuj. The ecclesiastical council — the principal authorities of the Yucatecan secular clergy — claimed that it alone could authorize any missionary activity. Its members cited, in particular, legal bases for the prohibition of the religious orders and the secular clergy to be in the same place at the same time. The only solution, they argued on December 16, was for Ursúa to withdraw the Franciscans from any activity on the camino real immediately.[66]

The ire of the secular clergy was directed in particular at Avendaño, who had departed on his second trip to the southern forests on December 13, just as the clerics in Mérida were anticipating the arrival of AjChan, the emissary and nephew of Ajaw Kan Ek'. The clerics were already certain that AjChan would declare that Ajaw Kan Ek' wished to surrender to Spanish control, and they were negotiating, in ways not revealed, for Ajaw Kan Ek' to request parish priests rather than Franciscan friars. Whether or not Ajaw Kan Ek' understood the significance of these disputes over Yucatecan religious jurisdiction, the ecclesiastical council was incensed that Ursúa had allowed Avendaño to depart for Nojpeten just as it was about to defeat Franciscan claims over any future Itza missions.

163

Silva, the Franciscan provincial, responded to the council's complaint on December 17, noting that Avendaño had been appointed by Ursúa himself. Reciting a long litany of earlier precedent-setting Franciscan activities on the southern frontier, including Itza territory, he argued that the Franciscans should control this area and that in any event it was simply too late to call Avendaño back.[67]

In the following two chapters we will see what transpired on two principal stages, oppositional yet intertwined, where the drama of the personal submission of Ajaw Kan Ek' to Spanish rule unfolded.

Part Three **THE PEACE SEEKERS**

AjChan was an important young Itza noble, the son of IxKante, a deceased sister of Ajaw Kan Ek', who said she came from Chich'en Itza in northern Yucatán.[1] In 1696 AjChan's father, known only as Chan, was married to another sister of Ajaw Kan Ek'.[2] In late 1696 or early 1697 the elder Chan, who was from Tipuj, died from a snakebite. AjChan, who was about thirty in 1697, said that he was born on the island of Nojpeten; his home, however, was at Yalain, the eastern provincial capital on Laguna Macanché. His marriage to a woman named Kowoj signified a classic alliance between competing noble families around Lago Petén Itzá.[3]

AjChan's social position enabled him to bridge some of the contentious political factions that plagued these regions on the eve of the conquest. He was both a close maternal relative of Ajaw Kan Ek' and a representative, through paternal ties, of the semi-Christian, Itza-colonized town of Tipuj. His residence at Yalain reinforced Itza control over a region secured years earlier by his father. Although his marriage several years before must have accompanied attempts to smooth over old Itza-Kowoj enmities, it had failed to prevent recent warfare that by 1695 threatened to tear apart the royal Kan family. By that year Ajaw B'atab' K'in Kante had declared war against the Itza ruler in an alliance with the Kowojs, now claiming control even over the Yalain region.

AjChan was not eligible to inherit the rulership from his mother's brother because he was a Chan, not an Ek'. Even so, when Ajaw Kan Ek' appointed AjChan in 1695 as his ambassador to take a message of peace and submission to the Spaniards in Mérida, the ruler drove the wedge between the warring factions even deeper. AjChan's diplomatic actions were clearly intended to maintain Ajaw Kan Ek' as the legitimate Itza supreme ruler — even if that meant colonial submission of the Itzas to the Spaniards. The ruler's uncle and the Kowojs, on the other hand, opposed

167

diplomatic negotiation with the Spanish enemy and must have viewed both the ruler and his nephew as traitors. Colonial officials, unaware that AjChan's diplomatic actions had intensified what already amounted to a state of war in central Petén, understandably failed to grasp that his representations in Mérida had no practical meaning.

AjChan offered his uncle's kingdom to the Spaniards. He received baptism in Mérida on December 31, 1695, and was given the name Martín Francisco in honor of his godfather, Martín de Ursúa y Arizmendi, and his patron, Francisco de Hariza, the alcalde of Salamanca de Bacalar, who sponsored his trip to the Yucatecan capital. From then on the Spaniards called him Martín Chan.[4]

Governor Ursúa and his political allies publicized AjChan's visit to Mérida at Christmastime in 1695 as a turning point in Yucatán's history. AjChan, they claimed, delivered official promises from his uncle, the Itza king, that at last the Itzas had submitted to the Spanish Crown and accepted Christianity as the one true religion. AjChan, previously unknown in Spanish circles, became an overnight hero and the subject of widespread admiration, gossip, and speculation. For a time the governor's principal preoccupation would be the political significance of AjChan's message of the Itzas' peaceful surrender. Ursúa was, at least for the moment, convinced that he was within sight of winning the great prize — tens of thousands of Itza souls and tribute payers who passively awaited the arrival of occupation forces. As we will see in later chapters, such hopes for a peaceful settlement would soon be dashed.

AjChan's first encounter with Spanish politics is a complex tale filled with intrigue, misrepresentation, and subsequent charges by Ursúa's enemies that AjChan was a "false ambassador" of the Itza "king." Because AjChan's personal legitimacy and goodwill were unquestioned by Ursúa — despite AjChan's later temporary abandonment of his new patrons — the governor touted throughout the empire his attainment of this Itza noble's sincere loyalty as one of his major political accomplishments. Ursúa and AjChan were to become uneasy friends and allies in an unlikely drama that ended in tragic events which neither could have predicted.

168   *The First Itza Delegation to Mérida*

On July 7, 1695, the alcalde of Bacalar-at-Chunjujub', Captain Francisco Hariza y Arruyo, wrote to Ursúa from the village of Saksuus, downstream from Tipuj on the upper Belize River. He was at last making progress in recontacting backsliding Mayas in this remote area, in particular Mopans named Musul:

> At the moment that I write this the water of holy baptism has been cast upon more than one hundred persons large and small, and I am actually having prayers taught to seven Indian leaders — each one of them over seventy years old, from a nation called Muzul, who have had no knowledge of Christianity — in order to cast upon them the water of holy baptism. I hope in God and the holiest Virgin of the Rosary that before long your lordship will have to sign the elections of the Indians of Tah Itza island, because I have sent an Indian ambassador with a letter and other explanations.[5]

Hariza had also appointed Tipuj's town council and planned to send its members to Mérida at the beginning of the year for the traditional annual confirmation of their "elections."

This was exciting news indeed. Hariza claimed that he had solidified Tipuj's loyalty to the Crown, that the Musuls were being converted, and that a Tipujan representative of his own choosing was on the verge of convincing Ajaw Kan Ek' that he should join the Spaniards.

Hariza's ambassador to Nojpeten was Mateo Wikab', a Tipujan "Indian of reason," who had gone there in April, carrying gifts and a letter from Hariza.[6] The Bacalar alcalde waited several months for him to return but was so keen to present the first fruits of his success to Ursúa in Mérida that he departed in August with, in Ursúa's words, "seven of the said Indians from Tipuj to render obedience, requesting confirmation of their elections and ministers . . . carrying clothing which they wear and trade with the said Noh Petens."[7] Hariza and his seven "Tipujans" stood before Ursúa in Mérida on September 7 with a gift of Itza clothing, and Ursúa confirmed their "elections." The governor wasted no time in requesting that the dean and ecclesiastical council — who were at the time governing all church matters until a successor to the recently deceased Bishop Cano could be named — appoint "evangelical ministers" whom Ursúa would ultimately send to Tipuj with a military escort of thirty soldiers in early January of the coming year.

The governor's confirmation of the Tipujans' offices was a standard requirement for Maya town councils throughout Yucatán, but the ceremony normally took place near the beginning of January. In his apparent haste to make official the Tipujans' long overdue acceptance of colonial status, Hariza had left Tipuj long before the required confirmation date. Clearly, he intended to accomplish something else by rushing these "Tipu-

169

jans" before Governor Ursúa. Only much later was his possible motive revealed. The names of the Tipujan leaders who visited Mérida in September were not mentioned in official correspondence. From other sources, however, we learn that some of them were not Tipujans at all but part of an advance party of Itzas sent by Ajaw Kan Ek' to explore peace terms with the Yucatecan Spaniards. The leader of this party was AjChan himself, who must have arrived at Tipuj during August with news from Ajaw Kan Ek' that the Itzas were prepared to begin negotiations of surrender with the governor of Yucatán. The publicized version of Hariza's visit to Mérida with "Tipujan" councilmen was simply a cover-up for the much more important advance delegation of Itzas sent by Ajaw Kan Ek'.

In sworn testimony a year later, Fray Andrés de Avendaño stated that upon his return to Mérida on September 16, 1695, after his first trip down the camino real,

> he found in this city four Indians from Tipu, jurisdiction of this province, who had come to request confirmation of their elections of alcaldes, regidors, and other *justicia* officers, to whom he spoke in his cell in the great convent of Señor San Francisco of this city. And on his second trip, having departed the said Itza for a distance of about ten leagues, he arrived at a town called Yalain, where they asked him about the said four Indians. And that having given news of them and their said names, they told him that they were the ones, two of whom he recalls were named Ah Chan and the other Ah Tek; and that the wife of this one, with the news that [Avendaño] had seen them, invited him to eat.[8]

In his detailed report of his trip to Nojpeten in January 1696 Avendaño reconfirmed that he had met with AjChan in Mérida the year before. At Yalain, he wrote, "the Yalain leader Chamach Xulu and others told him that four Tipujans had gone to Mérida in September to ask for 'ministers' of the gospel to administer to them the divine word and the holy sacraments."[9] Avendaño identified them precisely to his hosts — as AjChan, his younger brother, said to be named AjChant'an, and two others named AjTek and AjK'u — and told them that he had talked with them and had fed them in his monastery cell in Mérida. They had still not returned to Yalain.[10]

Who, then, were these other three men from Yalain who accompanied AjChan on this first trip to Mérida? AjChan's younger brother, AjChant'an, also known as Nikte Chan, was baptized Pedro Miguel Chan in Mérida on their return visit the following December; Spaniards later referred to him as don Pedro Nikte. AjTek also returned on that trip and was baptized Juan Francisco Tek. AjK'u apparently did not return with this group but was replaced by AjChan's sister's husband, who was baptized Manuel Chayax.[11] The remaining three Mayas in Hariza's party were "genuine" Tipujans who actually received their staffs of office. One of these was Andrés K'eb', the principal alcalde of Tipuj, who himself later made an official visit to Ajaw Kan Ek' on Hariza's behalf.[12]

This information enables us to reconstruct something of the September Itza mission to Mérida, recognizing that Hariza intentionally omitted any mention that Itza delegates accompanied the Tipujans. When the four men from Yalain reached Tipuj, they found Hariza there overseeing baptisms in the upper Belize River towns. Upon learning of their intention to travel to Mérida, Hariza quickly concluded that not only the Tipuj-area Mayas but also their allies, the Itzas, were on the verge of total submission to church and Crown. In secrecy he hurried them off to the governor.

THE TIPUJAN EMISSARY TO NOJPETEN

Once in Mérida, where they first met with Ursúa, the four Itzas waited, presumably at the governor's urging, in order to see Avendaño, who returned a week later from his journey along the camino real. During their meeting with the friar they invited him to visit Nojpeten via Tipuj and Yalain, where they told him that new houses would await him and his Franciscan companions. Alcalde Hariza set off shortly for Bacalar-at-Chunjujub' with the Itza delegation, the Tipujans, and a letter written by Ursúa to be delivered to Ajaw Kan Ek' himself. Finding no news awaiting him of the trip by Mateo Wikab' to Nojpeten, he sent another Bacalareño, Pablo Gil de Azamar, to escort AjChan and his six Maya companions back to Tipuj, which they reached on October 28. There Gil found Wikab' ill and with feet too sore to have made the trip to report to Hariza. Wikab' recounted the surprising news that when he had arrived at Nojpeten,

> the said Indians were preparing three or four thousand Indians to make war against some Spaniards, who they say consist of more than one hundred. These entered on horses, and having come into view of the town found thirty Indians, some in their milpas and others around the island, who when they saw [the Spaniards] went up to talk with them, without taking precautions in speaking with them. Then [the Spaniards] made war against them during which thirty Indians died and one was taken prisoner. The said Uicab says that he saw one who had been axed and struck in the middle of the

head with the butt of a musket; he returned to his town [with his wound] full of worms. Because of this the reyezuelo was found to be very upset.[13]

This encounter was the one with the Guatemalans under Captain Juan Díaz de Velasco that had taken place in April, described in chapter 5. The Spanish reports, however, failed to mention such substantial Maya casualties and placed the blame for the violence on the Itzas. The prisoner referred to was clearly AjK'ixaw, who was taken to Santiago de Guatemala to serve as a captive informant against his own people.

At Nojpeten Wikab' defended himself against charges that his visit was connected with this military encounter. Some Itzas refused to believe his innocence, but Ajaw Kan Ek' not only accepted gifts sent by Hariza but also made a stunning offer in poetic language that Ursúa was to quote many times as the first official Itza recognition of Spanish supremacy:

So tell that captain [Hariza] that I shall receive him with pleasure. And I promise to surrender myself at his feet with eighty thousand Indians that I have under my command, subdued and subjected, and that with a thousand affections I shall receive the water of baptism, I and all my vassals. And tell him also that he must not deceive me in order to kill me; that I promise his governor four thousand Indians for the city of Mérida, because I desire much to see his king. Tell him [Hariza] also that when he arrives at that town [an unidentified port town on the lake] he should send for me to call [on him], advising me by whomever, that at his dispatch I shall descend to see him, to know if it is he who grants me peace, because if he comes directly to my town, I shall make war.[14]

Wikab' then read the letter that Hariza had sent to Ajaw Kan Ek', in response to which, according to Gil, the ruler said "that everything was true and that the time of the prophecies had already arrived, and that he wished to see our governor, since he had offered him peace. 'Because the others (he says) wish not to conquer towns but only to kill us. And because of that we proceed to give them wars. But [he said] that to your governor I shall render vassalage, because my descent is from that province.'" Although now lost, it is apparent that Hariza's letter to Ajaw Kan Ek' included a request for an audience with the ruler, a proposal for his peaceful surrender and baptism by a priest who would accompany Hariza, and a statement concerning the significance of pending k'atun prophecies.

We may therefore conclude that shortly after the arrival of Wikab' at

Nojpeten in April, Ajaw Kan Ek' decided to send a delegation to Mérida, appointing AjChan and his Yalain companions as emissaries to meet with Ursúa. When these four arrived at Tipuj in August, they must have explained their purpose to Hariza and informed him of the desire by Ajaw Kan Ek' to explore terms of submission to the Spaniards. Their disguise as auxiliaries to the Tipujan town council simply provided a means to introduce them to Ursúa without causing public notice of their true identity.

After meeting with Wikab' at Tipuj in October, Gil decided to send the new alcalde of Tipuj, Andrés K'eb', as a second emissary to Ajaw Kan Ek'.[15] K'eb', accompanied by AjChan and his three kinsmen from Yalain, carried a machete and earrings as gifts for the Itza ruler and possibly Ursúa's letter to the Itza king as well. This was a difficult time for further negotiations at Nojpeten, because rumors were circulating among the people around Lago Petén Itza that the Guatemalans would return to kill them all, prompting even a group of one hundred Kowojs — rivals of Ajaw Kan Ek' — to journey to Tipuj to talk with Hariza. Wikab' had reported that a large number of towns had been abandoned all the way from Tipuj southward to Mopan and westward to the lake in response to these fears.[16]

Gil never reported the outcome of the October visit to Nojpeten by Andrés K'eb'. Nonetheless, we know that it resulted in the decision by Ajaw Kan Ek' to send his four representatives again to Mérida, where they would make a formal, public offer of peaceful submission. Gil urged Hariza to communicate the message from Ajaw Kan Ek' to Ursúa quickly, before the Guatemalans made further moves against the Itzas. He also offered to leave Tipuj with a group of Nojpeten representatives to Mérida before the end of November, promising that they would confirm the Itza peace offering. The messenger delivered a copy of Gil's letter to Hariza three weeks after it was written, on about November 23. Although delivered rapidly for those days, the letter gave Ursúa scarcely any time to plan for the upcoming events. Gil's letter gave him every hope that AjChan and his compatriots would return, as planned, in December. The governor was not to be disappointed.[17]

AUTHENTICITY IN THE VOICE OF AJAW KAN EK'

Did Pablo Gil's report of the visit of Mateo Wikab' to Ajaw Kan Ek' provide an accurate description of his speech to the Tipujan emissary? Or was Gil's quotation of the Itza ruler's words an artificial construction designed to further the interests of his patron, Francisco de Hariza? Consideration of this question is crucial, because the reporting of this message confirmed Spanish convictions that a peaceful solution to the Itza problem was imminent and that AjChan indeed represented the intention of Ajaw Kan Ek' to submit to the Crown.

A completely satisfactory answer to the question will always elude us. Closer examination of the rhetoric attributed to Ajaw Kan Ek' suggests, however, that the quotation probably approximated his own words closely. Wikab' would have reported to Gil in Maya, of course, but Gil's quotations differ strikingly from the style of his own prose correspondence, indicating his attempt to communicate not only the content of the message but its rhetorical style as well. The use of large multiples of twenty (eighty thousand subjects and four thousand to be offered to Mérida) reflects the vigesimal method of Maya counting.

The identification by Ajaw Kan Ek' of "others" who "wish not to conquer towns but only to kill us" referred to the Guatemalan Spaniards whom the Itzas had encountered in April. To them he recognized no obligation or kinship, because they represented a foreign province. Conquest — his perception of the Guatemalans' goal — was unacceptable to Ajaw Kan Ek', but he was willing to entertain a diplomatic solution to the governance of Nojpeten and the surrounding population. The legitimacy of his obligation to the governor of Yucatán is framed not only on the basis of his Yucatecan descent but also in prophetic terms: "The time of the prophecies had already arrived."

Wikab' was at Nojpeten between April and — at the latest — late October. The assertion that "the time of the prophecies had already arrived" could indicate that *in the view of* Ajaw Kan Ek' the turning of K'atun 8 Ajaw had occurred before Wikab' departed, probably in July or August. Other evidence suggests that others thought K'atun 8 Ajaw had arrived well before the emissary's visit to Nojpeten. As we learned in chapter 6, the Franciscans working in the Kejach area wrote in millennial language to their provincial on October 24, 1695, of Kejach reports from the Itzas over the previous six months that the time for friendship and trade with the Spaniards had arrived. If in fact the Itzas were referring to the turning of K'atun 8 Ajaw, this report would place the event sometime before late April, at about the time of the battles with the Guatemalan Spaniards.

If the Itzas were using the Mayapan calendar, the turning of the k'atun would not have occurred until mid-1697. Considering the growing intensity of local warfare and the threats of invasion, however, all parties must have been eager to resort to millennial exhortations. Whatever the precise date of the turning of K'atun 8 Ajaw, prophetic discourse was being widely disseminated throughout most of 1695. The message from Itza territory was clear: the time was at hand—the process already under way—for peaceful dealings with the Spaniards of Yucatán, but not with those of Guatemala.

The Second Itza Delegation to Mérida

On December 13, 1695, Avendaño set off from Mérida without military escort through Kejach territory, along the new camino real, on yet another journey to Nojpeten. He carried with him letters of patent from Governor Ursúa, an official letter from Ursúa to Ajaw Kan Ek', gifts for the Itza ruler, and zeal to claim Franciscan jurisdiction over the Itza missions. His experiences at Nojpeten, which he reached shortly after AjChan's heroic arrival in Mérida on December 26, will be the subject of the next chapter.

Even before Avendaño left Mérida, Pablo Gil was escorting the Itza representatives once again toward the Yucatecan capital. AjChan and his Itza companions had not tarried long at Nojpeten during November; they had already returned to the old site of Salamanca de Bacalar, on the long road to Chunjujub', on December 7. There the hardy Gil wrote to Hariza, who was awaiting their arrival in Chunjujub', that "there are here four Indians from the island of Noh Peten. One of them is the nephew of the monarch, who brought his uncle's crown in order to turn it over to your mercy and to the lord governor, [as well as] the other gifts that he brings. Your mercy should determine whether they should proceed there so that your mercy may speak with him and take them to Mérida. I am ready, thanks to God, to walk a thousand leagues."[18] In addition to AjChan and three other Itzas, Gil had with him several Mopans ("Muzuls") from the Tipuj area and the two Tipujan alcaldes (one of whom was certainly Andrés K'eb'), who were to serve as interpreters for the Itzas. In addition to the gifts brought by AjChan, Gil forwarded to Hariza the Itza clothing received by Mateo Wikab' on his earlier visit to Nojpeten.

The Itza ambassadors, along with Ajaw Kan Ek' and his advisers back at Nojpeten, were being required to evaluate conflicting signals. Who, they had to have asked themselves, were really the legitimate purveyors of Spanish authority? Avendaño and his humble Franciscan companions? The secular clergy? The ruthless officers who were building the new ca- **175** mino real? Or Francisco de Hariza and Pablo Gil from Bacalar? Could they trust any of their Spanish contacts, all of whom claimed to represent the governor of Yucatán? Were AjChan and his companions safe in the hands of the Bacalareños, who had long been enemies of the Itzas? Would they be well treated in Mérida, and would Spanish promises of peace be honored?

Not one of these questions had a simple, unequivocal answer, but once begun, AjChan's departure for Mérida was irreversible. On December 12 Ursúa received in Mérida the welcome news of the pending arrival of the Itza party. He immediately wrote a brief, ecstatic letter to the viceroy of New Spain: "I have just received a letter from Captain Francisco de Hariza, alcalde ordinario of the villa of Bacalar, with a note from Pablo Gil concerning his arrival from Tipu with four Indians from the great island of the Itzas, and among them a nephew of the petty king of that opulent nation, who comes in the name of his uncle to give obedience, in sign of which he carries his crown. Very singular news and of great pleasure for me as well as this entire city, reflecting that the hour has arrived that His Majesty our lord is served to bring so many souls to the pale of the holy church."[19]

This last sentence may reflect the millennarian thinking and rhetoric of Avendaño, who left Mérida the very next day, December 13, on his final trip to Nojpeten. He carried with him a letter in the Yucatec language written by Ursúa to Ajaw Kan Ek' only five days earlier. In it Ursúa gave the Franciscans major credit for their long-standing efforts to bring the Itzas to Christianity. Avendaño and Ursúa fully agreed that prophetic and millennarian forces were working in favor of the Franciscan spiritual conquest of the Itzas. Avendaño would attempt — although unsuccessfully — to capitalize on these principles in his meetings with Ajaw Kan Ek' and other Maya leaders a month later. Ursúa's loyalty to Avendaño and the Franciscans, however, was insincere.

The secular clergy, in this battle for Itza souls, were themselves to complain in due course about Ursúa's duplicity. Even while he awaited the Itza delegation in Mérida he was planning to appoint ten or eleven secular priests to accompany AjChan back to Tipuj and then, he hoped, on to Nojpeten. This, at least, was his public stance. In fact, he had already approved the Franciscan Avendaño's visit to Nojpeten, issuing his letter for the friar to carry to Ajaw Kan Ek' on December 8 and sending instructions two days later to Alonso García de Paredes, his field commander on the camino real, to allow Avendaño to proceed without military guard to Nojpeten.[20]

Avendaño later vigorously denied having had any knowledge of AjChan's pending arrival in Mérida before he left for Nojpeten; he also claimed that Ajaw Kan Ek' mentioned nothing to him about the emissary's second trip to Mérida. I believe Avendaño indeed knew of AjChan's imminent arrival, and his purpose in rushing off to Nojpeten at the moment when news of the delegation reached Ursúa was to undercut the secular clergy's claims to future Itza missions. The friar knew that the secular clergy would baptize AjChan and his companions in a public ceremony in the Mérida cathedral, an act that would seal secular claims to future Itza conversions. Unless he could reach Ajaw Kan Ek' quickly himself and accept on behalf of Governor Ursúa the ruler's offer of submission to Crown and church, Franciscan hopes of reaping the rewards of future Itza conversions would be lost.[21]

Mérida was a small town, and information spread quickly. The secular clergy had already filed a complaint to Ursúa for his support of the Franciscan missions on the camino real, and on December 16, only three days after Avendaño's departure for Nojpeten, the authorities of the secular clergy issued a formal protest to the Franciscan provincial, Fray Juan Antonio de Silva, demanding that Avendaño and the other Franciscans on the camino real be recalled immediately. Claiming that these appointments should have been approved by them, they were especially incensed by news that Avendaño and his companions were headed directly for Nojpeten. The seculars, after all, had already named missionaries for the Itzas.[22] Silva, however, refused to consider recalling Avendaño or the other missionaries, claiming that to do so would be to fail in his commitment to conversions already begun.[23]

Over the next few weeks each party raced against time in order to secure its plans and interests. Hariza hurried with AjChan and his delegation to Mérida so that their formal statement of capitulation could be recorded before Ursúa had to turn over his acting governorship to the returning Roque de Soberanis y Centeno.[24] The secular clergy hastened their preparation for AjChan's baptism in order to be able to claim their right to oversee further Itza conversions. Avendaño rushed to meet Ajaw Kan Ek' at Nojpeten before the seculars could leave Mérida for Tipuj with AjChan. By December 20 Ursúa was prepared for the official reception of the Itza delegation. It was to be a grand affair, involving as much of the Spanish elite of Mérida as possible. Ursúa hoped that these public rituals would symbolize for the Mayas of Yucatán the end of the free forest frontier and the beginning of full colonial control over the last independent Maya kingdom.[25]

The governor appointed the chief governmental secretary to prepare an official record of the Itza delegation's arrival, the attendant ceremonies, and the emissary's statement. This was to be an event fit for a king, and the record, of course, was intended for Carlos II himself. Meanwhile, the

ecclesiastical council of the cathedral was preparing for the religious ceremonies that would follow the official diplomatic reception. The council,
too, had appointed a secretary — the notary public of the ecclesiastical
tribunal — to prepare a parallel record of events.

DIPLOMATIC RITUALS

Christmas Day, 1695, fell on Sunday. While Francisco de Hariza waited
outside Mérida with AjChan and the rest of the Itza delegation, the secular
clergy celebrated Christmas masses in the city's magnificent cathedral and
offered prayers for the following day's events. The timing of the delegation's arrival could not have been more effectively arranged. On Monday
morning at about ten o'clock Governor Ursúa was notified of the approach of four Itzas, who were nearing the entrance to the city. Ursúa left
his offices immediately with the *escribano mayor* (the principal government clerk), Captain Francisco de Avila, and other officials to meet the
arriving group. By the time the greeting party stepped out of their carriages and dismounted their horses at the Franciscan Convent of La Mejorada on the outskirts of town, the visitors were already waiting.

There, in the convent church's patio, Captain Avila reported,

> preceding the courtesies, his lordship introduced [the Itza ambas-
> sador] into the carriage with him, and with all the said retinue and
> multitude of people who had crowded around to see the arrival of
> the said ambassador he took him to the holy cathedral church of
> this said city, from where, his lordship having made a speech, he
> came to the palace and royal dwellings, where I joined [them]. And
> in the presence of his lordship, the venerable dean and Cabildo Va-
> cant See, many clergy, priests of the Company of Jesus, the city
> council,[26] and other personnel already mentioned, the said ambas-
> sador took in his hands a crown that he carried, made of feathers of
> different colors in the style of a tiara, and he handed it over to his
> lordship, the said ambassador saying to him (according to the inter-
> pretation of Bachiller don Juan Pacheco . . .) these words:[27]
>
> Lord: Representing the person of my uncle the great Ah Canek,
> king and absolute lord of the Itzas, in his name and on his behalf, I
> come to prostrate myself at your feet and offer before them his
> royal crown, so that in the name of your great king, whose person
> you represent, you would receive and admit us into his royal service
> and under his protection, favor, and patronage; and that you would
> grant us fathers-priests who would baptize us, administer, and

teach the law of the true God. This is for what I have come and what my king requests and desires with the common sentiment of all his vassals.[28]

Ursúa then responded to the effect that he received the ambassador's message with gratitude and agreed to the request in the name of the Crown. Following these official exchanges "there entered and prostrated themselves in the presence of the said lord governor and captain general two Indians who came in the company of the said ambassador, from another nation who are called Muzuls, who through the said father-interpreter said to his lordship that they also came in the same submission, for themselves and in name of all the other Indians of their nation, to render obedience to him or as he who represents the person of His Majesty."[29] Ursúa presented a similar response to the presentation by the Musuls, following which "his lordship embraced them and regaled everyone with demonstrations of happiness."

The entire diplomatic ritual described thus far was carefully planned, precisely staged, and apparently well rehearsed. The visitors' entrance into the city was timed to the hour. AjChan's short speech was written for him; the choice of every word and phrase was that of a Spaniard knowledgeable in such matters. AjChan said to Ursúa exactly what Ursúa wanted him to say, using the phrasing that was legally necessary for the representative of a nation submitting itself to Spanish sovereignty. Ursúa had presumably forwarded the text of AjChan's speech directly to Hariza, who rehearsed it with the ambassador as they were traveling from Chunjujub' to Mérida. The speech also reflected the handiwork of the secular clergy, who wished to make certain that the phrase "and that you would grant us fathers-priests who would baptize us, administer, and teach the law of the true God" would be included. These "fathers-priests" (*padres sacerdotes*) were, of course, the secular clergy.

RELIGIOUS RITUALS

After AjChan was taken to the cathedral, mass was celebrated, following which Ursúa delivered a sermon, the message of which has not survived. The principals returned to the governor's residence, where additional greeting ceremonies were staged in honor of AjChan and his three Itza companions. The ecclesiastical notary recorded these ceremonies in eyewitness fashion:

> I see . . . the venerable lord dean and Council Vacant See assisting in the said reception with paternal love and rejoicing, accompanied by

the entire clergy and the pealing of the bells in the principal hall of the houses of the residence of the said lord governor, where also were [in attendance] the order of the Company of Jesus and that of Lord San Juan de Dios.

I saw that the said ambassador having entered, that they recognize [him by] his costume and the crown of different colors that he carried, and his three companions or assistants with the retinue referred to, and a numerous crowd of people; that the said ambassador had been moving through in midst of everyone with actions of polite courtesy and reverent obeisance toward the lords of the venerable cabildo. It appears that with special divine inspiration, upon coming up next to the lord dean, he kneeled down at his feet. His mercy took him in his arms with demonstration of charitable zeal and loving affection, engaging in a lengthy conversation with him in his own language.

And having seated him between the two heads [of the] ecclesiastical and secular cabildos, [the dean] ordered that the secretary of government be called to clear out the concourse of people, leaving the doors closed for about half an hour. When the bell had rung for the midday prayer, they opened the doors and the said gentlemen emerged, leaving the ambassador lodged in the said house.[30]

During all of these ceremonies, which were staged by the secular clergy, the Franciscans were conspicuously absent — except for the brief reception at the Franciscan Convent of La Mejorada. Neither the Jesuits nor the order of San Juan, who were invited to attend, were of much importance in Mérida, and their presence posed no threat to the credit that the ecclesiastical cabildo hoped to earn from its reception of the Itza emissary. The invitation list, however, was clearly intended to symbolize the secular clergy's defeat of the Franciscan effort to engineer the conversion of the Itzas.

AJCHAN'S DECLARATION

On Wednesday, December 29, Ursúa ordered AjChan to make a formal declaration in his presence before the government secretary and through the interpreter general, Nicolás Cardenia. Ursúa, as on other, similar occasions, delivered the questions himself. A satisfactory declaration would pave the way for AjChan's baptism, which would take place the following Friday. The questions were carefully worded. AjChan's answers indicate that he was being manipulated by the governor, who sought clear and unambiguous legal justification for his designs on the Itzas.[31]

Asked, "[W]ho sent him to this province and for what purpose?" AjChan repeated the major points of his speech delivered on Monday, stating that

> he came there under orders of the great Ah Canek, his uncle, king of the provinces of the Itzas, to make a covenant and establish peace between the Spaniards and [the Itzas], and likewise that they might be in communication with one another, ceasing all war, and also to solicit commerce and trade for the things that they needed; and that he should say to the lord governor that he [Ajaw Kan Ek'] sent him his crown and prostrated it at his feet, requesting of him that they drink of the same water and inhabit the same house, because the designated ending of the prophecies of his ancestors had been completed, as a result of which he and the four kings who obeyed him at once rendered the owed vassalage to the King our lord in order that with that they might secure his favor and patronage, and also that they might obtain fathers-priests to be remitted to them who would baptize them and teach the law of the true God.

It is doubtful that AjChan spoke in precisely these words; more likely he replied affirmatively, with minor additional details, to several subsidiary questions. This conclusion is inescapable when the wording of the reply is compared with a crucial section of Ursúa's letter of December 8 to Ajaw Kan Ek', which at this moment was being carried by Avendaño to Nojpetén: "And now also in the name of our great king don Carlos II, I ordered that you be given notice of all these things that I have said. And you, Ah Canek, have responded that if it is for peace and not war, you will surrender with all the Itzas to the obedience and service of our true king don Carlos, because the time has arrived in which your plate and your calabash might be one with the Spaniards, and in which you might be Christians."

In addition to confirming the offer made by Ajaw Kan Ek', as communicated by Mateo Wikab', the answer as stated — as well as Ursúa's letter — carefully noted that the offer of obedience was made with the understanding that war might cease and peace might reign between Spaniards and Itzas. AjChan's answer contained the additional understanding that peace would lead to the opening of trade between Yucatán and the Itza kingdom. This condition — that of peaceful conversion and the fostering of trade — was a primary requirement of the Spanish king's initial 1693 cédula to Ursúa, and the governor was eager to confirm that the Itzas understood and agreed to these terms. No less determined to avoid conflict had been

181

Avendaño himself, who repeatedly insisted that military action not be used against any of the forest Mayas. The metaphor of one plate, one calabash, and one house joining the Itzas and the Spaniards was an example of Franciscan thought, not the rationale of a worldly governor.

On the matter of the request by Ajaw Kan Ek' for missionaries, however, Ursúa orchestrated AjChan's testimony in order to justify his current plan to send secular clergy rather than Franciscans to Nojpeten. AjChan here requested "fathers-priests" — secular clergy — whereas in Ursúa's letter to Ajaw Kan Ek', carried by Avendaño, the governor emphasized that he had sent Ajaw Kan Ek' "fathers- preachers" (*padres predicadores*) — that is, Franciscans. The secular clergy had won Ursúa's support, and the letter carried by Avendaño was already out of date.

Ursúa went on to ask AjChan "what motives his king had for sending him on the embassy; if it was from fear that they [would] take the lands in which they dwell by force of arms, or if it has been voluntary and from the heart?" To this question AjChan referred to his previous answer, adding nothing more. The purpose of the additional question, obviously, was simply to reinforce Ursúa's peaceful intent. Probing further in order to confirm the legitimacy of AjChan's embassy, Ursúa asked him whether "for the embassy that he came to make in the name of his king, [the king] was unifying the wishes of the caciques and principal lords of his provinces." AjChan replied "that he knows, as one who was present, that before he came on the embassy his said king Ah Canek communicated with the reyezuelos called Citkan [Kit Kan], Ahamatan [Ajaw Matan], Ahkin [AjK'in], Ahcitcan [AjKit Kan], and Ahatsi [Ajaw Tzin], who is one of the principal Indians; and these with all the rest of the Indians, and in public, and all joined together agreed to it of their own will; and that one of the said reyezuelos already had his departure prepared with all his clothing solely to request the water of baptism."[32] As we learned in chapter 3, the four reyezuelos indicated by AjChan were the rulers of the four quarters of Nojpeten and of all of Itza territory. AjChan's claim that all four of them agreed in council to his role as emissary is implausible, but it was a necessity both for him and for Ursúa in order to legitimate his ambassadorial mission.

In reply to Ursúa's next question, concerning the number of provinces in the "kingdom," AjChan said that there were ten, "and each one of many towns; and that the largest of the [provinces] is the large island of the Itza, which is on an island in a large lake; and on [the lake's] shores many towns rich with people; that he is [not] able to comprehend the number of Indians that [the lake] has." Ursúa was clearly hoping to confirm the earlier report from Mateo Wikab' that Ajaw Kan Ek' ruled eighty thousand souls, a number of potential converts that staggered the Spanish imagination. AjChan, uninterested in citing population figures, offered little more than the idea of a numerous population, but in doing so he provided evidence of a complex territorial structure. Because of Ursúa's own lack of knowledge, this was one subject for which he found it difficult to manipulate or construct answers. Nor did AjChan's vague response to a follow-up question about neighboring "nations" of Indians provide further insights: "And he said that he had no information about additional nations other than those of the Mopans and Tipu, the Muzuls, and other forest Indians; that he does not know their numbers."

Ursúa next asked whether AjChan had "knowledge of the true God and of the holy Catholic faith." AjChan's reply again raised the issue of prophecy: "And he said that they have known of it for a long time in that region, and that by means of the writing of their prophets they knew that the time had arrived for requesting the said holy faith and Catholic religion, and that only his king and the priests understand the said prophecies."

We see once more the strong influence of Avendaño, both in the construction of Ursúa's question and in AjChan's reply. AjChan emphasized nonetheless that only their prophets — the "king and his priests" — could understand these prophecies. Although Avendaño would have argued that these men were inspired by God to seek Christianity, there is nothing in the testimony that buttresses such an interpretation. The source of knowledge about the meaning of the next stage of history is situated squarely in Itza sacred knowledge.

Turning to secular matters, Ursúa next asked "who gave them the knowledge of these provinces of Yucatán, and whether they have [this knowledge] from others of the dominion of the great king and lord of Spain." This knowledge, AjChan replied, was given to them "by the Indians of Tipu, and because his king reads it in his analtes [hieroglyphic books][33] they have knowledge of these provinces of Yucatán; and they do not have it from any others."

While granting that the Yucatecan Tipujans were a source of practical knowledge about colonial Yucatán, AjChan emphasized that prophetic insight belonged only to the Itza rulership. He then responded with a simple "no" to a follow-up question asking "whether they have or have had trade and contract with any Spaniards or other nation." Ursúa's purpose in asking these questions may have been to establish the legitimacy of Yucatán's claim over the conversion of the Itzas and their inclusion in the political and economic order of that province. The first of the questions was intended to establish the historical kinship of the Itzas with Yucatán and thus to rule out Guatemala's interests in Itza territory. AjChan's answer resolved any doubt about the historical basis for such jurisdiction: the Tipujans and the hieroglyphic books alone were the sources of Itza knowledge of Yucatán. And just as the hieroglyphic books were a source of divine knowledge, so too were they the authentic source of knowledge about the Itzas' historical ties to Yucatán.

AjChan could not have believed, of course, that only the Tipujans and the hieroglyphic books provided the Itzas with knowledge of Spanish Yucatán and the Spanish king. Trade items, including metal tools and silver and gold jewelry, had long been available to the Itzas. Itza history had been deeply affected by Yucatecan affairs since at least the early seventeenth century.

Finally, AjChan was asked "what fruits those provinces produce," to which he replied that "there is much cochineal, vanillas, honey, annato, cotton, and other vegetables; many wild and Castilian fowls; and that they have many canoes in which they come and go in order for the towns of the large island to communicate with those of the shores of the mainland." This last question elicited evidence for the economic value of the Itza undertaking, adding a footnote of no small importance to AjChan's assertion of the divine inevitability and historical precedent for Itza conversion and for their incorporation into the province of Yucatán.

Thus ended AjChan's testimony. The resulting document would satisfy the king and the Council of the Indies in every detail. Ursúa had carefully structured the testimony in order to legitimate AjChan as the true emissary of Ajaw Kan Ek', to provide theological and historical justification for the Itzas' conversion, to establish historical justification for their political incorporation into Yucatán, and, finally, to tantalize his superiors with hints of potential sources of colonial wealth. This document, among others, would be cited many times as a rationale for later military actions, because the Itzas did not subsequently behave as AjChan promised they would. AjChan's testimony became a primary textual source for the political and moral necessity of the violent conquest of the Itzas.

BAPTISMAL RITUALS

184 Over the next several days AjChan and his companions remained in the governor's residence, where they received religious instruction in preparation for their baptism and first communion. Joining them as pupils were two unconverted Kejach Mayas who had been sent separately to Mérida. These two were chosen as the first recipients of baptism on Friday, December 30. Their ceremony was the prelude to the climactic Saturday baptisms of the Itzas.[34] What became of the Musuls who traveled with AjChan is not recorded.

The ecclesiastical notary recorded that on Friday, at the ringing of the first bell, Governor Ursúa and a retinue of important personages arrived with two men from the "province of the Cehaches, newly pacified, from the area where the road has begun to be opened from this province to that of Guatemala." One of these, named K'u,[35] was said to be the cacique and principal leader of the "pacified" Kejaches; he arrived with his staff of office in his hands. His companion was named K'ixaw.[36] The greeting party at the door of the cathedral included the dean, the archdeacon, and the entire secular clergy. They were ready to stage an impressive ritual, dressed in their surplices and accompanied by organ, oboe,[37] and other instruments played by an ensemble of both men and women.

The priests took the guests to the baptismal chapel, where the archdeacon, Nicolás de Salazar, first baptized Cacique K'u, naming him Joseph.[38] Governor Ursúa served as his godfather. K'ixaw was then baptized, receiving the name Bartolomé. His godfather was Captain Joseph Fernández de Estenos, the Campechano who served as second-in-command of the troops who were opening the camino real; Fernández must have escorted these two men to Mérida.

Following the baptism the musicians played while the entire party moved to the altar of the Virgin next to the choir, where an additional ensemble of four black slaves belonging to Ursúa provided recorder music, joined by a group playing bugles and trumpets, accompanied by the beating of turtle shells and drums (*tunkul*s), "instruments which the Indians use." From there they moved to the presbytery, where the archdeacon presided over a mass in which the two newly baptized Kejach Mayas received their first communion. Following the ceremony they were returned to the governor's residence.

Their baptismal certifications described Joseph K'u as the cacique of the Kejach reduction town called Chan Pak'ek'em and Bartolomé K'ixaw as an inhabitant of the same town.[39] The actual census of Pak'ek'em, recorded six months later, listed both men, but neither held a position of authority there.[40] Captain Fernández may simply have grabbed two "willing" individuals to serve as symbolic representatives of the Kejach people. Who in Mérida was to know or care about a minor distortion of political reality?

The next morning an identical ceremony, with the same personnel and musical accompaniment, was carried out for the baptisms of AjChan and

185

his three Itza companions.[41] The ecclesiastical notary now described AjChan in impressive terms as "the ambassador of the great Ah Canek, monarch of the empire of the island of the Itzas in the forests." AjChan was baptized Martín Francisco in honor of his godfather, Martín de Ursúa. His brother, sponsored by Pedro de Garrástegui Oleada, the Count of Miraflores and treasurer of the Santa Cruzada, received the name Pedro Miguel Chan. His sister's husband was baptized Manuel Joseph Chayax in honor of his godfather, Sergeant Major Manuel Bolio, Ursúa's brother-in-law. Finally, AjTek, sponsored by Captain Juan Bernardo de Madrid, received the name Juan Francisco Tek. Garrástegui and Madrid were both major operators in the peninsula's repartimiento business, and Bolio, from a wealthy Mérida family of cattle ranchers, had served as Ursúa's residencia bondsman earlier that year.[42]

With the completion of the nominal Christian conversion of three important Itza personages, no further impediments could delay the conquest of this "infidel" nation. A fundamental principle in Spanish policies of conversion and conquest was that Crown demands for peaceful conversion could be overlooked once a people's leadership had come to recognize the true God. Ajaw Kan Ek', having now accepted Christianity through his sister's son, was no longer the ruler of an independent foreign nation. AjChan's baptism represented the moment at which the Itzas ceased to fall under the protection of Crown policies barring them from military conquest.

So began the final press for a military conclusion, even while the unknowing Avendaño made his way to deliver Governor Ursúa's now pointless letter to Ajaw Kan Ek'. The secular clergy had appropriated all future Itza conversions, and Franciscan claims to them were null and void.

Fray Andrés de Avendaño's well-publicized jour-
ney to Lago Petén Itzá and his encounters there in January 1696 with
Ajaw Kan Ek' and other Maya leaders comprise a crucial episode in this
history. His lengthy, meticulous report of the trip stands as the single most
important documentary source on the Itzas.[1] Yet because it is characterized by both religious and political bias, it must be interpreted with great
caution. Avendaño chose every word in order to address the issues that
concerned him personally; his writing is thus both self-conscious and au-
thoritative in tone.

Sometime in early December the Franciscan provincial, Fray Antonio
de Silva, had summoned Avendaño and announced that he could return
with his own and the governor's blessing to the camino real, forging ahead
to Nojpeten to meet Ajaw Kan Ek'. This was Avendaño's "great opportunity," and he was pleased to be able to make the trip without military
escort. When he departed Mérida on December 13, 1695, he had probably just learned of AjChan's imminent diplomatic mission. I believe he and
Silva realized that he had to leave for Nojpeten as soon as possible in order
to upstage AjChan's role as emissary. If Avendaño were to receive a personal statement of submission from Ajaw Kan Ek' himself, the Franciscan
battle for control over future Itza missions might be won.

That, however, is not how events ultimately transpired. Although the
Franciscan strategy was politically astute, Silva had waited too long to
send Avendaño back for a second try at reaching the Itzas. By the time
Avendaño arrived at Nojpeten on about January 14, the Itzas had already
delivered their public message in Mérida and had been baptized by the
secular clergy, with no Franciscans in attendance. Avendaño's interces-
sions with the Itza leaders were no longer needed or wanted in Mérida.

Although he had little time to prepare for the journey, he did insist upon
receiving a decree from Ursúa requiring Captain García de Paredes to

cooperate with his mission and provide whatever Avendaño asked for, including laborers, food, and horses. He also requested a second decree, again for García's benefit, which consisted almost entirely of a lengthy, detailed royal cédula issued in 1526 by Carlos V demanding that Indians be well treated in conquest situations. Both documents were signed by Ursúa on December 10, 1695, and are reproduced in Avendaño's account.[2]

Ursúa sent a suit of Spanish clothing for Ajaw Kan Ek', complete with a hat and staff of office. The intention was to dress the Itza ruler up as a typical Yucatán Maya alcalde, much as nineteenth-century native North American leaders were presented with European-style clothing as a means of co-optation. Ajaw Kan Ek' eventually accepted and wore this costume, although the people of Chak'an Itza attempted to keep it from Avendaño in order to prevent him from presenting it to the ruler. Other gifts for Ajaw Kan Ek' included a machete and sheath, a knife with a belt, and three yards of embroidered taffeta. In addition, Avendaño carried numerous smaller gifts, such as necklaces and knives, intended as general handouts. He also carried some items of fine Itza clothing that AjChan had brought on his trip to Mérida. These pieces had apparently arrived at Bacalar on December 7 with AjChan, his companions, and their Spanish escort, Pablo Gil de Azamar.[3] Silva later wrote that AjChan had brought along "tokens of the same clothing that Canek wore" and that these had been forwarded to Ursúa prior to AjChan's arrival in Mérida. Ursúa in turn handed them over to Avendaño, who was to take them with him to prove to Ajaw Kan Ek' that he was a genuine ambassador of the governor.[4]

Avendaño carried with him two documents addressed to Ajaw Kan Ek'. One was a letter, now lost, from Silva. The other letter would be of major importance for his upcoming meeting with the Itza leaders. Signed by Ursúa on December 8, before AjChan and his companions had reached Mérida, it was composed in Yucatec Maya and addressed to Ajaw Kan Ek'.[5] Although Avendaño did not mention it in connection with Ursúa's other two "instruments," as he called them, further along in his account he reported that he had tried, with little success, to read it to the assembled Itza leaders. The letter was intended to convince Ajaw Kan Ek' to confirm his message of submission sent via Mateo Wikab' and later forwarded to Ursúa. By delivering it to Nojpeten, Avendaño was therefore placed in a position of diplomatic sensitivity, and it was essential that he receive an official reply from Ajaw Kan Ek' that he could hand to Ursúa upon his return to Mérida. Letters to native leaders were generally intended to be read aloud by the messenger on the assumption that the recipient was illiterate. Both the content and style of this letter mark it as the written work of Avendaño.

Avendaño completed the written account of both his first, uncompleted mission along the camino real and this, his second mission, after he returned to Mérida on April 29, 1696. On May 3 he was called upon to testify under oath about the second mission at his order's Convent of La Mejorada in Mérida. On May 6 and 7 his two companions, Fray José de Jesús María and Fray Diego de Echevarría, added their oral depositions to the record.[6]

To Itza Territory

When Avendaño left Mérida on December 13 as "missionary commissary," he took with him one other priest: Fray Antonio Pérez de San Román, who had accompanied him on his last trip. He also took at least eight of the ten cantores who had also gone on that trip. Only four of these went with him to Nojpeten, and he left four with Fray Antonio at Chuntuki. Near Tzuktok' he stumbled upon Fray Joseph de Jesús María, who was on his way back to Mérida, sick and exhausted from months of excruciating work. Fray José, who had been preparing so assiduously for a trip to Nojpeten that never materialized, volunteered to accompany Avendaño despite his ill health.[7]

Joined also by Fray Diego de Echevarría and Brother Lucas, the party of Franciscans continued along the camino real to B'atkab', where on January 5 they found most of the army along with García de Paredes, Zubiaur Isasi, and the engineer, Sesere. There Avendaño must have presented Ursúa's decrees to García, who allowed them pass on toward the hamlet of Chuntuki without delay. Chuntuki was nothing more than about eight clustered houses and some dwellings scattered among the surrounding milpas.[8] At some point, perhaps at B'atkab', they picked up three Kejach guides who accompanied them on the rest of their journey.[9]

Traveling along the road for a little more than one and a half leagues south from Chuntuki, they found the narrow path heading toward the southeast that was believed to lead to Itza territory. Excited by their discovery, they began to run through the forest, "fearing no shipwreck" and calling out the prayer "*in exitu Israel de Egiptu,* in order to imitate the victory of the Israelites, who succeeded in making their way across the waves of the Red Sea." Following slash marks on the tree trunks, they crossed the river called Nojuk'um (near the headwaters of Río San Pedro) and reached a small lake, or aguada, called Yawilain.[10]

The path past Yawilain wound around low hills and aguadas before reaching a long barranco, or ravine, of difficult passage that extended for another winding one and a half leagues. This barranco, called Noj-jem,[11] was also known as "the hell of the Itzas," and in order to speed their passage they chose as its patron San Antonio of Padua. Here they were clearly beginning to cross the northern section of the karst hills southeast of La Palotada — "a great multitude of very steep ups and downs, entirely limestone hills and very high mountains."[12] At the highest ridge of this massive karst formation they could see "a great expanse of low forest, such that it seemed like another hemisphere, because even from above the trees we could not make out the other side or the altitude that corresponded to where we were, which we presumed without doubt we would find in the other new land and near the Itza nation where we were going."[13] They had reached the same place on the path reported in October by exploratory scouts who had believed they were looking out on Itza territory.[14]

After a precipitous descent from the karst hills they reached in about one and half leagues another aguada called Tanxulukmul, where they discovered some abandoned temple pyramids that astonished them by their size and height.[15] They found houses there that they believed to have been made by the Itzas, and of a type that they had seen frequently along the path. Although Avendaño was eager to destroy an "idol" reputed to be worshipped there, they were unable to find a way up the steep principal pyramid where they believed it to be. Tanxulukmul was also the name of a place "in the heart of the forest" where, according to the Book of Chilam B'alam of Chumayel, the Itzas of Yucatán had sought refuge in a prior K'atun 4 Ajaw and where in a K'atun 8 Ajaw they may have established the "cycle seat" of a new round of thirteen k'atuns. The ruin Avendaño found, still a site of rituals, was probably the same Tanxulukmul.

Standing water from the heavy rains made walking difficult beyond Tanxulukmul. They followed a "river" for some distance before coming upon their first sign of local life, a Chak'an Itza town on the south side. The river had to have been Río Acté, a headwater stream of Río San Pedro. Avendaño identified it as the Saklemakal, also the name of a town in this area and another on the eastern end of Lago Petén Itzá.[16] I suspect that the Chak'an Itza town was at or near the archaeological site of Kantetul.[17] The date of their arrival was January 13, 1695, the day of the Franciscan vesper celebration of the Holy Name of Jesus. They had arrived at the moment of vespers.

At Chak'an Itza and the Port of Nich

The three priests, four Maya cantores, and three Kejach guides — hot and filthy from seven days of hard walking — forded the stream and strolled directly toward the center of town.[18] They were a strange and shocking sight, the Franciscans with their brown robes and the singers wearing their cloaks. A woman and two children who were going to the river for water when they came up the path were so frightened that they ran back to town screaming for help. Several men rushed up carrying bows and arrows. These Chak'an men must have been startled when, according to Avendaño, the priests responded by "embracing them joyfully" and handing them "some things from Castile" — necklaces and "trinkets" for the women and knives for the men.

These peace offerings turned out to be popular items that they were forced to give out in large quantities. Avendaño took an immediate disliking to the people of Chak'an, whom he considered not simply inquisitive but indecently covetous. Demanding to see what else the loaded-down Maya singers carried in their backpacks, they succeeded in convincing Avendaño to open them. Out came the suit of clothes for Ajaw Kan Ek', other gifts for Itza leaders, and items for religious rituals. Avendaño was appalled that they wanted to touch and even carry off everything they had.

The visitors later learned that the woman with the two children was married to the "brother" of a "cacique" named AjKan, who Avendaño understood was a "close relative" of Ajaw Kan Ek'. This cacique, who with other leaders greeted the visitors with undrawn bows and arrows, was probably the provincial ruler of the north, Ajaw B'atab' K'in Kante.

That evening and into the night the Itzas hosted a spectacle that must have left the visitors trembling: "[W]ith such confusion of howls in their songs that even considering that they were savages of those rustic forests and those extravagant joys their custom, our hearts suffered some anxiety and grief, even more so when we took sight of those engraved, striped, and painted faces, done in the life and likeness of the devil."[19] The objects of this entertainment must have been terrified, for the Itzas had a reputation among Yucatecans, whether deserved or not, as practitioners of human sacrifice and cannibalism. The singing and dancing that night could have been, for all they knew, a prelude to their own demise.

Early the next morning the visitors were besieged with requests to see their possessions again, but this time the Chak'an Itzas promptly reached for the goods and supplies and carried most of them off. The priests were left with only their ritual items, the suit of European clothing, and a few trinkets. Avendaño bemoaned the fact that the cantores now had almost nothing to carry on their backs.[20]

It is impossible to reconstruct the "reality" of such a scene. We can imagine that the Chak'an Itzas did in fact help themselves to the goods — and that they did so, as Avendaño put it with rare sarcasm, "with great demonstrations of love." That is, they were friendly and verbally grateful as they took what they could. Their rationale for behaving in this way, however, might have been quite different from what Avendaño perceived. These people, living along the northern route to Yucatán, were experienced traders who had negotiated for beads and knives before, and they knew that possessing them would give them a commercial advantage in the region. Of equal interest to them, perhaps, was ensuring that Ajaw Kan Ek' and his allies not receive the more valuable gifts intended for them. As the days progressed it became apparent that the Chak'an Itza leaders and their Kowoj allies were doing all that they could to sabotage a growing relationship between Avendaño and the Nojpeten ruler.

The next morning the Franciscan party departed for the lakeshore, joined by a crowd dubiously described as "all of the Indian men from around Chak'an Itza with their wives and children, shouting joyfully in order to excite the others to join us."[21] All of this area was Chak'an Itza territory, the Itza northern province said to be at war with the principal Itza ruler. With this group of curiosity seekers they walked for four or five leagues across hilly, heavily forested terrain and some low, wet areas before coming out "at the wharf of the lake where one enters the said Peten Itza, on the shore of which is found a small town called Nich, which comprises about ten houses."

At Nich, or Nixtun, they had reached the very spot where about a year later Ursúa and his men would assemble the galeota that would carry the attack troops across the lake to Nojpeten. This was the principal port at the western end of the lake, also known from other sources as Ch'ich'. Because traders who plied their wares to and from the north came and went through this port, it was a place of major strategic importance. At this time the principal leader at Nich was the secondary ruler of Chak'an Itza, the trader and war captain B'atab' Tut. Nich, as well as Chak'an Itza, may be seen clearly on the map that Avendaño later drew to accompany his 1696 *Relación* (map 9).

Avendaño recalled being surprised by seeing an old man at Nich — older than any men he had yet seen among the Kejaches and would ever see again among the Itzas. Such a seemingly insignificant observation inserted at this point gave him the opportunity to cast aspersions upon the Itzas

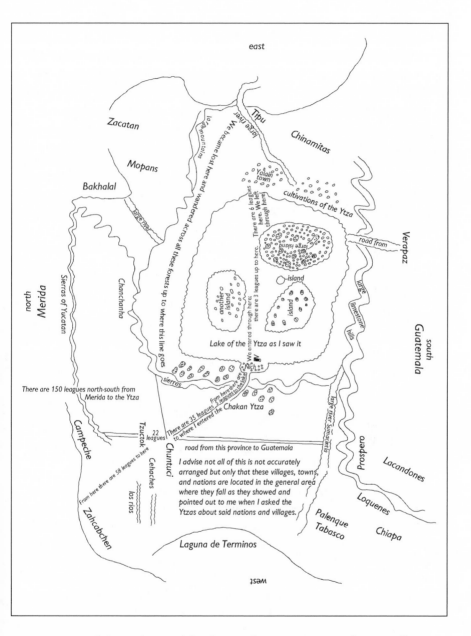

east

Zacatan

Tipu

Chinamitas

Mopans

We became lost here and wandered across all these forests up to where this line goes

large river

Bakhalal

to mountain

large river

Yalain town

cultivations of the Ytza

There are 6 leagues here. We left through here

Verapaz

road from

Sierras of Yucatan

Merida

north

Chanchanha

large island

island

large island

another island

there are 3 leagues up to here.

island

large limestone hills

We entered through here; there are 3 leagues up to here.

south
Guatemala

Lake of the Ytza as I saw it

Nich

sierras

There are 150 leagues north-south from Merida to the Ytza

from here there are 8 leagues to the lake

There are 35 leagues to where I entered the Chakan Ytza

22 leagues

There are 35 leagues to where I entered the Chakan Ytza

Campeche

Tzuctok

From here there are 58 leagues to here

Cehaches

los rios

Chuntuci

road from this province to Guatemala

I advise not all of this is not accurately arranged but only that these villages, towns, and nations are located in the general area where they fall as they showed and pointed out to me when I asked the Ytzas about said nations and villages.

large river Sumacinta

Prospero

Lacandones

Loquenes

Palenque
Tabasco

Chiapa

Zahcabchen

Laguna de Terminos

west

Map 9. English translation of sketch map of Lago Petén Itzá and surrounding regions drawn by Fray Andrés de Avendaño y Loyola, 1696.

whom he was about to describe: "[T]hey have the custom of decapitating them after they pass fifty years so that they will not learn how to be witches and kill them — except for the priests of their idols, whom they hold in great respect. This one must, without doubt, have been one."[22] One can imagine his having heard such things from his Kejach guides, who would have delighted in frightening the friars with tales of Itza cruelty.

At Nojpeten

The visitors spent only two hours at Nich, where they awaited a reply to a message sent to Ajaw Kan Ek' announcing their arrival.[23] From their arrival at noon until about two o'clock in the afternoon they were fed and entertained with musical instruments. Then the royal greeting party arrived:

> At least eighty canoes came, filled with Indian envoys dressed for war, with huge quivers of arrows (although all of them were thrown into the canoes [when they disembarked]), all of them escorting and accompanying the king, who with about five hundred Indians, stepped out to receive us. They put us on board with great impetuosity, paying no attention to the music of the *chirimías* [reed wind instruments] with which we greeted him, or the [message of] peace which, as its ambassador in the name of the King our lord (whom God may protect), I was taking to him. With most discourteous actions [going on] we were unable to execute it, because before they gave us a chance they suddenly began to embark, taking us across the lake.[24]

Expecting an official greeting, Avendaño had prepared a speech of his own, but Ajaw Kan Ek' remained in his canoe, paying no attention to the visitors. Instead, ignoring a fanfare of trumpet music and Avendaño's attempts to read his message, the Itzas led them directly on board and headed for Nojpeten. As they paddled off, the travelers lost sight of their remaining baggage, which remained on shore with their Chak'an hosts.

Avendaño did manage to present Ajaw Kan Ek' the machete and sheath and to give some "trinkets from Spain" to a nephew of the ruler's who stood by his uncle's side.[25] Unsatisfied with Avendaño's insignificant gift, the nephew twice asked him to give him the crucifix that he wore around his neck. When the friar refused, he grabbed the ruler's hand, pulled the new machete out of its sheath, and cut the string from which the crucifix hung, taking the object for himself. In reply to Avendaño's reprimand for

194

such an impolite act, the nephew, he wrote, responded, "[S]ince you have not wanted to give it to me, what do I have to do?" Ajaw Kan Ek', he recalled, rather than chastise his nephew, simply laughed, "and he began to chatter with me — things very inappropriate to that first meeting — with more vanity and pride than a Lucifer."[26]

Avendaño was put into the canoe with Ajaw Kan Ek'. As they plied the three leagues' distance across the lake to Nojpeten, he recalled, "a temptation occurred to the king, as if it had been inspired by the devil, and natural to his inhuman and cruel heart, to strike fear in me so that my own [heart] might suffer some affliction or upset."[27] Ajaw Kan Ek' could have done little to increase the already terrified Avendaño's heartbeat, and what he chose to do seems to have been little more than teasing or perhaps even a genuine expression of concern. He placed his hand over Avendaño's chest to feel his heart, asking the friar if he felt anxious. Avendaño, by his own account, then launched into a minor sermon:

> I, who early had been very pleased to see that my wishes and the labor of my footsteps were being realized, replied to him, "Why must my heart be disquieted? On the contrary it is very contented, seeing that I am the fortunate one [who] awaits the fulfillment of your own prophecies by which you must become Christians, which benefit will come to you by means of some bearded ones from the east who, according to those signs of their prophets, were we ourselves, by coming many leagues from the direction of the east, plowing the seas, for no gain besides, borne by the love of their souls, bringing them at the cost of much labor that favor which the true God prepared for them."[28]

This, like so many of Avendaño's sermonizing monologues to the Itzas, brought up the trope of prophecy that was so central to his rationale for negotiating at this time with Ajaw Kan Ek'.

In a canoe with Itza escorts dressed and armed for war, with Ajaw Kan Ek' pressing his hand on Avendaño's chest, and faced with conversing in the Itza language, which he knew only imperfectly, even a man as motivated and capable as Avendaño could hardly have constructed so elegant a speech. Throughout the history of colonial Yucatán, Franciscan missionary writers frequently inserted accounts, supposedly direct quotations, of long, on-the-spot sermons delivered under the most horrifying circumstances — usually situations in which they perceived themselves the objects of life-threatening or devil-inspired actions by bloodthirsty "savages." Their message — that God is conquering the devil's influences through inspired words — is almost always the same. Readers of the time must have understood that a deeper truth lay somewhere beneath the fiction of recorded verbatim language. Unimpressed with such details, the clerk who recorded Avendaño's testimony on May 2, 1696, omitted all of the quoted statements he presented in his formal account, apparently regarding them as no more than window dressing.[29]

Avendaño's statements permit few responses from his listeners; there is little conversation. Native people rarely speak in his report. For example, he wrote that when he finished the statement just quoted, he copied Ajaw Kan Ek' by putting his own hand on the Itza king's chest and asking him he if *he* were not upset. Ajaw Kan Ek' answered not with a speech of his own but with one word: "No." The friar then launched into another sermonette.[30] The purpose of these speeches was to legitimate the author as the sole authority who could describe the events that took place and explain their theological and worldly significance.

At this point in his narrative Avendaño claimed that Ajaw Kan Ek', again inspired by the devil, now tried to tempt the friar. Still paddling across the lake in the canoes, Ajaw Kan Ek' asked him if he were hungry. He was not, having only recently been fed at Nich. He was also convinced, recalling prior executions of friars who had visited Nojpeten, that this offer of food was part of a ritual that would end with his sacrifice and death the next day. Nonetheless, "so that his wickedness should not find any cowardice in me," he answered that he would eat some food if they had any. Ajaw Kan Ek' ordered all of the canoes to stop and had his attendants give Avendaño some "*chilaquiles* or vegetable tamales." Avendaño ate the food "anxiously" but asked if there was more, "to which he replied, 'Then it has pleased you.' 'Perfectly,' I told him. 'And I would eat more if there were any,' I said to him with some wit, at which they all laughed very earnestly. And they gave me another one, which I ate with the same relish, which I know they all admired in view of my coolness."[31]

Because all of his later experiences with Ajaw Kan Ek' indicated the latter's good will toward him, Avendaño, writing in retrospect, had no empirical evidence that his life had been in danger at that moment. The offer of food was clearly an act of hospitality, not a ritual prelude to human sacrifice. Avendaño nonetheless remained throughout his short visit to Nojpeten ready to interpret the slightest clue as evidence of that fearsome custom.

Once they reached the landing place on the island of Nojpeten, Avendaño performed a ritual in which he blessed the waters and exorcised the land in order to drive away Satan, who, in his view, had possessed the inhabitants from time immemorial.[32] This done, he immediately caught sight of the stone representation of Yaxcheel Kab' and AjKokaj Mut that looked out toward the west from directly in front of the house of Ajaw Kan Ek' (see chapter 3). Avendaño claimed, inexplicably, that he recognized this pair of supernatural beings from having already "read about it in their old papers and seen it in their *anahtees*" — hieroglyphic books in which "they have foretold their future events."

Elsewhere on the island there were other religious monuments or "idols" in view, including K'in Chil Kob'a and Itzimna K'awil. Avendaño later wrote that there were no "idols" inside any of the temples but that all were publicly displayed outdoors — an observation at conflict with claims made by the priests and officers who occupied the island on March 13, 1697, who said that the temples were overflowing with such works of the devil.[33] Aware of the fate of the Franciscans Fuensalida and Orbita, who had been chased out of town after Orbita destroyed what he took to be a religious representation of Cortés's horse in 1618, Avendaño restrained himself from damaging any of the images.[34]

Observing that there were "nine very large houses [that is, temples] constructed in the form of the churches of this province," he noted that these were all new. He saw signs of a devastating fire and was able to identify two buildings that had been rebuilt on the same spot. Indeed, as we will see later, AjKowoj had recently attacked Nojpeten, burning at least part of it to the ground — a fact of which Avendaño may have been aware. In his description of these buildings and their interior benches he was particularly struck by a "stone table" inside an anteroom in the house of Ajaw Kan Ek', described in chapter 3, which he was convinced was "the table of the sacrifice." He claimed to fear that he and his companions were to be put to death on it.[35]

Eventually the friars concluded that their lives were not in imminent danger and that, for the moment at least, the room was "the hospice for everyone." They were, of course, in a meeting house, not a temple of sacrifice. They had been led into the room by Ajaw Kan Ek' and possibly other leaders for the formal reception that had not been granted them at Nich but had simply been postponed until it could be carried out in the proper setting.

A GREETING RITUAL TRANSFORMED

The reception began with the presentation of a lukewarm maize beverage for the visitors to drink.[36] Avendaño overlooked the speech-making that must have gone on following the ritual drinking of the beverage, proceeding in his account to his request of Ajaw Kan Ek' that they all go outside where he could see to read the letters from Silva and Ursúa. Ajaw Kan Ek' led them to what Avendaño took to be a temple, situated about three blocks from the house of Ajaw Kan Ek' on or near the summit of the island. A noisy crowd of curious men, women, and children followed the new-comers, rushing ahead to look down on them as they climbed the hill.[37]

Although Avendaño would have preferred to remain outdoors, the in-terior of the temple was larger than the meeting room where they had been. He regretted that he and his companions did not examine more closely a suspended box or case in this room in which they thought they saw a large leg or thigh bone that looked like that of a horse. Their assumption that it was a relic of the animal that Cortés had left behind may or may not have been correct, but bones of this sort were found in one of the temple buildings on the day the island was captured by Spanish troops.[38]

Once they were all inside the temple Avendaño brought out his letters, called upon the noisy crowd to sit down and be quiet, and "made all of the priests, who are the teachers of the law, come before my presence, as well as all the caciques, captains, and *principales* of all of the divisions of that island or peten, and making them sit in their order next to the king, picking them out from the general populace where they were, I began to read the message that the governor had sent in writing in the name of the King our lord."[39]

To the contrary, it is more likely that Ajaw Kan Ek' or some other person of importance oversaw the seating of the officials and told Aven-daño when he could begin to speak. In any event, the audience paid little attention as he began to read the governor's letter. Asked why, they in-formed him that they did not understand him. Avendaño perceived the problem to be that the letter "was (although in their idiom) more cor-rupted than the old style in which they speak, which I had studied pur-posely." It is possible, of course, that the content of the letter was so foreign to his listeners, especially in its historical references, that little of it made sense to them. The letter itself was modeled partly on the *Requeri-miento*, a legally imposed declaration that was read aloud to populations about to be conquered; it was first brought to the Americas in 1514. This much later version, greatly embellished by more recent historical events and personal observations, retained the earlier declarations' warning that failure to accept Spanish domination peacefully might be met with appro-priate force.[40]

Only a Spanish version of the governor's letter has been found. Even though we do not know how far Avendaño progressed in his reading, seeing the letter in its entirety gives us some idea of the impression it might have created among its listeners:

> Don Martín de Ursúa, deputy of don Carlos — second of this name, king of Castile and of all these islands and lands that lie to its west, tamer of the barbarian people — his governor and captain general in this province of Mayapan, now called Yucatán.
>
> To noble Ah Canek, lord of the Itzas.
>
> I make known to you how our only true God, without beginning and end, created the heaven and the earth and created a man and a woman from whom you issue, we issue, and all the men of the world issue, and all who from now on may be born will issue, because many and without number are those who were born and issued from this man and from this woman from the time the world was created until now. It was necessary that these be divided among different islands and lands, because they could not be maintained or sustained together.
>
> Likewise our true God gave charge to one called San Pedro so that he might govern these men, so that he might be lord of all, wherever they might be, and so that every kind of people might obey him. He also handed over to him the entire world so that he might govern. And since He ordered that he might establish his seat in the great city of Rome, as the place most fit from where he would be able to govern all the world, He also told him that he could be in and establish his seat in whatever part that he might wish [in order] to govern the Christians, Moors, Jews, and other infidels. They named him Pope, which means lord of the world, because he is the lord governor of all men. Those who were living when they gave him the said charge received him as lord and king, and thus have all his successors been received until San Pedro Inocente, twelfth of this name, who today governs us. And thus will the rest be received until the end of the world.
>
> One, then, of these pontiffs that I mentioned, donated these islands and lands that are to the west of Castile, with all that they contain, to the great king named don Fernando and to his wife doña Isabel and to all their successors. By virtue of his donation our great king of Castile is thus king and lord of all these islands and lands, and he is your king and lord of all the people who inhabit them.
>
> For which reason, after all that I have said was made known they

199

received our great king and lord, and they serve and obey him with all goodwill as their true king and true lord. And likewise they obeyed the priests of the true God whom they had sent them in order to preach to them and to teach them the things of the holy faith. And all with goodwill were Christians. And for that our king ordered that no harm be done to them, and he loved them as he loves the rest of his vassals. And thus you are obligated to do the same.

And this is not the first notice that is given to you. Do not ignore it. It has been known for a long time, because when Montezuma, the ancient monarch who governed all these provinces, surrendered, he submitted to the obedience and service of the king of Castile. And likewise your great-grandfathers or ancestors surrendered when Hernando Cortés passed by that island of yours, and he left you a horse as a sign that he had to return to be with you. And he did not return because he had to return punctually to Mexico.

And not only this. In addition, when don Antonio de Figueroa was governor a little more than eighty years ago, the Canek who governed that island sent his ambassadors to this city of Mérida saying that the said Canek and all the Itzas had surrendered to the obedience and service of our great king. They were received with much rejoicing, and in the name of His Majesty they named them as justices and regidores. They returned to their town, and after some days had passed two priests named Fray Bartolomé de Fuensalida and Fray Juan de Orbita were sent to your island. And although it is true that they were well received by the Canek, after they said why they had gone they made them return, saying to them that the time to be Christians had not yet arrived.

And now likewise in the name of our great king don Carlos II, I ordered that you be given notice of all these things that I have said. And you, the Canek, have responded that if it is for peace and not war, you will surrender with all the Itzas to the obedience and service of our true king don Carlos, because the time has arrived in which your plate and your calabash might be one with the Spaniards, and in which you might be Christians. Your answer pleased me much. And the true God, creator of all things, knows. It is not my desire to harm you; rather my desire is to love you. Nor do I request anything else of you other than that you might know our true God and our true king and lord, and that you render him obedience. And as a sign that this is my intention and that I do not wish to make war against you in place of the peace that you request of me, in the name of our king and lord don Carlos II, I send you those fathers-preachers of Saint Francis in order that they might preach to you and teach Christianity and the mysteries of our holy faith, and remove you from your sufferings in the darknesses of the devil, who forfeits your souls and takes you to hell to suffer eternal torments. These will teach you the true road to heaven. And we fulfill that which our true God orders us so that our souls might be saved. For that reason love them very much as messengers of God and as your spiritual fathers-preachers.

This is my will and that of our King don Carlos. If you do so, you will do well, and you will do that which you ought to do. And I shall receive you in his name with all my goodwill, and I shall liberate you from your enemies, and I shall not allow any harm to come to you. And you, Ah Canek, shall answer this my letter so that I might know that you surrender completely to the obedience and service of our great king don Carlos with all the Itzas and how you receive the messengers of God, your spiritual fathers-preachers.

Finally, I require that you understand well all these things that I have said to you, and all that I wrote to you by the route of Tipu, in reply to that which you sent me: you [are to] state that you obey our mother the church, and the pope in her name, and our great king in his office as lord and king of all these islands and lands in virtue of the said donation. And otherwise I certify to you that with the aid of God with all my power I shall do all that our great king orders me, which I do not express in this my letter, as it is not necessary now. And if you issue any harmful protest, it will be through your fault, not that of our great king or my own.

And now I forward you a very fine machete with its sheath, its knife, and its broad belt, and three yards of embroidered taffeta, so that you might wear them in my name.

It was written in this city of Tihoo, which is Mérida, on the eighth day of the month of December in [the year] of the birth of Christ our savior four twenties that are counted for five[41] four hundreds with fifteen more.[42]

It is not difficult to imagine why Avendaño's audience reacted with restless boredom and complaints that they could not understand what he was saying. Avendaño's command of the Itza language was imperfect, and the contents and style of the letter were European, not Maya. From a Maya perspective the letter would have been rude, ignoring the proper conventions of a friendly and indirect introduction to its content and conveying a relentlessly authoritarian tone.

That Avendaño may have played a major part in writing portions of the letter is implied by the priority it gives to the religious element in the submission demanded of Ajaw Kan Ek', its heavy use of religious discourse and allusion, and its emphasis on earlier reports of Itza prophecies by the Franciscan missionaries Fuensalida and Orbita. Only one reference in the letter is made to Ursúa's earlier message to Ajaw Kan Ek' about submission: "because the time has arrived in which your plate and your calabash might be one with the Spaniards, and in which you might be Christians." Avendaño later repeated this statement to some visiting Kowoj leaders, saying that "the time had already arrived in which (according to what their prophets had announced to them) we would eat together from one plate and drink from one calabash, making ourselves one, the Spaniards with them."[43]

Avendaño, realizing that the governor's letter was not being well received, put it down and began to extemporize. Speaking, he claimed, in their "ancient dialect," he not only tried to explain the message but also, "with some fervor," expanded his remarks into a "spiritual discourse" about the benefits of Spanish friendship and law and of religious conversion.[44] Into this homily he inserted "some words about their prophecies, which were appropriate to the occasion." Such comments about prophecy would be central to most of his future remarks to his Itza hosts. Avendaño, again boasting of his command over the language, wrote that his listeners received his discourse "with pleasure, because they understood it completely." Their reply, however, was simply "kato wale," meaning "later"; they would have to think the matter over.[45]

ITZA HOSPITALITY AND CHRISTIAN RITUAL

By now it was almost night on the visitors' first day at Nojpeten. They were led, along with the crowd of onlookers, to a building about a block and a half from the house of Ajaw Kan Ek' where they were to stay and sleep. Individual households supplied them a steady stream of food, including a type of wide bean called *ib'*, black beans, squash, peccary, freshwater shrimp and other fish, and tortillas. Rules of hostly commensality were apparently quite specific: Their hosts — Ajaw Kan Ek' and others — watched them eat, and when they could eat no more they handed back the excess. The hosts then consumed their meal, with Ajaw Kan Ek' always the first to eat. In Avendaño's mind the one plate–one calabash prophecy was doubtless coming true.[46]

During the night, curious groups of people watched the friars constantly through the doorway as they tried to sleep, even following them as they went outdoors to relieve themselves. Their observers only laughed, wrote Avendaño, when they tried to shoo them away, and even chastisements by Ajaw Kan Ek' did no good. Before they went to sleep the friars said their customary mass, but they were impeded by those who kept crowding around them. When they sat down, people sat next to them, touching them from head to toe, "not excepting (if we gave them the chance) the most hidden recesses of a man." In order to say mass they seated this audience on the perimeter benches, performing the ceremony in the middle of the room. Whether mocking them or simply amused, the onlookers mimicked their every word and gesture.[47]

Not all of the Itza observers, however, were children and commoners. Ajaw Kan Ek' himself stayed with them almost constantly, day and night, "assisting us at our side." With him were two or three priests related to him, and over the course of the evening "all of the other priests" passed through their public guest room. At one point on the second night Avendaño learned that the priests were holding a meeting at a nearby "temple" where "they held their dances, idolatries, and songs on the nights we were there." He found them "all seated in a conference, along with others who were not priests, singing and dancing at their sides. Upon seeing me the priests rose, and he who could do so most quickly gave me the stool on which he was sitting for me to sit upon."[48] Shortly thereafter, however, Avendaño stated that there were only two Maya priests at this meeting with Ajaw Kan Ek' — a crucial piece of information, for it indicated that the meeting did not represent a large cross section of the governing council.

Ajaw Kan Ek', having left the other friars to join this meeting, took the lead in responding to the anxious Avendaño's request for an immediate reply to his "message." The answer would come later, he replied yet again. But taking Avendaño aside, he reportedly asked him what the friar actually wanted to hear from them. After Avendaño repeated the essence of his earlier discourse, emphasizing once more that the Itzas' own prophets had foreseen their imminent conversion and submission to Spanish rule, Ajaw Kan Ek' and the other two priests stated that they were willing to convert to Christianity but wanted to know how these baptisms that Avendaño proposed were to be performed. Citing an appropriate verse from Ezekiel, **203** Avendaño enthusiastically explained what baptism was all about.[49] The Itza leaders' final reply suggested that they would have to wait until the next day to decide.[50]

After the meeting, Ajaw Kan Ek' and the two priests spent the night with Avendaño and his companions. They were clearly determined to assay their guests closely, observing their every motion. Throughout his account, Avendaño fails to mention whether the four friars also shared their quarters with the four Yucatec singers and the Kejach guides, although we may assume that they did. These companions remain silent bystanders throughout his account of the visit.

Before dawn on the second morning of their visit, the customary maize beverage was delivered in calabash bowls to the guest quarters. Avendaño reported that he started in again with a sermon, but this time Ajaw Kan Ek' and the others interrupted, revealing their belief that the ritual of baptism involved "some shedding of blood or circumcision or the cutting of some part of their body." Their assumption, apparently, had been that baptism was a form of penis incision, which they presumably practiced. Ajaw Kan Ek', assured to the contrary, allowed Avendaño, assisted by one of his Maya cantores, to sprinkle baptismal water on several of his own children. Other children, who had been held in waiting nearby, were also allowed to undergo the ritual. Ajaw Kan Ek' then called upon others, "in particular those of his family and parcialidad, to bring their small children to receive their name (as this is what they call baptism), and he said to the priests who were present there, who were about three or four, 'It is a good thing for you bring all our children to receive the name and be washed.' "[51]

Over the next two days Avendaño performed nearly three hundred baptisms of children, with barely time to leave the "temple" where he carried out the rituals. Whether these children were of both sexes or only boys cannot be determined, because the term *hijos,* used to describe the children, remains ambiguous. Because of the initial Itza equation of baptism with penis mutilation, however, the possibility that they were only male children cannot be dismissed. The four Maya cantores served as godfathers for the baptisms, since they were the only available baptized adults other than the Franciscans.[52]

While the baptisms were going on, Ajaw Kan Ek' remained cordial to Avendaño, and he and "three other priests related to him" announced that they would "accept the Spaniards and their laws willingly" and that they were only awaiting word from two "caciques with their captains" (that is, two pairs of rulers from two quarters) before giving him a final, positive answer. Whereupon Avendaño, sensing that he would soon be departing, began to instruct the children "in the mysteries of our holy faith"—a remarkable feat for such a short stay.[53]

The visitors had arrived at Nojpeten on January 14 in the late afternoon. They waited for three and a half days before receiving an answer to their message, which would put the date of the events that are about to be described on their fourth and fifth full days, January 18 and 19. The nineteenth was to be their last day, for that night they were spirited across the eastern leg of the lake by Ajaw Kan Ek' and members of his family.[54]

DISPUTES OVER PROPHECY

In mid-afternoon of that last day an enemy of Ajaw Kan Ek', AjKowoj, arrived from the northern shore of the lake with his full retinue. This visitor was the leader who, in alliance with the ruler's uncle, Ajaw B'atab' K'in Kante, had only recently overseen the destruction by fire of much of Nojpeten. Avendaño, mistakenly thinking that these men were coming from the other nearby islands, went out to greet them as though he were the resident head of state:

> I found myself thus occupied [in baptizing and catechizing children] when on the said day some of the governors, captains, and heads of the other four petens, began to come, navigating across the lake, with their war officers and their standards, such as lances and stone knives a little less than a quarter [of a vara] long.[55] Instead of ribbons the said lances are decorated with feathers of many colors, very showy and all hanging down. I went out to receive them as a matter of courtesy, but the Indians of that peten went out only out of curiosity to see them arrive, painted and feathered, in war dress, their faces painted black. I embraced them and spoke to them in gentle words, and if I had anything to eat left over from what they had given me there, I shared it with them as recent arrivals, having them sit next to me and the king, who was always at my side.[56]

Convinced that his efforts had put the visitors at ease, Avendaño launched into his by now well-practiced speech about accepting Spaniards as friends and embracing their law. As a sign that they immediately accepted his "proposal," he noted that "they lowered their heads, [saying that] they would be pleased with the trade in axes and machetes that they would receive." Trade for metal tools had for some time been a motivation for increasing contact with the Spaniards, but this was hardly a sign of agreement.

Two leaders from the visiting party stood out from the rest. One was an old man with a double-bladed machete as his standard. The other was a younger man who carried a stone knife. They were "painted for war; their faces were as hideous as the evil purpose that they had in their hearts." The older man was AjKowoj; the younger one was probably his son. After Avendaño had recited his one plate–one calabash speech to them, AjKowoj replied sarcastically and "with a feigned laugh that this much gladdened him, to leave those forests in which he found himself and come with me to the province in order to retrieve some land titles that his ancestors had held and to live there in happiness with his elder brothers, the Spaniards, promising at the same time to accompany me with all his people before the presence of the governor as a sign of his true surrender."[57] Not fooled by such a clever reply, Avendaño smelled a rat.

Avendaño gave Ursúa a strikingly different version of his first encounter with these visitors prior to his return to Mérida: "At the end of three days they baptized many children, five petens or islands having been delivered up to the crown of our King and lord, the captains of each one having come to render obedience, as a sign of which they gave the [Itza] king two crowns of their own."[58] Ursúa reported this version of Avendaño's oral report on March 10 in a letter to King Carlos II, whereas Avendaño's final written report was signed on April 29. His claim that other leaders paid such homage to Ajaw Kan Ek' is highly dubious.

The visitors retired at about four o'clock to the house of "some confidant of theirs" and returned at about seven in the evening "to hear me discourse." After he finished his speech, Avendaño approached AjKowoj and his son, who stood at the back of the audience, embracing them yet again and informing them that he wanted to chat with them about "the old method of counting, equally days, months, and years, as well as ages, and to know what age was the present one (for them one age has only twenty years), and what prophecy the aforesaid year and age contained."[59] As a clarification, Avendaño provided his readers with a brief description of Maya hieroglyphic folding books, which he had obviously seen somewhere. He wrote in a now-famous passage that such books contained information about calendrical prophecy and ritual as well as explanations of how Maya Yucatán was governed by a system of thirteen political divisions structured by the intersection of time and space.[60] Avendaño was obviously well prepared to face knowledgeable local authorities.[61]

Avendaño regarded Ajaw Kan Ek', who had been close to him for more than three days, as "the principal priest and their teacher" and soon discovered that the other "priests and teachers" who surrounded him were equally well versed in the k'atun calendar. AjKowoj at first claimed not to understand Avendaño's computation, but the friar seemed to make some progress after Ajaw Kan Ek' and the other "priests and teachers" stepped in to listen to him try to convince them "how it was already the attained time (according to their prophets) at which they would become Christians." That Avendaño nearly won part of his argument is suggested by his statement that the final message the Itzas wished to send to the governor was that "thenceforth, at the [end of the] four months that were lacking for the said time to be completed, all the adults would receive baptisms."[62]

Avendaño had not, however, obtained agreement to his relentlessly repeated plea that they accept the Spaniards as their friends and embrace Spanish law. There was to be no eating from one plate and drinking from one calabash. Not only had he failed to gain agreement that adult leaders would be baptized before he left — the religious aspect of his mission — but he also failed to make headway on the diplomatic front. During the next twenty-four hours the extent of his failure would become increasingly apparent.

Following the announcement of the four-month delay, wrote Avendaño, the elder AjKowoj, despite his having agreed to the date, angrily denounced the agreement, saying, "What does it matter that the time when we would be Christians is found to be completed, if the sharp point of my stone lance has not been worn out?" To this eloquent question Avendaño replied that God was on his side alone, that he was willing to die, and that it was prophetically determined that AjKowoj and his people would become Christians. AjKowoj and his allies thereupon retired, leaving the friar, Ajaw Kan Ek', and the other priests to discuss the agreement further.[63]

The next morning — his last one at Nojpeten — Avendaño asked questions of his Itza hosts about agriculture, geography, and political organization. At this point his report takes an interesting detour from a preoccupation with prophecy and surrender to report on such innocuous subjects as cultivated food crops (maize, two kinds of beans, chilies, plantains, a chayote-like vegetable called *ch'un*, a little cultivated cacao and vanilla, some cultivated wild cabbage, and onions) and "commercial" crops (much cotton and two dyes, indigo and cochineal). He commented on the high quality of their multicolored cloth, which they bartered to Kejaches and the people of Tipuj in exchange for axes and machetes. The cloth was durable and feltlike, but the colors soon faded, because they did not, he supposed, know how to set the dyes.[64] Following some discussion about rivers and the lake's risings and fallings, which the Itzas denied occurred, he elicited the list of twenty-two districts, or parcialidades, discussed in chapter 3.

THE KING'S NEW CLOTHES

Despite his initial fears, by this last morning Avendaño had come to appreciate the hospitality of Ajaw Kan Ek' and to trust in his goodwill. He now claimed to respect his host, who ultimately saved his life, as a man of noble qualities but one whose personal pride was so resented by others that he failed as a ruler: "The king knows well that he is such by blood, because it is certain that he and his family possess a rare character and goodness. Being so good he boasts so much that all treat him with some disrespect, so that he is not the master who commands what he possesses. But to us he gave much attention and kindness, along with his family and ward [*parcialidad*], revealing to us the most hidden secrets about what was going on among the Indians and telling me . . . the good intention they had to become Christians and to admit the Spaniards and their law."[65]

On the other hand, he regarded AjKowoj as a wicked and dangerous man, possessed by Satan. By this time he seemed to have constructed a simple, uncompromised opposition between Ajaw Kan Ek' as a force of good and AjKowoj as the agent of evil. No doubt Ajaw Kan Ek' had contributed to this personification of his enemy, maintaining that AjKowoj had planned to kill the visitors as they passed through Chak'an territory. Avendaño claimed that the warm hospitality extended to him by the ruler and his "friends" reflected his own deep preparations for this meeting. He had surprised them by being the first outsider they had met who already knew "the language of their ancestors and their own," a feat that he credited to his having studied "their own papers" before leaving on his trip. So impressed were they, he claimed, that they called him "Chomach Ajaw, which means among them 'Great Lord, worthy of reverence,' and Citcaan, which means 'Father of Heaven.'"[66] Such self-congratulatory prose was in part couched in an admonition to others that they should be as sensitive to the Itzas as he was.

As events unfolded on this last day at Nojpeten, Avendaño became even more convinced that Ajaw Kan Ek' had become his mortal savior from certain death at the hands of AjKowoj. The first event was a "commotion" that broke out among a group of people, including a number of leaders. They vented their anger directly at Ajaw Kan Ek', saying "many disrespectful things" — meaning, apparently, that they cursed him. Avendaño reconstructed their complaints in a powerful passage: "What good did it do them to favor the friendship of the Spaniards and their law? If it was in order to have axes and machetes for their cultivations, they had never lacked anything with which to make milpa. Was it to clothe themselves with the goods and clothing of Castile, when, having very good things, they lacked none of that? If it was so that the Spaniards would defend them, when would the Itzalana nation be cowardly or be humiliated to anyone, as they had so many armed people to defend themselves and to destroy as many as ventured against them? It was a very bad action to receive them."[67]

Ajaw Kan Ek', by now foolishly dressed in the colonial costume and carrying the colonial baton of office, tried to defend himself, point by point, from these challenges. He purportedly took Avendaño's side on every point that the two had discussed and chastised the crowd for its call to arms. Ajaw Kan Ek' failed to satisfy his hecklers, who grew more excited. Some who had not spoken before called out "with very wrathful words and bold insolence." Clearly Ajaw Kan Ek' had lost every bit of ruling legitimacy he might have had before Avendaño's arrival. He had personally "sold out" to the Spaniards.

Realizing that matters were out of hand, Avendaño, the foreigner, came to the defense of the now-humiliated Ajaw Kan Ek'. He stood up next to the ruler and delivered a passionate speech that repeated nearly everything he had said on previous occasions, including the "one plate–one calabash" reference. At least one new element, the "Montezuma analogy," found its way into the speech: "And besides, heed how your great Montezuma, as soon as they gave him the news about how my king was such a great lord and how his empire was so extensive, presented him not only with his crown but also his person and his kingdom, going as he did personally to give it to him."[68] An expansion of a line from the Avendaño-authored letter from the governor, this slanted synopsis of the conquest of the Aztecs must have bewildered the audience, who made no claim to descent from sixteenth-century central Mexico.

Avendaño, if we are to believe that he actually said these things, made a serious tactical error at the end of his oration. Even though the agreement that he had reached made no mention of friendship with the Spaniards or political incorporation into their kingdom, the closing words of his oration contradicted these terms, indicating that Ajaw Kan Ek' had offered a complete capitulation:

> [T]he governor, who sends me, endeavors to take nothing from us [*sic*] nor from your king's lordship and rule, but instead he wishes that it [*sic*] remain with him, as is evident from that clothing I have placed upon him and by that baton I have placed in his hand, which among the Spaniards is a sign of lordship and rule. That which the governor wishes in the name of my king and lord is that you should also recognize him as your king, since we are all brothers and we are the priests of the true God, whose law we came to teach you (as

209

your ancient prophets have prophesied). All this being so, why do you raise this disturbance? Go, Itzalanos. Be ashamed. The agreement that you and your king have made with me is very good.[69]

As the crowd heard Avendaño say that Ajaw Kan Ek' had agreed to embrace the Spanish king in exchange for a suit of clothes and a staff of office, they must have looked upon their supposed "ruler" with disdain and disbelief. The symbolism of the clothing and baton was surely not lost on other leaders and the general population; some of them who had traveled to Yucatán knew perfectly well that their principal leader was now dressed in the formal clothing reserved for native leaders who had submitted to a colonial regime and that his baton was a sign of his tacit acceptance of Spanish law.

Ajaw Kan Ek' had apparently reached a separate, private agreement with Avendaño that he would be appointed "governor" of the entire Lago Petén Itzá region despite the refusal of other leaders to grant more than the initiation of adult baptisms four months hence. Avendaño had publicly exposed Ajaw Kan Ek' as a traitor to his own allies and people.[70]

Avendaño subsequently stated that at the council meeting "they voluntarily received the Spaniards' official message and, this being so, they asked me to return to see them at the end of the four months as stated above, by way of the town of Tipu, to which place the king, with all his people, promised to appear to receive me."[71] This version of the initial agreement again mentioned nothing about friendship or political accommodations. Although Tipuj apparently was still as much an Itza colony as a Spanish one, it seems unlikely that a royal delegation including Ajaw Kan Ek' would have gone there to meet Avendaño.

AVENDAÑO ON THE ITZAS

Avendaño's descriptions of these events contain brief digressions that continue to admonish his military readers that they should not use violence against the Itzas, that troops might well fail if they did try to use force, and that he and his fellow Franciscans could bring these people to a knowledge of God with no interference.[72] Before describing his departure from Nojpeten he also inserted more geographical information and some critical ethnographic interpretations.[73]

Avendaño was impressed by the Itzas' physical appearance, considering them well featured, light skinned like mestizos, and relatively tall. The men's body decorations, however, canceled their natural attractiveness. Some tattooed their faces in black, sometimes in stripes, to make them appear fierce, and others tattooed or painted their faces with designs of animals, which Avendaño took to be personal "auguries." In contrast, the women apparently stretched their earlobes so that they were unable — in contrast to the men, who wore silver and gold eardrops — to wear ear decorations.

These judgmental descriptions of gender differences in dress served only as an introduction to a commentary on what he perceived about Itza male sexuality — that is, on "sodomy," which was considered both a serious sin and a heinous crime by Spaniards. The men, he wrote, paid much attention to their personal appearance, not only tattooing or painting their faces but also rolling up their hair with tasseled cloth bands, made by themselves and woven in brightly colored designs. He considered their dress — including beautiful, brightly colored shirts or jackets into which stripes and other designs were woven — to be a sign of excessive vanity and effeminacy. He saw these traits in other male behaviors, too, including carrying small stools on which to sit, warming themselves at night as they sat with multicolored striped sheets, and drinking only lukewarm maize *posole* or *saka* but seldom the more manly "clear or cold water." In contrast, the women dressed plainly, wore nothing above their skirts, and put less time than the men into rolling up their hair. The men, he noted in passing, generally paid little attention to them.

All of this led him to the conclusion that, as "many judge," it was all a sign of the "sodomitic vice [*vicio nefando*] that prevails among them." He let this weakly supported accusation speak for itself, turning immediately to matters concerning his departure. He may have intended this digression on sexuality as further evidence that the Itzas were in dire need of conversion and moral reform, a theme that appears many times in his commentary. As we shall see in chapter 11, however, both Spanish military officers and secular priests used such accusations as justification for armed, not spiritual, conquest.

Departure from Nojpeten

The Itza leaders, well aware that Spanish troops were already advancing toward the lake, asked Avendaño to leave them "some sure signs or known token of friendship" that the Spaniards would honor and that, when displayed, would keep them from attacking. He chose to leave an open letter that he had already prepared three days earlier for the occasion of his departure:

I.M.I.

✝

Saint Paul the Apostle pray for us
Lords Captains of whichever of the two poles, north or south.

My dear Lords:
  Our Lord deigned to reveal his divine grace to us in order to succeed in obtaining that which for many ages was unattainable. (But nothing is impossible to the divine power, to whom glory may be given.)
  Because with [his grace] he has given opportunity to bend the neck of this invincible Itzalana nation, humbled at the first impulse of the evangelical ministers and sons of my seraphic father San Francisco, by promptly offering their children to the purest of washing, that of baptism, having baptized up to this time many of them with the sure hope of shortly baptizing them all, although their fathers and mothers, while docile and peaceable with us, still delay in giving up their idolatry. For this reason especially it is necessary [to demonstrate] moderation with great patience, so as to bear many such vexatious actions, as they are due to the darkness in which they have lived. In light of which I entreat your Graces to comport yourselves with much prudence (if by chance you should come to this nation of the Itzas, whose patron saint is San Pablo) so as not to quickly lose what has been so much desired and, thanks be to God, has been obtained. They remain instructed so that when your Graces appear they will receive you in peace and give you what supplies, etc. may be needed in exchange for axes, machetes, and other goods from Castile, which they much desire, but I do not know whether you will be well paid.
  This is as much as occurs to me now. After rejoicing in the good health of your Graces, to whose service I submit my own full [health], praying to our Lord asking our Lord to keep you many years, which I wish, in this town of Great San Pablo of the Peten Itza on the sixteenth of January of the year 1696. I kiss the hand of your Graces. Your most humble servant and chaplain, *Fray Andrés de Avendaño, Apostolic Missionary Commissary.*[74]

Avendaño wrote that he handed the letter to Ajaw Kan Ek' "in the presence of many principales and the greater part of the common people." He accompanied its ceremonial presentation with yet another oration, claiming that the letter would ensure that any arriving Spaniards, whether from Yucatán or Guatemala, would restrain from attacking them. Instead, because in the letter he assured future readers that an agreement of peace and friendship had been achieved, the people of Nojpeten would be able to go before visiting Spaniards in peace. All they had to do was show the visitors the letter, the Spanish clothes worn by Ajaw Kan Ek', and some crucifixes, rosaries, and other European items that he had presented them. Each such recorded speech, whether or not it was delivered, further reinforced for Spanish Yucatecan eyes Avendaño's case for having reached a successful agreement.

Captain Zubiaur Isasi later revealed that Avendaño's open letter had been brought to the encampment south of Chuntuki by two Kejaches whom García de Paredes had sent to Nojpeten to inquire about the friars. Because they arrived just after Avendaño left Nojpeten, he did not receive García's message, which undoubtedly would have informed him of the outcome of AjChan's visit to Mérida and of García's new instructions to march to Nojpeten in order to receive the formal surrender of Ajaw Kan Ek'. By the time the messengers arrived, Avendaño had already been forced to leave Nojpeten.[75]

THREATS AND POLITICS

Avendaño's open letter was accompanied by a certification of its truth and authenticity, written on April 28, 1696, by Fray Joseph de Jesús María, the apostolic notary who accompanied him. Confirming that the letter was delivered directly to Ajaw Kan Ek', Santa María added one piece of important new information: "[A]t the same time the king [Ajaw Kan Ek'] having said that if they would decapitate his enemy, the cacique Couoh, with all of his followers (who in all would be between sixty and seventy), he would hand over the petens that are in his charge."[76]

It is difficult to dismiss such a statement, which confirms that whatever political accommodation Avendaño had achieved, he had done so in a separate meeting with Ajaw Kan Ek' and possibly some of his friends and allies. The Kowojs, it appears, had steadfastly refused to participate. They probably had ample reason to believe that Ajaw Kan Ek' had already sold out his crumbling kingdom to the Spaniards and had called on them to side with him in a war against the Kowoj leaders and, presumably, Ajaw B'atab' K'in Kante, the Chak'an territorial ruler.

Avendaño had become fully aware of this conflict during his visit and manipulated it to his benefit by reaching an independent agreement with Ajaw Kan Ek'. Despite the crowd's jeering of Ajaw Kan Ek' on the mission's last day at Nojpeten, the friar continued to pretend that the Itza ruler still spoke on behalf of all his people. Avendaño, like Ajaw Kan Ek', blamed the entire event upon the Kowojs and their allies, the Chak'an Itzas. The latter were angry with him, he rationalized, because he had shamed them into giving back the Spanish suit and baton in which "I

213

myself dressed King Canek." Furthermore, Ajaw B'atab' K'in Kante had complained that by pouring baptismal water on his daughter, who had been presented to Avendaño by his nephew, Ajaw Kan Ek', the friar had harmed her. These, however, were small matters. What Avendaño did not admit was of far greater significance: that the Kowojs and the Chak'an Itza leaders were disgusted and angered by the private agreement he had reached with Ajaw Kan Ek'.[77]

Avendaño, forewarned by Ajaw Kan Ek' of the intentions of Ajaw B'atab' K'in Kante (AjKan in his text) and AjKowoj to have him killed if he retraced his steps through Chak'an Itza, became suspicious when these two leaders visited him in the house of Ajaw Kan Ek' on the last afternoon with a large calabash of maize beverage. He drank politely and listened to their offer to take back with them two ("who were the fattest") of his four carriers so that they could prepare food for him to his taste as they passed by "their house" on his way home. Avendaño refused the offer but feigned agreement to leave with them the next morning, certain all the while that as soon as they arrived in their town they would "prepare, without doubt, the *pib'* [cooking pit] or fire where the two fat Indians, whom they asked me for, were to be roasted, and the stakes on which we were to be spitted, as we found out later."[78] This dramatic but fanciful accusation was Avendaño's introduction to his marvelously constructed description of the friars' dramatic departure.

Ajaw Kan Ek', according to the account, confirmed for Avendaño that the Chak'an Itza ruler and AjKowoj not only intended to kill the visitors but also to follow the Kejach guides back to their home villages and kill them as well. The only choice, he advised, was to leave that very night so that the Franciscan party would be long gone by the time his enemies arrived in the morning. The ruler's wife, IxChan Pana, and her daughters supposedly offered them details of their intended fate, just as they were embarking in the canoes, saying, " 'They say that they are not going to kill you in any other way than by cutting you into little pieces,' and they made gestures with one hand over the other to show they were going to make hash and eat us."[79]

In oral testimony Avendaño presented a different version of this exchange, implying that IxChan Pana might have had a personal interest in the friars' murder and might have been in collusion with her husband's enemies. She tried, he said, to stop her husband from taking them off secretly in the direction of Tipuj by stating that the friars should not be afraid of foul play if they returned by the way they came — whereas Avendaño, and apparently Ajaw Kan Ek' as well, was convinced that AjKowoj planned to have them killed if they passed through Chak'an territory. Challenging his wife, Ajaw Kan Ek' put his hand on his machete, threatening to use it on anyone who questioned him and reminding her "that he alone was king and lord of all those lands and all his vassals."[80]

Because women's voices are all but absent in the record, Avendaño's attribution of these remarks to IxChan Pana and her daughter deserves our special attention. In his written report he mentioned only the remark about the intended fate of the friars and attributed it to both mother and daughters as a collective warning that the friars should escape as quickly as possible. His spoken testimony, however, distinguished between Ix-Chan Pana, who supposedly opposed her husband and wished to see them dead, and one of her daughters, about eighteen, who by her warning helped them to escape. This embellishment perhaps reflects an attitude we might infer on Avendaño's part that older women, especially the wives of native "royalty," were deceitful and untrustworthy. It seems likely that lineage rivalry among the nobility was at work in IxChan Pana's opposition to her husband.

DEPARTURE BY NIGHT

The departure took place at about nine o'clock at night following a session of "not a little grief and tears from the family of the king and his friends." Avendaño, the two other Franciscan friars, and his four cantores traveled in a single canoe, accompanied by Ajaw Kan Ek', his son-in-law, and his son — ten passengers in all. The transportation must have been one of the large Itza canoes capable of carrying a substantial load. The canoe was probably not navigated, as Avendaño claimed, by only the three Maya nobles, who would probably not have served in this capacity. Because that work must have been done by several paddlers, the canoe must have held as many as fourteen or sixteen persons.[81]

The canoe, by Avendaño's estimate, arrived at the eastern end of the lake between three and four o'clock in the morning. Avendaño recorded the parting words of Ajaw Kan Ek', delivered while "holding me lovingly embraced." They repeated an earlier motif: "See that you do not forget to tell your governor that I love him much and wish to be his friend and that of the Spaniards, and not to fail to decapitate my said rivals, the Chacan Itzas, for I am sure I shall deliver to him the petens which I rule. And do not fail to come to see us, as you say, and let it be by this Tipu road, so that I with all my people may come out to receive you."[82]

By the time he wrote his report, three months after these events, it was already too late; the opportunity had been squandered. If only García de

215

Paredes had killed the ruler's enemies when they visited his camp in search of Avendaño, "the entire nation of the Itzas would have been conquered and delivered to the King our lord, and at that moment they would have all been Christians without the said victory costing a shot of powder."[83]

The Bacalareño Francisco de Hariza later reported on an interview with a Tipujan who, following the February conflicts between Itzas and Spaniards detailed in the next chapter, had taken a gift from Hariza to Ajaw Kan Ek'. According to Ursúa's interpretation, Ajaw Kan Ek' told the Tipujan "how his vassals had risen up and that they wished to allow neither fathers nor Spaniards in their lands, although he, for his part, did wish so. He [the Tipujan] also declares that on the third day after the fathers arrived they decided to kill them. The king, knowing this, arranged with an Indian of his satisfaction to effect their escape, as he did so in the direction of said Tipu."[84] This statement confirms the thrust of Avendaño's contention that Ajaw Kan Ek' was loyal to the Spanish cause and had assisted in their escape. It also confirms that Ajaw Kan Ek' lacked support among even close members of the royal family. His effort to save the Franciscans' lives must have spelled the end of whatever political effectiveness he had enjoyed. From that point on, anti-Spanish factions appear to have dominated every sphere of Itza political life.

Once they had landed, probably near Saklemakal, Ajaw Kan Ek' sent his son and son-in-law as guides with Avendaño and returned immediately to Nojpeten. The group walked overland to Yalain, a town of "very few houses clustered together, but of many well-populated *milperías* [food cultivations] at a radius of one or two leagues." There he found, in addition to a number of Tipujans, a population dominated by people who he supposed were from Nojpeten but went to Yalain to make their milpas.

The visitors were taken to meet Chamach Xulu, "a priest who looks to be over fifty-four years old who rules this town . . . a close companion and confidant of the King Canek." He fed them and took them to a newly constructed thatch house that still lacked a finished floor, explaining that the house was "for us, the fathers they had requested."[85]

The people of Yalain, Avendaño wrote, asked about AjChan and his companions. They had not seen them, they said, since they had left for Mérida in August on their first trip to that city. Avendaño claimed to be puzzled by this information, because he recalled that they had departed Mérida at least twenty days before he left on his own journey on December 13. In fact they had left much earlier, arriving at Tipuj on October 28 — in plenty of time for them to make a full report of their trip to the

Nojpeten leadership — and, as Avendaño almost certainly knew, were approaching Mérida for the second time when he left in December.

The friars were treated well at Yalain for most of their stay. When Chamach Xulu, as Ajaw Kan Ek' had asked him to do, promised to give them a guide to take them to Tipuj, the ruler's son and son-in-law departed for Nojpeten. The guide was to be a Tipujan who had gone to Nojpeten while Avendaño was still there, but he failed to arrive at Yalain before they were forced to leave. Instead, disturbing news arrived at Yalain, carried by several people from Nojpeten, that "the peten had become excited due to the arrival from the location where we are [i.e., the lower camino real] of Indians from here, from the province [of Yucatán], and to having heard musket shots and rumors of Spaniards. I do not know if this was true, but what we experienced from then on from the Indians of this town where we were was that from then on they completely cooled off from that love which up to then they had shown us, treating us with a thousand contempts, doing nothing about giving us the guide we had requested."[86]

The Yucatecan party seen by the Itzas may have been the messengers and their escorts sent by García de Paredes to check on Avendaño and deliver the news of AjChan's visit to Mérida and of García's plans to march to the lake. Despite the uproar reported at Nojpeten, they must have been received politely and given Avendaño's letter to take back to the Spanish encampment.

Avendaño realized that he and his companions were in serious trouble during a meeting in which the participants not only became inebriated from *b'alche* (a ritual fermented beverage) but also "idolatrized" — carried out non-Christian rituals.[87] Avendaño was convinced that they would all be killed. Nonetheless — or so he claimed — he stepped into the meeting, took from them "the instruments of their fiesta," and reprimanded them for the "little constancy of their hearts." Always claiming to be successful in bringing the disloyal around to his side, on this occasion, he said, his words made them realize that "we knew the wickedness of their doings." They stopped their celebration, gathered peacefully around the visitors, and stayed with them for the rest of the night. At dawn, "remorseful, perhaps, of their sin," their behavior was as it had been before, and they gave the visitors a guide. Avendaño had again demonstrated his ability to turn the hearts of idolaters.[88]

The actual intentions of the people of Yalain, however, seem to have been to rid themselves of the friars as soon as possible. That morning, after the visitors were led to an orchard about half a league away, a priest called

Chamach Punab' — "Old Man" Punab' (but probably Pana), possibly a relative of IxChan Pana, the wife of Ajaw Kan Ek' — invited them to eat and "ordered that all of the Indian men and women in the vicinity be called to see us." The order, as it turned out, was for the women of the town to prepare food in their homes for the visitors. Once fed, they left on their journey with a crowd of people following along. Almost immediately, however, the people turned back to Yalain, leaving them with one man who accompanied them for only about two blocks further before showing them an "obscure path" that he said would take them in twelve days, walking from dawn until dusk, to Tipuj. They would have to cross a large river, he said, "but he did not tell us how or where." At that point the guide abandoned them. The possibility cannot be discounted that IxChan Pana had secretly encouraged her relatives at Yalain to abandon Avendaño and his companions this way, in the hope that they would die in the forests.[89] Their only food for the journey, claimed Avendaño, was twenty tortillas left over from their most recent meal — a lack of planning that strains credulity.[90]

LOST IN THE FOREST

Avendaño detailed the harrowing events that followed. After five days, subsisting only on the twenty tortillas, he and his companions reached the river. Thinking that they were nearing Tipuj, they followed the river for five more days. This was Río Mopán, the western tributary of the Belize River. They probably followed it into present-day Belize, reaching a point near its confluence with the Macal River, which joins the Mopán to form the Belize River just above the present-day town of San Ignacio del Cayo. At this point, unknown to them, they were only a few kilometers from Tipuj, which lay upstream along the Macal River.[91]

Realizing that they were now lost, they turned to the northwest, hoping to reach the then-deserted town of Chanchanja. They abandoned this plan after three days, supposing that they had missed Chanchanja (which was actually far to their north), and struck out on a new trajectory toward the west, using a needle and a magnet as their compass. Their hope was that they would ultimately meet the camino real, although they estimated the distance at sixty to seventy leagues. They walked for days and days across the vast Petén forests, savannahs, and wetlands, surviving on a sparse diet of palm nuts, sapotes, leaves, and occasionally honey. Eventually the other two priests and one of the Maya carriers, who traveled more quickly than the older Avendaño, struck out on their own to try to find the road.[92]

The remaining party entered hilly country in which they encountered an ancient ruin that might, from the description, have been Tik'al. Still many days from the road, they eventually found a well-traveled, marked path that they followed in a vaguely western direction. Too weak to go on, Avendaño instructed his remaining companions to leave him behind beneath a tree. There he prayed and prepared for death, but the very next day rescue came in the form of ten Mayas from the Yucatán Sierra town of Mani — workers on the camino real. The spot where he had been left was only an hour and a half from Chuntuki, to which they carried him in a hammock. His rescue came on February 19, precisely a month since his departure from Nojpeten.[93]

Avendaño on AjChan

Avendaño claimed that he did not learn of AjChan's December visit to Mérida until after he had returned to Yucatán. I believe, to the contrary, that he knew about AjChan's imminent arrival before he left Mérida. At the very latest, he would have learned about the event shortly after his rescue near Chuntuki. Such misrepresentation aside, we must consider another claim Avendaño made — that AjChan was a false emissary. That is, Ajaw Kan Ek' had not sent AjChan to Mérida, had given him no instructions to offer his submission, and had no prior knowledge of his activities there.

Avendaño had met with AjChan in Mérida in September. He also was fully aware of the message sent to Mérida the previous November via Francisco de Hariza purporting that Ajaw Kan Ek' was ready to receive Ursúa and deliver the Itzas over to Spanish control. When Avendaño read or summarized Ursúa's letter to Ajaw Kan Ek' and other leaders at Nojpeten, he made it clear that Ursúa had written in response to an offer of submission by Ajaw Kan Ek' himself. The audience's response, however, he reported as one of surprise and distress: "[L]ooking around at each other, the king doing so first of all — all of them acted surprised to hear about such a message; rather, with some commotion of their spirits they showed that their hearts were disturbed."[94]

He claimed to be convinced that Ajaw Kan Ek' had not sent the first verbal message that had been attributed to him and that the ruler had **219** known nothing about AjChan's supposed diplomatic mission in Mérida. He cited the "fact" that Ajaw Kan Ek' — despite his having shared personal "secrets" with Avendaño and having treated him with "such familiarity and love" — made no mention of having sent his nephew to Mérida.

He could not have forgotten to do so, Avendaño reasoned, considering the frequency with which they discussed the issues of Christian conversion and friendship with the Spaniards. Finally, and less convincingly, he argued that had Ajaw Kan Ek' sent AjChan to Mérida, the ruler would have kept Avendaño there as a hostage until he learned the outcome of his nephew's reception.[95] I think it likely that Avendaño constructed these rationalizations for the sole purpose of discrediting the outcome of AjChan's mission, in particular the secular clergy's newly assigned role as the future missionaries of the Itzas.

The evidence in support of the personal involvement of Ajaw Kan Ek' in his nephew's mission is too strong to dismiss. Many bureaucrats, military men, and churchmen (Franciscans and seculars alike) in Yucatán later challenged AjChan's legitimacy as an ambassador, their principal objective being to discredit Governor Ursúa for having naively accepted the message.[96] Nonetheless, their evidence against AjChan was only circumstantial, and in the last analysis the objections of Avendaño and others seem to have been little more than sour grapes.

The hostility with which the political enemies of Ajaw Kan Ek' treated Avendaño suggests that these men were fully aware of the ruler's prior overtures to the colonial government and to the Franciscans. Their opposition to Ajaw Kan Ek' had led to a recent attack on the capital by the Kowojs, probably between September and November 1695 (see chapter 13). Avendaño's visit, however, resulted in disclosure to a *public* audience just how deeply Ajaw Kan Ek' had committed himself to peace at any price with the Spaniards. The reaction, as we have seen, was one of outrage and dismay. The impact of Avendaño's disclosures, which further isolated Ajaw Kan Ek' from his internal enemies, was to increase rather than mollify Itza hostility against the Spaniards. As we are about to see, expressions of this hostility surfaced only a short time after Avendaño survived the ordeal of his journey out of Itza territory.

Part Four **PRELUDE TO CONQUEST**

Following AjChan's diplomatic encounter in Mérida at the end of 1695 and Avendaño's foreshortened visit to Nojpeten in mid-January 1696, a series of violent encounters between Itzas and Spaniards caused colonial officials in Yucatán to reconsider their initial assumptions about the authenticity of peace declarations by Ajaw Kan Ek'. This violence was to result in Ursúa's decision to move militarily against Nojpeten. Interim Governor Ursúa was about to be displaced by the returning Governor Soberanis, who would take office in late June,[1] and he had to move swiftly in order to complete his goal of incorporating the Itzas into the Spanish empire. He knew that Soberanis would make every possible effort to impede his plans and even to expel him from the province of Yucatán.

During 1696 and early 1697, evidence mounted that all was not well at Nojpeten. Avendaño, as we saw in the previous chapter, had himself experienced the bitter split between Ajaw Kan Ek' and the rulers of the north, who had declared war against the Itza ruler in alliance with the Kowojs. During the months following the March 1697 storming of Nojpeten, Spanish authorities at the new presidio built upon the ruins of the Itza capital finally began to reconstruct the extent of the political division. This reconstruction, although never synthesized by the conquerors, reinforces the interpretation that Ajaw Kan Ek' had been acting in his own interests by sending his nephew to Mérida. He was trying to stave off internal challenges to his authority by inviting Spanish support for his own cause.

This chapter recounts the Spanish experience with the Itzas during the critical weeks and months following Avendaño's hasty retreat from Nojpeten. The Spaniards' optimism that Ajaw Kan Ek' would lead his people to accept peaceful submission was premature and ill informed. Despite the good news brought by AjChan to Mérida at the end of 1695, efforts to cash in on promises of imminent Itza surrender proved disastrous. Ad-

223

vance parties from Yucatán and Guatemala met violent and aggressive opposition. Ursúa was forced to recalculate how he would bring the recalcitrant Itzas to their knees.

Ursúa Redefines His Strategy

As soon as AjChan and his kinsmen received baptism on December 31, 1695, Governor Ursúa proceeded to redefine yet again the project that had consumed him so completely for the past year. He now issued new orders to his field commander, Alonso García de Paredes, who had by then reached Río San Pedro beyond Tzuktok', eighty leagues past Kawich.[2] These new instructions sealed Ursúa's interpretation of AjChan's official mission to Mérida and his acceptance of baptism; they were to form the basis for Ursúa's defense of virtually every event and policy decision in which he participated over the next few years. Although the text of his actual orders has not been found, Ursúa's decree for their drafting does exist. He ordered that in light of the size and importance of the "lands of the great Itza" and AjChan's recent act of submission on behalf of Ajaw Kan Ek', a dispatch be prepared instructing García to

> set out immediately from the place where he is now and go and travel to the said lands of the great Itza and Muzuls. And . . . he declares that [García de Paredes] is to make known to the said great king Ah Canek and to the particulars who obey him, that they are under his obedience. . . . He is to take bodily and spiritual possession of the said lands of the said great Itza and Muzuls and the vassalage of its inhabitants for our Catholic king and natural lord with the positive actions that he might appropriately take, so that His Majesty might hold the said lands in an orderly and peaceful state, and with the vassalage of its inhabitants.[3]

In case García failed in this mission, Ursúa conceived another plan for demanding the physical surrender of the Itza nation. On New Year's Day, 1696, the day after AjChan had been baptized and Ursúa had drafted his new orders to García, the governor named the Bacalar alcalde, Francisco de Hariza, as military head of a company of thirty soldiers to escort the Itza delegation and a group of secular priests back to Tipuj. AjChan was presumably to travel via Tipuj to Itza territory in the company of the priests and soldiers to see his uncle, Ajaw Kan Ek', at Nojpeten. There Ajaw Kan Ek' would hear that he and his people were now Spanish subjects. Hariza was to recruit the soldiers himself, and Ursúa would pay their eight-peso monthly salary and all associated costs, most of which included food supplies and muleteers.[4] On the eve of Hariza's appointment, Ursúa also asked the secular clergy to supply the missionaries for this journey.[5]

Fray Andrés de Avendaño was already nearing Nojpetén himself, and the governor's messenger was running with the new orders to Captain García at Chuntuki. Ursúa was playing all of his cards, giving little heed to the possibility that any of the three parties — García and his troops, the secular clergy and troops at Tipuj, and the Franciscans under Avendaño — might fail. As we will see, they all failed more miserably than Ursúa could have predicted.

This was risky politics in the highly charged atmosphere of Mérida. Ursúa soon discovered that he had reignited the smoldering relations between the Franciscans and the secular clergy. His order for a division of ecclesiastical labor — Franciscans along the camino real and seculars to Tipuj — appeared at first to be a good solution. The Franciscan provincial, Fray Juan Antonio de Silva, was delighted that Ursúa asked his order to continue supplying the camino real with missionaries, responding that he was prepared to reinforce the seven Franciscans on the road with another six.[6] The secular dean and ecclesiastical cabildo, noting emphatically that Tipuj was in their own jurisdiction and that the first Itza delegation had come to Mérida through that town the previous September, promptly supplied Ursúa with the list of priests who would accompany Hariza back to Tipuj.[7]

The deeper ecclesiastical dispute over the potential Itza missions, however, had already exploded by the beginning of January. Ursúa's decision to send Avendaño and his Franciscan companions to Nojpetén had prompted the secular authorities to demand on December 15 that Provincial Silva cancel this expedition immediately. Silva, not about to be intimidated, replied at length that his order was beholden to no higher local ecclesiastical authority, citing an obscure 1689 royal decree that gave the regular clergy the right to appoint missionaries without the approval of bishops or archbishops.[8]

Silva and the secular clergy exchanged contentious letters during the second week of January. Each side used historical precedents and arcane legal arguments to justify its claim to jurisdictional authority. Each side claimed it alone had the right to the prospective Itza missions, and the seculars continued to insist that any Franciscan appointments required their approval.[9] Ursúa, caught in the middle of an embarrassing and volatile situation, tried to patch over the problem by issuing yet more unrealis-

225

tic instructions to García de Paredes. Upon taking possession of the territory of the Itzas, García was to divide it equally between the secular and
regular clergy. After all, Ursúa reasoned, AjChan had reported that this
territory comprised ten provinces with a capital town and a huge population surrounding the lake; there was enough for everyone. Besides, the
1693 cédulas had ordered Ursúa to divide any reductions and missions
between the seculars and the regulars.[10]

Armed Conflict at Lago Petén Itzá

In mid-January García de Paredes received his new orders from Ursúa at
the headwaters of Río San Pedro (the Nojuk'um), about five leagues south
of Chuntuki. García had only about ninety armed troops and some Maya
carriers and road workers at his camp. They had been temporarily sty-
mied from progressing further until they could finish building a *piragua*, a
longboat with oars, in which troops, horses, and armaments could cross
the river.[11] His men were running away in increasing numbers, fearing for
their lives as they approached the main Itza lake.

García had been encamped at B'atkab' when Avendaño passed through
there on January 6, but he had apparently moved his headquarters to the
terminus of the road when, a few days after Avendaño's January 19 departure from Nojpeten, a contingent of Maya leaders from the lake appeared,
seeking to talk with him. From the stories that he heard after his rescue
near Chuntuki, Avendaño concluded that these were none other than the
principal enemies of Ajaw Kan Ek', the Kowojs and their Itza patron, the
ruler of the north. They came with sixty armed men, and all were decorated with face paint and in full war regalia.[12]

The visitors claimed that Avendaño had sent them to pick up the vestments and other items that he had left packed in a chest at Chuntuki and
to take with them the friar who had been left in charge of them. This
priest, Fray Antonio de San Román, was waiting in Chuntuki for some
word from Avendaño, along with four Maya singers who had been left
behind. Avendaño, who believed that these were the men whom AjKowoj
had sent to kill him, was enraged to learn that García had welcomed them
with open arms, plying them with wine and aguardiente. Even worse, they
bore no message or personal messenger from Avendaño, a sure sign, he
concluded, of their evil intentions. Shortly after the visitors arrived at
Chuntuki they departed, without explanation, leaving behind the chest of
vestments.[13] The Kowoj and Chak'an Itza visitors had clearly been sizing

up the progress of the camino real and the extent of the Spanish military threat. They must have had a lengthy conversation with García de Paredes, who apparently learned from them that Avendaño had written an important "paper" at Nojpeten which the Spaniards should see.[14]

Avendaño's Kejach guides had left Nojpeten shortly after Avendaño fled there by night with Ajaw Kan Ek'. They arrived at the encampment about the same time as the Chak'an Itza and Kowoj visitors, giving García their own version of the outcome of Avendaño's mission. Before their appearance, however, the captain had sent two Kejach messengers to the lake to inquire after the friars. Reaching the lakeshore just after Avendaño left, they learned of the missionaries' precipitous departure.[15] These couriers, especially if they were accompanied by García's troops, could have been the source of the uproar reported at Yalain while Avendaño was there waiting for a guide to take him to Tipuj. The Itzas gave the messengers Avendaño's open letter, written on January 16, and as soon as they returned to the encampment, Fray Juan de San Buenaventura read it aloud to the troops. So impressed was Fray Juan by Avendaño's message of success that he and his companion were now more eager than ever to begin their own mission to Nojpeten.[16]

García de Paredes considered this news along with his new orders and decided — perhaps out of cowardice, a strong sense of survival, or even illness — to send one of his chief officers to deliver the indelicate demand for submission to Ajaw Kan Ek'.[17] He retreated back to Chuntuki while awaiting word of the outcome. His chief officer, the Campechano Captain Pedro de Zubiaur, took with him sixty musket-armed soldiers, including some Sajkab'ch'en Mayas, forty Maya carriers, and two Franciscans — San Buenaventura and a lay brother, probably Tomás de Alcoser. At Chuntuki, García first learned of the ensuing disaster from a Sajkab'ch'en musketeer and six other Mayas who, on February 3, ran breathlessly into his camp with the horrifying news that two days earlier they had escaped a battle in which the rest of Zubiaur's party had been killed. Zubiaur himself dragged into camp the following day with the welcome news that the fleeing Mayas had greatly exaggerated the casualties. The actual news, nonetheless, was grim. Reconstructed from several sources, what happened was something like this:[18]

On February 2, two armed Itza men, who said they were merely hunt- **227**
ers coming in peace, had approached the troops and missionaries along the road, striking up a conversation with them. Some days earlier, they said, the Itzas had had a confrontation with some people from Guatemala during which ten Spaniards and three Itzas had been killed.[19] The "hunt-

ers," who were clearly spies, told the Spaniards that they were now about eight leagues from the first Itza settlement, to which the party then proceeded. Either these men or other messengers brought Avendaño's "open letter" to Zubiaur along their route, which reassured them that the friar was safe and well.[20]

Once at the lakeshore they found at the port of Ch'ich' five or six canoes. The town had been abandoned by B'atab' Tut, who had been forewarned of the size of the approaching army and the extent of its heavy artillery. A large number of canoes—as many as three hundred by Zubiaur's estimate—soon approached the troops, carrying as many as two thousand men. San Buenaventura talked with some of the first to arrive, who assured him that they came in peace, that they were friends of the Spaniards, and that they would protect them from harm. He in turn told them that he was there to deliver an "message of peace to their king." While these Itzas mixed among the visitors without incident, more canoes—now filled with armed men—pulled up to the shore. Their passengers alighted and began to load the troops' supplies into the canoes, informing them that they intended to take one man in each canoe to Nojpeten to see their ruler. The visitors were terrified. Nonetheless, San Buenaventura asked to be put into a canoe with his lay brother companion and two of the soldiers. As many as a dozen more men were then forced bodily into the canoes, including one don Agustín de Sosa and the cacique of Sajkab'ch'en. The Itzas grabbed two carriers from Tek'ax and beat them to death with cudgels; their bodies were loaded onto another canoe. They beheaded Sosa on the spot.

As the troops opened fire, the canoes quickly departed, paddling toward Nojpeten. As they left the shore Fray Juan called out to Zubiaur, asking him to wait for them and saying, according to one account, "that he [Fray Juan] would send lashed canoes [for the horses] so that they could travel to the Petén." The witness went on to say that "having gone in the said canoe about the distance of a pistol shot, the said two religious wished to return, and they saw that the said Indians did not wish it. And [when] the said declarant called to the said religious that they should come back to shore, [Fray Juan] responded that the Indians did not wish it, that they did not know what they would do with them."[21] Zubiaur later intimated that San Buenaventura had been foolish in taking Avendaño's open letter as a green light for accepting the Itzas' invitation to get into the canoes. He commented that the friar had paid no attention to its early date—January 16—or to "the context in which it had been written."[22]

Zubiaur evidently remained cool even as he saw the friars, the captured men, and the dead bodies of the Tek'ax carriers and the Spaniard being paddled toward Nojpeten. He ordered his remaining men to regroup on an open savannah a short distance from the shore—the area behind and immediately to the west of the beach at Ch'ich'. A large number of Itzas— two thousand of them, Zubiaur recalled when he arrived back at camp— followed them there and attempted to disarm them and force them, too, into the canoes. During the commotion the Itzas captured another soldier, Francisco de Campos, who tried to escape by firing his musket. Campos was beheaded by his captors on the spot with a machete.[23] Seeing what was happening, the friars and the captives, now being paddled across the lake, called out for help. By now those on shore could do nothing, for they were under attack by Itza bowmen disembarking from canoes that had been hidden in the mangroves along the beach. The archers appeared to Zubiaur to number ten thousand. At some point during the confusion Zubiaur sounded the first order to fire; thirty or forty Itzas were killed in the ensuing mayhem.

Realizing the desperate situation of his outnumbered troops, Zubiaur sounded the retreat, leaving the kidnapped victims to their fate. He returned with his party to the base camp two days away without waiting to learn what happened to them. The seven Mayas who had first broken the news to García had escaped during the onset of the battle. As they ran away they heard the drum and bugle sound, but not a single gunshot. All of their companions, they assumed, were being massacred.

The road openers now worked overtime to reach the lake. Less than a month after this encounter another party arrived at the lakeshore armed with artillery pieces in addition to muskets. Their reported purpose was to pilfer maize from the milpas adjacent to the lake, but the racket they made as they cleared the last stretch of road in order to move the heavy weapons alerted the population well in advance. Not surprisingly, as they neared the lakeshore they saw "a great many canoes of Indians." The panicky troops, seeing that the Itzas "gave no signs of peace," fired their artillery pieces and some muskets. None of those in the canoes was reported killed, but four were captured. The rest retreated for some distance and raised a white flag. Some of them shortly returned and approached the Spaniards, who presented them with knives and machetes. The Spaniards asked about San Buenaventura and the others who had been taken. Pretending at first that they knew nothing, the Itzas "finally answered that they had been thrown out in the direction of . . . Tipu."[24]

Ursúa's immediate response was to recruit one hundred new Spanish and pardo troops to be led by Bartolomé de la Garma. He had authorized these troops in December, but now he realized that García needed reinforcements at once. Only about thirty of these men, who left Campeche in March, reached their destination; the other seventy mutinied near Tzuktok', returning to their homes in Campeche.[25] The instigator of the mutiny was later said to have been one of the officers, Alférez Juan de Baizabal.[26] He and the other "principal contrivers" were punished — by means left unspecified — under Ursúa's orders.[27] The mutiny was the result of fear generated by well-publicized, increasingly inflated reports of the ferocity and numbers of the Itzas whom they would ultimately have to face.

Ursúa wrote later that the two Franciscans and their dozen Spanish and Maya companions taken to Nojpeten had all been killed.[28] AjChan, in later testimony, also confirmed the murder of the Franciscans.[29] Although these assertions hardly constituted proof, the friars never appeared again, and their bones were reportedly discovered following the conquest. These two men — the only ones in García de Paredes's party who actually delivered a message of peace — seem to have been the first Franciscans martyred at Nojpeten since Delgado's violent death there in 1623, seventy-three years earlier.

AjChan Deserts the Spaniards

As these events unfolded, AjChan and his Itza companions set off once again for Tipuj in mid-January 1696, following their staged reception and baptisms in Mérida. Their initial "escort" consisted of only twelve Spanish soldiers commanded by the Bacalar alcalde, Francisco de Hariza,[30] and ten secular priests under the leadership of Bachiller Gaspar de Güemes.[31] With muleteers and supplies requisitioned from various Yucatecan towns and villages, they retraced the footsteps of the original "embassy," traveling via Chamuxub', Chunjujub', and the old location of Salamanca de Bacalar and arriving at Tipuj sometime later that month.[32] Now Hariza and the priests learned of Avendaño's forced departure from Nojpeten — but they stuck by their intention to accompany AjChan to present Ajaw Kan Ek' with Ursúa's demand for peaceful submission. (The secular priests, despite their prior complaints about the Franciscans' missions to Nojpeten, gave scarcely a moment's thought to visiting Ajaw Kan Ek' themselves.) At some point, perhaps before he arrived at Tipuj, Hariza sent a Bacalareño, Pedro de Mantilla, to deliver Ursúa's letter and some gifts to Ajaw Kan Ek' at Nojpeten.[33]

These plans ground to a halt when, a few days after their arrival,

AjChan (and, we may suppose, the kinsmen who had come with him) ran away from Tipuj. Hariza and the priests decided that it was now too dangerous to make the journey to Nojpeten on their own, and Güemes concluded that the priests should limit their missionizing activities to the Tipuj area. In less than two months Güemes and seven of his companions returned to Yucatán, claiming illness and leaving only two behind.[34]

AjChan was not seen again until March 10, 1697, when he appeared at Ursúa's camp on the western end of Lago Petén Itzá, only three days before the Spaniards stormed Nojpeten. There Ursúa questioned him about the circumstances of his sudden departure from Tipuj. His "testimony," the circumstances of which are discussed in chapter 11, was paraphrased and possibly corrupted by Ursúa, but some of his statements contain compelling and highly plausible details about the situation in which he had found himself at Tipuj. Ursúa's reconstruction of his testimony (which I quote showing Ursúa's voice in italics) reported that two weeks after AjChan arrived there, the cacique of Tipuj, named Sima, said to him, "What are you doing here? Why don't you go, [because] they will cut off your head?"

> *Asked what cause or motive the cacique Sima had to say that they would cut off his head and to tell him that he should run away or go, he said that:*
> The cacique Sima told him that on the peten they had caused injury and death to the Spaniards, and that [he] answered him that he had not been there and that he was not guilty.
> *Asked how it was that, not being guilty, and having received such news, he fled, he said that:*
> The same cacique frightened him and was the cause of his running away.[35]

Sima knew full well that as soon as Hariza learned of the Itzas' murders and kidnappings at Ch'ich' on February 2, he would accuse AjChan of having falsified or misrepresented himself in Mérida. AjChan did the only thing he could do under the circumstances—escape from Tipuj as quickly as possible. He went on to report that after leaving Tipuj he went home to Yalain, where he learned that other leaders had joined in armed opposition to Ajaw Kan Ek'. At that point he went into temporary hiding, continuing to fear, with good reason, that enemies of Ajaw Kan Ek' would kill him. 231

Although AjChan's desertion stimulated a flurry of speculation and accusations in Yucatecan circles that he was a false ambassador, all available evidence suggests that this was not the case. AjChan was a man caught between historical events over which he had, temporarily at least, lost control. We shall meet him again in subsequent chapters when, after a brief resurfacing of his interest in the Spanish cause, he finally deserted the conquerors in earnest, becoming a leader of independent resistance forces in southern Belize.

Guatemalans Return to Lago Petén Itzá

The only secure result of the ambitious Guatemalan entradas of early 1695 had been the "reduction" of Sakb'ajlan, which President Jacinto de Barrios Leal and his Dominican friars renamed Nuestra Señora de los Dolores del Lacandón. There, before he departed, Barrios built a fortification, armed it with a squadron of thirty troops, and left the Dominican Fray Diego de Rivas and his assistants in charge of converting the Chol Lakandons.[36] During the months that followed, the Dominicans managed to baptize several hundred persons and to make contact with other, neighboring Chol Lakandons.

Barrios himself tried to come to terms with Juan Díaz de Velasco's much-criticized retreat from his first armed encounters with the Itzas in April. The Guatemalans, apparently unaware of Ursúa's personal contacts with Ajaw Kan Ek', began during the second half of 1695 to plan a second entrada to Lago Petén Itzá. Armed with support from the viceroy of New Spain and a new royal decree congratulating him for his contributions to the Yucatán-Guatemala road project, Barrios wrote to Ursúa on October 26, 1695, that he now intended to recruit an additional 250 men to take up the unfinished tasks of the previous entradas. One hundred of these would travel via Huehuetenango in order to continue reductions around Dolores del Lacandón. The rest would pursue a route through Verapaz and Mopan territory with the goal of proceeding toward Lago Petén Itzá and reducing "the numerous nations that are on the said lake." The departure of the new forces was scheduled for early January 1696. Barrios — who, unlike Ursúa, always sought interprovincial cooperation — encouraged the Yucatecan governor to set out at the same time and asked Ursúa to send him three or four persons who could serve as interpreters in Mopan and Itza territory.[37]

Ursúa, however, wanted the Itzas for himself. The slow mails between the two provinces prevented either party from knowing exactly what the other was doing, but both Ursúa and the Guatemalans were aware of each other's general strategy and moved hastily to accomplish the ultimate task of Itza "pacification." The ailing and exhausted President Barrios died on November 12. Oidor Joseph de Escals, who had governed Guatemala during Barrios's first expedition, assumed acting control of the government. The Guatemalan audiencia named Oidor Bartolomé de Amésqueta to lead the Verapaz entrada and Jacobo de Alzayaga, a regidor of Santiago de Guatemala, to serve as military chief of the troops destined for Dolores.[38] Amésqueta, a level-headed, experienced, and intelligent civil servant, was to join Captain Díaz de Velasco at Mopan, where the core of the troops that had retreated from Lago Petén Itzá had been camped for nearly a year.[39]

Despite the hope for dry weather, Amésqueta and his troops and carriers suffered torrential rains on their thirteen-day journey from Cahabón through Chol territory to the town of Mopan, where they arrived on February 25, 1696, only three weeks after the Yucatecan debacle on the shores of Lago Petén Itzá.[40] No news had yet reached them of these events. Short of supplies owing to difficulties in recruiting Verapaz native carriers for the dangerous mission, Amésqueta found himself able to proceed only slowly. Twenty-five of his soldiers fell ill at their base camp at Mopan. He realized that it would be some time before he could lead his troops on to the lake.

Perhaps trying to recover his reputation after his embarrassing retreat the previous April, Captain Díaz thereupon volunteered, along with the Dominican Fray Cristóbal de Prada, to take twenty-five troops ahead to the lake while Amésqueta waited for the supply train. Uncertain of the wisdom of this option, Amésqueta sought advice in a general meeting. Finally he agreed that Díaz, Fray Cristóbal, and another Dominican, Fray Jacinto de Vargas, should proceed to Lago Petén Itzá. Their party departed Mopan on Ash Wednesday, March 7. On March 12, having left some ailing soldiers with supplies at the Savannah of San Pedro Mártir, they reached an advance road-clearing party of soldiers and native workers at Río Chakal. From there the combined remaining healthy forces, which included forty-nine soldiers and about thirty-four carriers and archers from Salamá, Verapaz, struck out for the Itza lake. The military men on this entrada were to serve merely as "escorts" for the Dominicans.

In addition to the missionaries, soldiers, and Verapaz Mayas, Díaz took with him the Itza noble AjK'ixaw, who had been captured the previous April and held prisoner in Santiago de Guatemala during the intervening months. AjK'ixaw would be useful as an interpreter and advance scout as they neared the lake. In addition, he was trusted to go on ahead to the lake as an "ambassador" once they had passed six leagues beyond Chakal to a

233

place called IxB'ol, near the lakeshore. He had been well instructed by the Dominicans "in all that he should say to his companions in order to pacify them and to bring them to our holy Catholic faith."[41] Also in their company was a Chol interpreter who spoke Mopan and could therefore communicate with the Itzas. Fray Cristóbal spoke Chol as a result of years of missionary work and understood a little Mopan as well.

In receipt of additional supplies back at Mopan, Amésqueta decided to follow after Díaz's party in the company of Fray Agustín Cano and eight or ten soldiers. He left on March 10, hoping to hear news on the way of AjK'ixaw's advance contact at Nojpeten, but when he arrived at Chakal a week later no message had been received. On the twentieth he set off to find Díaz's party himself, in company with thirty-six men.[42] He took only four days' supplies, for he was certain that he would find Díaz and his men only six leagues along the road, waiting for AjK'ixaw's report. During two days' travel, however, they covered more than eight leagues before finally meeting up with some of the Salamá carriers, whom Díaz had left behind. The heat was intense, and they slept the second night at the first Itza milpa with no water other than what they carried.[43]

On the third day of slow travel, passing signs of the missing party, they finally reached Lago Petén Itzá, "discovering in a short time three settlements, one on a large, very steep island, shaped almost like a sugar loaf, completely covered with houses, and on the highest point a very large one." Next to this large building were one or two smaller ones and a "promontory like a tower."[44] They saw a continuous settlement of houses on the shore opposite the island and, in front of their stopping place, a settlement of ten to twelve houses on a small island, behind which they could see hills on the mainland. From where they first stood — on the shore of Ensenada San Pedro opposite present-day Islote Grande — the main island was about two leagues away, and the distance to the opposite shore was about half a league. Further west they could see the broad opening into the main lake, about half a league from the island.[45]

Searching along the south shore of the lake, they again found signs that Díaz and his companions had been there before them. They walked out on the points of land that jutted into the lake, separating the inlets that scored the shoreline; through the tall grass they spied about thirty small canoes, ten of which followed them as they attempted to walk the shoreline toward the bay opposite the island.[46] As one of these drew near, Amésqueta called out to its occupants, "Quijan, Quijan, Padres, Capitán, Castilaguimic," the first terms K'ixaw's name and the last term his best approximation of the Itza word for Spaniards. The Itzas shouted something in reply, which he could not understand, and then took off toward the main island, calling before them as they paddled hurriedly on their way. Amésqueta, presuming that they were going to notify Díaz and the others of his arrival, led his men along the shore through thick vegetation and further signs of the lost Spaniards: the tracks of mules and various discarded items such as a leather bottle, mats and backcloths for the mules, saddlecloths, and bags of maize.[47] They stopped at another point of land, where they saw numerous canoes coming their way across the lake and other Itzas approaching them by land; these, however, came no closer than the opposite shore.

From here Amésqueta wrote to Díaz de Velasco informing him of his arrival and promising reinforcements. Most of all he wanted to know what had happened to them, what they had experienced, and whether they had seen the "ahau or cacique who they affirm knows how to read and write the Castilian language, because Kixan [AjK'ixaw] had said that on the island there was a redheaded man, resembling Sergeant Rodolfo Pérez, who was a Castelaguinic or Castilian who had come from other lands, who had come to the island, who had been married on it. He had two sons and a book that he read, resembling the books of hours or days that the Fathers carry. I hoped that this person was a Spaniard or a foreigner and that the cacique and he would read the letter." No other reports of the redheaded Spaniard or his breviary have been discovered — or that anyone at Nojpeten could speak and read Spanish.[48]

One of the soldiers tossed the note with a piece of candy to the nearby onlookers, one of whom who ran off with signs indicating that he would deliver the message. Several Itzas then approached the Spaniards. One of these had facial features like those of AjK'ixaw and, like him, was tattooed on his face, chest, and thighs.[49] This man, probably a person of high status, presented Amésqueta with two very large tortillas and three very small pieces of tortilla. In return, Amésqueta gave him some beef jerky, hardtack, and a knife. Struck by this man's friendliness, Amésqueta described their encounter in uncharacteristic detail: "He appeared to be very affectionate to me, embracing me and kissing me on the neck and repeating many times, 'utspusical,' which, as the Lacandones taught us, is the same as 'good heart.'[50] With signs he asked for a machete, but I did not want to give it to him. He indicated that he wanted to see a wide sword that Felipe Díaz had, and upon seeing it halfway unsheathed exhibited anger. He did the same when I pointed out some [musket] balls. He indicated that he was familiar with the musket. He did not wonder at the horses, the mules, the bugles, or the chests."[51]

Some of the soldiers presented other Itzas with small gifts, which were

235

reciprocated by a man who passed out posole from a calabash container. The Itzas, pointing to the island and saying, "Ajaw, Ajaw," insisted that they wanted the Spaniards to go with them in canoes, most of which would carry only three or four persons.[52] Placing their hands on their chests, they again communicated that "their heart was good."[53] With further signs they tempted the visitors with promises of food — even turkeys — once they arrived on the island.[54] The canoes, however, were at some distance from the inlet where they were standing, and the Itzas showed them a path they would have to take to the spot where they would embark.

This group soon left, apparently to recruit help. Four of them soon approached from the distance, insisting upon their arrival that they clear the path to the port ahead, using the Spaniards' machetes, so that they could take them in their canoes to the island. Refusing to loan them the machetes in fear that they would run off with them, the Spaniards repeated the words that described their lost companions, adding this time for good measure the term "Cristianos." Some of the Itzas pointed to the island, while others seemed not to understand the questions. When the officer Ramón Díaz asked one of the Itzas where the captain and priests were, the Itza became enraged and refused to respond.

Amésqueta directed his questions to the man who had earlier fed and embraced him, who in response said, "Kuman, kuman." At the time Amésqueta did not understand these words, but Fray Agustín Cano later told him that AjK'ixaw had said the previous year that any Spaniards who went to the island would be killed in the *kuman*. Cano did not know the meaning of the word, but after consulting with other priests who knew Maya languages, he concluded that it meant "palisade of small stakes."[55] Amésqueta and Cano did not know that many years earlier, in 1623, Bernardino Ek' and his Yucatee Maya companions were imprisoned in a similar stockade at Nojpeten in preparation for their murder.

Officer Tomás de Acevedo recalled later that one of this group appeared different from the others, "because he had curls and a sleeveless cotton shirt without designs like those of the others, and his ears were not pierced like those of the others; he was only in rags.[56] One of the apparently destitute man's companions was a Mopan who had accompanied Díaz de Velasco's party as a "soldier" the year before. Acevedo seemed to think that both men were Mopans and that they were trying to communicate to the Spaniards that the Itzas were up to no good.

By this time the Itzas had brought their canoes to the beach where the visitors stood, but Amésqueta, suspicious of their intentions, ordered his men not to enter them. Writing later about the situation, he recalled a passage in Remesal's history of Guatemala describing what the Lakandons had done, "bringing only their small canoes, hiding the large ones when they intended to kill the Spaniards who were embarked in them." He also remembered learning from Cano that AjK'ixaw had told him the Itzas had canoes capable of transporting forty men—but none of these were in view now. He even recalled reading somewhere that the Jicaques had killed some Franciscans who got into their canoes. His vision of the fate of Díaz's hapless party began to come into focus.[57]

AjK'ixaw, he surmised in his later assessment, had turned traitor, notifying the Itzas that now was the chance to capture the visiting Guatemalans. All the Spaniards must have embarked in the Itzas' small canoes, thinking they were being taken to the island. Perhaps in the middle of the lake the Itzas had overturned the canoes, forcing the thrashing victims into their large canoes and killing any who tried to escape. In another scenario, Amésqueta imagined they were all taken safely to the island but were there attacked and killed while ascending a steep street from the shore. Or they might have been forced into the stockade, unable to escape, with armed Itzas all around them. Even at the time it had occurred to him and some of the others that this island might not be "the peten" but a place called Petenja,[58] and that the main island was some distance beyond. In his wildest hopes he imagined that the lost party had battled the Itzas and retreated along the lakeshore to Tipuj, which he supposed was not far away. In any event, he was all but certain that his lost men were neither free nor alive on the island, "because being well received on the island and not to come to see us or to travel to us appeared totally impossible." His men, he wrote, had played their bugles and drums continuously, but there was no indication that their companions heard them.[59]

Amésqueta had written his letter at eleven o'clock in the morning and sent another at one o'clock. He waited until six in the evening but received no reply. While he waited he came to realize that he and his men were incapable of taking any action. Without canoes or rafts—and nothing with which to make them—they could not venture on their own to the island. They had no interpreters, and their food supplies would soon run out. The Itzas could set fire to the area where they were encamped. There was no choice but to leave without confirming the fate of Juan Díaz de **237** Velasco, the Dominicans Fray Cristóbal de Prada and Fray Jacinto de Vargas, and the others, even though "to return without knowing about those for whom I searched caused me no little anguish."

He left the lakeshore as nightfall approached, moving his party to a small hill about half a league away. They waited there until about two o'clock in the morning, aware that they were being closely watched but still hoping for a reply to Amésqueta's letter. At two in the morning, taking advantage of the cool night air, they began their retreat with the light of the moon and five torches. On the afternoon of Sunday, March 25, they arrived back at Chakal. Over the next six days Amésqueta prepared a long, detailed report to José de Escals concerning the disturbing events of the past two weeks. Convinced that he neither could nor should attempt an armed attack against the Itzas in order to rescue the lost party, he emphasized that he "came not with the authority to wage war, to invade, or to undertake [anything] against the Indians—but only to serve as an escort, with my men, for the religious. And if those, or my men, or the Christian Indians, or whoever, had actually been invaded by the pagans, I would certainly have used the arms entrusted in me in order to stop them and free [those who were attacked], if I could, from the difficulty and actual danger in which they found themselves."[60]

He was still reasonably convinced, however, that Díaz and the others had already been killed, and that any rescue mission would result only in disastrous warfare. Citing the ninth law of the Recopilación de las Indias, he rationalized his position legally by citing the requirement that any formal, open war against native populations must be preceded by notification to the Council of the Indies. He also cited the same impediments against the success of such an attack that had caused him to retreat from the lake in the first place: the difficulty, even futility, of trying to construct canoes and rafts to cross to the island; the lack of interpreters; the insufficient number of his troops; the lack of sufficient firearms; the danger of counterattacks by the Itzas on the island; and the problems caused by the carriers from Verapaz who ran away every time they approached Itza territory. The situation that he described appeared hopeless; in his view any imminent invasion of Nojpeten would be foolhardy and impractical.

Fray Agustín Cano, who remained with Amésqueta at Chakal—now christened San Joaquín de Chakal—agreed that there was no point in returning to the Itzas' lake. Equally convinced that "we have strong indications that they killed all of them with some great treachery and perfidy as is their custom and as those of this Ah Itza nation have done on other occasions," he commented dryly that "these Indians are not of a disposition to hear the word of the holy gospel." Besides, their only Itza interpreters were presumed dead, and the soldiers at Chakal were sick and incapable of mounting another entrada. The only immediate course of action, Cano concluded, was to retreat to their base camp at San Pedro Mártir.[61]

238

At Chakal the troops were nervous, convinced that they were surrounded by unseen Itza spies. Soldiers in charge of a supply train traveling from San Pedro Mártir to Chakal heard voices and whistles at four o'clock in the morning on April 6. Although believing these to be "Indians," they could see no one in the dark forest.[62] On the nights of the sixth and seventh the sentinels at Chakal heard people in the forest around their camp. They became increasingly anxious and, worried about an Itza ambush, sat awake all the night of the seventh with loaded muskets in their hands. Toward daybreak the sounds in the bush intensified, and in the distance they heard them "play instruments like trumpets." The sentinels began to shoot their muskets in order to frighten off the potential attackers. Soon the soldiers were arranged in military formation, and the musicians started beating their drums and playing their bugles. No attack was forthcoming, but Amésqueta realized that the dense jungles around Chakal—"serving them like a wall"—provided a military advantage for the guerrilla techniques of the enemy archers who, unlike the awkward, heavily clothed Spaniards, slithered through the forest "like snakes," nude except for their loincloths.[63] The muskets were all but useless except for long-distance shooting, in contrast to the efficient arrows of the Itzas.[64]

Amésqueta was particularly worried about reports that his supply camp at San Pedro Mártir, with its palm-thatched storehouses, might be attacked and burned. He did not trust the Mopans at San Pedro, or those who lived in the surrounding hamlets, because they "are like subjects or dependents of the Petenes and Ah Itzas, all of whom can (if God allows it) rob us of the relief of our provisions with great ease or inundate us with their multitude (and this is what they say)." To make matters worse, heavy rains were turning San Pedro Mártir into a swamp. His mules at Chakal were dying from rattlesnake bites, and most of his soldiers were sick.[65]

As if these trials were not enough to justify abandoning Chakal, Amésqueta cited still more reasons for giving up any effort to stay there and try to mount a serious rescue mission. He was under the impression that Ursúa had decided not to attempt another entrada from Yucatán toward Lago Petén Itzá in January. The last letter that he had seen from Ursúa had been written in December, before AjChan visited Mérida. Unaware of subsequent events, he believed that no one else had recently visited Lago Petén Itzá. Furthermore, confused sign-language communications with Itzas at the lakeside led him and his soldiers to believe that the lake had two major islands, one occupied by "Petenes" and the other, reputed to be much larger, by "Ah Itzaes." The latter was said to be called "Nojpeten," or "large island." Although we know that this intelligence was incorrect—

239

there was only one large island — the prospect of an even larger armed Itza island further fueled the fears of the men camped at Chakal.

On April 9 Amésqueta and his men abandoned Chakal. During their retreat they were struck by a severe hurricane, and heavy rainstorms pelted the pathetic train of sick and dying men all the way to San Pedro Mártir. They arrived at the supply camp on Friday the thirteenth.[66] There, on a savannah only nine leagues north of Mopan, Amésqueta would maintain his military base for the next several months.

His first actions at this new camp were to send out two small squadrons from Mopan, accompanied by friars, to explore the territory and to search out and bring back Mopans from the surrounding countryside. He hoped to use some of these as future interpreters. Finding that all the Mopans had fled deep into the bush in fear of the troops, he succeeded in rounding up no one. Amésqueta also sent out don Juan de Avendaño to find the Christian cacique of the Chol town of Chok Ajaw and a baptized man from Xokmo named Juan Kej, in the hope that they would take a letter to the "ahau of the Petenes." He hoped this way to learn what had happened to the lost men. The cacique, unimpressed with the gifts offered him, said that Juan Kej had run away.[67] Kej was eventually induced to go to Mopan, but he refused to carry out the mission to Nojpeten.[68]

Over the next few weeks Amésqueta continued his modest efforts to find a local interpreter who could be persuaded to carry a letter to the Itzas — he was still convinced that someone among them could read Spanish — or to accompany a squadron sent out to capture some "Peten or Ah Itza" from whom they could learn the fate of the lost party. He understood that the local Chols all spoke Mopan, but his efforts to bring in the "ahaus" of towns called Chok Ajaw, AjMay, Manche, and IxB'ol ended in failure. Now — still worried about being surrounded by hidden, uncooperative natives and despairing of ever learning the fate of his lost men — he wondered whether his troops' slow progress in constructing a fortification at San Pedro Mártir was worth the trouble.[69]

During his first week at San Pedro, Amésqueta finally learned from the new Guatemalan president, Gabriel Sánchez de Berrospe, of AjChan's December visit to Mérida and his offering the Itza ruler's crown to Ursúa.[70] This new information left Amésqueta more muddled than ever about the tragic events. Isolated at San Pedro Mártir, he attempted, without much success, to reconstruct the contradictory information now at his disposal. He supposed that the dramatic gesture of conciliation by Ajaw Kan Ek' was due to fear of the Spaniards and the realization that warfare with them would be futile, or that God had inspired him to accept a peaceful resolution.

But then why would Ajaw Kan Ek' have murdered the Guatemalans, when he must have realized that they were Christians just like "those of Campeche"? His answer to this self-imposed question, while unsatisfactory, revealed Amésqueta's inquiring intellect at work:

> Even though we concede that it is not known that all are vassals of one king, what is known very well are the many ladinos and allies that they have, especially the Spaniard or foreigner who is among them, who Kixan said resembled Rodolfo Pérez. This is added to what Kixan knew very well: that many of our people entered through Lacandon territory. And it is also clear to us that [Ajaw Kan Ek'] presumed that those whom I took with me were many more. From which the resulting difficulty can be inferred: that on one side being conquered, and on the other such a force coming against him, they ventured on such a great atrocity as to kill or capture all of our men, without anyone escaping.[71]

Amésqueta thus reasoned that Ajaw Kan Ek' might have been only one of several rulers around Lago Petén Itzá and that someone among his advisers and allies was a Spanish speaker who had provided good intelligence during the last months of increasing Spanish activities on the Itzas' borders. The only reason Ajaw Kan Ek' chose violence against the Guatemalans was his fear of violent attack from the south. Amésqueta was still puzzled about why the Yucatecans had not followed up on AjChan's message of submission by marching directly to the lake to demand the ruler's fulfillment of these terms. Had he known that they had in fact done so only a few weeks before the Díaz de Velasco tragedy, and that the results very nearly mirrored those experienced by the Guatemalans, his confusion would have been even deeper.

By repeating the report of the redhead at Nojpeten, Amésqueta revealed his continuing belief that some European had to be assisting Ajaw Kan Ek' in developing his defense strategy. A well-read man, Amésqueta must have been thinking of the parallel story of Gonzalo Guerrero, the Spaniard shipwrecked near Cozumel about 1511. At first held prisoner, he later adopted Maya culture wholeheartedly, taking a Maya wife with whom he had children and adopting Maya dress and body decoration. Guerrero was famous for the purported "fact"—the evidence was only circumstantial—that he ultimately became a *nakom*, or military chief, to the cacique of Chetumal. It was Guerrero's knowledge of Spanish military tactics, contemporaneous observers claimed, that enabled Chetumal to repel Francisco de Montejo's first attempt to conquer that town.[72]

The mysterious redhead, too, was said to be married to a Maya woman with whom he had children. He was also a close adviser to Ajaw Kan Ek', whom he may have taught the Spanish language. He carried about something resembling a priest's breviary — but who knows what this little book might have contained. The implication, however, was clear to Amésqueta: Ajaw Kan Ek' had direct advice from a traitorous Spaniard or some other enemy European, and this made him a much more dangerous and unpredictable enemy than he would have been if he were a simple pagan lord awaiting his first encounter with the Christian Spanish Crown. The myth of the redhead added depth and mystery to an already puzzling situation. But most of all it provided meaning and sense to what appeared to be a senseless, meaningless tragedy.

Both Amésqueta and Fray Agustín Cano found themselves helpless to accomplish anything at their disease-ridden, rat-infested camp at San Pedro Mártir. Surrounded by uncooperative Mopans and Chols, and unable to find interpreters willing to risk their lives by visiting Ajaw Kan Ek' directly, they saw no point in remaining there and continuing to build a fort.[73] Cano himself recommended that the Chols be relocated en masse to Belén in Alta Verapaz, near Rabinal, so difficult was it to administer missions in the area.[74] This unfortunate recommendation was accepted wholeheartedly by Sánchez de Berrospe, who by May 1696 had ordered that the presidio at San Pedro Mártir be abandoned.[75]

Amésqueta did dismantle the presidio, and at about the same time the president ordered the withdrawal of the Dominican missions among the Chols and their resettlement to Verapaz. The most vocal of Sánchez's opponents was the oidor José de Escals, who on June 13, 1697, registered his outrage in a letter to the Crown. The removal of the Chols, he claimed, was

> one of the most horrifying and abominable atrocities that has been heard of, inasmuch as he made many people enter the forests with lassos, and upon discovering any Indian they lassoed him, and thus tied up they took them away, dragging them, but due to the great horror and fear that they caused they succeeded in performing this cruelty on only two hundred Indians, because the others, intimidated, hid themselves in the innumerable, most concealed caves. They moved from one nation to another until reaching Tipu, a pagan nation adjoining Bacalar of Campeche, and they left all of

the lands of the Chols deserted. Most of the few that they took away died, and among those who experienced this wretched fortune was Domingo Cante, the principal cacique of the Chols, whom in every entrada we had regaled with gifts, dealt with kindly, and treated with great affection, because with his reduction the major goal — that of attracting the others — had been achieved, and a town had already been formed where he held watch, and by this means we would have succeeded in settling all of the Chols in towns.[76]

When this reduction began is not known, but it must have been during the first of the dry season in late 1696. Amésqueta himself later condemned the cruelty of the Chol removal to Belén in harsh terms.[77]

While Amésqueta was beginning his trip into Petén in February, the Guatemalans who had proceeded to Dolores del Lacandón were busy resettling and baptizing the Chol Lakandon population in that area. Quickly meeting with success, Captain Jacobo de Alzayaga and the two vigorous Mercederian priests who had accompanied him — Fray Diego de Rivas and Fray Antonio Margil — decided to try to reach the Itzas' lake on their own. They departed for the Río Pasión on March 3 in five large canoes with an escort of 150 heavily armed soldiers and an unknown number of native guides. By the seventeenth they had paddled some ninety leagues and believed that they were nearing Itza territory.[78] They ultimately reached as far as the savannah to the southeast of Lago Petén Itzá but, for unknown reasons, decided to turn back.[79] Had they actually followed Díaz's footsteps, they too would probably have perished.

Ursúa Inherits the Conquest

President Sánchez de Berrospe had received Amésqueta's report on the Díaz de Velasco disaster upon his arrival in the capital to assume office. He quickly called a war council at which a joint decision was reached that Amésqueta should remain at the Mopan presidio with his troops until the onset of the rainy season. Sánchez reported all of this to Ursúa, requesting details of the route he planned to follow from Yucatán and his specific strategies. Although he did so in the context of coordinating the Guatemalans' plans with those of the Yucatecans, he asked Ursúa to consider whether it might be best for the Guatemalans to suspend their military efforts altogether.[80] Without waiting for a reply, Sánchez almost immediately issued an order for the abandonment of the San Pedro Mártir

243

presidio, and with this retreat he closed the first chapter of Guatemala's participation in the conquest.

Ursúa now had a clear mandate to complete the Itza "pacification" single-handedly. He quickly responded to an earlier request by the now-deceased President Barrios for interpreters, sending three Franciscans directly to Guatemala. These friars had their own ideas about their mission and notified Sánchez that they wished to go immediately to Itza territory to search for the lost Guatemalan party. Their leader, Fray Domingo López, argued that he and his companions knew the Itzas' language and way of life well, having lived in the forests for extended periods. Sánchez, perhaps responding to sudden new Dominican or Mercederian interests in the Itza conversions, refused to grant the Franciscans license for the undertaking, and they returned "with great sorrow" to Yucatán.[81]

Ursúa and his second-in-command, García de Paredes, may have postponed revealing the news of the presumed Guatemalan massacre to their chief officers on the camino real. In depositions given by several officers on August 26, 1696, four months after the event, neither the questions framed by Ursúa nor the officers' responses provide any hint that the latter were aware of the Guatemalans' reports. One officer, Captain Pedro de Zubiaur Isasi, did know of a conflict between the Guatemalans and the Itzas, but he framed it only in the context of the road from Guatemala to Lago Petén Itzá, which Ursúa claimed had been completed. He confirmed that he knew that the southern portion of the road had been completed, "because some of the Indians from the lake told this declarant by means of the Maya language (which is that which they use), that there had been cattle on the other side, and that they had fought with the people of Guatemala, and that they killed nine Spaniards and [that the Spaniards killed] seven Indians, and that from where they live the road to Guatemala will be in midday [southerly] position."[82]

The number of Spanish casualties he reported was far smaller than the figure reported more reliably from the field. Perhaps the official transcript of Zubiaur's testimony was censored to make it appear that the number of deaths was small — or perhaps the Itza informant had lied. In any event, it appears that Ursúa withheld information about the massacre in order not to frighten the troops, carriers, and road workers. Once they were at the lakeside, about to attack Nojpetén, it would be safe, and even beneficial, for him to reveal the details. By that time the attack would be inevitable, and last-minute news about the "savagery" of the enemy would boost morale and fighting spirit.

chapter ten **THE COSTS OF THE CAMINO REAL**

T he Itza attacks on Yucatecans in February 1696 and on Guatemalans the following April contributed to intense political conflict in Mérida over Ursúa's increasing determination to strike a final blow against the Itzas. Soberanis, who returned to office in June, soon embarked on an all-out effort to discredit the project and even to terminate it. Threatened by Ursúa's domineering presence in Campeche, he even sought to have him bodily removed from the peninsula. The issue of Ursúa's right to remain and to continue the project was debated by the Audiencia of Mexico, and ultimately the Council of the Indies ruled in his favor. Amidst these altercations the secular clergy and the Franciscans continued to quarrel over their respective rights to missionize Kejach and Itza territories.

Nevertheless, the camino real continued to progress toward Lago Petén Itzá, and by September it touched the lakeshore. The operations were massive in scale, involving large sums of money and many hundreds of people: road workers, muleteers, soldiers, specialized craftsmen, a physician, and cooks. Working conditions were arduous and dangerous in the hot, tropical forests, and many people died, only to be replaced by others who were strong-armed into serving on the dreaded road. Maya villagers of Yucatán were the most oppressed, for they were given the most backbreaking tasks and were paid the least. Suffering in a different way, but perhaps no less, were the hundreds of forest Mayas — those known as Kejaches — who had been herded into the "mission" towns and placed under military guard.

As the camino real moved relentlessly forward during the second half of 1696 and the first weeks of 1697, little was heard from the Itzas themselves, who were in the midst of their own internal struggle for power. So great was the political chaos among the Itzas that their leaders found themselves unable to prepare an effective allied defense against the approaching forces of destruction. As the inevitability of attack became more and more apparent, however, a sense of foreboding — an anticipation that it would soon be over — possessed Nojpeten and the rest of the lake area population.

Ursúa Versus Soberanis

Governor Roque de Soberanis y Centeno, who had been excommunicated by Bishop Juan Cano y Sandoval in 1694, had waited out the investigation of the charges against him in Mexico City throughout the following year. Bishop Cano died on February 20, 1695, and the province of Yucatán was without a bishop until November 13, 1696, when an Augustinian, Fray Antonio de Arriaga, at last assumed the office. In the meantime the church in Yucatán was governed as a "vacant see" by the cabildo of the Mérida cathedral, whose members were the secular clergy.[1] During this period the secular church authorities apparently posed no opposition to Soberanis's pending exoneration, but they worked long and hard to gain as many favors as possible from Ursúa while he still served as governor. The most important of these, which they attempted to seal during AjChan's visit to Mérida, had been Ursúa's tacit support of their side in the secular-Franciscan battle over the status of future missions among the Itzas.

On February 10, 1696, Soberanis was at last absolved by the Inquisition Office.[2] He had begun the process of returning to Yucatán as early as November, but the viceroy, Gaspar de Sandoval, Count of Galve, had placed everything on hold until the absolution was official and and he could decide what to do about Ursúa.[3] Before and even after Soberanis's return to Yucatán on June 23, the viceroy, his fiscal or legal adviser, and the audiencia members struggled with the specter of the administrative chaos that might result from Ursúa's continued presence in Yucatán following his replacement by Soberanis as governor. This was a highly charged debate, fueled by petitions that Soberanis submitted in late 1695 requesting authorization to return to Yucatán immediately and take over the camino real project from Ursúa, who should be forced to leave upon his arrival. The viceroy and his closest advisers were sympathetic to Ursúa, and a series of edicts were issued from Mexico City that delayed Soberanis's return to office while giving Ursúa more time to extend the road and firm up his control over the project.[4]

In January the audiencia advised the viceroy that because Ursúa was nearing completion of his operation he should be able to finish it by the time Soberanis arrived to take over the government. If he did not manage to do so, then Soberanis would be expected to take over the project at his own cost, while Ursúa would have to leave the camino real via Guatemala and not return to Yucatán.[5] The fiscal, however, offered the counter recommendation that Ursúa be allowed to finish the task of converting all the inhabitants along the camino real and that Soberanis be ordered to cooperate with him. After all, he had already achieved major successes, most notably the Itza messenger's arrival in Mérida and the completion of so much of the road. Whichever resolution the viceroy adopted, it was likely to be difficult to execute, because Ursúa had numerous relatives and political supporters in Yucatán, particularly in Campeche. Whether the younger and politically weaker Soberanis would be able to govern under such circumstances remained an open question.[6]

In support of his case for finishing the project himself, Ursúa and his agents prepared a plethora of documentation for the viceroy and the audiencia members. One of the first of these documents contained certified accounts that by late January he had already spent 12,415 pesos of his own (and, according to his own later claims, his wife's) money on troop salaries, payments to Maya road workers, mules and muleteers, gunpowder and lead, food and wine, and gifts of cloth, ribbon, and beads for the forest Mayas.[7]

The viceroy issued his decision on February 10. If, when Soberanis reassumed the governorship, Ursúa had not completed "this operation," Ursúa would be required to take himself immediately down the camino real and continue extending the road through the end of March. At that time, whether or not the road was completed he was to return to Campeche immediately, without stopping along the road, and to depart from the province without visiting Mérida. Alternatively, he could leave the camino real directly via "the road from Guatemala" — although, in reality, no such road existed.[8] Soberanis was to offer Ursúa full cooperation within these limitations. The lowest blow of all to Ursúa's pride must have been the viceroy's instructions that Juan del Castillo y Toledo would be placed in charge of the project upon Ursúa's departure.

Ursúa could not accept these restrictions, regardless of the authority behind them. Time was on his side, and the viceroy delayed in allowing Soberanis to return to Yucatán. Ursúa's agent in Mexico, his brother Francisco de Ursúa, argued that the allotted time limit was too short.[9] The viceroy's fiscal, Baltásar de Tovar, who favored Ursúa's cause, recommended that Ursúa be allowed to remain in Tabasco or Chiapas until the project was completed, without returning to Yucatán.[10] On May 4 the

247

viceroy relented, impressed in particular by claims that the camino real had reached within eight leagues of the lake. He ordered that Ursúa be allowed to follow the project to its conclusion. Ursúa would not, however, be permitted to remain in Campeche but was to move to Ciudad Real in Chiapas or, of all places, the Guatemalan-governed Lakandon reduction town of Nuestra Señora de los Dolores (Sakb'ajlan). As an afterthought he added the possibility that Ursúa could retain his present military head-quarters at Tzuktok'. Finally, in what at first glance appeared to be a major victory for the Franciscans, he ordered that they be given the right to instruct the "infidel Indians," adding the nicety that children were not to be baptized against their will nor the adults baptized until they were fully catechized. This last order, however, appears to have been ignored except in the case of the already missionized Kejach towns.[11]

The viceroy was apparently unaware that communications between either Ciudad Real or Dolores and the existing camino real were nonexistent. The geography of the area was a mystery to officials in Mexico City, who were apparently still under the impression that Ursúa's road was leading to Dolores, where it would meet a road leading to Chiapas and Santiago de Guatemala via Huehuetenango. Because that had been the original plan Ursúa was supposed to follow, he and his agents did nothing to dispel these incorrect notions. On the other hand, Ursúa could accept no plan that would not allow him to retain the port of Campeche, where he had his political and financial support, as his ultimate home and head-quarters. At no point did he ever waver from his intention to stay in Campeche or to complete his project, regardless of orders received from Mexico.

These were Sandoval's last orders to Ursúa, for he now retired from his post and left Mexico City for Spain. His temporary replacement was Juan de Ortega Montáñez, the bishop of Michoacán, to whom Ursúa immediately wrote on May 12, describing in glowing detail the successes that he had achieved up to that point and pointedly omitting any mention of Itza-Spanish warfare on the shores of the main lake.[12] By this time the Council of the Indies had studied the conflict between Ursúa and Soberanis, and on May 29 it issued a cédula in Ursúa's favor. The short cédula was addressed to Soberanis as governor, although he had not yet reassumed the office. **248** The message was simple, strongly worded, and lacking in restrictions or qualifications: Soberanis, as governor, was to assist Ursúa in completing his project. If he failed to do so, his behavior would be judged a disservice to the king. The cédula included no requirements that Ursúa leave Yuca-tán or that he complete the task by a specified deadline.[13]

The cédula was not received in Mérida until December, nearly six months after Soberanis had returned.[14] By the time it arrived, he had done everything in his power to make Ursúa's life miserable, but he immediately acknowledged it and promised dutifully to abide by its terms, specifying what he would do to help Ursúa — providing titles for officers, writing orders on his behalf and for whomever he designated, and ordering payments for supplies, muleteers, and any other items he might request.[15] By now, despite the new governor's efforts to sabotage Ursúa's project, a road of sorts, although still barely passable, had been finished nearly all the way to Lago Petén Itzá. Ursúa's agent in Campeche welcomed the new spirit of cooperation, gladly taking Soberanis up on his offers of assistance.[16] For the next three months, up to the storming of Nojpeten in March, Soberanis granted, although unenthusiastically, his promised assistance.

Soberanis had already pursued a campaign to discredit almost every aspect of Ursúa's project. He collected testimony from friars, secular priests, distinguished citizens, soldiers, Maya supply carriers, and village officials and wrote scathing dispatches to the viceroy and the Crown. On July 20 he requested and shortly received information from the Franciscan provincial on the Kejach reductions.[17] On August 17 he took depositions from Franciscans working in the partido of Sierra in an attempt to gather information that would discredit the authenticity of AjChan's visit to Mérida and his submission to Spanish rule.[18] Three days later he recorded additional testimony from secular priests, soldiers, and citizens, both on the topic of AjChan and on working conditions on the camino real.[19]

Ursúa, who was constantly informed of Soberanis's strategy, responded by calling witnesses of his own in Campeche on August 26, defending himself from a growing list of complaints — including his failure to pay for labor and supplies, the poor condition of the road, the mistreatment of soldiers and workers, and the suffering and flight of the Kejach refugees in the mission towns along the road. His witnesses were his own officers, and even though the accomplishments of which they boasted were impressive, their denial of charges made by such a broad spectrum of Yucatecan society lacked credibility.[20] At about the same time Ursúa's agent, none other than the powerful Pedro de Garrástegui, count of Miraflores and treasurer of the Santa Cruzada, petitioned Soberanis to ask the dean and cabildo of the Mérida cathedral to take testimony from twelve secular priests concerning Ursúa's record of payment for the supply trains sent by Maya towns to the camino real and the Tipuj entrada.[21] The secular clergy, among Ursúa's closest allies and certainly eager to support Garrástegui, presented friendly testimonies, stretched out over the month of

September, that almost completely disclaimed the charges against him.[22] Ursúa himself denied all charges, including claims that mistreatment and nonpayment of carriers had caused the Mayas of the Sierra partido to abandon their towns.[23]

In a brilliant act of upstaging, Soberanis reacted quickly to the obvious conflict of interest involved in the testimonies by Ursúa's officers, ordering on August 29 that the caciques from every town in two partidos, Beneficios Bajos and Beneficios Altos, be summoned to Mérida to report to him on the number of animals and carriers supplied by their towns and payments received from Ursúa for the camino real project and the Tipuj entrada during which AjChan deserted the Spaniards.[24] The caciques gave mixed reports, but about half of those whose towns had provided men, animals, and supplies claimed that their townsmen had received incomplete payments or none at all.[25] Soberanis even acted to limit Ursúa's legal rights, ordering that he be disallowed to communicate with his local agent.[26]

The bulk of these accusations, defenses, and counteraccusations reached Mexico City by early September, further complicating the viceroy's dilemma over Ursúa's right to continue the project. In early September, responding to complaints by Ursúa that Soberanis was attempting to sabotage his project, the royal treasurer offered strong support for Ursúa to the viceroy.[27] The fiscal was more cautious, recommending that someone knowledgeable and impartial be commissioned to advise on whether the project should be suspended, postponed, or continued.[28] Ursúa's brother and agent in Mexico, Francisco, denied all of Soberanis's charges and said that it would be impossible for Ursúa to move his headquarters from Campeche to Tzuktok' or Dolores del Lacandón, as Soberanis was vehemently demanding.[29]

On September 20, by a suspicious coincidence of timing, four witnesses, apparently Itzas, appeared in Bacalar-at-Chunjujub' and provided testimony that seemed to settle once and for all the question of AjChan's authenticity as an agent of Ajaw Kan Ek'. Their depositions not only helped to clear Ursúa's credibility on this question but also led to the freeing of poor Pablo Gil de Azamar, who had been languishing in jail in Bacalar-at-Chunjujub' on charges of having fabricated AjChan's relationship to the Itza leader and his legitimacy as an ambassador.[30]

250 During October Ursúa stepped up his complaints about Soberanis's interference in a series of dispatches to the viceroy and the Crown.[31] By that time Soberanis had not only passed on a thick stack of condemnatory evidence against Ursúa and his associates but also articulated his obviously genuine concern about the harmful effects the project might have had on the social and economic life of the entire province of Yucatán.[32] Ursúa's hopes were nonetheless buoyed by receipt of the supporting cédula noted earlier and the October arrival in Mexico of a new viceroy, the Count of Montezuma, to whom he wrote a lengthy summary of the history of the camino real project, its successes, and the impediments that it currently suffered.[33]

Following Soberanis's receipt of the Crown's May 29 cédula these issues all became moot. Soberanis, finally cowed by the Council of the Indies, drew in his horns and proceeded to assist Ursúa. Modern scholars are fortunate, however, that the dispute grew to such proportions, because the paper it generated provides a wealth of information about some crucial issues related to the camino real project. Several of these issues are explored later in this chapter.

The Progress of Conquest

By early February 1696 García de Paredes had directed the road opening only as far as the upper Río San Pedro, although only a few weeks later a road of sorts was opened across the remaining fifteen leagues or so. Most of the road was not new but rather the preexisting route followed by traders and other travelers.[34] During the relatively dry month of March it was adequate for García's men to take heavy artillery across the karst hills southeast of Chuntuki all the way to the shore of Lago Petén Itzá, where they had the armed encounter with the Itzas described in chapter 9.[35]

In March or April the engineer, Captain Manuel Jorge Sesere, died while working on the camino real.[36] The loss of his able surveyor was yet another blow in a string of events that had dampened Ursúa's initial optimism that Ajaw Kan Ek' would quickly turn over his "kingdom" to García de Paredes in February.[37] The two armed encounters at the lake confirmed that the Itzas had taken up a stance of hostile defense. To add to his woes, Ursúa learned of the mutiny of seventy members of Bartolomé de la Garma's company near Tzuktok' in April. That same month, the rains had begun again in earnest, forcing the troops to languish at their encampment at Chuntuki, waiting anxiously for the periodic supply trains that brought them maize meal, beans, salted meat, and a few fresh pigs and chickens. Meanwhile, Soberanis was bombarding the colonial bureaucracy with growing evidence against the commander. Although Ursúa had hoped to leave his home at Campeche—known as Hacienda de Kastamay[38]—on June 25 in order to join García de Paredes on the camino real, he was forced to remain there to defend himself. As a result, García de Paredes and his troops remained divided between Tzuktok', Chuntuki, and their encampment at Río San Pedro for months waiting for new orders and a clearer, revised strategy.[39]

The small Tipuj garrison was in decline. By October all but one of the priests sent there had returned home, and the garrison itself had been reduced from fifty to twenty-one men.[40] Earlier visions of Tipuj as the gateway to the Itzas had vanished, and now it was a certainty that the Itza conquest would be pursued along the camino real. All that remained was to work out the details of an attack strategy. Ursúa now wrote of his intentions to construct more than one galeota, "in which it will be necessary to carry out the reduction of the great Itza."[41]

In October Ursúa asked the Crown directly to grant him a provision, in return for a twice-yearly payment (*media anata*) of one thousand ducats, that would prohibit the viceroy or the audiencia from interfering in his officially mandated project.[42] Once the empowering May 29 cédula was received in December, however, such an extraordinary measure became unnecessary. As soon as Ursúa heard the good news he began to enlist more experts and volunteers at Campeche—perhaps as many as 150. Soberanis ordered the governor of arms at the Campeche fort to arrange for the distribution of payments to soldiers, muleteers, and supplies. Native village officials throughout the partido of Campeche were to be instructed to provide Ursúa with mules, horses, and food supplies.[43] Ursúa in turn arranged for the purchase of stone mortars, muskets, powder, shot, cutlasses, and axes. Most important of all was the purchase of supplies and equipment for the construction of vessels to be used on the lake—nails, tar, pitch, burlap, tallow, nautical tackle, and other necessities. This task required him to employ carpenters, blacksmiths, porters, and sailors. Even the small boat built on Río San Pedro—now called a "war piragua"—would be transported to the lake.[44]

Although he still distrusted Soberanis, Ursúa praised the bishop, Fray Antonio de Arriaga, for his support of his project. With no more impediments in his way, he now hoped to be able to report soon that the camino real had been connected with the road from Verapaz and that his soldiers had gone all the way to Santiago de Guatemala.[45] Soberanis, Ursúa later complained, placed one further impediment in his way by refusing to provide an official notary or clerk (*escribano*) for his final entrada.[46] The absence of a notary, however, simply allowed him to tell the story of the conquest as he wished it to be entered in the official record.

On December 28 Ursúa sent ahead a garrison of troops and specialists to begin construction of the galeota. Two more garrisons, accompanied by Maya carriers, followed on January 7 and 17, 1697, respectively, carrying a variety of light and heavy arms, gunpowder and ammunition, and food supplies.[47] Ursúa himself departed from Campeche for the camino real on January 23, taking with him the remainder of the total of 130 soldiers sent on this campaign, in addition to more Maya muleteers.[48]

He and his troops were walking into a worsening situation on the camino real. On January 2 one of the captains had returned to Campeche with the news that "a considerable number of infidels from Chacan Itza (who inhabit the shore of that lake) had invaded the town of the Chans and carried off all of the domesticated Indian men and women with their children, numbering 316, and that they burned the church, and only two were able to escape."[49] The town was Pak'ek'em, at this point the larger of two remaining Kejach mission settlements on the road. The invaders were probably enemies of Ajaw Kan Ek', sent by his uncle, the ruler of the north, who was doing all in his power to discourage the forward movement of the troops. The Spanish officers stationed at Chuntuki, undoubtedly pressured by their ill and terrified troops, decided to abandon the town and return to Campeche. Before leaving, they buried their arms, ammunition, and other supplies, retiring back five leagues before sending Ursúa the news. Ursúa clearly believed now that he would be justified in using whatever force was required against the native population.

Between January 23 and March 22, nine days after the attack on Nojpeten, Ursúa apparently penned no official dispatches. Nor did he produce any other documents recording events or testimony until March 10, when he was already at the lakeshore preparing to sail the now-completed galeota across the lake. His march to the deserted encampment of Chuntuki and on to the "thatch fort" north of Lago Petén Itzá, as well as the work of moving the troops and the timbers for the galeota to Ch'ich' at the beginning of March, occupies only passing reference in his later correspondence. The probable reason for this black-out was the intensity of Ursúa's efforts to get the job done quickly, before his men lost their courage and mutinied.

The Fate of the Converts   253

Maintaining the Kejach mission towns, as small as they were, proved to be an impossible challenge. Their inhabitants became the wards of friars and soldiers, some of whom mistreated them, took advantage of their labor, and attempted to restrict their movements. As a result, some of them tried to run away, in response to which the officers assigned the Spanish-appointed "caciques" of these towns the unpleasant task of rounding them up from the forests. One officer, presumably a Yucatecan, was responsible for distributing to the caciques goods brought from Yucatán — maize and bean seeds, fowls, and pigs.[50] Such a service was clearly designed to make the mission towns more attractive than running away, because domesticated plants and animals were in short supply in the refugee forest communities.

The problem of desertion began at Tzuktok', whose inhabitants ran away in unknown numbers following the return of the troops in early 1696. Eighty-six troops had remained stationed there during December 1695 while García de Paredes recruited new troops in Campeche.[51] The presence of troops must have made conditions at this military headquarters intolerable for the Maya inhabitants. In May their "cacique," Diego Tz'ulub', was appointed to round them up. This task was significant enough to motivate Ursúa to issue an order not to mistreat or impede Tz'ulub' in his activities.[52]

The runaway problem was at first minimal at B'atkab' and Pak'ek'em. In early July 1696 Fray Nicolás Martín took complete censuses of these two towns with the assistance of Fray Diego de Salas. The total population of B'atkab' was 143, and that of Pak'ek'em, 348.[53] The friars had managed to hold onto most of the original population, estimated the previous November to have been 115 for B'atkab' and 350 for Pak'ek'em.

Assigned by their provincial to find out what had become of the small population of Tzuktok', which was now abandoned, Martín and Salas investigated a rumor that the people of Tzuktok' and others from B'atkab' had moved to Kantemo. On July 13 they went to Kantemo and found, in addition to the cacique of B'atkab', Cacique Diego Tz'ulub' of Tzuktok' with his family and two other runaways from the town. Tz'ulub', who had obviously failed to round up his townspeople, told them that four had gone to Jop'elch'en, three to Machich, and three to the partido of Sajkab'ch'en — all towns further to the north, under colonial control. As for the rest, he had heard reports that they had gone to the partido of Sajkab'ch'en and Yajb'akab'.[54]

254   When asked why the Tzuktok' inhabitants had fled, Tz'ulub' told the friars that illness, hunger, and mistreatment by the Spanish captain there had all contributed to their flight. When they complained to García de Paredes, he answered that if they found themselves aggrieved they should go to the partido of Sajkab'ch'en and IxB'akab' [i.e., Yajb'akab'].[55] What

choice did the people of Tzuktok' have but to flee? reasoned Fray Nicolás Martín. They were suffering not only death and hunger but also "the intolerable oppression with which the aforementioned Captain Mateo Hidalgo compelled them, holding them in excessive servitude as if they were slaves."[56]

This was not the first time García de Paredes had attempted to send the refugees at Tzuktok' to Sajkab'ch'en. He had tried to do the same thing the previous year while Avendaño was in the area, but was disallowed (see chapter 6). Whether the runaways actually accepted his "offer" on this occasion cannot be verified, but Tzuktok' remained totally abandoned for some time.[57]

Several weeks later Fray Nicolás Martín became ill and was taken by a group of seven men from B'atkab' to Mérida for medical care. He also apparently hoped to give these men the opportunity to address their complaints directly to the colonial authorities. Governor Soberanis, eager to obtain information that could be used to discredit Ursúa's project, set up a formal interrogation on September 4 during which all seven B'atkab' residents, now nominal Christians, presented their sworn depositions.[58] Leading the group was don Jerónimo Tun, the forty-year-old cacique of the town. The other men were all young, from nineteen to twenty-four.[59]

The men verified that B'atkab' and Pak'ek'em were now the only surviving mission towns along the road. Cacique Tun stated that B'atkab' had only ten married couples, "because the first time that the Spaniards attacked they killed twenty." Others, however, were quoted as saying that there were twenty married couples — closer to the friars' count of twenty-five only a few weeks earlier. Lucas Puk, presumably referring to their first encounters with troops, reported that the Spaniards had attacked them on two occasions, killing a total of about twenty married couples and twenty-five children.[60]

Soberanis, wanting to appear kind and solicitous, apparently treated these visitors well. Upon their departure he issued an order to all local officials in the towns through which they would pass on their way home — because they were "tormented and discontented outside their homeland" — to provide them with food and hospitality and with an alcalde or regidor to accompany them to the next town. Although he recorded none of their complaints, they must have made some, for he specifically instructed Captain Roque Gutiérrez, who was in charge of the B'atkab' region, to give them "good treatment, without allowing any grievance, harm, or ill-treatment to be done to them."[61] With Tzuktok' abandoned and B'atkab' beginning to follow suit, the tragedy noted ear-

255

lier struck Pak'ek'em in late December 1696 when a war party from Chak'an Itza attacked the town and kidnapped nearly everyone. By now the camino real was virtually deserted of its native inhabitants.[62]

The Camino Real and the Inhabitants of Yucatán

During the second half of August 1696, Governor Soberanis continued his investigation of the camino real project by calling before him in Mérida the "caciques" of native towns in the districts of Beneficios Bajos and Beneficios Altos. His purpose was to challenge evidence collected by Ursúa in support of claims that he had paid fairly and treated well the Mayas who had supplied pack and saddle animals, food, and men for both entradas to the camino real and for the expedition to Tipuj following Ah AjChan's visit to Mérida.[63]

The circumstances of the testimonies were hardly unbiased. Soberanis initially claimed that Ursúa had treated the towns of these two jurisdictions more fairly than others, presumably the Sierra towns. Ursúa, he argued, had attempted to whitewash the record by ignoring incriminating evidence from other towns, and Soberanis apparently chose to underscore his point by interviewing only the Beneficios caciques. If these men claimed to have been treated badly, the others could be presumed to have suffered even more.[64] Fifty-nine towns sent representatives to Mérida, some from a great distance, providing their depositions over a period of nearly two months, from August 31 through October 24. Soberanis contemplated, but never carried out, a similar investigation for the partidos of La Costa, Sierra, and Camino Real.[65]

Only seven of the reporting towns had sent supplies and animals to the camino real.[66] They had provided a total of thirty-one horses and 110 mules and supplied more than sixty cargas of maize meal, four cargas of beans, four live pigs, and an unspecified amount of maize seed, salted meat, and live chickens. These seven towns, of course, represented only a small portion of those that had participated in the supply trains to Chuntuki and Tzuktok'. Because Soberanis never fulfilled his plan to extend his inquiry to the southwestern partidos, where most of the suppliers would have been recruited, we can only estimate the full scope of the enterprise.

If these seven towns represented 5 percent of the total, not an unreasonable estimate, and had together supplied an "average" amount, the supply trains would have comprised more than six hundred horses and more than two thousand mules carrying great quantities of maize meal and beans. Nearly every animal was accompanied by a man, most often its owner, who walked alongside it — even if a soldier was riding the horse or mule. Following along behind the train were men on foot carrying live chickens and urging on small herds of stubborn, squealing pigs.

This was an arduous journey of about 165 leagues, probably taking over a month in each direction, with several days of rest at the destination point. Reimbursement for the use of the animal and the journey to Chuntuki was set at five pesos, about half a real per day. Only about half of the men had received their payments when they reported to Soberanis, and many of the remainder may never have been paid. Meals were supposed to be supplied along the way, but some complained that they were not properly fed. Considering the difficult conditions it is surprising that from this group of towns only two men and four animals, all from Tek'it, were reported to have died as a result of the journey.

The two barrios of Tek'it, a town about eleven leagues southeast of Mérida, serve as an example of the contributions of a middle-sized Sierra town to the supply trains. Five mules and five men carried beans and maize seed to Tzuktok', and twenty-eight mules and eight horses, accompanied by seventeen men, carried maize and flour meal, salted meat, and beans all the way to Chuntuki. In addition, the town supplied thirteen saddle horses for soldiers, and men to accompany them, as well as forty cargas of maize meal, four cargas of beans, chickens (carried by one man), four pigs, and two large jars of honey.[67]

While Soberanis was collecting this information, the secular clergy gathered countertestimony on behalf of Ursúa and his agent, Pedro Garrástegui y Oleado. During September an official visited the priests of ten towns in the partidos of Sierra and Beneficios, including two priests who had participated in the mission to Tipuj. The question they were required to "certify" was simple: Did or did not Ursúa still owe the Mayas for transport of supplies to Tipuj? The responses overwhelmingly supported Ursúa's claim that he owed the Maya muleteers nothing. Because several of the priests, however, were themselves responsible for overseeing the recruitment of men and the purchase of supplies, their testimony is suspect.[68]

As part of his investigation into the deception and abuse that he believed characterized the first two entradas, in August 1696 Governor Soberanis directed the following question to several Franciscan friars who worked in the partido of Sierra: "He was asked whether he knows that, with the occasion of the Indian people who have been taken away from the towns of this province — both for the opening of the said road as well as the transporting of provisions or fodder — some [of these towns] have been diminished and depopulated."[69]

Fray Gregorio Clareda of Oxk'utskab' responded that more than five hundred Mayas from that town alone had been recruited as road openers and muleteers. Others from the town, he said,

> had fled to the bush with their wives and children, out of fear that they would be obliged to do the same, leaving behind their empty houses, [their] milpas, and the mission church [*doctrina*] — and the worst thing of all, which the magistrates told him — lamenting that many milpas of those runaways had been eaten by the animals because their owners had not gone to take care of them, fearful of being captured if they went to the forests as a result of the terrors that had overtaken them when they encountered their dead companions on the roads. Of those who came back alive to their towns, some had died later on. He heard it said by reliable persons that more than 200 Indians had died in the forest, as a result of which there had been so few people in the said town of Oxkutzcab on festival days and Sundays during the course of the year. It caused wonder among all Spaniards and religious who attended on the said festival days when they saw the said town so deteriorated and the church without people, having been one of the affluent of the entire province, with more than 1,900 Indians, not including boys and girls.

Fray Andrés de Campo of B'olonch'en Tikul and Fray Pedro de Lara of Teab'o stated that their towns had also suffered population losses, and they repeated, in less detail, Cladera's despairing comments.[70]

Several days later additional witnesses, none of them Franciscans, were questioned in more detail about topics related to conditions on the camino real.[71] A secular parish priest in the Valladolid area, reported that he knew by hearsay of flight from the Sierra towns, of failure to pay workers and muleteers, and of the death of many of them on the road "without the holy sacraments." Julio Rentero, one of the soldiers who mutinied against Captain Bartolomé de la Garma at Tzuktok', had little to say in contradiction. Not only were he and his compatriots not paid for two and one-half months after receiving their first advance, but the food they received was inadequate: one calabash of maize beverage and two pieces of jerked beef every twenty-four hours. Because the Maya muleteers received nothing at all to eat, he shared his ration with the man who oversaw the mule team with which he traveled. Along the road before Tzuktok' he saw not only the skeletons of mules but also sixteen or seventeen crosses that marked graves of Mayas or Spaniards and a number of piles of stone that marked other burials.

Juan de Vargas, a particularly talkative "free pardo" who had served in Captain Mateo Hidalgo's company at Chuntuki, had suffered from malaria while he was there and had witnessed three men of his company die. He added a new perspective on the issue of flight from the towns of Yucatán, opining that not only had AjChan been a false representative but also that "upon the arrival of the said Indian he knows that the entire province was agitated by rumors, motivating the said lord don Martín [de Ursúa] to take away the arms from many Indians of this province." The questioner thereupon asked Vargas, "What rumors were those which he heard?" He replied that "he heard it said that [the rumors] were that the Indians wanted to rebel."

The next and last declarant, the secular priest Juan Tello, stated that these were more than rumors — that there was actually a movement among the Mayas to "conspire against the Spaniards." He confirmed that Ursúa had disarmed the native population. No other information about these purported incidents, unfortunately, has been discovered.

Diego de Avila y Pacheco, the absentee encomendero of Oxk'utskab', testified on August 29 on behalf of Ursúa, who sought to challenge the friars' charge that the camino real project had resulted in large-scale flight. He blamed the flight from Oxk'utskab' on excessive unpaid labor requirements by Fray Gregorio Clareda, the town's priest, especially his demand that the inhabitants cut timbers for a new church in the town and for the convent of St. Francis in Mérida.[72]

Ursúa's own military officers, who testified in his favor in October, did not deny that there had been hardships on the camino real. The conditions that they portrayed were far less dismal, however, than the horrors reported by the previous witnesses.[73] Captain Zubiaur Isasi stated that while the rainy weather had caused illnesses among both Spaniards and natives, only six men in all had died, and the military surgeon had been available at Chuntuki to treat the sick. One of those who died was the engineer, who had suffered from a long-term illness. Of the others, one died as the result of a urinary problem, and another suffered a snakebite. Two other captains, however, estimated that eleven persons had died — all, except for the snakebite victim and the engineer, from natural causes "originating from the moistures and the indispositions of unpopulated areas." Nine of these had been Spaniards, and only two, Mayas. The

259

officers, as would be expected, claimed that all workers had been fairly paid and that their services were voluntary, not forced. As we will see shortly, more detailed documentation about passive resistance on the part of the Mayas against serving on the camino real gives not only additional credence to their genuine fear of conditions in the forests but also evidence that they were impressed by local Maya officials against their will.

Soldiers, Craftsmen, Carriers, and Suppliers

Because of the survival of excellent accounting records, our knowledge about personnel and supplies on the last entrada, led by Ursúa to Lago Petén Itzá, is far more detailed than our knowledge about the first two entradas to the camino real.[74] The number and variety of people, supplies, and equipment was nothing short of impressive.

At the upper end of the social scale were thirteen "volunteers without salary." These were for the most part Campechanos, including the three principal captains — Alonso García de Paredes, José Fernández de Estenos, and Pedro de Zubiaur y Isasi. All but two of these men took their own arms and at least one horse, and several of them were each accompanied by a horse-mounted servant. García de Paredes had several servants and a small personal army of twelve men whom he fed and armed at his own cost. One of the volunteers, Bernardo de Aizuani Ursúa, was a relative of Martín de Ursúa's.[75]

The accounts also list payments made to a total of 136 soldiers assigned to the camino real and to several others who had recently returned from there and were collecting back pay. All of those listed had Spanish surnames, but we know from other sources that the troops were ethnically mixed. The illiterate Captain José Laines commanded a company of pardos and mestizos,[76] and several of the armed soldiers were Mayas from Tek'ax.[77] Most of the new recruits received two monthly payments of eight pesos each in advance; those with their own muskets received one additional peso each month. Several of the returning soldiers, who had served at Chuntuki, turned out to have been serving sentences of exile from Mexico, handed down by the audiencia. One of the squadrons was to escort a group that had been hired to build the galeota and piraguas. It comprised a master carpenter, five regular carpenters, and twenty-one sawyers — all with Spanish surnames. Four sailors were sent at the high monthly wage of forty pesos to man the as-yet-unfinished vessels. Ursúa's initial intention had apparently been to build two galeota, but only one galeota and a single piragua were completed. Seven male cooks, two with Maya surnames, also accompanied the troops, with wages of sixteen pesos per month.

Of equal interest are items of equipment and supplies purchased during January 1697 from a variety of people, including Campeche merchants and military officers participating in the entrada. These goods were transported in several stages, each time preceding by a few days the departure of a group of soldiers. Although the combined size of these mule and horse trains is not recorded, the bottom line of the paymaster's notebook indicated that about 665 pesos had been spent on pack animals and saddle horses. Some of the owners had been paid in full (at the rate of five and a half pesos for pack mules and three and a half pesos for saddle horses), but most had been paid only half this amount, with the rest to be paid upon the animal's return. Even the approximately 250 to 300 animals indicated by this amount were probably far fewer than the total number sent. Judging from the records of supplies, the number of mule loads must have exceeded one thousand, whereas only 152 mules are accounted for in the records. The items that appear on these accounts include, among other things, boat-building tools and supplies, supplies for the muleteers and for packaging cargo, religious supplies, arms and related equipment and services, powder and ammunition, cooking equipment, food supplies, alcoholic beverages, and even dogs.[78]

The merchants and other suppliers of Campeche fared well in supplying these goods, their receipts totaling about 3,750 pesos in January 1697 alone.[79] Sebastián de Sagüéz y Sabalsa, the major supplier for the final entrada (with receipts of 922 pesos, 4 reales), was not only a wealthy merchant but also alcalde ordinario of Campeche. He had been in charge of paying out the Campeche cabildo's small contribution to the camino real project — the salaries of twenty-five troops — ever since García de Paredes left on the first entrada in March 1695.[80] Even if these salaries had been paid regularly for the twenty-one months since the enterprise began, the cabildo's total outlay would have been no more than about forty-five hundred pesos; divided among the five members, individual contributions would not have exceeded nine hundred pesos. These costs were repaid, and then some, by the profits enjoyed by several of the cabildo members as suppliers of goods and services. Even though some of the goods sold were unique to the final entrada, especially the materials for boat construction, most were items that had had to be supplied regularly throughout the previous twenty-one months of the camino real operation.

In addition to this outlay, Ursúa spent several hundred pesos in salaries and 665 pesos toward the cost of freight transport. When amounts this size are taken into consideration, it is clear why the leading citizenry of Campeche was more than willing to support Ursúa's enterprise. By the end of January his total payments approached thirty thousand pesos, a large sum by the standards of the time. The camino real project, for all practical purposes, was underwriting the economy of Campeche. Meanwhile Ursúa was draining the rural Maya economy of its workers by taking men from their villages for months at a time in return for the low wages paid for road workers and muleteers and the paltry amounts paid for foodstuffs.

The Campeche import merchants, therefore, were those who stood to benefit from the camino real, and benefit they did — probably on the order of eight to ten times the total gross sales they enjoyed for the items listed in the accounts that have survived. Nor did the recorded Campeche accounts list of all of the materials taken for the final entrada. Ursúa had also noted that he intended to take with him other supplies for construction of the galeota — liquid pitch (*alquitrán*), burlap (*estopa*), and tallow (*sebo*) — along with blacksmiths and porters to carry items that would not be loaded onto pack animals.[81]

Conflicts of interest were the foundation upon which this enterprise was built. The cabildo members took credit for their contributions while padding their pockets with the sale of goods that supported the men whose salaries they paid. Sagüéz y Sabalsa not only collected and paid out these contributions and profited from the sales but also doubled as Ursúa's purchasing agent.[82] García de Paredes, the field commander, earned large profits from sales while claiming credit for contributing a substantial sum to the project.[83] Furthermore, as Avendaño had complained, he used his authority as a military administrator to send Kejach "converts" settled along the camino real to Sajkab'ch'en, where they were added to the minions who cut timber for his shipyards in Campeche. García, therefore, had every reason not to punish his officers and troops who abused and otherwise exploited the refugees of the mission towns.

Passive Maya Labor Resistance

Records of the recruitment of Maya road workers and muleteers for the final entrada clarify not only that such work was a form of forced labor but also that the Mayas could mount effective resistance to it. One fascinating example of the process of recruitment followed by passive resistance has survived:

At the beginning of January 1697 one of Ursúa's agents, Field Marshal Francisco de Salazar y Córdoba, requested that Governor Soberanis order Juan del Castillo y Toledo—who had fulfilled the same function on the first two entradas—to recruit, with power of authority, workers from several Sierra towns, including Tekax and Oxk'utskab'. The team of workers would be under the Maya "captain" of the Tek'ax company. Salazar y Córdoba recognized, although in an understated fashion, that the work was extensive, involving "not only the clearing of the said road—which, given the lapse of time [for it to have grown back], is judged to be somewhat difficult—as well as the transport of musket flints, salted meat, beans, lard, and the other items needed for the said enterprise."[84]

Soberanis refused to allow recruitment from the Sierra towns because they had been heavily exploited for this purpose during the first two entradas. Instead, he authorized Castillo to seek men from several Beneficios towns, since these people were "more rested and do not have hanging over them the continuation of providing Indians for the work shift (tanda) of this city"—the first indication that urban officials were also demanding Maya service. The four Beneficios towns in question were Sotuta, Yaxkab'a, Tixkakal, and Peto. Castillo, as usual, would meet with the caciques and town cabildos, listing specific demands for numbers of workers, muleteers, carts, and animals. He was ordered to pay them fairly and promptly and to keep complete accounts of all transactions. The numbers were modest, totaling fifty-nine mules, fifty-nine muleteers, and sixty road workers.[85] Castillo y Toledo was also occupied at the time making unauthorized demands for food supplies from the Sierra towns, including maize and beef. If he did not desist from such practices, threatened Soberanis, he would be deprived of his post as labor and supplies recruiter, forced to leave his home at Mani, and possibly banished from Yucatán.[86]

Castillo y Toledo sent his son, Juan del Castillo y Arrúe, to the four towns, where he ordered the caciques and cabildo members to provide the animals and workers specified by the governor. The road workers were to be paid three pesos monthly, plus their food and supplies, with no indication of the length of time they were to work. The muleteers would receive six pesos for their labor and the mule, plus food and supplies, and they would carry no more than half a load apiece. Castillo y Toledo guaranteed that they would be reimbursed for any mules that died on the road. Finally, he specified that those named to work be among the less fully occupied townspeople, whose absence would be less harmful to their families.[87] Such promises, of course, were cheap and could easily be broken.

In all, fifty road workers, forty-five muleteers, and fifty-one mules—

263

less than the total authorized — were immediately obtained from these towns.[88] These ninety-six men, including the captain, were to join up with a much larger mule train and parade of workers that would travel with Ursúa and his military escort for the long, brutal journey to Chuntuki.[89]

Over the next few days these men were expected to appear in Jop'elch'en. When the Tixkakal muleteers reached Peto, however, they ran away, obviously frightened and dismayed by the prospect of what lay ahead.[90] On the twenty-fourth Soberanis ordered that if the Maya authorities of Tixkakal did not provide replacements immediately they would be punished for noncompliance.[91] A number of others from the Beneficios group who had finally reached Jop'elch'en ran away as soon as they arrived there.[92] Orders for replacements seem to have been ignored, and the Maya authorities failed, or perhaps refused, to send all that had been promised. Time was of the essence, because Ursúa had left Campeche on the twenty-third, and replacements were needed in time for them to join the main supply train. Rather than replace them from the Beneficios towns, on February 3 Salazar y Córdoba requested and immediately received permission from Soberanis to recruit mules and muleteers from B'olonch'en Tikul and Jop'elch'en.[93]

Such incidents of passive resistance through refusal to serve must have been much more common than the surviving records indicate and perhaps had grown in intensity over the nearly two years since the camino real project had begun. Now that Soberanis, whose opposition to Ursúa and his project was well known, had taken charge of authorizing the recruitment of all supply trains and laborers, the Mayas were willing to count on the governor's legendary leniency in such matters. Ursúa no longer held any authority over them, and Castillo y Toledo, although known to be dishonest in his dealings with the rural population, would not dare carry out personally executed punishments in the Beneficios towns. Although Soberanis gave Castillo y Toledo the authority to collect the advances paid to the runaways, there is no indication that these sums were ever collected.[94]

In the space of only twelve days in early March 1697, Spanish troops and workers set up camp at Ch'ich', the lakeshore port, and completed and equipped the galeota that would be used to attack Nojpeten. Ursúa and his officers interviewed several Itza leaders at Ch'ich' and were visited by many Itza citizens. Although most of their encounters with local inhabitants were friendly, the Spaniards agreed in council on March 12 to row more than one hundred men across the lake in the heavily armed galeota in order to force Ajaw Kan Ek' to surrender. They carried out their mission on March 13, but the result was a massacre, not a surrender. This chapter recounts what can be reconstructed of the twelve-day period at Ch'ich' that led to that tragic event.

Ursúa had set out from Campeche on January 23, 1697, following the camino real, along which an advance party of troops, shipbuilders, supply trains, and artillery carriers had already marched during the past several weeks.[1] Accompanying him were his cavalry officers, his personal retinue, the recently appointed chaplain and his assistant, and the remaining members of the supply train.[2]

Captain Pedro de Zubiaur had left Campeche on December 28, instructed by Ursúa to march to a point two leagues from the lake, make a temporary camp, and cut timbers for the galeota and a "piragua menor." He took with him troops, artillery operators, ship carpenters and caulkers, and, of course, carriers.[3] Two more garrisons totaling 130 or 140 men and a large number of carriers left Campeche to join Zubiaur on January 7 and 17, transporting food supplies that were to last four months.[4] Ultimately, some three hundred to five hundred people must have occupied the new headquarters at Ch'ich', on the lakeshore beyond the temporary camp.

265

The Encampment at Ch'ich'

Ursúa arrived at the temporary headquarters, where the timbers for the galeota were being fashioned, on February 26, one month after departing from Campeche.[5] From there he sent an advance party of troops to assess the remaining two leagues of road to the lakeshore. The men found the town of Ch'ich' deserted—no doubt evacuated ahead of the occupying forces—and Ursúa immediately began moving his operation there in order to prepare the galeota for launching. His actions over the next two weeks indicate that he may have planned to use the threat of an armed attack on Nojpeten by water as a means of convincing the Itzas to surrender without a fight. In the end, however, strategies by both sides to avoid conflict failed, and the galeota became an attack vessel.

Ch'ich' sat at the western end of the lake on what was later known as the Ensenada de San Jerónimo (see map 4). The bay, which extends nearly two kilometers from north to south at its widest point and about one and a half kilometers from east to west, is bordered by a narrow, triangular point (Punta Nijtún) on its southern side and a steep slope on the north. Although Avendaño briefly described the town on this bay and included it on his sketch map, he assigned to it the name Nich. Today the long point on the southern side of the bay is called Punta Nijtún, suggesting that in the seventeenth century it was called Nixtun (*nix-tun*), meaning a stone ramp or slope. A ramp discovered by archaeologists in 1995 along the shore of Punta Nijtún, on the south side of the bay, was probably the one Ursúa and his troops constructed in order to launch their galeota, perhaps by modifying an earlier canoe ramp.[6]

On February 28, Maya workers and muleteers, escorted by sixty troops, began the arduous job of transporting the precut construction timbers, the artillery, and other supplies to Ch'ich'.[7] At the lakeshore they were attacked by Itza guerrilla forces but suffered no casualties. On March 1, wrote Ursúa, "they [Itzas] came with a considerable number of canoes in order to create warlike displays, situating their forces on the water, as they were accustomed to it; and seeing the little success that they achieved, they retreated. On the following day some canoes came secretly to the shore where I had established the headquarters, leaving behind the large number of people they had."[8] Although suspicious, Ursúa handed out gifts to the visitors. As soon as they departed, other Itzas arrived in a canoe, "saying that their heart was good, and that their experience told them that they should come only a few at a time." One of these visitors, he wrote, fired three arrows (toward Captain Pedro de Zubiaur, according to one account),[9] all of which landed in the water. This man quickly escaped, swimming out to the waiting canoes.

Every day following this event, Ursúa wrote, these "sons of treason" threatened them frequently, "joining in a movement to provoke me to attack, to which I never succumbed; I wished [nevertheless] to see whether I could achieve their reduction by peaceful means."[10] According to one of Ursúa's descriptions, following the attack by three arrows "they shouted and yelled. They have kept this up by communicating with one other with smoke. Ignoring these barbarous acts, I have received them every day with much love and affection, in order to determine whether they might be reduced and lured to the Catholic fold by handouts and gifts of axes, machetes, knives, and salt for the men, and likewise bead earrings, necklaces, and belts for the women. Although many Indian women have come in canoes by themselves, hearing the news spread from all over, and have been braided and regaled with necklaces, earrings, and belts,[11] they have been treated with the modesty that is owed the service of God."[12]

Ursúa had obviously miscalculated the enemy. These were not people to be bought off with trinkets, nor were their threats and smoke signals indicative of barbarity. As events unfolded, the sophistication of the Itzas' strategic response manifested itself in increasingly creative ways, especially in the form of sexual provocation by women — a topic I will return to later.

During the Spaniards' stay at Ch'ich', workers constructed a defensive wall or reinforced an existing one, within which they placed the heavy artillery.[13] Whether they also constructed thatch-roofed buildings or instead occupied buildings left by the Itzas is not recorded. The indigenous people, however, usually burned their villages when they abandoned them. Because the Itzas had ample advance warning of the Spaniards' arrival, it is unlikely that they left behind anything that would have made their enemies' lives easier.

The total number of officially armed men camped at Ch'ich' was at least 140, including Ursúa himself, 9 officers, 5 persons identified as Ursúa's *criados*, or relatives, and the balance of 125 regular troops.[14] The rest of the party included 4 sailors, 7 cooks, 6 carpenters, and 21 sawyers hired in Campeche, as well as 2 priests, the personal servants of Ursúa and his officers, and a host of muleteers, individual carriers, and other workers.

The officers who served during these days under Captain General Ursúa at Ch'ich' were Lieutenant Captain General Alonso García de Paredes, two infantry captains, three armored cavalry captains, two lieutenants, and a "commander of pardos and mestizos."[15] Bachiller Juan Pacheco de Sopuerta, a secular priest, was the official missionary of the "territories," bearing the title "curate and vicar general" as well as that of chaplain of the army. His lieutenant, Bachiller José Francisco Martínez de Mora, also served as chaplain to the troops.[16] Although there were four Spanish interpreters, no Yucatec Mayas were used for official testimony.[17]

Ursúa's orders had been to construct a galeota with a keel 25 cubits in length, or about 12 meters;[18] in its final form, however, its keel was 30 cubits, or about 14.4 meters.[19] A galeota (galliot) was a simple, small galley, a rowing vessel usually outfitted with a single triangular "Latin" sail. According to one source, the common galeota had seventeen oars on a side.[20] The cabin was customarily located on the raised stern of the vessel, from which flew the identifying flag. Such vessels are illustrated in a 1705 plan of Campeche, where they served as coast guard boats.[21] In an inventory document the Petén galeota was described as a "new piragua of thirty cubits, with its twenty-four oars and rudder with its iron screw."[22] This suggests that the vessel had twelve oars on a side and no sail. Although the vessel was small, it carried about 114 men and at least five artillery pieces on the attack on Nojpeten. The piragua menor, also identified as a *piraguilla,* was a longboat "of six oars," presumably meaning three oars on a side. It had a rudder but may not have had sails.[23]

Ursúa's accounts of this period require us to believe that between March 1 and March 12 workers completed the assembly, waterproofing, launching, and testing of the galeota, as well as the mounting of its artillery. In addition, they constructed a defensive wall around the encampment and may have built several thatch-roofed structures to protect men and equipment from the elements. We are left to conclude that the builders, designers, carpenters, and other craftsmen were men of great expertise who must have worked on the boat nearly around the clock. In addition, the Spaniards may have had to construct a new ramp to launch it, given that the existing wharf and landing area were designed only for canoes. Considering the depth of the galeota's keel, they may also have deepened the harbor itself. The speed with which this operation was accomplished indicates that Ursúa had set a deadline by which he intended to attack Nojpeten. In any event, he was obviously determined to complete the attack vessel as quickly as possible, despite minor distractions from Itzas intent on harassing the camp at Ch'ich'.

On May 9, when Ursúa finally departed from Nojpeten, he left an inventory of the material items that he was leaving there in the care of his officer-in-charge. This accounting indicates the military seriousness with which the Itza affair was undertaken, especially in terms of the artillery, shot, and gunpowder that were taken to the island between March 13 and May 9. These included three one-pound-caliber iron light cannons (*piezas*) mounted on carriages, four two-chambered iron stone launchers (*pedreros*), two double-chambered bronze pedreros, six bronze light artillery cannons (*esmiriles*), and fifty muskets of French and Dutch manufacture (plus at least six others belonging to soldiers).[24] There were also sixteen iron-tipped lances. The remaining shot, in addition to musket balls already in possession of the troops, included thirty stone and six lead balls for the piezas, thirty-eight sacks of stones for the pedreros, and several thousand musket balls.[25]

When the galeota left Ch'ich' to attack Nojpeten on March 13, the port was left defended by two piezas, two pedreros, and eight esmiriles.[26] There is no account of the total number of artillery pieces that had been taken to Ch'ich', but by comparing these numbers with the numbers that had been transported to Nojpeten by May 9, we can say that there was a total of at least three piezas, six pedreros, and eight esmiriles. By subtracting those left at Ch'ich' from this total, we can conclude that on its attack voyage the galeota carried at least one pieza and four pedreros, but possibly no esmiriles at all.[27] Moreover, Ursúa had purchased at least eleven hundred pounds of gunpowder in Campeche, and about half that amount had been expended by May 9. Almost no shot for the cannons remained. From this we may infer that large amounts of powder and shot were spent by heavy artillery and musket fire alike during the actual storming of Nojpeten — the only time when these weapons would have been extensively used.

The implications of such a heavy investment in weaponry and ammunition are that Ursúa had intended from the outset of his final entrada to take the island by force and that he anticipated a strong defense. This conclusion is further supported by the superb timing of his arrival at Zubiaur's encampment just as the galeota components were completed and by the rapidity with which the vessel was assembled and launched. There can be no doubt, notwithstanding his claims that he made every effort to seek the Itzas' peaceful surrender during the first two weeks of March, that Ursúa had planned all along to attack the island quickly and with all the firepower at his disposal.

Noble Visitors at Ch'ich'

On the morning of Monday, March 10, 1697, three delegations of Maya notables arrived successively at Ch'ich', each intending to assess Ursúa's attack plan and seek last-minute peace negotiations. Ursúa treated each of the encounters differently. In the case of AjChan, now nominally a Christian convert, he took sworn testimony through interpreters and before Spanish witnesses. Such formalities were put aside in what appears to have been a friendly meeting and conversational interchange with Chamach Xulu and the other men from Yalain. Finally, to AjK'in Kan Ek' Ursúa addressed a brief speech and posed a single question. The record of each visit forms a separate *diligencia,* or judicial formality, properly signed by the officers, interpreters, and other witnesses in attendance.

Despite their legal format, these diligencias should not be regarded as literal records of what transpired that day. They are, by their very nature, biased to represent the interests of the person in charge of the situation. When we hear what purport to be the Itza visitors' voices, we should be aware that their words have been translated, reinterpreted, modified, and possibly even falsified. Any conversation or negotiating speech that took place is lost to us, especially in the case of AjChan, in favor of an asymmetrical question-answer formula that supported Ursúa's political aims. For any contemporaneous reader of the official record, the written text served to disempower the political interests of the Maya party. Ursúa asked the questions and personally recorded, without the intervention of notarial assistance, the answers he heard.[28]

The first visitor was the long-missing and presumed renegade AjChan, who had last been seen before he ran away from Tipuj the previous September. No specifics of the circumstances of his arrival are immediately provided, only that "he came among others from the lake, apparently from the large peten that is seen to be populated." As the testimony unfolds, it appears that he arrived not from Nojpeten but from a temporary encampment of his own on the lakeshore south of the main island. He and his companions must have been the advance guard for the next two parties. We can assume that the series of visits had been carefully coordinated, probably by AjChan himself, who must have been playing the role of diplomatic go-between in an effort to avert an attack on Nojpeten.

AjChan, whom Ursúa identified by his baptismal name, Martín, and the honorific title "don," was the only visitor that day who said "that he knows that he is Christian," and Ursúa took from him a sworn testimony "by the sign of the Holy Cross." His testimony was also the longest, because it was constructed by Ursúa in order to extract his whereabouts and activities since his disappearance from Tipuj. AjChan spoke in the presence of the interpreters, Ursúa, the priests Juan Pacheco and José Martínez de Mora, Captain García de Paredes, Ursúa's "ayudante general," Gaspar del Castillo Cetina, Captain José Laines, "and many other persons who understand the Maya language" (which, of course, Ursúa did not).

At the end of AjChan's recorded declaration, Ursúa asked him, "[W]hy has he given me news that some canoes are coming? And the said don Martín says they are from Yalain and that in them are coming the cacique Chamay Zulu [commonly known as Chamach Xulu] with his *principales* and the declarant's brothers. This judicial procedure is [therefore] left in this state."

Ursúa's "conversation" with AjChan halted abruptly because the second party of visitors had showed up. It included five men from Yalain who were observed coming "from the lake, apparently from the large peten." They must have arrived in several canoes, accompanied by paddlers and other retainers, but none of them is mentioned. Nojpeten was directly visible from Punta Nijtún, but their point of embarkation was apparently not observed. Because they were all from the Yalain area, I surmise that these visitors probably came not from Nojpeten, as Ursúa guessed, but from AjChan's encampment on the mainland.

Ursúa immediately ordered "that the person of don Martín Chan be retained in this headquarters in case it is necessary to take him to the city of Mérida." Apparently deciding that he could use AjChan as a witness in future trials of the Itza leaders, as an informant who could supply useful information about the Itzas, and as a person who could assist in capturing leaders hiding in the forests, Ursúa simply arrested him. When Ursúa led his troops in the galeota to attack Nojpeten three days later, AjChan accompanied the Spaniards, calling out to the islands' defenders to surrender and reportedly killing one of them.

The five other visitors were also from Yalain. Ursúa, without explanation, took unsworn testimony from them as a group. Principal among them was their spokesman, Chamach Xulu, the "cacique" of Yalain whom Avendaño had met in 1696. Three of the Spaniards in attendance — Father Juan Pacheco, Captain Bartolomé de la Garma, and Diego Bernardo del Río — had attended the magnificent reception of AjChan in Mérida in December 1695. They recognized two of the younger men in the group, both of whom had been baptized along with AjChan. On this occasion, however, these two must have refused to answer in the affirmative Ursúa's standard but unrecorded question, "Do you know that you are Christian?" **271**

The four attendants with Chamach Xulu were recorded as "the one named don Pedro Nicte, brother of the said ambassador, and the other named don Manuel Chayax, who is declared to be married to the sister of said don Martín [Chan], and another named Chayax, relative of don

Manuel, and likewise another who said he was named Kin Octe and a relative of said don Martín Chan."[29] Don Pedro Nikte (Nikte Chan) was the same "brother" of AjChan who had been baptized Pedro Miguel Chan in Mérida.[30] Don Manuel Chayax, who was indeed AjChan's sister's husband, had been baptized Manuel Joseph Chayax on the same occasion.[31] The other two, the unidentified Chayax and AjK'in Okte, had not accompanied their kinsman AjChan to Mérida.

Ursúa's report of his meeting with the Yalain contingent was brief and in narrative form — not in the formal question-answer format of AjChan's sworn testimony. Its summary nature suggests that their stay was quite brief. Although Ursúa made no mention of it, Manuel Joseph Chayax remained behind with his brother-in-law, AjChan, and accompanied the Spaniards during the attack on Nojpeten three days later. As soon as the others from Yalain left, Ursúa wrote, "there appeared other canoes in squadrons that came directly from the large peten with a white flag, in which, the said don Martín Chan stated, came Kin Canek, who is the great priest, the brother of the petty king Canek. I immediately ordered *tomar armas*,[32] and he was received with chirimía music in company with another Indian who the said Martín Chan stated is named Kitcan and who is head of another province; and [he also stated] that Kin Canek is equal in power to the petty king [Ajaw Kan Ek'] in all things that are ordered."[33]

Ursúa's meeting with AjK'in Kan Ek' (the high priest) and the otherwise unidentified Kit Kan was apparently longer and more formal than his reception of the Yalain representatives. He posed specific propositions to AjK'in Kan Ek', whom he clearly regarded as a spokesman for the Itza government; he spoke in threatening terms, only thinly veiled by the niceties of procedure and diplomatic language.

The noble visitors, no doubt, were themselves intently assessing not only the potential strength of Ursúa's military machine but also his plans and intentions. If his descriptions are to be believed, Ursúa staged his reception of the second and third parties as something less than a formal diplomatic ritual, but with accompanying chirimía music, welcoming and departure formalities, refreshments, proper seating, and presentation of gifts. The particular ritual was foreign, to be sure, but such ceremony was hardly unknown to Itza leaders. At the same time, Ursúa was not interested in hiding his warlike intentions, and the visitors must have seen the artillery, the defensive wall, and the galeota.

As we will see, Ursúa manipulated these encounters of March 10 to his own ends. The purpose of his procedures was clearly to record proof that whatever future action he might take was justified in the light of what the "enemy" had stated. His descriptive accounts of the visits and his record of the questioning together form a single legal document that was intended, as a whole, to prove that he treated his visitors with great courtesy, established the probable guilt of the Kan Ek' cousins in the murders of Guatemalans and Yucatecans the previous year, offered them clear terms for surrender, and threatened to cause them all severe harm if they refused these terms.

AJCHAN'S TESTIMONY

Like his questioning of AjChan in Mérida over a year earlier, Ursúa's interview on this occasion was designed to confirm or justify his prior assumptions and to set the stage for anticipated events. The constructed record, that is, explicitly legitimated widely shared assumptions about the Itzas, justified Ursúa's belief that AjChan had been the rightful ambassador of the true ruler of all the Itzas, and provided such damning evidence for the deceitfulness of Ajaw Kan Ek' and other leaders that an attack on Nojpeten could have been his only responsible action.

A two-part variation on the standard first question put to a sworn Christian witness opens the testimony. AjChan's recorded responses usually begin with "that" or "and that," resulting in lengthy run-on sentences. Here I have removed these conjunctions, separated his statements for purposes of clarity, and translated the text loosely for readability. I have omitted the repeated phrase, "and this he replies," which served to close each response. Ursúa's questioning voice and commentary appear in italics, and AjChan's recorded responses in regular typeface.[34]

> *Asked what is his name, his age, and his occupation, where he is a citizen and native, and — as he says he is Christian — where and when he was baptized, he said:* His name is don Martín Chan, native of the large peten where the king is, son of Chan, native of Tipu, and of Cante, elder sister of Canek who governs these places. A snake bit his father, from which he died. He heard it said that his mother, who also died long ago, came from Chichen Itza. He [became] a Christian a year ago in the city.
>
> *And asked if it was [a city] of Spaniards, he replied that [it was] in the city where I had been and to which I took him to baptize [him].* He did not know how to say his age. He is married to an Indian woman named Couoh in Yalain. His father-in-law Couoh was in this bay and out of fear did not enter to speak in this royal encampment.
>
> *He did not know how to describe his occupation.*

273

In contrast to Ursúa's more general questioning of AjChan on December 29, 1695 (see chapter 7), on this occasion the standard opener revealed several important, previously unknown details about his birthplace and his closest kin. The question about the location of his baptism seems superfluous until we realize that Ursúa wished to prove to future readers that it was he himself who had brought about AjChan's baptism and that the high-status Christian, don Martín Chan, recognized this deed. The intrusion of Ursúa's voice in the first person simply reinforces this point.

Ajaw Kan Ek' is here portrayed, as he is throughout Ursúa's accounts, as the king who rules over all—"who governs these places." AjChan is seen by Ursúa as closely connected to the royal family, an important personage who carried the full legitimacy of a royal ambassador when he visited Mérida in December 1695. AjKowoj, on the other hand, is depicted as a coward, fearing even to visit Ursúa when he was in the bay at Ch'ich'.

This Kowoj, identified as AjChan's father-in-law, was the same leader who had challenged, even threatened, Avendaño during his visit to Nojpeten nearly a year earlier. As we have seen, however, he and the ruler's uncle were at war with Ajaw Kan Ek', partly over the issue of the willingness of Ajaw Kan Ek' to negotiate with the Spaniards. AjChan claims that AjKowoj had actually been in the bay, where he would have seen the encampment. His failure to visit was more likely out of fear of reprisal for the murders of Spaniards than an expression of refusal to negotiate.

The big surprise is AjChan's statement that his mother was from Chich'en Itza. Ajaw Kan Ek' himself later claimed that "[ever] since they came from Chichen Itza his ancestors attain the said lordship,"[35] but AjChan's statement is the only direct suggestion of a more recent genealogical connection between the Kan Ek' dynasty and people in northern Yucatán.

Ursúa's next questions addressed the circumstances under which AjChan made his trip to Mérida in December 1695:

> *Asked why he went to the city a year ago and who sent him, he said:*
> The king Ah Canek sent him (and three other Indians from Yalain, where he is a citizen, and where his wife, by whom he has a son, lives, went [with him]) with a message, giving them a crown of feathers so that he might offer it in his name and offer submission, as he wished to communicate with the Spaniards in order to join them in knowledge of the true God.

This "answer" was nothing more than a rewording of AjChan's testimony in Mérida—more likely words "put in his mouth" by Ursúa, to which he gave an affirmative reply. By extracting this response, Ursúa simply confirmed the authenticity of AjChan's original mission.

The next segment of the testimony, again containing no new information, further reinforced this purpose:

> *Asked from where he went to Mérida, how long he spent before he arrived to deliver his message, and what happened to him in the city, and what preparations had been made for him for his reception, and those [preparations] that were made for him in Yalain, he said:* Having departed Yalain he knows that he went with his companions via Tipu, where the Indians from the Muzul nation had been assembled. Although they were many, only two [of them] accompanied him. These told him that they wished to go with him for the same intention of requesting fathers-ministers, just as his uncle Canek had order him [to do]. Although he knows that they are savages and live barbarously, he took them with him.
>
> The preparation carried out in Yalain for the reception of the fathers who were to come consisted of the gift of food and all related large preparations, including a new, large house that is already constructed.
>
> From [Tipuj] he went with the aforementioned companions to the large town of the Spaniards, where he was received with much joy and with gifts from all of the Spaniards, on account of which he received with all his heart the law of God in the water of baptism.
>
> *So great was the love with which he was received that I seated him elegantly at my table. By this example he was made to understand. Once he had given his message and been cured of his illness caused by [the trip], I presented him with a gift of various things for Canek, [which] he left in Tipu. This declarant was also given various things, and the other Indians who went with him were provided with clothes.*

The preceding passage, which shifts abruptly to Ursúa's own first-person voice as he describes the good treatment that he accorded AjChan, suggests that Ursúa wrote most of it after their meeting. The choice of subject matter, the reaffirmation of AjChan's desire to seek missionaries, the reference to the house built for Avendaño (which the friar had himself described in sworn testimony), the epithets ("savages" and "barbarously") applied to the Musuls, and Ursúa's self-righteous praise for his own kindnesses all point to the probability that AjChan himself said very few of these things.

275

The next question concerned the good treatment that AjChan and his companions had experienced during their return trip to Tipuj, as well as the motive for AjChan's running away from the Spaniards there. This section, which contains important information and served as a means for Ursúa to establish AjChan's innocence in running away, was discussed in chapter 9.

Ursúa next addressed the issue that most concerned him — the identification of those who had killed the Guatemalan and Yucatecan "visitors":

> *Asked where he went to stay after [he left] Tipu, he said:* To his own town of Yalain, where the cacique is Chamay Zulu. The others told him that the Indians of Chacta [Chata] and those of Puc, along with the rest, joined in and united in disobedience to the king Canek. [These] joined together and committed the wickedness against those who came from Yucatán via this settlement as well as against those of Guatemala toward the area south of where we now are.

The first part of this passage is clearly AjChan's voice, for he mentions nobles (Chata and Puk) of whom Ursúa probably had no prior knowledge. Furthermore, having already established his own innocence by maintaining that he was in Tipuj when the Yucatecans were murdered, he also attempts to exonerate Ajaw Kan Ek' — hardly a claim that Ursúa would have been likely to accept. Ursúa further probed the matter:

> *Asked what they did with all the others and the fathers they captured from both territories and how many he has heard it said were from Guatemala, he said:* He heard it said that they killed those from Yucatán [who were] captured on this beach where we are, and [that] those from Guatemala [were] captured while they were sleeping in the savannah, and that they ate them and the pack animals. As for the religious fathers he cannot give account nor has he heard anything; because they are not accustomed to seeing fathers, they perceived them to be Spaniards like the rest. Although the king has gone about chasing after this evil deed, on account of having delivered his crown for peace, he has been unable to restrain these disobedient Indians. All of them tell lies.
>
> The Indians of Chata and the Pucs have distanced themselves one day by road from the peten. Some of them had been settled in the milperías [cultivations] by which we have come. One must not confide in anyone, because the king is unable to reach agreement with them. He also heard said that they killed those from Yucatán in the water and that none reached the peten.[36]

Now that AjChan has established his own innocence, he proceeds to implicate even more deeply the supposed enemies of Ajaw Kan Ek', Chata and Puk, who, with their followers, he continues to claim, had been the real perpetrators of the murders. "Chata" here may refer to Noj AjChata, *alias* Reyezuelo Tesukan (see table 3.7 and accompanying text). The head of the Puks may have been the "cacique" called Ayikal Puk (chapter 5), here identified as an ally of the warring faction of the north. The testimony claims that Ajaw Kan Ek', still true to his promises to the Spaniards, tried but was unable either to stop these renegades from committing the evil deeds or to punish them afterward. AjChan implies, however, that Ajaw Kan Ek' made their lives so difficult by sending armed parties after them that they relocated farther north from the lake along the very road taken by the Spanish troops. Although Ursúa's later actions indicate that he did not believe this account, I am inclined to think it was in most essentials correct.

Ursúa then proceeded to test AjChan by seeking his version of the motives of the murderers:

> *Asked what he has heard told concerning the motive of all of the Indians that made them commit the evil deed of killing the Spaniards from Yucatán and Guatemala, [in spite of] Canek's having sent a message that all wished to know the true God, he said:* What he has heard told is that they carried out the evil deed and that it would be by order of the demon that is in the idols. He does not know the motive.

This, presumably, was not what Ursúa expected to hear — or was it? If a demon inhabited the "idols" and gave orders through them, then it must have been the high priest, AjK'in Kan Ek', who was the perpetrator of the murders. By indirectly and perhaps unwittingly implicating the cousin of Ajaw Kan Ek', AjChan had shifted the blame back to the Kan Ek' ruler-priest pair. Ursúa, fascinated by the idea of talking idols, explored the matter further:

> *Asked if the demons in his town speak, and where they are, he said:* They do speak in the idols, and this declarant has spoken to them. When Canek appointed him to go to the city, one [of them] told him that his intention to go to see the Spaniards weighed heavily on him. Why had he gone unless he had been Spanish,[37] having come back already a Christian? What they [i.e., the idols] do seems very bad to him. Therefore, all of the Indians have looked upon the de-

clarant, like the rest who came back as Christians, with horror and
ill will. It also appears to this declarant that he has become repug-
nant to them and that they speak continually with the devil through
the idols.

Asked how many sections of idolatry the large peten has, he said:
Fifteen, and each one is a house or a large church. Only by seeing
the quantity of idols can they be counted, because he cannot describe it in any other way.

Using his own imagination, Ursúa could not have concocted better
evidence for the devil's handiwork: the Christian Martín Francisco Chan
and his companions in the faith were being persecuted by talking idols.
AjChan had implicated AjK'in Kan Ek' as the principal mortal enemy
of God, because Ursúa would have considered him to be the principal
spokesman for these images. The effect of his testimony was to help build
the case that Nojpeten was a place of idolaters (and, by implication, that
AjK'in Kan Ek' was the real enemy) and that therefore it had to be taken
by force. Ursúa, both in his own writings and through the testimonies that
he extracted from his officers, would later refer repeatedly to the Itzas'
paganism as a major justification for their military conquest. This is not to
say, however, that AjChan's testimony was bogus; other sources also indicate that Itza priests communicated through speech with ritual images (see
chapter 3).

The status of the next passage is much less ambiguous and may be
taken at face value:

Asked where he has been since he came from Yalain and what he has
been doing, he said: He left Yalain and in fear went to Motzcal,[38]
which is a small peten where there is only one house. He was there
with an Indian named Pana. Having been seen by the king's people,
the king sent for him, and he went to the water's shore. There he has
been afraid that the neighboring Indians would harm him.

[He has spent] all of these [past] days having to disperse squadrons [of war canoes], because the impostures of the Indians had
been those of war against the Spaniards. They say that they must
kill them. For four days he had brought over a defense watch so
that they would not come here.

AjChan had apparently gone directly from Tipuj to his hometown, Yalain,
on Laguneta Macanché. From there, according to this passage, he sought
hiding under the protection of one AjPana at the small island of Motzkal

(which may have been Islote Grande, just east of Nojpeten), close enough to have soon been discovered by "the king's people."

Upon being called for by Ajaw Kan Ek', AjChan moved his encampment to the lakeshore, but at an unspecified location, where he feared attack by his neighbors. By implication, he did not risk visiting Nojpeten itself. He had spent the past four days patrolling the bay against squadrons coming to attack the Spaniards.[39] Although the passage reads as if AjChan had gone alone with AjPana to Motzkal, and then alone to his new location on the lakeshore, this was certainly not the case. We can assume that he took a substantial group of followers from Yalain—in essence, a small army—to both places, setting up defensive encampments in each place.

Who were the squadrons from which he claimed to be defending the Spaniards? AjChan does not identify them, but we can assume that they were from Nojpeten. In the passage that follows he implicates Ajaw Kan Ek' himself in this activity:

> *Asked what preparations have been made recently on the large peten and on the other petens, he said:* Only on the large peten do they have defensive walls [*trincheras*]. These are built on low ground. On high ground there are none. They intend to fight.
> *Asked by whose order the said defensive walls were built, he said:* It will [*sic*] be that of Canek.

Ursúa had now established to his satisfaction that it was Ajaw Kan Ek' himself, in league with the high priest, who had determined to defend Nojpeten rather than to surrender. Their defenses, however, may have been intended to protect them as much from their Itza enemies of the north as from the Spaniards. Ursúa gave AjChan no opportunity to explain his uncle's ambiguous political position in the situation in which he found himself. Was he being held hostage by his own leaders, or had he reversed his earlier pro-Spanish stance and joined the Itza loyalists? Whatever the case, with a statement on record that Ajaw Kan Ek' was prepared to take on the Spaniards militarily, Ursúa would require little further justification for a decisive battle to gain control of the island capital.

Ursúa then turned his questioning to the issue of Itza political organization, which had long confused the Spaniards. AjChan's lengthy response was transformed by Ursúa into a series of brief intelligence statements:

> *Asked how many superiors there are on the petens, he said:* The superior of all is Ah Canek. Another is called Yahkin Canek [AjK'in

279

Kan Ek']. They are united and [have been] settled for a long time on the large island.

The cacique of Yalain [is] called Chamay Zulu. He heard it said that this [leader] and his people had wished to be Christians. It was by there that the fathers who were on the large peten went, and they treated them very well. They gave them gifts and sent them off. It will [*sic*] be by water. They live on one body of water.

[There is] another settlement, of the Couohs, one day's distance from this lake, whose Indians have split apart from each other. Their cacique is called Lax Couoh. Because they are carrying out war with those of this lake, the land road has been closed. Having fought with the people of Yalain, the said Couohs took away all their clothes and left them naked.

Near the road from Guatemala there is another small lake where the cacique Puc is located, inhabited by all the people of Chata and his [own people], who are many. The Spaniards will have noted that the lake does not have as many canoes now as before; [this is] as a result of their having left. The lake where the cacique Puc is now located is a day's distance from here; around it they have milperías.

Those of the peten have gone out armed with arrows, killing many of the runaway Indians, including the Chatas and Pucs. In recent days the Chatas and Pucs have come to the large main peten wishing to surrender. The declarant turned them away, not wishing to receive them, for which reason they have not been supported by Ah Canek. They [then] availed themselves of a remote place toward the north to which they have already gone.

AjChan apparently side-stepped Ursúa's first question, referring only to Ajaw Kan Ek' and his cousin, AjK'in Kan Ek'. The rest of his response spells out recent disruptions and relocations of other major political groups. His own people at Yalain under Chamach (also called Chamay) Xulu had recently been attacked by a splinter group of Kowojs under Lax Kowoj, who had resettled in the Lagunas Yaxhá and Sacnab area. Because AjChan's father-in-law, AjKowoj, is known from other sources to have attacked Nojpeten sometime during 1696 — presumably because of support by Ajaw Kan Ek' for Spanish interests — it is perhaps no surprise that his relative and presumed ally, Lax Kowoj, attacked the people of Yalain from his base around Lagunas Yaxhá and Sacnab, likely for the same reason. Regardless of his father-in-law's position, AjChan makes certain to point out that people of Yalain were Christian sympathizers and had supported both the visit by Avendaño and his own trip to Mérida.

The followers of Chata (possibly Noj AjChata) and Puk had run away from the western end of the main lake, seeking refuge, we may assume, from the advancing army. Some of them, according to an earlier statement by AjChan, had moved north, not far from the camino real; but others, he now states, escaped to the south, around Lagunas Oquevix and Ijá, where B'atab' Tut, who in 1696 was the second ruler of the north, also relocated — either at this time or at a later date.[40] Puk, it would seem, had since replaced Tut as the second ruler of the north or was another important Chak'an Itza leader. Some of this movement had occurred within the past ten days: the Spaniards, he says, should have observed a drop in the number of canoes in the area. Having suffered attacks from, presumably, the followers of Ajaw Kan Ek', a delegation from Chata and Puk had since visited Nojpeten seeking reconciliation.

The next statement — that the Chatas and Puks were turned away at Nojpeten by AjChan himself — casts AjChan as a supporter of Ajaw Kan Ek' against these renegades who, unknown to Ursúa, may have planned to kill the Itza ruler. AjChan must have set up his encampment on the main shore just south of Nojpeten, because there he could have confronted the Chata-Puk delegation, dealing with Ajaw Kan Ek' by courier. Unlike the Christian-sympathizing leaders of Yalain, the Puks and Chatas, the accused guilty parties in the murders, are portrayed as enemies of both the Spaniards and the ruler himself.

Stubborn to the end and wishing to implicate everyone possible in the murders, Ursúa asked AjChan yet again who did it:

> *Asked if he knows or has heard said if Indians [who] are now on the large peten were accomplices in the murders committed against those of both Yucatán and Guatemala, he said:* According to the conversations he has heard he can name no one, only that all have guilt in the murders that were committed in one or the other place.

Whether or not AjChan actually said that "all have guilt," he had previously made it clear that Ajaw Kan Ek' himself was not guilty. Although the Puks and Chatas had allies in committing the murders, Ajaw Kan Ek' also had a sufficient alliance, including the forces of AjChan, to require them to leave the environs of the main lake, to attack and kill some of them, and to refuse their negotiations of surrender. Had it not been for the protection offered the ruler by AjChan, the Itza king's enemies might have overthrown the dynasty before Ursúa could launch the galeota on March 13.

281

Still convinced that he was being tricked and misled, Ursúa began to
test AjChan with further questions, but the testimony was interrupted by
the arrival of the next group of visitors:

> *Asked for what cause or reason he left the gift in Tipu that was given
> to him in the city [Mérida] for Ah Canek, and if he has informed
> Canek of the gift that was given to him, he said:* He left the gift in
> the possession of Captain Hariza, with whom he came, because, as a
> result of the fear that the cacique Zima instilled in him, he left with-
> out giving notification. When he later left Motzcal, where he was
> hiding with Pana, he reported to Canek and his wife Pana and told
> them about the gift that had been given to each of them.
>   *And why has he given me news that some canoes are coming?*
> *And the said don Martín says:* They are from Yalain and that in
> them are coming the cacique Chamay Zulu with his principales and
> the declarant's brothers. This judicial procedure is left in this state.

THE DECLARATION OF CHAMACH XULU
AND HIS DELEGATION

Ursúa claimed that he received Chamach Xulu and the other four men
from Yalain "with much friendly attention, chirimía music, and embraces
[after which] they were provided refreshment, and after all this I took
pleasure in seeing them, the said Chamay Zulu said that he was happy to
see me because he had wished to do so."[41] AjChan had succeeded in
convincing Ursúa that Chamach Xulu was a good ally of the Spaniards.
What followed reads as if it were a monologue by the principal visitor in
which he catalogued his personal role in the early initiation of contact
with Mérida. He was the person who,

> by order of Canek, had sent don Martín Chan with the other In-
> dians from his town to the city, for which they were all called to the
> peten where the king gave him the order to send them. He [Cha-
> mach Xulu] had the authority to request fathers so that they would
> teach the law of the true God, to arrange the preparations of sup-
> plies and chickens to give them when they came to his town, and
> also to build a large new house in which to receive them. Later,
> when don Martín departed for Tipu to deliver his message, he initi-
> ated the construction of the house, and he still has it today, as it has
> not been more than a year since he built it.
>   [Following the arrival] of some fathers who left the peten, trans-
> ported by the [*sic*] Canek, he received them in Yalain, regaled them,

and gave them a guide to instruct them about the road. He told the fathers that he, along with all of his province, wished to be Christians and to know the true God, and now, once again, he says the same thing.

While all this may have been true, he failed to mention that the guide he provided to Avendaño deserted the friars, who quickly became lost in the forest.

Ursúa, pleased with "such good intent," responded with a speech in which he proffered "the great moderation with which he and all his province will be treated and the comfort that they will receive in their souls." The visit must have been a short one, because the visitors were quickly presented with the customary gift of axes and machetes for the men and belts and beads for their wives at home. Ursúa hurried them off "with every friendly attention, accompanied by music all the way to the embarkment; and they were very contented, leaving them [in this way] so that they would lose their suspicions, as [I] came *de paso y paz* in conformity with His Majesty's orders."

It was obvious to the Yalain visitors that this military encampment was no expression of a policy of "paso y paz," and they surely did not trust Ursúa's assurances of good treatment. This was, nonetheless, the first time that Ursúa had singled out in writing a particular Itza province and implied that he would pursue different policies of conquest in different political provinces. The next delegation, the object of his ire, was almost what he had been waiting for.

"NEGOTIATIONS" WITH AJK'IN KAN EK'

Ursúa had hoped to play host to Ajaw Kan Ek', but he received AjK'in Kan Ek' and one of the three provincial rulers called Kit Kan instead. Their arrival was an impressive sight, and they were greeted with the customary dignity. After the visitors were seated, AjK'in Kan Ek' was the first to speak, saying, reportedly, "that he was very pleased in his heart that his Indians were received in such a friendly manner."[42]

Nothing more of the speech by AjK'in Kan Ek' is recorded, but Ursúa took great pains to write a summary of his own aggressive response: "I responded that it pleased me to see him, and [I reminded him] that his people had already told him about the good treatment and friendship with which they had been received and regaled without any inducement, and [that] I was here by order of the King our lord don Carlos the Second (whom God may protect), to open, in peace and not war, a road and pass

283

on to Guatemala, and that he should understand this, because if they were to make and arrange war they would find it in me with punishment, and I would take them from under the earth to punish them; and if they wished peace they would have it, along with much love and affection and everything they might need." Ursúa's saber-rattling language gave AjK'in Kan Ek' few practical options. Ursúa was obviously already planning to execute punishment, and nothing short of full surrender—which he did not call for on this occasion—would have satisfied him.

But AjK'in Kan Ek', replying "that they did not wish war but peace, and that he was ready to keep it," immediately changed the subject to the camino real. His strategy was a long shot—to focus on the issue of the road in order to keep the Spaniards moving on to Guatemala, bypassing the lake altogether: "Having discussed the road from Guatemala he said, pointing toward the south, that it reached up to the water's shore at the other part of the lake. Having advised him that he assemble his Indians to open a solid land road to Guatemala, without crossing the lake, he responded that he would order his Indians to open it lower down at the west [end] where the lake terminates. He was then promised satisfaction."

Ursúa, of course, had no intention of abandoning the galeota and proceeding to Guatemala with his hundreds of men and large store of equipment. The high prophet, however, had much at stake in keeping the army at bay, so to speak, until it might take up the route to the south of an earlier traveler, Hernán Cortés. Cortés had headed an even larger army and retinue when he arrived at the lakeshore during K'atun 2 Ajaw, and the Itza leaders of that time must have feared that he, like Ursúa now, would attack and conquer them. Could AjK'in Kan Ek' have harbored the futile hope that history was about to repeat itself and this new general, too, would just go away? If Ursúa had any hint of such a hope, he chose to ignore it, changing the subject to the same topic he had posed to Chamach Xulu, that of the legitimacy of AjChan's trip to Mérida:

> *Asked what message was sent from the large peten a year ago now, by whose order, to what effect, and who was the messenger, he said:* This declarant [AjK'in Kan Ek'] and his brother the king ordered the message, and his nephew Chan carried it with a crown, requesting communication with the Spaniards and the law of the true God and padres to teach them. And said Chan was called with his brother Nicte from Yalain to the large peten, where he was given the message. Having also called Chamay Zulu, cacique of the said town of Yalain, they ordered him to inform and send via Tipu his

two nephews with other Indians and to prepare for their return a gift of food and a large new house in which to receive the padres. And to this end he knows that they built the house and that his nephews went to see the great one of the Spaniards and that they took the padres as far as Tipu.

Ursúa thereupon recorded, "It is appropriate for now not to touch upon the treacheries carried out by the Indians of this lake against Spaniards and Indians of Guatemala and Yucatán. Due to the malevolence of the matter it is not treated until it is seen whether the person of Ah Canek is obtained." That is, he had determined that the only person with whom he could have full diplomatic dealings would be Ajaw Kan Ek', whom he perceived to be the supreme ruler of the Itzas and thus responsible for the actions of his "vassals." This meeting, however, was not to take place.

Justifying Conquest

Ursúa and his officers sent this last set of visitors off with the usual set of gifts and formal words of departure. Over the next two days Ursúa pondered his situation and prepared a detailed "proposition" in which he reviewed long-past events and those of the last several days.[43] He read this paper to the assembled military officers on Monday, March 12, demanding their advice on the next step to be taken. The galeota was completed, and the troops were ready for an attack on Nojpetén. The council, or at least Ursúa's recording of its minutes, would further legitimate whatever action he decided to take.

The "proposition" was hardly that, for Ursúa proposed no specific action. Implicit, perhaps, was the assumption that the time for attack was at hand, but he was careful, in speaking from a written text, not to play his hand. By seeking opinions from his officers he would ultimately be able to show his superiors that everyone had agreed and that little choice remained but to use force against what he maintained was a cumulative Itza record of treachery.

Little in Ursúa's pronouncement at the royal encampment was new. He summarily reviewed the legal basis for his enterprise thus far and outlined the history of events that began with García de Paredes's first entrada to Kejach territory in 1695. Much of his account was skeletal and dispassionate. Even his description of the massacres of the Guatemalans and Yucatecans was cool and apparently "factual." His claim, however, that he himself was simply following royal wishes in coming to the region "de paz y de paso," for the sole purposes of reducing natives and opening the road to Guatemala, would have strained the credulity of any colonial readers familiar with the geography.

Ursúa contended that AjChan had been a legitimate representative of a genuine ruler when he visited Mérida in December 1695, an interpretation crucial to his own diplomatic and military strategy but doubted by many in local colonial circles. Yet even officials and encomenderos in Campeche and Mérida could not effectively challenge Ursúa's reports of his encounters with the Maya leaders on March 10 or, far more significantly, his reports of other encounters with the Petén Mayas in his war council report. The March 10 testimonies were clouded by ambiguities and complexities, compounded by Ursúa's obfuscation. His report of these other experiences with the local population, however—no matter how blatantly ethnocentric they may seem to a modern reader—would have been politically compelling, empirically straightforward, and emotionally distressing to almost any colonial official.

Ursúa's public rationale for his actions so far—sending García "to take possession of the islands and towns of the lake"[44] and displaying his arms and military prowess on the lake's principal western port—rested on the "truth" and validity of AjChan's diplomatic overtures in Mérida. If Ajaw Kan Ek' had sincerely offered peaceful surrender through his nephew, any action taken by Ursúa would be justified as a forceful claim to what had already been offered. Ursúa's strategy could not admit to the possibility that Ajaw Kan Ek' had lost his ability to rule and that AjChan's representations were no longer politically relevant.

Ursúa was not alone in creating the "paper trail" that justified his actions. On the afternoon of March 13, following the storming of Nojpeten, Bachiller Juan Pacheco de Sopuerta, the troops' chaplain, and his "lieutenant," Bachiller José Francisco Martínez de Mora, prepared a "certification" that further served the purpose.[45] They repeated Ursúa's claim that while at the encampment at Ch'ich' the captain general had made every effort to procure the friendship of Ajaw Kan Ek', citing the gifts, meals, music, and formalities provided the other visitors. Ursúa, they wrote, had offered secure passage to Ajaw Kan Ek' himself and had asked AjK'in Kan Ek' to assure the Itza king that Ursúa came in peace, merely passing on his way to Guatemala. Ajaw Kan Ek' himself, they wrote, was to have visited the encampment on March 12, bringing with him other leaders and his relatives. The two priests claimed that AjK'in Kan Ek' understood the nature of the invitation and promised that he would return with Ajaw Kan Ek' and his followers on the appointed day. Furthermore, AjK'in Kan Ek' had promised that on March 11, in return for axes and machetes, he would provide workers to begin the opening of the road to Guatemala along the southern side of the lake. Neither promise was fulfilled, and during the next two days canoes appeared near the shore of the encampment whose crews seemed hostile, convincing the priests that the Itza leaders had no peaceful intentions.

Female Visitors and Useless Gifts

In their certification the priests recounted that while these hostile canoe crews taunted the Spaniards on March 11 and 12, "many women at different times went to the royal encampment, without [our] having succeeded in discovering their intention,[46] and said lord [Ursúa] ordered that they be received with the modesty and dignity appropriate to the service of our Lord God, and that they be taken to the storehouse . . . [where they were regaled with] aguardiente and biscuit . . . , many-colored belts, strung beads for necklaces, and earrings, and they were sent off under guard to the landing place with the same modesty, still disallowing disrespectful conduct." Ursúa himself wrote, in his later account of these events to the Crown, "Many infidel women from this island came alone in canoes without [my] having been able to discover the pretext or diabolical scheme. After three days, during which they were received, beautified, adorned, regaled, and sent off with the restraint, decency, and modesty appropriate to the service of our Lord God, bearing in mind many examples of this quality."[47] These accounts of the women's visitations to the encampment differ only in the timing attributed to them. According to the priests, they arrived after the March 10 delegations of Maya leaders, whereas Ursúa wrote that they preceded the delegations, seemingly implying that their good treatment by the Spaniards influenced the Maya leaders to visit the encampment themselves.

We can accept both Ursúa's account of the order of events, which he repeated elsewhere,[48] and that of the priests. If both were correct, the camp was visited repeatedly by women, unaccompanied by men, for a period of about a week before the assault on the island. Both Ursúa and the priests claimed to have been unable to discern the purpose of these visits, although Ursúa opined that behind them must have been some "pretext or diabolical scheme." That he felt further compelled to state that they were treated with "restraint, decency, and modesty" suggests that these women were on an erotic mission and that he believed they had been sent by their own men to seduce the soldiers. He ordered his men, if his order is to be taken literally, to resist temptation and, instead, to limit their pleasure to braiding the women's hair and adorning them with jewelry and brightly colored belts.

The women's visits might be seen as part of a strategy by the Mayas at Nojpeten to lessen the threat of an imminent attack. To take the matter further and suggest, as Marshall Sahlins did for Hawaiian women's similar behavior toward European sailors in 1778, that the action reflected complex cultural responses to perceived foreign social power would certainly not be supported by such scanty information.[49] Whether the Maya women were sent to defuse a volatile situation, were acting on their own peace-making initiative, or were simply displaying a desire for Spanish trinkets cannot be known.

Ursúa's public strategy appears to have been to "win over" his nonelite visitors by presenting them with valuable gifts that their own leaders would have been unable to distribute. His intention was clearly to claim Nojpeten for the Spanish Crown, but perhaps, he argued, steel tools, salt, and jewelry would strengthen the commoners' disaffection for their own hostile leaders. He claimed that he had begun to achieve his goal when at last the official delegations arrived on the scene: "It appears that these circumstances were an incentive for luring Kin Canek (the king's brother) and Kitcan, Canek's lieutenant. Having been presented with gifts of axes, machetes, knives, and salt, just as for the other Indians, and having been received with the necessary solemnity and pomp, they were made to understand that I was pleased to see them."[50]

But Ursúa never offered these visitors the opportunity to discuss terms of surrender. Instead, he considered their visits only a prelude to an obligatory audience with their "king":

> After being invited to eat with me today, and [told] that they should come with the king Canek so that we might discuss matters convenient to our peace and the purpose of my coming — and also [told that] the said Kin Canek was obliged to drive his Indians later on to open a land road toward Guatemala without the need to cross this lake, their work being paid in axes and machetes — and because they have failed and fail in everything they say and propose, and [because] this morning when I waited for the said Ah Canek, Kin Canek, and Kitcan to eat with me, a number of canoes appeared, whose Indians came making warlike displays, provoking war de-

spite all that has been expressed, I found myself in the frame of mind of seeing whether the force of cajolery and gifts can lure these infidels to the obedience of the King our lord and to the profession of our holy faith.[51]

The preceding statement, a crescendo of bitter and angry frustration, climaxes with Ursúa's obviously facetious conclusion that he had been a fool to wait for "the force of cajolery and gifts" to herd such warlike barbarians into the corral of Christendom. The only alternative, although it is left unstated, must be war. All was in readiness, and all that he officially lacked for a direct attack on Nojpeten was his officers' support. Ursúa wrote, "whereas . . . the galeota is completely finished, and [inasmuch as] the Indian who this morning was falsely introduced as the ambassador of the Couohs for having three times found himself captured in the royal encampment declares through the interpreters that Kitcan has all of the provinces of the region united on the large peten to wage war, I, in view of that which all express, will determine myself what I judge to be most efficacious in the execution of His Majesty's orders. That which each one votes will be registered separately so that it will be clear."

Ursúa's final justification for attack demonstrated either his lack of knowledge of the civil war that gripped Itza territory or his refusal to recognize it. He refused to believe that his captive was in fact an ambassador for the Kowojs, although he gave full credence to his testimony that a Kit Kan was in charge of a united defense of Nojpeten. By implication, Ajaw Kan Ek' was now powerless, perhaps having already left Nojpeten in search of refuge from his own internal enemies. Ursúa, determined to mount an attack, decided to ignore political complexities and the opportunity for a negotiated settlement. His officers, as we now see, supported him fully.

War Council

Ursúa's records of verbal declarations, as we have seen so many times, are not literal renderings of speakers' words but rather his "interpretation" of what they said. As was so often his practice, the commander-in-chief served as his own clerk and scribe in recording the proceedings of the *junta de guerra*, or war council, held on March 12.[52] This is not to say, however, that the officers at this meeting did not express views similar to those that emerged in writing.

Ursúa's second-in-command, Captain Alonso García de Paredes, cited his long experience in the region, as if to say that no matter how long one waited for gifts and kindness to counteract idolatry, people controlled by the devil cannot be converted peaceably. On the basis of his twenty-five years of local experience (a record that complemented Ursúa's own lack of local knowledge), during which he had been

> carrying out entradas and domesticating the forest dwellers and rebels, and restraining their insults, [García de Paredes] finds that they attribute all their feelings to the idols, which keeps them apart from the knowledge of God's kindness. In the domesticated towns idolatries are found every day, and as sons of the lie they never profess something of truth by the gospel. The devil governs them. . . . Experience even teaches that ever since the original conquest, abhorring the divine cult, they go to idolatrize in the forests, and also that they have carried out their many rebellions on account of their natural aversion to Christianity.

To such visions of the moral depravity of the Mayas, this pragmatic soldier added a list of more practical motivations that would justify armed conquest: the value of opening the new road to Guatemala, the loss of security from closure of the fort of Santo Tomás in Honduras (a dubious argument), the agricultural promise of the region's fertile lands, and the possibility of unspecified future discoveries (presumably gold and silver).

As for AjChan's excuse that Ajaw Kan Ek' had been unable to control his "vassals" when they committed the recent massacres, García considered such a rationale "frivolous." Only "formal conquest" would "punish the aggressors of so much death carried out treacherously." A just punishment would be, in his closing words, "that the heads of all the false priests be cut off, as well as those of the old men who teach the idolatries; that their temples be demolished and in their place be erected the triumph of the Holy Cross in order to cast out the devil and to exalt our holy Catholic faith; and that God be washed where he has been offended so deeply." Such words were a call to holy war, a reiteration that only military conquest could free these unfortunates from the devil's control. Only the guiltiest parties, the priests who carried out the devil's wishes, were to be executed, as part of a cleansing that would eliminate all traces of idol-

290 atrous behavior. Once washed of such evil influences, the rest of the population would be ready to receive "our holy Catholic faith."

This was a top-down model of native religion that, except for its conviction that only violent destruction could eliminate evil, mirrored the Franciscan vision of a populace ready to accept the gospel if only the influences of a depraved priesthood could be eliminated. To the Franciscans, however, the means had to be peaceful, based on the voluntary, spiritual experience of the native leaders. Theirs was warfare of the soul, whereas the soldiers, pragmatic and impatient, believed that conversion could be speeded along by a clean sweep of the physical and political trappings of native ideology. Both models, of course, shared the ultimate goal of full colonial incorporation of the native population.

Captains Fernández de Estenos and Zubiaur Isasi spoke only briefly, seconding the statement of García de Paredes. Captain Nicolás de Aya, however, urged just enough caution to impart an impression that the meeting had more than one point of view. He stated that "knowing the pusillanimity of the Indians and in light of the completion of the galeota, he is of the opinion that before beginning warfare the islands or petens should be [visited] to see if some persons can be captured to carry peace messages to Canek, in order [to fulfill the] obedience to the King our lord, and to those [messengers] who deliver them no evil or any harm be committed against them. In the event they resist, the royal arms should enter, punishing and taking the lives of the false priests, commanders, and old Indian men, leaving the servants and small children." Otherwise, he said, he was in agreement with García.

Captain Diego de Avila Pacheco, on the other hand, agreed with García "to the letter," claiming on the basis of his experiences elsewhere in New Spain and New Vizcaya that "the Indians of every region are of the same nature, sons of the lie and of treason." Unlike the other officers, however, he distinguished between independent groups such as those whom they now confronted and the "domesticated" natives whose loyalty they threatened to undermine: "And the same domesticated [peoples] are excited to rebellion by their bad example, for which reason it is necessary to attack with blood and fire in order to punish such inhuman atrocities."

Captain Bartolomé de la Garma, applying legal reasoning, cited the massacres that followed AjChan's mission to Mérida as a form of "inhuman treason" that justified the "exemplary punishment" of Ajaw Kan Ek' and "all his allies." The massacres, he argued, had taken place following a legal agreement between Ajaw Kan Ek' and the colonial government and in a situation in which the visiting Spanish troops should have been offered full security. For this reason Ajaw Kan Ek' should bear full responsibility for the deaths. An attack on Nojpeten and the subsequent punishment of the murderers would therefore be the appropriate, justified action.

With brief affirmations of the need to apply a policy of "blood and fire" by the three remaining officers, Ursúa composed a closing statement to the

291

effect that in light of all of the recorded opinions the royal decrees demanding peaceful policies must nonetheless be taken into full account. To this end he ordered that no officer, soldier, or other person, on pain of immediate execution, break out arms against any defender "until receiving my order that I shall issue in the operations and occasions." Likewise, those who without orders set foot on land and entered native houses, "even if they see the doors open," would suffer equal punishment.

Such a statement—paying lip service to the royal policy (*de paz y de paso*) while openly anticipating the need to restrain his men in the event of attack on Nojpeten—indicated that Ursúa had already made up his mind. The attack was to be the very next day, and all preparations must have been completed by the time of the war council. The purpose of the meeting was not to assist the commander-in-chief in reaching a decision but rather to produce a written record that could prove the legitimacy of a violent attack.

Part Five **VICTIMS AND
SURVIVORS OF
CONQUEST**

chapter twelve **OCCUPATION AND INTERROGATION**

On the morning of Wednesday, March 13, 1697, Spanish troops under the command of Martín de Ursúa y Arizmendi stormed Nojpeten from the galeota constructed at Ch'ich'. After a brief, one-sided battle in which they inflicted heavy casualties on the Itzas defending the capital, the troops quickly occupied the island and began destroying much of what the defenders had left behind. They found Nojpeten all but deserted; those who had survived Spanish fire and were strong enough escaped by swimming to the mainland.

Within the space of a few hours, Nojpeten, seat of the last independent and unconquered Maya kingdom, was transformed into the presidio of Nuestra Señora de los Remedios y San Pablo, Laguna del Itzá. Its surviving inhabitants, many of whom were members of elite and ruling families, sought refuge in towns and hamlets throughout the region, recounting the loss of lives, property, and pride to their relatives and friends. Even in hiding, however, they were not entirely safe, because the Spaniards soon sent out search parties to capture and bring back the most important leaders. With the assistance of AjChan and the people of Yalain, the principal members of the family of Ajaw Kan Ek' were presented to Ursúa on March 31; other important captives were to arrive over the weeks and months ahead.

These events, the culmination of years of preparation, were only the beginning of a new, deeply troubled era for both the conquerors and the defeated. Isolated on their fortified island, the Spaniards found themselves lacking sources of food and surrounded by hostile Mayas. Scattered throughout towns and villages around the lakes, Itza leaders struggled to resurrect what they could of their political and social order, now in a state of collapse and confusion.

295

The Storming of Nojpeten

Two principal eyewitness accounts, both written on the day of the event, tell of the immediate preparations for and execution of the attack on Nojpeten. The first of these, signed by the military commanders and officers, was begun on the afternoon of March 13 but not completed until the next day. The second, authored by Fathers Juan Pacheco de Sopuerta and José Francisco Martínez de Mora, was completed that evening. These two records, in the form of "certifications" ordered by Ursúa, comprise nearly all that we know of the event.

The military report, Ursúa wrote on March 13, "exhibits sworn certification of that which happened today between the time I left the royal encampment until now, which would be five o'clock in the afternoon." In order to counter the officers' certification, which had a militaristic tone, he instructed the chaplains "to certify formally as soon as possible the peaceful efforts I have made ever since I set up the royal encampment on the lakeshore, with how many Indian men and women have come and gone to see me." These "peaceful efforts" were to include his ignoring provocative actions by squadrons of canoes that harassed the encampment and his treating all Itza visitors, including the women, with courtesy, generously plying them with trinkets.[1]

Although Ursúa's name was not attached to either "certification," both bear his style of writing and rhetoric, and it may be assumed that they were penned under his direct supervision. Particularly in the case of the chaplains' certification, Ursúa wished to suppress any information that would reveal the violence of the attack and the fact that he had lost control over his men during the fight. Despite the efforts Ursúa may have made to avoid bloodshed, we learn from other sources that his soldiers apparently seized the opportunity to commit a massacre.

Although the information contained in these two certifications differs in some points, the reports are complementary and do not contradict each other. Ursúa himself made certain of that. His own report to the king, written nine days later, contains even less information and avoids even more assiduously any direct indication that the attack resulted in massive loss of life.[2] Except where indicated, the account that follows is based directly on these reports.

Before dawn on the morning of Wednesday, March 13, Father Juan Pacheco offered mass to all who were encamped at Ch'ich'. Designated to remain behind were twenty-five soldiers under the command of Lieutenants Juan Francisco Cortés and Diego Bernardo del Río, three musket-armed Mayas from Tek'ax, and an unspecified number of carriers. Several of the heavy arms were left behind, ensuring that the encampment would be well guarded in the event of a Maya attack.

As dawn approached, the men appointed to the galeota began to board. They included, in addition to Ursúa and five of his personal servants, 108 armed men, the two priests, AjChan, AjChan's brother-in-law Manuel Joseph Chayax, and a bound captive from Nojpeten. Father Pacheco ordered the men to be silent while he offered a *salve* to Nuestra Señora de los Remedios, Ursúa's own patroness, for their success. After this prayer the men shouted, "Long live the law of God!" Ursúa then ordered Bernardo de San Juan to read his decree of the previous day that no man was to fire until receiving Ursúa's order.[3] Anyone who disobeyed this or other commands to exercise restraint would be executed. According to the officers' report, Pacheco then said "in a loud voice, 'Gentlemen, all of you who had pain in all your heart for having offended God and who begged him for forgiveness of your sins and mercy, raise your finger and say, "Lord have mercy on me." ' And all apparently having made the ritual statement in a loud voice, he made the sign of absolution."[4]

As the sun began to rise, the galeota set off, rowed by its crew on its maiden voyage, the two-league trip from Ch'ich' to Nojpeten. At the halfway mark they passed between two points of land, one from the mainland and one from an island—today's Punta Nijtún to their west and the point of Islote Lepete to their east.[5] There they sighted a canoe, which the officers believed to be that of a sentry, approaching them quickly. Then there appeared from the western shore "a great quantity" of canoes that stretched out in a wing across the bow of the galeota from one point of land to the other (a distance of about six hundred meters). As they approached the centerpoint of the arc of canoes they saw that the men in them appeared "arrogant," shouting aggressively. Ursúa ordered his pilot to row directly through the line of canoes on toward Nojpeten, a task easily accomplished.[6]

Approaching the island they saw a "multitude" of people along the shore, on the stone and mud fortifications, on the main part of the island, and on the roofs of buildings. The defenders, both on land and in the canoes, were shouting and moving about. Canoes coming from various points on the mainland were joining together to create, "with great effort," a half-moon formation, gradually closing around the galeota in a circle that joined the main island on one side. From this encirclement

297

arrows began to fly. In the midst of this situation, Ursúa claimed, he shouted, "Silence! And no one fire a shot, because God is on our side and there is no need to be afraid."

What followed was mayhem. AjChan, it was said by the officers and priests, spied from the galeota a small canoe near the shore to their north and identified the young man in it as belonging to the parcialidad, or urban quarter, of Ajaw Kan Ek'. He called to the person in the canoe, who paddled close to the galeota. Ursúa ordered AjChan to tell him to go to Ajaw Kan Ek' and "tell him on his behalf that he would give him three chances to make peace."[7] At that moment the defenders released volleys of arrows from the shore and the canoes. One arrow struck Sergeant Juan González in the arm. Another hit a soldier named Bartolomé Durán who, "perhaps as a result of the pain," fired his gun. At that point, according to Ursúa, González lost control of the infantry, as did the officer in charge of landing the galeota and deciding when to release the troops.[8]

The officers' reported that Sergeant González nonetheless

> restrained from firing the midship pieza and the four pedreros which, had they been fired, would have inflicted great mortality among the infidels, both because of their great number and because they would have caught them at the muzzle of the cannon. For this reason and so that not all would perish, we disembarked, leaving the galeota guarded by twenty men . . . ; and after we had charged the multitude of Indians several times, they fled impetuously — not only those in the canoes which the galeota had crossed but also the Indian men and women who were on land — all of them casting themselves into the water, even with their infants.[9]

Father Juan Pacheco confirmed this portrait of the retreat: "And having climbed up to the high point [of the island] we saw that those who were in the canoes had retreated, pushing off and abandoning many [of the canoes], and that the water was dense with the heads of Indian men and women who, fleeing from this island, swam toward the mainland."[10]

Nine days after the event Ursúa described the storming of the island in a letter to the king. His account of the effects of the Spanish attack on the defenders referred to native fatalities only in passing, turning the event into a metaphor for the opposition between "Indian" cowardice and Spanish courage. As he disembarked from the galeota,

> the men joined me with such courage that many were tossed into the water. As soon as the infidels heard the weapons and experi-

enced the courage of those who pressed them forward, they began such a cowardly retreat that those on land, both men and women, started swimming, filling up the water all the way across to the mainland. *I do not doubt that some would be imperiled by the assault, given what has since been recognized.*

I have collected more than 125 of the abandoned canoes and some Indian women and children. In light of the great multitude of infidels who defended the lake and the island from the water and those who crowned them [*sic*] on land, this victory, the joy of which was already obtained at eight in the morning, has been considered to be a great miracle.[11]

The italicized sentence constituted Ursúa's only admission, an indirect one at that, of substantial Itza mortality. What had "since been recognized" was, as we shall see, the large number of dead bodies left floating in the water — the remains of those fired on by the soldiers as they retreated. Ursúa and his men never again committed to writing any indication that they had killed a single defender that day. Ursúa did claim, however, that not a single Spaniard lost his life during the battle.[12]

The officers' report also accused the defenders of cowardice, observing that "[they are] so barbarous that as soon as they surrendered they wished to die. So great is their brutishness that an Indian from this island who was taken in shackles in the said galeota jumped overboard and drowned in the lake."[13] This inversion of the facts transformed the wanton killing of people trying to escape the gunfire by swimming toward the mainland into a portrayal of cowardly brutes who somehow invited their own death. The officers similarly remade the desperate escape attempt by their prisoner, who risked his life rather than face further humiliation and probable torture in the hands of his captors. In contrast, the officers wrote that the "Christian" AjChan, who was also aboard the galeota, "disembarked with us with such courage and valor that with a musket or *trabuco* that he requested and was given he killed one of the Indians who had started to swim away."[14] AjChan, of course, may have had his own reasons for choosing to kill that particular individual.

Later writers painted a rather different picture of the fate that befell the retreating Itzas. Although none of these writers was present during the storming of the island, they had all heard descriptions of the events from eyewitnesses. During a meeting in Santiago de Guatemala a year and a half later, Fray Diego de Rivas, a Guatemalan Mercederian with extensive experience in the Petén region, claimed that "so great was the number of those who challenged [Ursúa's attack] that the balls that our people shot killed such an innumerable quantity that the dead bodies of the Indians appeared as an island in the lake."[15]

In 1700 the Franciscan provincial of Yucatán, Bernardo de Rivas, who vigorously opposed the policies of Ursúa and the secular clergy, charged that the attack on Nojpeten had resulted in many deaths and the subsequent flight of most of the population.[16] Nine years later, commenting on the small native population of the Lago Petén Itzá area, President Toribio de Cosio of Guatemala blamed much of this decline on the great loss of life occasioned during the capture of Nojpeten.[17]

Although each of these individuals may have had personal reasons for claiming that the occupation of Nojpeten occasioned heavy Itza casualties, I believe that their statements should be considered seriously. Rivas, in particular, appears in his other writings and oral testimonies to have been a level-headed, intellectual missionary (in contrast, say, to Avendaño), whose style was not prone to exaggeration.

These few sources summarize all that we presently know about the massacre of March 13. The occupiers, however, were far more forthcoming about the excitement they experienced and the deeds they accomplished as they proceeded to take over and transform the Itza capital.

The Occupation of the Capital

In the midst of the Maya retreat, Ursúa, carrying his sword and shield, led his officers and the priests to the summit of the island. There, in an open place among what they called temples — "in which the majesty of God had been offended by idolatries" — he ordered his men to plant the banners of victory, among them the standards of "our sweet Jesus and our Lady of the Remedies" and the flag that displayed the royal arms of Spain.[18]

A small effigy of San Pablo had been found on the beach, perhaps dropped by the fleeing defenders.[19] In recognition of this small miracle, it was announced that Nuestra Señora de los Remedios y San Pablo would henceforth be the protectors of the newly conquered island. Few of those present would have known that San Pablo the Apostle had, indeed, been the patron of Nojpeten since 1618, when the Franciscans Fuensalida and Orbita designated him as such, naming the capital town San Pablo del Itza.[20] Fray Andrés de Avendaño was aware of the town's ancient epithet, dating a letter he wrote there as January 16, 1696, "in the town of the great San Pablo of Peten Itza."[21] Who had cared for the saint, which must have been the same statue left by the friars seventy-nine years earlier, and what he had meant to the people of Nojpeten, must remain a mystery.

Ursúa then offered a prayer of thanks for the "mercy" granted them by God, "knowing it was an absolutely certain miracle that the barbarians had not killed many of our people." No sooner had he finished this prayer than he and the priests began breaking "idols," and he soon ordered the officers and soldiers to continue the work. In one of the few such descriptions of Nojpeten before it was destroyed, the officers wrote that "in their horrid deformity and numbers [the idols] cannot be comprehended. In addition to twelve large houses that were filled with them, innumerable ones were found in all the houses of the Indians, because the said twelve houses and the nine tall ones are temples."[22] These nine "tall" buildings were described as such because they were constructed on top of stepped platforms. In the upper part of one of them, described as built "in the style of a castle," Alférez José de Ripalda Ongay discovered a "long bone" (*canilla*) that was "hanging by three multicolored ribbons made of fine cotton thread, and below it a small, narrow cloth bag about three-quarters [of a vara] long, in which there were small pieces of decayed bone which appeared to be from the said long bone. Below all of this there were three censers with *estoraque*[23] and some dried maize leaves which were wrapped around estoraque — something which was not seen or found with any of the other idols, [where there was] only copal. And above the said long bone in the upper part there was a crown."[24] The rest of the Spaniards crowded around to see this phenomenon. An old woman who was among several captured men, women, and children was asked what these pieces of bone had come from. According to the officers' report, she replied that they were the remains of "a horse that a king who passed through here long ago had left to be cared for. It was discovered that [this king] would have been don Fernando Cortés."[25] Apparently satisfied by this explanation, the Spaniards broke the long bone into pieces and threw it away.

The long-bone story, like other reported episodes of the day, is of unknown veracity but nonetheless tantalizing.[26] The officers were probably aware of the tale of Cortés's horse, which was familiar to anyone who had read or been told about López de Cogolludo's account of Fuensalida and Orbita's visits to Nojpeten in 1618 and 1619. They had probably also heard that Avendaño claimed that the Itzas still preserved a statue of the horse, although he did not actually see such an object.[27] Although they may have anticipated finding such evidence of continued "worship" of the famous animal, their report of the old woman's explanation cannot be entirely discounted.

The officers claimed that they and the soldiers spent the entire remaining part of the day, until about half past five, accomplishing nothing more than the breaking of idols, some of which they found arranged in pairs on top of small benches.[28] They found no objects of gold or silver, nor any clothing—"only the aforementioned idols and the beaches covered with arrows that the waves have washed to shore; and the galeota has collected and brought to shore many canoes that their owners abandoned."

The last statement of the officers' hurriedly written report was an incomplete sentence that summed up their impression of the place: "The town large, with a great many houses as well as temples, like a savage dwelling place, unswept and without a straight street." Ursúa expanded on this imagery of the savage town, its inhabitants possessed of devil-inspired idolatry, in his letter to the king: "I believe that these miserable people, deceived by the devil [and] lacking the true light, must have had no other activity than idolatrizing, as there was found no economical settlement pattern, but rather only the entire group of relatives living barbarously in one house."[29]

Ursúa ordered that the captive Mayas be treated well. He also lost no time in sending AjChan's "brother" Manuel with a message to Ajaw Kan Ek', offering the leader safe passage to come to the island with "his people" and promising that they would be received "with total love and kindness." This Manuel must have been Manuel Joseph Chayax, actually AjChan's sister's husband. He, it will be recalled, had visited Ursúa at Ch'ich' on March 10 with a party of men from Yalain. Ursúa probably retained him along with AjChan at the encampment, bringing him along in the galeto during the attack on Nojpeten.

Ursúa found himself in possession of only a small piece of land and no more than a dozen or so prisoners. Many of the island's resident leaders had fled or died in the fighting, while others had been in safe hiding before the attack. His only local allies were AjChan and his near relatives, whom he kept under close watch lest they slip away as they had a year earlier at Tipuj. Although he hoped that other leaders from Yalain would support the Spanish presence, he had no way of controlling their behavior in his isolation on Nojpeten. The next few weeks would be critical if he was to develop a strategy enabling him to maintain control over his fragile conquest.

302

GRISLY DISCOVERIES

On the day following the attack, Ursúa had sent out a party to search for the path that led southward from the lake toward Mopan. They found what he called "the road which was opened [by the Spaniards] from Guatemala," which in fact was a preexisting Maya path. Along it his scouts said they saw the footprints of the Guatemalans' pack mules — a dubious observation in a region where the first rainfall would have obliterated any such signs. On the same day they discovered on the mainland south of Nojpeten what they believed to be the ossuary containing the remains — "their skulls and bones macheted" — of the Guatemalan party that had been massacred the previous year. They also found "signs" of the presumably murdered Franciscans from Yucatán, Fray Juan de San Buenaventura and his lay assistant, including Fray Juan's walking staff.[30] Aside from the walking stick, these reports do not specify what objects were found with the bones that led the Spaniards to conclude that they belonged to the Guatemalan and Yucatecan parties.

Villagutierre, who saw a document that I have not found, wrote that Zubiaur found the bones of the friars from Yucatán on a small island. Ursúa ordered that their remains and those of the Guatemalans be brought to the presidio, where the occupying Spaniards buried the Guatemalans following a mass held in an Itza temple converted into a makeshift church. Ursúa later carried the remains of San Buenaventura and his companions back to Mérida, returning them to the provincial as Christian martyrs. Villagutierre reports that AjK'in Kan Ek' said that "he alone had bound them in the form of a cross, and had extracted their living hearts."[31]

The historian Francisco Ximénez, apparently referring to a report by Fray Agustín Cano, wrote that the two Guatemalan Dominicans, Fray Cristóbal de Prada and Fray Jacinto de Vargas, had met a similar fate. AjK'in Kan Ek' had tied them to poles in the X-shaped form of a Saint Andrew's cross. While they continued to preach, the Itza high priest cut them open and pulled out their hearts "to offer them to his idols." So loudly did Fray Cristóbal scream out as this was happening, wrote Ximénez, that "the barbarous executors of the wickedness fell stunned to the ground."[32] In other descriptions of such cases of priestly martyrdom, the victim also preaches until the bitter end.[33] The formulaic quality of such descriptions render them suspect, especially when there were no surviving Spanish witnesses to recall such details.[34]

No further mention of the discovery of the remains of Spaniards was made until four months later, when Lieutenant Diego Bernardo del Río wrote to the president of Guatemala that the troops had just that day discovered the bones of the two Dominican priests and three other Spaniards who had been killed "on this peten." Ursúa wrote around the same time that the bones had been identified by AjK'in Kan Ek' "on a nearby island, not without mystery separated from the rest."[35] Identification of

303

the remains, which were found in a cave, had been confirmed in testimony, presumably by Spanish soldiers. Río wrote that he was returning the bones to Guatemala in separate boxes, transported by native carriers.[36] It is particularly interesting that in none of these cases were signs of cannibalism mentioned, although later, questionable testimony would accuse the Itzas of wantonly consuming their victims.

CEREMONIAL POSSESSION OF NOJPETEN

The major event of Thursday, March 14, was a ceremony celebrating the formal possession of Nojpeten. Some time that day Ursúa called his officers together and read a statement, written for the occasion, that served as a prelude for the statement of possession itself.[37] This preamble, as was Ursúa's style, recited once more the historical background and acts of native treason and barbarity that justified his capture of the Itza capital.

Following his reading of this statement, Ursúa ordered the officers to call together the troops to hear his reading of the formal statement of possession of the island that would henceforth be known officially as Nuestra Señora de los Remedios y San Pablo, Laguna del Itza (or Petén del Itzá). Father Juan Pacheco de Sopuerta then blessed the island with holy water and offered mass in a "house" that had been designated as the temporary church.

The next eight days are nearly a blackout in the documentary record. We do know that four days after the attack, seventeen persons from Yalain visited Ursúa at Nojpeten, "offering their obedience" to the king of Spain. Among these was Pedro Nikte (AjChan's brother) and his wife and her sister. AjChan, Ursúa reported, had "behaved with inexpressible loyalty, and he has served me with much guidance and assistance." Recognizing the implications of AjChan's divided loyalties, Ursúa excused the fact that AjChan had not yet brought his own wife, owing to "the little physical security that he has among his own people." As a Kowoj, however, she may well have refused to join her husband with the Spanish enemy.[38]

During this period the Spaniards, with the assistance of twenty men from Yalain,[39] opened a road to connect the portion of the camino real from Yucatán with that which led from the south shore of the lake southward to Mopan. All that was now left to accomplish, Ursúa wrote, was "to subjugate these infidels." The road was, in fact, hardly more than a wide, muddy path on either side of the lake.

On March 23 or 24 Ursúa sent off all of the documents he had prepared, including his letter to the king of Spain, in the care of Captain General Alonso García de Paredes and Alférez Real José de Ripalda Ongay.[40]

These officers were to follow the difficult road, completely unknown to them, through the now-abandoned presidio of Mopan, south to Cahabón, and from there to Santiago de Guatemala. Knowing that he would receive no further assistance from Governor Roque de Soberanis in Yucatán, Ursúa hoped that the president of Guatemala would provide assistance in maintaining the presidio after the beginning of May, when the rains would begin in earnest, his men's contractual obligation would expire, and his supplies would run out. We will return to the officers' journey in the following chapter.

Capture and Testimony of the Royal Family

One of Ursúa's major goals during the next weeks and months was to capture the principal Maya leaders, discover which of them had participated in the previous year's murders of the Guatemalans and Yucatecans, and punish those whom he found guilty. Although some refugees from Nojpeten had been apprehended before García de Paredes left for Guatemala, the major prize did not appear on the island until a week later.[41] At about ten o'clock on Palm Sunday morning, March 31, Yalain loyalists brought several members of the Kan Ek' "royal family" before Ursúa. They included Ajaw Kan Ek', his wife and children, AjK'in Kan Ek', and various other male and female relatives and retainers of this elite family. One source states that along with them came "many Indian men and women both from the island and other areas." As was Ursúa's practice on such occasions, he made the event a spectacular celebration, greeting his prisoners of war "with great pomp of joy, music, and gifts," even, he claimed, inviting Ajaw Kan Ek' and AjK'in Kan Ek' to eat with him at his own table.[42]

Ursúa later implied that these people had come before him of their own free will.[43] The army chaplain, Juan Pacheco de Sopuerta, recalled that Ajaw Kan Ek', "although he fled from [the island town] when the said don Martín and the Spaniards entered it, a few days later, moved by the friendly approaches and promises which the said don Martín made him, he returned and gave him his obedience."[44] Considering what we know of later such roundups, however, it is possible that the message to Ajaw Kan 305
Ek' was that he either surrender or be attacked.

The people of Yalain had been given responsibility for apprehending the royal family. Although Ursúa had ordered Manuel Chayax, AjChan's sister's husband, to bring Ajaw Kan Ek' and his relatives to Nojpeten, other persons from Yalain received credit for the accomplishment. Chamach Xulu, Yalain's principal leader, was cited by Ursúa and his officers as having been the principal party responsible for the capture of Ajaw Kan Ek'.[45] Several of Ursúa's officers later testified, however, that it was actually AjChan who had brought Ajaw Kan Ek' and his family to the island.[46]

Accompanying the royal party was a large number of local people who had participated in the round-up.[47] This fact indicates that cooperation by the people of Yalain was solid and broad-based and that their method was capture rather than gentle diplomacy. Where they found the Kan Ek' family is unrecorded, but later information suggests that their headquarters were now west of the main lake, possibly in the vicinity of Laguna Sacpuy. Spanish soldiers did not accompany those who carried out this first such mission, an interpretation supported by Captain Diego de Avila Pacheco's remark that the apprehension was made possible "by means of mediation and infinite security provided by [Ursúa] to Chamach Xulu, cacique of the town of Yalain, and to many other Indians."[48] In the weeks and months to come, however, the military did provide cover for other, similar round-ups, suggesting that as time went on Maya loyalty to the occupying forces had grown weaker and that such search-and-capture missions required greater security.

The followers of Chamach Xulu, who had arrived to welcome Ursúa during the first week following the Spanish victory, were apparently eager to see the rulers brought before the Spaniards. AjChan and his brother-in-law, Manuel Joseph Chayax, had been retained at Ch'ich' on March 10, perhaps without their full consent, to assist Ursúa and to inform on other local leaders. Later reports that Christian conversion took an early hold among the relatives and allies of AjChan and Chamach Xulu (chapter 14) may indicate that at this early date the Yalain elites simply wanted to see the Kan Ek' family forced to accept Christianity—that they believed that a peaceful resolution with the Spaniards and with each other could be achieved only through conversion.

As soon as the royal captives been ceremonially presented to the new rulers of the island, Ursúa proceeded to interrogate Ajaw Kan Ek'. The testimony was unsworn, as was always the case with non-Christian declarants, but Ursúa stated that he did not use torture in order to extract a confession—in contrast to later interrogations. Ursúa presented the questions himself and recorded the responses without the assistance of a recorder, as he had when he questioned his Maya visitors on March 10. The interrogation was carried out in one of the houses now designated as the headquarters of the new presidio — perhaps part of the royal residential compound, which was later used as a barracks for the troops. The testimony of Ajaw Kan Ek' was also attended by three Spanish witnesses, three other Spaniards, and "many persons who understand the Maya language." No one, however, was appointed as official interpreter.

This was the moment that Ursúa had long awaited — the meeting of the man whom he believed to be the Itza head of state with the official representative of the Spanish king. Ursúa would have preferred that this meeting had taken place well before his own military action, a preference that perhaps indicates sincerity in his stated desire to avoid violence. He fully believed that the Maya leader's failure to accept his offer for diplomatic discussions at Ch'ich' signified an unwillingness to consider possible solutions to the growing crisis. This belief is clear from Ursúa's wording of the questions. Ursúa, however, had evidently not considered the alternative possibility that Ajaw Kan Ek' had not been informed of the invitation or that, even if he had received the message, powerful men in his midst had prevented him from accepting it. As the questioning progressed, his answers consistently supported this alternative interpretation. Claiming that he had lost control over his own leaders, Ajaw Kan Ek' repeatedly denied involvement in anti-Spanish activities.

Ursúa may have corrupted and misrepresented both questions and responses in constructing the written report. Nonetheless, that so many of the "defendant's" reported responses are clearly at odds with what Ursúa's questions anticipated allows us to assume that this is a reasonably accurate representation of what was said.

Ursúa opened the interrogation by asking Ajaw Kan Ek' the same stock question presented to AjChan at Ch'ich':[49]

Asked what is his name, age, and occupation, and where he is resident and native, he said: His name is Canek. He does not know how to state his age (he appears to be about forty-five years old). He is king and lord of this island and its territories, and he was born and has resided on it.

Asked if there is another king besides him and [if so] who that might be, he said: He was the only king and native lord.

It is hard to believe that Ajaw Kan Ek', who must have known how to **307** read Maya hieroglyphic writing, did not know his age. Ursúa may have been aware of the possibility that Ajaw Kan Ek' was not the only Ajaw in the region — primarily because of a report taken at Bacalar-at-Chunjujub' from Yalain-area informants over a year earlier, because of AjChan's statement in Mérida that there were four reyezuelos in addition to Ajaw Kan Ek', and because of AjChan's statement on March 10 at Ch'ich' that there were several "superiors in addition to Ah Canek."[50]

Ursúa, however, was still confused by the term *Ajaw*:

> *Asked how the title of king is [also] given to Kin Canek, he said:* They call all of their priests kings. This one is called this because he is both a priest and his father's brother's son, but he [Ajaw Kan Ek'] is the legitimate one.

By now Ursúa must have been puzzled by a term of "rulership" that could be applied not only to other rulers but also to priests. Trying to clarify the matter, he focused on this allusion to the concept of legitimacy through inheritance as a way of specifying among titular levels:

> *Asked if he has inherited this lordship from his antecedents, he said:* Yes. Ever since they came from Chichen Itza their descendants receive this lordship.

Much the way AjChan had revealed that his mother was from Chich'en Itza, Ajaw Kan Ek' now claimed for the Kan Ek' dynasty an unbroken descent from original ancestors there.

> *Asked how it can be that while he says there is only one native lord, don Martín Chan said there are four kings, he said:* The others are called kings because they are of his blood and have some authority and lordship.

By now Ursúa must have grasped that Ajaw Kan Ek' claimed to be both a supreme leader and a principal among principals. Now at least partially aware that Itza political leadership might not be as simple as he had assumed, he turned to the matter of the immediate family of Ajaw Kan Ek':

> *Asked if he is married and if he has children and [if so] how many, he said:* He is married. His wife's name is Chan Pana, and he has two children, a male and a female.

Ursúa probably concluded from this reply that Ajaw Kan Ek' had a male heir, although this young man would probably not have inherited the kingship. As for his children, we know that the ruler had two sons and probably two daughters.[51]

With matters of rulership at least partially answered, Ursúa turned his questioning to the matter of AjChan's visit to Mérida in December 1695:

Asked if it is true that just about one year and three months ago he sent his nephew Chan, who was called don Martín after he was baptized, with the message in which he [Kan Ek'] gave obedience to our great King and lord, and in which he asked for evangelical ministers who would administer and teach the law of the true God, he said: He did send him with the message and the crown, declaring his obedience by means of this sign of submission and surrender. He also requested fathers who would teach the law of the true God.

This was an exceedingly important matter for Ursúa to confirm, because so many accusations had been leveled in Spanish quarters that AjChan was a false emissary. Ursúa's next questions therefore further probed into the nature of the involvement of Ajaw Kan Ek' in this event:

Asked what persuaded him to send the said message and to request the said fathers, if it was because he was afraid of the Spaniards or some other motivation, he said: He was persuaded by the need for trade and to obtain axes and machetes, and that the request for the fathers was so that they would baptize them; and to prepare to receive them he ordered that they build a large house for them in Yalain, which is still there; and that he had no other goal or motive.

Ursúa had asked the same question of AjChan in Mérida, when the young emissary also told him that among other things, Ajaw Kan Ek' wished "to solicit commerce and trade in the things that they need." At that time, of course, AjChan also added, as expressed by Ursúa's translation, "fathers-priests, who would baptize them and teach the law of the true God."[52] The matter of the guest house at Yalain, which was already partially built when Fray Andrés de Avendaño was there in 1696, had also been mentioned by AjChan at Ch'ich' on March 10.

His next question was one that he also had put to AjChan in Mérida. AjChan had taken it as an opportunity to list the other "reyezuelos" and to emphasize the joint nature of the political decision to send the message attributed to Ajaw Kan Ek'.

Asked if he sent the said message with the approval of those who are called kings and of the other leaders, he said: He sent it after it had met with the approval of the said petty kings [*reyezuelas*] and the other leaders.

309

And on this occasion Ursúa wished to confirm whether the ruler's action was known beyond the ruling council:

Asked if all of his other subjects knew about this message, he said: All of his Indians knew about the said message.

Avendaño, however, had reported that in January 1696, people at Nojpeten were surprised and dismayed by the revelation of AjChan's mission to Mérida (chapter 8). Ursúa had read or heard Avendaño's statement, and we can only conclude that he now chose to put words in his respondent's mouth for purposes of political expediency.

His next question was all but an exoneration, a statement of faith in the sincerity and goodwill of Ajaw Kan Ek':

Asked if he once again gives his obedience to our great King and lord Charles the Second (whom God may protect), and if with all his heart and soul he wishes to be a Christian, he said: With all his heart and soul he had surrendered and had given his obedience to the majesty of Charles the Second (whom God may protect), and that likewise, with all his heart and soul, he wishes to be a Christian.

Ajaw Kan Ek' may have uttered words similar to these, either sincerely or in a desire to satisfy his questioner. In either case, that Ursúa recorded it indicates either that the general had softened his opinion of the Maya leader or, more likely, that he wanted legal proof that the ruler had indeed offered his surrender through AjChan.

Now Ursúa asked Ajaw Kan Ek' to explain the forced departure of the Franciscans:

Asked how it could be that while his ambassador was in Mérida or along the road I sent three religious of the order of lord San Francisco named Fray Andrés de Avendaño, Fray Joseph de Jesús María, and Fray Diego de Echevarría, and the said fathers arrived at this island and gave him the message that I sent in the name of His Majesty (whom God may protect) so that all of them [the Itzas] would give their obedience and be reduced to the brotherhood of our holy faith after being admitted to it, and after three days they made them return, seeing that his envoy was still in the province [of Yucatán], he said: They departed because his uncle and other principal leaders sought to kill the said religious, and that having discovered this he advised them and took them out himself over by Yalain along with a son-in-law of his and his brother-in-law, and that some of these are now dead, and the leader [*principal*], his said uncle,[53] now lives in retreat in a milpa.

This statement was a direct confirmation of Avendaño's own account of threats to his life by "AjKan" (Ajaw B'atab' K'in Kante) and AjKowoj. It also confirmed the circumstances of his precipitous departure under the personal escort of Ajaw Kan Ek'. Avendaño, however, had said that they were accompanied by the son and son-in-law of Ajaw Kan Ek' — a minor difference in accounts perhaps explainable by Avendaño's ignorance.

Ursúa continued to probe, in a series of further questions, the confusing matter of Avendaño's claim that Ajaw Kan Ek' had never mentioned AjChan's departure for Mérida while he was at Nojpeten:

Asked why he did not tell the fathers as soon as they arrived at this island that he had sent his nephew to the province to give obedience to His Majesty (whom God may protect) and to request evangelical ministers, he said: He soon told them how he had sent his messenger to the province and, questioning them through the great father [Avendaño], he [Avendaño] told him that he had seen him and fed him in the province.

Asked if he specified to the religious that he had sent the said ambassador to give obedience to His Majesty and to request evangelical ministers, he said: He told the said religious his purpose and motive for sending him and that in response they told him that when they [the friars] were ready to leave [Mérida], he [AjChan] had arrived and that they saw him and fed him; and having asked the said don Martín when he returned from the province if he had seen them and had been with them, he responded that he had never seen them.

Asked what relationship, and in what degree, he has with don Martín Chan, he said: He is his blood nephew, the son of his elder sister named Ix Cante.

Part of this passage is confusing and appears to conflate AjChan's September 1695 visit to Mérida, during which Avendaño claimed to have met and fed AjChan and others, with AjChan's official visit in December of that year. Ajaw Kan Ek' seems to be saying that AjChan did not see the friar on the latter occasion, which was in fact the case. Avendaño, however, denied learning of AjChan's December visit from the ruler, claiming that AjChan was a false ambassador.

We cannot know how Ursúa interpreted these contradictions or how much he knew about Avendaño's communications with Ajaw Kan Ek', because he apparently never committed his personal musings to paper. In any event, he was more concerned at this moment with establishing who had murdered the Spaniards from Yucatán and Guatemala. Changing the subject, he put this matter directly to his prisoner:

> *Asked how it was that, [Kan Ek'] having sent his message giving obedience to our King and lord, and Father Fray Juan [San Buena-ventura] de Chávez and forty Spaniards and some Indians having arrived from the province in peace, they deceitfully captured the said religious and the lay friar, two Spaniards, and eight Indians, killing them and wanting to do the same to the rest, he said:* Some Indians named Chata and Tut and the priest Kin Canek, along with an Indian named Izot [*sic*], another named Canek (his father's brother's son, who is a prisoner), and many other Indians who went out with them [did it], and he was unable to stop them, because they were not on the island.

AjChan, too, had blamed Chata, but he had identified the leader Puk, not B'atab' Tut, as Chata's partner in crime. The surprise comes in the ruler's accusation that AjK'in Kan Ek' and his otherwise unidentified cousin Kan Ek' (presumably a Kit Kan) were at fault; even his co-ruler, the high priest, had turned against him. We can never know with certainty whether Ajaw Kan Ek' was telling the truth in claiming that he had no part in the capture and murder of these people, although his claim is plausible, given the sum total of evidence suggesting that the ruler's political fortunes had been declining for more than a year.

His answer to Ursúa's next question was therefore a foregone con-clusion:

> *Asked why he did not then punish the evildoers, since they had acted without his order or mandate, he said:* He was unable to in-vestigate [the matter] with them because they paid him no respect or obedience and because they became so enraged that they threat-ened him and wished to kill him, and that this is why he did not proceed to punish them.

Ursúa must have expected Ajaw Kan Ek' to answer his next question in the same way, but this time he received even more information than he requested:

> *Asked how it was that when the people from Guatemala came in peace, they proceeded treacherously and deceitfully to kill them — How did it happen, how many were there, and did they kill them*

on the lake or on this island? he said: Those whom he named in the previous question and one Pana, along with a large number of Indians, killed them on the lake. Although he called to them, they did not hear him or pay attention to him or obey him. They wanted to kill them because he told them not to do it. They ate all of them — the ones from Campeche who came first as well as those from Guatemala, and as for how many there were he does not know.

The Pana in question may have been the brother of IxChan Pana, the ruler's wife. Again, Ajaw Kan Ek' was making the case that he had been isolated and abandoned by everyone. He not only claimed his powerlessness to stop the murders but also (if the transcript is to be believed) directed the worst possible accusation — that of cannibalism — against his adversaries. He did not claim that their eating the victims was part of a ritual of human sacrifice, but the Spaniards attributed such ritual practices to the Itzas. Ajaw Kan Ek' must have known from his long conversations with Avendaño that all native religious practices would have to be abandoned if the Itzas embraced Christianity. Human sacrifice was certainly at or near the top of Avendaño's list of prohibitions, and he also accused the Itzas of cannibalism.[54] Whether or not either or both practices had occurred on these occasions cannot be confirmed, but Ajaw Kan Ek' knew that to accuse his enemies of participating in them would raise his own credibility and reinforce his claims of innocence.

Ursúa, turning to the failure of Ajaw Kan Ek' to accept his invitation to meet him at Ch'ich', framed his question in sufficient detail to impress on future readers that he had made every effort at personal negotiation:

Asked how it was that when all my people arrived at the lakeshore northwest of this island and set up my headquarters, and when various invitations promising safe passage had been sent with the cacique Chamay Xulu, with don Martín Chan's brother and his brother-in-law don Manuel Choios [Chayax], with the priest Kin Canek, and many other Indians, stating that I came peacefully and gently in order to travel to Guatemala on orders of my King and that I did not want war, and asking that he come to see us in order to talk about said travel, he wished not to reply formally to any of these invitations, but rather from the time that I arrived made war **313** *preparations; and notwithstanding all of the protestations and warnings that I announced in the name of His Majesty in order that you not obstruct me or deny me free passage and withhold your arms and order your Indians not to shoot their arrows, what mo-*

tives did you have for doing it [anyway], when you had been invited to behave peacefully, he said: The Indians of this island and other provinces who carried out the first ambushes as well as the later ones were traders, and they did it without his knowledge, and the reason they did not go along with his appeals was that his own people did not allow him to do so.

Ajaw Kan Ek' did not say why he failed to respond to Ursúa's invitations, although Ursúa should have realized that even had he received them, he would not have been allowed to visit the encampment. In blaming the "ambushes" on traders he was probably referring to the followers of the Tuts, who controlled the province south of the main lake all the way to Río Pasión—the principal Itza trade route to Huehuetenango and the rest of highland Guatemala. This group had special reason to oppose the opening of a road to Guatemala that might threaten its own trade monopoly. The traders' principal complaint, however, would have been that the Spaniards had stolen the important lakeshore port of Ch'ich' from them, using it as a military headquarters. Their daily harassment of the troops at Ch'ich' was therefore a vain attempt to regain important territory.

Ursúa's last question was by now a mere formality, another opportunity for Ajaw Kan Ek' to claim that he had lost all authority and was in no way responsible for the use of arms against the Spaniards:

Asked how was it that if he wanted peace he had this island fortified with defensive walls and that on the morning that I traveled with my people to this island everyone was at war with a great many canoes on the lake from one side and the other, and these all approached my right-of-way in a half-moon formation and began to shoot their arrows from water and land; and notwithstanding all of this I sent with one of his Indians whom don Martín Chan knew to demand on the count of three to suspend his arms—that I came in peace and that if he made war the deaths and damages that would result would be his fault and not that of my King and lord (whom God may protect), he said: The situation with his Indians was such that he lost their obedience, and he was unable to obtain it despite his persuasions and efforts to stop them from constructing the defensive walls and likewise from going out in their canoes, and that his Indians told him that [the Spaniards] wanted to deceive them and that they were terribly afraid, so he was unable to do anything about it.

314

Itza fears of deception must have been fully understandable to Ursúa. Furthermore, why should they have trusted a general who had already informed them that he intended to make good on a promise of political surrender? Ursúa later wrote to the king that the testimony of Ajaw Kan Ek' had been given "voluntarily," interpreting it to mean that the Itza ruler had reaffirmed his loyalty to the Crown.[55] Whatever positive conclusions Ursúa might have drawn from the ruler's statements of political innocence and impotence were, however, about to be countered by a new series of events and revelations.[56]

Escape Plots and Interrogations

Shortly after the capture of the Kan Ek's, various persons from the lake region, including leaders from the Kowoj province, visited the conquered town. Some of these, Ursúa reported, "say that they are ready to receive the evangelical law. These I entertained and regaled with axes, machetes, beads, and other trifles, and they returned, pleased, to their towns."[57] Those who had come with the royal family, on the other hand, had all maintained their residences at Nojpeten, and the cultivators among them maintained their milpas on the mainland. Ursúa wrote that several days after their arrival some of these people sought his permission to go to their fields. Because they did not return, "I became suspicious and proceeded to investigate the motive. It was discovered to have been at the request and persuasions of the priest, who is the great magician and principal head of all the cruelties that have been carried out against both the people of [Guatemala] and those whom I sent last year."[58]

Ursúa had readied the galeota and some of his officers and troops to tour the northern shore of the main lake, which he knew to be the territory of the Kowojs. He later wrote that just as he was about to leave, "I found myself impeded by certain suspicions raised by Canek's restlessness. These [suspicions] were confirmed when don Martín Chan (always absolutely constant in his faithfulness and loyalty) affirmed [that they were correct]."[59]

Asserting that he had demanded on various occasions that they "bring their Indians to live on this island," and because he had heard rumors from "other Indians of this said island" that they were planning their own escape, on April 16 Ursúa took Ajaw Kan Ek', AjK'in Kan Ek', and the **315** ruler's other cousin, known only as Kan Ek', into heavily guarded custody and put them in shackles. In order to prevent their continued collaboration, Ajaw Kan Ek' was held in the storehouse (which also served as the general's house), and AjK'in Kan Ek' was watched over separately in the guardroom. The third cousin was presumably kept separate from both of them.[60] They were to remain prisoners on the island for more than two years.

Until this time the Maya leaders had apparently been treated well and given a certain degree of freedom, short of being allowed to leave the island. That Ursúa even invited them to eat at his table suggests that he had disbelieved their guilt in the murders of the Guatemalan and Yucatecan visitors.[61] Suddenly, upon learning that they had secretly forged an escape plan, his attitude changed. What might have been naiveté on Ursúa's part turned into anger and vengefulness. From this moment on he believed nothing they told him, and he also began to accuse them, often without apparent foundation, of treachery and guilt in the past incidents that had most deeply offended him.

TORTURE AND THE SHAMAN'S REVENGE

In one letter to the Crown, Ursúa stated that following AjChan's confirmation of his suspicions about the intentions of the Kan Ek' cousins, "I did it, and the facial expressions of both of them gave away their harmful intent."[62] I interpret the phrase "I did it" as Ursúa's admission that he had used torture in extracting the confession — the same interpretation Villagutierre followed in his reading of this passage.[63] Ursúa left a record of his interrogation of AjK'in Kan Ek',[64] but he left no judicial record confirming his implication that on this occasion he also requestioned Ajaw Kan Ek' under torture.

Following his imprisonment, AjK'in Kan Ek' exhibited a vocal anger that must have shocked even the most hardened Spanish soldiers. Ursúa later wrote that "he exhaled his venom like a man possessed, speaking indecent words against the infantry and officers, to the effect that he alone had killed and removed the hearts of the religious and the lay brother from this province. . . . In the declaration that I [later] took from him he despairingly denied that which had been proffered in the guardroom."[65] Sergeant Major Miguel Ferrer, who saw this behavior, later testified in Campeche that AjK'in Kan Ek' was clearly someone who could not be trusted, "as he was a man whom this witness saw call to the devils with many tremblings."[66]

Villagutierre's description of the priest's behavior was far more colorful than either of these sources:

> The general proceeded to arrange legal proceedings against them, and the false priest, like a man possessed and completely surrendered to the devil, executed incredible leaps, hurling himself several times like a fury in the prison where he was, and later he whistled.[67]
>
> Our men asked one of his female attendants, "What did that signify?" She replied, "to call the demons and idols of his province, who on certain occasions granted him as much he wished."[68]

Following his description of the high priest's interrogation, Villagutierre recounted the powers, as even the Spaniards perceived them, of this spiritually possessed shaman:

> When this confession or torture was finished, this devil-possessed priest said these words to our men: "You will see it before nightfall." And it was so, that around the time of the prayer [vespers] there arose such a terrible storm from the south that with great tempest and howling wind, lightning, and hail that island appeared to be nothing less than the veritable center of hell. The trees fell down, the houses broke apart, [the wind] tossing more than two hundred of those made of thatch and wood to the ground, destroying everything.
>
> Seeing themselves in such a terrible state, they turned to God in order to seek the intercession of their Holiest Mother of the Remedies. And praying the litanies before her image, with the priests exorcizing the storm, at three o'clock in the morning it began to calm down and the clouds to vanish, leaving half the island destroyed, the houses ruined, and everything in disorder.[69]

Unfortunately, these are among the few such accounts for which the original documentation that served as Villagutierre's source has not been discovered. I have found no confirmation of the storm, which must have been a hurricane, or of spiritual possession by AjK'in Kan Ek'. So specific are the details in Villagutierre's descriptions, however, that their having been based on a personal report or a document now lost cannot be discounted. Whoever presented the account of the priest's shamanistic leaps, shouts, and whistles, connecting them with the violent storm that followed, was probably convinced that this was a man who possessed great supernatural powers.

If AjK'in Kan Ek' had in a fit of anger claimed—for the first time—

to have singlehandedly committed the murders that Ursúa so wished to solve, the general's decision to interrogate him immediately would have been an understandable reaction. Even under torture, however, he refused to tell Ursúa what he wanted to hear.

NEW INTERROGATIONS

Ursúa had first demanded of AjK'in Kan Ek' why, following a meeting that he and Ajaw Kan Ek' had held with a large number of Itzas, he had decided to run away, and why he had persuaded Ajaw Kan Ek' to flee with him. AjK'in Kan Ek' denied that either of them had wished to run away and that "having surrendered once, he had not had to do such a thing."[70] When Ursúa asked why those who had left to go to their milpas had not returned, "he said that he did not know the reason why."

Ursúa, clearly angry, went right to the heart of the matter, asking if he had taken part in the murders of the visiting Guatemalans and Yucatecans. Again AjK'in Kan Ek' denied culpability, saying that "he was not an accomplice, and that those who were [accomplices] were the Tuts, Kin Chan Pana, the Chatas, Ah Canek (who is imprisoned), and the follower of the petty king Kixan [K'ixaw], along with a large number of Indians."

It will be recalled that Ajaw Kan Ek' had blamed the followers of Chata and Tut, AjK'in Kan Ek' himself, another cousin named Kan Ek', and a person named Itza, besides the "large number of Indians" who had gone along with them.[71] The Kan Ek' cousins all blamed one another in front of their conquerors (a third such accusation would be made presently), further convincing Ursúa that they were all guilty. K'ixaw, the brother of B'atab' Tut, was the man captured in 1695 by the Guatemalans, who escaped just before the Juan Díaz party was massacred in 1696.

Ursúa, although he still did not know who the people named by AjK'in Kan Ek' were or where they were located, must by now have been convinced that virtually all of the principal regional leaders, including the two ruling cousins, had participated in the massacres. We can presume that except for their blaming one another, they had corroborated their accounts in advance, well before they were imprisoned.

Did they eat their victims? Ursúa then asked. Yes, AjK'in Kan Ek' replied, but he denied participating in such behavior. How were they murdered? They beat them to death with sticks, he replied. Ursúa would later use this testimony and other such "evidence" for cannibalism as a means of discrediting the Itzas and justifying the conquest.

Ursúa's last question to his presumably tortured informant reflected again his desire to clear up the use of the title *rey,* or Ajaw:

Asked how, being priest, he says he is king, he said: He is priest and wise man for all of them. For that reason he is called king of these lands, and because he is father's brother's son to Ah Canek, who is the legitimate king of these lands.

Like Ajaw Kan Ek', AjK'in Kan Ek' must have used the term Ajaw as his own title, which would have left Ursúa as baffled as ever. The general did not understand that the two cousins ruled jointly.

At this point Ursúa concluded his interrogation of AjK'in Kan Ek' and proceeded to question the third Kan Ek' cousin. His questions, which opened with the customary inquiry into citizenship, occupation, and age that were missing in his interrogation of AjK'in Kan Ek', suggest that this man was not subjected to torture. He appeared to be about fifty, and he said that he had two wives. He was a "relative" of Ajaw Kan Ek' but "did not know how to state his occupation."

This Kan Ek' was more specific in his description of the murders but likewise claimed his innocence:

> The religious from Guatemala were killed by opening them up in the temple of the petty king Ah Can Ek — [by] the said petty king and Kin Canek. The Spaniards who came with them they killed on the water and took them to the island, many of them dying, where they finished killing them, and they ate them. Those from Campeche they killed the religious, soldiers, and Indians in the canoes on the lake, and they took them ashore and ate them as they had the others. The said declarant was present, but [he said] that he interfered in nothing.

So why, Ursúa asked, did he "wear that sign below his lip, and what does it signify?" To which he reportedly replied, "[H]e does not know why." And who were the killers? They were, he said, "the Tuts, Pucs, Itzas, Kixaw (he who came with the people from Guatemala), the Chatas, Ahau Canek, and many others, including Ah Kin Canek." The Tuts, he claimed, still had the chalices and ornaments brought by the various captured priests and of the firearms taken from the captured soldiers.

Finally, in preparation for his third and final interrogation, Ursúa asked him who the boy was "whom they captured with him," to which he replied that "he is named Kamal, and that he is from this island, and that he was in hiding where [the declarant] had been." This Mopan boy's testimony was to play a major role in Ursúa's claims concerning Itza cruelty.

319

Kamal, who stated that he was unmarried, appeared to be about seventeen. His father was also named Kamal, and his mother was dead. Asked to identify the principal murderers, he named the Tuts, the Chatas, AjK'ixaw, one Kan Chan, Ajaw Kan Ek', AjK'in Kan Ek', and the Kan Ek' who had just testified. His description of the murders was vivid: "They killed them on the water by tying up and macheteing them in the canoes, and after they were dead they took them to this island, and in one of the temples the petty king Ah Canek, and the priest Kin Canek opened them up and, among the Indians of this island, they ate some of them broiled and others of them boiled, and they had to kill them in order to eat them." This is the only time a person named Kan Chan was implicated in the murders, and one wonders if Kamal was referring to AjChan. AjChan might have been in Itza territory at the time of the Guatemalan affair, but he was on his return trip to Tipuj from Mérida during the conflict with the Yucatecans. Because other men would have had the same name, the possibility that Kamal was implicating him cannot be verified.

The specific reference to cooking methods and the claim that they killed their victims *in order to eat them* do not ring true, nor do some of the accusations that followed. Ursúa pursued the subject: Did they eat their enemies after they imprisoned them? Kamal replied, "[T]hey also kill and eat their captured enemy Indians with whom they are at war, and that he has seen it many times." In reply to the question, "Do they sacrifice live men and women to their gods during their festivities?" he said, "Those enemy Indian prisoners whom they capture they sacrifice alive, removing their hearts, and when they lack enemy Indians they sacrifice the fattest boys on the island." Did they "open up" the priests and other Spaniards in order to sacrifice them to their gods? He said, "[F]or that [reason] the priest opened them up. They took those from Guatemala alive to the island. One was the captain, and they took the others tied up to the island. They sacrificed them alive to their gods."

Then asked why AjK'in Kan Ek' and the Kan Ek' who had just testified were marked with a scar across their chins, he replied that "it is the sign by which those who are most identified in the murder of the Spaniards from Guatemala are recognized." While the scars on their chins may have been made following the murders, it seems more likely that these were identifications common to certain leaders. Kamal also stated that the Tuts held one of the chalices and various ornaments that had belonged to the murdered priests. Someone named Tzak had the other chalice and the soldiers' arms.

Who was this youth Kamal, whose supposed testimony gave Ursúa such potent ammunition concerning human sacrifice and cannibalism? He has to have been the same person later taken by Captain Bartolomé de la Garma back to his home in Campeche. Garma testified on July 1, 1697, that he had in his possession "an Indian youth sixteen or seventeen years old whom he is educating and teaching the Christian doctrine, whom he found on the said island and [who] was to be sacrificed on March 13, when [the island] was won; and he testifies that his father, mother, and brothers were also to have been sacrificed and eaten; and that in good time he will testify about what the said Itzas did to him and what they intended to do."[72] Kamal and his family may have been prisoners of war from an Itza battle with an unidentified Mopan group; Kamal was a Mopan name.[73] If he was about to have been sacrificed, he certainly would have been eager to tell his rescuers anything that would cast aspersions on the Itza rulers. It is impossible to know whether he was telling the truth or whether his testimony was exaggerated to begin with and then elaborated even further in Ursúa's writing. Kamal's claim that Itza boys from Noj- peten were sacrificed because of their fatness seems fanciful, and I suspect that Ursúa drew this example directly from Avendaño's similar claim. Such testimony, in any event, cannot be taken at face value, and there are ample reasons to doubt its accuracy.

Ursúa believed that his harsh treatment of his royal prisoners had yielded a positive outcome. On May 4 he wrote to President Sánchez de Berrospe of Guatemala that over the days following their imprisonment, "some, with their families, have begun to come [to the island]. Divine Majesty willing, all will be reduced to the brotherhood of our holy faith and to the obedience of our King and lord, although I consider that all those who are guilty and who were accomplices in the deaths of the Span- iards must be considered rebels."[74] He believed that he could identify "most or all" of the guilty ones, including AjK'in Kan Ek', by the scar across their chins, which he was convinced was "a trophy of their fury."[75] To Sánchez de Berrospe he mentioned, however, not a word about the accusations of human sacrifice and cannibalism. It would be another two months before he assembled and publicized his report on purported Itza savagery and degeneration.

Although Ursúa had by now satisfied himself that AjK'in Kan Ek' was, in the words of Captain Diego de Avila Pacheco, "the principal motor of as many evils and cruelties committed on that island as human malicious- ness can hold," he continued to treat Ajaw Kan Ek' as a royal prisoner of war, displaying the same friendliness and respect that he had exhibited

321

Victims and Survivors

before his interrogation of the high priest.[76] Ursúa kept Ajaw Kan Ek' at his side much of the time, retained him in his own house, and continued to feed him at his table.[77] He seemed to have felt a genuine affection for the Itza leader, hoping perhaps that he had misjudged his intentions and that it was AjK'in Kan Ek', not Ajaw Kan Ek', who was to blame for the deaths of his countrymen.

During the two years following the "conquest" of the Itzas, the tiny presidio of Spaniards on Nojpeten suffered not only from a shortage of food and supplies but also from isolation and fears of Itza reprisals. They attempted, with only a few successes, to hunt down the native inhabitants, most of whom skillfully avoided capture by seeking refuge deep in the surrounding forests. Although the Spaniards decisively punished those whom they perceived to be the major leaders, they were unable to effect a policy that would have created a new political order under colonial control. Soon abandoned by Ursúa, who was placed under house arrest by his nemesis, Governor Soberanis y Centeno, the troops remaining at the presidio turned for assistance to the Audiencia of Guatemala.

These two years were desperate ones for the occupying Spaniards, as well as for Itzas and Kowojs. Yucatecan authorities had appointed missionaries from the secular clergy who lacked the capability or courage to make sustained contacts with the increasingly restive, unconquered population. The food supplies were rotting, and the only choice for the troops was to rob the milpas of surrounding inhabitants, who deserted their towns when they heard the soldiers coming. Rumors of attack plagued the presidio, and the only friend of the Spaniards, AjChan, once again deserted them, raising new fears of a general rebellion.

The Kowoj Province and Its "Captain"

During early April, some two hundred people from the western Itza province and the Yalain area had visited Ursúa at the presidio.[1] Some of these had indicated an interest in becoming Christians, and Ursúa, who had no missionaries for them, had sent them back to their home communi-

323

ties loaded down with the usual gifts of axes, machetes, knives, belts, and beads.

During the same period a group of twenty-six representatives from Tipuj also arrived at the presidio, led by their "cacique," Mateo Wikab', and their "captain," Andrés K'eb'.[2] It will be recalled from chapter 7 that Wikab' and K'eb', at that time an alcalde, had separately made important journeys as Spanish-sponsored emissaries to see Ajaw Kan Ek' during 1695. On this occasion they were at the presidio not, presumably, to see Ajaw Kan Ek' but rather to present testimony to Ursúa concerning what they knew of the disposition of Ajaw Kan Ek' toward the Spaniards before AjChan visited Mérida in December 1695. They were escorted from Tipuj by two Spaniards from Bacalar, Juan de Medina and Antonio Guzmán, whose nickname was "Guatemala."[3]

Ursúa had sent an invitation to Captain Kowoj to visit him, but AjKowoj, rightly suspicious of the offer, in turn invited Ursúa to see him on his own territory. Ursúa had intended to carry out this trip to see for himself the towns along the northern shore of Lago Petén Itzá, but the rumors of rebellion that resulted in his interrogation of the Kan Ek' prisoners briefly delayed the trip. He had already appointed Captain Joseph Laines to ready the galeota to set out on the journey with forty men, "with the intention of punishing Captain Couoh, on whom the Indians of the island cast the blame for all their evil doings."[4] His interrogation of the Kan Ek' cousins had revealed little about AjKowoj's anti-Spanish activities other than his threats against Avendaño's life. Ursúa had heard enough to make him suspicious of AjKowoj, although he knew little at the time of the depth of enmity between many of the Itzas and the Kowojs and, therefore, the proclivity of the former to treat the latter as scapegoats in any dealings with Spaniards.

The galeota rowed off with its crew at nine or ten o'clock at night. The purpose of the mission, as Ursúa later wrote, was

> to look over the northeastern part of the lake, because I wanted to see the twelve towns that place to place adorn that shore. At one [of these towns], before that in which Captain Couoh lives, I woke up and recognized in the people who went to the shore unarmed the opposite of that which I was told on the island, [where they were] impugning him (due to their enmity toward him) as the principal accomplice in the very thing that they had [themselves] committed. I proceeded and arrived early in the day to catch sight of [Captain Kowoj's] town, and some of them tossed gifts of fruit up to me on

the galeota. The first thing that was sighted at that settlement was a new and beautiful holy cross, and everyone sweeping their houses in order to receive me. I found Captain Couoh happy in appearance — and not the castles and fortresses that those of the island had told me they had.[5]

Captain Laines recalled not only these aspects of their reception but also that a canoe approached them at AjKowoj's town bearing both a white flag and plantains. AjKowoj entertained the Spaniards in "a very well made and well swept house."[6] Captain Pedro de Zubiaur recalled that the soldiers disembarked at several towns where they were welcomed hospitably. At one of these towns a man actually swam out to the boat with a load of plantains.[7]

Ursúa and his men visited twelve towns on the northern shore, in the company of Captain Kowoj himself. AjKowoj's capital town, the first of those visited, was probably Ketz, whose population Father Juan Pacheco de Sopuerta later estimated to be about one thousand.[8] Various participants in the enterprise recalled the names of the other twelve towns: Chaltunja, Pop (or Poop), Sojkol, Yaxtenay, Tz'ola, Uspeten, AjB'ojom, Xililchi, B'oj, Chak'an Itza, and Saklemakal.[9] Each of these towns, which had obviously been well rehearsed for the Spaniards' visit, mimicked the theatrics displayed by AjKowoj, regaling the conquerors with foodstuffs and offering Ursúa their surrender.

Ursúa's complimentary references to AjKowoj, whom he always referred to as Captain Kowoj, resulted not only from this pleasant reception but also from information that emerged after his trip to the northern shore. Notwithstanding Captain Kowoj's hospitality and stated willingness to surrender to the Spanish Crown, Ursúa remained suspicious of his intentions, took him as a prisoner to the presidio, and had him shackled once he was on the island.[10]

Now with AjKowoj and his allies as well as the Kan Ek's cousins in his control, Ursúa apparently placed them all in the same room, forcing each of them to explain his previous actions toward the Spaniards in the presence of one another. The details of this verbal encounter are lost, but it resulted, at least in Ursúa's mind, in establishing the guilt of the Ajaw Kan Ek's and AjKowoj's innocence: "I found him not to be an accomplice in any previous cruelty but rather that, to the contrary, to have reproached the petty king, as on three occasions he sent him a warning that under no condition should he harm the Spaniards, which resulted in their falling out with each other, [with] those from the island killing Couoh's father and

325

brother, in revenge for which [AjKowoj] attacked the island with very few Indians, set fire to the houses, destroying half of them, although all of them went off with many arrow wounds."[11]

Captain Diego de Avila Pacheco later confirmed that AjKowoj had claimed he had attacked Nojpeten, burning down most of the houses "on account of the murder of the Spaniards and [on account of Ajaw Kan Ek'] not having wished to heed the three warnings [of AjKowoj] that he not harm the Spaniards."[12] Another witness recalled that AjKowoj had actually shown the Spaniards the scars from the arrow wounds he had received in the battle on Nojpeten.[13]

This war must have occurred two or three months before Avendaño's trip to Nojpeten in January 1696, because on that occasion he observed a number of newly constructed buildings on the island (see chapter 8). In all probability, AjKowoj attacked Nojpeten as soon as he heard rumors that during August or September Ajaw Kan Ek' had made contact with pro-Spanish representatives from Tipuj; he may even have been aware of AjChan's "secret" first trip to Mérida in September (chapter 7). Although there is ample evidence, already cited, that AjKowoj had been in league with Ajaw B'atab' AjK'in Kante, ruler of the north, in his efforts to depose the Itza ruler, Ursúa seems to have been either unaware of this alliance or unwilling to consider its implications. In any event, the alliance between AjKowoj and the ruler of the north was in shambles following the storming of Nojpeten. Ajaw B'atab' K'in Kante had disappeared from sight, possibly having taken refuge near Laguna Sacpuy, and the Kowoj leader was now on his own to negotiate with the Spaniards.

There is good reason, therefore, to doubt AjKowoj's claim that it was he, and not Ajaw Kan Ek', who wished to protect the Spaniards from harm. It was AjKowoj, after all, who had threatened Avendaño when face-to-face with Ajaw Kan Ek', the friar's protector as well as a treasonous Spanish sympathizer. Ursúa knew all of this from Avendaño's reports, but, for reasons that are unclear, he chose to accept AjKowoj's new version of these events. As it turned out later, AjKowoj, having deceived Ursúa, apparently intended to use the military power of his new "ally" as the principal means of defeating Ajaw Kan Ek' and his few remaining allies, for once and for all, before attempting to turn against and ultimately expel the conquerors.

As soon as Ursúa was convinced of AjKowoj's innocence, he had his shackles removed and set him free.[14] Captain Pedro de Zubiaur, in whose house AjKowoj was at first imprisoned,[15] had equally complimentary words for AjKowoj. He confirmed the Spaniards' belief that he was not only innocent but had also become an active ally and assistant in subsequent local roundups of resistant native forces:

> When they went to Cobox's [i.e., AjKowoj's] towns he was taken by señor don Martín to the island because they had always held him guilty in the cruelties committed on the lake, and when presented face-to-face with Canek and the priest not only was he found innocent but from then on he served as a guide and leader in bringing out from the forest the principal aggressors in the deaths and sacrifices committed against the people from Guatemala and from this province. The said Cobox, in the friendly company of don Martín Chan, [both] remained on the fortified island, assisting the men of the garrison with their wives, forsaking their native towns and homes.[16]

So zealous, stated Avila Pacheco, was AjKowoj in the pursuit of Itzas deemed guilty of the murders that he even killed those who resisted him.[17] Now AjKowoj joined his son-in-law, AjChan, in a new alliance against those whom they chose to blame for the previous murders of Yucatecans and Guatemalans. This was the first indication that AjChan was willing to turn against his uncle, Ajaw Kan Ek', in favor of supporting the now-favored AjKowoj. Just as AjKowoj was plotting to strike against the Spaniards, AjChan was, as we will see, reassessing his own support of the conquerors.

Ursúa's Departure

In late April, shortly after he had decided to free Captain Kowoj, Ursúa began plans for his own return to Campeche. On May 9 he completed all of the paperwork required for his departure, including a set of detailed instructions for Captain Joseph Fernández de Estenos, whom he left in command of the presidio.[18] Estenos's second-in-command was to be Lieutenant Juan Francisco Cortés, whose title was *alférez*. Of the original garrison he left only fifty men behind. They were housed in a palm-thatch barracks guarded by heavy artillery and plenty of ammunition. Also at their disposal were the galeota, a piragua, and a number of captured canoes. **327**

Fernández de Estenos was to keep Ajaw Kan Ek', AjK'in Kan Ek', and their cousin under guard. If the president of Guatemala agreed, as Ursúa had requested, to replace these fifty men, the arms and ammunition were to be turned over to the new garrison, and the Yucatecan troops were to return forthwith to Campeche. In high-sounding phraseology, Ursúa instructed Fernández to treat all of the natives of the area with "the gentleness and affection that is required, as in this way the reduction of the rest . . . will be achieved." He was to punish severely those Spaniards who abused their charges and to give special assistance and good treatment to don Martín Chan (AjChan) and Captain Kowoj and their followers. He should make sure the troops set a good example, including performing a nightly recitation of the rosary of Nuestra Señora de los Remedios.

At this point the native population of the island included the three Kan Ek' prisoners; AjKowoj; AjChan and his brother, Pedro Miguel Chan, and brother-in-law, Manuel Joseph Chayax; AjChan's close associate Juan Francisco Tek; and the wives, children, and other relatives of several of these men. In all there were about two hundred non-Spaniards, including children.[19]

Joining Ursúa and the returning troops was Father Juan Pacheco, who was subsequently questioned in detail in Mérida at the order of the bishop-elect, the Augustinian Fray Antonio de Arriaga.[20] Pacheco's departure, which infuriated Arriaga, left the presidio with no clerical presence whatsoever, because he had given his assistant, Bachiller José Francisco Martínez de Mora, permission to accompany Alonso García de Paredes on his trip to Guatemala. Although he had ordered Martínez de Mora to return to the presidio of Los Remedios, he had since learned that he had returned directly to Campeche.

Pacheco's excuse for abandoning his post was an illness so severe that he feared for his life. He appeared well enough, however, to the bishop, who ordered him to get back on his horse and return to his post via Campeche without delay.[21] Pacheco responded with pious calculation that he would follow the bishop's orders, even though he might die on the road. Eventually he was relieved from his obligations and, by October, another priest, Bachiller Pedro de Morales y Vela, had taken his place at Petén Itzá. Arriaga later sent Martínez de Mora back to the presidio to join him.[22]

Pacheco and Martínez de Mora had enjoyed few successes as missionaries to the Itzas. When later questioned about whether the conquered population had sought baptism or wished to receive Christian instruction, Pacheco replied that "they had done everything possible, not omitting a single effort, to achieve their reduction to the knowledge of the True God and the evangelical law, but that they had achieved nothing. They baptized only a girl about eight or nine years old who requested the water of baptism, being next to death, and two children of don Martín Chan and don Pedro Chan, Indians baptized in this city in 1695."[23]

Neither of these priests, whose primary responsibilities had been those of chaplains to the Spaniards, had been enthusiastic missionaries. Ursúa, furthermore, did little to encourage them in evangelical pursuits. Pacheco implied to the bishop that Ursúa had encouraged Martínez de Mora to join the group going to Guatemala and stated that Ursúa had not opposed his own wish to join the retreating soldiers. Their lack of success in obtaining converts clearly contradicted the claims of Ursúa and other military personnel that streams of eager Mayas were asking for baptism and religious instruction. Other colonial officials and church leaders in Mérida were to read into such contradictions the indication that Ursúa had little interest in the souls or the personal welfare of the conquered population.

A New Rhetoric of Depravity

Prior to his departure from the presidio, Ursúa and his officers had refrained from using derogatory language in describing the Itzas. Their descriptions of "idols" found on the island and their accusations of treachery on the part of Itza leaders notwithstanding, the texts produced between March and June exhibited not only moderation but even, on occasion, complimentary characterizations of people who were on the verge of becoming subjects of the Spanish empire.

All of this changed when Ursúa, upon his return to Campeche, found himself under fire for having disobeyed the royal instructions to which he had committed himself over the past four years. Soberanis issued a scathing attack on the violence of Ursúa's conquest of Nojpetén, to which Ursúa felt compelled to respond.[24] Ursúa's primary defense against such criticism was to develop a new rhetoric that portrayed the Itzas as a depraved, savage people whom he had had to conquer in the interest of God, the Crown, and the protection of civilized life.

Ursúa had arrived with his returning troops in Campeche in late May. Among his first acts was to request additional secular clergy, in addition to the two positions already assigned by the bishop. Despite Ursúa's claim that there were many souls to be attended to in the newly conquered regions and that his own funds were drying up, Bishop Arriaga's response was cool. He wrote that he could not fund the costs of transportation and **329** support of additional missionaries but demanded instead that Ursúa himself fund the costs of six or eight additional priests, including the price of chalices, ornaments, and the construction of churches and other ecclesiastical buildings. Should Ursúa be unable to meet these expenses, he could request them from the funds promised by the Guatemalan government. The bishop's denial of additional support, undoubtedly motivated in part by Father Juan Pacheco's testimony, as well as that of Soberanis, made matters even worse.[25]

Over the next month Ursúa strategized how best to make his case locally for the needs faced by the presidio. Although, as we will see shortly, substantial funds had been promised by the Audiencia of Guatemala, much more was needed. Governor Soberanis continued to question the legality of the conquest itself and was on the verge of placing Ursúa under arrest. Ursúa's immediate strategy to redeem his reputation and muster support for his cause was to try the familiar tactic of soliciting sworn testimony, this time from his own military officers.

He therefore called on his supporters in Campeche to sponsor a series of depositions. The petition for the calling of witnesses on Ursúa's behalf was presented by the alcalde of Campeche, Gregorio Carlos Sáenz, who had served as Ursúa's personal agent since mid-1696. Such conflict of interest was seldom an issue in the preparation of such evidence. The testimony was presented by nine witnesses, all military men, who came and went over a period of ten days (July 1–10). Their testimony was recorded by Agustín de Verganza, the public clerk of Campeche.[26]

Of the seven questions, which clearly were drafted by Ursúa, most dealt with "factual" matters concerning the preparatory activities that led to the conquest, the conquest itself, and the events following it. Although the lengthy, detailed wording of the questions constituted a flattering interpretation of Ursúa's valor, generosity, and fairness in all that he had done, there was little in them not detailed by Ursúa himself on other occasions. One question, however, invited the testifiers to expound on the perceived cruelty and even depravity of the Itzas. This question, and the witnesses' responses to it, was designed to reveal a people so barbaric that only the most hardened observer could doubt the importance of this conquest for the preservation of civilized life itself.[27] It read: "If they know from widely circulated information[28] that the nation of the Itzas had held these and the provinces of Guatemala in a state of terror by the cruelties that they had committed in removing the hearts of those they captured as sacrifices and in sustaining themselves on human flesh; and that as a result of what has taken place [i.e., the capture of Nojpeten] all of the towns have been pacified. Say what they know about this matter, have seen, or understood, etc."

Based mainly on Ursúa's interrogation of the youth Kamal and the forced testimony of AjK'in Kan Ek', the question invited the witnesses in

Campeche to speculate and to expand on rumors they had heard about sacrificial heart excision and cannibalism. Its linkage of these two supposed practices made it appear that human sacrifice necessarily involved the eating of human flesh. Linking cannibalism with sustenance, the question did not permit the understanding that it was primarily a ritual practice and not done to satisfy an appetite for human flesh. Like all such leading questions, there was only one answer, and that answer had to be confirmatory.

So tantalizing was the question that the witnesses introduced other accusations not even implied by it. The following are representative examples of their responses, presented in the order in which the witnesses spoke:

> [Captain Pedro de Zubiaur] said that the Itza nation had [the region] terrorized with the cruelties that they had committed, and it has been confirmed that they had extracted the living hearts from all of the Indians that they had captured in the towns and hamlets, which they sacrificed to their false gods with which the island was filled, sustaining themselves on human flesh, and other extremely lewd sins and other unspeakable and filthy matters, [too] contemptible to be written, and that having taken that infernal receptacle away from them these provinces and those of Guatemala have been secured.[29]

> [Captain Diego de Avila Pacheco] said that ... with this nation having laid waste to all of the Indians of the forest in order to make sacrifices to their gods and to sustain themselves on human flesh, and [the Spaniards'] having found on the island in possession of Kin Canek an Indian from the west, a boy [probably Kamal], who was to be sacrificed, as they had done to his father, mother, and brothers, ... he finds that a very particular service to the two majesties has been carried out.[30]

Sergeant Major Miguel Ferrer concluded his statement on human sacrifice by saying that "only he who had been there and has seen that sacrificial tool of Lucifer can describe it."[31] Squadron Corporal Francisco Antonio de la Joya, whose imagination may have been emboldened by Ferrer's description, said, "It was verified that they extracted the living hearts from those whom they sacrificed, and they chopped up their bodies and tossed them into pots, having separate female Indian cooks for this, and that after eating the human flesh they committed other very filthy sins in which the demon had his patrimony founded, with which it is seen to

331

have been of great consequence to have placed the house of God where similar evils were committed."[32]

Each response, some built upon the witness's listening to those who came before, added new elements, which climaxed in the absurd claim by Captain Nicolás de la Aya that the Itzas had eaten nearly everyone in the forests. So formulaic were the tropes describing the extraction of hearts, the lust for human flesh, the tossing of body parts into cooking pots, and the sin of sodomy (too filthy a word to be uttered in public) that we are led to question their truth or the evidence on which they were based. Even the limited testimony on human sacrifice collected in Yucatán by Fray Diego de Landa during the idolatry trials of 1562 appears moderate and measured by comparison.[33] That testimony, however suspect some of it might be, was based on individual, documented cases, whereas the 1697 accusations against the Itzas were generalized and hyperbolic in nature.[34]

Ursúa obviously intended that the testimony be used to reinforce a negative image of the Itzas and thereby justify the military actions he had taken against them. He wrote to the king in late July concerning his state of mind and the circumstances that had led to the incarceration of the Kan Ek' cousins and his use of torture to extract a confession from AjK'in Kan Ek'. His own prose had by now reached a new level of hyperbole, as in his reconstructed scenario of the fate of Captain Juan Díaz de Velasco and his party of Guatemalans in 1695; his inspiration for much of this description was the testimony he had taken in Campeche:

> [The Itzas] took them aboard and with sticks and machetes killed most of them in their canoes. They took Captain Juan Díaz and others, who were still alive, to the island, [where] between the petty king, his priest, and another barbarian, a follower [*deudo*] of theirs also named Canek, they removed the hearts of all of them. Having sacrificed them they cut up their bodies, which they ate roasted and boiled, this inhuman atrocity being a common practice among the infidels, who are so impassioned[35] by it that when they lacked a ready supply from among the inhabitants they had knocked off in the forests, they exacted the same cruelty upon the fattest boys of the island. Having already laid waste to the wild enemy nations, they descended to the domesticated towns, and in the daily absence of sacrificial material their own nation supplied and contracted it.[36]

Nearly two years later, in April 1699, after he had returned to the Petén Itza presidio, Ursúa, with the cooperation of his Guatemalan military counterpart, Melchor de Mencos y Medrano, administered a similar oral questionnaire. This time the witnesses included five priests and five military men. Although some of the responses were more detailed, the rhetoric had not changed substantially. The issues were still those of human sacrifice, cannibalism, and sodomy, and the language used to describe them was virtually identical to that recorded in Campeche in 1697.[37]

The two secular priests from Yucatán, Pedro de Morales and José Francisco Martínez de Mora (who had been present during the initial conquest), were the first to offer their responses, saying that "this island had been the patrimony of Lucifer, where all the infidels of these districts engaged in worshipping him (and in sacrificing the hearts of those whom they captured and killed in order to eat [them]) in many temples, caves, and vaulted rooms [*bóvedas*], whose ruins are evident."[38] The two priests offered no evidence for these claims, citing only the "innumerable idols" destroyed during the attack on Nojpeten and claiming that certain leaders "had wished to commit treason on three occasions." None of these occasions, however, each of which involved only attempts to escape or rebel against the Spaniards, involved human sacrifice or any other form of personal violence.

Fray Diego de Rivas, the Guatemalan Mercederian who had only recently arrived in Peten, also supported the claim of cannibalism. Ironically, however, he also noted that "this forest has been . . . the refuge of trouble-making Christian Indians from the province of Campeche," failing to see the contradiction in his assertion that people would seek refuge where they would be captured, killed, and eaten by their neighbors.[39]

The Dominican Fray Gabriel de Artiga, another newcomer, had recently been reassigned from Verapaz to the Itza reductions. He offered another contradictory observation — that the Itzas engaged in trade with the "untamed" forest peoples while terrorizing "all whom they can capture in the forest." He provided additional evidence for "other idolatrous abominations and the rest," specifically the island's "public atrium-enclosed houses of abomination (whose runes are patent)."[40] His term for these houses — "casas comunes nefandas apretiladas" — makes indirect reference to the "pecado nefando," the "sin of sodomy." Its walls were decorated with glyphs or pictures ("runes") that he claimed portrayed such activity.

Although a full critique of the sources for accusations such as these 333 cannot be presented here, it must be emphasized that all Spanish statements of the time must be carefully evaluated before their veracity is accepted. With that said, the cumulative evidence, which is considerable, does indicate that the Itzas, like the Mayas of Yucatán at the time of the conquest and most other Maya societies from Classic times on, practiced ritual human sacrifice and heart excision.[41] That the Itzas followed these practices, using primarily captives taken in raids, seems indisputable. The possibility of cannibalism among any Maya group, however, regardless of time period, is far weaker; to my knowledge there is no incontrovertible evidence for it.[42] Accusations of cannibalism were nearly always made by enemies, detractors, or conquerors and appear in most cases to serve as a means of decrying that group's savagery and inhumanity. Despite "admissions" that members of the Itza ruling nobility did practice the consumption of human flesh, we must remember that no interrogated Itza admitted to doing so *himself.*

The only claimed eyewitness account of the practice of cannibalism appears in a 1699 report by Nicolás de Lizarraga, the head of the first group of Guatemalan settlers in Petén.[43] Lizarraga, following an armed encounter with a group of Kowojs in which Spanish troops responded to a single arrow shot at them by killing thirty people, claimed that he and others saw "the parboiled chunks of arms and legs in a canoe." The victims were supposedly five native Verapaz workers who had been sent to gather firewood. Lizarraga gave his account under oath, but I have found much of his written prose to be exaggerated and untrustworthy.

In the absence of any reliable evidence of Itza cannibalism, Spanish accusations that the Itzas had an insatiable lust for human flesh, such that the forests were being depopulated, seem even more preposterous. Those who participated in ritual human sacrifice were the highest-ranking priests and nobility — a very small number. Spanish priests and soldiers, in exaggerating the number of sacrificial victims, grossly distorted human sacrifice into a means of obtaining food, whereas it was far more plausibly, as Linda Schele has shown for the Classic period, a highly ritualized practice heavy in blood symbolism and associated with nonterritorial raids on other communities.[44]

Whether or not Itza men engaged in same-sex activities on the universal scale suggested by Spaniards is equally impossible to determine with the evidence at our disposal. It will be recalled that Avendaño had alluded to such a possibility, although only on the basis of rumor and casual observations about male public behavior and dress. The presidio chaplain, Bachiller Francisco de San Miguel y Figueroa, made more specific reference to sexual behaviors in a 1702 letter to the Crown. In it he referred to a house surrounded by a wall into which young boys were invited for the purpose of having sexual relations with "ministers of the Demon," who wore women's skirts and made tortillas for the priests.[45]

334

This house would appear to have been one of Fray Gabriel de Artiga's "houses of abomination," of which Figueroa had observed or heard about only one. Here Figueroa described a transgender role that seems plausible, but because the accuracy of his statement cannot be independently confirmed, we can draw few conclusions.

It is a sad testimony to the record left by most observers that these men emphasized only what they viewed as the negative qualities of Itza life and seldom commented on positive ones. We almost never hear about families, the care of children, horticultural techniques, or medical curing, all of which were far more important aspects of everyday life for the vast majority of people than the subjects they chose to emphasize and denigrate. This imbalance might be simple enough to explain as reflecting the limited exposure of an occupying force that seldom saw or interacted with ordinary Itzas under normal conditions. What little experience they might have been able to report, however, was also intentionally omitted by Ursúa and his officers from a record that they designed primarily in order to defend military conquest and forced conversion.

The Kowojs Plot Rebellion

Despite the roundups pursued with the assistance of AjKowoj and AjChan, Captain Joseph Fernández de Estenos wrote to his friend the Guatemalan general Melchor de Mencos y Medrano on July 3 that many more fugitives were still in the forests, beyond the soldiers' grasp. Nevertheless,

> the Indians of three islands and another three towns, along with all the Indians of their territories, are quiet and peaceful. Whenever I call them they come punctually, which demonstrates recognition of the obedience that they have given to our King Lord Charles the Second. I omit some minor leaders of this island who, with troops of Indians that follow them, run about fugitive in the forests, whose obstinance and rebelliousness spring from their being the worst evildoers and the most guilty in the deaths that have befallen the Spaniards. I have made some forays in search of them, and, made aware by their spies, the bulk of them has always run away from me, abandoning the sites that they occupy and flying away. The cause of [my] not encountering them is their fear of being punished.

335

The rains were preventing additional forays, and there was little contact with the supposedly pacified natives, who lived scattered in small hamlets.

The two Yucatecan priests had also departed, "and we are serving here as vicars and sacristans, because they call on us to baptize when they consider it a terminal illness."[46]

A week later, his letter still unmailed, Fernández de Estenos added a shocking postscript:

> I discovered a treacherous act that the Cobox Indians wished to commit, and having imprisoned Captain Cobox, who had been the head or leader of the Coboxes, and taking his deposition, he confessed that it was true he, with the Indians of his town, had intended to come and kill us Spaniards at this presidio and that he had sent a message to the Indians of the forest and to all the other Indians of this nation to form an alliance and join together in order to kill us. But [he said] that there had been neither time nor place to receive an answer to his message and that he therefore does not know whether it had been received or whether it had appeared acceptable to them. The said treacherous act having been confirmed by the confessions of many witnesses, I ordered that he be shot, and afterwards I put him on a gallows in view of all of the Indians of this island.[47]

Even with AjKowoj dead, Fernández realized that the previous peacefulness of the Kowoj towns of the northern shore was suspect. Although he hoped that the execution of AjKowoj would create "horror and fear" and would quell the pending rebellion, he expressed his own fears to the president of Guatemala that the Kowojs "are very bloodthirsty and accustomed to killing Spaniards, not by the force of arms but with demonstrations of affection and friendliness, with submissiveness and humility with which they have always deceived everyone, pretending to have some kindness and affection in dealing and living with Spaniards. Besides previous examples, we are experiencing it now, as before, that they join together and plot some wickedness."[48]

Captain Kowoj was executed on Monday, July 8. He had revealed during his confession — or so it was said — that the devil had deceived him.[49] Shortly before he was executed he "received the water of baptism by the hand of the presidio's alférez, there being no priest in said places."[50] Captain Diego Bernardo del Río wrote to Melchor de Mencos on the day of AjKowoj's death that he was asked "whether or not he wished the water of baptism, that he should know that receiving it or not receiving it, he had to die, so that he might choose that which is best. He asked for the water very much from his heart. He died with great courage, and he asked for forgiveness from all of the Indian men and women of this island whom he had offended — that he might love the Divine Majesty, that he might die with complete repentance for having offended my [*sic*] God and Lord, and that his soul might depart to enjoy his glory."[51]

Del Río, who may have overstated AjKowoj's dying sentiments, lamented that this tragedy had occurred while there were still no priests at the presidio. Having raised the expectations of the native population through their teachings and initial baptisms, Satan would now undoubtedly seize his advantage. Considering Juan Pacheco's self-admitted lack of success in his evangelical efforts, del Río's observation that Christian teaching had achieved such a positive effect might be read as pure posturing. But everyone, he insisted, was now asking to be baptized. The evidence he cited suggests that an epidemic was already sweeping through the population and that some Itzas were indeed seeking alternative spiritual remedies: "Most of the Indian men and women are clamoring for fathers to baptize them, that they want to be Christians. The fathers and mothers of those who have just died come with their very sick sons and daughters, calling to the Spaniards that for the love of God might they cast the water on their child. The husbands do the same for their wives, and the wives for their husbands, seeing that they are very ill. May God touch the hearts of those fathers from Campeche that at least one might come."[52]

It would be some time before priests would arrive to minister to the dying Itzas. In the same mail packet, however, del Río enclosed a letter to President Sánchez de Berrospe saying that the bones of the two Guatemalan Dominicans and three of the Spaniards who had been captured in April 1696 had been found in a vaulted room (*bóveda*). He was sending these separately via Cahabón with a message to Fray García de Palomares requesting that "he place all of them in boxes, because these Indians wanted to carry them only in small bits, each piece separately." How he knew even this much about the five deceased men is not specified, but we may presume that their status was determined from their clothing. Del Río did not imply that the bodies had been mutilated or consumed cannibalistically, as others had maintained before their discovery.[53]

García de Paredes Begs in Guatemala   337

Only ten or eleven days after the assault on Nojpeten, Ursúa sent Alonso García de Paredes and José Ripalda Ongay to Santiago de Guatemala with a packet of documentation and instructions to request financial assistance for the new presidio. This journey along the unfinished road south of the lake to Mopan and from there to Cahabón turned out to be as difficult as might have been predicted. García and Ripalda left with the priest José Martínez, forty-five soldiers, and six unidentified "Indians," certain that they would find Spaniards encamped at the presidio of Mopan. They found it abandoned, sent thirty-five of the troops back to Petén Itzá, and arrived at Cahabón with the remainder on April 14, hungry and exhausted. There they were fed by the Dominican Fray García de Colmenares. The local cabildo gave them a few fresh food supplies for the Peten presidio, which García sent back to Petén Itza with the remaining troops and carriers.[54]

The two officers and the priest remained in Cahabón for only four days and then proceeded to Cobán, where García de Paredes sent a letter to President Sánchez de Berrospe informing him of their planned arrival in Santiago de Guatemala. Their appearance there on April 18 sparked a series of official meetings at which the two Yucatecans presented on Ursúa's behalf their petitions for assistance and answered questions from members of the audiencia, church officials, and other leading citizens.[55] Ursúa's letters to the president, in which he argued that he had fulfilled the terms of the 1693 royal cédula, requested fifty troops in order to maintain the presidio, to be paid from the royal treasury, as well as supplies, arms, and ammunition, which he had mistakenly believed would still be available at the presidio of Mopan.[56] The audiencia met on April 28 to consider the request and decided that a "general war meeting," attended by all who had experience in the recent reductions, should be called in order to discuss the matter.[57]

The meeting took place on May 1 and was attended by the six audiencia members, a fiscal, the bishop (a Mercederian), the two Yucatecan officers, the Mercederian provincial, the Dominican friar Agustín Cano, the royal accountant, nine military officers, and the public clerk.[58] The president read aloud Ursúa's communications and the relevant cédulas,[59] following which each person in attendance was given the opportunity to state his opinion on the request. The final resolution, voted on by all in attendance, was that the royal treasury would support the presidio with salaries for fifty soldiers but that Ursúa would have to provide the men from his own garrison. Not everyone voted in favor of the resolution, but the general consensus supported maintenance of what the Guatemalans had themselves been unable to achieve.

Following the meeting another fiscal and royal official, Pedro Velásquez y Valdez, wrote that they had already spent more than eighty-five thousand pesos of the Crown's money in the Chol and Itza entradas but had achieved only the deaths of two friars, Captain Juan Díaz, and the ninety-odd persons who had been captured with them. Furthermore, he reported that on May 13, 1696, shortly after this massacre, President Sánchez de Berrospe had issued an order that all further reduction efforts in the region be suspended. Notwithstanding these concerns, the fiscal recommended that Ursúa's request for troops be granted in light of the significance of the defeat of "the fortress that served these infidels as a sanctuary for their assaults, seditions, and resistance" and of the need to keep the new route between the two provinces open.[60]

The next day García de Paredes and Ripalda Ongay, who had been asked to detail their request for funds, handed the president a carefully justified budget totaling 13,672 pesos, 4 reales. This amount would cover the salaries of the fifty troops and their supplies for a fourteen-month period, at the end of which Ursúa was scheduled to resume the governorship of Yucatán.[61] Sánchez de Berrospe immediately approved the amount but determined that only half would be sent with the Yucatecan officers, who planned to return via Chiapas.[62] The royal treasurer advised him that seven months of support was all that could be afforded, and after that period payments could be made to Ursúa as might be necessary.[63]

On May 4 the messenger Juan Baraona departed for Mérida from Santiago de Guatemala with a letter from the president to Governor Soberanis and several to other persons from García de Paredes. He traveled the route that went to Ciudad Real (today San Cristóbal de las Casas) and then down into the tropical forests past Palenque, Petenekte on Río Usumacinta, and Sajkab'ch'en. He finally reached Mérida on May 27, presenting to Soberanis the president's letter informing him of his decision to support Ursúa's presidio but stating that the monies would be placed in a special account overseen by Pedro Velásquez y Valdez in Santiago de Guatemala. Soberanis was to have no control over the dispersement of the funds, a provision that García de Paredes must have requested on the assumption that Soberanis would have done all in his power to withhold them or to delay payment.[64]

Baraona was to return as far as Sajkab'ch'en and await answers to another packet of letters that the Guatemalan audiencia had sent to Ursúa at the Petén Itza presidio, on the assumption that he was still there. The 339 packet caught up with Ursúa just one day's travel from Campeche. He wrote thanking Sánchez de Berrospe for his generosity but could not resist boasting of the hardship he had suffered: "I have not only spent the patrimony of my wife and children but have also risked my life, placing it in calculated dangers that followed upon nearly intolerable toil." Some malcontents, he wrote, would of course deprecate the accomplishment, but he was certain that the president appreciated the importance of what he been doing in the name of God and the Crown. The principal naysayer went unnamed, but the president would have known from earlier correspondence and from his conversations with García de Paredes that this was Soberanis.[65]

Always as optimistic as he was boastful, Ursúa falsely assured the president that there was no danger of an Itza uprising, because the only region the Itzas appeared to "occupy" beyond the lake was that of the Mopans, who had already fled even further toward the east. And willing to stretch the truth to the breaking point, he claimed certain knowledge that the road from the main lake to Cahabón was perfectly passable. After all, García de Paredes and his party had gone across it with horses, even while "carrying their beds." (The messenger Baraona reported to Soberanis that he had been told that the road was virtually impassable and that García had been forced to cut through open country for much of the way.)[66] Ursúa had been assured by Diego Bernardo del Río, who had been along it as far as Cahabón, that the route was passable. As for the route from Yucatán to the lake, notwithstanding the swampy areas that appeared during the rainy season, it was a "very good road."[67]

García and Ripalda had not yet returned to Campeche when Ursúa wrote to the president on June 12, 1697. The Franciscan provincial later reported that all of those who went to Guatemala had returned via Tabasco, although Ursúa had believed they were to return through Chiapas.[68] Ripalda, at any rate, was back at the Petén presidio in his old post as alférez real in 1699.[69] Surprisingly, no information on Captain García's later activities appears in any documentation. He seems to have withdrawn entirely from the Petén Itza project, perhaps owing to illness. Because he was so deeply immersed in every aspect of the project, from its beginnings through the capture of Nojpeten, it is difficult to imagine that he withdrew intentionally after successfully petitioning the Guatemalan audiencia. Nor can it be explained why Ursúa, whom he had served with such apparent loyalty, never mentioned his ultimate fate.

The dispensing of the monies that Sánchez de Berrospe was to have sent to Yucatán for support of the presidio raised petty political rivalries that we cannot fathom today. Velásquez y Valdez, the Guatemalan official, said he would refuse to administer the funds, and the matter was still unresolved by August 1697. No money had yet been sent when the Guatemalan audiencia and a group of church leaders met that month to consider whether or not they should send missionaries to Petén Itzá. The president concluded that they were under no obligation to do so and that these should be supplied by Yucatán. No priests in Guatemala spoke the Itza language, and he wanted no conflict over ecclesiastical jurisdiction with the bishop of Yucatán. Guatemalan sympathy with Yucatán was strained by the lack of a resolution to the missionary question, and Sánchez wrote to Governor Soberanis that he had decided to send the funds directly to Ursúa for him to dispense, and that only in his absence would Soberanis be authorized to receive them.[70]

The funds finally arrived in October. Soberanis, believing that they would be received and administered by the royal treasurer, ordered on October 17 that new volunteer troops be recruited for the presidio of Petén Itza and that muleteers with forty mules be hired from the partido of La Costa to carry supplies.[71] The treasurer, however, true to his word, had refused to accept the money, which was now in Ursúa's hands. Ursúa, drained of his resources and hoping to live more inexpensively, planned to move with his family to Peto. Soberanis, however, was determined to exile him from Yucatán. While he strategized how to bring legal charges against Ursúa, he had him placed under house arrest in Jekelchak'an, also preventing his wife and children from leaving.[72]

The embittered Soberanis was critical of any plan to distribute any resources whatsoever to the Petén presidio. In writing to Sánchez de Berrospe he said, "I would like to know what spiritual benefit the Indians have received. Surely there are very few, or none at all, baptized or, in like manner, reduced. Surely Father San Buenaventura and a Franciscan lay religious or brother died under violent circumstances. I do not understand how they are reduced and are receiving the Catholic faith, which is associated with solid fundamentals and which is not resisted."[73] Soberanis was obviously uncertain what should be done next. He expressed no ideas about a future policy for the presidio and its relationship with the Itzas or about the future of missionary activities.

"A Glorious Task"

341

During the next months the issue of political control over Petén Itza became increasingly confused. Ursúa continued to complain in letters to the Crown about the impediments Soberanis placed in the way of his independent administration of the new territories. Recognizing the dangers facing the small garrison, he pleaded in September for Crown approval of additional forces and of families who could raise foodstuffs to support the troops.[74] He considered Guatemala's grant of funds to be tantamount to giving him administrative control over the presidio. He had now, he claimed, spent 46,300 pesos of his own and his wife's fortune and still owed more.[75]

The Spanish Crown's response to Ursúa's accomplishments and woes, although delayed by the mails and the complexities engendered by political conflict in Yucatán, was overwhelmingly positive. Juan de Villagutierre Soto-Mayor, who had been assigned to read the thousands of pages of documentation that was pouring into the court's offices, presented an oral summary and interpretation of these materials to the Council of the Indies in November. So favorable was his report that instructions were thereupon drawn up to draft a cédula expressing gratitude to Ursúa. Other cédulas, the most important of which would be directed to the viceroy and Soberanis, were to demand complete cooperation in all that Ursúa required in order to maintain the presidio and to continue reductions of the native population. Soberanis, whose objections to Ursúa's activities were completely ignored by the Council, was ordered yet again to cooperate and assist Ursúa, subject to punishment if he did not do so.[76]

The Crown, recognizing that his had been "a glorious task undertaken by your valor and zeal," finally granted Ursúa's earlier request to pursue his activities with complete independence from the governor of Yucatán. He was granted the title and authority of "governor and captain general of all the land and road that you might have subdued and shall subdue, subordinate to no one other than my viceroy in New Spain." This grant of authority, delimiting no fixed boundaries upon Ursúa's territory, apparently represented the first official recognition of the vast region that was later to become Petén. Potentially, however, the territory extended well into present-day Campeche, because Ursúa could claim that he had subdued all of the lands south of Kawich along the camino real. Less clear was the status of Ursúa's control over lands south of Lago Petén Itzá, because the lines of communication from there to Verapaz and Huehuetenango could well be claimed to have been established by the Audiencia of Guatemala. The purpose of such a grant to Ursúa seems to have been less that of establishing a new geopolitical territory than of freeing Ursúa from interference by Governor Soberanis.

The cédula, which offered no criticism of Ursúa's militarism, made

342

it clear that the previous policy of applying only "peaceful and gentle" means was no longer in effect. Ursúa and the president of Guatemala were to cooperate militarily in the final "subduing and reduction" of the region. Although Ursúa was instructed to establish a town with a fortified presidio that could be used for self-defense and against "apostates and rebels," its purpose was primarily to facilitate the conversion of the native population. Ursúa was to work toward the long-held goal of applying only "spiritual weapons" in attracting converts, but he was granted a wide latitude to define these limitations as he saw fit.[77]

In response to Ursúa's request for families to settle the newly conquered territories, the Crown ordered Soberanis to assist in finding settlers and granting them lands in villages on the camino real that were to serve as rest stops along the way. The viceroy was to send "the idle and hopeless people" from Mexico City to assist in defending the presidio and to settle in the new camino real villages. He was also to contact the governors of neighboring provinces, who were to send families to settle in the new territory.[78] These grandiose and impractical plans to establish *colonias* in Petén and along the camino real saw little action during the following years. A few ladino families from Guatemala did move to Nuestra Señora de los Remedios during 1699, and a few Sierra Mayas from Yucatán joined them in about 1702. Ultimately, however, disease and intolerable living conditions caused most, if not all, of the surviving civilian outsiders to leave.

AjChan Abandons the Spaniards

On September 24 a soldier at the presidio, complaining that he had not been paid, wrote that don Martín Chan had run away from the island with "all of the Indians," who would have included his brother, his brother-in-law, and other relatives. Ever since they had departed, every Spaniard had been anxious, on the lookout for attacks "con la barba sobre el hombro" — with his beard on his shoulder. The surrounding Itzas went about menacing the troops, presumably from canoes in the lake, in the hope that they would abandon the presidio altogether.[79] Apparently the native population on the island had grown considerably over the intervening months: AjChan was said to have slipped away in the night, silently and without alerting the guards, with more than five hundred people. The loss of the Spaniards' friend Martín Francisco Chan, who had served Ursúa, in the general's words, "as a light and guide for the capture of the principal island and as an inducement for the rest who gave themselves up," was an ominous sign. Although the Kan Ek' cousins remained imprisoned, AjChan was now in a position to mount a major resistance against the vulnerable presidio with the support of the eastern province and perhaps even with new allies among the Kowojs.[80]

AjChan sent a message from his old headquarters at Yalain, where he had sought refuge, that he had not run away but rather had gone there to wait until he learned more about a report that he and other native leaders were to be killed by the Spaniards. The supposed authors of the rumor, according to several Itza women who remained behind, were a group of "Chans" (i.e., Kejaches from around Pak'ek'em) along the camino real far north of Lago Petén Itzá. A few days later some "infidels" arrived along the mainland shore north of the island and called out to ask whether Ajaw Kan Ek' was still alive. When the Spaniards brought him out to display him to the visitors, "they demonstrated great happiness and began to dance." Several of them came over to the island and were told that Ursúa had already issued a general pardon in the name of the Crown.[81]

Immediately thereafter the sole priest at the presidio, Pedro de Morales, baptized Ajaw Kan Ek', his cousin AjK'in Kan Ek', and the others of their family who remained imprisoned. Ajaw Kan Ek' became don Joseph Pablo, and AjK'in Kan Ek' was given the name don Francisco Nicolás. The purpose of the baptisms was clearly to send a message to the followers of the Kan Ek' prisoners that their leaders had now offered their complete submission to the Spaniards. The act may have had its desired effect.

When Captain Pedro de Zubiaur Isasi went to Santiago de Guatemala in 1698, he reported that at the time he left Petén on January 21, about fifty Itzas from Yalain were building a house on the main island. Some of the estimated six hundred people of Yalain were coming and going peacefully to and from the island and had supplied Zubiaur with maize meal for his journey. The purpose of the building is unclear, because none of the runaways had returned to stay there, and only fourteen or fifteen native people — eleven women of various ages and three or four men (the Kan Ek' prisoners) — were actually living on the island.[82]

Morales also reported that continuing fears of the Spaniards' ill intent had caused the inhabitants of a small mission settlement he had established on the lakeshore half a league from the presidio to run away. While on another outing to collect foodstuffs from towns to the "north and northeast," he found other settlements abandoned. Even the inhabitants of nearby Ek'ixil had left their homes.[83] In 1699, as we will see in chapter 14, increased military interference in the form of forced maize requisitions led to even wider-scale flight from much of the region and Martín Chan's disappearance from Spanish eyes.

Zubiaur Isasi Begs in Guatemala

When the twenty-two-year-old Captain Pedro de Zubiaur Isasi left for Santiago de Guatemala in January 1698, he left behind a pathetic situation at the presidio. The garrison was all but under siege, unable to venture with safety into the surrounding native settlements. The few workers from Yalain came and went, and that town probably supplied the presidio with small amounts of produce. The troops that Ursúa had left behind had not yet been replaced, and no supplies or funds had arrived from Yucatán since the days before the occupation. Ursúa, still imprisoned in JeKelchak'an, had apparently been unable to hire the muleteers needed to deliver food, despite Soberanis's having approved the recruitment of Maya muleteers from La Costa the previous October.[84] With the garrison reduced to penury and hunger, and with no relief from Yucatán in sight, Zubiaur went to Guatemala seeking supplies, additional arms, and salary for the priests and troops. Part of his mission was to seek a shorter route to Verapaz, and Ursúa claimed that by so doing he had reduced the length of the trip from Peten Itza to San Agustín (located between Cobán and Cahabón) to thirty-five leagues.[85]

Accompanying Zubiaur were Alférez Juan Francisco Cortés, a recently arrived pilot or surveyor named Antonio de Carvajal, the two secular priests (Morales and Martínez de Mora), and an undisclosed number of soldiers and Maya carriers and road workers from Yucatán. When they arrived in Santiago de Guatemala, they were required to record formal depositions on the state of the presidio and the surrounding native populations. These depositions, taken in April in response to a only few pointed questions, are among the only records on the region for this time period.[86]

Zubiaur and Cortés both reported that although the two priests were sufficient for the small population on the island, more would be needed were they to "go out to catechize Indians in the places where they are found." Father Morales stated with calculated exaggeration that even sixteen missionaries would be insufficient to oversee the conversion of the surrounding natives. Of the "great number" of these, the priests boldly claimed, seventeen settlements, each with its "captain," had visited the

345

presidio to offer their submission. Many more had also offered submission on the several occasions when Zubiaur had traveled in the galeota around the lakeshore. The priests' knowledge of the surrounding area was still vague, but they were able to locate the principal areas of settlement as those around Yalain, Ek'ixil, the area north and northwest of the main lake (including the territory of the Kowojs), that to the west, and those elsewhere on the lake shore. Zubiaur estimated he had seen about five thousand people on Nojpeten when they stormed the island and, according to Martín Chan, more than twice that many lived near the mainland shores.

As for their present condition, Zubiaur had "heard it said publicly on the said Petén that there is an abundant number of Indians who have retreated to their milperías on all sides and that they are by nature deceitful, lacking permanent settlement, and untamed." Only by the use of force, he suggested, could such people in such large numbers be successfully converted. Juan Cortés had heard from the imprisoned rulers that many of those who had defended the island had retreated south to the headwaters of the river on which Dolores del Lacandón was located — most likely meaning Río Pasión.

Zubiaur clearly sought to convince the president that additional Guatemalan military support would be needed to complete the conquest and reduction. The promised results of his mission, however — stipends for the priests, travel expenses, some road-opening costs, and some food supplies — were extremely modest.[87] Zubiaur quickly returned to Cahabón, where he delivered the president's orders to the alcalde mayor of Verapaz, Diego Pacheco. With conditions worsening at the presidio, Captain Fernández de Estenos was thrilled to receive a letter from Zubiaur on May 30 saying that the supplies would be arriving soon. Two days earlier he had received a small shipment of beans and salt from Ursúa, with a letter indicating that a larger quantity of maize flour, salted meat, and lard would follow. Although he sent out scouts over the next two weeks to look for the new supply train, the food never arrived. It was assumed that the muleteers had run away, abandoning their cargo somewhere along the way.[88]

Finally, on June 25 Zubiaur and his companions returned to the presidio with the shipment of supplies from Verapaz. He wrote to the Guatemalan president that the trip had been a harrowing one. He had departed Cahabón with 676 carriers and road workers, 85 of whom had run away along the route, some with their cargo.[89] Many of the carriers had sickened, and five of them died. Road conditions were terrible, forcing the mules and horses to swim across some rivers. Most of the maize and beans with which they had started were delivered to the presidio, but of six mules, one had died and two had run away.[90] Zubiaur, exhausted and ill from his experience, left the presidio for Campeche on July 6.[91]

Prisoners of Conquest

By July, conditions at the presidio were rapidly deteriorating. Ursúa had notified Captain Fernández de Estenos that the president of Guatemala had agreed to pay him a monthly salary of sixty pesos and his second-in-command, Francisco Cortés, twenty-five pesos monthly. The other officers and the rank and file soldiers, however, had been assigned no pay and were, according to Fernández, "very disconsolate." Worms and rats had invaded the supplies of beans and hardtack, and the salted meat had rotted. At most they had only a three-month supply of food.[92]

Fernández, apparently having little faith that Ursúa would come through with needed assistance, wrote to President Sánchez de Berrospe pleading directly for relief. In addition to twenty-five more soldiers to reinforce the garrison, he needed a master mason with four assistants and two stonecutters to build a new stone fort with living quarters for the soldiers and a storage area for supplies and ammunition. The new building was crucial, because fire or wind and rain could easily destroy the present thatched structures.[93] The original Itza buildings, which they were still using, were deteriorating rapidly as well, and by mid-1698 roof leaks threatened the meager food supplies. The troops refused to make repairs, stating "that they do not know how to make houses, because most of them are maritime men, and those who are not are woodsmen."[94]

His list of requests, therefore, went on. He required five specialized craftsmen, including a carpenter, two sawyers, a blacksmith, and someone to maintain the galeota and the piragua. In addition, he would need quantities of tallow, tar, pitch, rope for the artillery, iron for making nails, nail extractors, and woolen devices for cleaning inside the heavy artillery barrels. Finally, he asked for both riding and pack horses, in the event that they might need to carry maize from the milpas of "rebel or fugitive Indians."[95] Eventually, as will be seen, the Spaniards' need to steal native food supplies became a harsh reality.

Just as Fernández had completed this letter he learned from a Kejach woman who had gone to the Kowoj capital of Ketz to see her daughter

347

that following Captain Kowoj's execution the inhabitants had abandoned their town and moved to Yaxja. Their new location, on Laguna Yaxhá, had not been seen by the Spaniards, who knew that it was quite far away.[96] Fernández realized that he was facing a long, difficult rainy season in the isolated squalor that now characterized the ruins of Nojpeten. With insufficient manpower to continue the conquest, surrounded by a hostile and unknown forest filled with enemies, and short of supplies, his situation must have seemed hopeless.

Threats of Rebellion

With no idea how he would be able to feed the presidio on the inadequate supplies from Verapaz, Fernández had already begun during June to send troops out to the nearby settlements to search for producing milpas. Finding various towns and milpas abandoned, he went with a garrison of men and the priest Martínez de Mora to Yalain, where AjChan and his followers had allowed a church to be constructed under the direction of Pedro de Morales about six months earlier. They discovered that the church and every house had been burned to the ground, and the crosses that had been erected had been chopped with axes and burned. The town was empty of people, but there was an ample supply of maize in the milpas, suggesting that the inhabitants had fled quickly as they learned of the troops' approach. Morales called out to them but heard only silence. He set up new crosses, and the troops stole from the milpas as much maize as they could take back to the presidio on several mules.[97]

Martínez de Mora had previously visited settlements toward the north and northeast seeking food for the presidio. He later visited them again with a few troops on a reconnaissance mission along the northern shore of the lake

> to see whether the said father could communicate with some Indians and trade with them for some food supplies. Disembarking at the abandoned settlements, they climbed to the top of the hill and found a fort, industriously constructed in such a manner, they say, that they would not be able to deal with it, even with artillery. But they found it abandoned [to the] northeast and north. From there they went directly north to the settlements of the Couohs, which they found completely burned. From there they went to another lake [Laguna Sacpuy], different from this aforementioned nation, located about

half a league from this large lake, finding on its shores all the canoes axed and with no fresh signs of the Indians. With this scene the said father returned with the men without achieving his good intention.[98]

The location of the fortification — the first of several that would be discovered — could have been anywhere along the northern shore, which had been largely abandoned by the Kowojs for areas in the interior. Martínez de Mora later went to Ek'ixil, again hoping to purchase food. Although he found newly planted milpas, the town was deserted — but not burned.[99]

On June 15 Fernández de Estenos wrote that he had managed to transport to the presidio some of the Yalain maize that his men had pilfered. His hopes dimmed, however, when

> I received news that all of the Indians of this nation were gathered on the shores of this lake in order to come to make war against us. I sent intelligence of this news to the said town of Yalain. When we united ourselves on the 14th, the Indians learned of this and retreated to their dwelling places, apparently leaving [occupied] only the parcialidad of the king. This King Canek and the other two prisoners told me that they wanted to bring the Indians together and settle them, and, initiating what they had promised, they began to build some houses with the help of Indians.
>
> God was served when their evil intention was exposed to me. According to the declarations of many Indians it was not an act of kindness but rather contained the idea of getting themselves together more quickly and uniting deceitfully in order to fall upon us. They also told us that they were going to attack at midnight, when it would have been darkest, and that the said prisoners had given them this advice and had incited them, sending them a supply of derisions stating that I had worthless captains or caciques.[100]

The "parcialidad of the king" turned out to be a settlement of "peten Indians" that, we learn, the priest Morales had formed earlier in 1698 on the lakeshore, half a league west of the main island.[101] It may have been on Punta Nijtún. Fearing that an attack on the small island garrison would result in the kidnapping of Ajaw Kan Ek' and the other prisoners, Fernández immediately sent the galeota to this community in order to release the five Itza prisoners who had informed the Spaniards of the plot. He gave orders to the commander that the troops were to remain on board, not fire on or disturb anyone, and allow the five Itzas go freely to their homes. When they arrived at the beach by the new settlement, "some

349

Indians went out to receive the Spaniards with much dissimulation," but the Itzas were released, and the galeota returned without incident.[102]

After returning to the presidio in late June, Morales reported that native informants and Martínez de Mora had told him that the people of this new settlement were the instigators of the supposed plot. When they became aware that the Spaniards knew of their intentions, they abandoned the community and had not been heard from since. After the burning and abandonment of Yalain was discovered, all attempts to talk with people seen walking through the forests were futile. The Itza population had completely withdrawn, and the frustrated priest returned to the presidio "with the knowledge that the said Indians are living in the vicinity of their milpas and availing themselves of their maize."[103]

After his return Morales learned more about both rumors of rebellion and patterns of flight from a thirteen- or fourteen-year-old native girl who had appeared alone on the lakeshore, calling to the Spaniards. She had come, she said, with two companions in response to the news that returnees would be well treated and because people in their settlements, separated from their own milpas, were suffering from lack of food. The three girls had been captured on their way by several native men whom she had overheard saying that the uprising would not stop until they had killed the Spaniards. Of the three girls, she alone escaped. According to her story, the inhabitants of a town called Pop on the northern shore were living in their cultivations along with a number of Kowojs. The people of Ek'ixil had fled directly north to join these others. Those of Ketz, the Kowoj center, also on the northern shore, had gone "to a hamlet called Tikal, which is directly northeast about two days by road from this peten."[104] This is, I think, the earliest reference to the name of the great Maya center still known as Tik'al.

Morales was optimistic that the rumors of rebellion would ultimately amount to nothing.[105] Given the ominous extent of flight from the principal native towns and rumors of attack, however, the men of the presidio were afraid to leave the island. During a meeting on July 2, called to discuss an order by President Sánchez de Berrospe for Zubiaur to take twenty soldiers and survey a possible road connection with Río Pasión and from there to Dolores, priests and officers alike spoke out against the idea. They argued that the weather was so rainy that they would be open to attacks by those living in the area southeast of the presidio. Arms would be useless under these conditions, and the entire garrison was needed to guard against possible attack on the island itself. The presidio still had no constructed fortification, and the number of sentinels had been doubled.[106]

The seriousness of the rumored threat against the Spaniards at the presidio may have been exaggerated; at any rate, nothing came of it over the next weeks and months. People from the surrounding region continued to come and go, primarily to talk with the Kan Ek' prisoners. The officers placed no restrictions on this communication, apparently believing that they were still able to counteract any plot that might be hatched in these meetings and that they would only worsen the situation by prohibiting free exchange among the Itzas. On the other hand, they remained fearful of venturing far from the main island and made no effort to search for, round up, or resettle people living in the forests. The rest of 1698 and the first months of 1699 were spent in a standoff between the Mayas and the Spaniards, the former remaining hidden, and the latter, all too visible, afraid to venture far beyond the confines of their island prison.

On August 11 Martínez de Mora set out once again with a military escort and an "Indian guide" for Laguna Quexil (Ek'ixil) "to see whether he could pick some spiritual fruit."[107] Captain Fernández reported the incident that occurred when they reached Laguna Quexil, offering it as testimony of the Spaniards' total failure in befriending the local population:

> Having reached the said lake, in view of the peten,[108] they saw an Indian in a canoe, whereupon the said father hid himself with the infantry. He told the guide to call to him, and because he saw that [the guide] belonged to his nation, he responded to the call, although with suspicion, asking if he had Spaniards. He answered no, saying over and over that the Spaniards were good people, that they had good hearts, and that the fathers loved the Indians very much. He answered from the canoe with a thousand opprobriums against all the Spaniards, especially with a thousand insults against the padres. Finally, on a spit of land, the guide having secured the canoe, the padre went out to embrace him. But he left the canoe and jumped into the water, not wishing to hear the padre.[109]

Two soldiers chased him in the canoe, but he managed to grab the paddle from them and swim to safety on the island. The priest, oblivious to the implications of the event, continued to call out to whoever might be on the island that they should bring canoes and take the Spaniards over to visit with them. Although it was now obvious that people had returned to settle Ek'ixil, the Spaniards had no idea how to make friendly contact with them.   **351**

Nor did the priests have much luck in communicating with the Itzas who came every day to visit the main island. They tried to talk with them, but, as Fernández wrote, "it goes in one ear and out the other. They come only to see the king and the imprisoned priest, and for the machetes and knives that the soldiers give them. There is no means by which they can be well settled [here]. They tell us that they will do it, but that day never comes."[110] The Kan Ek' prisoners, probably fully aware of the Spaniards' desperation, perhaps counseled their visitors to be patient. Fernández wrote in late October that "the Indians of these forests are undoubtedly believing that we must leave these lands and that we must abandon this place, [since] they are not coming to us." He was also certain that "the king and priest have counseled the Indians not to come [to the island] but, to the contrary, that they should retire to the forests. On other occasions they have counseled them that they should all come, but in order to make war against us and to kill us. Thus it shall be appropriate to remove them from here, because they are empowered by the devil and must be the cause of the Indians' not having been pacified."[111]

Contrary to the Spaniards' belief, Ajaw Kan Ek' and AjK'in Kan Ek' probably had little direct influence on the behavior of the surrounding population. Their power had been weakened even before the storming of Nojpeten, and they were not in a position to effect policies among the many people who had little interest in or respect for them. Nonetheless, their continued imprisonment must have had an empowering symbolic value that gave some Itzas hope.

For the Spaniards to kill the Kan Ek' leaders would have been to risk serious attack. Had they wished to do so, the Itzas could have set fire to the guardhouse and the food supplies, which by now had been moved to a separate building. Such a fire would have consumed the densely packed thatch-roofed houses, leaving those who survived with neither food nor shelter. As long as the Kan Ek' prisoners were alive on the island, even their enemies seemed loath to take such extreme measures.

Only outside settlers, additional priests, and, above all, military reinforcements could break this stalemate. By the end of 1698 the troops had been in residence on the island for nearly twenty-one months, with no hope of replacement. Ursúa and President Sánchez de Berrospe finally reached separate solutions to the crisis in early 1699, the outcome of which signaled the final conquest of the region. I will take up this last phase in the next chapter.

352

Sex, Work, and Marriage

Sánchez's patience with Ursúa's failure to take care of the presidio's needs was wearing thin. He insisted, despite the rains and Ursúa's imprisonment, that Ursúa go to the presidio himself before the task of even finding, much less rounding up, the surrounding population became impossible.[112] As for requests forwarded by Zubiaur for salary money for the languishing troops, he refused to provide any money until Captain Fernández de Estenos sent him a complete list of the men in question, with details on their rank, health, and previous salary payments. Among the issues that the priests had brought to the president was the moral turpitude that beset the isolated presidio society. Writing to Fernández he gave precise instructions on the matter:

> With regard to the governance of that peten, I have felt strongly that proper care has not been taken in separating the Indian women from the infantry, both because of the offenses against God that can result from this proximity as well as the hindrance in the reduction of the Indians, this ardor filling them with anger against the Spaniards. This imprudence is not a good method of proceeding with so many and such good Catholics.
>
> Therefore, Your Mercy is to remove immediately, instantly, however many Indian women there might be in the guardroom and to prohibit them from going in there. Your Mercy is to determine a location where they might grind [maize] and work and to post a fully satisfactory sentinel, [informing] him that he must have no communication with them. Your Mercy is to punish him who might harass them, and, if he does not mend his ways, Your Mercy is to send him to Campeche. Your Mercy is to understand that I will bring a most serious charge against you if I learn of any failure in this matter, believing that I cannot know about it. Your Mercy is to publish a proclamation in that presidio in my name so that this, so great a harm, might be avoided.[113]

It is hardly surprising that among fifty young soldiers, at least some had taken sexual advantage of the eleven Itza women held as virtual prisoners and separated from their husbands or families. The circumstances under which they were "employed" under terms known as "servicio personal" at the presidio are not known, but we can be certain that they were kept against their will.

Fernández later reported that he had carried out the president's orders almost completely. Because he had no building other than the guardroom that was large enough to store maize, he and the priests had agreed on a plan that would allow the women to grind maize in the guardroom during the day and to sleep and eat under guard in another house. Defending

353

himself against the president's charge that he had neglected his duty in allowing the women to sleep in the guardhouse, he stated that they were by nature mischievous and fickle and disliked living among Spaniards. In fact, they had very nearly managed to run away when they had been allowed to live elsewhere on an earlier occasion.

He had thought it better to keep his maize grinders in the guardhouse, where no one had any privacy, than to risk losing his primary source of tortillas. Food production was a far more critical issue than sex. His proposed solution was to replace local female labor with twenty-five native married couples who would be brought in to maintain the presidio, the men planting maize and beans and their wives preparing meals. If that were impossible, he suggested that the president could send fifteen black slaves "with their wives" for the same purpose. And if that option were unacceptable, could the president please send half a dozen Maya men or women to grind maize?[114]

Pedro de Morales, the priest, solved some of the problems of cohabitation later that year by performing seven marriages that joined Itza women with soldiers. By December, he claimed, news of how well the women were being treated had been so positively received in the forests that five families and three unmarried women had arrived at the presidio. Anticipating still more marriages and the arrival of more women, he asked the president to send him fifty *huipiles* (long overblouses) and fifty lengths of cloth in order to make skirts. In addition, he asked for thirty axes and machetes so that "some infidel Indians who wish to be reduced" could plant a milpa that would, in part, feed "some Indian women besides these, who, unless they are given a ration, are accustomed to leaving for the bush."[115]

Morales thus revealed a daunting logic. Because the Itza women wished to marry the soldiers, he could attract an increased number of them to the presidio by demonstrating that they would be presented not only with husbands but also with food. The families of these women would accompany them, resulting in an increase of the work force, the food supply, and the number of Christian converts. Immorality among the soldiers would be reduced by their marriages to the Itza women, and these men would be attracted to the option of remaining there as part of a nucleus of Europeanized settlers. Marriage was the magic glue that could initiate the pacification, Christianization, and economic stabilization of the new province. It was also the beginning of the "mestizoization" of Peten and would ultimately play a crucial part in the transformation of the region.

Sánchez de Berrospe had suggested to Zubiaur that the troops themselves be put to work making a milpa. After Zubiaur returned to the presidio he raised the question and met refusal in the form of excuses, including complaints that farm work, as well as the duties of gathering firewood and paddling piraguas, was "incompatible" with the duties of sentinels. The men, of course, would welcome the arrival of native men and women from Guatemala who could carry out such work, but they would have no part of it.[116]

By the end of 1698 the "conquest" was in a state
of collapse. All around Lago Petén Itzá people were abandoning their
towns. Itzas and Spaniards suspected each other of ill intentions. The missionaries, overwhelmed by their task, had made no headway in attracting
settlers to new missions. Their attempt to establish a church at Yalain, long
believed to be the town most sympathetic to the Spaniards and most receptive to Christian indoctrination, had failed. AjChan, the Spaniards' longtime "friend," had fled the presidio, taking his followers with him to
Yalain. In mid-1698 the inhabitants of Yalain had burned down the church
and their houses, axed the crosses, and disappeared into the forests.

Other towns within easy reach of the Spaniards, who had depended on
them for food, had moved inland from locations near the lakeshore.[1]
By the end of the year virtually all Itza settlements along the shores of
the major lakes were abandoned. Food shortages at the presidio persisted,
and morale among the tiny Spanish population deteriorated. Although
supplies reached Nojpeten occasionally from Guatemala, the poor condition of the road from Verapaz and the high cost of transportation made
shipments sporadic and undependable. Ursúa, under house arrest in Jekelchak'an, was virtually powerless to remedy the dismal situation. Governor Soberanis, who had opposed the project from its inception, did little
to accommodate the presidio's needs.

Finally, after lengthy deliberations, the Audiencia of Guatemala decided
to send a group of Spanish families to the presidio as settlers. Accompanied
by troops under the command of the aging general Melchor de Mencos
who would reinforce the beleaguered men from Yucatán, the settlers arrived in March 1699 following an arduous journey from Verapaz. They
found Ursúa, recently released from house arrest, already at the presidio;
he and Melchor de Mencos temporarily assumed joint governance of the
territory.

The new settlement was a failure, and many of the settlers died in a devastating epidemic brought with them from Verapaz. The soldiers themselves turned to a combined strategy of bartering for food in nearby villages and pillaging the Itzas' fields and food stores. The Itzá responded by burning and abandoning their settlements. Many of the soldiers sickened and died, and the lethal epidemic quickly spread to the indigenous settlements, killing many people. Within a few months the sick and starving Guatemalan troops withdrew from the presidio.

Nonetheless, the pattern of dual colonial control over Petén that was to characterize the governance of this area for decades to come was now established: Guatemala provided the military government, and Yucatán supplied the missionaries. Over the next several years troops and secular clergy worked hand in hand to force much of the surrounding population to return to the lakeshore and other nearby places where it could be controlled. Several new mission towns were established, usually at the locations of preconquest settlements, containing several thousand inhabitants altogether. Even these were unstable, not only in the sense that people frequently abandoned them but also in that they provided the Itzas an opportunity to plot rebellion. The decision by Ursúa and Mencos to send Ajaw Kan Ek' and his imprisoned kinsmen to Santiago de Guatemala at the end of April 1699 had little effect in reducing the strength of Itza enmity toward the Spaniards—its intended goal. Indeed, circumstances were building toward a brief but violent indigenous rebellion.

Reconquest Failed

The Council of the Indies, which was aware from the outset of Ursúa's inability to govern the territories he had "conquered," forwarded cédulas on January 24, 1698, to both President Sánchez de Berrospe and Governor Soberanis.[2] The cédula to the president ordered him to join in the effort to pacify and reduce the populations around Lago Petén Itzá, whereas the one addressed to Soberanis demanded that he provide full assistance to Ursúa in support of the same enterprise. Letters went back and forth between Ursúa and the president during this period, indicating that their plans were well coordinated. Ursúa even suggested that the Guatemalans send a secret advance escort to Petén Itzá in order to take Ajaw Kan Ek' and AjK'in Kan Ek' to Santiago de Guatemala, dressed in Spanish clothing as a disguise.[3] Ursúa wrote to Sánchez that he intended to depart for Itza territory at the beginning of January. There

357

he would meet the party of troops and twenty-five families of settlers from Guatemala.[4]

THE GREAT TRAIN FROM VERAPAZ

On November 14, 1698, Sánchez de Berrospe called a general meeting that included clergy and military, in addition to audiencia members, seeking advice on how best to fulfill the terms of the cédula. Suffering from ill health, he wished to avoid making the strenuous trip himself. In this he was supported by several people, including Fray Diego de Rivas, who argued that the president should not visit the region until the population was reduced and Christianized. Rivas wrote critically of Ursúa's violent methods of conquest and cited the inherent dangers of any entrada that would confront what he believed to be an extremely large population of unconverted natives.[5] Shortly thereafter Sánchez decided to absent himself from the entrada to Petén Itzá.

Rivas himself had only recently returned to Santiago de Guatemala, having earlier in the year attempted twice, unsuccessfully, to reach Lago Petén Itzá via Ixtatán and Dolores del Lacandón.[6] Rivas's failures and his dismal assessment of any potential road between Dolores and Itza territory must have been a decisive element in the president's decision to route the troops, settlers, and muleteers through Cahabón and the now-deserted town and presidio of Mopan. This was the long, arduous route followed by earlier parties of Guatemalans seeking Lago Petén Itzá and by messengers sent from the presidio to the Guatemalan capital.

The president ordered on December 2 that one hundred soldiers be recruited to go to Petén Itzá.[7] Two days later he announced that the seventy-four-year-old Melchor de Mencos y Medrano, then commissary general of the cavalry and until recently governor of Chiapas, was to be commander in chief of the troops. Mencos's captains were to be Marcelo Flores Mogollón, Cristóbal de Mendía y Sologastoa, and Marcos de Avalos; Estévan de Medrano y Solórzano was named sergeant major. Mencos's son, Juan Bernardo de Mencos y Coronado, accompanied him, bearing the title of *aventurero*, an unsalaried, voluntary position.[8] Their route at first was, as noted, to be through Dolores del Lacandón, not Verapaz,[9] but by the beginning of January the president decided that the bulk of the troops, which by then had increased to two hundred, should go via Verapaz with the families of settlers, while a company under Medrano y Solórzano were to attempt the Dolores del Lacandón route.[10]

According to Villagutierre, the train that traveled through Verapaz contained, besides the troops and the twenty-five families of intended settlers, a large number of Maya carriers and workers (*indios de servicio*); eight missionaries; much baggage and many supplies, arms, and ammunition; tools for masonry construction, carpentry, and ship caulking, and the craftsmen who would use them; gunsmiths; a forge and tools to repair the heavy weapons; and tools to make canoes. There was also a surgeon, an apothecary, and a supply of "simple and compound" medicines, as well as the obligatory supply of beads (*chaquiras*) and trinkets (*chucherías*) for the natives. They also took more than twelve hundred head of cattle and horses, including breeding stock, along with seeds and farming tools. Finally, they carried the overdue pay for the Yucatecan troops and priests at the presidio.[11]

The missionaries, the supply master, the troops, and presumably the families departed from Santiago de Guatemala on January 10, arriving twelve days later in Cahabón, where food supplies would be purchased and local workers and muleteers recruited; Mencos arrived some days later. One of the missionaries who participated in this massive undertaking, Bachiller Joseph de Lara, wrote a despairing and eloquent message to Mencos at Cahabón on February 2 about the disaster he perceived to be in the making.[12] Pondering his title of "missionary conqueror," he worried that too few supplies were being assembled too late to avert the starvation of the infantry at Petén Itzá and even that the pending reconquest of the Itzas was fundamentally immoral and wrong: "The reflection that I provide Your Mercy not only touches me but also breaks my heart with pain. . . . With what [little] has been provided to maintain the men (some of them, for a few days) . . . what will Your Mercy do when you see your soldiers exhausted from hunger and stressed by want, heading out to those forests, killing Indians with balls in order to take their poor sustenance from them, destroying their plantings and pillaging the milpas of those miserable people, and Your Mercy being unable to remedy all of this because hunger is the cruelest enemy?"[13]

Lara feared most, of course, that if the troops had to plunder in order to obtain food, the native inhabitants would run away and the missionary effort would have been in vain. "In two words," he concluded, "with the present supply of provisions the conquest is not only difficult but impossible."[14] Mencos apparently heeded Lara's warning, delaying the party's departure until more food supplies could be obtained.[15] Nonetheless, food **359** shortages plagued the massive entrada itself and continued to cause serious difficulties after its arrival at the presidio. Indeed, everything the priest feared ultimately came to pass.

In Cahabón, authorities counted thirteen Guatemalan "families" who

TABLE 14.1

Comparison of Three Censuses of Guatemalan Settlers Who Went to Petén, Indicating Effects of Epidemic Disease, 1699

No.	February 1699 (Cahabón)	May 4, 1699 (Petén Itzá)	September 6, 1699 (Petén Itzá)
Couples:			
1	Don Nicolás de Lizarraga Spouse 2 children	Don Nicolás de Lizarraga[a] Doña Francisca Lobo de Vargas 2 sons[b]	Living Died August 9 2 Living (ages 3, 5)
2	Don Gaspar González Spouse	Don Gaspar González Donis Doña Juana Lizarraga (daughter of no. 1)	Died July 10 Living
3	Don Domingo León de Moratalla (No spouse listed, assumed error) 4 children	Don Domingo de Moratalla Antonia de la Trinidad 3 daughters[c]	Living Died August 21 2 Living (ages 3, 5) 1 (Josefa) died July 20
4	Diego Barrejo Spouse 2 children	Diego Barrejo, silversmith María de Vargas y Castillo 2 daughters	Living Living 2 Living (ages 4, 8)
5	Alejandro Burguete Spouse 1 child	Alejandro Burguete, barber María del Socorro y Acuña	Living Living Died (no date)

6	Nicolás de Illescas
	Spouse
	6 children
		Nicolás de Illescas, saddler
		Apolonía de Ardón
		2 daughters, 2 sons,
		  1 unidentifed[d]
			Living
			Died July 26
			1 daughter living (age 4)
			2 sons living (ages 13, 14)
			1 daughter (Micaela) died
			  July 7
			1 unidentified died

7	Diego Marroquín Spouse 2 children	Diego Marroquín, saddler Magdalena de la Cruz 1 daughter, 1 son	Living Living 2 living (ages 2, 8)
8	Antonio Gómez (sic) Spouse 4 children	Antonio González Bernarda Sánchez 4 children	Died June 5 Died August 21 4 children died (no dates)
9	Simón de los Sánchez (sic) Spouse 1 child	Simón de los Santos, tanner Isabel María	Living Living 1 living adopted orphan son, age 4, child of no. 12
10	Diego Martín Spouse	Diego Martín, carpenter Dionisia de la Rosa	Living Living
11	Nicolás de Cabrera Spouse 1 child	Nicolás de Cabrera Nicolasa Sánchez 1 daughter (María)	Died July 26 Living Died July 17

TABLE 14.1
(continued)

No.	February 1699 (Cahabón)	May 4, 1699 (Petén Itzá)	September 6, 1699 (Petén Itzá)
12	Simón de Alvarado	Simón de Alvarado, tailor	Died July 14
	Spouse	María Ambrosio (deceased)	Died April 30
	2 children	2 sons	1 died July 20; see no. 9 for other son, adopted
13	Andrés Vásquez	Andrés Vásquez	Living
	Spouse	Francisca de la Cruz Bobadilla	Living
Others:			
	Not specified (child of couple 3)	Francisco de León	Living
	Not specified (child of couple 6)	Gertrudis de Illescas	Living
	Not listed	Not listed	Josefa Lorente, living[e]
	Not listed	Not listed	Antonia de la Cruz ("negra"), died May 5[f]
Demographic summary:			
	13 adult males	14 adult males	10 adult males (4 died after May 4)
	15 adult females	15 adult females (1 died 30 April)	10 adult females (6 died after May 4)
	25 children	21 children (2 died after February census)	12 children (9 died after May 4)
Totals:			
	53	50	32

SOURCES: February 1699: AGI, G 345, no. 20, Memoria de las familias de los trece pobladores que se hallan en este pueblo de Cahabon para pasar al Peten, n.d. (February 1699), ff. 311r–312r. May 4, 1699: G 151A, no. 1, Razón de las familias que hay en el Peten, 4 May 1699, ff. 135r–136v. September 6, 1699: G 343, no. 23, Memoria de las personas que . . . se hallan en esta isla y presidio del Peten Ytza de Nuestra Señora de los Remedios y San Pablo, 6 Sept. 1699, ff. 51v–57r; G 343, no. 23, Memoria de las personas que han muerto en este presidio desde el mes de abril hasta la fecha de esta, 6 Sept. 1699, ff. 57v–59v.

[a]Lizarraga, the head of the settler families, was in Cahabón seeking supplies at the time of the May 4 census. In several cases full names are reported only in the September 6 census.

[b]The May 4 census counts "hijos" as daughters and/or sons but designates the children as "hijas" if the couple has only daughters. The designation in this column does distinguish living sons from living daughters, on the basis of more complete information in the September 6 census.

[c]The fourth child was Francisco de León (see no. 14), who married Gertrudis de Illescas, daughter of couple no. 6.

[d]The sixth child was Gertrudis de Illescas (see no. 14), who married Francisco de León, the son of couple no. 3.

[e]Josefa Lorente, listed only on September 6, "came among the settlers."

[f]Antonia de la Cruz is listed only among the deceased on September 6.

awaited the departure for Petén (see Table 14.1). These were married couples, all with Spanish surnames, ten of whom had children with them, numbering from one to six per couple. In all there were fifty-three persons, including two single women. Each family received minimal rations — one pound of dried beef and one pound of hardtack (*biscocho*) per person — which must have been consumed long before their departure. Each also received a tiny sum of cash, in most cases a total of one and a half reales for husband and wife plus half a real for each child.

The origins of these families is unknown, although they were probably from Santiago de Guatemala. Three of the men, along with the wives of two of them, bore the titles don and doña, indicating that they were considered to be Spaniards; the rest, presumably, were ladinos or of another *casta*. Two single women, one a "negra" and presumably a servant, eventually joined the group on the trek to Petén Itzá. In a census taken of these families on May 4, after their arrival at the presidio, we learn that among the men were a silversmith, two saddlers, a barber, a leather tanner, a carpenter, and a tailor. The leader of the group was don Nicolás de Lizarraga, who spent much time during the months following their arrival in Petén attempting to procure food supplies from Cahabón. Lizarraga's daughter and son-in-law also joined them, and two children of other couples had married one another before the May 4 census was taken. Several other individuals with the same surnames may also have been related to each other. As we shall see later, the settlers did not fare well in Petén, where many of them died.

URSÚA'S RETURN

It was apparently widely known in Yucatán that the Crown had instructed Governor Soberanis to support Ursúa's return to Petén Itzá, where he would join the Guatemalans under Melchor de Mencos. Not until November 1698, however, did Soberanis issue a public proclamation announcing the royal cédula of January 24 of that year and encouraging volunteers to join Ursúa as settlers in the newly conquered lands. The announcement, issued in the plaza of Campeche with military trumpets and drums, offered whoever would be willing to go — whether Spaniard, mestizo, mulatto, or Maya — sufficient farmland to feed himself and, presumably, the military garrison as well.

Ursúa left Campeche sometime during January 1699, taking with him some fifty people, including various relatives, unidentified volunteers, and twelve Maya laborers from Campeche.[16] Among Ursúa's accompanying relatives was Bernardo de Aizvan y Ursúa, whom he appointed as chief commander of the presidio during his stay there.[17] South of Tzuktok' Ursúa found the Franciscan missions virtually abandoned and made desultory attempts to find some of the runaways in the vicinity of Pak'ek'em. At B'atkab' a messenger brought a letter from the president of Guatemala, dated January 8, with the first details of the supplies and people being sent from Verapaz and the troops coming to Petén Itza from Dolores del Lacandón.[18]

Ursúa finally arrived at the presidio on February 11, 1699, disappointed to find that the Guatemalans had not yet arrived. He found the troops' quarters in a state of disrepair and was himself forced to live in one of the barracks, which was repaired after his arrival.[19] He sent the twelve Mayas he had brought with him to the mainland to cut wood and palm thatch for a new building to house Mencos and the Guatemalan officers and priests. The rest of the Guatemalans, including the families of settlers, were to be housed in the by-now-dilapidated palaces of Ajaw Kan Ek' and AjK'in Kan Ek', which workers also set about repairing. Reconstruction of the crudely built church would have to wait until Guatemalan laborers had arrived.[20]

During the month while Ursúa awaited the arrival of the Guatemalans, numerous Itzas came and went from the island, their intentions not only to assess the new situation but also to sell produce to the troops. He sent two of them to Río Pasión to notify Fray Diego de Rivas and Sergeant Major Estevan de Medrano, who were to follow that route from Dolores del Lacandón, of his arrival. Messengers sent to look for the Verapaz party found them on March 5 at the Savannah of San Pedro Mártir, where they had arrived the previous day.

At this savannah Mencos's officers announced their refusal to go any further, citing the shortage of food. Mencos managed to convince them to continue the march after less than a day's rest by arranging a redistribution of their scarce resources.[21] The troops finally neared the lake on March 14, where they were greeted a league from the southern shore by Ursúa and his officers, who had taken the galeota across the short distance of water. The boat carried the most important of the newcomers to the island, where they were greeted by a spectacular salute of gun and heavy artillery fire.[22] The settlers, who had straggled along behind, arrived two days later.[23] They had suffered almost no mortality—two children at the most (Table 14.1). Medrano de Solórzano and his company finally arrived on April 1 with the Mercederian Fray Diego de Rivas and Rivas's companion, Fray Simón Galindo, after an difficult overland journey from Dolores del Lacandón.

Villagutierre described an amusing series of polite interchanges that supposedly took place between Mencos and Ursúa the day of the former's arrival. According to his description, the two men each insisted that the other should be the general in command, and only after several such back-and-forth exchanges did Ursúa finally resolve the problem by leaving the royal flag and posting the presidio's company in front of the house built for Mencos and then retiring to his own quarters. Even following this action, well-meaning exchanges — spoken and on paper — over who should be in charge continued into the next day. Villagutierre used this example to demonstrate Ursúa's and Mencos's generosity and goodwill; what better men could have been chosen to carry out the delicate ongoing task of conquering the Itzas?[24] Although Mencos's own description of this exchange confirms the tenor of Villagutierre's account, the final resolution, he wrote to the president, was their decision to share power equally until Sánchez de Berrospe gave Mencos specific orders.[25]

REDUCTION, TRADE, THEFT, AND VIOLENCE

Mencos and Ursúa jointly occupied the presidio for less than two months, a period during which promised supplies from Verapaz never arrived. Hunger and sickness forced the troops to seek food from surrounding Itza milpas, which in turn fostered increasing animosity and violence among the local population. The documents of this period portray conditions that, as they worsened, took on nightmarish proportions.

One of the first acts ordered by the generals was the preparation of a large cultivation, later known as the "king's milpa." The felling of the forest, probably with the labor of the Campeche Mayas, began on March 17.[26] Because the field would have had to dry, be burned, and be sowed, no crop would have been harvested for at least another four months. By then most of the troops had returned to Guatemala.

The two generals and the purveyor general of the Guatemalan troops, Alejandro Pacheco, who was stationed at San Pedro Mártir, exchanged a flurry of correspondence concerning why the mule train carrying the food supplies, payments for the Yucatecan troops at the presidio, and metal tools and other barter items for the Itzas had still not arrived from Verapaz by March 18.[27] On March 22 Pacheco reported that many of the Verapaz muleteers had run away and many of the mules had been left to wander with their cargoes. Although he wrote that he would send on to the presidio what he could, no supplies had appeared by the end of the month.[28]

On March 26 Mencos and Ursúa called a planning meeting of their principal military officers, except for Captain Marcos de Abalos y Fuentes, whom they had sent to Laguna Sacpuy four days earlier to search for food and runaway Itzas.[29] The issues were several: where the principal settlement and fortification should be located; how many troops would be needed for defense; how the road from Verapaz should be routed; and how continuing native labor for the king's milpa, which would someday feed both troops and settlers, should be provided in the absence of forty Maya families who had so far failed to arrive from Guatemala.

In their written opinions the officers agreed, surprisingly, that in order to avoid transporting people and materials to the island, the settlement and fortification should be on the mainland, at the location of present-day Santa Elena. This plan would ultimately turn out to be impractical and was never put into effect. The number of permanent troops needed would be eighty, forty of whom would be stationed at the presidio, with the rest employed in subjugating the surrounding population.[30] As for the road, Captain Abalos should be sent to survey a shorter route, along which settlements, bridges, and canoes would be stationed for ease of travel. Finally, the question of labor for the milpa, which still had not been burned (much less sowed), would be solved temporarily by putting to work on it fifty Itzas who had been brought to the presidio.[31]

None of these suggestions, however, could solve the principal problem of immediate food shortages that faced the presidio. By the end of March, half the troops were engaged in searching for produce and runaways in the surrounding areas, while the rest remained at work on the main island, improving the fortifications, the church, and the plaza. The Spaniards were already running out of trade goods, having bartered nearly all of the available machetes and axes, the most popular trade items; little choice was left but to take food by force of arms. Ayudante General Juan Francisco Cortés reported fears of attack, citing an earlier event — probably from before the arrival of Mencos and Ursúa — as evidence that the Itzas intended "to kill all of the Spaniards on this island and in Yalain." One night, when a number of Itzas were visiting the presidio, a baptized Itza woman warned the commander that the visitors meant harm. The commander thereupon ordered that three artillery pieces be fired, and the visitors quickly departed. "Proof" of their ill intentions was found in some cudgels or clubs (*macanas*) that they had dropped as they fled.[32]

During the last days of March, Ursúa and Mencos sent out three separate military parties to the countryside — to the western Itza province, to the Yalain region in the east, and to the Kowoj province in the northeast. The experiences of these three groups are detailed in a series of letters from the field that provide details not only about their efforts to secure food but also about the natives' responses to rapidly increasing threats to their autonomy and subsistence.

FORAY TO THE WESTERN PROVINCE

On March 21 Mencos and Ursúa sent out the first of the three parties, led by Captain Abalos y Fuentes and accompanied by General Mencos's son Juan, the Yucatecan priest Pedro Morales y Vela, and the head of the Guatemalan mission, the Mercederian Fray Gabriel de Artiga. They went west and on the twenty-second visited the island town of Sakpuy in the lake of that name, naming it Santa María de Sakpuy. There they were "well received," despite having told their hosts that they were there because their leader had not yet visited the presidio to offer submission. Their real motive, of course, was to procure maize, which they received in some abundance in exchange for knives, machetes, axes, silver coins, and salt.[33]

Abalos and his group continued to scour the countryside, finding "many and large settlements and milperías." Some of the houses were newly constructed, indicating that these areas had recently been populated by people who had fled their original towns. Appearances of friendly reception at these places turned out, however, to have been prematurely judged. On the night of March 26 the "cacique" of Joyop, on the southeastern shore of Laguna Sacpuy, "ran away . . . with great dissimulation, with all his Indians, his son-in-law Tebalam following him, setting all of the fields, granaries, and houses on fire, retiring to the west of Hoyop, the fire spreading everywhere."[34] Ursúa and Mencos responded by sending Abalos an officer with a reinforcement of twelve soldiers, along with extra powder and ammunition, forty baskets for the maize they had obtained, thirty metates, and thirty "Indians" who were to grind the maize on the spot. The maize that Abalos had already sent was found to be rotted and full of worms; soldiers apparently knew little about shopping for produce.[35]

On April 1 Abalos y Fuentes set out in search of the Joyop incendiaries, with the help of a guide named Kanek' who had been sent from the presidio along with the troops. They found the road toward the southwest blocked by a pile of palm fronds and recently cut green branches but passed beyond these to discover "a great many milpas and granaries that they say belong to a settlement called Chulte." The town itself was abandoned, but their scouts saw several people at a distance; at half a league beyond the town they came across a small lake where they camped that night.[36] The next day a scouting party of four men found a cluster of houses "hidden in the bush." They managed to capture three women and three small children, while the men in the hamlet ran off yelling into the forest.[37]

The women, whom they sent off to the presidio, claimed to be from Nojpeten. One of them, who had scars from old wounds on both arms, resisted and bit her captor. She said that she had received the wounds at the time of the storming of Nojpeten and that she was the aunt of the "Indian youth Canek,'" the guide said by Abalos to be the nephew of Ajaw Kan Ek'.[38] He believed that this was the principal refuge area for those who had fled Nojpeten. According to his captives, even IxChan Pana, the wife of Ajaw Kan Ek', had passed that way.[39]

The three captive women and their children were sent to Joyop, where Spanish soldiers was overseeing the shelling of the maize. All but nine of the thirty Itzas sent from the presidio to assist in this task had run away. The small garrison, who nervously watched smoke signals in the distance, feared attack. They recognized their vulnerability, because all signs — the many milpas, granaries, roads, and hamlets — indicated that they were surrounded by a large population.[40] By April 6 Abalos had given up his attempt to find the incendiaries, although he did meet and converse with four Itza men on his return via Laguna Sacpuy. Three of these claimed to be the husbands of the captured women, but the captain refused to believe them. He left the four men alone but took the three women as prisoners to Ch'ich', where he waited on April 6 for the piragua to take them to the presidio.[41] Women, who could grind corn and provide sexual services, were the only desirable prisoners.

FORAY TO THE YALAIN PROVINCE

While Abalos y Fuentes was scouring the western province in search of maize and arsonists, Captain Cristóbal de Mendía y Sologastoa, with thirty soldiers and three Itza prisoners as guides, was searching for AjChan, Chamach Xulu, and other leaders of the Yalain province to the east of the lake. They had left the presidio on March 27 with orders from Ursúa to resettle those whom they could capture at the now-abandoned town of Yalain. Their axes and machetes already spent, the only gifts the Spaniards could now offer were beads. If they were unable to capture anyone, they were to take whatever maize they could find and send it to the presidio. They were accompanied by Manuel Chayax, AjChan's sister's husband, and were to be assisted by twenty-one Tipujans and two "men," presumably Spaniards, who had apparently sent messages that they would be coming along the road from Tipuj. Manuel Chayax had been held prisoner

367

at the presidio for two years; fearing that he would try to escape, his captors had him bound and leashed with a lasso.[42]

Captain Mendía apparently found no one in the vicinity of Yalain and marched east until he arrived on March 31 at IxTus, a settlement of fifteen houses just to the west of Laguna Yaxhá. Manuel Chayax, who was the son of the principal head of the town, climbed a hill and called for people to come out of hiding. A number of them then appeared, bringing gifts of tortillas and atole. These people said they had been in hiding for eight days as a result of being told by the leader, "Panub" (Pana?), that their women, like several who had been captured by "the two young men from Campeche" would be taken off to the presidio where "they would serve" the Spaniards. This man had been particularly angry, because one of the captured women was his wife. Clearly, several parties of Spaniards had been scouring the countryside for female captives; this could not have been the group captured by Abalos's men; they were taken prisoner on April 2.[43]

So frightened were the inhabitants of IxTus that before escaping into the forest they had destroyed their milpas and even broken their pottery vessels so that the Spaniards would have nothing in which to transport maize. Even as the inhabitants began to return, conditions at IxTus appeared like those of a refugee camp, with as many as twenty-five children and adults living in one house. IxTus was clearly a place of last refuge from the Spaniards for the people of the Yalain area, and food supplies were so scarce that the troops were unable to find enough to eat. One of the women there was the wife of Juan Chayax, perhaps the brother of Manuel Chayax; she was put to work making tortillas. Manuel Chayax's father, the leader of IxTus, was reported to be deeply upset by seeing his son "tied up with a lasso."[44]

At IxTus the Spaniards also learned that the inhabitants of Chinoja (also called Nojchija), located five leagues to the east, probably on Laguna Sacnab, had also abandoned their town and that their leader was probably AjChan. AjChan's brother Pedro Miguel (Nikte) appeared at the Spanish camp with his wife and family, claiming, inexplicably, that he would help the Spaniards capture AjChan and take him to Ursúa. Captain Mendía sent six soldiers and two men from IxTus to round up the runaways from Chinoja, including AjChan, and to meet up with the Tipujans who had been sent from the presidio.[45] On April 3 the party from Tipuj found that Chinoja had been deserted and burned four or five days earlier, although some maize remained in the yards. The inhabitants had fled further east and were reported to be still on the move; nothing was known of AjChan's whereabouts.[46]

The troops at IxTus complained of increasing sickness and hunger as more refugees arrived. By April 4 there were about two hundred of them, mostly children and a few old people. Although they protested the captain's suggestion that they relocate at Yalain, he was heartened by signs that "the Indians . . . desire the faith." He wrote: "The day we set up a tall cross was the first [sign]. The Indian don Manuel soon ordered an Indian to carve two crosses in his arms, with no little pain and blood. And whenever the rosary is said they very quickly kneel down." Although a prisoner, don Manuel still had sufficient influence among his people to convince this man to inflict customary self-mutilation, now expressed in an innovative fashion, to convince the Spaniards of his Christian sympathies. Mendía y Sologastoa wrote that he regretted that he had no priest with him who could take advantage of these presumed signs of faith.[47]

Ursúa and Mencos responded on April 8 to the captain's dismal reports by sending reinforcements and a small amount of beans; his sick men were to return with the local natives who carried the beans. They instructed Mendía to punish the Itza men, by unspecified means — their crime having been to run away after previously offering submission. The women and children were to be held under close custody, and every effort should be made to capture AjChan, Chamach Xulu, and, additionally, AjK'ixaw — an odd object for this chase, because AjK'ixaw had not previously been associated with these leaders. In what seems to have been an irrational strategy under the circumstances, the generals also ordered Mendía to "set fire to all the maize found in granaries and milpas," because the milpas were the source of sustenance for those who sought refuge in the forest.[48]

Aided by men from IxTus, Mendía's soldiers captured Chamach Xulu, "with much peace," somewhere in the vicinity of Chinoja; he was taken to see the captain at IxTus. Chamach Xulu's wife was later sent to join him from Chinoja. On April 12 Mendía went to visit Chinoja himself but discovered that the Tipujan party had given up its search for AjChan and returned home; he had no more leads to follow.[49] He expected another of AjChan's brothers, the unbaptized Tz'ib'it Chan, soon to join his wife at Chinoja. The inhabitants rejected all of the captain's efforts to convince them to move back to Yalain, and he restrained himself from forcing them to do so.[50]

Before leaving IxTus the captain questioned Chamach Xulu and Pedro Miguel (Nikte) Chan as to the cause of their flight and the arson. He was told that "an Indian from the peten named Kali Canek, the brother of the large Indian who is imprisoned on that island, told them that he was running away because the Spaniards had come firing many gunshots and

369

that they had come to kill them. Therefore, they fled and set fire to their houses."[51] I suspect that Kali Kan Ek' and his brother were both Kit Kans, sons of the former ruler. Mendía could not explain this report, because he had come in "total peace" and had punished no one, notwithstanding the generals' orders. As we shall see presently, other groups of Spaniards who had not behaved with such restraint were likely the cause of these fears.

One of the Guatemalan Mercederian friars, Simón de Mendoza y Galindo, ventured out from the presidio with a companion in search of the troops, finally arriving at Chinoja on about April 9 after seven days of walking. They had first passed by IxTus, which he named San José and where he confirmed the population estimate of two hundred souls. He described Chinoja, which he designated Nuestra Señora de los Dolores, as "very pleasant and attractive," its three hundred inhabitants living on a small lake with houses all along the shore and with cultivations, including cacao, nearby. The inhabitants were distressed by threats that they would be moved closer to the main lake but expressed their willingness to submit to Spanish authority. He was particularly struck by a "very well decorated cross" that he saw in the house of one of the "caciques" — a house in which he found both the cacique and some children sick. This was the first report of an illness, apparently spread by the Spanish troops, that would ultimately claim many native lives.[52]

Still unable to locate AjChan, Mendía asked permission to return to the presidio, but Ursúa and Mencos refused his request on April 19, listing the names of various persons who the native messengers from Chinoja reported still remained in the forest with their families.[53] He was to remain until everyone had been accounted for, and when he returned to the presidio he was to bring with him Chamach Xulu, don Pedro Miguel (Nikte) Chan, one Felipe Puk, and all of the other leaders of IxTus and Chinoja.[54] The captain must have disregarded the orders that he remain until everyone was rounded up, for he was back at the presidio by April 29. He did manage to bring Chamach Xulu and fourteen others with him. AjChan was still at large.[55]

FORAY TO THE KOWOJ PROVINCE

The third, last, and quickest of these military entradas departed from the presidio in the galeota on April 2. Captain Marcelo Flores Mogollón was to take forty men to the port of Saklemakal at the east end of the lake and search on land for settlements, people, and cultivations associated with that town.[56] From there they were to carry out their major mission: to discover the whereabouts of one Kulut Kowoj and his followers and, presumably, bring him to the presidio.[57] Kulut Kowoj, also known as Captain Kowoj, was probably the son of the Captain Kowoj whom the Spaniards had executed at the presidio in July 1697 (chapter 13). The Spaniards continued to regard the Kowojs as a particularly dangerous, well-organized group, in contrast to people of the Yalain province, whose Christian sympathies and pacific dispositions they seemed to admire.

The energetic, boastful Captain Flores landed at Saklemakal and immediately began a march extending more than twelve leagues inland. By the next day, April 3, he was back at Saklemakal, which now bore the name Puerto Nuevo de San Antonio del Itzá. At the first of the settlements that he and his men passed during their march they captured Kulut Kowoj's son, merely a boy. Along the road he claimed to have garnered more than ten thousand fanegas of maize and other produce to send to the presidio, with no indication that he paid anything for what was taken. He described the road as a well-traveled trade route that connected the region with far distant places — as far, in fact, as the Ríos Pasión and Usumacinta to the west and Cobán, Sacapulas, and San Agustín in Verapaz to the south. So many natives were there in the region that their numbers alone justified "having captured the peten."[58]

Flores now explored the area around Saklemakal, "enjoying a location on the shores of the lake."[59] He described an extensive region of settlement: "[F]rom the vestiges and ruins of houses it is known that it was a very extensive and large town, as I was made more certain when I landed at this place and marched inland with thirty men; I marched fourteen leagues toward the southeast and in three crossings noticed many milperias and thatch or palm houses."[60] His path then apparently followed a loop, beginning around Saklemakal, curving toward the northwest, and finally returning in a southwesterly direction toward the lakeshore, where he arrived at "Abujon" (probably AjB'ujon, also known as B'oj and Tib'oj).[61] Because this town was probably at Playa Blanca, about fifteen kilometers (just over four leagues) west of Saklemakal, I believe that Flores had rapidly explored the entire northeastern coastal and interior region — the heartland of the Kowoj province. After returning to the presidio he reported that all of the shoreline settlements were abandoned, but he commented on the large number of settlements in the interior that had been hurriedly constructed by those who had fled.[62]

Captain Flores Mogollón and his men concentrated their brief efforts on stealing food, not collecting and resettling people. He failed to capture

Kulut Kowoj or any important person other than Kulut Kowoj's young son. It would be several years before the Spaniards would "pacify" the Kowoj province.

MALNUTRITION, SICKNESS, AND DEATH

Ursúa and Mencos called another general meeting on April 9, including both missionaries and military officers. Although the principal alarm was the growing shortage of food, the generals used the meeting to administer a brief questionnaire designed to solicit information about the region's potential for settlement and agriculture, the past and present savagery of the Itzas, and the number and extent of the surrounding population. The replies were recorded over a period of twelve days as the priests and officers dragged in from their forays into the countryside. They provide, notwithstanding their redundant rhetoric on cannibalism and human sacrifice, valuable information about Itza culture and economy.[63]

Ursúa and Mencos collected this information in full awareness that they would have to evacuate the bulk of the troops quickly in order to avoid mass starvation and mortality. Continued correspondence from the purveyor general at San Pedro Mártir indicated that supplies from Verapaz were nowhere in sight, and conditions at the presidio were already desperate. On April 8 Mencos had written to President Sánchez de Berrospe that the troops at the presidio had subsisted on half rations since their arrival, while those who went out on forays had to subsist on what they could barter or pillage.[64] Finally, on April 23 Mencos and Ursúa called another meeting of all military and religious personnel at which they proposed an evacuation of troops back to Guatemala, leaving only the families of settlers and enough men to maintain a small garrison at the presidio. The retreating army would take with them Ajaw Kan Ek', his son, AjK'in Kan Ek', and the other Kan Ek' prisoner.[65] The officers, secular priests, and Mercederian missionaries all concurred.

According to the Yucatecan priest José Francisco Martínez de Mora, most of the two hundred troops on the island were by now sick and starving. Six men had already died, and he had given last rites to at least six others who were on the verge of death.[66] The surgeon, Teodoro O'Kelly, had earlier reported that eighty-eight men were sick, two had died, and he himself was so ill that he needed to leave in order to seek medical assistance.[67] Captain José Fernández de Estenos also requested permission to go to Guatemala for treatment, complaining that he had been extremely ill for some days. Although O'Kelly, he wrote, "has performed various evacuations on me, I have great gastric putrefaction with extremely life-

372

threatening humors."[68] His symptoms might be interpreted as an extreme form of diarrhea, an ailment from which others were probably also suffering and that ultimately accompanied the deaths of those who were most weakened.

Although Mencos initially opposed the withdrawal, on April 28 he and Ursúa jointly ordered the evacuation of the Guatemalan troops before the increasing rains made their return trip impossible. The four Kan Ek' prisoners would accompany them — the fulfillment of Ursúa's long-standing desire to see these leaders, whom he regarded as the fundamental cause of native rebellion and unrest, bodily removed from the presidio. On the same day Alférez Ramón de Abalos y Fuentes, the brother of Captain Marcos de Abalos y Fuentes, also died.[69] Two days later Juan Francisco Cortés was named chief commander of the presidio, replacing the ailing Fernández de Estenos.[70]

On May 5 the galeota carried Mencos and his troops to the mainland shore, and they began their march that day, leaving Mencos's second-in-command, Sergeant Major Estévan de Medrano y Solórzano, at the presidio to bring up the rear guard within a few days. On the next day Ursúa ordered that the Kan Ek' prisoners be turned over to Medrano y Solórzano.[71] The exchange of prisoners took place on the island at about four o'clock in the afternoon and was recorded in a formal, witnessed "receipt" that described them in unemotional detail as "the persons of the reyezuelo Ah Canek, named don Joseph Pablo Canek, with two pairs of secured shackles; and likewise his son Canek with another two pairs of secured shackles; the false priest and cousin of said reyezuelo named don Francisco Nicolás with a pair of shackles; and another named don Francisco Antonio Canek, also cousin of the said reyezuelo, with another pair of shackles."[72]

Preparations for the withdrawal of the final company of Guatemalans, who waited on the lakeshore with Captain Abalos y Fuentes, stretched on for several days. Food became so short that Captain Cortés had to plead on May 9 that they leave as soon as promised supplies were received at Río de los Dolores, along the road to the Savannah of San Pedro Mártir.[73] At six o'clock on the morning of May 11, Cortés and Medrano y Solorzano boarded the galeota with the four royal family members, who were tied with ropes. They crossed the short distance of water and delivered the prisoners to Captain Abalos y Fuentes. Alférez Manuel de Tapia, who was to serve as their guard, received the eight pairs of shackles, which he was to place on them each night along the long march ahead.

Ursúa left Petén shortly after the Guatemalans' departure; he was back in Campeche by June 20. Governor Roque Soberanis y Centeno had died in office earlier in the year, and Ursúa assumed the governorship upon his return to Yucatán.[74]

The Fate of the Royal Prisoners

Nicolás de Lizarraga, the Guatemalan settler who had been placed in charge of the other families of settlers at the presidio, wrote in about 1708 that the four persons taken as prisoners from the presidio were "King Canek, the two princes, and the Pope [*Papaz*, i.e., AjK'in Kan Ek']."[75] Although Lizarraga considered both "princes" to be the king's sons, from the previously cited list of prisoners and other sources it appears more likely that one of them was the second known cousin of Ajaw Kan Ek', Francisco Antonio Kan Ek'.[76] Lizarraga commented that AjK'in Kan Ek' "burst out in anger upon seeing that they had taken him from the forest. Manuel Tapia, I don't know why, ordered that the prince don Juan be shot with two balls to his body. On this retreat many soldiers died of hunger." The "don Juan" whom Tapia ordered executed was probably Francisco Antonio Kan Ek'; Lizarraga may simply have been mistaken in calling him "Juan." Although Lizarraga did not say that the soldiers killed AjK'in Kan Ek' as well, we learn from other sources that he, too, died before reaching the capital. As we see later, other evidence confirms that of these four, only Ajaw Kan Ek' (Joseph Pablo) and his son (later baptized Francisco IxK'in) survived the journey to Santiago de Guatemala.

Villagutierre either knew nothing of these two deaths or chose to ignore such information. Fortunately, however, he had access to a report that described the reception given to the two survivors, first in Verapaz and shortly afterward in the Guatemalan capital. Undoubtedly elaborating on the information in this report, he wrote,

> When the Guatemalan troops arrived at the settled area of Verapaz, news of the prisoners who had been taken from the island gener-ated great interest as a result of the continuous rumors about what had happened to them over the preceding years and because they all wanted to see the personages created by such scandal and rumor in those forests.
>
> They came out from all of the towns to see them, and many even followed the troops from town to town in order to slow them down and to see, wherever they stopped, the respectful and gentle treat-

ment given to them, which conformed to the orders that the generals had issued, ignoring their natural inconstancy, disposed [as they are] to live in the idolatrous freedom of their forefathers — except that, although barbarians, theirs had been the best blood among them, and they had occupied the highest ranks during their gentility.

Even larger was the concourse that came out to see them in the city of Guatemala, reflecting the large population [of that city], everyone wanting to be first and all succeeding; having entered the city, the prisoners were taken to the houses of the same General don Melchor de Mencos, where they were lodged, dealt with, and attended with every exactness and propriety.[77]

Melchor de Mencos y Medrano recorded in 1701 that many of his soldiers, including his own son, had died in the retreat from Petén Itzá, "and among them two of the four Indians, who were the great priest of the said infidels and the cousin of the said reyezuelo." He said nothing of the circumstances of their deaths. Mencos had arrived on June 4 at Cahabón, where, nearly dead himself from illness and exhaustion, he received last rites. The two surviving royal family members must have been kept with him there until his health improved. Finally he set off with them for Santiago de Guatemala, arriving there on June 28 — forty-nine days after Ajaw Kan Ek' and his son had crossed Lago Petén Itzá for the last time.

Mencos, despite the fact that Ajaw Kan Ek' had already been baptized at the presidio, arranged for both men to be further instructed "in the mysteries of our holy faith." He had Ajaw Kan Ek' rebaptized and his son baptized for the first time in the city's cathedral on October 4, 1700. Doctor Gregorio Carrillo and Licenciado Pedro de Eguaroz Fernández de Ijar, both oidores on the royal audiencia, served as their padrinos.[78] Why the son was allowed to keep his Itza name, IxK'in, rather than receive a Christian name is still unclear.[79]

Captain Marcos de Abalos y Fuentes also confirmed that two of the four people named Kan Ek' placed under his charge on the trip from Lago Petén Itzá died before reaching Santiago de Guatemala, but that Ajaw Kan Ek' and his son survived the trip and lived for some time in his own house. There he observed that although Ajaw Kan Ek' spoke Spanish well, he had little knowledge of Christian doctrine. If a person of such importance had been so poorly instructed, he concluded, the rest of those baptized in Petén must have understood almost nothing about the meaning of the faith.[80]

Joseph Pablo Kan Ek' and his son, Francisco IxK'in Kan Ek', were shortly transferred to a boarding house in the capital operated by Antonio de Andino y Arze. In late 1704 or early 1705 Andino claimed that he had been providing them meals, room, and instruction in religion and reading and writing for the past six years, at his own expense until the past five months, when the audiencia began to cover his costs. One day Andino was called upon by a constable who took him before the audiencia, apparently in response to complaints of mistreatment expressed by Joseph Pablo. Andino recounted the precipitating event, in which Joseph Pablo had insisted that he be joined at mealtime by another resident of the house who he said was his first cousin (*primo hermano*); nothing more is known of this person's identity. He usually stayed at the royal hospital and was apparently living at Andino's boarding house temporarily. When Andino refused the request, Joseph Pablo (who, he confirmed, spoke Spanish fluently) abused him verbally, and an angry exchange followed that led to Andino's brief apprehension.[81]

Andino, who said that a total of six Itzas lived in his house, complained that neither Joseph Pablo nor Francisco IxK'in, both of whom he addressed as "don," took his Christianity seriously, having forgotten most of what he had known and refusing to pray even once a month — and then only with angry reluctance. The two had behaved well, he said, for six years and had only recently begun to abuse him verbally. Now Joseph Pablo insisted that they be allowed to make a trip outside the city, for a destination that Andino did not specify. Andino suggested that their behavior could be improved by sending father and son to the Colegio de Cristo Crucificado for several days of what would have amounted to "sensitivity training."[82]

Andino's guests enjoyed considerable freedom to come and go, and Joseph Pablo Kan Ek' and Francisco IxK'in Kan Ek' must have been familiar faces on the streets of Santiago de Guatemala. In 1702 Fray Diego de Rivas, at his quarters in the Mercederian convent, interviewed the two of them and "other boys," who may have been the four other Itzas staying at Andino's boarding house.[83] The circumstances of the subsequent removal of other Itzas to the capital are poorly known. All that can be added is that in 1717 two secular priests testified in Mérida that by then the native population in Petén had suffered a major decline owing to more than one smallpox epidemic (see chapter 15) and to the removal of "many other natives" to Guatemala and "other areas" by the officers who had been governing the presidio.[84]

This is all that is presently known of Ajaw Kan Ek', his son, and the other Itzas who were removed to Santiago de Guatemala. Future documentary research will likely produce additional information about them.

The Epidemic of 1699

As we have seen, illness, combined with malnutrition, had already taken a considerable toll on the Spaniards by the time of the May 1699 retreat of the Guatemalan forces. More troops died on the return march, and over the next several months an epidemic — though we do not know precisely what disease it involved — took an even greater toll at the presidio itself. Evidence indicates that it also had a devastating effect on the indigenous population in the surrounding areas.

According to two *memorias* dated September 6, 1699, of the sixty-seven soldiers who had been formally enlisted to continue serving the presidio on May 10, six had died between the end of May and September 5. Five of these were Guatemalans; the other was a Campechano. Between April 5 and May 11, the day on which the last company of Guatemalans departed, ten other Guatemalan soldiers had died. Twenty-seven Guatemalan soldiers remained behind, too ill to make the trip. Of these, ten had died, the last on August 11.[85]

Because the total number of Guatemalan troops who had initially arrived at the presidio is unknown, the significance of these figures cannot be calculated. But because all sources agree that many more men died on the return trip to Verapaz, we can assume that loss of life among the Guatemalans was high. In contrast, the Yucatecans apparently suffered very few deaths.

The Guatemalan settler Nicolás de Lizarraga later wrote that while Mencos's troops had waited for two months for supplies in Cahabón prior to advancing to Petén Itza in March 1699, "most of his men" had died of hunger and sickness. On the march itself, Lizarraga claimed, 214 soldiers and 319 "Christian Indian tributaries" died before reaching Lago Petén Itzá.[86] Although these figures appear to be exaggerated, they indicate that the Guatemalans brought the epidemic with them from Cahabón.

As for the settlers themselves, on May 4, the day before Mencos's departure, Captain Diego Bernardo del Río, the official notary, carried out a full census of the families of nonindigenous Guatemalans who were then residing at the presidio. It revealed that one married woman among the original group had died only a few days earlier (on April 30) and that at some point two children had also died (see Table 14.1). Fortunately for historians, yet a third census was made on September 6, allowing a full analysis of the mortality that had occurred between February and September. Because a full list of those who had died was included in the third census, the accuracy of the figures is extremely high.

Between February and May 4, two of the twenty-five children counted in Cahabón had died; two others had married each other, changing their status to that of "adult." Until April 29, all of the adults were still alive. Between April 29 and September 6, twenty of the forty-nine persons who had survived the trip had died, including four adult males, seven adult females, and nine more children. In other words, of the original twenty-five children listed at Cahabón, nearly half had died. The frequency of deaths at the presidio increased during the second half of July and tapered off during August. Not included in these figures is the death on June 21 of a Cahabón Maya settler named Joseph, married to Juana K'ek. Because the number of native settlers is not known, his death cannot be included in the calculation of total mortality.

The settler families had probably camped apart from the troops at Cahabón and had made the trip to the presidio behind the main body of soldiers. The epidemic apparently struck the troops first, with the first wave of deaths beginning at Cahabón in March and continuing unabated through the march back to Verapaz in May. Although the settlers may also have contracted the disease at Cahabón, they suffered the highest mortality during the months following their arrival at the presidio. Surely, more died after the September 6 census. Four years later, of only four remaining families of Guatemalan settlers at the presidio, three were headed by remarried men whose spouses had died during the epidemic. An unrecorded number had been allowed to return to Guatemala.[87]

Mortality was high among the Mayas at this time, too. Fray Simón de Mendoza y Galindo, as noted earlier, had reported finding a cross in the house of one of the "caciques" of Chinoja as early as April 10, 1699. The cacique was ill, as were small children in his house; the cross, by implication, had been set up to ward off further infection or death.[88] The illness had probably been introduced by troops who had arrived at IxTus, six leagues to the west, on March 31; from IxTus the disease would have been carried by local inhabitants to Chinoja. Although this is the earliest indication of the epidemic in an indigenous local community, it probably had also been carried to the western Itza province, where troops had already been in close contact with local residents. Local intersettlement movement of infected individuals would have spread the disease quickly throughout the entire region. Although burning and abandoning their houses may have been primarily an Itza response to Spanish incursions, the possibility that they were also attempting to destroy infected places cannot be discounted.

On September 6, 1699, twenty-seven baptized Itza female workers and children (their own and others) were living at the presidio, some of them captives from the western Itza province. In addition, there were male Maya cooks and four male Maya "forced" laborers from Campeche. Unfortunately for us, Captain Cortés, commander of the presidio at this time, did not record how many such inhabitants of the presidio died during the epidemic.[89]

That Itzas were affected by the epidemic, however, is confirmed by additional information provided by Cortés. On July 5 thirty-nine Itza men were brought from an unspecified location to the presidio as laborers; they had presumably been captured. Six of them died while there, and fourteen became too ill to work. Those who remained healthy accompanied the troops on several maize-pilfering trips to the mainland to the north and east; they also went three leagues inland from Ch'ich' to cut palm for the presidio jail. On August 18 the twenty healthy Itzas, and presumably the sick ones as well, escaped their captors.

On August 22, 1700, Fray Diego de Rivas, who was still at the presidio, responded to a letter from President Sánchez de Berrospe that complained of Ursúa's lack of sympathy for the widespread deaths that had occurred in Petén. Ursúa, Rivas wrote, "does not see the justification with which the Christian piety of Your Lordship weeps lamentations over the deaths that have occurred along these roads, nor that Your Lordship, in whom resides the obligation to look after the Indians, must lament with greater compassion."[90] Not only had the epidemic spread "along these roads," a metaphor for the wider region, but it also continued to devastate the population of the presidio. Rivas was "disquieted and afflicted," he wrote, by the "continued deaths of this peten" and thanked God for having remained healthy so that he could attend to the sick and dying.[91]

The epidemic also affected the two Chol reduction towns far to the southwest, Dolores del Lacandón (or Sakb'ajlan) and San Ramón Nonato. There the population had risen from 700 when counted by Rivas in October 1696 to about 800 in early 1698.[92] By 1701 the number had dropped to 460, the rest, according to Fray Antonio Margil de Jesús, having died. Although Margil attributed only some of these deaths to the 1699–1700 epidemic,[93] the period over which this 42.5-percent population decline occurred fell squarely within its worst phase. The loss of population is close to that experienced by the Guatemalan settlers during mid-1699, about 40 percent.

Far to the northeast of Lago Petén Itzá, the epidemic also made itself felt at the Franciscan mission of Santa Rosa de la Pimienta, located at the town of Chanchanja. In June 1700 Franciscan officials complained to the Crown that the inhabitants of Chanchanja were running away both because they were compelled to provide beeswax for illegal repartimientos and because they were experiencing the effects of the epidemic ("la peste").[94] Chanchanja, unlike Dolores and San Ramón, was not under military control, so they could choose flight as one means of escaping both forced labor and disease. It was a poor strategy for avoiding contagion, however, for its effect was to spread the disease beyond its place of origin. The appearance of the epidemic at Chanchanja by mid-1700 suggests that this was precisely how it arrived there — that is, carried by people fleeing ever farther from the regions north and east of Lago Petén Itzá.

This was not, it will be recalled, the first epidemic to strike the native populations of Petén. Itzas visiting the presidio as early as June 1697 — only three months after the capture of Nojpeten — asked the military officers, in the absence of a priest, to baptize their severely ill and dying children, wives, and husbands.[95] Although the nature and degree of impact of this earlier epidemic are not known, it probably resulted in considerable mortality. We might guess that by 1701 the Itza population had been reduced to less than half its preconquest size.

Other than the brief symptoms noted by Fernández de Estenos ("great gastric putrefaction with extremely life-threatening humors"), the only description of the illness was produced by Nicolás de Lizarraga, who sickened during a return trip from Cahabón, where he had gone in May 1699 to obtain supplies for the starving presidio population.[96] He had left Cahabón on August 7 with seventy-five carriers from that town and twenty-five from San Agustín. A number of the carriers sickened, and the rest ran away, leaving the cargo in the forest; Lizarraga was left alone with only one companion, a boy named Gaspar Cho from Cahabón.

He and the boy carried what they could to an unidentified rancho, where, he wrote, they both became ill. His own symptoms were those of a severe upper respiratory ailment, in which "I came down with a facial affluxion which affected my nostrils so much that from my eyes to my mouth it became a rotten sore, as is widely known."[97] He was still suffering when he arrived at the presidio on August 26, where he discovered that his wife and his daughter's husband had both died in the epidemic. On September 7, when he wrote to President Sánchez de Berrospe of these circumstances, his two small sons were "very ill," and his own illness had become so serious that he considered requesting permission to go to the capital for medical treatment.

These descriptions of the illness or illnesses that so severely affected the populations in Petén are inadequate to identify the disease. It might have been a form of influenza, in which case the most susceptible individuals — children, those most weakened by fatigue and hunger, and those with no previous exposure to the virus — would also have been the most vulnerable to secondary infections that resulted in pneumonia and, for some, death. Those who survived underwent lengthy periods of convalescent rest. Such a scenario would account for the high mortality among the exhausted and underfed Guatemalan troops, the settler women and children, and the indigenous population as a whole. The Yucatecan troops and officers, the Guatemalan officers, and the missionaries, on the other hand, weathered the epidemic quite successfully. The Yucatecan troops were in reasonably good physical condition when first exposed to the disease, and the Guatemalan officers and missionaries were presumably better fed than the infantrymen.

Internecine Warfare

During the three years following the May 1699 departure of the bulk of the Guatemalan troops, the Itzas in the surrounding regions suffered not only severe mortality from a relentless epidemic but also a high degree of internal violent strife. Open warfare among various groups killed more people, further displaced communities and individuals, and broke down already weakened political alliances. Although the full complexity of this intergroup violence eludes us, new and old factions among those who sought accommodation with the conquerors and those who pursued anti-Spanish strategies appear to have been the important factors.

The Spaniards remaining at the presidio on Nojpeten, who by June 1699 had given up their efforts to "reduce" and relocate the indigenous population, first learned of this intergroup strife during their continuing trips into the countryside to barter or pillage for food. The presidio commander, Captain Juan Francisco Cortés, wrote in early September that since the departure of the Guatemalans in May he had already sent out several groups of troops and laborers — most of whom were local captives — five times to Chacha in the western Itza province, once to Tzunpana, probably north of Yalain, and once to the Kowoj province. The

381

results of these missions were poor, with only eighty-one fanegas of maize obtained by barter around Chacha and none at all in the other areas. The populace, except for those who were willing to trade for the few goods the Spaniards had to offer, was now planting most of its milpas well beyond the reach of scavengers.[98]

The trip to Kowoj territory resulted from a lead offered by a captive from the area, who said that he could take them overland to milpas that were about four leagues inland from Saklemakal.[99] When they reached the area, however, this guide signaled to a party in hiding, which ambushed them with volleys of arrows from both sides of the path. Two Spaniards and a Maya from Cobán were wounded; the guide escaped. Hand-to-hand combat followed, but the attackers shortly fled, leaving behind arrows with points made of iron, stone, and fire-hardened wood.[100] Intelligence resulting from this encounter enabled Cortés to draw this portrait of a united, fiercely anti-Spanish Kowoj province: "This nation of the Couohs is allied with the Ketzes, Poopes,[101] and Saclemacales, and subjugating them would mean the reduction of the entire wilderness, as these are the most powerful [people] in any part of it. They are so rebellious that they have never let themselves be seen, apart from peace messengers whom they have sent."[102]

The Kowojs, however, were no more united and warlike than were the followers of the war captain B'atab' Tut of the northern province. Some of them made an armed visit to Chacha on September 6, 1699, for the reported purpose of removing the town's inhabitants to their own territory. When some resisted, fighting broke out, leaving one inhabitant dead and another wounded.[103] Over the next three years B'atab' Tut gained a reputation as a vicious fighter who roamed far and wide attacking Itza towns. One of his principal allies was his famous brother AjK'ixaw, the leader who was captured by Juan Díaz de Velasco in 1695, released in 1696, and blamed for the subsequent murders of his Guatemalan kidnappers. B'atab' Tut sometimes made his headquarters at Kontal, which was probably located on Laguna Oquevix, south of Lago Petén Itzá.[104]

The followers of the native war captains apparently concentrated their attacks on groups that demonstrated friendliness toward the Spaniards. Chacha, for example, not only sold food to the presidio but also, from its location near Laguna Sacpuy, maintained close social relationships with the troops. Several Chacha women actually married soldiers at the presidio, and some of their relatives and acquaintances ultimately went to live there.[105] By 1702 B'atab' Tut had extended his range of attack all the way to Mumunti, a Mompana town northeast of the eastern end of Lago Petén

Itzá — evidently because Mumunti had several months earlier established friendly relations with the Spaniards.[106]

Fray Diego de Rivas confirmed in August 1700 that some Itza groups remained cooperative with the Spaniards and were even willing to help convince others in his Christianization efforts. His efforts were hampered, however, by "the other opposed Indians, because this wilderness is divided. Some want [Christianity], and others do not. These go about making war [against] them, because they have the Spaniards' friendship. . . . Those who are [our] friends have recently been attacked by enemies, and some have been killed. It appears that this type of opposition among them will facilitate the subjugation of all."[107] That is, left to their own devices, the indigenous people, already devastated by the epidemic, would eventually reach exhaustion and give themselves up willingly.

This model of Itza warfare — anti-Spanish groups pitted against friendly, peaceful ones — may account for much of the violence, but it is probably both too simple and too Eurocentric in its perspective. By all accounts, intergroup violence was widespread and devastating, and some Spanish observers believed that it involved questions of regional political control and succession. The secular priest Bachiller Francisco de San Miguel described the warfare as that of king against king.[108] Nicolás de Lizarraga assembled a long list of Itza towns and groups of allied communities, describing each of them briefly in terms of their warlike or peaceful disposition.[109] His underlying purpose in doing so seems to have been to assess who were friends and who were enemies of the Spaniards. Yet the large number he described by phrases such as "risen up in revolt" (*alzado*), "rebel people" (*gente rebelde*), "warriors" (*guerreros*), "bold and bloodthirsty" (*osado y carnicero*), "restless" (*andariego*), and "feared by all" (*todos los temen*) indicates a region at war not so much with Spaniards as with itself. Of the forty-four lake-area groups on Lizarraga's list, twenty-nine bear such descriptions, whereas only six are typed as friendly; the remaining nine are either unclassified or accorded an intermediate status.

In several cases Lizarraga indicated that groups were at war internally or with others, and he specified others that had established or were seeking wider intergroup alliances.[110] Of the five such groups that he listed, the most important had its headquarters at a placed called Chun Ajaw ("Seat of the King").[111] This place had "the major portion of forest people, as it **383** was there that the king and pope and their priests were crowned." It had never been seen by Spaniards.

Another name for this place may have been Chun Mejen ("Seat of the Son of the Father"), and it was here the new Ajaw resided.[112] Although he was said to be the "brother" of Ajaw Kan Ek',[113] there is no other record that the ruler had a brother. Therefore, the new Ajaw may have been the exiled ruler's father's brother's son, in which case he was probably one of the three brothers, each an Ajaw B'atab', who bore the titles Kit Kan and Tz'o Kan. These three, I proposed in chapter 3, were the sons of the previous ruler, who was possibly the uncle (father's brother) of Ajaw Kan Ek'. Reference to a "pope" surely meant a new co-ruling high priest, whose identity is not known.

Several years later (about 1710) Lizarraga wrote that "this Chumexen was the first who was crowned king after the imprisonment of Canek, and he created in his territory a new Jerusalem with his pope, although the rest were opposed to the crown, making war against him, and each one was being crowned in his own province. But he always continued his Jerusalem and pope where they all go to consult their priests as they did before during the time of King Canek."[114] This new ruler's two principal caciques, he wrote, were Joyop and Sakpuy, which he noted had already been discovered. Apparently he meant that these were the towns where the principal caciques had their headquarters. Sakpuy was surely located on Laguna Sacpuy, and Joyop, as suggested earlier, was on the southeastern shore of the same lake. The new Ajaw's headquarters may have been north of Laguna Sacpuy, perhaps at B'alamtun.[115]

The four other newly created or recreated provinces that Lizarraga mentioned in this later document, which is the legend for a now-lost map that he had prepared, were "El Tute," "El Chan," "El Mompaná," and "El Cobox," that is, Tut, Chan, Mompana, and Kowoj. The Tut province was marked with a black line "and borders upon the south and west with the provinces of Verapaz and Huehuetenango, letters D. C., and it includes a large portion of the Lacandons from the hills to Huehuetenango. The leaders and caciques that have been discovered are Chachulte, Chans, Buenavista, Chatoco, and Yxmucuy." Except for "Chans," these were all names of towns, not leaders, as in the previous case. The region controlled by AjTut could not have been this extensive, but it is likely that it did include the area between the main lake and Río Pasión.

Lizarraga's Chan province, demarcated by the eastern border of his map and by a green line, "borders upon the entire Gulf coast, letter B, and with the mountains of Verapaz, and he who is crowned as king is don Martin Chan, nephew of the king Canec, who had been a Catholic from Tipu (and he who deceived don Martin de Ursua as ambassador of the said King Canec), who apostated and was crowned as a very powerful king. He includes in his territory the Mopans and Chols of the Gulf Coast, and he has as leaders and caciques Muquixill, Paliac, Oaxal, Chacha, Quejaches, Yalayn, Sinoxá, and Ystús [Muk'ixil, Paliak, Waxal, Chacha, K'ejaches, Yalain, Sinoja, and IxTus]."[116] AjChan had become the ruler of what is today southern Belize; Paliak is known to have been a Chol-speaking town in that region, probably on Río Grande. Ich Tutz, possibly another rendering of IxTus, was the name of a seventeenth-century village that Thompson believed to be on the Sittee River, then called Xoyte. "Oaxal" or Waxal is possibly a mistranscription of Yaxal, which was the name of the Moho River.[117]

Mompana, marked by a purple line, bordered on the north with the province of Campeche (i.e., Yucatán). Its principal towns were Mumunti, Balamtun, and Chanchanja, and the people were known collectively as "Monpanaes." I suspect that the name Mompana or Monpana was from Moan Pana, presumably the principal leader or ruler of the region.

Despite Lizarraga's tendency to exaggerate, it is difficult to disregard such specific references to the formation of new and redefined independent political territories, to the appearance of new rulers, and to inter-group warfare over issues that must have included political succession and territorial control. His accounts are particularly plausible when viewed in light of evidence, discussed in earlier chapters, of a war between Ajaw Kan Ek' and Ajaw B'atab' K'in Kante in 1695 and 1696. Indeed, these later wars were likely an extension and regionwide expansion of that conflict, during which the ruler's uncle apparently enlisted AjKowoj to set fire to Nojpeten and to terrorize the Yalain province.

Some towns constructed large fortifications that, under the circumstances, were as likely to have been defenses against attacks by other indigenous groups as defenses against Spaniards. In 1698 Spaniards discovered in the hills above the northeastern shore of Lago Petén Itzá a fort, presumably made of wood, that was said to be capable of withstanding even artillery fire.[118] Another was described by the Yucatecan captain Pedro de Navarrete, who saw and occupied it in April 1702 while he was opening a new road from Chanchanja to Lago Petén Itzá. According to him, it was a "very strong fortification of slender stakes in the form of an O, with very astutely constructed entrances and exits."[119] Navarrete found that all roads from the town toward the lake had been closed or camouflaged for a distance of two leagues. Navarrete told Juan Francisco Cortés that the stockade was large enough to hold five hundred men.[120]

The stockaded town, which belonged to the Kowojs, was located about three leagues from the port of Saklemakal, probably in a northeasterly direction. Navarrete, who had twenty-two soldiers with him, claimed that

385

after running away the inhabitants returned voluntarily, bringing gifts of food and promising to obey whatever they were ordered to do. He took at least two leaders back to the presidio to offer their formal submission.

If Navarrete is to be believed, not a shot was fired when the troops occupied the town — the result of strict orders from Ursúa. The inhabitants had run away as the Spaniards approached, making no use of the circular stockade.[121] To all appearances, the stockade was a defense against native attack, not against the firepower of the Spaniards. Although Cortés and Navarrete seemed to think that the roads toward the lake had been closed because of the Kowojs' fears of Spanish attack, they probably had more to fear from the followers of B'atab' Tut, who would also have approached them from the south, passing by the eastern end of the lake.

Although the stockaded town was reputed to be in one of the most rebellious areas of the wilderness surrounding the Spaniards, it had fallen without a whimper.[122] The presidio commander, Cortés, feared that groups were plotting a nighttime attack on the island, but there is little evidence that the surrounding population contemplated any large-scale action against the Spaniards.[123] At this time they simply were too weakened, divided, and exhausted from disease and internecine warfare to mount an attack on the heavily armed island presidio.

In 1704, however, continuing rumors of pending attack on the presidio very nearly materialized in an abortive rebellion by missionized Itzas and Kowojs. As we will see, this final expression of hostility against the Spanish occupiers was too late and too little. It resulted in little more than stepped-up security measures that further separated the handful of Spanish troops at the former Itza capital from the remote hinterlands where so many of the "conquered" towns continued to seek refuge.

Τhe establishment of mission towns around Lago Petén Itza by the secular clergy of Yucatán had been long delayed as the presidio, soon known by the shortened name of Los Remedios, struggled to survive. At last, in the early years of the eighteenth century, the missionaries, aided by troops stationed at the presidio, began to make intermittent headway. According to Spanish reports, many Itzas and Kowojs, already devastated by epidemics and internal warfare, at first offered little resistance to being relocated. In 1704, however, scarcely two years after the founding of the first mission, an anti-Spanish rebellion broke out, in which several soldiers died. The immediate cause of this uprising was fear that a census of the towns heralded the imposition of tribute payments; evidence suggests that this was a justifiable worry and that it was Ursúa, now governor in Mérida once again, who hoped to benefit from the tribute income. Threatening the very existence of the small garrison on Nojpeten, this rebellion, had it succeeded, would have resulted in the native recapture of the Itza capital. Its failure left the Spaniards at the center of a region over which they still had little control.

The 1704 rebellion ended in the abandonment of most of the original mission towns, but renewed military activities rounded up many among the refugees, as well as new souls who were herded into both old and new mission towns. During the years that followed, the presidio commander forced captured runaways, both men and women, as well as men judged guilty of participating in the rebellion, to work as virtual slaves at Los Remedios. The population of the mission towns quickly increased, only to be cut in half later in the first decade of the century, primarily by a devastating smallpox epidemic.

The closing years of the conquest were less a time of celebration in colonial circles than a period of discouragement, dismay, and disagreement over how to govern what little had been gained.[1] In the final pages of this chapter we meet yet again a man who appears to have been AjChan, who, following repeated capture by and escape from the Spaniards, served in his old age as cacique of San Luis, formerly Mopan. He had most recently been "king" of independent Mayas in southern Belize, but he was, apparently, captured one last time and forced to live up to the commitments he had made as a young man in Mérida at Christmastime 1695.

The First Missions, 1702–3

By mid-1701 the only missionary left at the presidio was the Yucatecan secular priest Pedro de Morales. The Guatemalan friars had left not long after the Guatemalan troops in 1699, and Fray Diego de Rivas had returned to Santiago de Guatemala in early 1701.[2] Morales became ill and left for Campeche along the camino real in mid-1701; he died along the road at Nojb'ekan on June 23, many leagues from his destination.[3] A new head of the Itza missions, Bachiller Francisco de San Miguel, finally arrived at the presidio on February 11, 1702. His partner, Bachiller Marcos de Vargas Dorantes, joined him later that month to minister to the needs of the presidio.[4] The intrepid Rivas returned in late 1702 or early 1703.[5] Although Rivas's health was failing and he apparently accomplished little over the next year or so, San Miguel was a man of great energy who claimed much of the responsibility for establishing the first successful Itza missions during 1702 and early 1703.

The missionary successes of this period, however, would have been impossible without an even more energetic Yucatecan, Captain José de Aguilar y Galeano. In early 1702 Governor Ursúa appointed him to carry out a dual mission: first, to travel to Chanchanja, then to Tipuj, and from there to the central coastal area of Belize, where he was to round up native apostates. Once he had accomplished this, he was to return to Chanchanja and set out for Petén in order find and capture AjChan, who had run away from the Spaniards in 1698 and been in hiding ever since. By means unknown, Aguilar handily accomplished the first of these tasks by April 25, capturing thirty-eight apostates in Belize and delivering them to the Franciscan friar at Chanchanja. He then went to Los Remedios, arriving on May 20 with twenty-one troops and more than twenty Maya "warriors" from Chanchanja. He had just captured not only AjChan but also his wife and children.[6] AjChan told Aguilar that he had run away from the Spaniards for the second time because he had heard rumors that Ursúa planned to execute him.[7] Since his escape from the presidio he had become the leader of the sizable Yalain province, which since 1699 had been nearly spared from Spanish aggression.

Ursúa agreed with Aguilar's suggestion that AjChan be pardoned for his errors and that, given the long history of their relationship, this prodigal godson should be sent to Mérida to live with him, lest AjChan inadvertently set off new unrest in the Petén wilderness.[8] By December, unaware that AjChan had attempted to escape yet again, Ursúa had reconsidered the matter, thinking it might be better to send AjChan to live with Melchor de Mencos or in another household in Guatemala.[9]

At this time the governance of the presidio was in disarray. The presidio commander, Juan Francisco de Cortés, had failed to pacify the Itzas and had barely managed to feed and support his troops, receiving virtually no assistance from either the Guatemalan or the Yucatecan government. Ursúa now took matters into his own hands, instructing Cortés on December 15, 1702, to cooperate with Captain Aguilar and Father San Miguel in what was to be a nonviolent reduction of the native population into mission settlements.[10] Aguilar, however, with Ursúa's obvious prior blessing, had already initiated this undertaking, although using armed military, not peaceful, tactics to capture indigenous leaders.

The two surviving accounts of the process by which Aguilar and San Miguel succeeded in establishing the new missions during 1702 and 1703 were written independently by the two secular priests—San Miguel himself and Vargas Dorantes.[11] Their "certifications" differed markedly. San Miguel, the missionary, emphasized the importance of his own role as a gentle and persuasive missionary, giving credit to Aguilar for little more than his assistance in settling people in the mission towns. Vargas, the presidio's parish priest, gave no credit at all to San Miguel's missionary efforts and produced instead a paean to Aguilar's military valor and his successes in capturing native leaders and settling them into the mission towns. The following narrative attempts to make sense of these two contrasting accounts, noting where their differences are especially striking. Because Vargas, in contrast to San Miguel, made no attempt to downplay the military aspects of mission formation, I tend to place somewhat more credence in his version of history when the two writers differ. The locations of these early missions, as well as later ones, are indicated, some precisely and others less so, on map 10.[12] In chronological order of their founding, the new missions were Arcángel San Miguel, Nuestra Señora de la Merced, San José, San Jerónimo, San Martín, San Antonio, San Andrés,

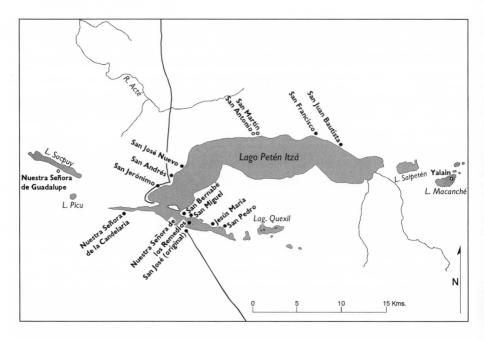

Map 10.   Early eighteenth-century missions in the vicinity of Lago Petén Itzá.

San Francisco, San Juan Baptista, San Pedro, Nuestra Señora de Guadalupe, and Nuestra Señora de la Candelaria.

ESTABLISHING THE MISSIONS

In early May 1702, Francisco de San Miguel, the missionary, proposed to
Captain Cortés that they together establish a mission on the lakeshore
near the presidio where they would attract people running away from
internecine warfare. Three such families arrived at the presidio during
these discussions, their heads named B'ak Tz'ib', Nikte Tz'ib', and Tanche
Pana. San Miguel and Cortés agreed to locate the mission a "musket shot"
north of the main island, where they built four houses for the newcomers
with the help of Spanish and Itza residents of the presidio. They were given
maize, axes, and machetes as inducements to clear and plant a milpa.

390   Forty-one additional families, unidentified by name, were later "acquired," placed in twenty-four additional new houses, and given similar
inducements. San Miguel began giving them religious instruction, oversaw the building of a church, and on Easter Sunday baptized and married
some of the residents. He "founded" the town as Arcángel San Miguel on

May 12, which he said was the customary date of celebration of that saint.[13] San Miguel remains today the name of the shoreline community directly north of Flores.

When Aguilar y Galeano arrived on May 20 he already had AjChan and his family in his possession. They were immediately placed in San Miguel, where AjChan was made "cacique" as a means of attracting others to join him. This was a rational choice, considering his identification with Yalain, the probable origin of the first families to arrive. All but six or seven of the forty-four original families, however, had already run away, and AjChan immediately disappeared with everyone else on May 23. Aguilar chased them all down again and brought them back, including AjChan, presumably leaving them under heavier guard.[14]

Sometime later Aguilar went with his Spanish troops and Chanchanja archers to capture the infamous B'atab' Tut, who was living under constant guard at Kontal, eight leagues away. The crafty war captain evaded capture, but Aguilar imprisoned his wife, children, and brother, who were sent to live at San Miguel.[15] This was an odd choice for their settlement, because B'atab' Tut and AjChan were old enemies. San Miguel, which must still have been heavily guarded, could not have been a happy place.

On June 12 Captain Aguilar left the presidio to find and capture AjK'ixaw, the brother of B'atab' Tut, who was in hiding at Petmas, said to be twenty leagues away. He chased AjK'ixaw and captured him along with one hundred of his followers. According to Father Vargas's account, AjK'ixaw was imprisoned at the presidio, and the rest were forced to settle at a new lakeshore mission called Nuestra Señora de la Merced.[16] Father San Miguel made no mention of this mission, whose location Vargas did not reveal. Its captive inhabitants probably escaped soon thereafter; the mission is never heard of again.

Father San Miguel wrote that the next mission, San José, was founded at the end of July and was populated by twenty-one families brought by Aguilar from Kowoj territory. Vargas's report noted that these people were from a town called Kitis that had recently been viciously attacked by allies of Kulut Kowoj. Aguilar convinced them that they were in danger of being attacked again and should relocate voluntarily.[17]

According to Father San Miguel, these families asked that they be settled on the lakeshore and that their town be named for "their saint" — **391** implying that at some point they had come into possession of an image of San José. The place chosen for them was "about one musket shot" southwest of the main island and "as much more" from San Miguel — probably on the eastern side of the peninsula that protrudes from present-day San

Benito. This is not the location of the later mission known as San José Nuevo, which has been a community along the northern main shore of the lake, east of San Andrés, since at least 1750.[18]

In late September, according to San Miguel, sixteen families from settlements whose principal inhabitants were named Tzin came to the presidio to tell him that they had been attacked by other Itzas and wished to be settled on the lakeshore; they knew of twelve other families who wished to join them. Before the conquest B'atab' Tzin had been the second ruler of the eastern province (see chapter 3), and it appears that his followers had fled west following the capture of Nojpeten. Cortés and San Miguel took them to settle on "a point that protrudes into the lake one league from the island in the area toward the west."[19] This description suggests that the new mission, named San Jerónimo, was located on Punta Nijtún. By about 1734, however, it had been moved to a location a short distance west of another mission, San Andrés.[20] The date of the town's founding was the day of San Jerónimo (Doctor), which is celebrated on September 30.[21]

Other groups from distant settlements continued to visit San Miguel at the presidio, according to his account, and he sent them back with messages promising that all would be well treated and pardoned for their old crimes against the Spaniards. His messages bore the threat, however, that if they did not come voluntarily they would be attacked. The result of his entreaties, he claimed, was the arrival on November 11, the day of San Martín Obispo,[22] of eighteen families from the Kowoj settlements and as many more from the settlements identified with the name K'ixab'on. They were taken to the location they requested, on the northern shore three leagues from the island, and it was named San Martín for the day of their arrival.[23]

The "real" story of the establishment of San Martín, however, may have been quite different. According to Vargas, Captain Aguilar had set out to capture the principal Kowoj leader, Kulut Kowoj. After ten days of searching he caught Kulut Kowoj asleep at midnight, along with two of his brothers and their wives, children, and other relatives—seventy persons in all. He released all of these except Kulut Kowoj and his wives and children, whom he took back to the presidio, where he kept Kulut Kowoj a prisoner. He exhorted the others to settle on the lakeshore (at an unspecified location). Cortés released Kulut Kowoj after four months on the condition that he bring his followers who were still in the forest to settle on the lakeshore. It was this group that settled at San Martín.

After Kulut Kowoj was settled at San Martín, according to Vargas's account, he brought a group of K'ixab'on families to relocate at a spot next to that mission. Once they were settled, Vargas wrote, they "built a church in imitation of the settlers [who were already there] so that in it they could be instructed in the law of God."[24] From events that transpired during the rebellion of February 1704 it is apparent that this mission, immediately adjacent to San Martín, was known as San Antonio. Most later reports failed to mention the new San Antonio as a mission separate from San Martín.

The next mission to be founded was that of San Andrés. San Miguel wrote that on the day of the Apostle San Andrés (November 30),[25] some thirty families from the Chanchanja settlements arrived on the lakeshore at a spot about one league northwest of the main island. They made their settlement there, and this has remained the location of San Andrés ever since. In later years San Andrés was populated primarily by people with Itza and Kowoj names and become the principal mission on the northern shore of the lake.

In January 1703, according to San Miguel, fifteen families from another settlement of Kowojs came out of the forests. They were settled one and a half leagues east of San Martín in a mission called San Francisco, apparently named for Saint Francisco de Sales, whose day of celebration is January 29.[26]

Vargas reported that after Kulut Kowoj was transferred to San Martín he went to the place where one of his relatives was hiding in the forest in order to convince him to relocate with his numerous followers. All of them did so and became the first settlers of San Francisco.[27]

Also during January nine families appeared from a settlement of people named Tz'ib'.[28] They were settled at a place about one league east of San Francisco.[29] The town's avocation, San Juan Baptista, "appeared by chance," not on either of the saint's celebration days.

In late February some Itzas from a settlement of people with the patronym Pana appeared on the lakeshore one league east of the main island, apparently near their original location. San Miguel named it in honor of his personal patron, San Pedro, whose solemnity is celebrated on June 29.[30]

In early March some twenty families from settlements identified with the surname Chab'in were placed on the two islands of Laguna Sacpuy and assigned the name of Nuestra Señora de Guadalupe. The Laguna Sacpuy region was the new headquarters of the successor to the Itza throne, who may have been a Kit Kan (see page 384). This mission, far from the reach of the presidio and in a region particularly hostile to Spanish control, is never mentioned again and may have been soon abandoned.

393

One final mission, Nuestra Señora de la Candelaria, was mentioned by neither San Miguel nor Vargas. Rivas, however, reported that it was in existence, with seventeen houses, by June 1703.[31] Established one league along the shore from San Jerónimo, it was probably situated on the southern shore of the western arm of the main lake, four kilometers west of the tip of Punta Nijtún, near the place today called Candelaria.[32]

EARLY DEMOGRAPHY OF THE MISSIONS

Fray Diego de Rivas had returned to the presidio on May 17, 1703, with instructions from the Guatemalan audiencia to prepare a report on the current condition of the Itza reductions.[33] His June 20 report provided the number of houses in each of nine identified mission towns. Of the original twelve missions, Nuestra Señora de Guadalupe and Nuestra Señora de la Merced had already ceased to exist, and San Martín and San Antonio

TABLE 15.1

Numbers of Mission Families at Founding (Late 1702– Early 1703) and of Mission Houses in June 1703

Mission	Number of Families	Number of Houses
N. S. de la Candelaria	—	17
N. S. de Guadalupe	20	0
N. S. de la Merced[a]	20	0
San Andrés	30	63
San Francisco	15	28
San Jerónimo	16	36
San José	21	24
San Juan Baptista	9	32
San Martín/San Antonio	36	42
San Miguel	44	31
San Pedro	—	8
Total	211	281

SOURCES: For mission families at founding, AGI, EC 339B, no. 15, Certification of Br. Francisco de San Miguel y Figueroa, 1 July 1703, ff. 5r–8r, and no. 28, Certification of Bachiller Marcos de Vargas Dorantes, 10 July 1703, ff. 18r–21r. For houses in June 1703, EC 339B, no. 28, Certification by Fr. Diego de Rivas, 23 Dec. 1703, ff. 34r–35r.

[a]Vargas Dorantes estimated the total population that was moved to Nuestra Señora de la Merced at more than one hundred. The estimate of twenty families is based on a 5:1 ratio of total population to number of families.

TABLE 15.2

Reconstruction of Mission Population Growth, 1702–3

Source and Date	No. Families	No. Houses	Total Population
San Miguel/Vargas (late 1702–early 1703)	*±220*	83	*1,100*
Rivas (June 1703)	*750*	281	*3,750*
Rivas (Dec. 1703)	*800*	300	*4,000*
Varaya (Dec. 1703)	800	*300*	4,000

SOURCES: For late 1702–early 1703, AGI, EC 339B, no. 15, Certification of Br. Francisco de San Miguel y Figueroa, 1 July 1703, ff. 5r–8r, and no. 28, Certification of Bachiller Marcos de Vargas Dorantes, 10 July 1703, ff. 18r–21r. For June 1703, EC 339A, Consulta de Fr. Diego de Rivas y Capitán Alejandro Pacheco, 20 June 1703, ff. 142v–152v. For December 1703, EC 339B, no. 28, Certification by Fr. Diego de Rivas, 23 Dec. 1703, ff. 34r–35r, and no. 26, Gaspar Reymundo de Varaya to governor of Yucatán, 17 June 1704, ff. 7r–10r.

NOTE: The documented total of founding families is shown in Table 15.1 to be at least 211. The larger estimate of ±220 given here incorporates an additional estimated number for the uncounted towns of Nuestra Señora de la Candelaria and San Pedro. Reconstructed data are in italics.

were considered to be a single community. When Rivas's figures are compared with rather different data provided by San Miguel and Vargas, it appears that most of the towns had grown, some considerably, since their foundation (Table 15.1). Rivas observed that a number of settlers had only recently been added and that many of the houses contained three or four "families," including many children.[34]

In late December 1703 Rivas reported that there were ten mission settlements on the lakeshore with a total population of about three hundred "families."[35] He apparently extracted this figure from a complete census ordered that month by the new presidio commander, Captain Aguilar y Galeano, which accounted for at least four thousand persons, including eight hundred "families," who were "already reduced" in *eleven* mission towns.[36] This marked difference in the number of "families" (300 versus 800) suggests that Rivas had inadvertently substituted "families" for houses or households.

Table 15.2 compares and extrapolates from information provided for the missions by Rivas, San Miguel and Vargas, and Gaspar Reymundo **395** Varaya, an officer at the presidio who took a census in December 1703. Calculating from this information, the ratio of total population to number of families appears to have been 5.00 to 1; the ratio of total population to number of houses 13.33 to 1; and the ratio of families to houses 2.67 to 1.

Extending these ratios back to the earlier censuses enables us to estimate the total population of the missions at the time of their founding in late 1702 and early 1703 (approximately 1,100) and in June 1703 (approximately 3,750). During 1703, therefore, the mission population had quadrupled in size.

The large size of individual households (averaging more than thirteen people) confirms Rivas's observation that houses contained multiple, presumably extended, families. Such a high average number of household members is predictable under the existing conditions, in which large numbers of people would have been squeezed into a few newly constructed houses. While large extended-family households were the norm prior to the 1697 conquest, the rapidity with which these missions were constructed suggests that the houses were smaller than earlier ones had been and that the populations suffered from overcrowding.

THE PROCESS OF MISSION FORMATION

Although Father San Miguel emphasized that most of the missions were settled voluntarily, it is clear from Vargas's report that Aguilar and his troops had captured many of the settlers, forcing them into the towns militarily. The captain's use of force seems to have been aimed primarily at those whom he considered the major anti-Spanish leaders still at large: AjChan, AjTut, AjK'ixaw, and Kulut Kowoj. As he scoured the countryside, fear of attack must have led other, smaller groups to decide voluntarily to move to the lakeside and accept Spanish protection before they were attacked themselves.

Although other Itza leaders seem to have been lower on Aguilar's "most wanted" list, he captured at least three of them — Kali Kan Ek', Tz'ib'it Kan Ek', and Tzutz Masa — apparently hoping to discover in their possession the chalice of the Yucatecan friars who were murdered in 1696.[37] He not only captured them and found the chalice but also extracted confessions from them that they had participated in the killings.[38]

Nearly all of the groups that moved to the missions, either voluntarily or involuntarily, comprised "families" from a single hamlet or "ranchería." Each ranchería and its inhabitants, in turn, was usually known by the name of its leader, presumably the head of the dominant lineage. The Spaniards apparently did not place these kinship groups haphazardly in randomly located towns. To the contrary, they often asked the returnees where they wished to settle and allowed them to exercise that choice. With the exception of Arcángel San Miguel and San José, which were situated next to the presidio for obvious security reasons, the missions were probably all located on or near the sites of towns abandoned only three or four years earlier.

Certain of the missions grew rather quickly, probably drawing in former residents of the abandoned towns. Other missions disappeared, their members either joining relatives in nearby larger missions or escaping back to the forests. The process of mission formation entailed, at least for a short time, the reconstitution of previous, abandoned towns through the reassembling of their scattered parts. It must be assumed, however, that this process could not have operated perfectly. Spanish officials undoubtedly forced mission communities to accept undesired or unrelated refugees and may have forced others to join larger towns for purposes of administrative convenience. The decline in the number of mission towns, as we shall see, indicates that freedom of locational choice declined significantly as time progressed.

The Rebellion of 1704

The immediate risk that the Spaniards assumed by initiating the reconstitution of Itza society was that the leaders of towns would seek to repair and restructure intertown political alliances that had been weakened by years of warfare and physical displacement. This risk manifested itself in a short-lived but dramatic rebellion that broke out on February 7, 1704, resulting in the deaths of six Spanish soldiers, the execution of six important indigenous leaders, and the flight of most of the recently settled mission inhabitants back into the forests.[39]

Sometime in January 1704 the presidio commander, Captain Juan Francisco Cortés, resigned his post and left Los Remedios with his two daughters and an escort of six soldiers for a brief stay in Mérida. Following the death of his wife during the 1699 epidemic, he had married the widow of one of the Guatemalan settlers who had also perished.[40]

Fray Diego de Rivas had returned to Los Remedios on May 17, 1703, with instructions from the Audiencia of Guatemala to assess the state of the Itza reductions.[41] He returned to Guatemala the following January with an escort of six more soldiers from the presidio and Nicolás de Lizarraga, the original head of the small band of Guatemalan settlers.[42] By this time only four families of settlers remained at the presidio, three of them headed by remarried men whose first spouses had died during the epidemic. Several others had been allowed to return to Guatemala.[43]

By the end of January 1704 the departure of these two escorts had

397

temporarily reduced the presidio garrison of fifty soldiers by twelve. In addition, four others had gone to Yucatán to bring back a group of Maya laborers who were to carry out repairs on the camino real. A few soldiers, perhaps three or four, were routinely posted to guard the royal milpa and the estancia, which had about two hundred head of cattle and forty horses.[44] At this time, therefore, no more than about thirty soldiers were in residence to guard the presidio itself. In addition, Francisco de San Miguel had also returned to Yucatán, leaving Marcos de Vargas as the only missionary. Although several other Spaniards on the island also owned firearms, the presidio was clearly in a state of defensive vulnerability when Captain Aguilar y Galeano assumed command at the beginning of 1704.

Sometime during January Aguilar decided to bring to the presidio a number of Maya men from each of the missions for a general meeting. At this gathering he announced that work was about to begin on the construction of a new church that would replace the existing small, dilapidated building. Each town was expected to procure timbers and palm thatch, which would be picked up at the beaches in canoes sent from the presidio. In addition, each town in rotation would provide laborers for two or three days at a time to frame, roof, and prepare the lime for plastering the structure.

In his speech to this assembly, apparently delivered in Maya, he emphasized that because there would be many workers, neither their work in providing materials nor their contribution to the construction itself would exhaust them. Although he later claimed that the men had unanimously and with great willingness agreed to these tasks, they clearly had little choice in the matter. He also claimed that he had offered to wait eight days before beginning the work so that they could plant their milpas. The men replied, however, that they would rather complete the work for the church before beginning their planting. Aguilar apparently did not understand that, given the time of year, they had probably not finished cutting the forest for their milpas, much less burned them in preparation for planting. Therefore, they would supply the timbers and palm leaves from the forest that they were already in the process of cutting.

As they departed, Aguilar handed out salt, beads, and other unspecified gifts. The dates of each community's labor shift, as well as the general deadline for supplying the building materials, had been announced. When the villages sent notification at the beginning of February that the materials were ready, he sent every available canoe from the presidio to pick them up. The canoes were few, however, and it soon became apparent that three or four trips would be required.

On February 7, according to Aguilar's accounts, he sent the galeota with ten soldiers and the boat's captain to San Martín, located on the northern shore of the lake, in order to pick up the first scheduled labor crew and to load timbers that had not yet been transported. Maya oarsmen must also have been on board, but their presence or subsequent behavior is not acknowledged in any of the reports. From San Martín the loaded boat went to San Antonio to advise its inhabitants when their labor shift would begin.[45]

In a later report, the officer Gaspar Reymundo Varaya offered a different account of the crew's February 7 itinerary. According to him they went first went to San Juan and San Francisco to pick up the workers, who included Kulut Kowoj and members of his family. The soldiers asked the galeota's captain to stop at San Martín in order to purchase some food items, which he did.[46] This was in fact the case; Aguilar himself complained in describing the events of this day that when his soldiers visited the towns they habitually asked for such items as plantains, camotes, and "other delicacies" (*otras golosinas*).[47]

If Varaya's is the correct account, Kulut Kowoj had moved or been moved from San Martín, where Aguilar had first sent him after his release from imprisonment in 1702. San Juan and San Francisco were located along the shore east of San Martín, indicating that the galeota first beached or anchored at the farthest mission, San Juan, before turning around and stopping again at San Francisco. The troops apparently picked up the intended Kowoj workers from both towns.

In either event, the descriptions of what followed are in essential agreement. When the galeota reached the twin community of San Martín-San Antonio, the inhabitants called to the crew, offering them fresh produce. Five of the soldiers accepted the invitation and were escorted by townspeople to five different houses, where, apparently, they had been told that they could pick up their foodstuffs. The soldiers' foolishness in allowing themselves to be separated, Aguilar noted, amounted to "allowing themselves to be deceived like children" and was in disobeyance of all prior orders.[48]

The five other soldiers and the captain stayed on board with Kulut Kowoj, the other workers, and, presumably, the oarsmen, waiting for them to return. Other townspeople attempted to lure these Spaniards to a nearby house, offering them food as well, but they wisely rejected the offers and remained on board. From this vantage point they saw twenty or so townsmen simultaneously enter each of the houses to which the five trusting soldiers had been taken. Quickly disarmed and overpowered, the

399

soldiers screamed for help but were killed immediately. At some point another group of attackers ran toward the galeota, yelling loudly. A fight ensued, in which the others on board may have joined against the Spaniards. All five soldiers were seriously wounded by arrows and had to defend themselves with their machetes, because their guns would not fire.[49]

During what must have been a vicious battle, the Spaniards inexplicably managed to recapture their vessel. They returned immediately to the presidio, presumably manning the oars themselves, and reported to Aguilar that their five companions were dead. Although none of the accounts explicitly considered what the attackers' goals had been, it seems obvious that they intended to kill all the Spaniards and seize the galeota. The loss of the boat, which probably still carried at least one heavy artillery piece, would have crippled all efforts to control the mission towns and would have made further reductions virtually impossible. In possession of the galeota, a combined Itza-Kowoj force would have been able to mount a credible attack on the presidio. That the Maya attackers failed to achieve fully what they had intended enabled the Spaniards to put a quick end to the rebellion.

On the same day, Aguilar had sent a canoe with three Spaniards to San Martín, precisely where these events were unfolding. These three included the son of Juan Francisco Cortés, the former presidio commander; Nicolás de Lizarraga, son of the principal Guatemalan settler of the same name; and Sergeant Diego de la Garza. Upon arriving at the town, unaware of what had happened, Garza and one the others disembarked and walked up the beach toward a group of men whom they assumed to be a greeting party. Garza was immediately struck by an arrow and attacked from behind, his gun wrested away. Then, according to early reports, another attacker struck him in the neck with a machete that severed his head.[50] A later report stated simply that after he was hit by the arrow a large number of men fell on him, finishing him off.[51]

Seeing his companion felled, the other Spaniard mortally stabbed the attacker with his bayonet. The third defender quickly jumped out of the canoe and shot and killed another attacker. In the ensuing scuffle other Mayas were also wounded. The two surviving Spaniards quickly boarded the canoe and returned to the presidio, by which time the survivors from the earlier attack had already returned in the galeota.

Shortly thereafter, probably late the same day, Aguilar sent twenty or twenty-five troops and their commanding officer to San Martín and San Antonio, where they were to observe conditions and bring back the bodies of the dead. He did not go himself, because he did not wish to leave the presidio without command. There was little left to command, however; six of the thirty or so soldiers left at the presidio were now dead, and five more were wounded. The scouts returned a day later, reporting that they had found the towns completely deserted and had been unable to capture anyone. They brought back all six bodies, which had stab wounds to the hearts.[52] The deceased were later buried at the presidio.

On the day after the attacks Aguilar reported that four other towns had also joined the rebellion. Two of them must have been San Juan and San Francisco, and we later learn that the other two were San José and San Jerónimo, both located near the presidio. Even though these were said not to have been involved in the murders, most or all of their inhabitants abandoned their towns.[53] Bachiller Bernabé de Herrera, who arrived from Mérida on March 22 to take up his duties as "provincial vicar and ecclesiastical judge of these forests,"[54] wrote on April 3 that by then twenty-two of the runaway families had returned voluntarily. When interviewed they stated that they had fled out of fear that they would be punished for or be accused of the acts committed at San Martín and San Antonio. Herrera hoped that others would continue to come back, although there appeared to be little chance that those from San Martín and San Antonio would do so.

Within a few days Aguilar sent ten soldiers with two light cannons to guard the "king's milpa," after receiving intelligence that the Itzas planned to burn the maize stored there. The milpa lay four leagues from the presidio, probably along the road toward the south.[55] One night attackers shot three arrows at the soldier on watch in the sleeping quarters. They apparently missed him, and the guards responded by charging them and firing the cannons. The attackers fled, and no Spaniards were wounded.[56]

IDENTIFYING THE CONSPIRATORS

About twelve days after the attacks Aguilar apprehended the "cacique" of San Jerónimo, don Pedro Tzin, who was believed to be one of the conspirators. The Spaniards had considered Tzin, he wrote, to be "one of the good Indians," "the best liked of them all,"[57] but they now realized that he had deceived them all along. Aguilar imprisoned Tzin along with others from San Jerónimo. Following his questioning of Tzin, Aguilar wrote, it was determined that he, along with the unnamed cacique of San José and four others from that town, was the initial conspirator who had called together the other towns in order to plan and coordinate the attacks.[58] As

401

a result of Tzin's testimony, other suspects were apprehended and interrogated, although how and when this was done appears in none of the reports of the rebellion.

Varaya later wrote that it had been determined that the principal organizer of the uprising was Kitam Kowoj, who had been captured in 1702 and appointed cacique of San José; Pedro Tzin, the San Jerónimo cacique, was determined to be his principal co-conspirator. Aguilar sentenced both men to death by shooting. He also ordered that four others be executed in the same manner. The three of these who were identified were Kulut Kowoj himself, the K'ixab'on cacique, and the unnamed cacique of San Antonio. The K'ixab'on leader was probably the cacique of San Martín. Although they also questioned don Martín Chan (still cacique of San Miguel), as well as individuals from San Andrés, these were found innocent of any prior knowledge of the murders and were set free.[59]

Nothing else is known about Kitam Kowoj, the San José cacique, although the first families brought to San José were from a settlement identified by the Itza surname Kitis that had recently been attacked by Kulut Kowoj for responding positively to Spanish overtures. Some people named Kitis, however, had lived well within Kowoj territory and were allies of the Kowojs.[60] Considering their location, people from San José may well have been those who attacked the king's milpa shortly after the attacks at San Martín and San Antonio. Two of the other three named conspirators — Kulut Kowoj and the cacique of San Martín — were from Kowoj territory, and the K'ixab'on cacique might have been associated with the Chak'an Itza province, which was allied with the Kowojs at the time of the conquest. Pedro Tzin, whose lineage name had been associated with the Itza eastern territory, probably did not belong to a group that had been part of the preconquest alliance between the Kowojs and Chak'an Itza.

The identities of the bulk of the rebellion's leaders, therefore, indicate that the 1704 rebellion had important roots in the conquest-period alliance between the Kowojs and the rulers of the north. The net effect of the vicious civil war among hostile Maya parties described in the previous chapter may well have been to set the stage for the rebellion by eliminating, insofar as that was possible, any sentiments by either Itzas or Kowojs to submit peacefully to Spanish control. The civil war's most important leader, as we learned earlier, was AjTut, the B'atab' of the north. The Spaniards considered AjTut to be their principal enemy, but they had been unable to capture him and had to satisfy themselves with capturing his brother AjK'ixaw and placing numerous K'ixab'on followers in the missions.

Except for a few families from the Yalain region, most of the early missions were populated by Kowojs and Itzas affiliated with the former rulers of the north. Some, we are told, came willingly, while others were captured. Those who came willingly may well have been encouraged to do so by the newly installed Itza ruler in the hope that once native presence had been reestablished on the lakeshore, it would be only a matter of time before the Spanish forces could be attacked, defeated, and even annihilated. At that point Nojpeten could be reclaimed by the Kan Ek' rulers, and a new era of anti-Spanish military cooperation with the Kowojs could begin. If this was indeed the new ruler's plan, the organization for the upcoming rebellion was already under way in 1702 as the missions were first being formed.

If such a widespread conspiracy existed, the first stage would have been to kill all ten soldiers who had gone to San Martín. The Mayas would then have held the galeota, its armaments, and the soldiers' weapons and ammunition. Had this been successful, the next obvious step would have been to kill the guards at the king's milpa and capture their weapons, ammunition, and the two light cannons in their possession. At this point fewer than twenty regular troops would have been left to defend the presidio. They could have been easily overcome by surprise attack at night, and the rest of the small Spanish population could have been massacred. A sufficient number of Mayas had probably observed the firing of the heavy armaments to enable them to operate them and, consequently, to mount a defense against any future Spanish attempts to recapture the island.

Aguilar wrote that throughout their questioning the accused leaders told him repeatedly that they had intended not to leave a single Spaniard alive, including the mail couriers, whom they intended to ambush as they came or went along the roads to Yucatán and Guatemala. Marcos de Abalos y Fuentes, the Guatemalan captain who had participated in the disastrous 1699 entrada, wrote that one of his soldiers who had remained for some time at the presidio used words like these to describe the state of the mission towns prior to the rebellion: "He answered me that they are growing weary. Indeed the same Indians say they do not want the Spaniards to settle in. [They say,] 'So we will be here. In the meantime they go or we kill them.' "[61]

Although neither claims such as these nor the hypothetical scenario just **403** sketched demonstrate conclusively that the rebels intended to annihilate the Spaniards and recapture Nojpeten, such an intent offers the only satisfactory explanation for why they risked their lives at San Martín and San Antonio on February 7. Had they succeeded, Nojpeten would have become the capital of the new Itza political order. The long-held wish of the rulers of the north and their Kowoj allies to win control over Nojpeten during K'atun 8 Ajaw would have at last been accomplished.

OTHER PRECIPITATING FACTORS IN THE REBELLION

Spanish explanations of the rebellion omitted any mention of such political aspirations on the part of its leaders. During the trials, Aguilar wrote, the defendants offered two related "reasons" for their decision to rebel. First, a rumor had spread that the Spaniards intended to remove them all to Guatemala and Yucatán. Second, they feared that they would be subjected to the same tribute demands and heavy labor requirements (*tequío*) that they knew natives in those areas had to pay.[62] Varaya reported that the second rumor had resulted from the census of the mission towns carried out some weeks earlier by Aguilar, the priests, soldiers, and other officials. Censuses had always been the colonial method by which tribute requirements were determined, and the indigenous population was well aware of it.[63] This census had been ordered by Ursúa, who had received a royal cédula, presumably at his request, authorizing that it be taken.

The fact that four years later Ursúa petitioned the Crown for an annual rent of four thousand ducats (equal to fifty-five hundred pesos) to be paid by the reduced natives of Petén confirms that the rumor connecting the census with tribute was well founded.[64] This tribute was of the same magnitude as the population counted in the census: about four thousand souls of all ages. Although his petition was never approved, it would have been most unusual to assign tribute amounts on the basis of total population rather than the number of able-bodied adults.

Captain Aguilar suggested yet another reason for the rebellion — that the eight towns in question resented that the Spaniards were still holding the "lords" (*señores*) of their lands as prisoners at the presidio.[65] Although we do not know who, other than K'ixaw, these nobles were, Aguilar insisted that the imprisonment of potential troublemakers among the regional leaders was the only solution to future anti-Spanish uprisings. In a letter to the president of Guatemala, in which he pleaded for fifty more soldiers and additional weapons and ammunition, he also made a case for increased restraints for future prisoners. He asked for "two hundred chains one vara in length, with large foot rings with which we will secure the family heads and leaders — and especially some that have a parted opening."[66] His confusing but vivid rationale for chaining prisoners paints a grim picture of the treatment they had probably already received:

The vices of killing one another while drunk are very inveterate, having three or four wives apiece, something to which we cannot consent. What is worse is that they [the wives] are sisters to each other, and in separating them they are sorry and then become angry. And [when] they [the men] are at their word, they stay or they leave, and by having them imprisoned we can be masters of their persons and wills, and they will be indoctrinated at pleasure and with complete security. Thus restrained they will be taken to make their milpas and houses, because they are lazy and do not wish to work, even for themselves.[67]

High-ranking Itzas and Kowojs who were almost certainly unaccustomed to manual labor were now treated as forced laborers, a practice that continued for at least several more years.

Workers and Captives

Over the next several years Aguilar y Galeano continued to retain certain captives as prisoners at the presidio, holding them for a period of time before releasing them to live in the mission towns. Some of these had been runaways, whom he punished with whippings as well as confinement. As late as 1709 he still held as prisoners twenty to twenty-five Itza men who had been captured after the 1704 rebellion and found guilty of participating in the murders of the Spanish soldiers. He had sentenced them to two years of personal service, which consisted primarily of carrying stones, shoveling soil, and burning lime — probably for the construction of the church. For a while they assisted in dyeing thread, which Aguilar apparently sold for his own income.[68]

In 1709 Aguilar reported that it was not unusual for him to have twenty or thirty Itza women working in his kitchen, grinding maize; women who were "idle" (*de baldío*) he put to work spinning cotton and weaving. For the most part these women had been married to captives, who had from three to as many as seven wives; some co-wives, as he had indicated, were sisters. When he freed a male prisoner, he allowed him to take with him only his "first and legitimate wife," retaining the others as workers.[69]

Shortly before the 1704 rebellion Aguilar and the resident priest, Marcos de Vargas, had clashed over the treatment and assignment of Itzas who worked in their respective households. In one case Vargas objected to the

405

captain's decision to release a young man from duty as a cook in Aguilar's kitchen. The youth's uncle, who lived at the mission of San José, asked Aguilar to allow him to return there in order to help him in his milpa. When Aguilar agreed, Vargas reacted angrily, claiming that the youth should remain so that he could continue to be taught the Christian doctrine. When, during a heated argument over the matter, Vargas threatened to excommunicate Aguilar, the captain replied (as he recalled saying), "I was here at war, with weapons in my hand and the enemy in sight, [and] that his mercy could not excommunicate me."[70] The young man, presumably, went to live at San José.

Vargas himself, according to Aguilar, retained individuals at the presidio for reasons other than religious instruction. He required two women to make a tablecloth for him in the elaborate Itza style of weaving, forcing them to carry out the work in his own house without supplying them sufficient thread. Another Itza woman, whose husband was required to work for the Spaniards, accused Vargas of dragging her from her house by the hair to serve for a week as his live-in cook — despite the fact that she had broken her arm and was unable to grind maize. Vargas, who had a vicious temper, once punished Aguilar's male and female Itza workers for failing to attend evening prayer sessions at his house. He and Aguilar argued over their respective rights to the labor of boys and girls whom they employed shelling maize and working in their kitchens.[71]

New Reductions

During the few years following the 1704 rebellion the Spaniards at Los Remedios not only succeeded in recapturing many of those who had run away but also managed to increase substantially the numbers of "reduced" Itzas. Almost no details of how this was accomplished appear in the documentary record, which is exceedingly thin for this period. Summary census figures, however, indicate a steady rise in the mission population, as indicated in Table 15.3.

These figures indicate that in 1706, two years after the 1704 rebellion, the total mission population was still less half what it had been just before the rebellion, and the size of a "family" had declined precipitously from an average of 5.0 persons in 1703 to 2.4 persons in 1706. The small sizes of families, which were customarily identified as married couples and their children, suggests both a high proportion of widowed or absentee parents and a significant decline in the number of children. The best expla-

TABLE 15.3
Population Change in the Mission Settlements, 1703–16

Date	No. Towns	No. Houses	No. Families	No. Baptized Persons	Total
Founding	11	*83*	*±220*	—	*1,100*
June 1703	9	281	750	—	*3,750*
Dec. 1703[a]	9	300	800	—	4,000
March 1704	3	—	300	—	*1,500*
Oct. 1706	5	—	700	320	1,686
June 1707	7	—	1,200	2,600	5,000
Dec. 1707[b]	7	—	—	3,161	5,360
Oct. 1708	9	—	—	4,972	6,000
1711	15	—	—	—	3,027
May 1712	16	—	—	2,677	3,728
1715[c]	18	—	—	—	4,423
Oct. 1717[d]	18	—	—	—	+5,000
1766[e]	8	—	—	+1,167	+1,471

SOURCES: For founding, AGI, EC 339B, no. 15, Certification of Br. Francisco de San Miguel y Figueroa, 1 July 1703, ff. 5r–8r, and no. 28, Certification of Br. Marcos de Vargas Dorantes, 10 July 1703, ff. 18r–21r. For June 1703, EC 339A, Consulta de Fr. Diego de Rivas y Capitán Alejandro Pacheco, 20 June 1703, ff. 142v–152v. For December, 1703, EC 339B, no. 28, Certification by Fr. Diego de Rivas, 23 Dec. 1703, ff. 34r–35r, and no. 26, Gaspar Reymundo de Varaya to governor of Yucatán, 17 June 1704, ff. 7r–10r. For March 1704, EC 339A, Informe del Capitán José de Aguilar Galeano, to president of Audiencia of Guatemala, 28 March 1704, ff. 67r–73r. For October 1706, EC 339B, no. 27, Ursúa to Crown, 12 Oct. 1706, ff. 1r–3v. For June 1707, M 889, José de Aguilar Galeano to Crown, 26 June 1707, and EC 339B, no. 27, Br. Bernabé de Herrera to Crown, 25 Oct. 1707, ff. 5r2D6r. For December 1707, EC 339B, no. 27, Ursúa to Crown, 24 Jan. 1708, ff. 12r–15. For October 1708, EC 339B, no. 27, José de Aguilar y Galeano to Crown, 9 Oct. 1708, ff. 19r–21v. For 1711, G 186, Consulta by Consejo de Indias, 5 July 1716. For 1712, G 224, no. 19, Certificación del Br. D. Bernabé de Herrera, 17 May 1712. For 1715, M 702, Memorial del Lic. Luis Coello Gaytán al Rey, no date. For 1717, M 1032, Autos and testimony on the state of the reductions and doctrinas of Peten Itza, administered by the secular clergy of Yucatán, Oct. 1717. For 1765, G 859, Testimonio de los autos seguidos sobre el pre de dos reales diarios que se dan a los presidarios del castillo de Peten Ytza, 1771.

NOTE: Reconstructed data are in italics. See text for explanation.

[a]Rivas noted that there were ten towns, although he listed only nine. One of these, San Martín, apparently included San Antonio, which is not listed separately. Varaya noted eleven towns, possibly in error.

[b]The five lakeshore towns were Jesús María, San José, San Jerónimo, San Miguel, and San Andrés. The other two towns were Nuestra Señora de los Dolores and San Francisco Xavier, located on the southern road to Guatemala.

[c]The source of this information, Lic. Luis Coello Gaytán, presented his memorial directly to the Council of the Indies, which first reviewed it on Feb. 5, 1716. A secular priest who had been serving in Petén, he claimed that the reduced population had been as high as eight thousand but was cut in half by an epidemic of smallpox, a disease that, he surmised, was previously unknown to the region.

[d]Smallpox epidemics, it was reported, had reduced the population.

[e]These eight towns include San Luis and a number of cattle ranches. The total is based on the reconstruction of the indigenous population explained in the text.

nation for these phenomena might be epidemic disease, although the earliest source referring to epidemics after 1702 did not appear until 1715, when priests who had worked in Petén noted that over previous years smallpox and other epidemics had taken a high toll among the indigenous population.

The growth of the population to a total of six thousand by October 1708 indicates that more than three thousand persons had been "reduced" during 1707 and 1708. At least thirteen hundred of these were Mopans who had twice been forced to relocate. In about 1706 Guatemalan troops rounded up Mopans who had fled eastward into Belize, settling them in the towns of San Luis, Dolores, Santo Toribio, and San Francisco Xavier, located along the camino real. In 1707 Miskito slave raiders, known then as "Sambos," acting as mercenaries for British slavers along the eastern coast of Honduras, attacked these newly reduced Mopan settlements. In response to this new threat, in August 1707 Aguilar forced the approximately thirteen hundred already reduced Mopans to relocate yet again, nearer the lake, with the assistance of forty armed troops and four hundred Itza archers.[72] This last move, however, seems to have been short lived, because the original reduction settlements were soon reestablished.

Another reduction during this period was precipitated by Ursúa, who in September 1707, in preparation for leaving Yucatán to become governor of the Philippines, wrote to the king requesting that Captain José de Aguilar y Galeano be granted the title of governor and captain general of the Itza territories.[73] One of his duties was to remove the population of Tipuj to a new settlement in the vicinity of the presidio. Tipuj had already been attacked by the English, who captured some of its inhabitants as slaves.[74] Before the end of 1707 it had been attacked again, this time by "Musuls," referring to Mopans, who killed the "cacique" of Tipuj, his "lieutenant," and as many as fifteen town leaders. Aguilar sent twenty-five soldiers and about two hundred "reduced" Itzas to capture the aggressors, whom they apprehended as they were returning yet again to Tipuj. At this time the troops apparently brought the remaining Tipujans back to Petén Itzá.[75] By early 1708 there was already a settlement somewhere near the presidio known as the town "of the Tipujans" (*de los Tipues*). Its location and fate, however, are unknown.

408 The pace of such reductions apparently slowed over the next few years; further increases were slight. The 50-percent drop in population between 1708 and 1711 was probably caused primarily by a smallpox epidemic, along with other, unspecified epidemic diseases.[76] One missionary reported that the total mission population had reached more than eight

thousand before smallpox wiped out nearly half of it, explaining why there were only 4,423 mission inhabitants in 1715.[77] Increases in the rate of flight from the missions may have contributed to these losses as well. Moreover, the priests complained that "many other natives" had been removed to Guatemala and Yucatán by various governing commanders.[78]

The most detailed census of the native population for this period was produced by the priest Bernabé de Herrera in 1712 (Table 15.4). Of the sixteen towns in this census, including the presidio, the six lakeshore missions comprised 61.7 percent of the Maya population. Several of the towns on the roads to Yucatán and Cahabón still had high percentages of adult catechumens who were not yet considered ready to take communion, indicating that these communities had only been recently reduced.

Although the number of Spanish-controlled rural towns in Petén was reported in about 1715 to be eighteen — four of them recently reduced — only six of these had resident secular clergy; these were San Andrés, San Martín, San Xavier, San Pedro, San Antonio, and Los Dolores. Of these six, however, only three had town councils and churches; these would have been San Andrés, San Martín, and Jesús María.[79] Jesús María, which I have not seen in earlier sources, appears on one map just east of San Martín, which had been relocated to the mainland immediately north of the presidio.[80] This was not the same San Martín shown on Table 15.4 along the road to Yucatán.

The Political and Religious Governance of Petén

On January 24, 1698, the Crown had granted Martín de Ursúa y Arizmendi the title of governor and captain general over the newly conquered Petén territories, with responsibility to the viceroy of New Spain and none to then-governor Soberanis of Yucatán.[81] Ursúa never returned to Petén, however, except for the several months during 1699 when he and Melchor de Mencos resided and governed jointly at Los Remedios. As time passed, it became apparent that Ursúa was more interested in furthering his career elsewhere and in obtaining monetary and political rewards for his role in the conquest than in governing the conquered territory.

Some rewards came to him quickly. In 1700 he was awarded a knighthood in the Order of Santiago, and in 1705 the new Bourbon king, Felipe V, who had taken office in 1700, granted him the title Conde de Lizárraga, a town in his native Navarra.[82] According to Robert Patch, Ursúa had purchased the title with profits from his repartimientos.[83] In 1701 or 1702

TABLE 15.4

Census of the Maya Population of the Colonial Towns of Petén, 1712

| | Adults | | | | | Children | | | | |
| | Christians | | Catechumens | | | | | | | |
Towns	Married[a]	Single or Widowed	Married	Single	Unspecified	Pupils[b]	Others	Total Adults	Total Children	Total
Lakeshore towns:										
San Andrés	324	36	0	0	3	138	232	363	370	733
San Jerónimo	236	37	0	0	0	52	97	273	149	422
San Miguel	218	35	0	0	4	72	81	257	153	410
San José	186	30	0	0	21	46	89	237	135	372
Jesús María	132	26	0	0	2	51	28	160	79	239
San Bernabé	62	11	4	6	0	34	–	83	43	126
Subtotal	1,158	175	4	6	30	393	536	1,373	929	2,302
Presidio:										
Petén del Itzá[c]	67	20	0	0	12	65	4	99	69	168
Towns on Cahabón road:										
San Juan	18	3	6	6	0	5	4	33	9	42
Santo Toribio	34	12	4	10	0	18	10	60	28	88
Dolores	68	46	24	34	0	39	11	172	50	222
San Francisco Xavier	32	35	30	42	0	51	19	139	70	209
San Luis	74	21	12	16	0	26	27	123	53	176
Subtotal	226	117	76	108	0	139	71	527	210	737
Towns on Yucatán road:										
San Martín	122	26	14	6	0	87	6	168	93	261
San Antonio	28	12	0	0	0	0	11	40	11	51
Concepción	16	7	0	0	0	0	10	23	10	33
San Pedro	10	9	64	51	0	0	42	134	42	176
Subtotal	176	54	78	57	0	87	69	365	156	521
Total	1,627	366	158	171	42	684	680	2,364	1,364	3,728

SOURCE: AGI, Guatemala 224, no. 19, Certificación del Br. D. Bernabé de Herrera, vicario provincial y juez eclesiástico de la provincia del Petén, 17 May 1712.
[a] The original document lists married couples as "familias cristianas" to describe converted married couples or "familias catecúmenas" to classify married couples who were presumably "reduced" only recently and were not yet baptized. The number of married individuals is calculated by doubling the number of familias.
[b] "Pupils" are labeled in the original document as "muchachos y muchachas de doctrina," or children who were receiving religious instruction.
[c] This row includes, among the married Christians at the presidio (identifed as "Peten del Itza"), 41 females identified as "mujeres de ladinos," presumably

he petitioned the Crown for the title of Castillo, receiving it in 1705 as well.[84] By 1706, while still governor of Yucatán, he had been named future governor of the Philippines, and he requested that his governing authority over Petén be turned over to Captain José de Aguilar y Galeano, who had actually commanded the presidio since 1704.[85] None of these titles satisfied his desire for immediate financial rewards, which he requested from the Crown in the form of the title "adelantado of the new province of the Ytza," which would be accompanied by tribute payments from the conquered subjects in the annual amount of four thousand ducats.[86] Receipt of this title, with its origins in the sixteenth-century New World conquests, would have amounted to a lifetime income. As we have seen, his plan to request tribute payments had already begun four years earlier, when he authorized a census of the mission towns.

Within three days of penning and mailing his bold request, Ursúa must have come into possession of a letter sent the previous October by the vicar of Petén Itzá directly to the king. In this letter, Bernabé de Herrera, who clearly knew of Ursúa's intentions, recommended that Petén natives be freed of tribute obligations for ten years following their baptism. He explained that the people were poor and had to buy proper clothes to wear at religious services. Furthermore, freedom from tribute would make them realize that the Spaniards were there to save their souls, not to profit from them. Faced with payments that they had no way of making, the natives would respond by running away to the forests.[87] Recognizing that his proposal was doomed, Ursúa immediately wrote again to the king, this time echoing the vicar's request. To the best of my knowledge, the matter of tribute was never raised again, and the Petén Mayas remained free of at least that form of colonial exploitation.[88]

Captain José de Aguilar, left in full and virtually independent command over the presidio following Ursúa's departure for the Philippines in early 1708, soon found himself in serious trouble with the government of New Spain over accusations of monetary fraud and mistreatment of both the presidio soldiers and the reduced native population.[89] Complaints about Aguilar's behavior by Toribio de Cosio, who had recently become president of Guatemala, resulted in the viceroy of New Spain's decision in 1709, pending final royal approval, to place the governance of Petén directly under the Audiencia of Guatemala.[90]

411

Soon after this change in governance took effect, Aguilar attacked an "English" encampment, probably somewhere along Río Mopán. Reportedly, the foreigners were handing out arms to local native inhabitants whom they paid to capture "other Indians" who were to be sold as slaves in Jamaica. There were even rumors that Miskito mercenaries employed by the slavers planned to attack Los Remedios. He captured nineteen English men and one woman, ten black slaves, and six "indios." Of the English prisoners he released all but two, one of whom was Catholic and the other of whom claimed a desire to convert. These and the other prisoners he took back to the presidio. With additional soldiers sent by the president of Guatemala, Aguilar later attacked the English encampment again and this time took fourteen English prisoners to Los Remedios.[91]

Despite Aguilar's successes against the British slavers, complaints about his autocratic and corrupt behavior increased to the point that Toribio de Cosio decided to remove him from office. His replacement, field marshal (*maestre de campo*) Juan Antonio Ruíz de Bustamante, was to send him to Guatemala or some other distant place. No sooner had he arrived at Dolores, however, than Ruíz learned that Aguilar had already fled to Yucatán with his family and the black slaves whom he had captured.[92]

Aguilar's departure from Petén closed the final chapter on Ursúa's direct political legacy there. From now on Petén would be governed by political-military appointees from Guatemala, whereas Yucatán would have virtual control over the religious affairs of the province. The Crown's decision in 1716 to give the secular clergy of Yucatán continued rights to administer at least some of the Petén missions followed upon an official visit to the Council of the Indies in Madrid by Bachiller Luis Coello Gaytán during the previous year. Coello, who had served as second-in-command under the vicar of Petén Itzá for the past ten years, bore instructions and a letter of introduction from the secular clergy's ecclesiastical council in Mérida, which had long opposed any other group that sought to preach the gospel in the newly conquered territory.[93] Its principal opposition, apparently, was to a royal cédula issued in 1713 that would have turned the Petén missions over entirely to the Jesuit order, which had representatives in both Guatemala and Yucatán.[94]

The outcome of Coello's representations left matters in an ambiguous state. In its advice to the king, the Council of the Indies noted that the bishop of Yucatán had earlier opposed the presence in Petén of Dominicans from Guatemala but that the Crown had ordered him to cooperate with them. By 1716 Dominicans had been forced out of Petén by the bishop of Yucatán,[95] and Coello now proposed that civil governance and religious authority over the province be shifted to the governor and bishop of Yucatán, respectively. As to the 1713 cédula, he offered the compromise that the three secular priests then serving in Petén should administer the

412

six missions located near the main lake, whereas members of the Jesuit order should serve the twelve other towns and villages scattered at considerable distances away from the presidio. The council's advice, which may or may not have resulted in a follow-up cédula, was to grant the secular clergy only three missions and to distribute the other fifteen among Jesuits, whose salaries would be paid by the Guatemalan government.[96] The Franciscans of Yucatán had long ago given up any hope, or perhaps even desire, of preaching the gospel in Petén.

Four Jesuits were ready to leave the Guatemalan capital for Petén in August 1716, long before any outcome of the Council of the Indies' recommendations could have been received.[97] The secular clergy of Yucatán reacted with dismay at the Guatemalan president's order that they withdraw their priests, and even the Guatemalan governor of Petén considered the plan to be a mistake.[98] By October 1717 Jesuits still had not arrived in Petén, and the ecclesiastical council collected formal testimonies in Mérida from secular priests who had worked there, an action designed to counter accusations that they had been so inept that they needed to be replaced.[99]

At least one Jesuit did work in Petén. This man, Antonio Valtierra, trained Itzas to preach the gospel at two towns, one of which was San Francisco Xavier on the camino real. As late as 1755 the matter was still being discussed, the archbishop of Yucatán recommending to the Crown that Jesuits be sent to Petén in place of the secular clergy.[100] The secular clergy of Yucatán, however, continued to serve in Petén until at least the end of the colonial era.[101]

Renewed Resistance, 1750–66

The first recorded instance of renewed native resistance after the rebellion of 1704 occurred around 1750 at Santo Toribio. It consisted only of a purported plot to murder two priests and certain ladinos during mass on Holy Thursday night of Holy Week.[102] Five or six years later another, more ominous plot was discovered, reported by the vicar of Petén in 1766:

> Sergeant Major don Joseph Citcan of the town of San Joseph arrived at this headquarters, taking every precaution, in order to report that an Indian named Couoh from the town of San Bernabé had called together all of the towns of this district to revolt during Holy Week of that year, on the pretense of coming down to this

413

headquarters in order to celebrate.[103] With this news the said castellano [Francisco García de Monsabal] and the vicar [Bachiller Pedro Meneses] went to the town of Santa Ana to apprehend [Couoh], finding him there pursuing his calling of people together. They in fact manacled him and took him prisoner. Upon confirming what had happened, they punished him publicly in this headquarters, leaving out of the question other [future] revolts, which, as I have learned from the old settlers, they had attempted in previous years and had not carried out due to respect for this garrison.[104]

Plots such as these may have been exaggerated inventions, but there is a ring of truth in this report of an intended attack on the inhabitants of the presidio. That the plot was reported by an Itza named Kitkan, whose name (from Kit Kan) suggests association with the royal matrilineage of Nojpeten, in order to implicate a Kowoj suggests that old Itza-Kowoj wounds were still festering more than half a century after the conquest.

The same vicar who reported these incidents also made the questionable but interesting claim that the Campeche Maya (later known as Jacinto Kanek') who led the Kisteil rebellion in northern Yucatán in 1762 had lived in San Andrés two years earlier. There he had attempted to convince the inhabitants, who kept him hidden, to rebel — demonstrating, according to the vicar, that they were not to be trusted. The vicar feared that more than five hundred refugees from Kisteil, whose ears had been cut off as punishment for participating in the rebellion, were reportedly living in the vicinity of the camino real to Yucatán. These, it was believed, might at some time organize a rebellion among the local native inhabitants.[105]

Not all indigenous leaders received harsh treatment. Those who assisted Spaniards in rounding up other Mayas fared best, receiving modest rewards for their efforts. For example, a title granted to don Bernardo Chata as governor of San Andrés in 1713 indicates that as "cacique" of the town he had accompanied colonial troops to the Kejach region over the past several years in order to capture rebel apostates. His duties as governor included working with the town council, seeing to it that children and adults attended mass and religious instruction, overseeing subsistence cultivation, and making certain that "in their houses the natives have images, rosaries, clothing, and fowls, and that they have separate houses with no more than two married persons living in each house . . . and that among them they not engage in concubinage, vices, idolatries, or other public sins . . . and also that they take care to attract and bring together the pagan Indians that wander scattered and fugitive in those forests."[106]

The marriage registers for San Andrés (which include nearby San José and adjacent San Jerónimo) for the period between 1751 and 1766 confirm that up to this time few who were not Petén natives lived in this cluster of communities.[107] A handful of the names appear to be of Mayas from Yucatán, and another handful are Spanish. All but two of these latter are men, some perhaps soldiers from the presidio who married local Maya women but others probably criminals or political prisoners sent from Guatemala to live in exile in the Petén forests.[108]

Population Decline

In December 1765 the alcalde mayor of Chiapas ordered a detailed report on the state of Petén. In response, the "castellano" (presidio commander) of Petén Itzá submitted the following year a set of individual reports by the five secular clergy (the vicar and four priests) who were then working in the area.[109] Each of them had carried out censuses of towns and cattle ranches under their authority (Table 15.5). Because most children were omitted from these *padrones,* the total nonpresidio population of 1,450 (from Table 15.5, 1,865 minus the 415 for Petén Itza) is too low. For the towns in which children were counted, however, we see that the ratio of indigenous children to adults was low indeed: 1 to 1.8 for San Andrés, 1 to 1.6 for San José, 1 to 1.6 for Dolores, and 1 to 1.3 for Santo Toribio — or a ratio of 1 to 1.6 for the combined populations of these four towns. At the presidio, which would have been almost entirely nonindigenous, the ratio was even lower (1 to 3.0), in part owing to a subpopulation of unmarried soldiers. Even taking into account that some small children went uncounted at San Andrés and Dolores, these figures indicate that the Petén population was in a state of severe decline. They suggest in particular that infant and child mortality had been very high — high enough to account for most of the precipitous population decline over the past half century.

Assuming a conservative overall child-to-adult ratio of 1 to 1.6 among the indigenous population of Petén (based on the average for the four previously mentioned towns) and a total adult indigenous population of 905,[110] there would have been about 566 children in 1766, and a total indigenous population of about 1,471.[111] Based on these calculations, the **415** "mission" population of Petén would have declined 75.5 percent in fifty-eight years, from a peak of about 6,000 in 1708 (See Table 15.3). Following a substantial population recovery by 1717, to a total of about 5,000, the population had again dropped — this time by 70.1 percent in a space of

TABLE 15.5

Population of Petén Towns and Cattle Ranches, 1766

Town/Partido	Leagues from Presidio	Adults	Children	Total	Cattle Ranches (Leagues from Presidio)
Peten Itza[a]		312	103	415	
San Bernabé	0.5	37	—	+37	
Santa Ana	9.0	—	—	186	Nisam (1)
					Dolores (3)
					Sapote (2)
					Sumb'ob' (4)
					IxKoxol (3)
					Cholo (5)
					Ain (4)
					Muknal (6)
					Chachaklum (5)
					San Juan de Dios (6)
					Chilonche (8)
					San Pablo (8)
San Andrés[b]	1.5	164	+92	+256	Petenil (7)
					Gwakut (Kwakut?) (9)
					Sakluk (9)
					Yalkanix (4)
					Yalxut (9)
					Pachayil (8)
San Andrés ranches		68	—	+68	
San Andrés ladinos		24	—	+24	
San José	2.5	68	+42	+110	
San Jerónimo	1.5	21	—	+21	
Dolores	25.0	293[c]	180	473	
Dolores ladinos		23	—	+23	
Santo Toribio[d]	18.0	79	61	140	Santa Rosa
					San Felipe, Hacienda del Rey (20)
Sto. Toribio ladinos		15	—	+15	
San Luis	40.0	—	—	97	
Indigenous subtotal		+730	+375	+1,388	
Ladino subtotal		374	+103	+477	
Total		+1,104	+478	+1,865[e]	

SOURCES: AGI, Guatemala 859, Testimonio de los autos seguidos sobre el pre de dos reales diarios que se han a los presidarios del castillo de peten Ytza . . . , 1771.

NOTE: Town/partido names in italics are parish headquarters. Distances from the presidio of Petén Itzá are as given in this document. Numbers in italics indicate nonindigenous (i.e., "ladino") populations.

[a]There were probably a few adult female Mayas living at the presidio. In a 1744 census of the presidio, eighteen such women were counted, of whom all were married to non-Mayas (AGCA, Padrón remitido a esta capitañía general por el gobernador del presidio del Peten de Itza de las familias avencidados en el [y los] solados de su guarnición, 1744. Genealogical Society of Utah, Microfilm Roll 9763388).

[b]San Andrés had 92 children "de confesión," not including an unspecified number of younger children. The same comment applies to children listed for San José.

[c]These were "personas de comunion" and probably included individuals not yet married.

[d]The figures for Santo Toribio include the ranches. The 79 in the first column were "personas de comunión." The 61 in the second column included 30 "personas de confesión" and 31 "párvulos."

[e]The grand total of 1,865 is greater than the sum of the rows, owing to the absence of breakdowns for either adults or children from Santa Ana.

forty-nine years. Not since 1706–7, just after the rebellion, had the indigenous population dipped below 3,000.

There are indications that the indigenous population of Petén stabilized after 1766. A 1778 census of Petén records the indigenous population as 1,358, out of a total population of 1,604.[112] Because this number did not include small children (*párvulos*), we might conjecture that the total indigenous population was somewhat more than 1,500, a marginal increase over the 1,471 estimated for 1766. Unfortunately, later censuses did not distinguish indigenous and nonindigenous persons. The total population in 1823 was said to be 2,555. How much of this growth reflected increases, if any, in the indigenous population is unknown.[113] By 1845 the total population was 5,203, of whom 4,178 lived in rural areas outside Flores; this number was little changed as late as 1921, when the rural population was 6,101.[114]

Not until the 1950s did Petén experience rapid population growth, a phenomenon due almost entirely to migration from other areas of Guatemala. Although the total estimated population of the department was three hundred thousand in 1986, the population that could still be identified as "Itza"—the descendants of the original natives—had declined to only a few dozen families, mostly at San José.

In 1750 the bishop of Yucatán, Fray Francisco de San Buenaventura, carried out an official inspection visit to Petén, where he learned that small numbers of natives from the mission towns were continuing to escape to the forests. He was especially perturbed by reports that the military government at Los Remedios was preventing local Maya officials from chasing after runaways from San Martín and Dolores.[115] His continued complaints resulted in a 1753 royal cédula demanding a full accounting from the Guatemalan president on the state of the Petén reductions. The president in turn ordered the governor of Petén, José Monzabal, to investigate the matter. The final report, apparently completed in 1758 and spurred on by an additional cédula written in 1756, included reports of testimonies taken by Monzabal as well as information from a number of different sources.[116]

Much of the report concerns flight and reduction in the Chol regions of Verapaz, southern Petén, and Belize. Monzabal admitted that people had run away from San Martín on Lago Petén Itzá, including 140 families who deserted the town in 1746 and were now living on Río Usumacinta in Tabasco—where he had no authority to recapture them.[117] Despite the extensive nature of the accompanying testimony, witnesses reported few instances of flight and offered little indication that large uncontacted or

417

apostate Mopan or Itza-speaking populations lived in the Petén forests. Monzabal, however, had every reason to make it appear as if the Petén reductions had been successful. For this reason, we might assume that the numbers of runaways and apostates were much higher than the report indicates.

The governor and the secular priests of Petén reported in 1766 that some Mayas still lived independently in the forests, but they were unable to estimate their numbers. One priest had heard rumors of two towns of "barbarian Indians" north of the main lake and of others around Río Usumacinta.[118] Another reported seeing signs of others — fires, pottery vessels, comals for cooking tortillas, and "idols" — in the nearby forests. Since 1739, however, only twenty-five forest dwellers had been captured, all of whom had earlier run away from the missions.[119] Such information, although vague and inadequate, suggests that by the mid-seventeenth century the forest population was smaller than that under colonial control.

AjChan, King and Cacique

What, during all these years of Maya reduction, resistance, and waning fortunes in Petén, had become of AjChan, the nephew and former emissary of Ajaw Kan Ek' and the on-again, off-again ally of the Spaniards? Recall that not long after being absolved of any wrongdoing in the 1704 rebellion AjChan had deserted the Spaniards yet again, renouncing his position as cacique of San Miguel and reassuming his role as a leader of Mayas living beyond Spanish control. What subsequently happened to him can be only partially reconstructed, but even the bare outlines that the documents provide tell an evocative story.

Between 1705 and 1710 Nicolás de Lizarraga produced a multicolor map of the "forest of Peten Itza." The map itself has been lost, but his detailed legend, written on a foldout folio, has survived.[120] In one section of this legend he describes a native "province" that he calls "El Chan," where don Martín Chan, alias AjChan, had been made king over Mopans and Chols. He undoubtedly had Itzas among his followers as well. Lizarraga's geographical description of El Chan clearly identifies it as the southern coastal plain of Belize, a region known to have been occupied by Chols and Mopans.

Apparently AjChan had been accompanied to this region by his followers. On a 1770 map, across the region between Verapaz and the Belize River, is written the phrase "Tierras yncultas havitadas de Yndios Gentiles Ytzaes" ("uncivilized lands inhabited by Gentile Indians, Itzas").[121] AjChan would therefore have been the leader of a multiethnic population comprising Itzas, Mopans, and Chols. These were people who had apparently put aside any previous enmities, perhaps convinced by AjChan himself that their only hope for continued independence was to join forces in this relatively remote region.

In a memorial written to the king in 1708 Lizarraga wrote that forty leagues from Los Dolores there were two towns founded by five native youths from Petén.[122] Melchor de Mencos had taken them with him to Santiago de Guatemala when he left Petén in 1699 and had kept them in his own home to teach them Christian doctrine. They had been baptized, and he arranged that they be taught to read and write under the tutelage of a Jesuit, Antonio Valtierra. One of the pupils was named Juan Chab'in, indicating that he was an Itza; his companions must have been Itzas as well. Chab'in was so talented that Valtierra started to offer him instruction in grammar, and all five learned how to take confession and offer communion in the absence of a priest.

In 1707 these five young men, according to Lizarraga, sought and received government permission to teach the gospel among their "companions" in the forest. Mencos and Lizarraga gave them money to buy religious instructional materials, and the Jesuits presented them with images of Nuestra Señora del Carmén and San Francisco Xavier. Their mission, as it turned out, was twofold: named as captains, they succeeded in rounding up seven hundred families to settle in two communities, and as missionaries, they taught the reduced settlers something about the gospel and saw to the construction of portions of two churches. Their military mission, moreover, had another facet: they led battles against "the rest of the forest Indians, in particular with don Martín Chan, apostate and Prince among them."[123]

According to Lizarraga, the two towns founded by these Christian Itzas were forty leagues from Peten Itza, a few leagues north of Mopan or San Luis. One of them was surely San Francisco Xavier, which according to reports was established when military raids caused Mopans to flee east into Belize.[124] Because the "battles" that led to their establishment were with AjChan, his headquarters must have been in this area when they occurred.

Lizarraga told only part of the story, and his motive for doing so was to **419** assert that he had helped, along with Mencos, in contributing the instructional materials that the young missionaries used in the field.[125] These 1707 reductions were probably part of a larger Guatemalan effort to "protect" the Mopan population of southern Petén and Belize from Miskito raids by gathering them into defensible towns. The young men were probably also participating as minor functionaries in a wider Guatemalan effort to reduce and convert those Mopans, Chols, and other Itzas who were under the influence of AjChan, their king—"apostate and Prince among them."

In October 1757 a sixty-year-old Mopan named Francisco Sumkal ("Sun-Kal"), identified as the cacique of San Luis, testified at Los Remedios that about ten years earlier, while hunting wild pigs, he had seen signs of "infidels" (*infieles*) near his town. He said simply—and no more—that although the San Luis cacique of that time, one Martín Chan, "intended to follow the said signs, he never did it."[126]

Spaniards had estimated AjChan's age in 1697 to be about thirty. He would therefore have been about eighty when the event described by Francisco "Sun-Kal" occurred. This Martín Chan, who refused "to follow the said signs," may have been the same AjChan who had spent his adult life tortured by personal conflicts over his loyalty to his own people versus their conquerors. At some point in his middle or old age, Spaniards and their native allies had, we might infer, captured him one last time and placed him once again in a position of authority in a native mission town, this time San Luis. As an old man in about 1767, one of his last acts as an Itza leader over his Mopan, Itza, and Chol subjects and allies may have been to ignore the signs indicating that others among his people still enjoyed their independence.

The mission towns established in Belize in 1724 had been largely abandoned, their populations apparently removed by Spaniards to San Luis and other towns along the Verapaz road. Mopans, Itzas, and Chols probably continued to live in small numbers in the Toledo District, but, if so, we have no record of them at this time. We do know, however, that the eighteenth- and early nineteenth-century inhabitants of San Luis bore a mixture of Mopan and Itza names, which is exactly what we would expect had AjChan and his followers reestablished themselves there.[127] One of the most common of these names was Chan.

In 1883 a group of families from San Luis, "irked by constant taxation and military service" imposed by the Guatemalan government, decided to establish a new community in what was then British Honduras. About one hundred of these San Luiseños settled first at a place known today as San Antonio Viejo but soon moved their main settlement to the town that still bears the name San Antonio.[128]

J. Eric S. Thompson described a series of events that took place following the establishment of San Antonio, during which the people of the new town raided San Luis in the dark of night and took away the images of their former neighbors' saints and the church bells. Their crops had been poor, and "fever was rife"; having the saints, they hoped, would improve their fortunes. Invaders from San Luis subsequently tried to retrieve their possessions but were captured and taken as prisoners to Punta Gorda on the coast. British authorities released them, but the saints and bells have remained in San Antonio to this day.[129] I heard a similar version of this account in San Antonio while doing fieldwork there in July 1965.

When Thompson visited San Antonio in 1928–29, he recorded the old Itza names Kanche, Tek, and Tzib' ("Tzip").[130] Today the Itza name Kante ("Canti") and the Mopan name Jola still survive there.[131] Such names at San Antonio and San Luis, in addition to the evidence from church registers from the eighteenth and nineteenth centuries, indicate that some members of these communities are still in all likelihood the descendants of Itzas and Mopans who sought refuge from the Spaniards in southern Belize with AjChan, nephew of the last Itza who ruled at Nojpeten. The present-day "Mopan" language — the descendant of seventeenth-century Mopan-Itza — is still spoken as a principal language in these towns, despite more than two centuries of intermarriage with increasingly dominant numbers of K'ek'chi-speaking peoples from Verapaz. This fact is profound testimony to the strength of ethnic survival among the people devastated by the conquest of 1697 and its three centuries of aftermath, as is the recent renewal of ethnic identity among the Itzas of the old mission town of San José on Lago Petén Itzá.

REFERENCE MATTER

Notes

The archives referred to in the notes are abbreviated as shown in the following list:

AAICFP   Archivo Apostólico de la Iglesia Católica de Flores, Petén (Guatemala)

AGCA   Archivo General de Centro América, Guatemala City

AGI   Archivo General de Indias, Seville. This abbreviation is followed by a second one, indicating a section of the archive, part of the full signature of a document:

C   Contaduría

EC   Escribanía de Cámara

G   Audiencia de Guatemala

M   Audiencia de México

P   Patronato

NL   Newberry Library, Chicago

Spelling and Pronunciation in Mayan Languages

1. Hofling with Tesucún, 1997.
2. Barrera Vásquez et al., 1980.
3. Hofling with Tesucún, 1997, pp. 4, 6; see also Hofling, 1993.

Introduction

1. Villagutierre, 1701. This work, reissued twice in Spanish (1933, 1985), has been published in English (1983). See also Means, 1917, on these materials.

2. J. Eric S. Thompson (1951) wrote a brief article on the Itzas that suffers from the absence of any citations as well as from a rather uncritical reading of the sources. This article has been the modern source perhaps most widely cited by subsequent authors. Carmack's synthesis of Itza social and political organization (1981, pp. 388–93) is far more useful, although my own (chapter 3) is quite different. Bricker's summary of the events leading up to and encompassing the conquest of the Itzas (1981, pp. 21–24) is situated in a comparative context of

other conquest activities in the Maya region. My own previous book (Jones, 1989) provides extensive background for this one. Farriss's magisterial work (1984) is an excellent introduction to the colonial history of the Mayas of Yucatán.

3. Hellmuth, 1972, 1977.

4. For preliminary reports on the work of Proyecto Maya Colonial see Rice et al., 1995, 1996, and Sánchez Polo et al., 1995.

5. No mention is made in this book of a previously reported secret visit by Fray Andrés de Avendaño y Loyola to Nojpeten in late 1694 or early 1695 (Jones 1991, 1992, 1994). These publications contain transcriptions, translations, and commentary on a document known as the Canek Manuscript, previously thought to have been written by a lay friar who accompanied Avendaño. Hanks (1992) has written a linguistically informed textual analysis of the manuscript, and Pendergast and Jones (1992) have analyzed evidence concerning material culture described in it. Subsequent close examination of this manuscript, comparing it with others with similar characteristics, has led me to agree with Prem and colleagues (Prem et al., 1996) that the Canek Manuscript is in all probability a forgery. At the time of writing I am working with Prem on this issue, and he and I intend to issue statements in an appropriate academic journal in which we detail the evidence regarding this apparent forgery. The analysis of Avendaño's activities at Nojpeten contained in this book, in contrast to my above-cited publications, assumes that his purported early visit there, based on information in the Canek Manuscript, never took place.

Chapter 1: The Itzas and Their Neighbors

1. Kaufman (1976, p. 111; q.v. for other sources on the diversification of Mayan languages) asserts that the four branches of "common Yucatecan" (Yucatec, Itzaj, Yucatec Lakandon, and Mopan) broke up about A.D. 1000, but he does not address the degree of later differences among these speech varieties. The Spanish suggests that the Itza language of the late seventeenth century differed little from the Yucatec language recorded in the sixteenth-century Spanish dictionaries. Fray Bartolomé de Fuensalida, who visited the Itzas in 1618 and 1619, reported that they spoke the same language as that of Yucatán (López de Cogolludo, 1971, vol. 2, bk. 9, ch. 14, p. 256; first published as López de Cogolludo, 1688). In 1695 official interpreters in Mérida apparently had no difficulty translating the speech of the Itza emissary AjChan (see chapter 7). In that year President Jacinto Barrios Leal of Guatemala asked that Ursúa send him interpreters who spoke the language of Yucatán so that they could assist and teach missionaries who would work with the Itzas (AGI, G 151A, no. 4, Auto by Ursúa, 3 Dec. 1695, ff. 44v–45v). Spanish military officers from Campeche testified in 1696 that they were able to communicate in Maya (i.e., Yucatec) with Itzas whom they encountered at the main lake and that this was the language which the Itzas spoke (AGI, G 151A, no. 3, Testimonies presented on behalf of Ursúa, 26 Aug. 1696, ff. 69r–104v).

Only one source contradicts such evidence that Yucatec and Itza were virtually identical. Fray Andrés de Avendaño y Loyola, describing his 1696 visit to Nojpeten, claimed that the Itzas had great respect for him because he had learned the "language of their ancestors and their own" (*lengua de sus antepasados y suya*). They marveled at his ability, he claimed, because they had never encountered other Mayas or Spaniards who spoke their language, which was not "*usable*" in northern Yucatán (Avendaño, NL, Ayer Collection, Fray Andrés de Avendaño, Relación de las dos entradas que hize a la conversión de los gentiles Ytzaex y Cehaches, 29 April 1696, f. 39r; 1987, p. 44). While the Itzas probably did speak in a way that seemed antiquated to those who spoke the seventeenth-century language of northern Yucatán, Avendaño certainly exaggerated the differences.

Numerous sources also confirm that Itza and Mopan were mutually intelligible in the seventeenth century. During 1695 and 1696 Guatemalan missionaries and soldiers were informed by Chols and Mopans alike that Mopan and Itza were one and the same language (see AGI, G 153, no. 2, Juan Ruíz de Alarcón to president of Guatemala, 17 Nov. 1695, ff. 132r–v, 153r–v; G 152, ramo 3, Fr. Agustín Cano to Jacinto Barrios Leal, 15 May 1695, ff. 370v–81r; G 153, no. 1, Bartolomé de Amésqueta to Gabriel Sánchez de Berrospe, 26 April 1696, ff. 138r–49v; G 153, no. 1, Fr. Agustín Cano to Gabriel Sánchez de Berrospe, 31 March 1696, ff. 64r–66v; G 151A, no. 3, Bartolomé de Amésqueta to José de Escals, 31 March 1696, ff. 14r–40v; G 505, Diligencia by Fr. Agustín Cano, including account of Manche Chols by the late Fr. Cristóbal de Prada, 16 April 1696, ff. 109v–20r).

2. For further background on Tz'ul Winikob' see Jones, 1989, pp. 41–44. In contemporary Itzaj *tz'ul* means a patron, rich man, or boss (Hofling and Tesucún, n.d.). Yucatec dictionaries generally translate it as "foreigner" and "Spaniard"; it may have signified territory under the Itza or Mopan sphere of influence.

3. Bricker, 1981, pp. 36–38; Thompson, 1938.

4. On the Chols around Sakb'ajlan see Vos, 1980. The final conquest of this region in 1695, only alluded to in this book, is described in Houwald, 1979.

5. Scholes and Roys, 1948, 1968, provide a detailed history of the Akalan Chontals.

6. On trade between Verapaz and the central Petén region see AGI, G 151A, no. 1, Marcelo Flores to Martín de Ursúa and Melchor de Mencos, 3 April 1699, ff. 69v–70r (also in AGI, G 344, ramo 3, ff. 102r–3v); AGI, G 151A, no. 1, Parecer by Fr. Gabriel de Artiga, 10 April 1699, ff. 84r–85v.

7. Thompson, 1938, pp. 592–93.

8. The sole reference that I have found to Suyuja (Zuyuha) Peten Itza is in AGI, P 237, ramo 1, Razón individual y general de los pueblos, poblaciones, y rancherías de esta provincia de Zuyuha Peten Itza, 6 Jan. 1698, ff. 80r–84v. The Itza ruler and the high priest apparently intended that the full name should apply to the entire Itza territory, not simply to the island capital. It is for this reason that I have translated *peten* here as "province," not island; both meanings are applied to

this word in the colonial Yucatec dictionaries. Colonial Yucatec Maya dictionaries gloss *suy* as *remolino* (whirl), as in *u suy haa'* (whirlpool).

Edmonson considers the name Zuyua, as it usually appears in the Maya chronicles, to be from the Nahuatl for "bloody water" (Edmonson, 1982, p. 220; 1986, p. 309). For a discussion of the mythological significance of "Zuyua" see Barrera Vásquez and Morley, 1949, p. 27. In a questionnaire or ritual recorded in the Book of Chilam B'alam of Chumayel, *zuyua* refers to a particular type of riddlelike speech or language used to test the genealogical legitimacy of town officials: their "answers are called the 'language of Zuyua,' and Zuyua, a legendary Nahuatl place name, was the symbol of the Mexican origin of the ruling class in Yucatán. The implication seems to be that only the descendants of the Zuyua people should hold important offices and not the autochthonous population" (Roys, 1943, p. 151). The association of Yucatecan elites with Suyua or Suyuja, however, probably refers not literally to their Mexican origins but simply to their historical legitimacy as rulers.

A k'atun wheel in the Book of Chilam B'alam of Chumayel, the chronicle of the Itzas, records that a place toward the south called "Zuyua" was where a K'atun 3 Ajaw was seated (Roys, 1967, p. 132; Edmonson, 1986, p. 112). Edmonson associates this occurrence with the seating of this k'atun in 1618 (1982, p. 16). Apparently the reference was to Nojpeten, a matter of some significance in light of the fact that the Itza rulers were contacted by Franciscans at this time (see chapter 2).

The background to my suggestion that the name written by Spaniards as "Itza" was actually Itza', translatable as "Sacred-Substance Water," is as follows: Barrera Vásquez and Rendón suggested some time ago (1948, p. 29) that "Itzá es un compuesto de dos elementos: *its + a'*. El primero, *its*, lo tomamos por brujo o mago y *a'* por agua. El nombre Itzá, pues, se traduce por Brujo-del-agua" (Itzá comprises two elements: *its + a'*. We interpret the first, *its*, as witch or magician and *a'* as water. The name Itzá, then, is translated as Witch-of-the-water). They also conclude that in northern Yucatán *itz* referred not only to the various liquid substances named in the colonial dictionaries (milk, tears, sweat, sap, resin, etc.) but also to rain and water in general, especially when associated with the supernatural powers of Itzamna as god of water or rain (pp. 29–31). The primary meaning of *itz* in the Itzaj language today is sap or resin (Charles A. Hofling, personal communication, 1996).

Freidel, Schele, and Parker have argued that *itz* can best be translated as "blessed substance" and that *itzam* refers to "shaman," one "who opens the portal [of the sky] to bring *itz* into the world" (1995, p. 51; see also pp. 210–13). They also see *itz* as sacred "cosmic sap" that had the power to be "magic" when used ritually by shamans in their encounters with the "Otherworld" (pp. 222–24), and they seem to agree with Barrera Vásquez and Rendón that *itz* can also be glossed as "sorcerer" or a related concept even without the additional agentive suffix -*am* (p. 411).

Such questions of etymology are by their nature speculative. It is worth

428

noting, however, that in Yucatec the morpheme *itz* alone is apparently nowhere glossed as shaman, magician, or witch — only *itzam,* the agentive form, describes a human who uses *itz* for magical or supernatural purposes. In Cakchiquel Maya, however, *itz* or *aj-itz* can refer to a shaman.

9. Hofling (personal communication, 1996) has noted that *taj* in Itzaj place names is a contraction of the locative preposition *ti'* ("to" or "at") and *aj* (designating a group of people or a person). In the sixteenth century Díaz del Castillo recorded the name of the island capital as "Tayasal," whereas Hernán Cortés wrote it as Taiza, apparently from TajItza (see chapter 2). I have found Tayasal nowhere in the seventeenth- and eighteenth-century documentation and suspect that it was adopted by scholars in the twentieth century, when this name was used to designate the peninsula just north of the main island and the archaeological site on that peninsula. Atran has offered *t-aj-itza-il* ("at the place of the Itza[s]") as another interpretation of Tayasal (Atran, 1993, p. 638).

Another Itza place name of this sort is TajMakanche (Tahmacanche), referring to a place on Laguneta Macanché (AGI, EC 339A, Memoria on Peten Itza by Fr. Diego de Rivas, 26 May 1702, ff. 31r–3v). In this case *makan-che'* refers to an arbor or shelter (ramada) covered over with wood or branches, possibly a religious shrine (although in contemporary Itzaj it is a wooden granary). The Books of Chilam B'alam of Chumayel and Tisimin make several references to such town names in Yucatán: TajKab', TajAak, TajKumchak'an, and TajWaymil (Roys, 1967, pp. 70–71, 146; Edmonson, 1982, pp. 112, 167; Edmonson, 1986, pp. 83, 86, 305). In each case Edmonson translates *taj* as "division."

10. In 1698 the Mercederian missionary Fray Diego de Rivas found extensive cultivations by people he identified as Itzas, apparently located along Río Subín, a major tributary of Río Pasión (AGI, G 345, no. 20, Parecer of Fr. Diego de Rivas, 15 Nov. 1698, ff. 200r–210r). In 1702 a Guatemalan settler in Petén, Nicolás de Lizarraga, identified a town named Sakyaxche, which he wrote had "mucha gente muy osadas" (many very bold people) (AGI, EC 339B, no. 7, Lista y memoria de los pueblos y parajes de los indios vecinos de la Laguna del Peten, 1702 [undated], ff. 15r–17r). This may have been the same place as the town named Yaxche, identified by the Itza ruler and his son in 1702 as occupied by people named Tut (AGI, EC 339A, Memoria on Peten Itza by Fr. Diego de Rivas, 26 May 1702, ff. 31r–33v). I believe that it was also at the present location of the town of Sayaxché, whose name is probably derived from it, on Río Pasión a short distance upstream from its conjunction with Río Subín. Lawrence Feldman (personal communication, 1995) has informed me that there were Chol-speaking people in this area in the early seventeenth century. The presence of Itzas there at the end of the century does not mean that Chols necessarily ceased to occupy the **429** region as well.

11. Sharer, 1994, p. 387. Except where indicated, this brief background on Chich'en Itza and Mayapan is based primarily on Sharer's recent interpretations (1994, pp. 348–49, 384–412).

12. The identity of a people called Putun and their proposed expansion into the rest of the Maya lowlands was first articulated by Thompson (1970, pp. 3–47).

13. Ringle, 1990, p. 239.

14. Ringle, Bey, and Peraza, 1991.

15. Schele, Grube, and Boot, 1995, p. 16.

16. Ibid., pp. 7–8.

17. Edmonson, 1986, pp. 58, 61. See also Schele, Grube, and Boot, 1995, pp. 9–10; Roys, 1967, pp. 140–41, 179–80. Interpreters of this passage disagree about whether these events occurred during the thirteenth or the fifteenth century. It is Edmonson (1986, p. 61) who interprets a passage to mean that Tanxulukmul was the "cycle seat" of the Itzas of Petén, although K'atun 8 Ajaw would probably have been the end, not the beginning, of the cycle of thirteen k'atuns known as the *may* (1986, p. 9).

18. Schele, Grube, and Boot (1995, p. 10) also suggest that Chak'an Putun, mentioned frequently in the chronicles as place of both early settlement and periodic retreat of the Itzas, was actually Chak'an Peten, perhaps a miscopying of the latter name. Most scholars have associated Chak'an Putun with Champoton on the Gulf coast. Although the name Chak'an Peten appears nowhere in the documentation on the Itzas of Petén, the region around the northwestern shore of Lago Petén Itzá was known as Chak'an Itza ("Savannah of the Itza") during the late seventeenth century.

19. Ringle, Bey, and Peraza, 1991, p. 2.

20. Sharer, 1994, pp. 408–10. See also Roys, 1962. Ringle (1990) has identified the Kokom name glyph at Chich'en Itza.

21. Roys, 1957.

22. AGI, G 151B, no. 2, Declaración del reyezuelo Ah Canek, 31 March 1697, ff. 39v–45v; AGI, P 237, ramo 3, Gil to Hariza, 30 Oct. 1695. The second of these sources states only that his ancestors were from Yucatán, not from Chich'en Itza in particular.

23. AGI, G 151B, no. 2, Declaración de don Martín Chan, 10 March 1697, ff. 4r–11v (also in P 237, ramo 11).

24. AGI, EC 339B, no. 18, Declaración que hace el Capitán don Marcos de Abalos y Fuentes de lo que ha habido, hay, y puede haber en la Provincia del Itza, 10 March 1704, ff. 28r–60v. Abalos, who spent several months in Petén in 1699 as part of a Guatemalan military force, while confirming other statements by the Itzas that they are from Chich'en Itza, is the only source for the time and place of origin of the Kowoj migration. He wrote, "The Couohs are almost one and the same with the Itzas, because they are located in the region to the north of the shores of their lake. Both are descended from Yucatán, the Itzas from Chichen Itza and the Couohs from Tancab [*sic*], ten or twelve leagues from this city. These [the Couohs] retreated at the time of the conquest, the others much earlier."

The location of "Tancab" clearly refers to Mayapan, which is about fifty kilometers (about 12.4 leagues) south of Mérida. Tancab is apparently a copyist's error for "Tancah" (Tankaj), a name frequently applied as a description of Mayapan (Roys, 1967, pp. 84, 149, 153, 164, 167). Edmonson translates Tankaj as "capital" ("front town") (1982, p. 143).

25. The location of this place is unknown, and I have found no mention of it in other sources.

26. López de Cogolludo, 1971, vol. 2, bk. 9, ch. 14, pp. 256–57. See another translation of this passage in Roys, 1962, p. 67.

27. Roys, 1962, pp. 70, 72, 76, 78–81.

28. Roys, 1957, p. 127; 1962, p. 48. Saki, named for an "idol" located there, had a pyramidal temple that was still in use when the Spaniards arrived. A powerful war captain named NaKajun Noj ("Nacahun Noh") resided there, and the principal lord, or B'atab', of the town was named Tzuk (or possibly Tz'ul) Kupul. None of these names at Saki appears among the Itzas of Petén, but others in the region do, including B'atab' Kamal at Sisal and the regional ruler named Ob'on Kupul at Tik'uch (probably the same provincial ruler who resided at Chich'en Itza).

29. Ringle, 1990, p. 235; López de Cogolludo, 1971, vol. 2, bk. 9, ch. 12, p. 250.

30. López de Cogolludo, 1971, vol. 2, bk. 9, ch. 12, p. 250. K'awil Chel, a priest mentioned in the Book of Chilam B'alam of Chumayel, also bore this name as a surname or title (Roys, 1967, p. 165).

31. Roys, 1967, p. 69.

32. For a stimulating recent discussion of Maya prophetic history see Farriss, 1987.

33. For a more detailed discussion of Maya calendrics see Edmonson, 1986, pp. 7–14. We would create the same problem that the Mayas did in omitting the b'ak'tun if we were to drop the number that indicates where a century falls in relation to a fixed point in our own calendar. For example, reference to the "nineties" could refer to the ninth decade of any century past or present.

34. Edmonson (1986, p. 9) explains the coefficients as follows: "The period of the *katun* (7,200 days) divided by 13 gives 553 cycles of 13 and a remainder of 11. Thus the sequence of the coefficients of the Ahau days that ended (or, later [in colonial times], began) the *katun* followed the order 13, 11, 9, 7, 5, 3, 1, 12, 10, 8, 6, 4, 2." He refers to the initial date k'atun calendar as the Mayapan calendar, which was used in Yucatán from 1539 to 1776. The previous Tik'al calendar identified a k'atun by its ending date as opposed to its beginning date, and the Mayapan calendar included a two-day adjustment to accommodate this change. The last k'atun in the Tik'al calendar, K'atun 13 Ajaw, began in 1539.

Edmonson (1988, p. 56) regards the Mayapan calendar as the innovation of the Itzas of Yucatán, who may have invented it shortly after the fifteenth-century fall of Mayapan but did not formally inaugurate it until 1539. He is uncertain about the calendar used by the Itzas of Petén (p. 266). Given the close identification of the southern Itzas with Yucatán, however, it is reasonable to assume that they also used the Mayapan calendar.

431

35. Hofling (1993, p. 164) has demonstrated that patterns of "cyclicity in cosmology and discourse structure are systematically related in modern Itzaj Maya narrative."

36. These are only a few of many examples of statements concerning K'atun 8 Ajaw in the various chronicles. They are quoted from the translation by Roys, 1967, pp. 136–37, 140, 160.

37. In the original, Roys used angled brackets in place of square brackets in this translation.

38. Although the Kowojs and Itzas were clearly distinct political and territorial groups, I point out later that the former were allied with one Itza faction at the time of the 1697 conquest. I suspect that this was a late development and that in earlier years the two groups were in a chronic state of hostility, perhaps broken by periods of peace.

39. These events, described by Landa and others, are examined by Tozzer, with numerous references to original sources, in Landa, 1941, pp. 54–56. See also Roys, 1957, pp. 63–66; Roys, 1962, pp. 47–48. Edmonson, in particular, has stressed the historical importance of the east-west division of Yucatán between the Xiws and the Itzas and its implications for conflicts over calendrical matters. Whereas the Book of Chilam B'alam of Tisimin is written from an Itza perspective, that of Chumayel reflects Xiw sympathies and Mexican-influenced linguistic conventions (Edmonson, 1982, pp. xvii–xix; 1986, pp. 2–3).

40. López de Cogolludo, 1971, vol. 2, bk. 9, ch. 14, p. 259. *Ma' winik-o'ob'* would mean "not men/people."

41. Thompson, 1977, p. 13. *Tulum-kij* would be "trap of henequén" in modern Itzaj, and *tulum* refers specifically to a U-shaped fish trap made of stones.

42. López de Cogolludo, 1971, vol. 2, bk. 9, ch. 8, p. 223. Fray Andrés de Avendaño, who visited Nojpeten nearly eighty years later, included the "Tuluncies" as part of the Itza "nation," in his attempt to estimate the total population of the Lago Petén Itzá area (Avendaño, Relación, 1696, f. 42v; 1987, p. 47).

43. Thompson was surely incorrect in locating the Chinamitas southwest rather than east of Nojpeten, where Fuensalida placed them (Thompson, 1977, p. 13). Thompson was looking for an actual cordillera, as specified by Fuensalida. The friar, however, knew little about the geography of areas that he had not seen, and we need not accept this geographical feature as a reality.

44. AGI, P 237, ramo 1, Razón individual y general de los pueblos, poblaciones, y rancherias de esta provincia de Zuyuha Peten Itza, 6 Jan. 1698, ff. 80r–84v. The alternative spellings in brackets are from another copy of this document in AGI, G 345, no. 20, ff. 121v–29v. Villagutierre (1933; 1983, bk. 9, ch. 4) cited the same testimony but garbled most of the spellings. The name written as "Ahoacob" (that is, AjTz'akob') is presumably a mistranscription and should have been "Ahtzacob" (AjTzakob').

45. Ximénez, 1971–77, vol. 29, bk. 5, ch. 58, pp. 319–21. Cano also

mentioned all of these in addition to an individual named Tus B'en (1942, p. 66; see also Cano 1984, p. 9).

46. AAICFP, Santo Toribio, Baptismal Register, 1709–49. The patronyms at Santo Toribio that appear with the greatest frequency for the period 1709–30 are Musul (15.8 percent), Tzak (13.4 percent), Kischan (10.6 percent), Tesukun (9.7 percent), Yajkab' (5.2 percent), K'in (4.5 percent), and K'ixab'on (3.2 percent). Early nineteenth-century baptismal records for San Luis exist, but I have not yet studied them. Of the certain Mopan names identified in the Kan Ek' list of 1698 and the Santo Toribio baptismal registers, Ch'em ("Chen"), Tzak ("Tzak") and Tesukun ("Tesecum") were still found at San Luis in the late 1920s. Other names are either of K'ek'chi or Chol origin (Thompson, 1930, p. 85).

47. An interesting piece of archaeological evidence suggests that the name Mopan had ancient association with the San Luis area. Among the numerous Classic-period painted inscriptions in the cave of Naj Tunich, located northeast of San Luis and just west of the Guatemala-Belize border, is a glyph sequence which MacLeod and Stone read as "mo-o-pa-na" and interpret as the toponym "mo'-pan." Pana was a patronym used by Itzas and may have Mopan origins. See MacLeod and Stone, 1995, pp. 165, 169.

48. The following is the principal additional evidence for this reconstruction of Mopan territorial distribution:

In 1677 the Guatemalan Dominican Fray Joseph Delgado, accompanied by three Spaniards who had cacao and anatto cultivations on the Moho River, set out from Manche, near the town of Mopan, crossing southernmost Belize and working his way north and then back again through native settlements located inland from the coast all the way to the Belize River. Although Delgado noted that most of this area was inhabited by Chols, there were many Mopans as well. Within what is today the Toledo District, in the area roughly between the Moho River and present-day San Antonio, he identified people with the Mopan patronyms Yajkab', Tzak, K'in, and Chikuy. Another name, Tz'ununchan, was either Mopan or Itza. Several baptized town leaders along the rivers to the north also had the Mopan patronyms Yajkab' and Musul. The northernmost town, on the Belize River a day and a half from Tipuj, was headed by a Musul. From the Spaniards he knew of a town called Tisonte, which may have been around present-day Poptun, north of the town of Mopan (San Luis). The large population there was said to have moved from elsewhere to escape the Itzas; many more were hiding in the forests. See Thompson, 1970, pp. 22–29; the original documents, both in the Bibliothéque Nationale de Paris, are Memoria de los parajes y ríos que ay desde el pueblo de San Miguel Manche hasta los indios Ahizaes, el camino y indios, 1677; and Viaje de Bacalar, y encuentro de los de Bacalar, los nombres están en el derrotero que día a V.P.M.R., el de la canoa se llama Alonso Moreno, 1703 (?). For translated versions see Bunting, 1932, and D. Stone, 1932, pp. 259–69.

The Mopans who were known as Chinamitas or Tulumkis were said in 1698 to be located nine days by foot travel in an easterly direction from Nojpeten. Such a distance would be well into Belize, east or southeast of Tipuj (AGI, P 237, ramo 1, Razón individual y general de los pueblos, poblaciones, y rancherias de esta provincia de Zuyuha Peten Itza, 6 Jan. 1698).

Spaniards reduced a group of Musuls around Saksuus on the middle Belize River in 1695 and captured and reduced other Musuls around Tipuj the following year (AGI, P 237, ramo 10, Francisco de Hariza to Ursúa, 7 July 1695, ff. 568v–69v; G 151A, no. 3, Ursúa to Juan de Ortega Montañez, 10 May 1696, ff. 45r–47v). In 1697 the Musuls were said to inhabit the forests toward the Belize coast, east of Tipuj. In 1707 Musuls attacked Tipuj, killing several people. Those attackers who were captured by the Spaniards were probably taken to Santo Toribio, where Musul was a common name (AGI, EC 339B, no. 27, Ursúa to Crown, 24 Jan. 1708, ff. 12r–15r).

49. The name "Tziquin Tzakam" appears on a modern map adjacent to the Flores-Belize highway, where the road passes by a bend in the Río Mopan southeast of these lakes (Guatemala 1:50,000, 1973, Hoja 2367 III). The name is likely a corruption of Itzk'in Tzakwan, a double name comprising a Yucatec day name (also used by Mopans at Santo Toribio) and a common Mopan patronym. It may well be a modern survival of an earlier Mopan settlement at this location.

50. AGI, G 151A, no. 3, Bartolomé de Amésqueta to José de Escals, 31 March 1696, ff. 14r–40v. He claimed, in fact, that he had been told that "the Mopan language . . . is said to be the same as [that of] the Petenes [i.e., Itzas]" (*la lengua Mopan . . . se dice ser la misma de los Petenes*).

51. Cano, 1942, p. 66 (my translation); see also Cano 1984, p. 9.

52. When in 1695 Ursúa spoke of taking possession of "the said lands of the great Itza and Muzules," he must have been referring in like manner to Itza claims that their larger territory included that of the Mopans (AGI, G 151A, no. 4, Auto by Ursúa, 31 Dec. 1695).

53. Spaniards working along the camino real even called Pak'ek'em the "Town of the Chans," thus confirming the core status of this lineage. Thompson (1977) was so struck by the frequency of the name Chan (a Cholan variant of the Yucatec name Kan, "Serpent"), which is widely distributed from Kejach territory through the central lakes region all the way to Tipuj in western Belize, that he called this the "Chan Maya Region." Although this name was widely distributed among Yucatec speakers throughout Petén and western Belize, it certainly did not define a single, culturally unified region.

Chapter 2: Itza-Spanish Encounters, 1525–1690

1. Cortés, 1976, p. 241. The published accounts give "Taica," but surely "Taiça" was intended.

2. In his own account of this entrada Díaz del Castillo called the island town "Tayasal" (Díaz del Castillo, 1977, vol. 2, pp. 209–10).

3. Unless otherwise indicated, this summary of the background and first part of Cortés's journey is based on the account by Scholes and Roys (1968, pp. 88–122). The original accounts, which I later refer to in detail, are Cortés, 1976, and Díaz del Castillo, 1977, vol. 2, pp. 188–230.

4. Thomas, 1993, pp. 595–96.

5. Cortés, 1976, p. 222.

6. Ibid.

7. Doña Marina spoke Nahuatl and knew at least one Mayan language, presumably Chontal, which apparently served as the principal regional trade language. Tozzer believed that she spoke Chontal but cited Roys as suggesting, presumably on the basis of a statement by Landa, that she spoke Yucatec (Landa, 1941, p. 16 and 16n92). As Cortés's interpreter and mistress she had soon learned Spanish (Martínez, 1990, p. 162). The common language that made it possible for her to interpret at Nojpeten, therefore, may have been Chontal or, less likely, Yucatec.

8. *Pax-* was an honorific prefix in Chontal, like *aj-* in Yucatec and Itza. B'olon was clearly a surname, but the status of Acha is not certain; it was probably a surname.

9. Itzam K'anak was written "Ytzam Kanac" (with its full name rendered "Acalan Ytzam Kanac") in the merits and services of don Pablo PaxB'olon (AGI, M 138). See Scholes and Roys, 1968, following p. 366 (f. 71 of the Chontal text facsimile).

10. Ibid., p. 236. Scholes and Roys make this point on the basis of Cortés's claim that Chakujal on Río Polochic in northern Guatemala had the most impressive civic-ceremonial plaza that he had seen since leaving Akalan (ibid., p. 54; Cortés, 1976, p. 254). Itzam K'anak has been tentatively identified archaeologically as the site of El Tigre on the Candelaria River. For descriptions of this site, see Piña Chan and Pavón Abreu, 1959; Pincemin, 1987.

11. Scholes and Roys, 1968, p. 54.

12. During his stay at Itzam K'anak Cortés received rumors of a plot by the Mexica rulers who accompanied him to attack and kill him and the other Spaniards. Although those accused denied any such intent, Cortés executed Cuauhtemoc and Tetlepanquetzatzin on February 28, 1525, by hanging them; he released others implicated in the plot.

13. Díaz del Castillo (1977, vol. 2, p. 207) described the area as Los Mazatecas, which he translated as "towns or lands of deer." Kejach, the Yucatec name for the region, means much the same thing (from *kej*, deer, and *-ach*, a suffix that may indicate quantity).

14. Cortés (1976, p. 240) described the fortified town as having "only one unobstructed entrance, and it is completely surrounded by a deep ditch and after the ditch a chest-high wooden breastwork, and after this wooden breastwork an encirclement of very thick planks up to two *estados* [over 4 meters] tall, with embrasures [*troneras*] all along it from which to shoot their arrows, and at inter-

vals along the wall some tall watchtowers that extended above the wall another estado and a half, likewise with their towers with many stones on top in order to fight from above; and all of the houses of the town had their own embrasures on top and from the inside as well as embrasures and barriers facing the streets. I would say that the order and arrangement could not have been better, given the arms with which they fight." Díaz del Castillo wrote a similar description (1977, vol. 2, pp. 206–7).

15. Cortés, 1976, p. 240.

16. Díaz del Castillo, 1977, vol. 2, p. 207.

17. Cortés, 1976, p. 240.

18. Ibid., p. 241; Díaz del Castillo, 1977, vol. 2, p. 208.

19. Díaz del Castillo, 1977, p. 209. The Spanish original of the last portion of the text, which I have translated almost literally, reads, "y blanqueaban las casas y adoratorios de más de dos leguas que se esparcían y era cabecera de otros pueblos chicos que allí cerca están." In his biography of Díaz del Castillo, Cerwin (1963, p. 60) quotes part of the passage in exaggerated phraseology: " 'Its houses and lofty temples,' " said Bernal, " 'glistened in the sun and they could be seen two leagues away.' "

20. They had walked ten or twelve kilometers, first following the savannah above Ensenada San Jerónimo (the area of the wide road) and then crossing the karst hills that drop down to the arm of the lake (the narrow portion of the road). Although it would not have been necessary for them to walk through the marsh in order to reach dry shore, they apparently chose to do so in order to avoid giving themselves away before finding canoes.

21. Cortés, 1976, p. 241.

22. They would have had to cross around Punta Nijtún in these canoes and move up the arm of the lake to the shore near the Spanish encampment, which was probably between the present-day causeway that crosses the western end of the arm of the lake and the escarpment that begins to rise about one kilometer to the north. Cortés estimated that the encampment was "two good leagues" from Nojpeten; later on, Ajaw Kan Ek' told him that the distance was about three leagues.

23. Díaz del Castillo made no mention of the arrival of the Itza spy's canoe but instead recalled that Cortés sent the smaller of the canoes captured that night to Nojpeten with six of the newly captured Itza men and two Spaniards, who carried gifts for the ruler and instructions that he send additional canoes to the "river" so that the expedition could cross it. Díaz's account indicates that the next morning he and Cortés walked from their encampment to the shore of the "river," sending the remaining canoe the short distance from the estuary to join them. There they found the "cacique" and numerous other important individuals from Nojpeten waiting for them, bearing a gift of four fowls and maize. Díaz's account apparently telescopes events recorded in more detail by Cortés.

24. Cortés, 1976, p. 242. The phrase referring to defeat in three battles may well have been a rhetorical formula.

25. Ibid.

26. I have interpreted "certain red shell beads" (*ciertas cuentas de caracoles coloradas*) to have been necklaces of flat spondylus shells.

27. Díaz del Castillo wrote that Cortés took thirty crossbowmen with him (1977, vol. 2, pp. 209–10).

28. Ibid., p. 210.

29. The Franciscan historian López de Cogolludo recounted two versions of the legend. The first, whose source he did not cite but which was possibly one of two versions recorded by Bartolomé de Fuensalida, recounts that the horse soon died despite the Itzas' every effort to care for it. Fearing Cortés's anger, Ajaw Kan Ek' called his leaders together to determine what they should tell Cortés when he returned. They decided to make a replica of the horse out of wood in its memory, eventually worshiping it as one of their gods. By 1618, when the Franciscans Fuensalida and Orbita visited Nojpeten, it was the Itzas' principal "idol," occupying "the most preeminent place of the principal temple, above the rest of the abominable figures of idols that they worship" (*la parte mas preheminente del templo principal y superior á las demas abominables figuras de ídolos que adoraban*) (López de Cogolludo, 1971, vol. 1, bk. 1, ch. 16, pp. 59–60).

The second version, ostensibly based explicitly on Fuensalida's account, has it that because the Itzas thought that the horse was an "animal of reason" they fed it chicken and meat and presented it with bunches of flowers, as was customary in honoring important people. The horse died of hunger, and they decided to make a statue of it out of lime and stone in case Cortés returned to claim it. In 1618 the statue was in one of the twelve or more temples on the island, although the temple is not specified as being the most important one. The Itzas called it Tzimin Chak, "which means horse of thunder or lightning" (*caballo del trueno ó rayo*), the name signifying the Itzas' supposed belief that the noise and light created by the guns of Spaniards on horseback were actually caused by the horses (ibid., vol. 2, bk. 9, ch. 9, pp. 230–31).

Both versions enable the storyteller to emphasize the essential illogic in the reasoning power of the Itzas. For other interpretations of the horse legend see comments and citations in Martínez, 1990, pp. 438–40. I am also grateful to W. George Lovell for pointing out B. Traven's (1966) imaginative story about Cortés's entrada.

30. Hofling and Tesucún, 1992. Reports still circulate that the statue of the horse may be seen on the bottom of the lake but that all attempts to retrieve it end in failure (Soza 1970, pp. 395–96; see also Borhegyi, 1963). For other nineteenth- and twentieth-century citations of the legend see Villagutierre, 1983, pp. 401–2, n. 1312.

437

31. Díaz del Castillo, 1977, vol. 2, p. 210.

32. The sources offer no hint concerning these cultivations, which may have been cacao in addition to cotton.

33. Cortés (1976, p. 244) wrote "Amohan." Hofling (personal communica-

tion, 1996) has pointed out that this name in modern Itzaj would be Aj Mujan, "hawk." This may be the same name usually written "Moan" in the seventeenth century.

34. This was probably the place known in the late seventeenth century as Chakal, a short distance from the seventeenth-century Mopan mission community of Santo Toribio, which has survived as a town to the present day.

35. Díaz del Castillo, 1977, vol. 2, p. 211. Cortés, however, called this place "Tahuytal" (TajWital?), the same name he had given to an earlier place (Cortés, 1976, p. 245).

36. The name given by Cortés to this "province" was AjKukulin ("Acuculin"). Its "ruler" was AjKawil K'in ("Acahuilguin"). He may have confused a local town head (the former) with a provincial ruler (the latter). Although later observers noted that the Manche Chol–speaking populations to the north and northwest were dispersed, that may not have been the case in this region, which was apparently independent of Itza intrusions or colonization.

37. See Martínez, 1990, pp. 448–49.

38. The name Chetumal is probably a Spanish corruption of the original Maya name Chaktemal (see Roys, 1957, p. 159).

39. Jones, 1989, pp. 25–41.

40. Bacalar is a Spanish corruption of the original Maya name, which Roys suggested was B'ak'jalal, "Surrounded by Reeds" (1957, p. 159). "Multitude of Reeds" or "Four Hundred Reeds" (*bak'jalal*) might be alternative meanings. I use the Spanish spelling throughout, as it had become the name of a Spanish town.

41. Jones, 1989, pp. 41–53.

42. Graham, Jones, and Kautz, 1985; Jones, Kautz, and Graham, 1986; Graham, Pendergast, and Jones, 1989.

43. I developed this theme in some detail throughout a previous work (Jones, 1989).

44. Scholes and Roys, 1968, pp. 492–93. Their full account of these entradas (pp. 492–502), based on documentation in AGI, is far more detailed than the summary given here. I have omitted secondary quotation marks when quoting from original documents reproduced in this source.

45. Ibid., pp. 494–95. Although Scholes and Roys estimated that they were near Itza territory, the principal widening of Río San Pedro Mártir — probably the "bay" described in the accounts — is far to the northwest of Lago Petén Itzá, upstream from the archaeological sites of El Naranjo and Maktum. This point is about ninety airline kilometers from Nojpeten, a journey of several days. On the other hand, a Maya informant, Pedro Uk, reported that the expedition had reached within a day of Nojpeten. He may have been referring to advance parties sent out by Bravo, not to the main expedition.

46. Ibid., p. 493.

47. Ibid., p. 496.

48. Ibid., p. 497.

49. AGI, M 2999, libro D3, Reales cédulas to Nuño de Cháves Figueroa, alcalde mayor of Tabasco; Luis de Velasco, viceroy of New Spain; and president and oidores of the Audiencia of Guatemala, 22 June 1592.

50. Scholes and Roys, 1968, pp. 251–98; Jones, 1989, pp. 128–31.

51. The circumstances of Orbita's first visit to Nojpeten are discussed in more detail in Jones, 1989, pp. 133–34. See also Bricker, 1981, p. 21; López de Cogolludo, 1971, vol. 2, bk. 9, ch. 2, p. 192; Villagutierre, 1933, 1983, bk. 2, ch. 1; Lizana, 1893, p. 115.

52. López de Cogolludo, 1971, vol. 2, bk. 9, ch. 8, p. 224.

53. The 1618 journey to Nojpeten by Fuensalida and Orbita is described in detail in Jones, 1989, pp. 135–49. The principal source is López de Cogolludo, 1971, vol. 2, bk. 9, chs. 6–11, pp. 212–238. López de Cogolludo based his account on an original copy of Fuensalida's account, now lost. A recently published manuscript presents a rather different account of both the 1618 and 1619 missions of Fuensalida and Orbita, also said to be based on Fuensalida's original account (San Buenaventura, 1994, pp. 107–33). The authenticity of the manuscript is highly suspect, and I have declined to rely on any part of it as a source of information. For a recently published debate on this topic see Prem et al., 1996, and Solís Robledo, 1996.

54. The composition of Tipuj's early sixteenth-century population is uncertain, but I suspect that it may have been predominantly Mopan.

55. I suspect that Chaltunja was part of a string of settlements at the eastern end of the main lake in the vicinity of the archaeological site of Ixlu, one of which was Saklemakal. There are more specific references to this region in subsequent chapters.

56. López de Cogolludo, 1971, vol. 2, bk. 9, ch. 9, p. 230.

57. Ibid., p. 231. The original meaning of *tzimin* was tapir, an animal native to the region.

58. This is one of several instances in which a patrilineal principal of succession is cited for inheritance of Itza rulership.

59. López de Cogolludo, 1971, vol. 2, bk. 9, ch. 10, p. 235. Fuensalida's claim that the present ruler was the son of the ruler whom Cortés met in 1525 is plausible. We do not know the ages of either ruler in either 1525 or 1618, but the difference of 93 years between these two dates would not make such a relationship a biological impossibility.

60. Ibid., ch. 13, p. 252.

61. Ibid., pp. 253–55.

62. This section is a summary of a much longer account of these events in Jones, 1989, pp. 155–87, 313–19. The principal sources include AGI, M 141, Documentos respectivos al servicio que prometió hacer a S.M. el Capn. Francisco Mirones y Lezcano, 1622 (transcribed in Scholes and Adams, 1936–37, pp. 160–73; translated in Scholes and Adams, 1991, pp. 18–29), and López de Cogolludo, 1971, vol. 2, bk. 10, chs. 2–3.

439

63. Ximénez, 1929–31, vol. 2, bk. 4, ch. 5, p. 24. See also León Pinelo, 1960, p. 262; 1986, p. 8.

64. Ximénez, 1929–31, vol. 2, bk. 4, ch. 68, p. 210.

65. Except where indicated, this section is based primarily on the introductory summary in Scholes and Adams, 1960, pp. 7–19.

66. Tovilla, 1960, p. 179.

67. Ibid.

68. Ibid., pp. 181, 185.

69. León Pinelo, 1960, p. 265; 1986, pp. 10–11.

70. Tovilla, 1960, pp. 178, 185.

71. Ibid., p. 185. Scholes and Adams, who edited Tovilla's lengthy account of the history of Verapaz, doubted the entire veracity of the supposed Itza planned attack and the discovery of the items they left behind. In particular, they doubted that the Itzas would have carried so many idols and ritual paraphernalia into battle; other evidence exists, however, that the Itzas did carry such items in times of war (López de Cogolludo, 1971, vol. 2, bk. 9, ch. 14, pp. 258–59).

72. Tovilla, 1960, pp. 226–27.

73. Ibid., pp. 233–35.

74. Ibid.

75. Ximénez, 1929–31, vol. 2, bk. 4, ch. 68, pp. 210–11. See also Tovilla, 1960, p. 267; 1986, pp. 11–12.

76. Ximénez, 1929–31, vol. 2, bk. 4, ch. 70, p. 222.

77. AGI, M 360, Luís Sánchez de Aguilar et al. to governor, 20 Sept. 1638.

78. Cárdenas Valencia, 1937, p. 97.

79. López de Cogolludo 1971, vol. 2, bk. 11, ch. 12, p. 500.

80. Graham, Pendergast, and Jones, 1989. On syncretism at Tipuj see also Graham, 1991.

81. AGI, M 369, Bishop of Yucatán to Crown, 5 March 1643.

82. Although commonly written Lamanay in the colonial documentation, the archaeological site is known today as Lamanai.

83. López de Cogolludo, 1971, vol. 2, bk. 11, ch. 13, p. 507.

84. Ibid., ch. 14, pp. 514–15.

85. Ibid., bk. 12, ch. 12, p. 635; AGI, M 158, Méritos y servicios del Capitán Francisco Pérez, 1661.

86. The Chunuk'um matrícula is discussed in Jones, 1989, pp. 233–39, and, with a full transcription, in Scholes and Thompson, 1977.

87. Jones, 1989, p. 237.

88. Why the three married Itza couples brought with them a group of twenty-three presumably unmarried Itza women is not clear but may have signified a form of sexual hospitality toward the visiting Spaniards. Cortés wrote that when he was in Tabasco on his way to Mexico he was presented with twenty-one women, including doña María (Cortés, 1976, p. 242). A similar practice appeared on the eve of the 1697 conquest of Petén, discussed in chapter 11.

89. Jones, 1989, pp. 246–47.

90. Patch, 1993, p. 47.

91. Avendaño, 1987, p. 54; Relación, 1696, f. 49v.

92. AGI, P 237, ramo 1, Razón individual y general de los pueblos, poblaciones, y rancherías de esta provincia de Zuyuha Peten Itza, 6 Jan. 1698, ff. 80r–84v.

93. AGI, G 151B, no. 2, Declaración de don Martín Chan, 10 March 1697, ff. 4r–11v.

94. Ibid.

95. The patronym Chan does not appear on the list of Itza elites in the 1655 Chunuk'um matrícula, but several Chans appear among the Christianized Tipujans.

96. Villagutierre (1983, p. 129, n. 129) states that Ximénez "insisted that no one remembered anything like this happening," but he provides no location in Ximénez for this statement, nor have I found it.

97. Scholes and Roys, 1968, pp. 25–26, 445–46. The town still appears on modern maps as Canizan.

98. AGI, G 151A, no. 1, Ursúa to Gabriel de Sánchez de Berrospe, 25 Aug. 1698, ff. 11r–20v.

99. AGI, G 151A, no. 5, Testimony of Alférez Blas Felipe de Ripalda Ongay, 2 July 1697, ff. 35–50.

100. AGI, EC 339B, no. 18, Declaración que hace el Capitán don Marcos de Abalos y Fuentes . . . , 10 March 1704, f. 52r.

101. For Itza attacks on Mopan see AGI, P 237, ramo 1, Razón individual y general de los pueblos, poblaciones, y rancherías de esta provincia de Zuyuha Peten Itza, 6 Jan. 1698, ff. 80r–84v.

Chapter 3: Itza Society and Kingship on the Eve of Conquest

1. The literature on Maya and other Mesoamerican quadripartite cosmology, some of it concerning political organization and architectural patterns, is extensive. Some treatments of various aspects of this complex topic may be found in Ashmore, 1989; Bey and Ringle, 1989; Coe, 1965; Coggins, 1980; Freidel, Schele, and Parker, 1995; Gossen, 1974; Marcus, 1973, 1976; and Schele and Freidel, 1990.

2. Although I cannot deal with such comparisons in detail here, it should be pointed out that each of these quadruple and dual structures (as well as a triple one, in the case of the three ruling brothers to be noted shortly) are found elsewhere throughout Mesoamerica, most notably at Tenochtitlan, the Aztec capital. Tenochtitlan was also divided into cardinally oriented quarters, each divided by north-south and east-west canals (Zantwijk, 1985, pp. 59–81). Dual rulership and the existence of senior-junior pairs were also characteristics of Aztec political organization (ibid., pp. 22, 94–95, 142–45, 177, 222–23). The similarities be-

441

tween Itza and Aztec social organization are striking, and further research on these commonalities is in progress. See Gillespie, 1989, for an extended discussion of such structural elements in Aztec political and social organization.

The ethnohistorical model presented in this chapter, as well as material presented in chapter 1, differs in significant ways from that summarized in Rice, Rice, and Jones, 1993. These differences stem from extensive additional documentary analysis and from frequent communication with the Rices regarding both the results of the first two seasons of fieldwork by Proyecto Maya Colonial and my own ongoing ethnohistorical work.

3. The Spanish term for "town" was ordinarily *pueblo*. Hofling (personal communication, 1996) has pointed out that these three types in modern Itzaj would be *noj-kaj* ("big town"), *kaj* ("town"), and *kajital* ("village, settlement, rancho"), with the third type often occupied seasonally.

4. Spanish estimates of the populations of specific towns (not including militarily "reduced" communities) are rare. The only ones I have found are the following. In 1697 a secular priest from Yucatán testified that by his own estimate one of the twelve Kowoj towns on the shores of Lago Petén Itzá had as many as one thousand persons of all ages (AGI, G 151A, no. 3, Declaration by Juan Pacheco de Sopuerta, 14 June 1697, ff. 402v–406r). I believe that he was referring to Ketz. In testimony taken in 1699, Spanish observers estimated that the population of Chacha, an Itza town two or three leagues southwest of Nojpeten, was two hundred persons, supported by a rural population of one thousand more, based on observations of hamlets and cultivations (AGI, G 151A, no. 1, Parecer of Fray Diego de Rivas, 14 April 1699, ff. 81v–84r; Parecer of Esteban de Medrano y Solorzano, 11 April 1699, ff. 86r–88r). On the same occasion, a Dominican friar estimated the population of the town of Sakpuy, which apparently occupied the two islands in the western end of Laguna Sakpuy and probably the western shoreline as well, at four hundred persons between the ages of twelve and twenty-five. These were apparently all males, because the figure did not include "eight or ten Indian women" and other women, children, and older people who were apparently in hiding elsewhere. Therefore, the total population of Sakpuy must have been at least twice that which he actually saw (Parecer of Fr. Gabriel de Artiga, 10 April 1699, ff. 84r–85v).

5. Although the Itzas identified their towns with their core elite lineages, we can be certain that other lineages also lived in them.

6. Spanish sources do not provide a Maya term for this council.

7. AGI, G 151A, no. 1, Marcos de Abalos y Fuentes to Martín de Ursúa and Melchor de Mencos, 27 March 1699, f. 63r–v; G 151A, no. 5, Testimony of Capitán Diego de Avila Pacheco, 1 July 1697, ff. 23–35.

8. *Bata* and *bataa* in the original: Ximénez, 1929–31, 1971–77, bk. 5, ch. 65. This reading is not absolutely certain.

9. The Itzaj equivalents would be *chal-tun-ja'* ("white-earth water"), *chi'*

noj-ha' ("shore of the big water"), and *peten-ja'* ("island-lake"); *nab'a'* ("incense tree, balsam"), *nek' noj-che'* ("seed of great tree"), *säk-le'-mäkäl* ("white-leaf cassava"), and *ti'-puj* ("at reeds"); *pol ayim* ("head of alligator/crocodile"), *tz'unu'un-witz* ("hummingbird hill"), and *job'on-mo'* ("hollow macaw"); and *b'alam-tun* ("jaguar stone"), *ich tun* ("among stones"), and *ajLa'-la'-'ich* ("old-old face").

10. Much less is known about the composition of and relationships between towns and hamlets than might be desired. Following the conquest of 1697 the native population soon abandoned most of their towns, in many cases moving some distance away from them to live nearer their cultivations. This meant that Spanish observers, who first began to explore the interior countryside intensively in 1699, in most cases saw only the overgrown ruins of towns and evidence of hamlets in the form of cultivations and scattered homesteads. The most notable exception to this pattern was the exploration by Ursúa and others of the Kowoj-occupied northern shoreline of Lago Petén Itzá only a few weeks after the conquest, when they saw twelve thriving "towns" there (see chapter 14).

11. Avendaño (1987, p. 54; Relación, f. 49v) described Yalain as an agricultural town occupied by people from Nojpeten who went there to cultivate their plots. It is more likely that people in this area were permanent residents who cultivated foodstuffs for consumption by elites at the capital.

12. Sánchez Polo et al., 1995, pp. 712–13.

13. Ibid., pp. 711–12.

14. For Kulut Kowoj at both Ketz and the Saklemakal area see AGI, P 237, ramo 1, Razón individual y general de los pueblos, poblaciones, y rancherías de esta provincia de Zuyuha Peten Itza, 6 Jan. 1698, ff. 80r–84v; G 151A, no. 1, Orden al don Juan Guerrero por Martín de Ursúa y Melchor de Mencos, 2 April 1699, f. 65r–v. For Captain Kowoj at Ketz (unspecified, but apparent by context) see G 151A, no. 5, Testimonies of Capitán José Laines and Capitán Nicolás de la Aya, 6 July 1697, ff. 75–99. There was another town called Saklemakal in the Chak'an Itza region.

15. The archaeological site of Chachaklun, surveyed in 1994, is situated on flatter land above the hills along the northern shore of the lake. Larger and more densely settled than sites surveyed adjacent to the shore, it displays probable Postclassic architecture and may have been occupied in historic times (Sánchez Polo et al., 1995, pp. 712–13).

16. One set of testimonies taken in Petén in 1699 contains numerous statements referring to extensive populations west, southwest, and east of the main lake (AGI, G 151A, no. 1, Auto, questionnaire, and pareceres on Petén Itza region, 4 April to 3 May 1699, ff. 78r–98r).

17. Avendaño, 1987, pp. 47–48; Relación, f. 42v.

18. Lutz, 1994, Table 2, p. 67. A conversion factor of about 4.0 persons per *tributario entero,* applied here, is a conservative one. I have not located population figures for Ciudad Vieja (Almolonga) during this period.

443

19. Lutz, 1994, p. 264, n. 49 (for San Pedro de las Huertas, also known as San Pedro del Tesorero [p. 38]); p. 77 (for San Juan del Obispo, based on age pyramid).

20. Petén did not again enjoy such a large population until the late nineteenth century. It rose from 25,207 in 1869 to 64,129 in 1879 (Schwartz, 1990, p. 11, Table 1:1). This late rapid growth may have been the outcome of migrations resulting from the Caste War of Yucatán.

21. AGI, EC 339A, Memoria on Petén Itzá by Fr. Diego de Rivas, 26 May 1702, ff. 31r–33v.

22. See Ringle and Bey, 1992.

23. Díaz del Castillo, 1977, p. 209.

24. AGI, G 505, Auto by Bartolomé de Amésqueta, with attached declarations, 27 March 1696.

25. López de Cogolludo, 1971, bk. 9, ch. 9, p. 228.

26. Avendaño drew attention to world tree symbolism in his description of images that he called Yaxcheel Kab' and AjKokaj Mut, which were merged in a basal platform and column situated directly in front of the center of the house of Ajaw Kan Ek', looking out directly across the short open distance to the western shore (Avendaño, Relación, 1696, f. 29r–v; see also Avendaño 1987, p. 32). The column, if Avendaño was correct, was the symbol of a tree with a mask depicting the supernatural lord, the "first son," also called AjKokaj Mut. The latter may be related to the "idol" of sixteenth-century Yucatán known as Yax Kokaj Mut, to whom, according to Landa (1941, p. 145), priests made offerings and sacrifices during the Wayeb' ceremonies for Muluk years.

27. Avendaño, 1987, p. 34; Relación, f. 29v. The 1987 translation is incorrect in translating "media cuadra," or half a block (Relación, f. 29r), as "half a quarter of a league" (1987, p. 32).

28. Avendaño, 1987, p. 34; Relación, f. 29v.

29. See also Rice, 1986.

30. López de Cogolludo, 1971, vol. 2, bk. 9, ch. 9, p. 230.

31. López de Cogolludo, 1971, bk. 9, ch. 9, p. 229.

32. López de Cogolludo, 1971, bk. 9, ch. 9, p. 230.

33. Nojpeten had been burned in an attack by the Kowojs just before Avendaño's January 1696 visit.

34. That is, they were 1.5 varas in both height and thickness—about 1.25 meters.

35. Avendaño y Loyola, 1987, p. 34; Relación, f. 30r. My rather loose translation of this difficult passage differs considerably from that in the 1987 translation.

36. AGI, P 237, ramo 1, Testimonies of Fr. Andrés de Avendaño and two other religious who visited the Peten of the Itzas, May 1696, ff. 24r–41v. This recorded oral testimony suggests that the bench was attached to the center of the wall rather than standing freely. This is probably an error of interpretation.

37. Such structures were presumably of the type known as "open halls" by archaeologists. See, for example, Proskouriakoff, 1962, and Rice, 1986.

38. AGI, G 151B, no. 2, Certificación de los cabos y oficiales de guerra, 14 March 1697, ff. 30r–35v. Ursúa's first report of the conquest to the king simply summarized the officers' report, noting that there were twenty-one temples in all (AGI, P 237, ramo 11, Ursúa to Real Acuerdo, Guatemala, 22 March 1697, ff. 629r–635v). AjChan, on the other hand, specified that there were fifteen "places of idolatry" on the island, each of which was "a house or a large church" (AGI, G 151B, no. 2, Declaración de don Martín Chan, 10 March 1697, ff. 4r–11v).

39. Villagutierre, 1933, bk. 8, ch. 13, p. 386, my translation. For a slightly different translation and interesting notations see Villagutierre, 1983, pp. 313–14.

40. For an interpretation of the *pretil* as a parapet, see Villagutierre, 1983, bk. 8, ch. 13, p. 313, n. 1130. *Pretil* is an architectural term with several specific meanings, including a masonry pedestrian railing of the type found on bridges or along riverbanks, a battlement or breastwork, a stone bench, and a parapet (but one in which the stone wall, the actual *pretil*, protects people from falling).

41. Avendaño, Relación, 1696, f. 49v; 1987, p. 54.

42. The "given" names have a wide variety of meanings but are easily distinguished from the day names, which are virtually identical to the Yucatecan names for the twenty named days in the 260-day calendar cycle known as the *tzol k'in* (order of the day/sun). We can presume that every child was named for the day on which he or she was born. With a repertoire of only twenty days, however, only an additional name would ensure unique identification. In many cases a person was identified by only two names — in any combination, but almost never omitting the patronym. I have found no recorded case of an individual's complete set of four names. The use of three names was common — sufficient, presumably to distinguish any individual from another, especially if the individual bore a title.

43. Itza "given names" are probably equivalent to what Roys (1940, pp. 38–39, 45–46) labeled as "boy names" in Yucatán, although it is difficult to distinguish such names from possible matronyms. The Chunuk'um matrícula confirms his belief that females also bore such names. Xok may be from IxOk, which would signify a day name.

44. Fox and Justeson, 1986, provide one of the best recent overviews of the hieroglyphic evidence (focusing on Piedras Negras) for Classic Maya dynastic kinship alliance and succession. While recognizing alternative interpretations, they hypothesize "that royal succession was founded upon regularly maintained dynastic alliances: that systematic matrilateral parallel-cousin and/or patrilateral cross-cousin marriage joined ruling families, with a ruler's son-in-law the heir to his throne and his fraternal nephew the heir at a politically affiliated site; and that at the core of these alliances was a single royal matriline whose husbands ruled" (p. 7). That is, they argue that the rulers were the husbands of a descent line of women who belonged to a core matrilineage.

In their review of the Postclassic and colonial evidence, Fox and Justeson

445

recognize that father-son and brother-brother succession was the usual pattern in the Maya lowlands. They see some evidence, however, indicating the practice of matrilineal as well as patrilineal descent (p. 27). Schele and Freidel also read a number of hieroglyphic texts from both Classic and Postclassic Maya centers as indicating the possible importance of matrilineal principles, notwithstanding evidence for patrilineal succession as well (1990, pp. 270–71, 360–63, 366, 502). Philip Thompson (1978, n.d.) has offered an intriguing analysis of both kinship terms and succession to office in an eighteenth-century town in Yucatán that strongly suggests the presence of both matrilineal and patrilineal succession principles even at that late date.

The literature on this complex topic is highly technical and sometimes dependent on incomplete and insufficient data. Among others who favor a double descent model are Coe (1965, p. 104) and Joyce (1981). Marcus (1983, p. 470) has suggested bilateral descent among Maya elites, distinguishing them from a generally patrilineal population. Haviland (1972, 1977) and Hopkins (1988) argue against a matrilineal or double descent model. For a brief review of the topic see Sharer, 1993, pp. 99–100.

45. Documentation for marriage avoidance between individuals with the same patronym is found most clearly in the mid- and late-seventeenth-century marriage registers of San Andrés and San José, as well as in the early-seventeenth-century baptismal registers of Santo Toribio, which represent a dominantly Mopan population with a smaller number of Itzas and Kowojs. For San Andrés and San José see AAICFP, San Andrés, Libro de matrimonios, años 1751–1808 (Genealogical Society of Utah, Salt Lake City, Microfilm roll 1220087). For Santo Toribio see AAICFP, Santo Toribio, Baptismal Register, 1709–49 (not microfilmed, original consulted).

46. López de Cogolludo, 1971, vol. 2, bk. 9, ch. 14, pp. 257–58.

47. Avendaño, Relación, 1696, passim. The English translation of this work (Avendaño, 1987) transcribes the royal name as "Canek," although examination of a photocopy of the original document shows that Avendaño or his copyist clearly separated the two names, giving Ek a capital *E*.

48. Landa, 1973, pp. 41–42. My quite literal translation differs slightly from those of Roys (1972, p. 37) and Tozzer (Landa, 1941, pp. 97–98).

49. By labeling the father's *apellido* or patronymic surname the "proper" name, Landa apparently meant that it was the individual's principal or most important name. By calling the mother's name "appellative" he was using a specific sense of the term *nombre apelativo* as a *sobrenombre*, a "name which is sometimes added to the apellido [i.e., the surname inherited from the father] in order to distinguish two persons who have the same one." Here I have relied on the definitions in *Diccionario de la lengua castellana*, 1914, pp. 716, 946 (the quotation). These are more complete than in some later editions..

50. Roys, 1972, pp. 37–38.

51. Ibid., p. 38. Only one early colonial dictionary, the so-called Motul II,

specifies that *tz'akab'* means "direct succession from the mother's side, descending in lineage" (*generación por vía recta de parte de la madre, descendiente en linaje*). Omitting this detail, Motul I offers the definition "abolorio, casta, linaje o generación" — all of which refer to descent, lineage, and/or inheritance, understood in Spanish culture as patrimonial in nature. The Motul I entry for *ts'akab'* includes five Maya-language sentence examples with Spanish translations, each glossing the term as *casta*, which bears the additional connotation of multigenerational "purity" of descent. Each of four of these sentences offers one example of what could be passed on to individuals through the ts'akab', namely, having the office of B'atab' (translated as "cacique"), exhibiting evil qualities, being an "idolater," or being a priest. Motul I's Maya consultant, that is, made it clear that it was through the ts'akab' — a matrilineal descent group according to Motul II — that titles of nobility, sacred cult identifications, priestly offices, and even personal qualities could be passed on to successive generations (see Barrera Vásquez et al., 1980, for such entries).

Several early colonial dictionary definitions of *ch'ib'al* specify that the term referred to descent in the male line. They use the same and similar terms (*casta, linaje, genealogía,* and *abolorio* — as well as *nación*) applied to tz'akab'. Whereas, however, Motul I's sentence examples for tz'akab' specify that an individual received specific qualities or positions through membership in such a kinship group, the dictionary's examples for *ch'ib'al* place emphasis on the characteristics of the group. According to these examples, one "comes" from a *ch'ib'al* of caciques (B'atab', B'atab'il), "principales" (*almehenil*), wise people, or thieves. From this distinction it appears that while *inheritance* of a high-ranking position was effected through matrilineal descent in a tz'akab', individuals who inherited such positions matrilineally also belonged to a patrilineal ch'ib'al.

Such a principal of double descent may be expressed by the colonial Yucatec term for a person of noble, high-ranking political status: *al-mejen,* in which *al-* refers to the child of a woman and *mejen* refers to the child of a man. An al-mejen, according to Motul I, was at the same time a child "respecto de padre y madre" (with reference to father and mother) and an "hidalgo, noble, caballero ilustre por linaje y el señor o principal del pueblo así" (a person of noble birth, a noble, an illustrious gentleman by lineage and therefore the lord or highest-ranking person of the town) (Barrera Vásquez et al., 1980, p. 14). Other dictionaries extend *almehen* to mean all men and women of noble ancestry — people of *buena casta,* or "good descent."

The Itzás presumably used the term *almehen* in this way, although only *mejen* is recorded in the Spanish documents. The title Ajaw Mejen (king, son of the father) was applied to the successor of Ajaw Kan Ek' in about 1700, confirming **447** patrilineal inheritance of the kingship. The ruling Itzá dynasty, however, reproduced itself through descent in both the Kan matrilineage and the Ek' patrilineage; only successive marriages between the "principles" of female descent and male descent could ensure the continued identity of kings.

52. Roys, 1972, p. 37.

53. The *naal* names compiled by Roys from colonial sources, with the number of occurrences of each name in parentheses, are B'atun (13), B'ich (1), Chan (39), Chi (8), Itza (1), Jaw (29), Kab' (2), Kajum (1), Kajun (4), Kamal (4), Kan (7), Kowoj (3), K'uk' (1), May (10), Mo (5), Ob'on (1), Pol (1), Pot (8), Puk (24), P'ol (1), Tz'ay (1), Tz'imab'un (1), Tz'ul (5), and Um or Un (10) (Roys 1940, pp. 44–45). An apparent *naal* name, Tzin (also an Itza name), is also found in Roys's list of "unclassified" names (from Na-Tzin Yab'un Chan, in which the significance of the middle name is unclear). Of these, only B'ich, Ob'on (from NaOb'on Kupul, the sixteenth-century ruler of Chich'en Itza), and Tz'imab'un do not appear on his list of patronyms (pp. 42–44).

54. *Kan* is "serpent," the principal meaning of the name. *Kän* means "four," and *kaan* means "sky" or "heaven," allowing for punning on the name. *Ek'* is "star." *Eek'* is "black" or "dark" and, in colonial dictionaries, a "secular priest," the markings on animal pelts, and fat produced by cooking. In addition, it is the Yucatec name of the logwood or dyewood tree (*Haematoxylon campechianum*), which grew plentifully in lowland coastal regions (see Roys, 1931, p. 240).

55. When Chan does appear as the first name in double names, as in the case of IxChan Pana, the wife of Ajaw Kan Ek', it was likely a matronym.

56. AAICFP, San Andrés, Libro de matrimonios, años 1751–1808 (Genealogical Society of Utah, Salt Lake City, Microfilm roll 1220087).

57. Avendaño may have been referring to such naming practices when he wrote the following concerning the Ajaw's name: "This reign comes to him by inheritance, so their kings are always Ah Can Eks. But this does not mean that all Can Eks are of royal blood or relatives, because all people from his town or district are called Can Eks, and this does not mean that they are his relatives, since besides and in addition they also have their own legitimate surnames [*apellidos*] and have that one [i.e., Can Ek] because of the head person who rules them" (Relación, 1696, f. 38v; see also Avendaño, 1987, p. 44). Later in his account Avendaño wrote that at Yalain there were "many Indians called Can Eks like the king of the peten, but they are not his relatives but rather natives of his district who (as I have said) take the names of those who govern said districts, although they might have, as they have, their own surnames from father and mother, each one" (f. 49v; see also 1987, p. 54).

If Avendaño was correct, this means that at least some of the surnames recorded by Spaniards, including those that appear in the eighteenth-century church marriage registers (such as Kanchan, Kanek' Kante, K'ixabon, and perhaps Kowoj), were taken from governing nobility and not from parents. Some individuals in the San Andrés and San José marriage register appear, in fact, to have assumed the titles as well as the names of governing rulers, including Chan Eb' ("Chaneb'"), Kan Yokte ("Kanyokte"), K'in Yokte ("Kinyocte"), and Noj K'ute ("Nokute") (see Table 1.1). All such names were treated as patronyms in the marriage registers, suggesting that patrilineages may have been defined by association with a particular local branch of the nobility as well as by descent in a local male line.

58. The name Kan Chan appears in three western Itza towns. See AGI, EC 339A, Memoria on Peten Itza by Fr. Diego de Rivas, 26 May 1702, ff. 31r–33v.

59. See Table 3.1 for Kawil Itza. For Kab'an Kawil see Ximénez, 1971–77, vol. 29, bk. 5, ch. 65, p. 358.

60. Both instances of the name are spelled with *c* in original, not *k*.

61. AGI, EC 339B, no. 28, José de Aguilar Galeano to Toribio de Cosio, president of Guatemala, 30 April 1709, ff. 6r–16v. Sororal polygyny among captured leaders is described in AGI, EC 339A, Informe del Aguilar Galeano, to president of Guatemala, 28 March 1704 (see chapter 15).

62. AGI, G 151A, no. 1, Cristóbal de Mendía y Sologastoa to Martín de Ursúa and Melchor de Mencos, 1 April 1699, ff. 65v–67r.

63. The form that such large households might have taken is nowhere described in the documents. However, considering the importance that I believe the elite Itzas placed upon maternal kinship principles, it would not be surprising to find elite households in which maternal kin lived together. Their households may have been similar to those of the Chontal Mayas of the Tabasco reduction town of Tixchel, for which a household-by-household census was recorded in 1569 (Scholes and Roys, 1968, pp. 470–90). This census suggests "a strong tendency toward matrilocal residence," indicated by a high percentage of daughters of the household head couple who had brought their husbands to live with them. In addition, households often had other men related by marriage to the male household head, as well as his nephews (ibid., pp. 474–75) — all patterns that could point toward matrilineal descent or, more likely, a dual descent system similar to that which I describe in this chapter for the Itzas.

64. One man was well equipped to have reached such an understanding: the Mercederian Fray Diego de Rivas, who spent considerable time at Nojpeten following the conquest and who interviewed Ajaw Kan Ek' and his son in Santiago de Guatemala in 1702. By then he was tired and infirm, and it may be that he left only his one known record of an interview with the ruler.

65. Marcus, 1993, p. 115.

66. Ibid., pp. 133–37. Marcus's model relies heavily on Roys's conceptualization of three types of polities in northern Yucatán at the time of conquest (pp. 118–21; see Roys, 1965a, p. 669). The first, ruled by a single individual (an Ajaw or Jalach Winik) who hereditarily controlled subservient elites bearing the title B'atab', was the most hierarchical. In the second type, a group of related individuals with the title B'atab' shared power and authority over towns within a territory, without a central ruler. The third type had little political cohesion and was **449** found along the fringes of more stratified political provinces. Marcus argues, however, that these were not "types" per se but rather evidence of the several levels of hierarchical cohesion and dissolution that characterized the dynamic histories of Yucatec Maya polities (p. 121). I believe that this assessment is fundamentally

correct, although there may have been other historical processes that also contributed to such variation.

67. Marcus, 1983, p. 125.

68. Ringle and Bey, in their excellent discussion of segmentary states (1992), conclude that such pyramidal, hierarchical societies, while ideologically oriented around a king and a central capital with such cosmic associations as divine rule and the city as *axis mundi,* are beset by administrative weaknesses that can lead to the hiving off of segments as a result of political conflicts (p. 3). I am not arguing that the Itzas, who fit most of the characteristics of a segmentary state, did not experience such difficulties but rather that their rulers seem for a time to have dealt successfully with the problem through policies of expansionary conquest (see also Fox, 1987, 1989).

69. Fray Agustín Cano supplied the name Yajkab' (Cano, 1984, pp. 9–10).

70. That is, *kaj jol* ("town of the port"), *ma'-kooch' eb'* ("not-wide stairway"), and *noj-peten* ("big district [or island]"). The 1929–31 edition of Ximénez's *Historia* records the names of the four wards as Canc, Cohoh, Macacheb, and Nojpeten, while the usually more dependable 1971–77 edition lists them as Canc, Cahoh, Macucheb, and No peten (Ximénez, 1929–31, bk. 5, ch. 65, vol. 3, p. 55; 1971–77, vol. 29, bk. 5, ch. 65, p. 356). My readings of Cohoh/Cahoh and Macacheb/Macucheb are highly tentative, but it may be significant that there was a town identified elsewhere as Jolka, probably *jol-kaj,* "town of the port" (see Table 3.1).

71. Avendaño, Relación, 1696, f. 38r; 1987, p. 43.

72. Avendaño, Relación, 1696, f. 38r–v; 1987, p. 43.

73. Both *tz'akan* and *tz'akab',* the term for mother's lineage, apparently come from the same root *(tz'ak)* meaning to multiply or augment. I am grateful to Charles A. Hofling for pointing out this connection (personal communication, 1996).

74. Tedlock, 1985, pp. 72–73; Freidel, Schele, and Parker, 1995, pp. 59, 73–75, passim.

75. The Nahuatl kinship term of reference for older brother, male speaking, was *-teachcauh* (Lockhart, 1992, p. 74).

76. Zantwijk, 1985, pp. 276, 295.

77. Ibid., p. 122.

78. Schumann, 1971, pp. 18–19.

79. Hassig, 1988, p. 29.

80. Ibid., p. 47.

81. B'aka was described in 1702 as a place with many people "where the kings descend" *(donde descienden los reyes).* B'aKa's location is unknown. In 1697 a town named IxPop was under Kowoj control; it is probably the same place as present-day Ixpop on the eastern end of Lago Petén Itzá.

82. His text reads "en una sima de un mogote" (Avendaño, Relación, 1696, f. 29v). The image, probably small, may have been in a pile of stones at one of the town entrances, left there from recent Wayeb' ceremonies. The translated passage in Avendaño, 1987, p. 33, is incorrect in situating it "on the top of a hillock."

83. See Roys, 1957, pp. 32–33. Roys translated K'inchil Kob'a as "sun-eyed chachalaca," and Thompson offered "Chachalaca Bird of the Sun" (Barrera Vásquez et al., 1980, p. 324). K'in Chil may in the Itza case be associated with the name of a town, Kob'a, that was probably located in the Yalain region. The Ach Kat with this name and title might have been the priest of the cult of this image and might have represented this town. The only reference to the town of Kob'a is in AGI, G 151A, no. 3, Declaration of four Indians from Peten, 20 Sept. 1696, ff. 237v–40r.

84. Roys, 1965a, p. 669; Okoshi Harada, 1995, p. 22; Quezada, 1993, pp. 50–56.

85. The remaining Ach Kat–related titles provide no direct hints concerning military organization. AjMatan (which could mean "receiver of a privilege" as well as "beggar") suggests a general honorific, and K'ayom could be a "priest-singer." Both could certainly have applied to Maya military officers, some of whom may well have had priestly functions, which I discuss later in this chapter.

86. The author of the sixteenth-century Motul dictionary defined *jol pop* as "leader of the feast; the caretaker-proprietor of the house called *popol na,* where they gather together to discuss matters of government and to be taught to dance for the town fiestas" (Barrera Vásquez et al., 1980, p. 228).

87. Ajaw AjKan Ek' made an indirect reference to AjK'in Kante as his uncle, identifying him as the one who tried to kill Avendaño in 1696. See AGI, G 151B, no. 2, Declaración del reyezuelo Ah Canek, 31 March 1697, ff. 39v–45v, and chapter 12.

88. Zantwijk, 1985, p. 296; see also Karttunen, 1983, p. 34. Gillespie (1989, p. 133) notes that because *coatl* also has a second meaning, "twin," the "two offices of *tlatoani* [the principal ruler] and *cihuacoatl* thereby conjoined the (male) ruler and his 'female' counterpart" in a manner reflected elsewhere in the Aztec pantheon. Alternatively, and less satisfactorily, Kit Kan might be a misreading of *kit kaan,* "father of sky," in which *kit* has a less commonly cited meaning as an honorific for father. Nowhere, however, is it written as Kit Kaan.

89. AGI, P 237, ramo 1, Razón individual y general de los pueblos, poblaciones, y rancherías de esta provincia de Zuyuha Peten Itza, 6 Jan. 1698, ff. 80r–84v.

90. An ambiguity appears in the Spanish commentary for column IV, which states that there were four kings and four caciques—whereas in fact it lists five kings, including Ajaw Kan Ek'. One version of this document (in AGI, G 345, as cited in Table 3.6) lists all five, while the other version (in AGI, P 237) omits the first Reyezuelo Kit Kan. I believe that the first of these is correct, and that the copyist for the second version incorrectly attempted to solve the discrepancy by omitting this individual. **451**

91. Avendaño, Relación, 1696, f. 27v; 1987, p. 30 (in which AjTut is mistranscribed as "Ahtul").

92. According to López de Cogolludo, Fuensalida called two Itza rulers—

AjChata P'ol and Ajaw Puk—by the term "captain" in 1618 (1971, vol. 2, bk. 9, ch. 8, pp. 223, 227; bk. 9, ch. 12, p. 250). This P'ol he later referred to specifically as Nakom P'ol (bk. 9, ch. 13, p. 253).

93. For Classic-period hieroglyphic forms of the title Ajaw see Schele and Freidel, 1990, p. 54. These authors describe the title as emerging as that of the "high king" during the Late Preclassic period (p. 57). As they also note (p. 419, n. 1), the sixteenth-century Motul dictionary glosses Ajaw as "rey o emperador, monarca, principe o gran señor" (king or emperor, monarch, prince, or great lord). For a discussion of the distribution of the title in Late Postclassic northern Yucatán see Roys, 1967, p. 189. Roys observed that the title was not used by the Xiw rulers of Mani, who preferred the title Jalach Winik. Ajaw, therefore, may in later times have been used only by the Itzas.

94. The Spanish original reads, "Este rey era entre ellos como emperador, pues dominaba sobre todos los demás reyes y caciques que en su lengua llaman batabob, y esta parcialidad declaran ser la mayor."

95. AGI, P 237, ramo 3, Declaración de un indio que dijo llamarse Ah Chan, 29 Dec. 1695, ff. 191v–96v.

96. Colonial dictionaries glossed *peten* as both island and "comarca, región o provincia" (Barrera Vásquez et al., 1980, p. 648).

97. Roys, 1965a, p. 669; Quezada, 1993, pp. 50–58.

98. Recall that in the 1620s the town of IxPimienta had four leaders, each called B'ob'at, "prophet" (chapter 2). The sixteenth-century Chontal Akalan capital of Itzam K'anak was also divided into four quarters, each of which had a ruling head, with a supreme ruler standing above the rest. All five of these rulers, as well as heads of other towns, bore the title Ajaw (Scholes and Roys, 1968, pp. 54–55).

99. AGI, P 237, ramo 1, Razón individual y general de los pueblos, poblaciones, y rancherías de esta provincia de Zuyuha Peten Itza, 6 Jan. 1698, ff. 80r–84v.

100. AGI, G 151B, no. 2, Declaration of Ah Kin Can Ek, 10 March 1697, ff. 13v–15v.

101. The Kowojs may also have practiced joint rulership, although the evidence is ambiguous. Following the execution of "Captain" Kowoj in July 1697 this leader was succeeded by his son "Captain" Kulut Kowoj. Kulut may be a title meaning deity-twin, from *k'u* (deity) and *lot* (twin), which would suggest a similar relation as that shared by the joint Itza rulers.

102. Avendaño, 1987, pp. 28, 50–52; Relación, ff. 25v, 45v–48r.

103. AGI, G 151A, no. 3, Declaration of four Indians from Peten, 20 Sept. 1696, ff. 237v–40r.

452 104. Avendaño, 1987, p. 30; Relación, f. 27v.

105. Coe, 1965.

106. Ibid. These rituals are described in Landa, 1941, pp. 136–53. See also Roys's discussion of directional rituals (1965b, pp. xiv–xv).

107. AGI, P 237, ramo 1, Razón individual y general de los pueblos, poblaciones, y rancherías de esta provincia de Zuyuha Peten Itza, 6 Jan. 1698, ff. 80r–84v.

108. Roys, 1965a, p. 669.

109. Avendaño, 1987, p. 39; Relación, f. 35r–v. The translation is my own.

110. Edmonson, 1982, pp. 3, 15, 21; see also Love, 1994, p. 25.

111. On matters of royal policy see AGI, G 151A, no. 5, Testimony of Capitán de Caballos Nicolás de la Aya, 6 July 1697, ff. 86–99; G 151B, no. 2, Declaración de don Martín Chan, 10 March 1697, ff. 4r–11v.

112. The "dance of sacrifice" noted in this quotation refers to an "idol" reported by Fuensalida called Job'on ("Hobo"), before which, according to Fuensalida, the Itzas danced while sacrificing a person in a ritual accompanied by drumming, playing of flutes, and singing (López de Cogolludo, vol. 2, bk. 9, ch. 14, pp. 258–59). Job'on, meaning "hollow" and possibly bearing a relationship with the Itza surname Ob'on, may have been another name for an object that Fuensalida called Moloc (probably from Muluk, a year-bearer day). This is described in unlikely terms as a hollow bronze figure of human appearance, open at the shoulders with arms extended. The sacrificial victim was supposedly placed in it and roasted alive over a fire. Such salacious descriptions of sacrifice by torture are found nowhere else and should be considered suspect.

113. One colonial Yucatec term for "war captain" was *aj-chun k'atun*. The more familiar term for war captain, *nakom*, referred both to a military leader and to a priest who carried out human sacrifices, confirming that war captains were indeed priests who consulted supernatural forces for military guidance.

114. Roys, 1965a, p. 669.

115. Roys, 1967, p. 137; for his English translations of passages in all three chronicles see Roys, 1962, pp. 72 (Tisimin), 74 (Mani, in which the k'atun is not clearly indicated), and 76 (Chumayel). For the original passage from the Chumayel chronicle see Roys, 1967, p. 49. Barrera Vásquez offered a translation based on a compilation of all three versions: "8 Ahau . . . was when Ichpa-Mayapan was abandoned and destroyed by those without the walls, those without the fortress because of the joint government of Mayapan" (Barrera Vásquez and Morley, 1949, p. 38).

Edmonson disagreed with the translation of *mul tepal* as "joint government" and offered "crowd rule" instead. His translation of the same passage from the Chilam B'alam text reads, "8 Ahau there occurred/The stoning/Inside the fort/Of Mayapan,/Because it was behind the ramparts,/Behind the wall,/Because of crowd rule/Inside the city of Mayapan there" (Edmonson, 1986, p. 54). The original passage is ambiguous about whether the battle was an attack from outside or an uprising from within. In any event, "crowd rule," which suggests an uncontrolled riot, is far different from "joint government," which implies an organized civil war. He translated the similar passage in the Tisimin chronicle to read, "8

453

Ahau [1461]/There was/Crushed stone inside the walls/Of Mayapan/Because of the seizure of the walls/By crowd rule/In the city/Of Mayapan" (Edmonson, 1982, p. 10).

The colonial dictionaries noted that *mul,* when used with nouns, specified that the item indicated was produced by or belonged to a community in common, as in *mul ixi'im,* "common maize" or "maize of the community." *Tepal* was commonly translated as referring to a supreme ruler, even equivalent to the title Ajaw. It is on this basis that the term *mul tepal* has been interpreted as joint governance. See Barrera Vásquez et al., 1980, pp. 785–86.

116. Roys, 1962, pp. 56–63 (a compilation of extended quotations from Landa, 1941, and from Herrera y Tordesillas, who apparently worked from the now lost full manuscript by Landa). The tradition of three ruling brothers at Chich'en Itza mirrors the statement noted earlier that three brothers also ruled the Itzas of Petén (p. 62). It may or may not be relevant that the Kokoms, who ruled Mayapan for an extended period, "were so rich that they possessed twenty-two good pueblos" (p. 61). This is the same number that Avendaño recorded as *parcialidades,* or provinces, among the Itzas.

117. Schele and Freidel, 1990, pp. 360–61.

118. Ibid., pp. 361, 371.

119. Ibid., p. 361.

Chapter 4: Power Politics

1. His full name appeared as Martín de Ursúa Arizmendi y Aguirre in the royal cédula naming him Conde de Lizárraga on 14 April 1705 (Elorza y Rada, 1958, p. 32).

2. This petition is recorded in AGI, G 151A, no. 6, Real cédula to president and oidores of Guatemala, 24 Nov. 1692, ff. 1r–3r.

3. AGI, G 151A, no. 6, Real cédula to president and oidores of Guatemala, 24 Nov. 1692, ff. 1r–3r. Villagutierre discussed this cédula in 1933, bk. 3, ch. 7, pp. 148–49; 1983, pp. 124–26.

4. The copyist mistakenly substituted "los Lacandones" for Verapaz in this passage.

5. The following section is based on Elorza y Rada, 1714, pp. 218–21. This work was translated and published in facsimile (Elorza y Rada, 1930). See also Fontavelli, 1943, and Elorza y Rada, 1958.

6. Carrillo y Ancona, 1895, vol. 2, pp. 83–84.

7. Soberanis y Centeno was named governor and captain general of Yucatán and Campeche in 1690. His successor was to be Diego de Villatoro, who in turn named three individuals, all apparently Basques, who could serve in his place: Martín de Ursúa y Arizmendi, Juan José de Veytia, and Juan Andrés de Ustariz. It was Ursúa who ultimately succeeded Soberanis (Magdaleno, 1954, p. 711).

8. Martín de Ursúa's relationship to Pedro de Ursúa, however, is not known.

9. *Enciclopedia Universal,* 1907–c.1930, s.v. "Ursua, Pedro de"; Orti-guera, 1968.

10. Elorza y Rada, 1714, p. 209. The Conde de Jerena was also captain general of the armada, lord of the palaces of Ursúa, Nas, and Utalcoa in Alta Navarra, and knight of the Order of Santiago. He made twenty-seven voyages to the Americas, taking with him various other Ursúas who remained there as residents (Elorza y Rada, 1958, p. 33).

11. Elorza y Rada, 1714, p. 209; 1958, p. 33.

12. Elorza y Rada, 1714, p. 209; 1958, pp. 33–34. One of the most important of the descendants of these marriages was Antonio María Bucareli y Ursúa, who was named viceroy of New Spain in 1771.

13. Elorza y Rada, 1714, p. 208.

14. Carrillo y Ancona, 1895, vol. 2, p. 659.

15. Carrillo y Ancona, 1895, vol. 2, p. 660.

16. The identities of the members of the Council of the Indies who so strongly supported Ursúa's cause have not been positively established. One of them, according to Bishop Carrillo y Ancona, quoted earlier, was said to be the brother of Bernardino de Zubiaur, who served as one of Ursúa's major officers on the final entrada to Lago Petén Itzá. Another may have been Manuel García de Bustamante, also a member of the Order of Santiago, whose "Approbation" of Villagutierre's book was included in the material prefatory to it (Villagutierre, 1933, p. 2; found in 1701 edition on p. 13 of the prefatory material). To these influential contacts may possibly be added Enrique Enríquez de Guzmán, who, after having served as president of Guatemala, was serving in 1689 in the royal court at Madrid and may well have advised Ursúa to propose the road-building project (Villagutierre, 1933, bk. 3, ch. 7, p. 148).

17. In 1708 Ursúa petitioned for the title of *adelantado* and income in the amount of four thousand ducats annually from the "reduced" peoples of Petén (AGI, EC 339B, no. 27, Ursúa to Crown, 21 Jan. 1708, f. 17r–v).

18. Patch, 1993, pp. 81, 83, 126–27, passim. For a discussion of repartimiento in Yucatán see also Farriss, 1984, pp. 43–45. I have related the repartimiento to the continued flight of Mayas from the towns of Yucatán to the southern frontiers of the peninsula (Jones, 1989, p. 125).

19. Patch, 1993, p. 81.   20. Patch, 1993, p. 83.
21. Patch, 1993, p. 82.   22. Patch, 1993, p. 127.

23. Ursúa's letter to the Crown, from which most of this information is taken, was sent from Mexico City on June 30, 1692. The original of this letter of petition has not been found but was partially quoted by Villagutierre, 1933, 1983, bk. 3, ch. 8; the date of Ursúa's memorial is noted in AGI, P 237, ramo 3, Real **455** cédula to Ursúa, 26 Oct. 1693, ff. 173r–175r. This cédula is also quoted in Villagutierre, 1933, 1983, bk. 3, ch. 9. Ursúa included a *memorial* (petition) with this letter, summarized by Villagutierre. That Ursúa was alcalde ordinario of Mexico City in 1694 was reported by a member of the Audiencia of New Spain (Houwald,

1979, vol. 2, p. 132). See AGI, P 237, ramo 3, Auto and certification pertaining to the absolution of Roque de Soberanis y Centeno, Feb. 1696, ff. 238r–2 42r. For details on charges against Soberanis see AGI, G 151A, no. 6, Roque de Soberanis y Centeno to Jacinto de Barrios Leal, Dec. 1694, ff. 5v–7r.

24. One of their sons, Joaquín, became governor of Yucatán (Carrillo y Ancona, 1895, vol. 2, p. 660).

25. Patch, 1993, p. 84.

26. For vague information on Ursúa's kinship network in Yucatán see AGI, EC 339B, no. 18, bishop of Yucatán to Crown, 14 March 1704. One of his relatives, probably his brother, was Francisco de Ursúa, who lived in Mexico City and served as Martín's agent there in 1695 and 1696 (AGI, P 237, ramo 3, Memorial, with fiscal's response, by Francisco de Ursúa, on behalf of Martín de Ursúa y Arizmendi, Nov. 1695, ff. 116r–118v; G 151A, no. 3, Memorial by Francisco de Ursúa, c. 1 Dec. 1696, f. 244r–v; Petition by Francisco de Ursúa to viceroy of New Spain, c. 18 Sept. 1696, ff. 108r–112r).

27. Villagutierre, 1933, 1983, bk.3, ch. 8.

28. Ibid. Here and elsewhere the translation of this letter, Villagutierre's commentary on it, and the cédula of 26 Oct. 1693 directed to Ursúa is largely my own, but amply informed by Robert D. Wood's translation (Villagutierre, 1983, pp. 126–30).

29. I have not been able to locate this cédula. For more on Castillo y Toledo, see Jones, 1989, pp. 250–68, 328–30.

30. AGI, G 151A, no. 4, Real Cédula to President and Oidores of Audiencia of Guatemala, 22 June 1695, ff. 35r–36v. The original (AGI, M 924, Méritos y Servicios de Castillo y Castillo, Petition by Juan del Castillo y Toledo) is undated, and I previously reasoned, apparently mistakenly, that it was written in 1696 (Jones, 1989, p. 328, n. 29).

31. The enmity between Ursúa and Castillo y Toledo softened over the years, for Castillo served as Ursúa's supply master and hiring agent during the second entrada to Petén. In 1699 Castillo served as the guarantor of the surety bond of six thousand pesos that Ursúa, like all outgoing governors, was required to post against the costs of his *residencia,* an investigation into his activities as governor by his successor (Patch, 1993, p. 125).

32. Villagutierre, 1933, bk. 3, ch. 8, p. 150.

33. For example, AGI, EC 339B, no. 27, Petition from Ursúa to Crown, c. April 1709, ff. 7r–8r.

34. Villagutierre, 1933, bk. 3, ch. 8, p. 150.

35. AGI, G 151A, no. 6, Real cédula to president and oidores of Guatemala, 24 Nov. 1692; Real cédula to governor of Yucatán, 24 Nov. 1692, ff. 2v–3r.

36. AGI, P 237, ramo 3, Real cédula to Ursúa, 26 Oct. 1693. This cédula also appears in Villagutierre, 1933, 1983, bk. 3, ch. 9.

37. AGI, P 237, ramo 3, Real cédula to Ursúa, 26 Oct. 1693.

38. AGI, G 153, no. 1, Real cédula to president and oidores of Audience of

Guatemala, 26 Oct. 1693, ff. 77v–79v; P 237, ramo 3, Real cédula to Conde de Galve, 26 Oct. 1693, ff. 177v–79r; G 151A, no. 4, Real cédula to Franciscan provincial of Yucatán, 26 Oct. 1693, ff. 69v–70r. The cédula to the Bishop of Yucatán is reproduced in Carrillo y Ancona, 1895, vol. 2, pp. 624–25. The Count of Galve was Gaspar de la Cerda Sandoval, Silva y Mendoza (Villagutierre, 1983, p. 129, fn. 517).

39. Jacinto de Barrios Leal to Soberanis y Centeno, 17 Nov. 1694, in Houwald 1979, pp. 129–31; AGI, G 151A, no. 6, Soberanis y Centeno to Barrios Leal, Dec. 1694, ff. 5v–7r.

40. Ancona, 1878, vol. 2, p. 272.

41. Ibid.

42. Ibid., p. 273. The original reads "cercenado las medidas del maíz."

43. See also Carrillo y Ancona, 1892, vol. 2, p. 605.

44. Ancona, 1878, vol. 2, p. 278.

45. AGI, G 151A, no. 6, Jacinto de Barrios Leal to Roque de Soberanis y Centeno, 13 Aug. 1694, ff. 4r–5v.

46. Soberanis's letter has not been located but is acknowledged in Barrios Leal to Soberanis y Centeno, 17 Nov. 1694, in Houwald, 1979, pp. 129–31; it is also noted in Barrios Leal to Sandoval, bishop of Yucatán, 17 Nov. 1694, in Houwald, 1979, pp. 131–33. Barrios addressed his letter to Soberanis "or the person who might be in charge of the government of the province of Yucatán."

47. Coordination difficulties were already becoming apparent, owing to perceptions of differing climatic conditions in Yucatán and Guatemala. Soberanis had said that during the "summer" (the dry season, beginning in January or February) there was insufficient water for drinking and that the Yucatecans could not possibly set out then. Barrios stated that during only three months (late February through early May) was the region dry enough for this sort of travel (Barrios Leal to Soberanis y Centeno, 17 Nov. 1694, in Houwald, 1979, pp. 129–31).

48. Barrios Leal to Sandoval, Bishop of Yucatán, 17 Nov. 1694, in Houwald, 1979, pp. 131–33.

49. Houwald, 1979, vol. 2, pp. 132–33.

50. AGI, P 237, ramo 3, Memorial, with fiscal's response, by Francisco de Ursúa, Nov. 1695; P 237, ramo 3, documents related to Martín de Ursúa's petition, Dec. 1695, ff. 121r–148r. Ursúa later indicated that Saraza had assisted him in obtaining copies of official correspondence early on in his residence as interim governor (G 151A, no. 3, Ursúa to Conde de Montezuma, 24 Oct. 1696, ff. 246v–250r).

51. Avendaño, Relación, 1696, f. 1r.; 1987, p. 2.

52. AGI, P 237, ramo 3, Auto and certification pertaining to the absolution of Soberanis y Centeno, Feb. 1696; AGI, G 151A, no. 3, Ursúa to Juan de Ortega Montáñez, 23 June 1696, ff. 48v–49r. **457**

53. AGI, G 151A, no. 4, Ursúa to Jacinto de Barrios Leal, 1 Dec. 1695, ff. 36v–40v.

54. AGI, P 237, ramo 10, Auto by Ursúa, 24 Feb. 1695, f. 517r–v.

55. Avendaño (Relación, 1696, f. 47v.; 1987, p. 52) described García de Paredes as a supplier of timber for ships. Campeche had become an important center for the building of small trade vessels that brought in imports and carried local products — cotton textiles, beeswax, logwood, and salt — to the port of Veracruz. See Patch, 1993, pp. 36 and 235–236, for more information on Campeche's commercial trading and shipbuilding.

56. García de Paredes's "rancho" was one of three in the Sajkab'ch'en partido (AGI, C 920, Matrícula del pueblo de San Antonio de Sahcabchen, 15 May 1688.) His encomienda, granted to him in 1689, comprised the three villages of Usulab'an, Mamantel, and China, which in 1695–96 generated an annual income of about forty mantas, indicating an adult tributary population of 160 or 320 persons, depending on whether one applies a manta-to-tributary equivalency of four to one or eight to one (AGI, G 151A, no. 3, Certification of payment of tributes of the real de manta and acabala de los tercios for 1695 and half of 1696, Partido de la Costa, 30 Aug. 1696, ff. 58v–65r). Usulab'an and Mamantel had originally been part of the partido of Tixchel, later renamed the partido or curacy of Popola. China, also included in his encomienda, was located a short distance southeast of Campeche. At its height the Tixchel district had included the towns of Tixchel, Usulab'an, Chek'ub'ul, Chiwoja, Cheusij, Tik'intunpa-Mamantel, and Popola. Originally Chontal Maya territory, the Tixchel district had been an unstable region since the mid-sixteenth century, when reductions were carried out both under Spanish auspices and by the colonial Chontal leader don Pablo PaxB'olon. The complex and fascinating history of this area is the primary subject of a classic and thorough study by Scholes and Roys (1968).

57. This was the route over which messages between Guatemala and Yucatán were carried. Sajkab'ch'en, a major stop on the route, was "the beginning point of the jurisdiction of Yucatán" and under García de Paredes's paramilitary jurisdiction (AGI, G 151A, no. 7, Petition by Francisco de Salazar y Córdoba, c. 15 Oct. 1697, ff. 42r–43v).

58. AGI, P 237, ramo 10, Auto by Ursúa, 21 Jan. 1695, ff. 516r–517r.

59. AGI, G 151A, no. 7, Certification by Pedro Enríquez de Novoa, contador, 15 Dec. 1696, ff. 6v–7r. His title was teniente de capitán general y justicia mayor.

60. AGI, P 237, ramo 10, Auto by Ursúa, 21 Jan. 1695, ff. 516r–517r.

Chapter 5: The Birth of the Camino Real

1. AGI, G 505, Auto by Amésqueta, 24 April 1696. Saraus's role on this entrada is briefly mentioned by the secular clergy in AGI, P 237, ramo 8, Auto by dean and ecclesiastical cabildo of Mérida, 4 Dec. 1695, ff. 431r–432v; Cabildo eclesiástico de Mérida de Yucatán to Crown, 10 May 1696, ff. 418r–423r; Auto by dean and ecclesiastical council, Mérida, to provincial, 9 Jan. 1696, ff. 446r–452r; Fr. Juan Antonio de Silva et al. to Ursúa, 17 Jan. 1696, ff. 469r–483v;

Notification of delivery of real cédula to dean and ecclesiastical council of Mérida, 3 Jan. 1696, ff. 444r–445r.

2. The distance of forty-three leagues is estimated on the basis of information in AGI, P 237, ramo 3, Itinerario diario of Franciscan missionaries, 12 June 1695 to 24 Oct. 1695, ff. 148r–156v, and in Avendaño, Relación, 1696, ff. 2v–6r; 1987, pp. 5–9.

3. AGI, P 237, ramo 10, Auto by Ursúa, 2 May 1695.

4. Villagutierre, 1933, bk. 4, ch. 6; 1983, p. 183.

5. AGI, G 151A, no. 4, Ursúa to Barrios Leal, 1 Dec. 1695.

6. Avendaño, Relación, 1696, ff. 12r, 13v; 1987, pp. 15–16.

7. Villagutierre, 1933, bk. 4, ch. 6; 1983, p. 184.

8. Villagutierre, 1933, bk. 4, ch. 9; 1983, p. 191.

9. Villagutierre, 1933, 1983, bk. 4, chs. 4–5, 7–8.

10. Villagutierre, 1933, 1983, bk. 4, ch. 7–8.

11. Villagutierre, 1933, bk. 8, ch. 6. AGI, P 237, ramo 10, Declaration of Captain Diego Bernardo del Río, 23 June 1695, ff. 541r–542v; see also Houwald, 1979, vol. 1, p. 400.

12. Villagutierre, 1933, bk. 4, ch. 17; 1983, p. 177. AGI, G 152, ramo 3, Fray Agustín Cano to Barrios Leal, 2 April 1695, ff. 369v–370v.

13. AGI, P 237, ramo 10, Declaration of Captain Diego Bernardo del Río, 23 June 1695, f. 541v.

14. AGI, EC 339B, no. 6, Testimonio de la consulta y consejo de los R. padres misioneros, 24 April 1695, ff. 18r–19r.

15. The others were Fray Joseph Delgado, Fray Lorenzo Rodríguez, and Fray Joseph Guerra (AGI, EC 339B, no. 6, Testimonio de la consulta y consejo de los R. padres misioneros, 24 April 1695).

16. AGI, G 180, Fr. Agustín Cano to Crown, 14 Nov. 1686; Fr. Juan Bautista Alvarez de Toledo et al. to Crown, 5 Aug. 1687.

17. Villagutierre, 1983, p. 176, n. 704; Houwald, 1979, vol.1, p. 474.

18. Villagutierre (1933, bk. 4, ch. 17; 1983, p. 176) claimed that they encountered large numbers of Manche Chols, some five hundred of whom were placed in reduction communities under the administration of Dominican missionaries.

19. AGI, G 152, ramo 3, Cano to Barrios Leal, 2 April 1695, ff. 369v–370v. The four Mopan caciques in addition to Taxim Chan were, according to Cano (1942, p. 66; 1984, p. 9), Tzak ("Zac"), Tus B'en ("Tuzben" in 1984, "Zuhben" in 1942), Yajkab' ("Yahcab"), and Tesukun ("Tesecum" in 1984, "Texcum" in 1942). All but Tus B'en are also mentioned by Ximénez, 1973, vol. 29, bk. 5, ch. 58, pp. 319–21.

20. AGI, G 152, ramo 3, Cano to Barrios Leal, 2 April 1695, ff. 369v–370v; also in Houwald, 1979, vol. 1, pp. 400–401.

21. García Peláez stated that Cano cited Taxim Chan's town as the largest Mopan settlement, with five hundred inhabitants and "an idol with mother-of-

pearl eyes" (Houwald, 1979, vol. 1, pp. 400–401; cited in Villagutierre, 1983, p. 177, n. 71).

22. AGI, G 152, ramo 3, Cano to Barrios Leal, 15 May 1695, ff. 370v–381r.

23. AGI, EC 339B, no. 6, Captain Juan Díaz de Velasco to President Jacinto Barrios Leal (Rio de los Itzáes), 17 April 1695, f. 11r–v; Testimonio de la consulta y consejo de los R. padres misioneros, 24 April 1695.

24. This account is based on a detailed reconstruction prepared by Fray Agustín Cano (AGI, G 152, ramo 3, Cano to Barrios Leal, 15 May 1695, ff. 370v–381r) and on the field diary of Captain Juan Díaz de Velasco (recorded in Ximénez, 1971–77, vol. 29, bk. 5, ch. 65, pp. 353–60).

25. AGI, G 152, ramo 3, Cano to Barrios Leal, 15 May 1695, ff. 370v–381r. See also AGI, EC 339B, no. 6, Velasco to Barrios Leal (Rio de los Itzáes), 17 April 1695, f. 11r–v; Velasco to Jose de Escals (Savana del Axiza), 25 April 1695, ff. 17v–18r.

26. Ximénez, 1971–77, vol. 29, bk. 5, ch. 65, p. 355.

27. For a discussion of these names see chapter 3.

28. Ximénez, 1971–77, vol. 29, bk. 5, ch. 65, p. 356. Ximénez believed that the statement was an exaggeration intended "to induce fear."

29. Ximénez, 1971–77, vol. 29, bk. 5, ch. 65, pp. 356–57.

30. The original reads "con orejas o cuernos hechos a mano."

31. Ximénez, 1929–31, vol. 3, bk. 5, ch. 65, p. 56; 1971–77, vol. 29, bk. 5, ch. 65, p. 357.

32. Ximénez, 1929–31, vol. 3, bk. 5, ch. 65, p. 56; 1971–77, vol. 29, bk. 5, ch. 65, p. 357. I have edited the names to conform to the most likely form in standard colonial spelling. Adding to the difficulty of interpreting names poorly transcribed by Guatemalans who were unfamiliar with Itza or Yucatec, the transcriptions of names from Ximénez's original manuscript differ in the two published editions. In most cases the 1929–31 edition seems more reliable, but I have used my best judgment in deciding on the more likely forms.

The following compares the spelling that I have adopted with that found in each edition (the 1921–31 edition and the 1971–77 edition spellings are in that order, in parentheses). Personal names: Chan (Chan, Chen), K'in Chan (Quin Chan, Quien Chen), IxPuk (Xpuc, Xpuc), Kuch Pop Kit Kan (Cuxpop quitcam, Cuxpop Quitcam), Ayikal Chan (Aicalchan, Aicalchán), Ayikal Puk (Aicalpuc, Aicalpuc). Towns: Tixb'ol Pululja (Tixbol pululhá, Tixbol Pululhá), Nojpeten (Noj-peten, Noj Petén).

33. Ximénez, 1929–31, bk. 5, ch. 65, p. 57; 1971–77, vol. 29, bk. 5, ch. 65, pp. 357–58; AGI, EC 339B, no. 6, Velasco to Escals 25, April 1695; Testimonio de la consulta y consejo de los R. padres misioneros, 24 April 1695, ff. 18r–19r. See also AGI, G 152, ramo 3, Cano to Barrios Leal, 15 May 1695, ff. 370v–381r. Cano's later account, written in 1697, telescopes these encounters with the Itzas, providing less detail. He stated that the advance scouts actually reached the main lake and saw Nojpeten (Cano 1942, p. 87; 1984, p. 10).

34. Ximénez, 1929–31, vol. 3, bk. 5, ch. 65, p. 57; 1971–77, vol. 29, bk. 5, ch. 65, p. 357–58.

35. The following compares the spellings that I have adopted with those found in each edition of Ximénez's *Historia* (the 1921–31 edition and the 1971–77 edition spellings are in that order, in parentheses). Personal names: K'ixaw (Quixan, Quixán), Ajaw Kan Ek' (Ahau Canec, Ahau Canec), PakLan (Paclan, Paclan), PakNek (Pacnec, Pacnec). Towns with names of their "caciques": B'atab' Sima (Batazima, Batazima), Kab'an Kawil (Cahan Cahil, Cabon Cabil), AjChak Tun (Ah Catun, Achactun), AjK'ixaw (Ah Quixam, Aquixán), Ach Kat Chan or Ach Kaj Chan (Achcachan, Achcachan), B'atab' AjK'u or B'atab' Ajaw (Bataahcu, Bataaheu), K'eyan Chan (Queyan chan, Queián Chan). Town with a descriptive name: Tib'ayal (Itzaj *ti'-bäyäl*, "at the basket tie-tie vine") (Tibuyal, Tibayal).

The variation in recorded pronunciations of K'ixaw or Kixan appears to have reflected local dialectical differences. For consistency I have adopted the former spelling throughout this book.

36. AGI, EC 339B, no. 6, Velasco to Escals, 25 April 1695.

37. Juan Díaz de Velasco to Jacinto de Barrios Leal, 16 May 1695, in Houwald, 1979, pp. 410–17.

38. AGI, P 237, ramo 1, Razón individual y general de los pueblos, poblaciones, y rancherías de esta provincia de Zuyuha Peten Itza, 6 Jan. 1698, ff. 80r–84v.

39. On his baptism see AGI, G 151A, no. 4, Certification of baptisms of Martín Francisco Chan and others, 31 Dec. 1695, ff. 62v–63r.

40. AGI, EC 339A, Ursúa to Juan Francisco Cortés, 15 Dec. 1702, ff. 58r–64v; EC 339B, no. 28, Certification by Fray Diego de Rivas, 23 Dec. 1703, ff. 34r–35r.

41. AjK'ixaw arrived with the retreating forces at Rancho de los Sapos ("Hamlet of the Toads"), north of Mopan, on April 26. There he told Delgado that on Nojpeten there were "four very large idols and another in a cave, [and] that they stand up with their arms and mouths open, and that they had spoken to them. The one in the cave is called Pecoc" (Ximénez, 1929–31, vol. 3, bk. 5, ch. 66, p. 61; 1971–77, vol. 29, p. 362). After arriving at Mopan on May 7, AjK'ixaw was further questioned and provided additional information about the Itza political order. He reported that one Kit Kan was "the principal cacique or reyezuelo" and that he was "very tall and fat," never left the island, and did not have (as AjK'ixaw presumably did) pierced ears. He listed the "other caciques, who are like governors of the island," as "Canec, Mata, Unzauyal, [and] Quil" and claimed that there was a xiquipil (eight thousand) of houses on the island and that three large towns and many smaller settlements were along the lakeshore. The caciques of these were "Paná, Bolóm, Pachá, Chatá, Tibolom, and Belaic." (The transcription of the last set of names is taken from the 1929–31 edition of Ximénez, vol. 3, bk. 5, ch. 66, p. 62.)

These lists are a confusion of individuals and place names. "Canec" of course was Ajaw Kan Ek'. Chata, Matan, and Pata were Itza names associated with the nobility. "Tibolom" (Tib'olon), "Unzauyal" (Junsawyal?), "Quil" (K'il), and "Belaic" (B'elaik) were all probably place names.

42. AGI, EC 339B, no. 6, Testimonio de la consulta y consejo de los R. padres misioneros, 24 April 1695.

43. Ibid.

44. Díaz and Cano must have realized the possibility of their being misled by Itza informants on this question. Although the two prisoners, AjChan and AjK'ixaw, said that there were no other troops were in the area, had the facts been otherwise they would have been foolish to reveal them to Díaz.

45. Sources on the condemnation of the retreat by Díaz include AGI, G 152, ramo 3, Cano to Barrios Leal, 15 May 1695, ff. 370v–381r; Velasco to Barrios Leal, 16 May 1695, in Houwald, 1979, pp. 410–417; and Cano 1942, 1984.

46. AGI, P 237, ramo 10, Auto by Ursúa, 2 May 1695.

47. AGI, P 237, ramo 10, Dispatch by the cabildo of Campeche, 7 May 1695. The eight-peso salary was to be paid to all of the non-Maya enlisted men (AGI, G 151A, no. 3, Testimonies presented on behalf of Ursúa, 26 Aug. 1696, f. 70r).

48. AGI, P 237, ramo 1, Ursúa to Conde de Galve, 10 March 1696, ff. 257r–261r; AGI, P 237, ramo 3, Itinerario diario of Franciscan missionaries on camino real, Cauich to Chuntuqui, 12 June 1695 to 24 Oct. 1695, ff. 148r–156v. Pedro de Zubiaur Isasi was twenty-two in 1698.

49. Although the documents ordering the recruitment of this group of fifty Mayas do not specify the town from which they were to come, later information makes it clear that they were from Sajkab'ch'en. See Avendaño, 1696, f. 6r–v; 1987, pp. 9–10; AGI, P 237, ramo 3, Itinerario diario of Franciscan missionaries, 12 June 1695 to 24 Oct. 1695; P 237, ramo 8, García de Paredes to Ursúa, 4 Feb. 1696.

50. AGI, P 237, ramo 10, Auto by Ursúa, 11 May 1695, ff. 521v–522v.

51. AGI, P 237, ramo 10, Auto by Ursúa, 12 May 1695, f. 522r–v.

52. Avendaño, Relación, 1696, f. 1v; 1987, p. 2. See also AGI, P 237, ramo 10, Auto by Ursúa, 12 May 1695, f. 522r–v.

53. Avendaño, Relación, 1696, f. 9v; 1987, p. 13.

54. AGI, P 237, ramo 10, Auto by Ursúa, 12 May 1695, ff. 522v–523r. His actual title was "teniente de capitán general de su señorío y justicia mayor de las montañas."

55. AGI, P 237, ramo 10, Dispatch by Ursúa, 11 May 1695, ff. 534v–536v.

56. AGI, P 237, ramo 10, Diligencia by Juan del Castillo y Toledo, 21 May 1695, ff. 536v–537r.

57. AGI, P 237, ramo 10, List of Mayas sent to the montaña from Tek'ax, 22 May 1695, ff. 537r–538v.

58. AGI, P 237, ramo 10, Diligencia by Juan del Castillo y Toledo, 23 May 1695, ff. 538v–539r; List of Mayas sent to the montaña from Oxkutzcab, 24 May 1695, ff. 539r–540r.

59. AGI, G 151A, no. 3, Testimonies presented on behalf of Ursúa, 26 Aug. 1696.

60. AGI, P 237, ramo 10, Auto by Ursúa, 27 July 1695, f. 547r–v.

61. AGI, P 237, ramo 3, Informe dado por mi, el Capitán Manuel Jorge de Zever [*sic,* i.e., Sesere], ingeniero militar de esta provincia, 23 Nov. 1695, ff. 166v–167v.

62. AGI, P 237, ramo 10, New instructions to Alonso García de Paredes from Ursúa, 24 June 1695, ff. 543v–546v.

63. Ibid.

64. Ibid.

65. Ibid.

66. The fort at Chuntuki is mentioned in AGI, P 237, ramo 1, Ursúa to Crown, 12 May 1696, ff. 18r–21r; Ursúa to Crown, 27 Oct. 1696, ff. 43r–48r; and G 151A, no. 3, Testimonies presented on behalf of Ursúa, 26 Aug. 1696. The headquarters located two leagues from the lake was established for the purpose of cutting timbers for the galeota that was to attack Nojpeten. The boat was assembled at Ch'ich', on the western shore of the lake, just before the final attack. Ch'ich', therefore, served as the final headquarters. See AGI, G 151B, no. 2, Junta de guerra, 12 March 1697, ff. 16r–25v.

Chapter 6: Franciscans on the Camino Real

1. AGI, P 237, ramo 10, Auto by Ursúa, 18 May 1695, ff. 527v–529v.

2. AGI, P 237, ramo 10, Petition by Fray Antonio de Silva, Provincial, c. 30 May 1695, ff. 532r–534r.

3. Silva did not mention de Vargas by name but wrote only that this group would include "another donado" (AGI, P 237, ramo 10, Petition by Silva, Provincial, 30 May 1695). That he was part of the group, however, is confirmed in Avendaño's later report of this mission (Avendaño, Relación, 1697, f. 2r; 1987, p. 3).

4. Avendaño, Relación, 1696, title page; 1987, p. 1.

5. AGI, P 237, ramo 10, Auto by Ursúa, directed to Fray Antonio de Silva, 1 June 1695.

6. The "sonorous trumpet" (*sonoro clarín*) quotation is from Avendaño, Relación, 1696, f. 2r; 1987, p. 3.

7. Avendaño, Relación, 1696, f. 2r; 1987, p. 4.

8. Avendaño, Relación, 1696; 1987.

9. AGI, P 237, ramo 1, Testimonies of Avendaño and two other religious who visited the Peten of the Itzás, May 1696; AGI, G 151A, no. 6, Declarations of Franciscan *guardianes* from the Partido de la Sierra y Bolonchen, 17 Aug. 1696.

463

10. Comparato thought that Avendaño meant Telchaquillo (Avendaño, 1987, p. 4, n. 19), but this town was not on Avendaño's route. Telchaquillo, located near Mani, was, to my knowledge, never called Telchak, and its proper Maya name was Tichak (Roys, 1957, p. 67).

11. Collins has argued that the three *maestro* positions held by village Mayas (maestro cantor, maestro de capilla, and *maestro de escuela*) were different titles for a single position that involved, among other responsibilities, leading prayers, teaching children prayers and chants, and actually chanting (Collins, 1977, p. 243). Avendaño here clearly distinguishes between two of these. I have decided to translate the terms literally.

12. Avendaño, Relación, 1696, f. 3r; 1987, p. 4.

13. The headquarters was to have been at B'olonch'en Kawich, but Avendaño makes a clear distinction between these two nearby communities.

14. Avendaño, Relación, 1696, f. 3r.; 1987, p. 5. There are two folios numbered 3.

15. AGI, P 237, ramo 3, Itinerario diario of Franciscan missionaries, 12 June 1695 to 24 Oct. 1695.

16. He even recorded what he regarded as a miracle that occurred on their first night past Kawich at a place called Job'onmo. During a violent thunderstorm, a deadly poisonous snake crept onto the sleeping mat of his servant, Francisco K'u, but did not bite him when he awoke, saw it, and jumped up. The snake was thereupon killed by his Maya companions (Avendaño, Relación, 1696, f. 3r–v; 1987, p. 5).

17. Avendaño, Relación, 1696, f. 3v; 1987, p. 6. In the treatment of Avendaño's text I have quoted from Bowditch and Rivera's translation (Avendaño, 1987), with occasional editings of their text based on a reading of the original. See also the excellent Spanish edition by Temis Vayhinger-Scheer (1996).

18. Avendaño, Relación, 1696; ff. 3v–4r; 1987, p. 7.

19. AGI, P 237, ramo 3, Itinerario diario of Franciscan missionaries, 12 June 1695 to 24 Oct. 1695. *Conga* may be translated as "hutia," a ratlike rodent of the genus *Capromys*. The second party of Franciscans set up crosses at a number of places along their route where they saw that people had been living.

20. Jesús María mentioned another abandoned town, not noted by Avendaño, called Yoxjalek' or Yochjalek', which would have been about six and a half leagues (twenty-six kilometers) north of Temchay. The second group did not mention Temchay (AGI, P 237, ramo 3, Itinerario diario of Franciscan missionaries on camino real, 12 June 1695 to 24 Oct. 1695).

21. Avendaño, Relación, 1696, f. 5r; 1987, p. 8. The distance is the sum of Avendaño's place-to-place estimates. At this point they were probably about twelve kilometers south of present-day Constitución, which is on Highway 186 east of Laguna Siviltuc. As the crow flies, they had traveled about one hundred kilometers almost due south from Kawich, and Avendaño calculated that the walking distance was about thirty-three leagues, equivalent to some 132 kilometers.

22. Avendaño, Relación, 1696, f. 5v; 1987, p. 9. Although Avendaño says that the trees were "limones," they were almost certainly limes.

23. AGI, P 237, ramo 3, Itinerario diario of Franciscan missionaries on camino real, 12 June 1695 to 24 Oct. 1695.

24. Nojt'ub' was probably located at or near "Pueblo Viejo Conhóas," on the path south of Constitución. Jesús María estimated that the sarteneja held "more than thirty *botejas* of water" (AGI, P 237, ramo 3, Itinerario diario of Franciscan missionaries on camino real, 12 June 1695 to 24 Oct. 1695).

25. AGI, P 237, ramo 3, Itinerario diario of Franciscan missionaries on camino real, 12 June 1695 to 24 Oct. 1695.

26. Ibid.

27. Avendaño, Relación, 1696, f. 6r; 1987, p. 6.

28. Avendaño, Relación, 1696, ff. 6v–9r; 1987, pp. 10–13. Some of these events are also noted in AGI, P 237, ramo 3, Itinerario diario of Franciscan missionaries on camino real, 12 June 1695 to 24 Oct. 1695.

29. AGI, P 237, ramo 10, Auto by Ursúa, 27 July 1695.

30. AGI, G 151A, no. 3, Testimony of Captain José Laines, August 29, 1696; Testimony of Captain Pedro de Zubiaur Isasi, 29 August 1696. The Spanish captains seem to have considered the entire area that they were traversing to be part of the Kejach territory. The friars, however, were clear on the matter, considering Kejach to begin south of Tzuktok'.

31. Avendaño, Relación, 1696, f. 10v; 1987, pp. 13–14. For details on Fray Cristóbal Sánchez see Scholes and Roys, 1948, pp. 310–11.

32. Avendaño, Relación, 1696, f. 11v; 1987, p. 15. Avendaño, 1987, omits the phrase that describes the meeting. The second captain is not specified but would surely have been Fernández de Estenos, García de Paredes's second-in-command. In Avendaño, 1987, the name of the friar who delivered the sermon is mistranscribed as "fr Jua Erchales;" it should be "fr Jua Chaves."

33. Avendaño, Relación, 1696, ff. 12v–13r; 1987, p. 16. There is some confusion in Avendaño's account about whether the Sajkab'ch'en troops had occupied only one or perhaps all three of the dispersed hamlets comprised by Chunpich. The three hamlets were on the shores of a kidney-shaped lake, about 1.5 kilometers in length, located about 13 kilometers north of the present-day Guatemalan border. Avendaño commented that from Chunpich itself the lake appeared so large that "it stretches out of sight." A short distance to the west of this lake, called Laguna Chunpich to this day, are two lakes of similar size—Laguna el Civalón and Laguna la Amapola—that must also have been inhabited in 1695. Chunpich itself was on the east side of the lake, whose waters were "very good" (Avendaño, Relación, 1696, f. 14r; 1987, p. 16).

34. AGI, G 344, ramo 3, Miguel de Pineda y Useche to Ursúa and Melchor de Mencos, 3 April 1699, ff. 106–108r.

35. Avendaño, Relación, 1696, f. 13v; 1987, p. 16.

36. Avendaño received this letter at a large aguada one and a half leagues **465** south of Chunpich, today called Laguna Mangüito. He heard that there was a large abandoned town called IxB'am three "long leagues" from there, which would be on the south end of Laguna Paixbán, or Paisbán, on or near the Guatemalan border.

37. Avendaño, Relación, 1696, f. 15r; 1987, p. 1. My translation differs considerably from that in Avendaño, 1987.

38. See Avendaño, Relación, 1696, f. 47v; 1987, p. 52; p. 458n.

39. Avendaño, Relación, 1696, f. 15v; 1987, p. 18.

40. Avendaño, Relación, 1696, f. 16v; 1987, p. 19.

41. San Buenaventura, writing from Chuntuki, also reported that the Mayas at Tzuktok' were not to be sent after all to Sajkab'ch'en (AGI, P 237, ramo 3, Fr. Juan de San Buenaventura to provincial, 22 Sept. 1695, 22 Sept. 1695, ff. 156v–158r).

42. Avendaño, Relación, 1696, f. 16v; 1987, p. 19.

43. Ibid.

44. AGI, P 237, ramo 3, Itinerario diario of Franciscan missionaries on camino real, 12 June 1695 to 24 Oct. 1695. The reduction at B'atkab' is also discussed by military officers, who offered no significant details (AGI, G 151A, no. 3, Testimonies presented on behalf of Ursúa, 26 Aug. 1696).

45. AGI, P 237, ramo 3, Itinerario diario of Franciscan missionaries on camino real, 12 June 1695 to 24 Oct. 1695.

46. AGI, G 344, ramo 3, Pineda y Useche to Ursúa and Mencos, 3 April 1699.

47. AGI, G 344, ramo 3, Melchor de Mencos y Medrano to Gabriel Sánchez de Berrospe, 8 March 1699, ff. 80r–90r.

48. AGI, P 237, ramo 3, Informe dado por mi, Manuel Zever, ingeniero militar de esta provincia, 23 Nov. 1695.

49. AGI, P 237, ramo 3, San Buenaventura to provincial, 22 Sept. 1695.

50. AGI, P 237, ramo 3, San Buenaventura et al. to provincial, 24 Oct. 1695. Jesús María, a recent arrival in Yucatán, spoke no Mayan.

51. Ibid.

52. Ibid.

53. AGI, P 237, ramo 3, San Buenaventura to provincial, 22 Sept. 1695; San Buenaventura et al. to provincial, 24 Oct. 1695.

54. AGI, P 237, ramo 3, San Buenaventura to provincial, 20 Nov. 1695, ff. 162v–166v.

55. AGI, P 237, ramo 3, San Buenaventura et al. to provincial, 24 Oct. 1695.

56. AGI, P 237, ramo 3, San Buenaventura to provincial, 20 Nov. 1695.

57. Ibid.

58. AGI, P 237, ramo 8, Fr. Juan Antonio de Silva, Provincial, to dean and ecclesiastical council of Mérida, c. 17 Dec. 1695, f. 436v.

59. AGI, P 237, ramo 1, Barrios Leal to Ursúa, 26 Oct. 1695, ff. 167v–173r; AGI, G 151A, no. 4, Ursúa to Barrios Leal, 1 Dec. 1695.

60. AGI, G 151A, no. 3, Testimonies presented on behalf of Ursúa, 26 Aug. 1696. The Spaniards sometimes made a distinction between Kejaches and Chanes, although the latter was actually the name of the predominant lineage at Pak'ek'em

(AGI, G 151A, no. 6, Matrícula del pueblo de Pakekem, 9 July 1696, ff. 14v–21r). These names did not refer to separate ethnic groups. The Franciscans also made a matrícula of B'atkab' (AGI, G 151A, no. 6, Matrícula del pueblo nuevo de Batcab, 7 July 1696, ff. 11r–14v).

61. AGI, G 151A, no. 4, Ursúa to Barrios Leal, 1 Dec. 1695. One company among these was commanded by Captain Mateo Hidalgo. Of the forty-nine men of this company, eighteen were from an unidentified place written as "Sixntun," under the command of one Antonio Franco; the others were pardos from Mérida. The basic payment of the rank and file, paid and armed by Ursúa himself, was eight pesos monthly; Franco received twelve pesos per month. See AGI, P 237, ramo 10, Auto by Ursúa, 2 Nov. 1695, f. 548v; Auto by Ursúa and payment of military recruits, 5 Nov. 1695, ff. 548v–550r.

62. AGI, P 237, ramo 3, Ursúa to Conde de Galve, 2 Dec. 1695, ff. 182r–187r.

63. AGI, G 151A, no. 3, Testimonies presented on behalf of Ursúa, 26 Aug. 1696. Garma's full name was Bartolomé de la Garma Alzedo y Salazar.

64. AGI, G 151A, no. 3, Testimonies presented on behalf of Ursúa, 26 Aug. 1696; AGI, G 151A, no. 4, Auto by Ursúa, 23 Feb. 1696.

65. AGI, P 237, ramo 8, Auto by dean and ecclesiastical cabildo of Mérida, 4 Dec. 1695. For background to this dispute see Ayeta, 1693.

66. AGI, P 237, ramo 8, Auto and recaudo by dean and ecclesiastical council of Mérida, 16 Dec. 1695, ff. 433v–434v.

67. AGI, P 237, ramo 8, Silva to dean and ecclesiastical cabildo of Mérida, c. 17 Dec. 1695, ff. 435r–437r.

Chapter 7: *The Itza Emissaries*

1. The name Kante is a known patronym among the Itzas, but I suspect that IxKante inherited this name from her mother. It is likely that she and Ajaw Kan Ek' were half siblings, children of the same father and different mothers.

2. AjChan's father may have been Ach Kat K'in Chan (see Tables 3.4 and 3.5).

3. AGI, G 151B, no. 2, Declaración de don Martín Chan, 10 March 1697, ff. 4r–11v; G 151A, no. 3, Declaration of four Indians from Peten, 20 Sept. 1696, ff. 237v–240r; P 237, ramo 3, Ursúa to Conde de Galve, 29 Dec. 1695, ff. 203r–204v; Declaración de un indio que dijo llamarse Ah Chan, y ser sobrino del rey Canek que lo es de la nación de los Itzáes, 29 Dec. 1695; P 237, ramo 1, Ursúa to Crown, 31 Dec. 1695, ff. 9r–10r; Razón individual y general de los pueblos, poblaciones, y rancherías de esta provincia de Zuyuha Peten Itza, 6 Jan. 1698, ff. 80r–84v; G 151B, no. 2, Declaration of Ah Kin Canek, 10 March 1697, ff. 13v–15v; Junta de guerra, 12 March 1697, ff. 16r–25v; G 345, no. 20, Br. Pedro de Morales y Veles to Gabriel Sánchez de Berrospe, July 1698, ff. 64r–67v; EC 339B, no. 28, Certification of Bachiller Marcos de Vargas Dorantes, 10 July 1703, ff.

467

18r–21r; EC 339B, no. 18, Declaración del Br. don Gaspar de Güemes, 29 Nov. 1703, ff. 3r–6r; EC 339A, Ursúa to Fr. Diego de Rivas, 12 May 1702, ff. 40v–44r.

4. Villagutierre, apparently believing (despite all evidence to the contrary) that AjChan was in the relationship of brother's son to Ajaw Kan Ek', transformed his name into "Ah Can" or Martín Can. His name was always recorded as Chan, however, in the primary sources that Villagutierre consulted.

5. AGI, P 237, ramo 10, Francisco de Hariza to Ursúa, 7 July 1695, ff. 568v–569v.

6. In March or April 1697 the same Mateo Wikab' appeared at the recently conquered Itza capital to visit Ursúa (AGI, G 151A, no. 5, Testimony of Capitán de Caballos Nicolás de la Aya, 6 July 1697, ff. 86–99). The surname Wikab' was shared in the 1655 matrícula of Chunuk'um by five individuals from Tipuj and Saksuus: three married men named Juan and two women (one married, the other single) named María. One Juan Wikab' was married to Andrea Chan, who was probably a relative of AjChan's. Mateo Wikab' may well have been their son—the ideal emissary to represent "Spanish" Tipuj to the Itza ruler.

7. This section is based on AGI, G 151A, no. 4, Auto by Ursúa, 7 Sept. 1695, ff. 49v–50v (same as AGI, P 237, ramo 10, Auto del Ursúa, 7 Sept. 1696, ff. 569v–571r).

8. AGI, G 151A, no. 6, Declarations of Franciscan *guardianes* from the Partido de la Sierra y Bolonchen, 17 Aug. 1696.

9. Avendaño, Relación, 1696, f. 50r; 1987, p. 54.

10. A marginal notation in Avendaño's manuscript confuses these names by indicating that "these Indians who came [to Mérida] were called the two Ah Chan brothers, the third Ah Chant'an Ah Tek, and the fourth Ah K'u" (*llamabanse estos indios que vinieron los dos hermanos Achanes, el tercero Achanthan Ahtec y el quarto Ahku*). The notation incorrectly conflates AjChant'an (a misrecording?), one of the two brothers, with AjTek (Avendaño, Relación, 1696, f. 50r; 1987, p. 54, n. 167).

11. This situation is not clear. Two Kejach men baptized in Mérida the day before AjChan's group received the names Joseph K'u and Bartolomé K'ixaw. Both of these were from Pak'ek'em; K'u was said to be the cacique of that town. This K'u might have been the AjK'u who went with AjChan on his September trip to Mérida, although this seems unlikely. For Manuel Chayax's relationship to AjChan see chapter 11.

12. Andrés K'eb and Mateo Wikab' visited Ursúa at the newly occupied Itza capital in March or April 1697 (AGI, G 151A, no. 5, Testimony of Nicolás de Aya, 6 July 1697).

468 13. The report by Wikab' to Gil is described in AGI, P 237, ramo 3, Pablo Gil to Francisco de Hariza, 30 Oct. 1695, ff. 196v–199r.

14. Ibid.

15. The 1655 Chunuk'um matrícula lists two persons named K'eb: Catalina K'eb of Tipuj (married to Pedro Tamay) and Pedro K'eb' of Saksuus (married

to María Wikab'). The Wikab'-K'eb' intermarriage suggests that Mateo Wikab' and Andrés K'eb' may have been relatives.

16. AGI, P 237, ramo 3, Gil to Hariza, 30 Oct. 1695. These towns included Tab'in Chan, Sakpeten, Mopan, Tzok, Wikab', Nojpolol, Ichtun, and Sakche between Tipuj and Lago Petén Itza. Tab'in Chan and Wikab' would have been names of town leaders. This Mopan would not have been the town of that name which is today San Luis in southern Petén. Around the lake the following towns were being abandoned: Sakpuy, Motzkalek', Ek'ixil, Sakpeten, B'oj (AjB'oj), P'ich, Ain (probably Yalain), Kantetul, and Mas K'in (a person's name).

17. AGI, P 237, ramo 10, Auto del gobernador Ursúa, 23 Nov. 1695, ff. 572v–573v. Hariza received Gil's letter of 30 October at Chunjujub' on 18 November, sending it immediately to Ursúa (AGI, G 151A, no. 4, Hariza to Ursúa, 18 Nov. 1695, f. 52r–v).

18. AGI, P 237, ramo 10, Pablo Gil de Azamar to Francisco de Hariza, 7 Dec. 1695 (about) ff. 576v–577r.

19. AGI, P 237, ramo 3, Ursúa to Conde de Galve, 12 Dec. 1695, f. 187r–v.

20. Avendaño, 1987, p. 21.

21. Ursúa was equally eager for Avendaño to reach Nojpeten, owing to his concern that Roque de Soberanis y Centeno would return to office before he could record officially the Itza ruler's personal submission to the Crown. In a letter to Jacinto de Barrios Leal, the president of Guatemala, Ursúa stated that he had sent Avendaño to Nojpeten with a letter and gift for Ajaw Kan Ek', "so that he may begin to catechize them until I am able personally to go to the said provinces." He had to go to Nojpeten, he explained, before Soberanis's return, which he expected shortly; he wished not to have to give up control over the Itza enterprise, considering his efforts to date and the heavy financial costs he had incurred personally (AGI, G 153, no. 1, Ursúa to Barrios Leal, 22 Dec. 1695, ff. 71v–73r).

22. AGI, P 237, ramo 8, Auto and recaudo by dean and ecclesiastical cabildo of Mérida, 16 Dec. 1695.

23. AGIH, P 237, ramo 8, Fr. Juan Antonio de Silva, Provincial, to dean and ecclesiastical council of Mérida, c. 17 Dec. 1695, ff. 435r–437r. This was a weak claim on Silva's part, because the Franciscans' mission so far had reached only the distant frontiers of Itza territory. The "ambassador" in question was the lay friar Lucas de San Francisco, who had gone in October to meet some Itzas in a town south of Chuntuki. Sixty-seven of these later went to Chuntuki to see the commissary, Fray Juan de San Buenaventura Chávez (AGI, P 237, ramo 3, San Buenaventura et al. to provincial, 24 Oct. 1695).

24. Ursúa wrote to the Crown and the viceroy during this period, as he had to the president of Guatemala, expressing concern for the future of his accomplishments with the Itzas in light of Soberanis's return to office (AGI, P 237, ramo 1, Ursúa to Crown, 21 Dec. 1695, ff. 7r–v; P 237, ramo 3, Ursúa to Conde de Galve, 21 Dec. 1695, ff. 176v–177v; G 153, no. 1, Ursúa to Barrios Leal, 22 Dec. 1695). **469**

25. AGI, G 151A, no. 4, Auto by Ursúa, 20 Dec. 1695, ff. 57r–58r.

26. That is, "justicia y regimiento," the city's governing cabildo comprising an alcalde and several regidores.

27. Pacheco was a secular cleric appointed as interpreter for this occasion.

28. AGI, P 237, ramo 3, Recibimiento del indio Ah Chan, 26 Dec. 1695, ff. 187v–191v.

29. Ibid.

30. AGI, P 237, Certification by Diego de Carvajal Frío, 26 Dec. 1695, ff. 440v–441r.

31. AGI, P 237, ramo 3, Declaración de un indio que dijo llamarse Ah Chan, y ser sobrino del rey Canek que lo es de la nación de los Itzaes, 29 Dec. 1695.

32. Ibid.

33. Avendaño used the similar word "anahte" [*anajte*] (his plural *anahtees*) to refer to the Itzas' hieroglyphic books (Avendaño, 1696, f. 29v). Either form may be related to the Nahuatl *amatl*, meaning both the book made from bark paper and the tree from which the bark is taken (Barrera Vásquez et al., 1980, p. 16).

34. Except where noted, information about the Kejach baptismal ceremony is from AGI, P 237, ramo 8, Certification by Diego de Carvajal Campo Frío, 30 Dec. 1695, ff. 441r–442r.

35. The name is written "Kumu" in AGI, P 237, ramo 8, Certification by Diego de Carvajal Campo Frío, 30 Dec. 1695, ff. 441r–442r, but all other sources indicate that his name was K'u.

36. His name is written Ciyau in AGI, P 237, ramo 8, Certification by Diego de Carvajal Campo Frío, 30 Dec. 1695. Other sources make it clear, however, that his correct surname was K'ixaw.

37. The instrument that I have translated as "oboe" was the *chirimía,* or flageolot.

38. Salazar's title, in addition to archdeacon, was "chantre y comisario de los tribunales de inquisición y cruzada in Yucatán." He carried out the baptisms himself because of the advanced age of the dean.

39. AGI, G 151A, no. 4, Certification of baptisms of Ah Chan and others, 31 Dec. 1695.

40. AGI, G 151A, no. 6, Matrícula del pueblo de Pakekem, 9 July 1696. The cacique of Pak'ek'em appears in the census to have been don Marcos Puk.

41. AGI, P 237, ramo 8, Certification by Diego de Carvajal Campo Frío, 31 Dec. 1695, ff. 442r–443r. The baptismal certifications are recorded in AGI, G 151A, no. 4, Certification of baptisms of Chan and others, 31 Dec. 1695.

42. Patch, 1993, pp. 126, 191.

Chapter 8: Avendaño and Ajaw Kan Ek'

1. Avendaño, Relación, 1696, ff. 17r–66r; 1987, pp. 20–66.

2. Avendaño, Relación, 1696, ff. 18r–22r; 1987, pp. 21–24.

3. AGI, P 237, ramo 10, Azamar to Hariza, 7 Dec. 1695.

4. AGI, P 237, ramo 8, Silva et al. to Ursúa, 17 Jan. 1696.

5. The letter from Silva is mentioned in Avendaño, Relación, 1696, f. 30v; 1987, p. 34. A Spanish version of Ursúa's letter to Ajaw Kan Ek' is in AGI, P 237, ramo 3; see note 40, this chapter.

6. AGI, P 237, ramo 1, Testimonies of Avendaño and two other religious, May 1696. The content of the recorded deposition indicates that Avendaño either read his written account aloud or simply turned it over to the clerk, who omitted certain information in his final transcript. The other two friars presented shorter oral accounts that added little new information. All three also responded to several follow-up questions.

7. Avendaño, Relación, 1696, ff. 17v, 46v–47r, 66r; 1987, pp. 20, 51, 66. The phrase "misionero" is mistranslated in 1987, p. 20.

8. Avendaño, Relación, 1696, ff. 22v–23r; 1987, pp. 24–25.

9. Avendaño, Relación, 1696, f. 26r; 1987, p. 28.

10. Avendaño called this body of water a *sib'al.*

11. *Nohem* in the original, from *noj-jem*, large valley.

12. Avendaño, Relación, 1696, f. 24r; 1987, p. 26. Avendaño's distances appear to be greatly exaggerated as he crossed these karst hills, even allowing for the winding nature of the path.

13. Avendaño, Relación, 1696, f. 24r–v; 1987, p. 26.

14. Ibid.

15. Avendaño, Relación, 1696, f. 24v; 1987, p. 27. Edmonson translates Tanxulukmul as "facing final mound" (*tan xuluk mul*). This section of Avendaño's itinerary is highly confusing, making it difficult to locate where he saw the ruin. In a subsequent paragraph he clearly redescribes the trip across the karst hills, this time calling the pond Ichmuxan (possibly from Itzaj *ich muxan*, "among muxan palms"). The realization that parts of these two paragraphs offer different descriptions of the same portions of the trip — about four leagues across the karst hills and then a passage of about one and a half leagues before coming to the pond — finally helped me make sense of his route. Tanxulukmul and Ichmuxan were almost certainly the same place, but perhaps the different names reflect different memories of those who contributed to Avendaño's account.

It appears that they descended from the karst hills at about kilometer 20 along the present road, three kilometers east of Hacienda Papactún. About five kilometers farther south is the archaeological site of Acté, also the name of the river to its south, which at its headwaters is called Arroyo Cantetul. Acté may therefore be Tanxulukmul, although this possibility has yet to be investigated.

16. Avendaño, Relación, f. 25r–v; 1987, pp. 27–28.

17. Teoberto Maler visited Kantetul in 1895, noting that it was in a savannah of the same name. He was unimpressed with the size of the mounds and learned that no "sculptured stones" had ever been seen there by the inhabitants of nearby San Andrés (Maler, 1910, pp. 132, 152).

18. The edge of the town was, Avendaño calculated, four blocks from the riverbank.

19. Avendaño, Relación, 1696, f. 26v; 1987, p. 29. Unless otherwise indicated, the translations from the Relación are my own.

20. Avendaño, Relación, 1696, ff. 26v–27r; 1987, p. 29.

21. Avendaño, Relación, 1696, f. 27r–v; 1987, pp. 29–30. Apparently the path first followed Río Acté (or Saklemakal) toward the east to a point around the present-day settlement of Acté, and then turned south, crossing Río Ixkonob on the way toward the lake.

22. Avendaño, Relación, 1696, f. 27r; 1987, p. 29. As we see later, Ajaw Kan Ek' hoped that the Spaniards would behead his enemies. Beheading of political captives and enemies was an ancient Maya practice.

23. The advance message is mentioned only in AGI, P 237, ramo 1, Testimonies of Avendaño and two other religious, May 1696.

24. Avendaño, Relación, 1696, f. 27r; 1987, p. 30. Avendaño, 1987, mistakenly gives the number of canoes that arrived as eight instead of eighty. AGI, P 237, ramo 1, Testimonies of Avendaño and two other religious, May 1696, gives the number of canoes as "more than four hundred."

25. Avendaño did not specify how he knew that this person was the nephew of Ajaw Kan Ek'.

26. Avendaño, Relación, 1696, ff. 27v–28r; 1987, p. 30.

27. Avendaño, Relación, 1696, f. 25r; 1987, p. 30.

28. Avendaño, Relación, 1696, f. 28r–v; 1987, p. 31.

29. AGI, P 237, ramo 1, Testimonies of Avendaño and two other religious, May 1696.

30. Avendaño, Relación, 1696, f. 28v; 1987, p. 31.

31. Avendaño, Relación, 1696, f. 29r; 1987, p. 31.

32. Avendaño, Relación, 1696, f. 39r; 1987, p. 44. Avendaño states that he carried out the blessing and exorcism "luego que llegué a dicho Peten," suggesting that it was the first thing he did upon arriving.

33. Avendaño, Relación, 1696, f. 31v; 1987, p. 36.

34. Avendaño, Relación, 1696, ff. 29v–30r; 1987, p. 33.

35. Avendaño, Relación, 1696, f. 33r–v; 1987, p. 34.

36. This beverage was identified by Avendaño as *posole,* which today refers to the dough used to make both tortillas and *atol,* the actual drink.

37. Avendaño, Relación, 1696, ff. 30v–31r; 1987, p. 34.

38. AGI, P 237, ramo 11, Ursúa to Real Acuerdo, Guatemala, 22 March 1697, ff. 629r–635v.

39. Avendaño, Relación, f. 31r–v; 1987, p. 35.

40. The Spanish version of the letter is AGI, P 237, ramo 3, Ursúa to Canek de los Itzaes, 8 Dec. 1695, ff. 199r–203r. There is no descriptive material associated with it. Avendaño's discussion of the letter is in Relación, 1696, f. 31v; 1987,

p. 35. For discussion and examples of sixteenth-century *Requerimiento* texts, including bibliographic references, see Moroles Padrón, 1979, pp. 331–47.

41. The date was in error and should have had four four hundreds, not five, which would yield 80 + 1,600 + 15, or the year 1695. This was probably a copyist's error, because Avendaño, the presumed author of this letter, would not have made such a mistake.

42. AGI, P 237, ramo 3, Ursúa to Canek de los Itzaes, 8 Dec. 1695.

43. Avendaño, Relación, 1696, f. 34v; 1987, p. 38.

44. Avendaño, Relación, 1696, f. 31v; 1987, p. 35.

45. Ibid.

46. "Frijoles" were presumably black beans, and "carne de puerco del monte" was probably peccary (Avendaño, Relación, 1696, f. 33r; 1987, pp. 36–37).

47. Avendaño, Relación, 1696, f. 32r; 1987, p. 36.

48. Avendaño, Relación, 1696, f. 32v; 1987, p. 35.

49. Avendaño, Relación, 1696, ff. 32v–33r; 1987, p. 36. The complete passage from Ezekiel 36:25 is cited in Avendaño, 1987, p. 36, n. 124.

50. Avendaño, Relación, 1696, ff. 32v–33r; 1987, p. 36. Their answer he recorded as " 'ba valac a toca [i.e., *cota*] *vale*,' " which he translated, " 'so it will be when dawn comes tomorrow and we see it.' "

51. Avendaño, Relación, 1696, f. 33v; 1987, p. 37.

52. Avendaño, Relación, 1696, f. 46r; 1987, p. 50.

53. Avendaño, Relación, 1696, ff. 33v–34r; 1987, p. 37.

54. AGI, P 237, ramo 1, Testimonies of Avendaño and two other religious, May 1696.

55. A quarter of a vara would be about twenty-one centimeters.

56. Avendaño, Relación, 1696, f. 34r; 1987, p. 38.

57. Avendaño, Relación, 1696, f. 34v; 1987, p. 38.

58. AGI, P 237, ramo 1, Ursúa to Conde de Galve, 10 March 1696.

59. Avendaño, Relación, 1696, f. 35r; 1987, p. 39.

60. Avendaño, Relación, 1696, f. 35r–v; 1987, p. 39.

61. Avendaño, Relación, 1696, f. 35r–v; 1987, p. 39.

62. Although this literal translation is awkward, it conveys Avendaño's effort to demonstrate that the new k'atun had already begun.

63. Avendaño, Relación, 1696, f. 36v; 1987, p. 41.

64. Avendaño, Relación, 1696, f. 37r; 1987, p. 42. Cochineal was actually an insect that was attracted to a cultivated cactus plant.

65. Avendaño, Relación, 1696, f. 38v; 1987, p. 44. This translation differs significantly from that in Avendaño, 1987.

473

66. Avendaño, 1696, f. 39r; 1987, p. 44.

67. Avendaño, Relación, 1696, f. 39r; 1987, p. 45. This is a very free translation of this passage.

68. Avendaño, Relación, 1696, f. 40v; 1987, p. 45.

69. Ibid.

70. Ibid.

71. Avendaño, Relación, 1696, f. 43r; 1987, p. 48.

72. Avendaño, Relación, 1696, ff. 37v, 40v–41r; 1987, pp. 43, 45–46.

73. The following section is drawn from Avendaño, Relación, 1696, ff. 42v–43r; 1987, p. 48.

74. Avendaño, Relación, 1696, ff. 43v–44r; 1987, p. 49. This letter also appears in AGI, P 237, ramo 3, Open letter from Avendaño, 16 Jan. 1696, ff. 256v–257r (with another copy in AGI, P 237, ramo 8).

75. AGI, G 151A, no. 3, Testimonies presented on behalf of Ursúa, 26 Aug. 1696, Testimony of Zubiaur, 29 August 1696.

76. Avendaño, Relación, 1696, ff. 44r–v; 1987, p. 49.

77. Avendaño, Relación, 1696, ff. 45v–46r; 1987, p. 51. Avendaño claimed that Ajaw Kan Ek' had at first agreed to the friendship pact with the Spaniards and later reneged. This seems most unlikely, given the rest of the scenario that he reported.

78. Avendaño, Relación, 1696, f. 46v; 1987, p. 51.

79. Ibid.

80. AGI, P 237, ramo 1, Testimonies of Avendaño and two other religious, May 1696. In this version Avendaño attributed the comment about plans to chop the friars up into pieces only to a daughter of Ajaw Kan Ek', who he said was about eighteen years old. Comparato noted this report of IxChan Pana's apparent treachery in Avendaño, 1987, p. 51, n. 147, and in Villagutierre, 1933, bk. 7, ch. 2, p. 251, n. 960.

81. Avendaño, Relación, 1696, ff. 46v, 48v–49r; 1987, p. 53.

82. Avendaño, Relación, 1696, f. 49r; 1987, p. 53.

83. Avendaño, Relación, 1696, f. 48r; 1987, p. 52.

84. AGI, P 237, ramo 1, Ursúa to Conde de Galve, 10 March 1696.

85. Avendaño, Relación, 1696, f. 50r; 1987, p. 54.

86. Avendaño, Relación, 1696, f. 50v; 1987, p. 55.

87. The drink is not mentioned but is referred to as "their beverage" (Avendaño, Relación, 1696, f. 50v; 1987, p. 55).

88. Avendaño, Relación, 1696, ff. 50v–51r; 1987, p. 55.

89. Following the conquest, AjK'in Kan Ek', by then a prisoner of the Spaniards, implicated a "Panau" (Pana?) in the murders of soldiers and friars from Guatemala and Yucatán that occurred following Avendaño's departure. This accusation was also made by a relative of the ruler's named Kanek' (with the spelling "Panao"). AGI, G 151B, no. 2, Declarations of Ah Kin Canek, Canek (relative of Ah Canek), and the youth Camal, 16 April 1697, ff. 45v–47r, f. 46v.

90. Avendaño, Relación, 1696, f. 51r–v; 1987, p. 55.

91. Avendaño, Relación, 1696, f. 51v; 1987, p. 56.

92. Avendaño, Relación, 1696, f. 52r; 1987, p. 56.

93. Avendaño, Relación, 1696, ff. 52v–63v; 1987, pp. 56–64. I have considerably condensed his description of this period of time.

94. Avendaño, Relación, 1696, f. 64r–v; 1987, p. 65.

95. Avendaño, Relación, 1696, ff. 63v–66r; 1987, pp. 65–66.

96. See, for example, AGI, G 151A, no. 6, Declarations of Franciscan *guardianes* from the Partido de la Sierra y Bolonchen, 17 Aug. 1696; Declarations of additional witnesses concerning the Itza enterprise, 20 Aug. 1696; G 151A, no. 3, Consulta from Roque de Soberanis y Centeno to Viceroy, 28 Aug. 1696, ff. 119r–125r; Petition by Pablo Gil de Azamar, c. 19 Sept 1696, ff. 235v–237r. Pablo Gil de Azamar was imprisoned for five months in Bacalar by Captain Francisco de Hariza after AjChan's escape from Tipuj, where he had been taken by Spanish troops and secular missionaries following his visit to Mérida at the end of 1695. Gil was accused of falsely representing AjChan as the nephew and personal representative of Ajaw Kan Ek'. Eventually he was released following testimony in support of AjChan's legitimacy presented by several representatives of the Yalain province on September 20, 1696 (AGI, G 151A, no. 3, Petition by Azamar, 19 Sept 1696; Declaration of four Indians from Peten, 20 Sept. 1696).

Chapter 9: Itza-Spanish Warfare

1. AGI, G 151A, no. 3, Ursúa to Ortega Montáñez, 23 June 1696.

2. See AGI, G 151A, no. 3, Testimonies presented on behalf of Ursúa, 26 Aug. 1696.

3. AGI, G 151A, no. 4, Auto by Ursúa, 31 Dec. 1695, ff. 63v–64v. Summarized in Villagutierre, 1933, bk. 6, ch. 5, p. 277.

4. AGI, G 151A, no. 4, Auto by Ursúa, 1 Jan. 1696, f. 65r.

5. AGI, P 237, ramo 8, Auto by Ursúa to dean and ecclesiastical cabildo, 1 Jan. 1696, ff. 443v–444r.

6. AGI, G 151A, no. 4, Auto by Ursúa, 3 Jan. 1696, ff. 70r–71r; Respuesta del padre provincial, Fray Juan Antonio de Silva, 3 Jan. 1696, ff. 71v–72v.

7. AGI, P 237, ramo 8, Notification of delivery of real cédula to dean and ecclesiastical cabildo of Mérida, 3 Jan. 1696.

8. AGI, P 237, ramo 8, Auto and recaudo by dean and ecclesiastical cabildo of Mérida, 16 Dec. 1695.

9. AGI, P 237, ramo 8, Auto by dean and ecclesiastical council, Mérida, to provincial, 9 Jan. 1696; Fray Antonio de Silva, provincial, to dean and ecclesiastical cabildo, 9 Jan. 1696, ff. 452v–454v.

10. AGI, G 151A, no. 4, Auto by Ursúa, 14 Jan. 1696. The secular clergy–regular clergy dispute continued unabated throughout January and February 1695. See AGI, P 237, ramo 8, Silva et al. to Ursúa, 17 Jan. 1696; Diligencia by Pedro Rangel, secretary, ecclesiastical cabildo of Mérida, 25 Jan. 1696, ff. 458v–459r; Auto by dean and ecclesiastical cabildo, 31 Jan. 1696, ff. 459r–467r; Auto by dean and ecclesiastical cabildo of Mérida, 13 Feb. 1696, ff. 485r–40v. Ursúa at

one point pronounced that the Crown would ultimately have to resolve the conflict over the Itza missions. In the meantime, each party would consult with him individually in order to work out temporary solutions, and the Franciscan missions in the Kejach and Chan areas would continue with license from secular authorities, in accordance with the 1689 cédula presented by Silva.

11. AGI, G 151A, no. 3, Testimonies presented on behalf of Ursúa, 26 Aug. 1696.

12. Avendaño, Relación, 1696, f. 47r; 1987, p. 51. Avendaño, who knew the ruler of the north only as AjKan, is the only source for this episode.

13. Avendaño, Relación, 1696, ff. 47r–48v; 1987, pp. 52–53.

14. AGI, G 151A, no. 3, Testimony of Zubiaur Isasi, 29 Aug. 1696.

15. AGI, G 151A, no. 3, Testimonies presented on behalf of Ursúa, 26 Aug. 1696; Testimony of Zubiaur Isasi, 29 Aug. 1696.

16. Ibid.

17. Ursúa stated that García de Paredes did not go because he was ill (AGI, P 237, ramo 1, Ursúa to Conde de Galve, 10 March 1696). In the same dispatch he said that the troops went to the lake only to pilfer maize from the milpas adjacent to the lake.

18. This reconstruction is based on AGI, P 237, ramo 3, Zubiaur Isasi to Ursúa, 4 Feb. 1696, ff. 255r–256r; G 151B, no. 2, Junta de guerra, 12 March 1697; P 237, ramo 8, Paredes to Ursúa (?), 4 Feb. 1696; and G 151A, no. 3, Testimonies presented on behalf of Ursúa, 26 Aug. 1696.

19. This episode is unreported elsewhere and may have been an attempt by the Itzas to convince the Spaniards to return.

20. AGI, P 237, ramo 1, Ursúa to Crown, 12 May 1696. The description that follows is reconstructed from Ursúa to Crown, 12 May 1696, and AGI, G 151A, no. 3, Testimonies presented on behalf of Ursúa, 26 Aug. 1696. Where details differ, I have depended primarily upon Zubiaur's description.

21. AGI, G 151A, no. 3, Testimonies presented on behalf of Ursúa, 26 Aug. 1696.

22. AGI, G 151A, no. 3, Testimony of Alonso García de Paredes, 29 Aug. 1696, f. 76r.

23. In later testimony Zubiaur suggested that Campos was not killed (AGI, G 151A, no. 3, Testimonies presented on behalf of Ursúa, 26 Aug. 1696), but other reports confirmed the beheading (AGI, P 237, ramo 1, Ursúa to Crown, 12 May 1696, ff. 18r–21r; AGI, P 237, ramo 8, Paredes to Ursúa (?), 4 Feb. 1696, ff. 424v–427r).

24. This was reported to Ursúa by "one of the captains" (AGI, P 237, ramo 1, Ursúa to Crown, 12 May 1696; Ursúa to Conde de Galve, 10 March 1696).

25. AGI, G 151A, no. 3, Testimonies presented on behalf of Ursúa, 26 Aug. 1696, ff. 69r–104v. The muster roll for Garma's company appears in AGI, G 151A, no. 4, Auto by Ursúa, 23 Feb. 1696, ff. 74v–75r.

26. AGI, G 151A, no. 6, Declarations of additional witnesses concerning the Itza enterprise, 20 Aug. 1696, testimony of Julio Rentero.

27. AGI, G 151A, no. 3, Ursúa to Ortega Montáñez, obispo virrey, 12 May 1696, ff. 45r–47v; P 237, ramo 1, Ursúa to Crown, 12 May 1696.

28. AGI, G 151B, no. 2, Junta de guerra, 12 March 1697. The murder of the two Franciscans was also confirmed later by Governor Soberanis (AGI, G 151B, no. 8, Soberanis to Sánchez de Berrospe, 20 Oct. 1697).

29. AGI, G 151B, no. 2, Declaración de don Martín Chan, 10 March 1697.

30. These were later reinforced by another group of soldiers (AGI, EC 339B, no. 18, Declaración de Güemes, 29 Nov. 1703). Ursúa wrote that a total of thirty soldiers eventually went to Tipuj (AGI, M 363, Ursúa to Crown, 31 Jan. 1696), although later reports stated that there were only twenty-five (G 151A, no. 3, Certifications by secular priests regarding Indian carriers, Sept. 1696, ff. 221v–224v).

31. The number of secular priests was reported on some occasions as eleven, but a later report stated that there were ten. The original list of eleven priests included Lorenzo Pérez de Güemes (Jomun), Francisco de San Miguel y Figueroa, Manuel Méndez, Manuel Valencia, Salvador de Solis, Diego Rajón, Felíz Sánchez, Juan Francisco del Canto, Manuel Martín, Gaspar de Güemes, and Tomás Pérez (AGI, P 237, ramo 8, Notification of delivery of real cédula to dean and ecclesiastical cabildo of Mérida, 3 Jan. 1696; Auto by dean and ecclesiastical cabildo of Mérida, 4 Dec. 1695; Real cédula to bishop of Yucatán, 26 Oct. 1693; Cabildo eclesiástico de Mérida de Yucatán to Crown, 10 May 1696).

Some of these apparently did not participate. Known to have been included in the final list were Gaspar de Güemes, Manuel de Valencia, Pedro Martín Negrón (*cura* of Bacalar), and Francisco Gómez (*cura* of Peto) (AGI, EC 339B, no. 18, Declaración del Güemes, 29 Nov. 1703; P 237, ramo 8, Auto by dean and ecclesiastical council of Mérida, 11 Jan. 1696; G 151A, no. 3, Certifications by secular priests regarding Indian carriers, Sept. 1696; Petition of Conde de Miraflores, Pedro de Garrástegui Oleaga, to dean and ecclesiastical cabildo of Mérida, c. 29 August 1696, f. 220r–v).

32. AGI, G 151A, no. 3, Certifications by secular priests regarding Indian carriers, Sept. 1696; AGI, EC 339B, no. 18, Declaración del Güemes, 29 Nov. 1703. PWaltok' is written Valtok in the original source.

33. AGI, P 237, ramo 8, Diligencia by Pedro Rangel, secretary, ecclesiastical cabildo of Mérida, 25 Jan. 1696, ff. 458v–459r.

34. AGI, EC 339B, no. 18, Declaración de Güemes, 29 Nov. 1703.

35. AGI, G 151B, no. 2, Declaración de don Martín Chan, 10 March 1697.

36. AGI, P 237, ramo 1, Barrios Leal to Ursúa, 26 Oct. 1695; P 237, ramo 10, Declaration of Bernardo del Río, 23 June 1695.

37. AGI, P 237, ramo 1, Barrios Leal (president of Audiencia of Guatemala) to Ursúa, 26 Oct. 1695; see also Villagutierre, 1933, bk. 6, ch. 2, p. 268.

38. Villagutierre, 1933, bk. 6, ch. 2, p. 269.

39. Cano, 1942, p. 71; 1984, p. 14.

40. Unless otherwise indicated, the following account of this entrada is based on Amésqueta's long report to Escals (AGI, G 151A, no. 3, Bartolomé de Amésqueta to José de Escals, 31 March 1696, ff. 14r–40v). Villagutierre's summary of this report may be found in 1933, 1983, bk. 6, ch. 7–10.

41. AGI, G 505, Fray Agustín Cano to Bartolomé de Amésqueta, 9 April 1696, ff. 103v–105v. See also Cano, 1942, p. 72; 1984, p. 15.

42. See also AGI, G 505, Auto by Bartolomé de Amésqueta, with attached declarations, 27 March 1696, ff. 66v–91r.

43. The milpa, they surmised from information provided earlier by K'ixaw, was called IxB'ol. At this point they were four leagues from the lake, near the location of present-day Juntecholol.

44. AGI, G 505, Auto by Amésqueta, with attached declarations, 27 March 1696.

45. Ibid.

46. Ibid.

47. Ibid.

48. J. Eric S. Thompson surmised (1954, p. 154) that the redhead was an Englishman from Belize, but Amésqueta seemed to think he was a Spaniard.

49. Amésqueta described these as "labores que se estampan," which might also be interpreted as scarifications.

50. That is, *uts-puksik'al*, literally "good heart" or "kind heart."

51. AGI, G 151A, no. 3, Bartolomé de Amésqueta to José de Escals, 31 March 1696, ff. 14r–40v.

52. They had seen only one larger canoe with a capacity of seven or eight persons.

53. AGI, G 505, Auto by Amésqueta, with attached declarations, 27 March 1696.

54. Ibid.

55. Cano himself indicated in a letter to President Sánchez de Berrospe that the proper meaning was "a stockade of thick stakes" and confirmed K'ixaw's warning that any visiting Spaniards would be taken to it and killed there (AGI, G 153, no. 1, Fray Agustín Cano to Gabriel Sánchez de Berrospe, 31 March 1696, ff. 64r–66v). *Kuman* in colonial Yucatec could be used to mean "detained" and apparently here meant "imprisoned."

56. AGI, G 505, Auto by Amésqueta, with attached declarations, 27 March 1696.

57. Young Manuel de Zavaleta, who was posted in a tree during all this, counted fifty-nine canoes in the lake and about three hundred Itzas on land and water (AGI, G 505, Auto by Amésqueta, with attached declarations, 27 March 1696). Remesal's history is published as Remesal, 1932.

58. Petenya in original.

59. According to Cano (1942, pp. 73–74; 1984, pp. 16–17), the Itzas who

first met Díaz's party on the lakeshore told them that Franciscans were at Nojpeten and invited them into their canoes. The Guatemalans apparently believed that any such friars would have been Avendaño and his companions, having had no news of the outcome of Avendaño's mission. Fearing a trap, the Guatemalans sent a message to the supposed friars with the Itzas, receiving in reply only a rosary as "proof" that they were there. Still suspicious, they looked across the water to see men dressed "in the clothes of the priests whom they had killed a few days before, and they made signs from the Island and called to our men — at this it appears they had no further cause for doubt." The men in these clothes, however, were Itzas (Cano, 1942, p. 73; 1984, p. 16).

At this point Díaz, the other soldiers, the two Dominicans, and "two other young men" embarked in the canoes, leaving the thirty native carriers on the mainland to watch after the mules and their loads. A struggle ensued in which the Itza paddlers upset some of the canoes and killed and wounded a number of the soldiers, taking the wounded back to the shore and finishing them off there. The canoe carrying Díaz, the two priests, and the two unidentified young men was not overturned, owing to its large size. As this group neared Nojpeten, the Spaniards jumped ashore, where all but Díaz were seized without resistance. Díaz defended himself with his sword, killing, according to Cano, about eighty Itzas before being mortally wounded by arrows. They killed the two young men immediately. The two Dominicans, only wounded by arrows, were reportedly beaten with sticks by AjK'in Kan Ek', the high priest, and tied to X-shaped wooden crosses, where they remained in a vertical position for some time. While in this position Fray Cristóbal de Prada preached to his torturers in Itza and Chol, while Fray Jacinto de Vargas prayed to God and the Virgin Mary even as the high priest cut open their chests and removed their hearts. Back on the mainland the Itzas killed every one of the native carriers.

In all, according to Cano, the Itzas killed eighty-seven members of the expedition, including the two priests, fifty soldiers, thirty natives, "and four young men and a Christian Chol Indian who went on account of his language." Their murderers, he claimed, ate every one of them, leaving the bones of all but the captain, the priests, and the two young men killed on Nojpeten on the mainland. They placed the bones of the others in a cave on Nojpeten, where they were later found by the conquerors and returned to Santiago de Guatemala.

Cano's sources for this account, he stated, included "information given by the Chol Indians as well as through information made public by the people of Yucatán" — that is, García de Paredes and the others who went to Santiago de Guatemala shortly after the 1697 conquest. There were, however, no surviving Chol eyewitnesses to the events, and few of these details appeared in confessions **479** extracted following the conquest. Most of the account, except for the excessive claims of cannibalism, is plausible but can be neither confirmed nor disconfirmed on the basis of reliable independent evidence.

60. AGI, G 151A, no. 3, Amésqueta to Escals, 31 March 1696.

61. AGI, G 505, Cano to Amésqueta, 9 April 1696, ff. 103v–105v.

62. AGI, G 505, Auto by Amésqueta, with testimonies, 7 April 1696, ff. 96r–102r.

63. AGI, G 153, no. 1, Amésqueta to Gabriel Sánchez de Berrospe, 18 April 1696, f. 130r. The term translated here as loincloths is "guruperas" (*gruperas*), the meaning of which is "crupper," the leather strap that stabilizes a horse's saddle when it is looped under the animal's tail. These, then, were cloths that were wrapped under the man's crotch and tied around his waist.

64. AGI, G 153, no. 1, Amésqueta to Sánchez de Berrospe, 18 April 1696.

65. Ibid.

66. AGI, G 505, Auto by Amésqueta, 9 April 1696, f. 106r; Auto by Amésqueta, 13 April 1696, ff. 106r–107r.

67. The text states that Kej and the cacique of Chok Ajaw had died, but it is apparent that this is a copyist's error.

68. AGI, G 153, no. 1, Amésqueta to Sánchez de Berrospe, 18 April 1696.

69. AGI, G 153, no. 1, Amésqueta to Gabriel Sánchez de Berrospe, 26 April 1696, ff. 138r–149v.

70. The following paragraphs are based on AGI, G 153, no. 1, Amésqueta to Sánchez de Berrospe, 26 April 1696.

71. AGI, G 151A, no. 3, Amésqueta to Escals, 31 March 1696.

72. See Jones, 1989, pp. 27–28, 33, 298, n. 7.

73. AGI, G 153, no. 1, Amésqueta to Sánchez de Berrospe, 26 April 1696.

74. AGI, G 505, Diligencia by Cano, including account of Manche Chols by late de Prada, 16 April 1696.

75. AGI, P 237, ramo 2, Jose de Escals to Crown, 16 May 1696, ff. 90r–100r. In these dispatches José de Escals referred to the abandonment of a presidio at Mopan rather than San Pedro Mártir. These locations were apparently considered synonymous, although the town of Mopan proper was about nine leagues from San Pedro Mártir.

76. AGI, P 237, ramo 2, Jose de Escals to Crown, 13 Jan 1697, ff. 102r–110r.

77. AGI, P 237, ramo 8, Cabildo eclesiástico de Mérida de Yucatán to Crown, 10 May 1696, ff. 418r–423r.

78. AGI, P 237, ramo 2, Escals to Crown, 16 May 1696, ff. 90r–100r.

79. AGI, P 237, ramo 11, Junta general de guerra (Guatemala) and attached pareceres, 1 May 1697, ff. 643v–679v, parecer of José de Escals.

80. AGI, G 151A, no. 3, Sánchez de Berrospe to Ursúa, 17 April 1696, f. 17.

81. AGI, P 237, ramo 2, Escals to Crown, 16 May 1696; AGI, P 237, ramo 1, Barrios Leal to Ursúa, 26 Oct. 1695. The other two Franciscans named as interpreters were Fray Miguel de Loaysa and Fray Francisco del Búrgos (AGI, G 151A, no. 4, Auto by Ursua, 3 Dec. 1695, ff. 44v–45v).

82. AGI, G 151A, no. 3, Testimonies presented on behalf of Ursúa, 26 Aug. 1696.

Chapter 10: The Costs of the Camino Real

1. Carrillo y Ancona, 1895, vol. 2, pp. 617 ff.

2. AGI, P 237, ramo 3, Report by Lic. Baltásar de Tovar to Conde de Galve, 20 Jan. 1696, ff. 205r–220r; Parecer del real acuerdo, 23 Jan. 1696, ff. 220r–224r. Details concerning the inquisition charges, not considered here, may be found in AGI, P 237, ramo 3, Auto and certification pertaining to the absolution of Soberanis y Centeno, Feb. 1696, ff. 238r–242r.

3. AGI, P 237, ramo 3, Soberanis y Centeno to Conde de Galve, 11 Feb. 1696, ff. 232r–234v. The viceroy was Gaspar de Sandoval Cerda Silva y Mendoza, Conde de Galve.

4. See Villagutierre, 1933, 1983, bk. 7, ch. 6. I have studied only portions of the extensive original documentation for these issues and have relied heavily on Villagutierre for this section.

5. AGI, P 237, ramo 3, Parecer del real acuerdo, 23 Jan. 1696, ff. 220r–224r. See Villagutierre, 1933, 1983, bk. 7, ch. 6.

6. AGI, P 237, ramo 3, Report by Tovar to Conde de Galve, 20 Jan. 1696.

7. AGI, P 237, ramo 3, Certification of Ursúa's expenditures in the opening of the road to Guatemala, 21 Jan. 1696, ff. 224r–225v.

8. AGI, P 237, ramo 3, Decree by Conde de Galve, 10 Feb. 1696, ff. 227r–232r; Mandamiento de Gaspar de Sandoval Cerda Silva y Mondoza, Conde de Galve, 13 Feb. 1696, ff. 243r–252r.

9. AGI, P 237, ramo 3, Mandamiento de Sandoval Cerda Silva, 13 Feb. 1696. Francisco de Ursúa's relationship as brother of Martín is recorded in AGI, G 151A, no. 3, Petition by Francisco de Ursúa to viceroy of New Spain, c. 18 Sept. 1696.

10. AGI, P 237, ramo 3, Respuesta del fiscal, 20 April 1696.

11. AGI, P 237, ramo 3, Decree by Conde de Galve, viceroy of New Spain, 4 May 1696, ff. 273r–275v. It is not clear when the headquarters were moved from Chuntuki back to Tzuktok'.

12. AGI, G 151A, no. 3, Ursúa to Ortega Montañez, obispo virrey, 12 May 1696. He simultaneously sent the same information to the Crown, adding, however, news of the Itza-Spanish conflict (AGI, P 237, ramo 1, Ursúa to Crown, 12 May 1696).

13. AGI, P 237, ramo 1, Real cédula to Roque de Soberanis y Centeno, 29 May 1696, and supporting documents on behalf of Ursúa, ff. 53r–58v.

14. AGI, G 151A, no. 3, Ursúa to Ortega Montañez, 23 June 1696; P 237, ramo 1, Ursúa to Crown, 16 Dec. 1696, ff. 50r–52r. Ursúa mentioned receiving another empowering cédula, but its contents are unknown (AGI, G 151A, no. 3, Ursúa to Conde de Montezuma, 24 Oct. 1696, ff. 246v–250r).

15. AGI, P 237, ramo 1, Auto by Roque de Soberanis y Centeno, 3 Dec. 1696.

16. AGI, P 237, ramo 1, Juan Jerónimo Abad to Roque de Soberanis y Centeno, 7 Dec. 1696.

17. AGI, G 151A, no. 6, Auto by Governor Roque de Soberanis y Centeno, 20 July 1696, ff. 7r–8v; Notification of delivery of auto de ruego y encargo to provincial, Fray Juan Antonio de Silva, 23 July 1696, ff. 10r–11r.

18. AGI, G 151A, no. 6, Auto by Governor Roque de Soberanis y Centeno, 13 Aug. 1696, ff. 22v–23r; Declarations of Franciscan *guardianes* from the Partido de la Sierra y Bolonchen, 17 Aug. 1696.

19. AGI, G 151A, no. 6, Declarations of additional witnesses concerning the Itza enterprise, 20 Aug. 1696.

20. AGI, G 151A, no. 3, Testimonies presented on behalf of Ursúa, 26 Aug. 1696.

21. AGI, G 151A, no. 3, Petition of Conde de Miraflores, Pedro de Garrastegui Oleaga, to dean and ecclesiastical council of Mérida, c. 29 August 1696.

22. AGI, G 151A, no. 3, Certifications by secular priests regarding Indian carriers, Sept. 1696.

23. AGI, G 151A, no. 3, Ursúa to Dr. Juan de Ortega Montáñez, 14 Oct. 1696, ff. 241v–243v. Ursúa, however, indirectly admitted to underpaying the carriers and suppliers by stating that in September or October he had remitted monies to the secular priests "in the partidos closest to the entrada so that the supply trains [*cabalgaduras*] might be paid [both] when they make [the journey] and on their return, [when] they carry less."

24. AGI, G 151A, no. 6, Auto by Governor Roque de Soberanis y Centeno, 29 Aug. 1696, f. 44r–v.

25. AGI, G 151A, no. 6, Declarations by caciques and justicias of Beneficios Bajos and Altos, 31 Aug. 1696–24 Oct. 1696, ff. 45r–72v.

26. AGI, G 151A, no. 3, Ursúa to Ortega Montáñez, 14 Oct. 1696.

27. AGI, G 151A, no. 3, Velásquez to viceroy of New Spain, 2 Sept. 1696.

28. AGI, G 151A, no. 3, Respuesta del fiscal, Lic. Baltásar de Tobar, 12 Sept. 1696, ff. 112r–118v.

29. AGI, G 151A, no. 3, Petition by Francisco de Ursúa to viceroy of New Spain, c. 18 Sept. 1696.

30. AGI, G 151A, no. 3, Petition by Azamar, c. 19 Sept 1696; Declaration of four Indians from Peten, 20 Sept. 1696, ff. 237v–240r.

31. AGI, G 151A, no. 3, Ursúa to Ortega Montáñez, 14 Oct. 1696; Ursúa to Montezuma, 24 Oct. 1696; AGI, P 237, ramo 1, Ursúa to Crown, 27 Oct. 1696.

32. AGI, G 151A, no. 3, Consulta from Soberanis y Centeno to viceroy, 28 Aug. 1696; Governor Roque de Soberanis to Juan de Ortega Montáñez, 18 Sept. 1696, ff. 56v–58r.

33. AGI, G 151A, no. 3, Ursúa to Conde de Montezuma, viceroy, 24 Oct. 1696, ff. 246v–250r.

34. Ursúa noted the antiquity of the road himself (AGI, P 237, ramo 1, Ursúa to Crown, 26 Sept. 1697, ff. 67r–69v).

35. Ursúa wrote in May that the road was by then completed to the lake; the months of March and April would have been spent improving it (AGI, P 237, ramo 1, Ursúa to Crown, 12 May 1696).

36. AGI, G 151A, no. 3, Ursúa to Obispo Virrey Ortega Montáñez, 12 May 1696.

37. Sesere had built the fort at Campeche and was known as a mathematical expert (AGI, P 237, ramo 1, Ursúa to Crown, 27 Oct. 1696).

38. AGI, G 151A, no. 3, Ursúa to Montezuma, 24 Oct. 1696.

39. Once he had finished building a piragua in order to cross Río San Pedro, García de Paredes had so little to keep his troops occupied that sometime in July or early August he sent twenty-nine of his soldiers, with a thirty-day supply of food, to search for the source of the river. He also sent some of his workers to improve the road across the hills toward the lake, but the rains forced them to stop and build a "thatch fort" eight to ten leagues from the lake. This encampment, occupied at that time by forty troops and defended with heavy artillery, was probably located at the aguada north of the Acté River that Avendaño had called Ichmuxan, only three leagues north of the first Chak'an Itza town. See AGI, G 151A, no. 3, Ursúa to Juan de Ortega Montáñez, 20 Aug. 1696, ff. 54v–55v.

Ursúa wrote that the fort was located sixteen leagues from the lake, which would have placed it at the southern foot of the high hills north of the lake, perhaps at the lake or aguada that Avendaño called Tanxulukmul (see chapter 8). By October the estimate of the distance had grown still greater, to eighteen leagues from the lake (AGI, Guatemala 151A, no. 3, Ursúa to Montezuma, 24 Oct. 1696). The closer location, however, seems more likely as a base camp for the fashioning of the timbers for the galeota.

40. AGI, P 237, ramo 1, Ursúa to Crown, 27 Oct. 1696, ff. 43r–48r.

41. Ibid.

42. Ibid. He cited a similar provision granted to Diego de Vera Ordoñez de Villaguirán in a cédula dated 29 March 1639.

43. AGI, G 151A, no. 7, Auto by Governor Roque de Soberanis y Centeno, 14 Dec. 1696, f. 6r–v.

44. AGI, P 237, ramo 1, Ursúa to Crown, 16 Dec. 1696, ff. 50r–52r. Recruiting sailors for what would ultimately be only a single galeota proved somewhat difficult, because all available seamen were needed to protect the coasts (AGI, G 151A, no. 7, Juan Jerónimo Abad to Governor Roque de Soberanis y Centeno, 26 Dec. 1696, f. 7r–v).

45. AGI, P 237, ramo 1, Ursúa to Crown, 16 Dec. 1696.

46. AGI, G 151B, no. 2, Auto by Ursúa, 10 March 1697, ff. 3r–4r.

47. AGI, P 237, ramo 1, Ursúa to Crown, 22 Jan. 1697.

48. Villagutierre gives Ursúa's date of departure as January 24 (1933, bk. 8, ch. 3, p. 24).

49. AGI, P 237, ramo 1, Ursúa to Crown, 22 Jan. 1697.

50. AGI, G 151A, no. 6, Mandamiento by Ursúa, 21 May 1696, f. 11r.

51. AGI, G 151A, no. 4, Ursúa to Barrios Leal, 1 Dec. 1695, ff. 36v–40v.

52. AGI, G 151A, no. 6, Mandamiento by Ursúa, 21 May 1696.

53. B'atkab' was known as a Kejach town, whereas Pak'ek'em had always been the "town of the Chans," because a large number of its inhabitants bore the name Chan. An equally large number, however, were Puks. These two patrilineages far outnumbered the others. A similar social pattern characterized B'atkab', whose dominant families were Puks and K'ixaws. The population of B'atkab' included 98 "adults" and 45 children ten years and younger; that of Pak'ek'em, 207 "adults" and 141 children.

54. AGI, G 151A, no. 6, Certificación de los padres comisarios de las nuevas poblaciones, 13 July 1696, ff. 21r–22v. The identity of Yajb'akab', also recorded as IxB'akab', is unknown.

55. AGI, G 151A, no. 6, Certificación de los padres comisarios de las nuevas poblaciones, 13 July 1696.

56. Ibid.

57. See AGI, G 151A, no. 6, Declarations of Franciscan guardians from the Partido de la Sierra y Bolonchen, 17 Aug. 1696, which consists of depositions by several Franciscans serving in the Partido of the Sierra and B'olonch'en, by demand of Soberanis. Three of those testifying knew that Tzuktok' had been abandoned. One of them, Fray Andrés de Campo, stated that there had been only about twenty adult Mayas living there before the abandonment. Soberanis, however, wrote that there had been two hundred living there (AGI, G 151A, no. 3, Consulta from Roque de Soberanis y Centeno to viceroy, 28 Aug. 1696).

58. AGI, G 151A, no. 6, Auto by Governor Roque de Soberanis y Centeno, 2 Sept. 1696, f. 76v.

59. The six men were Ventura Kawich (age 20), Agustín Tz'ul (24), Lucas Puk (25), Alonso B'atun (19), Juan K'ixaw (20), and Gabriel Jaw (20). All of them appeared on the B'atkab' matrícula.

60. AGI, G 151A, no. 6, Declarations by Indians from Batcab, 4 Sept. 1696, ff. 76v–79v.

61. AGI, G 151A, no. 6, Auto by Governor Roque de Soberanis y Centeno, 6 Sept. 1696, ff. 79v–80r.

62. When Ursúa's final entrada reached Tzuktok' in early 1697, he learned of the further fate of the Kejach converts. He discovered that the cacique of Tzuktok' had moved some of the inhabitants three leagues from the town's original location because of "its bad climate." Others were now living at Jop'elch'en, B'olonch'en Kawich, and Sajkab'ch'en. Since all these towns were "administered" by García de Paredes and Castillo y Toledo, it is unlikely that their move had been voluntary. At B'atkab' Ursúa learned that some of the kidnapped inhabitants of Pak'ek'em had escaped from the Itzas and returned, only to run away from the approaching Spanish troops. Thirty were later rounded up and taken to him at the new headquarters established by Zubiaur two leagues from the lake. The inhabitants of B'atkab' had moved two leagues from their original location, but 120

people of Chunpich had relocated at a distance of four leagues in the bush. Ursúa handed out gifts to the people of Pak'ek'em, instructing them to try to convince those of B'atkab' and Chunpich to return to their original locations (AGI, P 237, ramo 11, Ursúa to Real Acuerdo, 22 March 1697; Villagutierre's interpretation of this letter is an excellent example of his proclivity to exaggerate and embellish information included in the original document [1933, bk. 8, ch. 3, p. 347]).

63. AGI, G 151A, no. 3, Testimonies presented on behalf of Ursúa, 26 Aug. 1696, ff. 69r–104v; Declaration of Diego de Avila y Pacheco, encomendero of Oxkutzcab, 29 Aug. 1696, ff. 104v–107v.

64. AGI, G 151A, no. 6, Auto by Soberanis, 29 Aug. 1696, f. 44r–v.

65. AGI, G 151A, no. 6, Auto by Governor Roque de Soberanis y Centeno, with attached certification and list of cabeceras and visitas in the partidos of Costa, Sierra, Camino Real, Campeche, and jurisdiction of Valladolid, 31 Oct. 1696, ff. 73r–76v.

66. Two of these — Tek'it and Mama — were actually located in the partido of Sierra, while the rest were in Beneficios Bajos. Twenty-seven towns had supplied the Tipuj entrada — five in Beneficios Bajos, twenty in Beneficios Altos, and two in Valladolid. Assignment of the district affiliation of the towns is based on Gerhard, 1979. Because these boundaries changed from time to time, all of these may have been considered Beneficios towns at the time.

67. The twenty-seven towns that reported supplying the entrada to Tipuj provided a total of 143 horses and fifteen mules, in addition to modest amounts of maize meal.

68. AGI, G 151A, no. 3, Petition of Conde de Miraflores, Pedro de Garrástegui Oleaga, to dean and ecclesiastical council of Mérida, c. 29 August 1696; Auto by dean and ecclesiastical council of Mérida, 29 August 1696, ff. 220v–221v; Certifications by secular priests regarding Indian carriers, Sept. 1696, ff. 221v–224v. The priests were from the towns of Jomun, Jokab'a, Joktun, Santiago Tekoj, Mama, Tixkakal, Sakalaka, Yaxkab'a, Peto, and Bacalar (i.e., Chunjujub').

69. The friars' testimony, not cited again in this section, is from AGI, G 151A, no. 6, Declarations of Franciscan *guardianes* from the Partido de la Sierra y Bolonchen, 17 Aug. 1696, ff. 24v–35r.

70. Fray Andrés de Avendaño, also called upon to testify, had nothing to say about this subject, presumably because his administrative duties in Mérida prevented him from knowing what had transpired in the rural missions.

71. AGI, G 151A, no. 6, Declarations of additional witnesses concerning the Itza enterprise, 20 Aug. 1696.

72. AGI, G 151A, no. 3, Declaration of Avila, 29 Aug. 1696, ff. 104v–107v.

73. These depositions are from AGI, G 151A, no. 3, Testimonies presented on behalf of Ursúa, 26 Aug. 1696.

74. See AGI, G 151A, no. 7, Accounts of payments to soldiers and suppliers, including muster rolls, for the journey to Peten Itza, Jan. 1697, ff. 15v–25r. In contrast to the absence of payment records to Maya, mulatto, and Spanish

participants on the first two entradas, payments for Ursúa's own, final entrada to the camino real was meticulously documented. Governor Soberanis delegated the responsibility of keeping these records to Juan Jerónimo Abad, the governor of arms at Campeche. Countersigned by the public clerk, they provide a detailed roster of many of the players and their duties on the final expedition to Chuntuki and, ultimately, to Ch'ich' on the shores of Lago Petén Itzá. They also record in great detail the materials and food supplies required for such an ambitious undertaking. Although the extant records are not complete — they extend only from December 22, 1696, through January 11, 1697 — their contents are quite specific.

75. The spelling of this Basque name is uncertain. It appears as Aysucion (AGI, G 151A, no. 7, Accounts of payments to soldiers and suppliers, Jan. 1697, ff. 15v–25r), Aizvam (AGI, G 151B, no. 2, Certificación de los cabos y oficiales de guerra, 14 March 1697, ff. 30r–35v), and Ayzuani (Villagutierre, 1983, bk. 10, ch. 5, p. 373). I follow Villagutierre's spelling with a slight modification.

76. AGI, P 237, ramo 10, Auto by Ursúa, 27 July 1695.

77. AGI, G 151B, no. 2, Certificación de los cabos y oficiales de guerra, 14 March 1697. Two of the fifty-two soldiers who remained on Nojpeten after Ursúa's departure in May had Maya surnames (AGI, G 151A, no. 3, Lista de la gente de guarnición del reducto del Peten de Nuestra Señora de los Remedios y San Pablo, 9 May 1697, ff. 307v–309v).

78. More specifically, the items include tools for building the boats (1 anvil, 4 hammers, 4 tongs, 1 drill, files, 2 axes) and supplies for their construction (2,000 framing nails, 400 nails for the principal support beams [*clavos de escora mayor*], oarlocks [number unspecified], 1.5 quintals of iron and an unspecified amount to make rudders, 19 pounds of steel, deerskin to make bellows, 2 boxes of pitch, 1 saw, 1 flag for the galeota, 1 sisal rope 5.5 inches thick and 81 fathoms (about 143 meters) long, 2 small lengths of sisal tackle, pulleys [*motonoes vigotas*], and friction material [*rozamento*, probably used to sand wood]). In addition there were supplies for muleteers and for packaging cargo (72 leather carrying bags, 1 bundle plus 72 individual tie-ropes [*lías*], 1 bundle of rope for tying animals together in the train [*reata*], 30 empty jars, jars for storing dried chicken, 12 bags [*costales*] with tie-ropes for storing salted meat, 384 bags [*costales*], 6 sacks [*sacas*], and 2 bundles plus 137 individual palm-mats [*petates*] for bagging). Religious supplies comprised 1 chest for vestments and 2 arrobas of decorative wax candles (*cera labrada*) for celebrating mass.

There were also arms and related services (12 long rifles [*espingardas*], 12 muskets, and charges for gun alignment by the *armeros*) as well as powder, ammunition, and related supplies (1,690 musket balls, 912 pounds of gunpowder, 2

reams of paper for cartridges, 4 pounds of agave for cartridges, 100 musket flints for the long rifles, and 2 empty chests for carrying gunpowder bags [*frasqueras*]).

Cooking equipment and food and alcoholic beverages included 6 iron griddles (*comales*); 1 large pan or kettle (*paila*); 1 long-handled iron pan (*sartén*); 4 cauldrons; *bizcocho* cutters; 68.5 arrobas of salted meat; 9 fanegas of salt; 8 jars of honey; 400 hens to be dried and stored in jars; 98 cargas of maize to be ground into meal; 294 cargas of maize meal (carried by a fleet of 50 mules); 102 mule-loads (*tercios*) of bizcocho, wheat flour, salted meat, salt, etc.; 8 additional arrobas of white bizcocho in a box; 1 carga of wheat flour to make bizcocho; 118 arrobas of jerked beef; 20 arrobas of chocolate; 15 arrobas of sugar; 100 bundles of tobacco; 2 jars of vinegar; 2 pounds of saffron; 8 pounds of black pepper; 7 pounds of cinnamon; 1.5 pounds of nutmeg; 32 arrobas of fish (*róbalo*); 3 arrobas of oil; aguardiente (40 pesos worth plus 1 cask [*pipa*] [180 pesos]); and 1 cask of wine (also used for the mass).

Finally, there were 21 dogs, 8 large wax candles (*hachas*), 80 candles, 1 crystal lantern, 1 balance, and 1 2-pound weight (for the balance).

79. The Campeche sellers and their receipts in January 1697 were as follows: don Sebastián de Sagües y Sabalsa (922 p. 4 r.), unidentified suppliers (895 p.), don Bernardino de Zubiaur Isasi (557 p. 6 r.), Captain Alonso García de Paredes (355 p. 1 r.), Captain Francisco Guillén (226 p. 7 r.), José Pintado (180 p.), Captain Juan Ramos Sarmiento (150 p. 2 r.), Francisco Rodríguez (121 p. 4 r.), don Jerónimo de Solis (79 p. 3 r.), Manuel de los Santos (78 p.), Captain Antonio Fernández (54 p. 4 r.), Captain Juan de Frías Salazar (40 p.), Alonso Palomino (30 p. 5 r.), the Armeros of Campeche (29 p.), and José de Sintla (3 p.). The amounts add up to 3,746 pesos 4 reales.

80. AGI, P 237, ramo 10, Dispatch by the cabildo of Campeche, 7 May 1695, ff. 518v–520r.

81. AGI, P 237, ramo 1, Ursúa to Crown, 16 Dec. 1696.

82. AGI, P 237, ramo 3, Certification of Ursúa's expenditures in the opening of the road to Guatemala, 21 Jan. 1696.

83. AGI, P 237, ramo 1, Ursúa to Crown, 27 Oct. 1696.

84. AGI, G 151A, no. 7, Petition from Francisco de Salazar y Córdoba to Governor Roque de Soberanis y Centeno, c. 1 Jan. 1697, f. 8r–v.

85. AGI, G 151A, no. 7, Auto by Governor Roque de Soberanis y Centeno, 4 Jan. 1697, ff. 8v–9v.

86. AGI, G 151A, no. 7, Auto by Roque de Soberanis y Centeno, 17 Jan. 1697, f. 12r–v.

87. AGI, G 151A, no. 7, Statement by Captain Juan del Castillo y Toledo, 8 Jan. 1697, f. 27r–v.

88. AGI, G 151A, no. 7, Statement by Castillo, 8 Jan. 1697; Statement by Captain Juan del Castillo y Toledo, 9 Jan. 1697, ff. 27v–28r; G 151A, no. 7, List of Maya road workers assigned to the journey to the montaña, 9 Jan. 1697, ff. 28r–29r; List of Maya muleteers assigned to the journey to the montaña, 20 Jan. 1697, ff. 29r–30v.

487

89. Mules and muleteers were even recruited from Mérida (AGI, G 151A, no. 7, Petition from Francisco de Salazar y Córdoba, c. 10 Jan. 1697, f. 10r; Auto by Roque de Soberanis y Centeno, with attached account, 12 Jan. 1697, ff. 10v–11r).

90. AGI, G 151A, no. 7, Petition of Francisco de Salazar y Córdoba, c. 24 Jan. 1697, f. 11r–v.

91. AGI, G 151A, no. 7, Auto by Roque de Soberanis y Centeno, 24 Jan. 1697, ff. 11v–12r.

92. AGI, G 151A, no. 7, Auto by Roque de Soberanis y Centeno and list of runaway road workers and muleteers, 28 Feb. 1697, f. 32r–v.

93. AGI, G 151A, no. 7, Francisco de Salazar y Córdoba to Governor Roque de Soberanis, 3 Feb. 1697, ff. 30v–31r; Roque de Soberanis to Francisco de Salazar y Córdoba, 7 Feb. 1697, f. 31r–v.

94. AGI, G 151A, no. 7, Auto by Soberanis and list of runaway road workers and muleteers, 28 Feb. 1697.

Chapter 11: The Eve of Conquest

1. AGI, P 237, ramo 1, Ursúa to Crown, 22 Jan. 1696, and ramo 11, Ursúa to Real Acuerdo, 22 March 1697, give the departure date as January 23. Villagutierre, 1933, bk. 8, ch. 3, p. 347, indicates, apparently incorrectly, that it was the twenty-fourth. In AGI, P 237, ramo 11, Ursúa to Real Acuerdo, 22 March 1697, Ursúa gives the figure of 130 "hombres y gastadores" (men and carriers) who had already been sent before he left Campeche.

2. This section is based on Villagutierre, 1933, bk. 8, ch. 3, pp. 346–49.

3. Villagutierre, 1933, bk. 8, ch. 3, p. 346.

4. AGI, P 237, ramo 1, Ursúa to Crown, 22 Jan. 1696; G 151B, no. 2, Junta de guerra, 12 March 1697.

5. The precise location of this camp is not known, but it may have been either near the place identified on modern maps as Bonxajan, just below the descent from the karst hills northwest of Ch'ich', or at Aguada Kantixal to the southeast of Bonxajan.

6. Don S. Rice and Prudence M. Rice, personal communications, 1995. The question of the identity of Nich as opposed to Ch'ich' has not been completely resolved. These may have been alternative names for the same place, or there may have been two separate embarkments on the bay. Several people from Chak'an Itza who visited Bacalar in September 1696 reportedly extended an invitation to the Spaniards there to come to the lake in order to defeat Ajaw Kan Ek', whom they described as their traditional enemy. They further offered to make five boats that they would put "in a place named Chich, where they specify that the Spaniards should embark in order to pursue their intention, as it is the most adequate and secure place found there for the operation." See AGI, G 151A, no. 3, Declaration of four Indians from Peten, 20 Sept. 1696. In another source Ch'ich' (Itzaj, "fine gravel") is called the "embarcadero de Chichi," indicating that it, like Nich, was also on the shore (AGI, G 343, no. 23, Memoria de las personas que . . . se hallan en esta isla y presidio del Petén Ytzá de Nuestra Señora de los Remedios y San Pablo, 6 Sept. 1699, f. 54v).

7. AGI, P 237, ramo 11, Ursúa to Real Acuerdo, 22 March 1697; G 151B, no. 2, Junta de guerra, 12 March 1697.

8. AGI, P 237, ramo 11, Ursúa to Real Acuerdo, 22 March 1697.

9. AGI, G 151B, no. 2, Junta de guerra, 12 March 1697.

10. AGI, P 237, ramo 11, Ursúa to Real Acuerdo, 22 March 1697.

11. Other accounts indicate that braiding the women's hair would have been in line with other acts of "adornment."

12. AGI, G 151B, no. 2, Junta de guerra, 12 March 1697.

13. AGI, G 151B, no. 2, Certificación de los cabos y oficiales de guerra, 14 March 1697. This wall is described as a "trinchera de la custodia de dicho real" (defensive wall for the protection of the said encampment). The term *trinchera* in this and other, related documents refers to a defensive wall of stone or timbers, not to a trench alone. During the 1995 excavations carried out by Proyecto Maya Colonial, three ditch-wall complexes as well as a boat-launching ramp were discovered at the extensive site of Nixtun-Ch'ich' that cut the peninsula from north to south. At least one of these must have been the defensive wall or walls constructed (or perhaps reinforced upon an earlier wall) by the Spaniards. Single gunflints were found in three partially cleared structures at the site (Don S. Rice and Prudence M. Rice, personal communications, 1995; see also D. Rice et al., 1996, pp. 177–224).

14. AGI, G 151B, no. 2, Certificación de los cabos y oficiales de guerra, 14 March 1697, provides the total number of troops on March 13.

15. The officers, listed according to rank, were as follows: Lieutenant Captain Alonso García de Paredes; infantry captains José Fernández de Estenos and Pablo de Zubiaur Isasi; armored cavalry captains Nicolás de la Aya, Diego de Avila Pacheco, and Bartolomé de la Garma Alcedo y Salazar; lieutenants Juan Francisco Cortés and Diego Bernardo del Río; and José Laines, commander (captain) of pardos and mestizos. In addition, five volunteers referred to as Ursúa's *criados* (i.e., relatives) held what amounted to honorary titles. Three of these — Gaspar del Castillo Cetina, Bernardo de Aizuani Ursúa (a known relative of Ursúa's), and Blas Felipe de Ripalda Ongay — were *alférezes,* and Castillo Cetina held the additional honorific of *ayudante general,* or aide-de-camp. Ursúa named Juan González and José de Heredía as sergeants. Information on these officers comes mainly from AGI, G 151B, no. 2, Junta de guerra, 12 March 1697, and Certificación de los cabos y oficiales de guerra, 14 March 1697. On Laines's position see AGI, P 237, ramo 10, Auto by Ursúa, 27 July 1695.

16. AGI, G 151B, no. 2, Certificación de los capellanes del ejército, 13 March 1697, ff. 25v–30r.

17. The official interpreters were Ignacio de Solis, Sergeant José de Heredía, Sergeant Luis Ricalde, and Juan Bautista de Salazar (AGI, G 151B, no. 2, Auto by Ursúa, 10 March 1697). **489**

18. The "common or geometric" equivalent of the *codo,* or cubit, is 42.8 centimeters, the equivalent of 0.5 *vara.* The *Enciclopedia Universal Ilustrada* (c. 1907–30, s.v. "codo") provides conversions suggesting that the nautical cubit was

48 centimeters. I have used this last equivalence in estimating the length of the galeota.

19. AGI, G 151B, no. 2, Junta de guerra, 12 March 1697; P 237, ramo 11, Ursúa to Crown, 22 March 1697.

20. *Enciclopedia Universal Ilustrada,* c. 1907–30, s.v. "galeota"; Kemp, p. 336.

21. "Plano del Ing. Luis Bouchard de Becour en 1705" (fig. 37 in Piña Chan, 1977, p. 85).

22. AGI, G 151A, no. 3, Memoria y razón de lo que . . . Martín de Ursúa y Arizmendi me ha entregado de armas, municiones, y otras cosas para la guarnición del reducto que en este Peten del Ytza deja formada y su defensa a mi cuidado, by José Fernández de Estenos, 9 May 1697, ff. 305r–307r.

23. AGI, G 151A, no. 3, Instrucción dada por Ursúa al Cabo José Fernández de Estenos, que quedó en el Peten del Ytza, 9 May 1697, ff. 303v–305r; Memoria y razón by José Fernández de Estenos, 9 May 1697.

24. AGI, G 151A, no. 3, Lista de la gente de guarnición del reducto del Peten de Nuestra Señora de los Remedios y San Pablo, 9 May 1697.

25. AGI, G 151A, no. 3, Memoria y razón by José Fernández de Estenos, 9 May 1697. There were 1,780 counted musket balls plus 4 quintals. In addition to what was already in the hands of the troops, there were 62 cartridges of gunpowder for the no.s, 2 quintals (200 pounds) plus 3 barrels (200 lbs.) of fine and semifine gunpowder, 1 barrel (50 pounds) plus 1 *botija* (50 pounds) of bombard gunpowder, and 160 musket flints.

26. AGI, G 151B, no. 2, Certificación de los cabos y oficiales de guerra, 14 March 1697.

27. One or more piezas and one pedrero aboard the attacking galeota are mentioned by Ursúa, but not in the form of an inventory. AGI, P 237, ramo 11, Ursúa to Crown, 22 March 1697.

28. The testimonies are found in AGI, G 151B, no. 2, Declaración de don Martín Chan, 10 March 1697; Declaration of Chamach Xulu and others from Alain, 10 March 1697, ff. 11v–13r; and Declaration of Ah Kin Can Ek, 10 March 1697. Another copy of the testimonies includes a brief portion of AjChan's testimony that was omitted by the copyist from the G 151B copy just cited (see AGI, P 237, ramo 11, f. 714ff.).

29. AGI, G 151B, no. 2, Declaration of Chamach Xulu and others from Alain, 10 March 1697.

30. Further information on don Pedro Nikte appears in AGI, G 151A, no. 1, Cristóbal de Mendia y Sologastoa to Ursúa and Melchor de Mencos, 1 April 1699, ff. 65v–67r; Cristóbal de Mendia y Sologastoa to Ursúa and Mencos, 16 April 1699, ff. 100v–101r; Cristóbal de Mendia y Sologastoa to Ursúa and Mencos, 12 April 1699, ff. 98r–99r; Ursúa and Mencos to Mendia y Sologastoa, 19 April 169; and no. 6, Declarations of Franciscan *guardianes* from the Partido de la Sierra y Bolonchen, 17 Aug. 1696. Records of his baptism as Pedro Miguel

Chan appear in AGI, G 151A, no. 4, Certification of baptisms of Chan and others, 31 Dec. 1695, and in P 237, ramo 8, Certification by Carvajal Campo Frío, 31 Dec. 1695. His baptism is also mentioned much later in AGI, G 151A, no. 3, Declaration of Sopuerta, 14 June 1697.

31. Further information on Manuel Chayax is found in AGI, P 237, ramo 8, Certification by Carvajal Campo Frío, 31 Dec. 1695; G 151A, no. 1, Mendia y Sologastoa to Ursúa and Mencos, 1 April 1699; Orden por Ursúa a Mendia y Sologastoa, 27 March 1699, ff. 61r–62v; Cristóbal de Mendia Sologastoa to Ursúa and Mencos, 4 April 1699, ff. 71r–72v; no. 2, Certificación de los capellanes del ejército, 13 March 1697; Declaración del reyezuelo Ah Canek, 31 March 1697; and no. 4, Certification of baptisms of Chan and others, 31 Dec. 1695.

32. That is, to stand at attention with guns on their shoulders.

33. AGI, G 151B, no. 2, Declaration of Ah Kin Canek, 10 March 1697. Although most sources identify AjK'in Kan Ek' as father's brother's son of Ajaw Kan Ek', Ursúa here stated, probably due to a mistranslation, that they were brothers.

34. AGI, G 151B, no. 2, Declaración de don Martín Chan, 10 March 1697.

35. Ibid.

36. This question is incorrectly placed at an earlier point in the AGI, G 151B version. This is the location as it appears in AGI, P 237, ramo 11. The copyist of the G 151B version made several apparent errors that changed the meaning of the responses. I have followed the P 237, ramo 11 version throughout.

37. This translation is tentative. The original reads, "para que iba sino era Español."

38. Written Motzkal here and Motzcal later in the document, this is probably the same place called Matzkalek' elsewhere (AGI, P 237, ramo 1, Razón individual y general de los pueblos, poblaciones, y rancherías de esta provincia de Zuyuha Peten Itza, 6 Jan. 1698, ff. 80r–84v).

39. Villagutierre embellishes his account of AjChan's answer: "[L]os embustes de los indios, eran todos de guerra contra los españoles, y decían, los habían de matar, sacrificarlos á sus dioses y comerlos" (1933, bk. 8, ch. 4, p. 353).

40. In 1698 AjTut's headquarters were ten leagues south of Nojpeten on these lakes (AGI, G 345, no. 20, Ursúa to Gabriel Sánchez de Berrospe, 28 Sept. 1698, ff. 151r–158v).

41. This section is based on AGI, G 151B, no. 2, Declaration of Chamach Xulu and others from Alain, 10 March 1697.

42. This section is based on AGI, G 151B, no. 2, Declaration of Ah Kin Canek, 10 March 1697.

43. This section is from AGI, G 151B, no. 2, Junta de guerra, 12 March 1697.

491

44. Ibid.

45. AGI, G 151B, no. 2, Certificación de los capellanes del ejército, 13 March 1697.

46. The Spanish phrase is "sin haberse podido penetrar el intento."

47. AGI, P 237, ramo 11, Ursúa to Real Acuerdo, 22 March 1697.
48. AGI, G 151B, no. 2, Junta de guerra, 12 March 1697.
49. Sahlins, 1981, pp. 33–37.
50. AGI, G 151B, no. 2, Junta de guerra, 12 March 1697.
51. Ibid., f. 20v.
52. Ibid., ff. 21v.–25r.

Chapter 12: Occupation and Interrogation

1. AGI, G 151B, no. 2, Auto by Ursúa, 13 March 1697, ff. 25v–26r. The two reports comprise AGI, G 151B, no. 2, Certificación de los capellanes del ejército, 13 March 1697, and Certificación de los cabos y oficiales de guerra, 14 March 1697. Although the officers' report is dated March 14, Ursúa's instructions to the priests indicate that it had already been drafted by the previous afternoon. The priests wrote most of their report on the evening of the thirteenth, but the last section indicates that it was not completed until the next day.

2. AGI, P 237, ramo 11, Ursúa to Real Acuerdo, 22 March 1697.

3. AGI, G 151B, no. 2, Certificación de los cabos y oficiales de guerra, 14 March 1697.

4. Ibid. A similar version of this statement appears in AGI, G 151B, no. 2, Certificación de los capellanes del ejército, 13 March 1697.

5. These modern place names are not mentioned in the report, but they are obvious from the description: "And having reached halfway, where there are two points, one from the mainland and the other from an island . . . " (AGI, G 151B, no. 2, Certificación de los cabos y oficiales de guerra, 14 March 1697).

6. See also AGI, P 237, ramo 11, Ursúa to Real Acuerdo, 22 March 1697.

7. The original reads "y le dijese de su parte que le requería una, dos, y tres veces con la paz" (AGI, G 151B, no. 2, Certificación de los cabos y oficiales de guerra, 14 March 1697). Ursúa's later, simplified description of this episode, part of his report to the king, differed from that of the officers and the priests in that he made no mention of AjChan's interchange with the young man in the canoe or of his own attempt to send a message to Ajaw Kan Ek'. Finding himself encircled, he ordered the rowing to stop and instructed his interpreters "to tell them that I came not in war but in peace and friendship" and that he would give them three chances to give up their fighting (AGI, P 237, ramo 11, Ursúa to Real Acuerdo, 22 March 1697).

8. In his letter to the king describing the event, Ursúa did not admit to losing control of his men, as had been claimed by his own officers. Rather, he claimed to have himself ordered that the galeota be rowed to the shore (AGI, P 237, ramo 11, Ursúa to Real Acuerdo, 22 March 1697).

9. AGI, G 151B, no. 2, Certificación de los cabos y oficiales de guerra, 14 March 1697.

10. AGI, G 151B, no. 2, Certificación de los capellanes del ejército, 13 March 1697.

11. AGI, P 237, ramo 11, Ursúa to Real Acuerdo, 22 March 1697. Italics added.

12. Ibid.

13. AGI, G 151B, no. 2, Certificación de los cabos y oficiales de guerra, 14 March 1697.

14. Ibid.

15. AGI, G 345, no. 20, Parecer of Fray Diego de Rivas, 15 Nov. 1698, ff. 200r–210r.

16. AGI, G 180, Fray Bernardo de Rivas, provincial, et al. to Crown, 26 June 1700.

17. AGI, EC 339B, no. 29, Toribio de Cosio, president of Guatemala, to viceroy of New Spain, 26 Sept. 1709, ff. 21r–29v.

18. AGI, G 151B, no. 2, Certificación de los cabos y oficiales de guerra, 14 March 1697.

19. The discovery of the effigy of San Pablo is mentioned in AGI, G 151B, no. 2, Certificación de los capellanes del ejército, 13 March 1697, and Documents confirming Spanish possession of Nuestra Señora de los Remedios y San Pablo, Laguna del Itza, 14 March 1697, ff. 35v–39v.

20. Fuensalida and Orbita had first decided to name both San Pablo the Apostle and his companion, San Bernabé, as the patrons of Nojpetén, but upon leaving they designated specifically only San Pablo (López de Cogolludo, 1971, vol. 2, bk. 9, ch. 9, p. 228; bk. 9, ch. 10, p. 236).

21. Avendaño, 1987, p. 49. He also noted the town's name in another account of this trip (AGI, P 237, ramo 1, Testimonies of Avendaño and two other religious, May 1696).

22. The illogical construction of this sentence is preserved from the original. The two priests described the "idols" in a similar fashion: "[N]ot only were the many temples filled [with them] but also all of the houses of this island, of much deformity."

23. *Estoraque* usually refers to the resin of the storax tree (*Styrax officinalis*), which has a vanilla-like odor. It may also refer to liquidambar, from the sweet gum tree (*Liquidambar styraciflua*), which is what Thompson supposed this to be (1951, p. 395; see also Comparato's comment in Villagutierre, 1983, p. 314, n. 1134).

24. AGI, G 151B, no. 2, Certificación de los cabos y oficiales de guerra, 14 March 1697.

25. Ibid.

26. The same account was repeated by Ursúa in his letter to the king (AGI, P 237, ramo 11, Ursúa to Real Acuerdo, 22 March 1697).

27. See Avendaño, Relación, 1696, f. 29v; 1987, p. 33.

493

28. Ursúa claimed that the idol-smashing went on continuously from eight o'clock in the morning until five o'clock in the afternoon. In fact, it must have started later in the morning, because the ceremonies at the summit of the island would have taken at least an hour (AGI, P 237, ramo 11, Ursúa to Real Acuerdo, 22 March 1697).

29. Ibid.

30. Ibid.; G 151B, no. 2, Documents confirming Spanish possession of Nuestra Señora de los Remedios y San Pablo, Laguna del Itza, 14 March 1697.

31. Villagutierre, 1933, bk. 8, ch. 11, p. 375; 1983, p. 300.

32. Ximénez, 1971–79, vol. 29, bk. 5, ch. 77, p. 422.

33. Jones, 1989, pp. 177, 180.

34. Thompson accepted these descriptions without questioning their source (1951, p. 393), suggesting that the X-shaped crosses were of Mexican origin.

35. AGI, M 895, Ursúa to Crown, 30 July 1697.

36. AGI, P 237, ramo 11, Diego Bernardo del Río to Gabriel Sánchez de Berrospe, 10 July 1697, f. 700r–v.

37. AGI, G 151B, no. 2, Documents confirming Spanish possession of Nuestra Señora de los Remedios y San Pablo, Laguna del Itza, 14 March 1697.

38. AGI, P 237, ramo 11, Ursúa to Real Acuerdo, 22 March 1697. The precise day on which the delegation arrived is provided in AGI, G 151A, no. 5, Certification by Br. Juan Pacheco de Sopuerta, 9 May 1697.

39. AGI, G 151A, no. 5, Testimony of Sargento Mayor Miguel Ferrer, 3 July 1697, ff. 50–63.

40. The date of their departure is given both as April 24 (AGI, P 237, ramo 11, Ursúa to Gabriel Sánchez de Berrospe, 4 May 1697, ff. 697v–699v) and as April 23 (Alonso García de Paredes to Sánchez de Berrospe, 20 April 1697, ff. 641r–642r).

41. AGI, P 237, ramo 11, García de Paredes to Sánchez de Berrospe, 20 April 1697.

42. AGI, G 151A, no. 5, Testimony of Pacheco, 1 July 1697.

43. AGI, P 237, ramo 11, Ursúa to Sánchez de Berrospe, 4 May 1697.

44. AGI, G 151A, no. 3, Declaration of Br. Juan Sopuerta, 14 June 1697.

45. AGI, G 151B, no. 2, Declaración de don Martín Chan, 10 March 1697.

46. AGI, G 151A, no. 5, Testimony of Nicolás de la Aya, 6 July 1697, and Testimony of Avila Pacheco, 1 July 1697.

47. AGI, G 151B, no. 2, Declaración de don Martín Chan, 10 March 1697; AGI, G 151A, no. 5, Testimony of Diego de Avila Pacheco, 1 July 1697.

494

48. AGI, G 151A, no. 5, Testimony of Avila Pacheco, 1 July 1697.

49. This interrogation is found in AGI, G 151B, no. 2, Declaración del reyezuelo Ah Canek, 31 March 1697, ff. 39v–45v. I have edited the interrogation like those in chapter 11.

50. AGI, G 151A, no. 3, Declaration of four Indians from Peten, 20 Sept. 1696; AGI, P 237, ramo 3, Declaración de un indio que dijo llamarse Ah Chan, y ser sobrino del rey Canek que lo es de la nación de los Itzaes, 29 Dec. 1695; G 151B, no. 2, Declaración de don Martín Chan, 10 March 1697.

51. That Ajaw Kan Ek' had two sons at this time is reported in AGI, EC 339B, no. 12, Memorial by Nicolas de Lizarraga to Crown, 1708 (about), ff. 16r–18v. In his report on his 1696 visit to Nojpeten, Avendaño observed that IxChan Pana, the wife of Ajaw Kan Ek', had more than one daughter (see Avendaño, Relación, 1696, f. 46v; 1987, p. 51). In his oral testimony, however, he mentioned only one daughter about eighteen years old (AGI, P 237, ramo 1, Testimonies of Avendaño and two other religious, May 1696).

52. AGI, P 237, ramo 3, Declaración de un indio que dijo llamarse Ah Chan, y ser sobrino del rey Canek que lo es de la nación de los Itzaes, 29 Dec. 1695, ff. 191v–196v.

53. This is the only reference to the kinship relationship between Ajaw Kan Ek' and B'atab' Ajaw K'in Kante.

54. Reference to Avendaño's belief that the Itzas practiced cannibalism appears in Chapter 8, p. 214 (with citation in n. 78, p. 474).

55. AGI, M 895, Ursúa to Crown, 30 July 1697.

56. Villagutierre opined that Ursúa knew that what Ajaw Kan Ek' told him was untrue but pretended to believe him (1983, bk. 8, ch. 16, p. 324). I have taken a rather different position here, seeing no evidence in Ursúa's writing that he disbelieved what he heard.

57. AGI, P 237, ramo 11, Ursúa to Sánchez de Berrospe, 4 May 1697. For information on these visitors, see AGI, G 151A, no. 5, Testimony of Laines, 6 July 1697.

58. Ibid.

59. AGI, M 895, Ursúa to Crown, 30 July 1697.

60. AGI, G 151A, no. 5, Testimony of Ripalda Ongay, 2 July 1697; Testimony of Laines, 6 July 1697; G 151B, no. 2, Declarations of Ah Kin Canek, Canek (relative of Ah Canek), and the youth Camal, 16 April 1697; P 237, ramo 11, Ursúa to Sánchez de Berrospe, 4 May 1697.

61. AGI, G 151A, no. 5, Testimony of Avila Pacheco, 1 July 1697.

62. AGI, M 895, Ursúa to Crown, 30 July 1697.

63. Villagutierre 1983, bk. 8, ch. 17, p. 327.

64. AGI, G 151B, no. 2, Declarations of Ah Kin Canek, Canek (relative of Ah Canek), and the youth Camal, 16 April 1697.

65. AGI, M 895, Ursúa to Crown, 30 July 1697.

66. AGI, G 151A, no. 5, Testimony of Sergeant Miguel Ferrer, 3 July 1697. **495**

67. The translation "he whistled" is from "silvaba," apparently a misprint of *sivlaba* or *siblaba*. This is the translation offered in Villagutierre, 1983, p. 327.

68. Villagutierre, 1933, 1983, bk. 8, ch. 17. My translation.

69. Ibid. My translation.

70. This interrogatory is found in AGI, G 151B, no. 2, Declarations of Ah Kin Canek, Canek (relative of Ah Canek), and the youth Camal, 16 April 1697.

71. AGI, G 151B, no. 2, Declaración de don Martín Chan, 10 March 1697.

72. AGI, G 151A, no. 5, Testimony of Capitán Bartolomé de la Garma Alzedo y Salazar, 10 July 1697, ff. 99–110.

73. In 1699 a Chamay Kamal was being sought in the area of the town of Chinoja, which was probably on or near Laguna Sacnab (AGI, G 151A, no. 1, Ursúa and Mencos to Mendia y Sologastoa, 19 April 1699). The name also appears in the eighteenth-century baptismal records from San Andrés.

74. AGI, P 237, ramo 11, Ursúa to Sánchez de Berrospe, 4 May 1697.

75. Ibid.

76. AGI, G 151A, no. 5, Testimony of Avila Pacheco, 1 July 1697.

77. AGI, G 151A, no. 5, Testimony of José de Ripalda Ongay, 2 July 1697, and Testimony of Laines, 6 July 1697.

Chapter 13: Prisoners of Conquest

1. These included leaders from Yalain and three islands in Lagunas Sacpuy and Quexil. People from the Kowoj town of Saklemakal had also reportedly visited (AGI, G 151A, no. 5, Testimony of Laines, 6 July 1697). Questions prepared by Ursúa suggested that numerous other Kowoj towns also sent representatives (G 151A, no. 5, Questions for interrogation of witnesses presented by Ursúa, 1 July 1697), but other reports indicate that these probably came as a result of Ursúa's subsequent visit to the northern shore.

2. AGI, G 151A, no. 5, Testimony of Captain Nicolás de la Aya, 6 July 1697, ff. 86–99. Ursúa noted that, according to these visitors, they actually came from two towns with a total population of four hundred (AGI, P 237, ramo 11, Ursúa to Sánchez de Berrospe, 12 June 1697).

3. AGI, G 151A, no. 5, Certification by Sopuerta, 9 May 1697; Testimony of Avila Pacheco, 1 July 1697; Testimony of Miguel Ferrer, 3 July 1697. See also AGI, P 237, ramo 11, Ursúa to Sánchez de Berrospe, 4 May 1697.

4. AGI, G 151A, no. 5, Testimony of Captain José Laines, 6 July 1697.

5. AGI, M 895, Ursúa to Crown, 30 July 1697.

6. AGI, G 151A, no. 5, Testimony of Captain Nicolás de la Aya, 6 July 1697.

7. AGI, G 151A, no. 5, Testimony of Capitán Pedro de Zubiaur Isasi, 1 July 1697, ff. 13–23.

8. In 1698 Ajaw Kan Ek' and AjK'in Kan Ek' told the Spaniards that Kulut Kowoj was from Kets. This is the principal basis for assuming that Ketz was the Kowoj capital (AGI, P 237, ramo 1, Razón individual y general de los pueblos, poblaciones, y rancherías de esta provincia de Zuyuha Peten Itza, 6 Jan. 1698). For

the population of Kets see AGI, G 151A, no. 3, Declaration of Sopuerta, 14 June 1697.

9. AGI, G 151A, no. 5, Certification by Sopuerta, 9 May 1697, and Questions for interrogation of witnesses presented by Ursúa, 1 July 1697. The spellings vary considerably among the several sources.

10. AGI, G 151A, no. 5, Testimony of Captain José de Laines, 6 July 1697; M 895, Ursúa to Crown, 30 July 1697. According to Captain Laines, all of the Kowoj towns had also rendered their submission to the Spanish Crown.

11. AGI, M 895, Ursúa to Crown, 30 July 1697.

12. AGI, G 151A, no. 5, Testimony of Captain Diego de Avila Pacheco, 1 July 1697. The account of AjKowoj's attack on and burning of Nojpeten is also found in G 151A, no. 5, Testimony of Ripalda Ongay, 2 July 1697; Testimony of Laines, 6 July 1697; and Testimony of Nicolás de la Aya, 6 July 1697.

13. AGI, G 151A, no. 5, Testimony of la Aya, 6 July 1697.

14. AGI, G 151A, no. 5, Testimony of Laines, 6 July 1697.

15. AGI, G 151A, no. 5, Testimony of Ripalda Ongay, 2 July 1697.

16. AGI, G 151A, no. 5, Testimony of Zubiaur Isasi, 1 July 1697.

17. AGI, G 151A, no. 5, Testimony of Avila Pacheco, 1 July 1697. An account of AjChan's participation is also found in AGI, G 151A, no. 5, Testimony of Ripalda Ongay, 2 July 1697; Testimony of Ferrer, 3 July 1697; and Testimony of la Aya, 6 July 1697.

18. AGI, G 151A, no. 3, Instrucción dada por Ursúa al Estenos, que quedó en el Peten del Ytza, 9 May 1697; Memoria y razón de lo que . . . Ursúa me ha entregado de armas, municiones, y otras cosas para la guarnición del reducto que en este Petén del Ytzá deja formada y su defensa a mi cuidado, by José Fernández de Estenos, 9 May 1697, ff. 303v–305r; Memoria y razón de lo que . . . Ursúa me ha entregado de bastimientos y otras cosas para la manutención de cinquenta hombres con que quedó en este Peten y reducto de guarnición, 9 May 1697, f. 307r–v; Lista de la gente de guarnición del reducto del Peten de Nuestra Señora de los Remedios y San Pablo, 9 May 1697, ff. 307v–309v.

19. AGI, G 151A, no. 3, Declaration of Br. Juan Pacheco Sopuerta, 14 June 1697.

20. Ibid.

21. Ibid.

22. Ibid; AGI, G 151A, no. 3, Fray Francisco Ruiz, provincial, to Franciscan comisario general, 22 Oct. 1697, ff. 437r–439r.

23. AGI, G 151A, no. 3, Declaration of Sopuerta, 14 June 1697.

24. For Soberanis's criticisms of Ursúa's enterprise, see AGI, P 237, ramo 1, Roque de Soberanis y Centeno to Gabriel Sánchez de Berrospe, 5 June 1697, ff. 70v–75r. Bishop Arriaga of Yucatán tried to remain neutral in this dispute, which he detailed in P 237, ramo 14, Bishop Fray Antonio de Arriaga y Agüero to Crown, 2 Sept. 1697, f. 869r–v. Guatemalan colonial and church officials also criticized

Ursúa's methods and goals, though less vehemently than Soberanis. See AGI, G 343, no. 21, Junta de guerra, Guatemala, 8 Aug. 1697; P 237, ramo 11, Junta de teólogos, Guatemala, 20 August 1697, ff. 776r–778r; and Sánchez de Berrospe to bishop of Mérida and Tabasco, 22 August 1697, ff. 789r–790r.

25. AGI, P 237, ramo 14, Auto by Bishop Fray Antonio de Arriaga, 2 June 1697, ff. 878v–880r.

26. The questions put to the witnesses are found in AGI, G 151A, no. 5, Questions for interrogation of witnesses presented by Ursúa, 1 July 1697.

27. The immediately preceding question included garbled information that the Itzas had attacked and burned a town in the Kejach region shortly before the troops had passed through their territory in early 1697 on their way to Lago Petén Itzá.

28. AGI, G 151A, no. 5, Questions for interrogation of witnesses presented by Ursúa, 1 July 1697. The original phrase, common in such legal instruments, is "por público y notorio pública voz y fama."

29. AGI, G 151A, no. 5, Testimony of Pedro de Zubiaur Isasi, 1 July 1697.

30. AGI, G 151A, no. 5, Testimony of Avila Pacheco, 1 July 1697.

31. AGI, G 151A, no. 5, Testimony of Ferrer, 3 July 1697. He used the term *sacrificadero,* apparently referring to the by-now-legendary slab upon which victims were said to have been killed and their hearts removed.

32. AGI, G 151A, no. 5, Testimony of Laines, 6 July 1697.

33. Scholes and Adams 1938; see also Clendinnen, 1987 (especially pp. 88–92, 176–82), in which the author examines the issues of human sacrifice, including crucifixions, during the Franciscan-sponsored 1562 trial and investigation.

34. Beneath the hyperbole there was probably some degree of truth to some of these descriptions. Although there is no direct evidence for Itza human sacrifice, it is highly likely that it was practiced, although not on the scale claimed by these witnesses.

35. That is, "cebado," a term used here to refer to the desire for human flesh once tasted.

36. AGI, M 895, Ursúa to Crown, 30 July 1697.

37. AGI, G 151A, no. 1, Auto (including questionnaire) by Ursúa and Melchor de Mencos, 9 April 1699, ff. 78r–79v.

38. AGI, G 151A, no. 1, Parecer by Br. Pedro de Morales and José Francisco Martínez de Mora, 10 April 1699, ff. 79v–81v. *Bóvedas* are rooms in ruins.

39. AGI, G 151A, no. 1, Parecer by Morales and Mora, 10 April 1699.

40. AGI, G 151A, no. 1, Parecer by Fray Gabriel de Artiga, 10 April 1699, ff. 84r–85v.

498   41. See, for example, Clendinnen, 1987; Edmonson, 1984; Robicsek and Hales, 1984; and Schele, 1984.

42. One possible exception may be the reports by Landa and Cervantes de Salazar that Jerónimo de Aguilar, one of several members of a shipwrecked party who came ashore on the eastern coast of Yucatán in 1511, told Hernán Cortés that

some of his companions were sacrificed and eaten and that he and the rest were held in a cage, where they were to be fattened for the same fate. He and Gonzalo Guerrero escaped, and he was rescued by Cortés at Cozumel (Landa, 1941, pp. 8, 236 [extract from Cervantes de Salazar, who wrote in 1560]). Landa also claimed that in Yucatán sacrificial victims were eaten, but Tozzer, in a dispassionate review of other sources, notes that other colonial sources denied that any form of cannibalism was practiced (Landa, 1941, p. 120, including n. 547).

43. AGI, G 344, Declaración de Nicolas de Lizarraga, 16 May 1699, ff. 234v–235v.

44. Schele, 1984. See also Clendinnen, 1987, pp. 176–82.

45. AGI, EC 339B, no. 16, Br. Francisco de San Miguel y Figueroa to Crown, 12 March 1702, f. 55r. The original passage reads, "Lord, the perversity of this miserable people reached such a point [that] next to one of their principal temples they had a walled-around large house of very decorous construction solely for the habitation of the acquiescents, into which entered all of those who wished to have their sodomitic copulations, especially those who are very young, so that they could learn there, these ministers of the Demon wearing women's skirts and occupying themselves only in making bread for the priests and in their obscenities."

46. AGI, P 237, ramo 11, José Fernández de Estenos to Melchor de Mencos, 3 July 1697, ff. 772v–774v.

47. AGI, P 237, ramo 11, Estenos to Mencos, 3 July 1697.

48. AGI, P 237, ramo 11, Estenos et al. to Sánchez de Berrospe and Audiencia of Guatemala, 10 July 1697.

49. AGI, P 237, ramo 11, Diego Bernardo del Rio to Mencos, 9 July 1697, ff. 775r–776r.

50. AGI, P 237, ramo 11, Declaración de Juan de Barahona, Correo, 1 August 1697, ff. 760v–763v.

51. AGI, P 237, ramo 11, Bernardo del Río to Mencos, 9 July 1697.

52. Ibid.

53. AGI, P 237, ramo 11, del Río to Sánchez de Berrospe, 10 July 1697.

54. AGI, P 237, ramo 11, García de Paredes to Sánchez de Berrospe, 20 April 1697; Ursúa to Sánchez de Berrospe, 4 May 1697.

55. AGI, P 237, ramo 11, Ursúa to Sánchez de Berrospe, 22 March 1697, ff. 639r–640v; Respuesta del fiscal, Lic. José Gutiérrez de la Peña, Audiencia de Guatemala, 30 April 1697, ff. 635v–638v; Junta general de guerra (Guatemala) and attached pareceres, 1 May 1697; Auto by Sánchez de Berrospe, 2 May 1697, ff. 679v–681v; Memorial by Alonso García de Paredes and José de Ripalda Ongay, 2 May 1697, ff. 682r–684v.

56. AGI, P 237, ramo 11, Ursúa to Sánchez de Berrospe, 22 March 1697; **499** Ursúa to Sánchez de Berrospe, 12 June 1697.

57. AGI, P 237, ramo 11, Ursúa to Sánchez de Berrospe, 12 June 1697.

58. Those in attendance included the following persons: President Gabriel Sánchez de Berrospe; Bishop Fray Andrés de las Navas y Quevedo (Mercederian);

oidores Lic. José de Escals, Lic. Manuel de Baltodano, Dr. Bartolomé de Amésqueta, Pedro de Ozaeta, and Juan Jerónimo Duardo; José Gutiérrez de la Peña, fiscal; Fray Agustín Cano (Dominican); Fray Diego de Rivas, provincial (Mercederian); Captain Alonso García de Paredes; Alférez José de Ripalda Ongay; Manuel de Medrano y Solorzano, royal accountant; Postmaster (*correo mayor*) and Field Marshal José Agustín de Estrada y Azpeitia; Sancho Ordóñez de Avilez; Captain Juan de Lan García, Knight of the Order of Alcántara; Sergeant Major Francisco López de Aluisuri; Captain Juan Jerónimo Mejía Céspedes; Captain Pedro de Orozco; Governor Estévan de Medrano y Solorzano; Captain Juan López de Ampuero; Alférez Juan de Alarcón; and the public clerk (*escribano público*), not identified in my notes.

59. Two of these cédulas would have been those addressed to Ursúa and to the president and Audiencia of Guatemala granting Ursúa the patent to open the camino real between Guatemala and Yucatán; these were dated October 23, 1693. In addition, he read a cédula dated June 22, 1696, charging him with completing the reduction of the "infidels of Chol and Lacandon" (AGI, P 237, ramo 11, Real cédula to Sánchez de Berrospe, 22 June 1696, ff. 693r–693v). As a result of the obvious contradiction between the recent cédula and his decision to grant financial support to Ursúa in order to maintain the Petén presidio, the president shortly thereafter decided to rescind his previous order to suspend the Itza reductions (P 237, ramo 11, Auto by Sánchez de Berrospe, 10 May 1697; Respuesta del Fiscal, Valdez, 8 June 1697).

60. AGI, P 237, ramo 11, Ursúa to Sánchez de Berrospe, 12 June 1697; Auto by Sánchez de Berrospe, 10 May 1697, ff. 693v–695r; Respuesta del fiscal, Pedro Velásquez de Valdez, 8 June 1697, ff. 695r–697r.

61. AGI, P 237, ramo 11, Memorial by Paredes and Ripalda Ongay, 2 May 1697.

62. AGI, P 237, ramo 11, Auto by Sánchez de Berrospe, 2 May 1697.

63. AGI, P 237, ramo 11, Pedro Velásquez de Valdez to Sánchez de Berrospe, 4 May 1697, ff. 691v–692r.

64. AGI, G 151A, no. 7, List of dispatches sent from Guatemala with the messenger Juan Baraona, 4 May 1697, ff. 35v–37r; Sánchez de Berrospe to Roque de Soberanis y Centeno, 4 May 1697, ff. 37r–38r.

65. AGI, P 237, ramo 11, Ursúa to Sánchez de Berrospe, 12 June 1697.

66. AGI, G 151A, no. 7, Declaration of Juan Baraona, messenger from Guatemala, 27 May 1697.

67. AGI, P 237, ramo 11, Ursúa to Sánchez de Berrospe, 12 June 1697. See also AGI, G 151A, no. 5, Questions for interrogation of witnesses presented by Ursúa, 1 July 1697, question 2. This source states that the messenger Baraona returned to Guatemala via the Petén Itza road.

68. AGI, G 151A, no. 3, Fr. Francisco Ruiz, provincial, to Franciscan comisario general, 22 Oct. 1697; P 237, ramo 11, Ursúa to Sánchez de Berrospe, 12 June 1697, ff. 705r–711v. The provincial wrote that they had brought seven

thousand pesos with them from Guatemala. Other sources indicate that the money arrived late, probably in October. Perhaps they had stayed in Santiago de Guatemala until the funds were freed.

69. AGI, G 151A, no. 1, Recibo de presos, 6 May 1699, f. 137r–v.

70. AGI, P 237, ramo 11, Junta de teólogos, Guatemala, 20 August 1697; Auto by Sánchez de Berrospe, 31 August 1697, ff. 782v–783r; Sánchez de Berrospe to Ursúa, 22 August 1697, ff. 783r–789r; Sánchez de Berrospe to bishop of Mérida and Tabasco, 22 August 1697; Sánchez de Berrospe to Soberanis y Centeno, 22 August 1697.

71. AGI, G 151A, no. 7, Auto by Roque de Soberanis y Centeno, 17 Oct. 1697, ff. 43v–45r. No further hiring of muleteers from the Sierra partido would be permitted, because Soberanis believed they had already suffered too much on previous supply missions.

72. AGI, P 237, ramo 1, Ursúa to Crown, 14 April 1698, f. 78r–v; G 151B, no. 8, Roque de Soberanis y Centeno to Sánchez de Berrospe, 20 Oct. 1697.

73. AGI, G 151B, no. 8, Soberanis y Centeno to Sánchez de Berrospe, 20 Oct. 1697.

74. AGI, G 151B, no. 8, Soberanis y Centeno to Sánchez de Berrospe, 20 Oct. 1697; P 237, ramo 1, Ursúa to Crown, 12 Nov. 1697, ff. 70r–73r; Ursúa to Crown, 25 Nov. 1697, ff. 75r–76v.

75. AGI, P 237, ramo 1, Ursúa to Crown, 12 Nov. 1697.

76. AGI, P 237, ramo 1, Note by the Consejo de Indias, 3 Dec. 1697, ff. 61r–66v. Copies of these three cédulas, all dated January 24, 1698, were reproduced by Villagutierre (1933, 1983, bk. 9, ch. 4). Another, prepared on the same day, was sent to the president of Guatemala: AGI, G 345, no. 20, Real cédula to Sánchez de Berrospe, 24 Jan. 1698, ff. 81v–85r.

77. Villagutierre, 1933, 1983, bk. 10, ch. 4.

78. Villagutierre, 1933, 1983, bk. 9, ch. 4.

79. AGI, G 151B, no. 8, Mederos to Aguilar, 24 Sept. 1697.

80. AGI, P 237, ramo 1, Ursúa to Crown, 12 Nov. 1697.

81. Ibid.

82. AGI, G 343, no. 21, Declarations concerning Petén del Itzá, presented in Guatemala by Zubiaur Isasi et al., 16 April 1698.

83. AGI, G 345, no. 20, Pedro Morales y Veles to Sánchez de Berrospe, July 1698.

84. AGI, G 151A, no. 7, Auto by Soberanis y Centeno, 17 Oct. 1697. Ursúa complained that Soberanis had prevented him from hiring muleteers and road workers from Tek'ax and Oxk'utzkab' (AGI, G 151B, no. 8, Soberanis y Centeno to Sánchez de Berrospe, 20 Oct. 1697; P 237, ramo 1, Ursúa to Crown, 12 Nov. 1697 and 25 Nov. 1697).

85. AGI, P 237, ramo 1, Ursúa to Crown, 14 April 1698, f. 78r–v.

86. The following section is based on AGI, G 343, no. 21, Declarations concerning Petén del Itzá, presented in Guatemala by Zubiaur Isasi et al., 16 April

501

1698. Morales held the title "vicario y juez eclesiástico y capellán nombrado de la infantería," and Martínez de Mora was his "ministro compañero." Morales stated that he had left Petén Itza on March 24, 1968, which would have been two months after Zubiaur's departure. He also reported that there had been a third priest at the presidio, Domingo de Gronca, who had become ill and returned to Campeche. They had apparently taken with them to Santiago de Guatemala a written summary of depositions given by Ajaw Kan Ek', AjK'in Kan Ek', Captain Kulut Kowoj, and AjChan on the topic of the territorial and political organization of the entire region around Lago Petén Itzá (AGI, P 237, ramo 1, Razón individual y general de los pueblos, poblaciones, y rancherías de esta provincia de Zuyuha Peten Itza, 6 Jan. 1698, ff. 80r–84v). Father Morales's testimony was partially based on this document.

87. AGI, G 343, no. 21, Junta de Hacienda, Guatemala, on payment of missionaries to Petén Itzá, 25 April 1698, ff. 163r–164v; Auto by Sánchez de Berrospe, 25 April 1697, ff. 164v–166v; Sánchez de Berrospe to Ursua, 28 April 1698, ff. 166v–169r; Sánchez Berrospe to Fernández de Estenos, 28 April 1698, ff. 170v–172v. See also Villagutierre, 1933, 1983, bk. 9, ch. 4.

88. AGI, G 345, no. 20, Fernández de Estenos to Sánchez de Berrospe, 15 June 1698, ff. 58r–60r; Morales to Sánchez de Berrospe, July 1698.

89. The carriers from two towns, Tamaxu and Salamá, had complained to him that the alcalde mayor had not provided them with sufficient food for the entire trip. Zubiaur sent them back to Cahabón for supplies, but they never returned (AGI, G 345, no. 20, Zubiaur Isasi to Sánchez de Berrospe, 3 July 1698). Others turned back to Cahabón on the grounds that they were ill (AGI, G 345, no. 20, Diego Pacheco to Sánchez de Berrospe, 20 July 1698, ff. 77r–78v). Diego Pacheco, the alcalde mayor of Verapaz, wrote that some of the runaways were being sought in order to punish them and recover their four-peso advance and the stolen goods. Pacheco claimed to have spent 7,293 tostones, 2 reales on the purchase and shipping of supplies from Verapaz to Petén Itzá and an additional 1,162 tostones in removing 225 Chols from the forests (AGI, G 345, no. 20, Petition by Alejandro Pacheco on behalf of Diego Pacheco, August 1698, ff. 80v–81v).

90. AGI, G 345, no. 20, Morales y Veles to Sánchez de Berrospe, July 1698; Zubiaur Isasi to Sánchez de Berrospe, 3 July 1698.

91. AGI, G 345, no. 20, Zubiaur Isasi to Sánchez de Berrospe, 3 July 1698; Receipt for supplies received at presidio of Petén Itzá, 4 July 1698, f. 77r.

92. AGI, P 237, ramo 11, Fernández y Estenos et al. to Sánchez de Berrospe and Audiencia of Guatemala, 10 July 1697. Note that Fernández's signature in the documents sometimes reads Fernández y Estenos, rather than *de*.

93. Ibid.	94. Ibid.
95. Ibid.	96. Ibid.

97. AGI, G 345, no. 20, Morales y Velez to Sánchez de Berrospe, July 1698; José Fernández de Estenos to Sánchez de Berrospe, 15 June 1698; Zubiaur Isasi to Sánchez de Berrospe, 3 July 1698.

98. AGI, G 345, no. 20, Zubiaur Isasi to Sánchez de Berrospe, 3 July 1698.

99. Ibid.

100. AGI, G 345, no. 20, Fernández y Estenos to Sánchez de Berrospe, 15 June 1698. The last phrase, in the original, reads "enviándoles recaudos de mofa, diciendo que capitanes o caciques de borondanga tenía." *Borondanga* is the equivalent of *morondanga,* and the phrase *de morondanga* is applied to something that is worthless, despicable, lowly, etc.

101. The settlement, which is known by no other name, would have been just south of Isla Pedregal, on the western end of present-day San Benito.

102. AGI, G 345, no. 20, Fernández y Estenos to Sánchez de Berrospe, 15 June 1698, ff. 58r–60r.

103. AGI, G 345, no. 20, Br. Pedro de Morales y Veles to Sánchez de Berrospe, July 1698.

104. Ibid.

105. Ibid.

106. AGI, G 345, no. 20, Testimonies concerning proposed entrada from Petén Itza to Nuestra Señora de los Dolores del Lacandon, 2 July 1698, ff. 73–77r.

107. AGI, G 345, no. 20, Fernández y Estenos to Sánchez de Berrospe, 14 Sept. 1698, ff. 111v–114v.

108. There are actually two small islands in Laguna Quexil.

109. AGI, G 345, no. 20, Fernández y Estenos to Sánchez de Berrospe, 14 Sept. 1698.

110. Ibid.

111. AGI, G 345, no. 20, Fernández de Estenos to Sánchez de Berrospe, 22 Oct. 1698, ff. 161r–164r.

112. AGI, G 343, no. 21, Sánchez de Berrospe to Ursúa, 28 April 1698, ff. 166v–173v.

113. Ibid.

114. AGI, G 345, no. 20, Fernández de Estenos to Sánchez de Berrospe, 4 July 1698, ff. 60v–164r.

115. AGI, G 345, no. 20, Br. Pedro de Morales y Veles to Sánchez de Berrospe, 30 Dec. 1698, ff. 248r–249v.

116. AGI, G 345, no. 20, Zubiaur Isasi to Sánchez de Berrospe, 3 July 1698.

Chapter 14: Reconquest, Epidemic, and Warfare

1. Some reports indicate that Spaniards actually purchased maize and beans from the towns, but whether with currency (for which the Itzas would have had little use at this early date) or by trading goods, particularly metal axes, is not specified. See, for example, AGI, G 345, no. 20, Morales y Veles to Sánchez de Berrospe, July 1698. As more towns were abandoned, troops took what they could from partially harvested milpas.

2. AGI, G 345, no. 20, Real cédula to Sánchez de Berrospe, 24 Jan. 1698, ff.

81v–85r. The cédula to Soberanis is summarized in Villagutierre, 1983, bk. 9, ch. 9, p. 362; see also bk. 10, ch. 5, p. 374.

3. Villagutierre, 1983, bk. 9, ch. 9–10, pp. 361–64. Villagutierre provides information on these topics that appears to be from documents that have been lost or misplaced in the Archivo General de Indias.

4. AGI, G 345, no. 20, Ursúa to Sánchez de Berrospe, 28 Sept. 1698, ff. 151r–158v.

5. Various written opinions by those who attended the meeting comprise a fascinating commentary not only on the president's dilemma but also on the larger issue of the degree to which Guatemala should support Ursúa's enterprise. See, for example, AGI, G 345, no. 20, Pareceres of Bartolome de Amésqueta and Fr. Diego de Rivas, 15 Nov. 1698.

6. For information on Rivas's attempts to reach Petén Itza between March and June see AGI, G 345, no. 20, Fray Diego de Rivas to Gabriel Sánchez de Berrospe, 2 March 1698, ff. 46v–47v; Rivas to Sánchez de Berrospe, 4 April 1698, ff. 47v–50r; Rivas to Sánchez de Berrospe, 5 June 1698, ff. 50r–53v; Declaración de Blas Fernández de Miranda, 10 June 1698; Sánchez de Berrospe to José Fernández de Estenos, 12 June 1698, f. 22r–v; Sánchez de Berrospe to Zubiaur Isasi, 12 June 1698, ff. 22r–23v; Rivas to Sánchez de Berrospe, 13 June 1698; G 234, no. 20, Sánchez de Berrospe to Br. Pedro de Morales, 12 June 1698; AGI, Mapas y planos, Guatemala 13, Mapa de lo reconocido por el Padre Fray Diego de Rivas en el Peten Ytza, 13 June 1698.

7. AGI, G 345, no. 20, Decreto by Gabriel Sánchez de Berrospe, 2 Dec. 1698, ff. 238v–239r.

8. Mencos y Medrano's age and the fact that his son accompanied him are recorded in AGI, G 256, Memorial ajustado por el comisario general de la caballería don Melchor de Mencos y Medrano, Caballero del Orden de Santiago, Santiago de Guatemala, 3 Feb. 1701, in Confirmación de una encomienda de 180 pesos a favor de doña Ana de Mencos y por su falta doña María de Guadalupe, vecinas de Guatemala, 29 Aug. 1704.

9. AGI, G 345, no. 20, Razón naming Melchor de Mencos as cabo principal, 4 Dec. 1698, f. 240r–v.

10. Villagutierre, 1983, bk. 9, ch. 10, p. 363.

11. Villagutierre, 1933, bk. 9, ch. 10, pp. 455–56; 1983, p. 363. AGI, G 151A, no. 1, Parecer del Lic. José de Lara, 2 Feb. 1699.

12. AGI, G 151A, no. 1, Parecer del Lic. José de Lara, 2 Feb. 1699, ff. 145r–147v.

13. AGI, G 151A, no. 1, Parecer del Lara, 2 Feb. 1699.

14. Ibid.

15. AGI, G 256, Memorial ajustado por el comisario general de la caballería don Melchor de Mencos y Medrano, Caballero del Orden de Santiago, Santiago de Guatemala, 3 Feb. 1701.

16. Villagutierre, 1933, bk. 10, ch. 2, p. 462.

17. AGI, G 256, Memorial ajustado por . . . Mencos y Medrano, 3 Feb. 1701.

18. AGI, G 151A, no. 1, Auto by Ursúa, 12 Feb. 1699; Villagutierre, 1983, bk. 10, ch. 1, p. 366.

19. That is, "tienda de compaña." The translation of this section in Villagutierre, 1983, is in error in stating that Ursúa and the troops were living in tents or in open-air situations (bk. 10, ch. 1, p. 367); see Villagutierre, 1933, p. 462.

20. Villagutierre, 1933, bk. 10, ch. 1, pp. 462–63.

21. AGI, G 256, Memorial ajustado por . . . Mencos y Medrano, 3 Feb. 1701

22. Villagutierre, 1983, bk. 10, ch. 2, p. 369.

23. AGI, G 344, ramo 3, Mencos to Sánchez de Berrospe, 8 March 1699. The date on this letter is incorrect, possibly a copyist's error. The correct date, based on the context of the letter, is probably April 8, 1699. Nicolás de Lizarraga, who was placed in charge of the families of settlers, later claimed that Mencos's son, Juan Bernardo de Mencos y Coronado, had advanced him 3,150 pesos in payment for leading the troops and supplies, in addition to 2,270 pesos in payment for food supplies. Before the train reached the presidio, he claimed, 214 soldiers and 319 Christian natives had died (AGI, EC 339B, no. 12, Memorial by Lizarraga to Crown, c. 1708).

24. Villagutierre, 1933, p. 466; 1983, bk. 10, ch. 2, p. 369.

25. AGI, G 344, ramo 3, Mencos to Sánchez de Berrospe, 8 March 1699. This arrangement of power sharing remained in place until Mencos departed in May. Villagutierre continues his description of the arguments over joint leadership in 1983, bk. 10, ch. 3, pp. 370–71.

26. AGI, G 256, Memorial ajustado por Mencos y Medrano, Caballero del Orden de Santiago, Santiago de Guatemala, 3 Feb. 1701.

27. Villagutierre, 1983, bk. 10, ch. 5, p. 372. Alejandro Pacheco was the nephew of the governor of Verapaz (Villagutierre, 1983, bk. 6, ch. 11, p. 240).

28. Villagutierre, 1983, bk. 10, ch. 5, p. 372.

29. I did not record the documentation for this meeting, which will be found in AGI, G 151A, no. 1, preceding Parecer del Ayudante General Cortés, 26 March. See also AGI, G 344, ramo 3, Mencos to Sánchez de Berrospe, 8 March 1699, in which Mencos reports on this meeting.

30. Mencos, however, wrote that sixty men would be sufficient (AGI, G 344, ramo 3, Mencos to Sánchez de Berrospe, 8 March 1699).

31. Villagutierre, 1983, bk. 10, ch. 5, pp. 374–76.

32. AGI, G 151A, no. 1, Parecer del Ayudante General Cortés, 26 March 1699; Villagutierre, 1983, bk. 10, ch. 3, p. 370. Villagutierre reports this event as if it occurred during the period reported in this section; it had probably happened during 1698.

505

33. AGI, G 344, ramo 3, Marcos de Avalos to Ursúa and Mencos, 22 March 1699, ff. 96v–97r; G 151A, no. 1, Ursúa to Estevan de Medrano y Solor-

zano, 25 March 1699, ff. 47r–48v; G 256, Memorial ajustado por . . . don Melchor de Mencos y Medrano, 3 Feb. 1701.

34. AGI, G 151A, no. 1, Ursúa and Melchor de Mencos to Marcos de Abalos y Fuentes, 28 March 1699, ff. 62r–63r. The term translated here as "fields" is *rancherías* in the original. Usually meaning "hamlets" or a cluster of houses, the context suggests that it refers here to the milpas.

35. AGI, G 151A, no. 1, Ursúa and Mencos to Abalos y Fuentes, 28 March 1699; Abalos y Fuentes to Ursúa and Mencos, 27 March 1699, f. 63r–v.

36. This indicates that Ch'ulte was half a league east of Laguneta El Sos. Abalos y Fuentes located Ch'ulte three leagues southwest of Joyop, placing the latter off the southeastern shore of Laguna Sacpuy.

37. AGI, G 151A, no. 1, Abalos y Fuentes to Ursúa and Mencos, 2 April 1699, ff. 67v–68v.

38. Ibid.

39. Ibid.

40. AGI, G 344, ramo 3, Miguel de Pineda y Useche to Ursúa and Mencos, 3 April 1699.

41. AGI, G 151A, no. 1, Abalos y Fuentes to Ursúa and Mencos, 6 April 1699, ff. 72v–73r.

42. AGI, G 151A, no. 1, Orden por Ursúa a Cristóbal de Mendía y Sologastoa, 27 March 1699. The circumstances of the arrival of the Tipujans are unclear. It is possible that the two "men" in question had been sent out from the presidio to bring the Tipujans back there.

43. AGI, G 151A, no. 1, Mendía y Sologastoa to Ursúa and Mencos, 1 April 1699.

44. Ibid.

45. AGI, G 151A, no. 1, Mendía y Sologastoa to Ursúa and Mencos, 1 April 1699. Amusingly, Mendía y Sologastoa referred to the Tipujans as "Arizas," referring, of course, to Francisco de Hariza, the Bacalareño who had long held sway over that town. On this occasion, however, the Hariza who accompanied the Tipujans was Juan de Hariza, possibly Francisco's son.

46. AGI, G 151A, no. 1, Juan de Hariza to Mendía y Sologastoa, c. April 1699, ff. 70v–71r.

47. AGI, G 151A, no. 1, Mendía y Sologastoa to Ursúa and Mencos, 4 April 1699.

48. AGI, G 151A, no. 1, Ursúa and Mencos to Mendía y Sologastoa, 8 April 1699, f. 73r–v.

49. The generals replied to this report that don Martín Chan was, upon his capture, to be told that he would be granted full pardon (AGI, G 151A, no. 1, Ursúa and Mencos to Mendía y Sologastoa, 14 April 1699).

50. AGI, G 151A, no. 1, Mendía y Sologastoa to Ursúa and Mencos, 12 April 1699.

51. Ibid.

52. AGI, G 151A, no. 1, Fray Simón de Mendoza y Galindo to Ursúa, 10 April 1699, f. 100r–v. The epidemic apparently spread from the Valley of Guatemala, where Molina documented "pestilence" that year (Molina, 1943, p. 172; cited in Lovell, 1992, p. 247).

53. AGI, G 151A, no. 1, Ursúa and Mencos to Mendía y Sologastoa, 19 April 1699. They listed the following names: AjItzk'in, AjChak May, Chak Itza, YumKuk Tut, Chamach Chab'in, Chamach Kamal, Chamach Tek, NojTut, Chamach Chiken, and Kuk Xiken. Also missing were the children of the "parcialidad de Chamach Xulu, and doubtless many others."

54. AGI, G 151A, no. 1, Ursúa and Mencos to Mendía y Sologastoa, 19 April 1699.

55. AGI, G 151A, no. 1, Parecer of Cristóbal de Mendía y Sologastoa, 29 April 1699, f. 97r–v.

56. These forty men apparently included paddlers, because he later reported that he took thirty men with him to the inland region (AGI, G 151A, no. 1, Parecer by Marcelo Flores Mogollón, 14 April 1699, ff. 88r–95r).

57. AGI, G 151A, no. 1, Orden al don Juan Guerrero por Martín de Ursúa y Melchor de Mencos, 2 April 1699, ff. 65r–v. Juan Guerrero was the pilot of the galeota.

58. AGI, G 151A, no. 1, Flores to Ursúa and Mencos, 3 April 1699, ff. 69v–70r; another copy is in G 344, ramo 3, ff. 102r–103v. He identified the rivers as those of "Los Dolores y los de Los Achotales [Ah Chontales]" and claimed that he met seven natives from San Agustín.

59. That is, "gozando de estar a orillas de la laguna."

60. Ibid.

61. In a *parecer* written on April 14, after he returned to the presidio, Flores Mogollón stated that he traveled for fourteen leagues to the southeast (AGI, G 151A, no. 1, Parecer by Mogollón, 14 April 1699). This must have been a copyist's error, because the places he visited besides Saklemakal would all have been along the northeastern shore of the lake (see also AGI, G 151A, no. 1, Auto [including questionnaire] by Ursúa and Mencos, 9 April 1699, ff. 78r–79v).

62. AGI, G 151A, no. 1, Parecer by Mogollón, 14 April 1699.

63. AGI, G 151A, no. 1, Auto (including questionnaire) by Ursúa and Mencos, 9 April 1699; Parecer of Fray Simón de Mendoza, 3 May 1699, f. 98r.

64. AGI, G 344, ramo 3, Mencos to Sánchez de Berrospe, 8 March 1699. Apparently some few food supplies had arrived from Verapaz prior to April 8, but Mencos described them as rotten and inedible.

65. The principal document on the junta is not recorded in my notes; it appears in AGI, G 151A, no. 1, just before Parecer of Mora, 24 April 1699, f. 112r–v. See also Villagutierre, 1983, bk. 10, ch. 11, p. 390.

66. AGI, G 151A, no. 1, Parecer of Mora, 24 April 1699.

67. AGI, G 151A, no. 1, Memorial by Teodoro O'Kelly, surgeon, April 1699, ff. 124v–125r.

68. AGI, G 151A, no. 1, Memorial by José Fernandez y Estenos, teniente de capitán general, April 1699, f. 112v.

69. AGI, G 151A, no. 1, Auto by Ursúa and Mencos, 28 April 1699, ff. 125r–126r. Other information on the state of sickness may be found in AGI, G 151A, no. 1, Ursúa to Sánchez de Berrospe, 24 April 1699, ff. 119r–123r, and Ursúa to royal officials of Guatemala, 26 April 1699, ff. 123v–124v. Their orders were repeated on April 30 (AGI, G 151A, no. 1, Auto definitivo by Ursúa and Mencos, 30 April 1699, ff. 131–134). For Mencos's reasons for opposing a hasty withdrawal, see Villagutierre, 1983, bk. 10, ch. 13, pp. 394–95.

70. AGI, G 151A, no. 1, Junta para nombrar cabo del presidio, 30 April 1699, ff. 128–131.

71. AGI, G 151A, no. 1, Auto para el entrego de presos, by Ursúa, 6 May 1699, ff. 136r–137r.

72. AGI, G 151A, no. 1, Recibo de presos, 6 May 1699. The receipt was prepared by Alférez Real Joseph de Ripalda Ongay, who countersigned it as official notary or clerk. Mencos later wrote that he took the Kan Ek' prisoners with him when he began his march on May 5. Although the rear guard forces may have caught up with him later, the prisoners departed with this latter group no earlier than May 10.

73. AGI, G 151A, no. 1, Auto by Juan Francisco Cortés, 9 May 1699, ff. 137r–137v.

74. AGI, G 151A, no. 1, Auto by Ursúa, 20 June 1699, ff. 147v–48v. According to Comparato, Soberanis died of yellow fever (Villagutierre, 1983, p. 125, n. 511).

75. AGI, EC 339B, no. 12, Memorial by Lizarraga to Crown, c. 1708.

76. This person would therefore have been a Kit Kan, one of the sons of the Kan Ek' who ruled before the present one. We do know, however, that Ajaw Kan Ek' had two sons; Juan may have been the second one, not mentioned by other sources on these events.

77. Villagutierre, 1933, bk. 10, ch. 13, p. 506 (author's translation); cf. 1983, p. 400.

78. AGI, G 256, Memorial ajustado por el comisario general de la caballería don Melchor de Mencos y Medrano, Caballero del Orden de Santiago, Santiago de Guatemala, 3 Feb. 1701.

79. His name was spelled Yxquin and Exquin in the documents. This name may be equivalent to the Yucatec day name Ix (*ix k'in* = *ix* day).

80. AGI, EC 339B, no. 18, Declaración que hace el Capitán don Marcos de Abalos y Fuentes . . . , 10 March 1704, f. 54r.

81. AGCA, 1.12–11, Exp. 39, Leg. 3, Petition by Antonio de Andino y Arze, n.d. (1705).

82. Ibid. Andino submitted two additional petitions to the audiencia in 1707, in which he stated that he had offered room, board, and instruction since 1680 to "infidel Indians" from the eastern Chol towns of Kan Pamak (Kam-

pamak), Tzun Kal (Tzuncal), and Chok Ajaw (Chocohau), as well as Petén Itzá. The purpose of these petitions was to seek monetary reward for services that he could no longer personally afford. He noted that one of his guests, unidentified, had been sent to prison for throwing drinking glasses at him during a meal. His guests, he claimed, were free to come and go as they pleased (AGCA A.1.5, Exp. 3695, Leg. 181, Two petitions by Antonio de Andino y Arze, 1707).

    83. AGI, EC 339A, Memoria on Petén Itza by Fr. Diego de Rivas, 26 May 1702, ff. 31r–33v.

    84. AGI, M 1032, Autos and testimony on the state of the reductions and doctrinas of Petén Itza administered by the secular clergy of Yucatán, Oct. 1717.

    85. AGI, G 343, no. 23, Memoria de las personas que . . . se hallan en esta isla y presidio del Peten Ytzá de Nuestra Señora de los Remedios y San Pablo, 6 Sept. 1699; Memoria de las personas que han muerto en este presidio desde el mes de abril hasta la fecha de esta, 6 Sept. 1699, ff. 57v–59v.

    86. AGI, EC 339B, no. 12, Memorial by Lizarraga to Crown, c. 1708.

    87. AGI, EC 339B, no. 18, Declaración que hace el Capitán don Marcos de Abalos y Fuentes . . . , 10 March 1704.

    88. AGI, G 151A, no. 1, Mendoza y Galindo to Ursúa, 10 April 1699.

    89. AGI, G 343, no. 23, Memoria de las personas que . . . se hallan en esta isla y presidio del Peten Ytza de Nuestra Señora de los Remedios y San Pablo, 6 Sept. 1699.

    90. AGI, G 343, no. 22, Rivas to Sánchez de Berrospe, 22 Aug. 1700.

    91. Rivas was by now sufficiently discouraged by his work in the area that he requested a transferral to Tipuj.

    92. AGI, EC 339A, Memoria on the mission of Dolores del Lacandón, c. 1701, f. 30r–v; G 180, Fray Diego de Rivas to Crown, 23 Dec. 1696. The later memoria, certified by Fray Antonio Margil de Jesús, is in error in stating that Rivas had counted 500 people at these two towns three years earlier. In fact, he counted 500 at Dolores and 200 at San Ramón in 1696. San Ramón was a new reduction settlement, formed that year from two small villages. The exact date of the 1698 census is uncertain but is deduced from the fact that Rivas returned to Dolores early that year, from where he attempted unsuccessfully to reach Petén Itzá (AGI, G 345, no. 20, Rivas to Sánchez de Berrospe, 4 April 1698; Rivas to Sánchez de Berrospe, 5 June 1698).

    93. Although some of the population loss at Dolores and San Román may have been due to flight, the fact that the settlements were under military security would have reduced the possibility of escape. Margil attributed all of the population loss to death from illness.

    94. AGI, G 180, Fray Bernardo de Rivas, provincial, et al. to Crown, 26 June 1700.

    95. AGI, P 237, ramo 11, Diego Bernardo del Río to Mencos, 9 July 1697.

    96. AGI, G 343, no. 23, Lizarraga to Sánchez de Berrospe, 7 Sept. 1699, ff. 45v–48v.

509

97. Ibid. The original, translated loosely here, reads, "me cayó una flucción a la cara y me cargó en las narices de tal calidad que están de los ojos a la boca hechas una llaga de podridas, como es notorio."

98. AGI, G 343, no. 23, Memoria de las personas que . . . se hallan en esta isla y presidio del Peten Ytzá de Nuestra Señora de los Remedios y San Pablo, 6 Sept. 1699.

99. The reference was to the Kowoj port (*embarcadero*) located near the archaeological site of Ixlú, at a place then known as Saklemakal. The inland milpas, which turned out to have been only recently planted, probably lay in a northern direction from the eastern end of the lake.

100. I tentatively interpret "buscojol" (from *buts' kojol* ["smoke aim"]), as fire-hardened wooden arrow points. Cortés was so impressed by the quality of the arrows that he sent six of them to President Sánchez de Berrospe (AGI, G 343, no. 23, Memoria de las personas que . . . se hallan en esta isla y presidio del Peten Ytzá de Nuestra Señora de los Remedios y San Pablo, 6 Sept. 1699).

101. Or "los Quetz y Popes" in the original.

102. AGI, G 343, no. 23, Memoria de las personas que . . . se hallan en esta isla y presidio del Peten Ytzá de Nuestra Señora de los Remedios y San Pablo, 6 Sept. 1699.

103. AGI, G 343, no. 23, Cortés to Sánchez de Berrospe, 7 Sept. 1699, ff. 48v–51v.

104. AGI, EC 339B, no. 28, Certification of Vargas Dorantes, 10 July 1703. In 1702 AjK'ixaw was living at Petmas, said to be twenty leagues from Nojpeten. The distance was probably an exaggeration, and the location is unknown.

105. AGI, G 343, no. 23, Cortés to Sánchez de Berrospe, 7 Sept. 1699; AGI, EC 339A, Consulta de Rivas y Pacheco, 20 June 1703.

106. AGI, EC 339A, Cortés to Sánchez de Berrospe, 12 March 1702, ff. 9r–12r.

107. AGI, G 343, no. 22, Rivas to Sánchez de Berrospe, 22 Aug. 1700.

108. AGI, EC 339B, no. 16, San Miguel Figueroa to Crown, 12 March 1702.

109. AGI, EC 339B, no. 7, Lista y memoria de los pueblos y parajes de los indios vecinos de la Laguna del Peten, 1702 (undated), ff. 15r–17r.

110. Examples include the following: Tzunpana comprises many towns and "is very bold and bloodthirsty even among themselves" (*es muy osado y carnicero hasta entre ellos*); Xalal, "being at war, seeks the support of other towns" (*estando de guerra piden favor con otros pueblos*); Saklemakal and Nab'a are allied with the Kowojs; the Chans are feared by all; and the Tuts are par-ticularly feared, because "the [*sic*] Tut is the principal enemy of as many Indians as there are in the forests. He is a very high-ranking head. He constantly goes about making wars and tricking the Spaniards. What is certain is that he is very bold and bloodthirsty" (AGI, EC 339B, no. 7, Lista y memoria de los pueblos y parajes de los indios vecinos de la Laguna del Peten, 1702 [undated]). Lizarraga later wrote

that at this time the Kowojs were also enemies of the Tuts (AGI, EC 339B, Mapa y descripción de la montaña del Peten Ytza, c. 1710, ff. 19r–20v).

111. This name is written "Cunagau" in AGI, EC 339B, no. 7, Lista y memoria de los pueblos y parajes de los indios vecinos de la Laguna del Peten, 1702 (undated), ("Cuñahau" in another copy, AGCA, A 1.12–11, Exp. 3155, Leg. 4061). Lizarraga later wrote it as "Chumaxau" (AGI, EC 339B, Mapa y descripción de la montaña del Peten Ytza, c. 1710). In modern Itzaj *chun* means "base," and in colonial usage it could also refer to the foundation of a building (*chun pak'*), a tree trunk (*chun che'*), etc. Its precise meaning in the case of Chun Ajaw and Chun Mejen is not clear, but I assume that it refers to the place where the king exerted his authority, perhaps to the location of the mat of governance. The English word "seat" seems most appropriate in conveying this meaning.

112. Lizarraga wrote this name "Chumexen" (AGI, EC 339B, no. 7, Lista y memoria de los pueblos y parajes de los indios vecinos de la Laguna del Peten, 1702 [undated]; AGI, EC 339B, Mapa y descripción de la montaña del Peten Ytza, c. 1710). *Mejen* is a term of reference meaning "son," from the father's perspective.

113. AGI, EC 339B, Mapa y descripción de la montaña del Peten Ytza, c. 1710.

114. Ibid.

115. Ibid. In the earlier document Lizarraga lists B'alamtun, Chun Ajaw, Saksel, Sakpuy, Joyop, Nek'nojche, and Gwakamay (El Guacamayo on modern maps) in that order—all apparently towns in the same western region around Laguna Sacpuy.

116. Ibid. The last three names would have been Yalain, Chinoja, and IxTus, all names of towns in the old Yalain province. Either Lizarraga was in error in including them or towns of the same names had been reestablished elsewhere.

117. The best discussion of these place names is in Thompson, 1972, pp. 21–32 and foldout map.

118. AGI, G 345, no. 20, Pedro de Zubiaur Isasi to Gabriel Sánchez de Berrospe, 3 July 1698, ff. 67v–73r.

119. AGI, M 1014, Pedro Navarrete to Ursúa, 16 May 1701.

120. AGI, M 1014, Cortés to Ursúa, 5 May 1701. Unlike the much more elaborately fortified towns described by Hernán Cortés in Mazatlan in 1525, the houses in the Kowoj town were apparently all outside the perimeter of the stockade.

121. Navarrete may have had as many as eighty "warriors" with him from Chanchanja (AGI, EC 339A, Juan Francisco Cortés to Gabriel Sánchez de Berrospe, 2 Feb. 1701, ff. 1v–2v).

122. The Kowojs appeared open to religious overtures. Navarrete left a simple wooden cross, made on the spot, before he left the stockaded town, leaving it inside "the house where they have their meeting." When he returned on his way back to Chanchanja, he found the building decorated and the cross "adorned with its own arches and branches, which led us to conclude that they had been venerating it" (AGI, M 1014, Navarrete to Ursúa, 16 May 1701).

123. AGI, EC 339A, Juan Francisco Cortés to Gabriel Sánchez de Berrospe, 1 Feb. 1701, f. 1r–v. An apparent plot to attack Spaniards at IxPapaktun in March 1712 was blown out of proportion by Cortés, who concluded that this western town was the center of a pending large-scale rebellion. In a short fight, Spaniards killed five individuals and wounded one. See EC 339A, Cortés to Sánchez de Berrospe, 12 March 1702.

Chapter 15: Missions, Rebellion, and Survival

1. In sorting out the topics that I should include here, I have relied indirectly on Norman B. Schwartz's chapter on the colonial-period social history of Petén (1990, pp. 31–76). Because I slight the later colonial years, interested readers should turn to his work for a fuller exposition of the history of the entire colonial period in Petén, and for his excellent coverage of the nearly two centuries of independence that followed.

2. AGI, EC 339A, Cortés to Berrospe, 1 Feb. 1701; Fray Diego de Rivas to Gabriel Sánchez de Berrospe, 6 March 1701, ff. 2v–4v.

3. AGI, EC 339A, Juan Francisco Cortés to Gabriel Sánchez de Berrospe, 15 July 1701, ff. 6v–8v.

4. AGI, EC 339A, Consulta de Rivas y Pacheco, 20 June 1703; EC 339B, no. 15, Certification of Br. Francisco de San Miguel y Figueroa, 1 July 1703, ff. 5r–8r.

5. AGI, EC 339A, Consulta de Rivas y Pacheco, 20 June 1703.

6. AGI, EC 339B, no. 28, Certification of Vargas Dorantes, 10 July 1703.

7. AGI, EC 339A, Ursúa to Rivas, 12 May 1702.

8. Ibid.

9. AGI, EC 339A, Ursúa to Cortés, 15 Dec. 1702.

10. Ibid.

11. AGI, EC 339B, no. 15, Certification of San Miguel y Figueroa, 1 July 1703; no. 28, Certification of Bachiller Marcos de Vargas Dorantes, 10 July 1703, ff. 18r–21r. Although Cortés wrote a third report on these events, it was almost word-for-word a duplicate of Vargas's report (AGI, EC 339B, no. 28, Certification of Capitán don Juan Francisco Cortés, 10 July 1703, ff. 22r–25r).

12. The locations of missions on map 10 is based both on textual descriptions as noted and on several eighteenth-century maps. Because several of the first missions were short lived or abandoned early as the result of the 1704 rebellion, they cannot be precisely located; two or three of the later missions are also unlocated. The most useful maps of which I am aware are "Plano de la Provincia de Yucathan...," c. 1734; "Descripción plano hidrographica...," c. 1770; and Diez Navarro, 1771. In addition, a watercolor bird's-eye view of the main lake and its environs shows a number of missions (AGI, Mapas y planos, Guatemala 26, Mapa de la provincia del Peten y del Castillo de su nombre, 1740). This painting was not intended to be a precise map, and artist's license has distorted distances and loca-

tions. It has been reproduced in Reina, 1966; Cano, 1984; and Rice, Rice, and Jones 1993.

13. AGI, EC 339B, no. 15, Certification of San Miguel y Figueroa, 1 July 1703. The actual date of the appearance of San Miguel is May 8; see Thurston and Attwater, 1963, p. 699.

14. AGI, EC 339B, no. 28, Certification of Vargas Dorantes, 10 July 1703.

15. Ibid.

16. Ibid.

17. Vargas reported that after Aguilar captured Kulut Kowoj, allies of the prisoner attacked the town known as Kitis, killing its leader and his wife and children. Aguilar unsuccessfully pursued the guilty parties and, returning through the same town, brought the remaining inhabitants with him to settle at San José.

18. All known eighteenth-century maps indicate that San José was adjacent to San Andrés (to its east), where it remains today. San Jerónimo was also adjacent to San Andrés (to its west). The earliest of these maps is dated about 1734 ("Plano de la Provincia de Yucathan," c. 1734).

19. That is, "una punta que sobresale en la laguna una legua del cayo a la parte occidental."

20. The later location is confirmed on an early map, "Plano de la Provincia de Yucathan . . . ," c. 1734. It appears there on later maps as well, and is described as being next to San Andrés in AGI, G 859, Informe de Br. Juan Antonio Moreno de los Reyes, vicario de San Andrés, 12 March 1766, in Testimonio de los autos seguidos sobre el pre de dos reales diarios que se dan a los presidarios del castillo de Peten Ytza, informes, y demás instruido en virtud de los resuelto por la Real Junta de Hacienda, 1771, ff. 92v–101r.

21. Thurston and Attwater, 1963, vol. 4, p. 693.

22. That is, Saint Martin of Tours (ibid., p. 697).

23. Fray Diego de Rivas and Captain Alejandro Pacheco located San Martín two leagues east of San Andrés, which would place it near present-day Chachaklum (AGI, EC 339A, Consulta de Rivas y Pacheco, 20 June 1703).

24. AGI, EC 339B, no. 28, Certification of Vargas Dorantes, 10 July 1703. The location of this K'ixab'on church and settlement is not entirely clear; Vargas said only that it was "adjacent to" (*junto al*) San Martín; he used the same phrase in describing the location of San Francisco, which was probably more than a league from San Martín.

25. Thurston and Attwater, 1963, vol. 4, p. 682.

26. Ibid., p. 690.

27. AGI, EC 339B, no. 28, Certification of Vargas Dorantes, 10 July 1703.

28. The term translated as "settlement" in San Miguel's report is "ranchería." **513**

29. San Miguel is the source for San Juan Baptista, San Pedro, and Nuestra Señora de Guadalupe. This is not the same San Pedro established later near Santo Toribio.

30. Thurston and Attwater, 1963, vol. 4, p. 701.

31. AGI, EC 339A, Consulta de Rivas y Pacheco, 20 June 1703.

32. Punta Nijtún itself has also been known as Punta de Candelaria, probably a survival of the mission's name.

33. AGI, EC 339A, Consulta de Rivas y Pacheco, 20 June 1703. The date of his return is recorded in EC 339B, no. 18, Capitán José de Aguilar y Galeano to bishop of Yucatán, 8 Feb. 1704, ff. 23r–25r. Although his report, dated June 20, was cosigned by Aguilar y Galeano, it exhibits Rivas's personal style.

34. AGI, EC 339A, Consulta de Rivas y Pacheco, 20 June 1703.

35. AGI, EC 339B, no. 28, Certification by Rivas, 23 Dec. 1703. The tenth mission may have been San Antonio, which was included with San Martín in the June report.

36. AGI, EC 339B, no. 26, Gaspar Reymundo de Varaya to governor of Yucatán, 17 June 1704, ff. 7r–10r. The identity of the eleventh mission is unknown.

37. We cannot be sure whether their names were Kanek' or Kan Ek', but in most cases I assume that nonmembers of the royal extended family bore Kanek' as a patronym. Their "first" names may be "given" names.

38. AGI, EC 339B, no. 28, Certification by Rivas, 23 Dec. 1703. Masa was probably from the Laguneta El Sos region southwest of Laguna Sacpuy (AGI, G 151A, no. 1, Abalos y Fuentes to Ursúa and Mencos, 2 April 1699; Parecer by Artiga, 10 April 1699). Kali Kan Ek' was probably a close relative of Ajaw Kan Ek' (G 151A, no. 1, Mendia y Sologastoa to Ursúa and Mencos, 12 April 1699).

39. The sources for the 1704 rebellion comprise five documents. Aguilar y Galeano first reported the event to the bishop of Yucatán the day after the murders of the six soldiers. Although his report was quite detailed, information that turned out to be erroneous was revised in later reports (AGI, EC 339B, no. 18, Aguilar y Galeano to bishop of Yucatán, 8 Feb. 1704).

The next extant report was written by Aguilar to the president of Guatemala on March 28, following the trial and execution of six indigenous leaders (EC 339A, Informe de Aguilar y Galeano, to president of Audiencia of Guatemala, 28 March 1704). This was followed almost immediately, on April 3, by a second report to the president of Guatemala, written by the recently arrived Yucatecan secular priest, Br. Bernabé de Herrera (EC 339A, Herrera to Juan Jerónimo Duardo, president of Audiencia of Guatemala, 3 April 1704, ff. 91r–92v). Herrera's account was largely a duplicate of Aguilar's March 28 report and was clearly written at the behest of the captain, who sought additional military support from Guatemala.

On June 17 Gaspar Reymundo de Varaya, an officer from the presidio who had been absent from there when the events occurred, wrote a fairly detailed account of the rebellion and subsequent related events to Ursúa (EC 339B, no. 26, Varaya to governor of Yucatán, 17 June 1704). Although his account parallels for the most part those by Aguilar and Herrera, it contains a few details that were omitted in the earlier accounts.

Finally, Fray Diego de Rivas, who had left the presidio for Santiago de Guatemala prior to the rebellion, summarized what he had learned about it in a letter written to Ursúa on July 20 (EC 339B, no. 26, Rivas to Ursúa, 20 July 1704, ff. 11r–12r). Probably his only sources of information were the letters previously written by Aguilar and Herrera to the president of Guatemala. Because there is much overlap in these accounts, I have not cited specific references in this description of the rebellion except in cases where there is conflicting evidence.

40. AGI, EC 339B, no. 18, Declaración que hace el Capitán don Marcos de Abalos y Fuentes . . . , 10 March 1704; no. 26, Varaya to governor of Yucatán, 17 June 1704. Aguilar y Galeano wrote that Cortés hoped to find husbands for his daughters in Guatemala. He was probably back in Santiago de Guatemala by March 1704 (AGI, EC 339B, no. 18, Aguilar to bishop of Yucatán, 8 Feb. 1704).

41. AGI, EC 339A, Consulta de Rivas y Pacheco, 20 June 1703.

42. AGI, EC 339B, no. 12, Memorial by Lizarraga to Crown, c. 1708; no. 26, Varaya to governor of Yucatán, 17 June 1704.

43. AGI, EC 339B, no. 18, Declaración que hace el Capitán don Marcos de Abalos y Fuentes . . . , 10 March 1704.

44. Ibid. A few years later Lizarraga claimed, with wild exaggeration, that the estancia had more than six thousand head of cattle and forty-five hundred horses (AGI, EC 339B, no. 12, Memorial by Lizarraga to Crown, c. 1708).

45. AGI, EC 339B, no. 18, Aguilar y Galeano to bishop of Yucatán, 8 Feb. 1704; EC 339A, Informe de Aguilar y Galeano, to president of Audiencia of Guatemala, 28 March 1704.

46. AGI, EC 339B, no. 26, Varaya to governor of Yucatán, 17 June 1704.

47. AGI, EC 339A, Informe de Aguilar y Galeano to president of Audiencia of Guatemala, 28 March 1704.

48. Ibid.

49. This is the account provided by Varaya (AGI, EC 339B, no. 26, Varaya to governor of Yucatán, 17 June 1704). According to Aguilar, when the men on board the galeota became suspicious after the others did not return, they began to yell at people on shore; it was at this point, he wrote, that the fighting began (EC 339A, Informe de Aguilar y Galeano to president of Audiencia of Guatemala, 28 March 1704).

50. AGI, EC 339B, no. 18, Aguilar y Galeano to bishop of Yucatán, 8 Feb. 1704.

51. AGI, EC 339A, Informe del Aguilar y Galeano to president of Audiencia of Guatemala, 28 March 1704.

52. The original reads, "me trayeron dichos cuerpos que quebraban los corazones" (AGI, EC 339A, Informe del Aguilar y Galeano, to president of Audiencia of Guatemala, 28 March 1704). The first reports indicated that all, including de la Garza, had been decapitated (EC 339A, Informe de Aguilar y Galeano to president of Audiencia of Guatemala, 28 March 1704). This apparently was not the case, nor could the soldiers waiting in the galeota have known how their

515

companions had been murdered. Decapitation was surmised by Spaniards to be a favorite method of killing among the Itzas, as was the ritual removal of hearts and subsequent consumption of the bodies. None of the 1704 victims suffered such a fate.

53. Aguilar's later report stated that these four towns joined the rebellion several days after the initial attacks, a statement that conflicts with the report written on February 8, the day after the attack.

54. That is, "vicario provincial y juez eclesiástico de estas montañas" (AGI, EC 339A, Herrera to Duardo, 3 April 1704).

55. According to Varaya, twelve soldiers were guarding both the milpa and the estancia in mid-June (AGI, EC 339B, no. 26, Varaya to governor of Yucatán, 17 June 1704).

56. They charged with a "carga cerrada," a close formation charge with swords or bayonets.

57. That is, "el más querido de todos" (AGI, EC 339A, Informe de Aguilar y Galeano to president of Audiencia of Guatemala, 28 March 1704).

58. Ibid.

59. AGI, EC 339B, no. 26, Varaya to governor of Yucatán, 17 June 1704.

60. Lizarraga later identified a Kitis as a Kowoj leader (AGI, EC 339B, Mapa y descripción de la montaña del Peten Ytza, n.d., c. 1710).

61. AGI, EC 339B, no. 18, Declaración que hace el Capitán don Marcos de Abalos y Fuentes . . . , 10 March 1704.

62. AGI, EC 339A, Informe de Aguilar y Galeano to president of Audiencia of Guatemala, 28 March 1704.

63. AGI, EC 339B, no. 26, Varaya to governor of Yucatán, 17 June 1704.

64. AGI, EC 339B, no. 27, Ursúa (Conde de Lizárraga) to Crown, 21 Jan. 1708, f. 17r–v. This was twice the amount he had requested in 1696 (chapter 10).

65. AGI, EC 339A, Informe del Capitán Aguilar y Galeano to president of Audiencia of Guatemala, 28 March 1704.

66. Ibid.

67. Ibid.

68. AGI, EC 339B, no. 28, Aguilar y Galeano to Toribio de Cosio, president of Guatemala, 30 April 1709.

69. AGI, EC 339B, no. 28, Aguilar y Galeano to Cosio, 30 April 1709. Sororal polygyny among captured leaders is described in AGI, EC 339A, Informe del Capitán Aguilar y Galeano to president of Audiencia of Guatemala, 28 March 1704.

70. AGI, EC 339A, Informe del Capitán José de Aguilar y Galeano to president of Audiencia of Guatemala, 31 March 1704, ff. 73r–79 (f. 74v).

71. Ibid. Vargas, for his part, complained that Aguilar mistreated his troops and other Spaniards (EC 339B, no. 24, Br. Marcos de Vargas Dorantes to oficiales reales of Guatemala, 28 Feb. 1704, ff. 19v–22r).

72. AGI, G 299, Gaspar Reymundo de Varaya to Fray Juan del Cerro,

24 August 1708 (f. 9r); José de Aguilar y Galeano to Fray Juan del Cerro, 24 August 1708 (f. 13r), in Testimonio de los autos fhos sobre la entrada del Sambo en los pueblos del Peten y providencias dadas para efecto de remitir a el de Consejo de las Indias, 1708. By 1704 most of the southern Mopans had fled east, presumably into Belize (AGI, EC 339B, no. 18, Declaración que hace el Capitán don Marcos de Abalos y Fuentes . . . , 10 March 1704, ff. 50v–51r). Within the next two years a presidio was reestablished at Mopan (San Luis), from where Guatemalan troops made forays into Mopan territory; the details of these reductions have not emerged in the documentation. According to Ursúa, two thousand Mopan families had agreed that year to be relocated at a place called Los Zinzontles on the camino real, presumably in the vicinity of Mopan (AGI, EC 339B, no. 27, Ursúa to Crown, 12 Oct. 1706). The settlements that resulted from the Mopan reductions were San Luis, Santo Toribio, San Francisco Xavier, and Dolores (G 299, Gaspar Reymundo de Varaya to Fray Juan del Cerro, 24 August 1708, in Testimonio de los autos fhos sobre la entrada del Sambo en los pueblos del Peten, 1708, f. 9r).

73. Fernando de Meneses Bravo de Sarabia took possession of the office of governor of Yucatán in September 1707 (AGI, M 889, Bravo de Sarabia to Crown, 20 Sept. 1707).

74. AGI, EC 339B, no. 27, Ursúa to Crown, including real cédula (24 Jan. 1698), 12 Sept. 1707, ff. 23r–29v.

75. AGI, EC 339B, no. 27, Ursúa to Crown, 24 Jan. 1708.

76. The population count noted for 1711 in Table 15.3 was carried out by Juan Antonio Ruíz de Bustamante, whom the Audiencia of Guatemala appointed in 1710 to investigate Aguilar's governance. According to this *minuta,* Ruíz personally visited fifteen towns, which were widely spaced from one another. For further information see AGCA A3.1, Exp. 11545, Leg. 559, Autos hechos para la venta y remate de los nueve negros que envió Juan Ruía de Bustamante y lo demás en ellos contenido, 1710; A2.3–2, Exp. 6833, Leg. 301, El maestre de campo don Juan Antonio Ruíz de Bustamante es nombrado proveedor del presidio del Peten, 1710; A.1.12, Exp. 7044, Leg. 334, Providencias acerca de la mejor organización de la reducción de los infieles del Peten, 3 April 1710; A.1.12, Exp. 7045, Leg. 334, Razón que dan los oficiales reales de las cajas de Guatemala de lo gastado en la reducción de los infieles del Peten, 1 Sept. 1710; A1.12–11, Exp. 3785, Leg. 185, Juan Antonio Ruíz de Bautamante to President Toribio de Cosio, 2 Feb. 1712.

77. AGI, M 702, Memorial del Lic. Luis Coello Gaytán al Rey, n.d. (written in Spain in late 1715 or early 1716 and seen by the Consejo de Indias on 5 Feb. 1716). This must have been the smallpox epidemic that struck Santiago de Guatemala in 1708, which was followed immediately by another, unspecified epidemic that devastated the Maya towns of the Valley of Guatemala through 1711 (Lutz, 1994, pp. 247–48; see also MacLeod, 1973, pp. 98–100, and Lovell, 1992, p. 149). Lutz notes "a series of smallpox and measles epidemics that killed many more Indians and poor castas than Spaniards" in Santiago between 1690 and 1710 (1994, p. 93).

78. AGI, M 1032, Autos and testimony on the state of the reductions and doctrinas of Petén Itzá, administered by the secular clergy of Yucatán, Oct. 1717.

79. AGI, M 702, Memorial del Lic. Luis Coello Gaytán al Rey, n.d. (ca. 1715). A report submitted by the president of Guatemala in 1724 stated that at that time there were six towns on the shores of Lago Petén Itzá, all within a little more than a league from Los Remedios; their church and houses were all roofed with palm thatch. Of these the report named only three, with population figures, all said to be "indios" and probably including only adults: San Miguel (50), Jesús María (40), and San Jerónimo (40). The report named eight towns along the road to Verapaz, with intermediate distances: Santa Ana (8 leagues from Los Remedios), San Juan (5 or 6 leagues further), Santo Toribio (2 leagues further), "Chinaco" (5 leagues from Santo Toribio and not on the road), Dolores (6 leagues from Santo Toribio on the road), San Francisco Xavier (4 leagues further), San Luis (6 leagues further), and Santa Isabel (14 leagues further, the last town on the road). The journey from Santa Isabel to Cahabón took fourteen days over a difficult road that went through uninhabited territory.

The towns and distances along the road to Campeche, according to this report, were Santa Rita (12 leagues from Los Remedios), San Martín (8 leagues further), San Felipe (17 leagues further), Concepción (11 leagues further), and San Antonio (12 leagues further, the last town under Petén jurisdiction). The distance from San Antonio to "Chivalche" (possibly Sib'alch'en, known on maps), the first town in Campeche, was 12 leagues through uninhabited territory.

This report is found in Det Kongelige Bibliotek (København), NKS 348, Breve resumen y noticia del descubrimiento de la Nueva-España, demarcacion, y descripcion de aquellas provincias divididas en las cinco audiencias que la goviernan . . . , 1750, ff. 449–51. The report itself is entitled "Razon del Presidio del Peten," and a marginal notation indicates that the information was provided by the president of Guatemala, don Francisco de Rivas, in June 1724.

80. The map on which Jesús María appears is "Plano de la Provincia de Yucathan . . . ," c. 1734. It does not appear on maps drawn in the second half of the century. One map of questionable accuracy has the mission named Concepción at this location (AGI, Mapas y planos, Guatemala 26, Mapa de la provincia del Peten . . . , 1740).

81. AGI, EC 339B, no. 27, Real cédula to Ursúa, 24 Jan. 1698, ff. 23r–27r.

82. Elorza y Rada, 1958, p. 32. He had anticipated the countship for some time (AGI, EC 339B, no. 18, bishop of Yucatán to Crown, 14 March 1704, ff. 61r–68).

83. Patch, 1993, p. 126.

84. AGI, EC 339B, no. 18, Auto by bishop of Yucatán, Fray Pedro Reyes de los Ríos y la Madrid, despatched to Captain Marcos de Avalos, 4 Nov. 1703, containing Real Cédula to Bishop, 20 Sept. 1702; no. 27, Petition from Ursúa to Crown, no date (c. 1709).

85. AGI, M 889, Ursúa to Crown, 29 May 1706; EC 339B, no. 27, Ursúa to Crown, 12 Sept. 1707, ff. 27r–29v; Ursúa to Crown, 24 Jan. 1708, ff. 12r–15r.

86. AGI, EC 339B, no. 27, Ursúa to Crown, 31 Jan. 1708, f. 17r–v.

87. AGI, EC 339B, no. 27, Br. Bernabé de Herrera to Crown, 25 Oct. 1707, ff. 5r–6r.

88. AGI, EC 339B, no. 27, Ursúa to Crown, 24 Jan. 1708, ff. 12r–15r. In an undated printed petition from Ursúa to the Crown, he summarized his accomplishments and reiterated his request for the title of adelantado and encomienda tribute "en perpetuidad" in the amount of four thousand ducats, to be adjusted if the population decreased (AGI, EC 339B, no. 27, Petition from Ursúa to Crown, no date). The Council of the Indies received the petition on May 11, 1709, suggesting that they had refused to review it earlier. It must have been written no later than January 1708, because Ursúa is identified in it as still serving as governor of Yucatán, a post that he seems to have left around the end of that month.

89. AGI, EC 339B, no. 29, Testimonio de la junta general fecha por el señor virrey de la Nueva España, 31 Aug. 1709, ff. 1v–9r; Duque de Albuquerque, viceroy of New Spain, to Toribio de Cosio, president of Guatemala, 4 Sept. 1709, f. 1r.

90. AGI, EC 339B, no. 29, Testimonio de la junta general fecha por el señor virrey de la Nueva España, 31 Aug. 1709, ff. 1v–9r; Duke of Albuquerque, viceroy of New Spain, to José de Aguilar y Galeano, 4 Sept. 1709, f. 15r–v; Toribio de Cosio, president of Guatemala, to viceroy of New Spain, 26 Sept. 1709, ff. 21r–29v.

91. These events are detailed in AGI, G 186, Consulta by the Consejo de Indias, 5 July 1716. This *consulta* is based on an analysis of a large *expediente,* not yet located, sent to Spain by the president of Guatemala in 1712.

92. Ibid.

93. Coello Gaytán's letter of introduction to the Council of the Indies is AGI, M 1032, Cabildo Eclesiástico de la Santa Iglesia Catedral de Mérida to Crown, 4 April 1715.

94. This cédula is noted in AGI, M 1032, Dispatch by Sancho del Puerto, maestre escuela of Mérida Cathedral, on behalf of Juan Gómez de Prada, bishop of Yucatán, 9 Dec. 1716. The background to the Crown's desire to send Jesuits to Petén is unclear. As early as March 8, 1705, cédulas were sent to the viceroy of New Spain and the Jesuit provincial in Mexico ordering that they recruit Jesuit priests to go to Petén. These two cédulas are recorded in AGI, EC, no. 26, and are cited in no. 27, Ursúa to Crown, 12 Oct. 1707.

95. The expulsion of the Dominicans is alluded to in the Council of the Indies' document summarized here and is specifically mentioned in AGI, M 1032, Minuta by the Consejo de Indias, no date (about 1755).

96. AGI, G 186, Consulta by the Consejo de Indias, 5 July 1716.

97. AGI, M 1032, Auto by Sancho del Puerto, maestre escuela of Mérida Cathedral, on behalf of bishop of Yucatán, 10 Dec. 1716. The auto includes a quoted portion of a letter, dated 14 Aug. 1716, from Maestre de Campo Juan An-

tonio Ruíz de Bustamente, who then governed the presidio of Petén but wrote from Santiago de Guatemala, to Br. Marcos de Vargas Dorantes, the vicar of Petén Itzá.

98. Ibid.; see also AGI, M 1032, Dispatch to Crown by Sancho del Puerto, maestre escuela of Mérida Cathedral, on behalf of Juan Gómez de Prada, bishop of Yucatán, 9 Dec. 1716.

99. AGI, M 1032, Autos and testimony on the state of the reductions and missions of Peten Itza, administered by the secular clergy of Yucatán, Oct. 1717.

100. AGI, M 1031, Archbishop of Yucatán to Crown, 18 March 1755. In reaction to the archbishop's recommendation, the fiscal of the Council of the Indies opined that Dominicans would be a better choice than Jesuits to serve in Petén (AGI, M 1032, Statement by fiscal, Consejo de Indias, 5 June 1756).

101. Oddly missing from the contemporaneous sources on the Petén missions is any mention of the obvious linguistic advantage that the bilingual Creole secular clergy of Yucatán enjoyed in their knowledge of Yucatec Maya.

102. AGI, G 859, Informe del vicario del Peten, Manuel de Santiago y Betancurt, 20 Feb. 1766, in Testimonio de los autos seguidos sobre el pre de dos reales diarios . . . , f. 81r–v. The date is uncertain, said to have been when the vicar first arrived in Petén. One of the threatened priests, Juan Antonio Moreno, was serving at San Andrés between 1754 and 1766 (Libro de matrimonios, San Andrés [also San José and San Jerónimo], 1751–1808, Genealogical Society of Utah, microfilm roll 1220087).

103. San Bernabé, according to all early maps, was located west of San Martín on the Tayasal Peninsula.

104. AGI, G 859, Informe del vicario del Peten, 20 Feb. 1766.

105. Ibid., ff. 82v–83r. Br. José Estanislao de Sousa of San Andrés made similar claims in his informe, dated 28 Feb. 1766 (f. 91r). He made the further claim that Jacinto Kanek' had testified during his trial in Mérida that he had earlier lived in Petén.

106. AGCA, A1.24, Expediente 10224, Legajo 1580, Título de Gobernador del Pueblo de San Andrés de la nueva provincia del Hitza a don Bernardo Chatha Casique y Principal, 15 May 1713.

107. ACFPAA, San Andrés, Libro de matrimonios, años 1751–1808.

108. Among the 368 partners in 184 marriages that I recorded for these years, the following names represent likely immigrants from Yucatán or Tipuj or their offspring (total = 24): Chab'le (1 male), Chay (1 male, 1 female), Chen (1 male), Koil (1 male), Kawich (1 male, 4 females), Kech (1 male), Kumil (1 male, 2 females), Moo (4 males, 2 females), Naa (1 male), Poot (1 female), Tzel (1 male), and Tzuk (1 male). Ten men and three women have Spanish names. The earliest report that I have seen regarding convicts or others sent as exiles to Petén is dated 1755 (AGI, M 1031, Archbishop of Yucatán to Crown, 18 March 1755).

109. AGI, G 859, Testimonio de los autos seguidos sobre el pre de dos reales diarios que se dan a los presidiarios del castillo de Peten Ytza . . . , 1771. The reports by the priests comprise ff. 75r–104v.

110. This total requires reconstructing the adult populations of Santa Ana and San Luis, which, given the 1-to-1.6 child-to-adult ratio suggested here, would have been about 115 (with 71 children) for Santa Ana and about 60 (with 37 children) for San Luis.

111. Norman Schwartz, who also summarized these data, reported a total indigenous population of 1,168 and a total nonindigenous population of 419. The major difference between our calculations appears to be his omission of reported children (*párvulos*) (Schwartz, 1990, p. 52, Table 2:2).

112. Schwartz, 1990, p. 53, Table 2:3. I have not seen this census from AGI, reported by Lawrence Feldman; the reference in Schwartz bears no signature or title.

113. Ibid.

114. Ibid., p. 106, Table 3:10.

115. AGI, M 1031, Fr. Francisco de San Buenaventura y Tejada, bishop of Yucatán, to Crown, 10 June 1750; Certification by Manuel de Santiago, vicar of Petén Itzá, 16 Feb. 1750.

116. AGCA, A.12–11, Exp. 3799, Leg. 185, Autos hechos en virtud de la Real Cédula de su Magestad . . . Año de 1754. This *expediente* was published by the government of Guatemala in 1936, and I have taken all page references from that edition. The years actually covered by the document are 1754 to 1758. For a brief commentary on this expediente see AGI, M 1031, Archbishop of Yucatán to Crown, 18 March 1755.

117. Guatemala, 1936, pp. 261–62.

118. Ibid.; Informe del vicario del Peten, Manuel de Santiago y Betancurt, 20 Feb. 1766, f. 83r.

119. Ibid.; Castellano of Petén Itzá to ?, f. 70; Informe del Br. Juan Antonio Moreno de los Reyes, vicario de San Andrés, 12 March 1766, f. 100r.

120. AGI, EC 339B, Mapa y descripción de la montaña del Peten Ytza, n.d. (ca. 1708–10), ff. 19r–20v.

121. "Descripción plano hidrographica de la provincia de Yucathan Golfo de Honduras y Laguna de Terminos," c. 1770.

122. This section is based on AGI, EC 339B, no. 12, Memorial by Nicolás de Lizarraga (to Crown), no date (ca. 1708), ff. 16r–18v.

123. Ibid.

124. In 1724 San Francisco Xavier was located six leagues north of San Luis, four leagues south of Dolores, and about thirty-one leagues south of the Petén Itzá presidio (see note 79, this chapter). The distance from Petén Itzá to San Luis had been reduced from about forty-five leagues in 1695 to thirty-seven leagues by 1724 (AGI, G152, ramo 3, Fr. Agustín Cano to Jacinto Barrios Leal, 15 May 1695, ff. 370v–381r). Lizarraga's estimate of forty leagues from Petén Itzá to San Francisco Xavier would have been quite accurate in 1708.

125. Lizarraga's reports were written as defenses against claims that he owed the Guatemalan government two hundred pesos advanced to him in 1698.

He was apparently in prison for his debts when he wrote the documents quoted in this section.

126. Guatemala, 1936, p. 279.

127. I am indebted to Scott Atran for providing me a copy of his notes on eighteenth-century baptismal and marriage registers from the Archivo Apostólica de la Iglesia Católica de Flores Petén; I was unaware of the existence of some of these (from San Luis and Dolores) when I worked there (Atran, personal communication, April 1997). Daniel Ruggiero, a Davidson College student, carried out an analysis of San Luis baptismal registers for the period 1801–8 in which he demonstrated the presence and intermarriage there of Itzas, Mopans, Chols, and K'ek'chis (from Cahabón) (Ruggiero 1997; see AAICFP, San Luis Baptisms, 1801–16 [Genealogical Society of Utah, Salt Lake City, Microfilm roll 1220088]). K'ek'chi migration to San Luis apparently began in the 1770s, resulting in gradual assimilation with the local dominantly Itza-Mopan population. Although San Antonio and San Luis have in recent years been commonly identified as "Mopan," their origins are in an ethnically mixed population.

128. Thompson, 1930, pp. 38–39.

129. Ibid.

130. Ibid., p. 85.

131. Missy Garber, personal communication, February 1997.

Glossary

Ach Kat.   Title of Itza nobility whose holder probably had military and religious responsibilities.

Adoratorio.   Spanish term applied to an indigenous, non-Christian temple.

Aguada.   Seasonal water hole in tropical forest environment.

Aguardiente.   Distilled cane liquor.

Aj-.   Prefix for a man's name and certain noun classes.

Ajaw.   Title of the principal Itza ruler, always a Kan Ek'.

Ajaw B'atab'.   Probable title of the second level of Itza rulership, represented by four individuals.

AjK'in.   Title designating a priest.

Alcalde.   Principal magistrate and administrator of a cabildo (q.v.); also *alcalde ordinario.*

Alcalde mayor.   Spanish official who governed a district called an *alcaldía mayor.*

Annatto.   Achiote (*Bixa orellana*), a small tree whose seeds were used as a red dye and food coloring.

Audiencia.   Court and governing body of a region or the area of its jurisdiction.

Ayikal.   Itza title of respect, which in colonial Yucatec meant "rich."

B'ak'tun.   Calendrical period of 20 k'atuns (q.v.), or 400 tuns (q.v.), a total of 144,000 days.

B'atab'.   Among the Itzas, a title of the nobility for the third level of rulership, represented by four provincial rulers; in Yucatán the head of a *b'atab'il.*

B'atab'il.   In Yucatán, the district governed by a *b'atab'.*

B'ob'at.   Maya priest-prophet.

Cabecera.   Principal town of a colonial province or region.

Cabildo.   City, town, or village council; also the governing body of a cathedral chapter.

Cacicazgo.   Town or territory governed by a cacique.

Cacique.   Indigenous local or territorial leader; a term used primarily by Spaniards.

523

Cantor. Lay indigenous church officer with ritual duties, lit. "singer"; see *maestro.*

Casta. Social category referring to persons of mixed racial or ethnic ancestry.

Cédula. Written royal order.

Chayote. Pear-shaped fruit resembling a squash.

Classic period. The epoch of Maya civilization between about A.D. 250–1000, including the Terminal Classic period.

Cochineal. *Cochinilla* or *grana,* an insect (*Coccus cacti*) attracted to a cultivated cactus plant, used to manufacture a red dye.

Copal. Resinous incense from the copal tree.

Cue. Spanish term for an indigenous, non-Christian temple.

Cycle seat. Location where a *may* (q.v.) was ritually installed.

Encomendero. Holder of an encomienda.

Encomienda. Royal grant to a Spaniard for right of tribute from a specified native population, usually one or more towns.

Entrada. Expedition, military and/or religious, into an indigenous region not under colonial control.

Escribano. Colonial notary or clerk.

Estado. Measurement of 2 varas (q.v.).

Estancia. Cattle ranch.

Fiscal. Offical government attorney.

Galeota. Galliota; a small galley with oars and usually one sail.

Holy Crusade (Santa Cruzada). Church institution for the sale of indulgences, also applied in Maya towns.

Indigo. Plant (*añil, Indigofera anil*) used to make a blue dye.

Ix-. Prefix for a woman's name and certain noun classes.

Jalach Winik. In Yucatán, a territorial ruler of a *kuch kab'al* (q.v.); among the Itzas, probably a senior military commander.

Jol Pop. In Yucatán, a position associated with council governance (lit. "head of the mat").

Juez de grana. Spanish overseer of cochineal production.

Justicia. Cabildo alcalde or alcaldes.

Kuch kab'al. In Yucatán, the entire territory administered from a central town under a single Jalach Winik (q.v.).

Kuch Pop. Itza title, lit. "bearer of the mat," in essence the head of government affairs.

K'atun. Calendrical period of 7,200 days, or 20 tuns (q.v.).

League. Measure of distance, usually approximately four kilometers.

Logwood. Small thorny tree (*Haematoxylon campechianum*) used to make a purple dye.

524

Maestro. Native lay church officer assigned responsibility for religious instruction, sacramental duties, and ritual performance (also called *maestro cantor* and *maestro de capilla*).

Matrícula. Village or town census, often taken for tribute purposes.

May. Calendrical period of 13 k'atuns (q.v.), or 260 tuns (q.v.), also known as the k'atun cycle.

Mestizo. A casta (q.v.) social category comprising descendants of indigenous people and Europeans.

Milpa. Indigenous subsistence cultivation, frequently a swidden plot.

Milpería. Small horticultural settlement or hamlet, often seasonally occupied.

Multepal. In Yucatán, term usually interpreted as referring to a confederated system of government, especially at Mayapan.

Nakom. In Yucatán, a title for war captain.

Oidor. An audiencia official; a judge.

Parcialidad. Colonial designation for a town ward or a district; see also *partido*.

Pardo. A casta (q.v.) social category comprising descendants of Africans and indigenous people or Europeans and indigenous people.

Partido. Colonial designation for a political-geographical province, usually an indigenous one.

Peten. Among Itzas, an island, peninsula, or local territory.

Pieza. Light cannon.

Piragua. Pirogue; long-boat with oars.

Piragua menor (*piraguilla*). Small *piragua* with three oars on a side.

Popolna. Building serving as center of council governance, lit. "mat house."

Postclassic period. The epoch of Maya civilization from about A.D. 1000 to the time of the Spanish conquest.

Presidio. Militarily defended post or town.

Principales. Colonial term for high-ranking indigenous political leaders.

Provincial. Governing superior of a religious order.

Ramada. Arbor or shelter covered over with wood or branches, often a religious shrine.

Ranchería. Small horticultural settlement or hamlet, sometimes seasonally occupied; also the horticultural fields themselves.

Rancho. Small horticultural settlement or hamlet.

Reduction (also *congregación*). A community established as a result of resettlement of indigenous populations by colonial agents.

Regimiento. Members of a cabildo (q.v.), especially *regidores*.

Regular clergy. Members of a religious order, such as Franciscans, Dominicans, and Mercederians.

Repartimiento. Labor draft, represented in Yucatán by advances of cash or goods in return for demands of native-produced foodstuffs, crafts, or natural products.

525

República de indios. Colonially mandated governing council of an indigenous town; equivalent to *cabildo* (q.v.).

Residencia. Official inquiry into a colonial governor's activities, usually by his successor.

Reyezuelo.   Usually translated "petty king," a term given by Spaniards to principal indigenous rulers.

Sacristán.   A lay religious officer responsible for the condition of the church's religious objects.

Sakb'e.   Maya stone causeway.

Secular clergy.   Priests under the direct authority of the Vatican and its local representatives; not members of a religious order.

Señor.   Colonial title of respect, equivalent to "lord."

Servicio personal.   Work for Spaniards required of indigenous people by authorization of colonial authorities.

Tun.   Calendrical period of 360 days.

Tzol k'in.   Calendrical period of 260 days, comprising thirteen named months and twenty named days.

Tz'akab'.   Probable term in Yucatán for a matrilineal descent group.

Tz'o Kan.   Probable title for the sons of the former Ajaw Kan Ek', the Itza ruler.

Vara.   Measurement of about 33 inches, or 84 centimeters.

Villa.   Town serving as local seat of colonial government, subordinate to the provincial or viceregal capital.

Visita.   Subordinate town of a parish; also, a tour of towns by a civil or church official, sometimes for the purpose of imposing fines or collecting contributions.

Visitador.   Offical royal investigator who usually examines a governing official's behavior in office.

Xiquipil.   Unit of measure (Nahuatl), equivalent to eight thousand cacao beans.

Zontle.   Unit of measure (Nahuatl), equivalent to four hundred cacao beans.

Zuyua.   Riddle-like elite speech in Yucatán; also a legendary Nahuatl place name, the symbol of Mexican influences on the ruling class in Yucatan, and possibly the source for the Itzas' name of their own territory.

References Cited

Ancona, Eligio. 1878. *Historia de Yucatan desde la época más remota hasta nuestros días.* 3 vols. Merida: Imprenta de Manuel Heredia Argüelles.

Ashmore, Wendy. 1989. "Construction and Cosmology: Politics and Ideology in Lowland Maya Settlement Patterns." In William F. Hanks and Don S. Rice, eds., *Word and Image in Maya Culture: Explorations in Language, Writing, and Representation,* pp. 272–86. Salt Lake City: University of Utah Press.

Atran, Scott. 1993. "Itza Maya Tropical Agro-Forestry." *Current Anthropology* 34(5): 633–700.

Avendaño y Loyola, Fray Andrés de. 1987. *Relation of Two Trips to Peten: Made for the Conversion of the Heathen Ytzaex and Cehaches.* Ed. Frank E. Comparato; trans. Charles P. Bowditch and Guillermo Rivera. Culver City, Calif.: Labyrinthos.

Ayeta, Francisco de. 1693. *Crisol de la verdad, manifestada por el R. P. Fr. Francisco de Ayeta . . . en defensa de dicha su provincia, sobre el despojo, y sequestro de las 31. doctrinas, de que la removió el reverendo obispo D. Juan de Palafox, siendo visitador del reyno. En contravencion de los sagrados privilegios, que los sumos pontifices la concedieron a instancias de los señores reyes, como delegados apostólicos de la Indias. . . .* Madrid.

Barrera Vásquez, Alfredo, Juan Ramón Bastarrachea Manzano, and William Brito Sansores, eds. 1980. *Diccionario maya Cordemex: Maya-español, español-maya.* Mérida: Ediciones Cordemex.

Barrera Vásquez, Alfredo, and Sylvanus Griswold Morley. 1949. "The Maya Chronicles." In *Carnegie Institution of Washington Contributions to American Anthropology and History,* vol. 10, Contribution 48, pp. 1–86. Washington, D.C.: Carnegie Institution of Washington.

Barrera Vásquez, Alfredo, and Silvia Rendón. 1948. *El Libro de los Libros de Chilam Balam.* México, D.F.: Fondo de Cultura Económica.

Bey, George J., and William M. Ringle. 1989. "The Myth of the Center: Political Integration at Ek Balam, Yucatan, Mexico." Paper presented at the fifty-fourth annual meeting of the Society for American Archaeology, April 1989.

527

References Cited

Borhegyi, Stephan F. de. 1963. "Exploration in Lake Peten Itza." *Archaeology* 16: 14–24.

Bricker, Victoria Reifler. 1981. *The Indian Christ, the Indian King: The Historical Substrate of Maya Myth and Ritual.* Austin: University of Texas Press.

Bunting, Ethel-Jane W. 1932. "From Cahabon to Bacalar in 1677." *Maya Society Quarterly* 1: 112–19.

Cano, Agustín. 1942. "Informe dado al Rey por el Padre Fray Agustín Cano sobre la entrada que por la parte de la Verapaz se hizo al Petén en el año de 1695, y fragmento de una carta al mismo, sobre el proprio asunto." Sociedad de Geografía e Historia, *Anales*, vol. 18, pp. 65–79. Guatemala.

———. 1984. *Manche and Peten: The Hazards of Itza Deceit and Barbarity.* Ed. Frank E. Comparato; trans. Charles P. Bowditch and Guillermo Rivera. Culver City, Calif.: Labyrinthos.

Cárdenas Valencia, Francisco de. 1937. *Relación historial eclesiástica de la provincia de Yucatán de la Nueva España escrita en el año de 1639.* México: Editorial Porrúa.

Carmack, Robert M. 1981. *The Quiché Mayas of Utatlán: The Evolution of a Highland Guatemala Kingdom.* Norman: University of Oklahoma Press.

Carrillo y Ancona, Crescencio. 1895. *El obispado de Yucatan: Historia de su fundación y de sus obispos desde el siglo xvi hasta el xix.* 2 vols. Mérida: Imprenta de R. B. Caballero.

Cerwin, Herbert. 1963. *Bernal Díaz, Historian of the Conquest.* Norman: University of Oklahoma Press.

Clendinnen, Inga. 1987. *Ambivalent Conquests: Maya and Spaniard in Yucatan, 1517–1570.* New York: Cambridge University Press.

Coe, Michael D. 1965. "A Model of Ancient Community Structure in the Maya Lowlands." *Southwestern Journal of Anthropology* 21(2): 97–114.

Coggins, Clemency C. 1980. "The Shape of Time: Some Political Implications of a Four-Part Figure." *American Antiquity* 47: 727–39.

Collins, Anne C. 1977. "The *Maestros Cantores* in Yucatán." In Grant D. Jones, ed., *Anthropology and History in Yucatán*, pp. 233–47. Austin: University of Texas Press.

Cortés, Hernán. 1976. "Quinta carta-relación de Hernán Cortés al Emperador Carlos V, Tenuxtitan, 3 de septiembre de 1526." In Hernán Cortés, *Cartas de Relación*, pp. 219–83. México: Editorial Porrúa.

"Descripcion plano hidrographica de la provincia de Yucathan Golfo de Honduras y Laguna de Terminos." C. 1770. In *Cartografía de ultramar*, 1955, vol. 2 (*Atlas*), no. 123. Madrid: Imprenta del Servicio Geográfico del Ejército.

Díaz del Castillo, Bernal. 1977. *Historia verdadera de la conquista de la Nueva España.* 2 vols. México: Editorial Porrúa.

Diccionario de la lengua castellana. 1914. 4th ed. Madrid: Imprenta de los Sucesores de Hernando.

Diez Navarro, Luis. 1771. "Plano de la Laguna de el Peten, Pueblos y terreno inmediato, siendo de Bosque mui cerrado mucho mas de lo que representa el Plano." In *Cartografía de ultramar,* 1955, vol. 2 (*Atlas*), no. 127. Madrid: Imprenta del Servicio Geográfico del Ejército.

Edmonson, Munro S. 1982. *The Ancient Future of the Itza: The Book of Chilam Balam of Tizimin.* Austin: University of Texas Press.

———. 1984. "Human Sacrifice in the Books of Chilam Balam of Tizimin and Chumayel." In Elizabeth P. Benson, org., and Elizabeth H. Boone, ed., *Ritual Human Sacrifice in Mesoamerica,* pp. 91–99. Washington, D.C.: Dumbarton Oaks.

———. 1986. *Heaven-Born Mérida and Its Destiny: The Book of Chilam Balam of Chumayel.* Austin: University of Texas Press.

———. 1988. *The Book of the Year: Middle American Calendrical Systems.* Salt Lake City: University of Utah Press.

Elorza y Rada, Francisco de. 1714. *Nobiliario de el Valle de la Valdorba, ilustrado con los escudos de armas de sus palacios, y casas nobles con el extracto de la conquista de el Ytza en la Nueva España.* Pamplona: Francisco Antonio de Neyra, Impresor del Reyno.

———. 1930. *A Narrative of the Conquest of the Province of the Ytzas in New Spain.* Paris: Editions Genet. (Part I contains introduction and English translation by Phillip A. Means; Part II is a facsimile of the 1714 edition.)

———. 1958. *Nobiliario del Valle de la Valdorba con los escudos de armas de sus palacios y casas nobles; y Relación de la conquista de Itza en la Nueva España por el Conde de Lizárraga por el Doctor don Francisco de Elorza y Rada.* Madrid: Sociedad de Bibliofilos Españoles.

Enciclopedia Universal Ilustrada Europeo-Americana. 1907–c. 1930. Madrid: Espasa-Calpe.

Farriss, Nancy M. 1984. *Maya Society under Colonial Rule: The Collective Enterprise of Survival.* Princeton: Princeton University Press.

———. 1987. "Remembering the Future, Anticipating the Past: History, Time and Cosmology among the Maya of Yucatan." *Comparative Studies in Society and History* 29(3): 566–93.

Fontavelli, Vicente. 1943. *Conde de Lizárraga-Bengoa: Conquista del Ytzá en la Nueva España.* Valencia: Universidad Literaria de Valencia, Facultad de Filosofía y Letras.

Fox, James A., and John S. Justeson. 1986. "Classic Maya Dynastic Alliance and Succession." In Victoria Reifler Bricker, gen. ed., and Ronald Spores, vol. ed., *Supplement to the Handbook of Middle American Indians,* 4 (*Ethnohistory*). Austin: University of Texas Press.

Fox, John W. 1987. *Maya Postclassic State Formation: Segmentary Lineage Migration in Advancing Frontiers.* Cambridge: Cambridge University Press.

———. 1989. "On the Rise and Fall of *Tuláns* and Maya Segmentary States. *American Anthropologist* 91(3): 656–81.

References Cited

Freidel, David, Linda Schele, and Joy Parker. 1995. *Maya Cosmos: Three Thousand Years on the Shaman's Path*. New York: William Morrow.

Gerhard, Peter. 1979. *The Southeast Frontier of New Spain*. Princeton: Princeton University Press.

Gillespie, Susan. 1989. *The Aztec Kings: The Construction of Rulership in Mexican History*. Tucson: University of Arizona Press.

Gossen, Gary H. 1974. *Chamulas in the World of the Sun: Time and Space in a Maya Oral Tradition*. Cambridge: Harvard University Press.

Graham, Elizabeth. 1991. "Archaeological Insights into Colonial Period Maya Life at Tipu, Belize." In David Hurst Thomas, ed., *Columbian Consequences*, vol. 3, *The Spanish Borderlands in Pan-American Perspective*, pp. 319–34. Washington, D.C.: Smithsonian Institution Press.

Graham, Elizabeth, Grant D. Jones, and Robert R. Kautz. 1985. "Archaeology and Ethnohistory on a Spanish Colonial Frontier: An Interim Report on the Macal-Tipu Project in Western Belize." In Arlen F. Chase and Prudence M. Rice, eds., *The Lowland Maya Postclassic*, pp. 206–14. Austin: University of Texas Press.

Graham, Elizabeth, David M. Pendergast, and Grant D. Jones. 1989. "On the Fringes of Conquest: Maya-Spanish Contact in Colonial Belize." *Science* 246: 1254–59.

Guatemala 1:50,000. 1973. 1st ed. Guatemala City: Instituto Geográfico Nacional.

Guatemala, Archivo General de Gobierno. 1936. "Autos hechos en virtud de la Real Cédula de su Magestad, en que se ordena a este Superior Gobierno, que serciorado del estado en que se hallan las reducciones de Indios de la Provincia del Petén, aplique los medios correspondientes para que se saquen de los montes los Indios que se han huido, y retirado a ellos, y que se agreguen a los Pueblos que han desamparado, solicitando tambien todos aquellos que permanecen en la gentilidad. Año de 1754." Guatemala, Archivo General de Gobierno, *Boletín* 1(3): 257–93.

Hanks, William F. 1992. "The Language of the Canek Manuscript." *Ancient Mesoamerica* 3: 269–79.

Hassig, Ross. 1988. *Aztec Warfare: Imperial Expansion and Political Control*. Norman: University of Oklahoma Press.

Haviland, William A. 1972. "Principles of Descent in Sixteenth-Century Yucatan." *Katunob* 8(2): 63–73.

———. 1977. "Dynastic Genealogies from Tikal, Guatemala." *American Antiquity* 42: 61–67.

Hellmuth, Nicholas M. 1972. "Progreso y notas sobre la investigación etnohistórica de las tierras bajas mayas de los siglos XVI a XIX. *América Indígena* 32: 172–244.

———. 1976. *Maya Archaeology: Tikal Copan Travel Guide, 1978*. St. Louis: Foundation for Latin American Anthropological Research.

———. 1977. "Cholti-Lacandon (Chiapas) and Petén-Ytzá Agriculture, Settlement Pattern and Population." In Norman Hammond, ed., *Social Process in*

Maya Prehistory: Studies in Honour of Sir J. Eric S. Thompson, pp. 421–28. London: Academic Press.

Hofling, Charles Andrew. 1991. *Itzá Maya Texts with a Grammatical Overview.* Salt Lake City: University of Utah Press.

———. 1993. "Marking Space and Time in Itzaj Maya Narrative." *Journal of Linguistic Anthropology* 3(2): 164–84.

Hofling, Charles Andrew, and Fernando Tesucún. 1992. "El caballo de Cortés: una relación Itzá." *Winak: Boletín Internacional* 7(1–4): 41–60.

———. 1997. *Itzaj Maya–Spanish–English Dictionary, Diccionario Maya itzaj–español–inglés.* Salt Lake City: University of Utah Press.

Hopkins, Nicholas. 1988. "Classic Mayan Kinship Systems: Epigraphic and Ethnographic Evidence for Patrilineality." *Estudios de Cultura Maya* 17: 87–121.

Houwald, Götz Freiherr, von, ed. 1979. *Nicolás de Valenzuela: Conquista del Lacandón y conquista del Chol.* 2 vols. Berlin: Colloquium Verlag.

Jones, Grant D. 1989. *Maya Resistance to Spanish Rule: Time and History on a Colonial Frontier.* Albuquerque: University of New Mexico Press.

———. 1991. *El Manuscrito Can Ek: Descubrimiento de una visita secreta del siglo XVII a Tah Itzá (Tayazal), última capital de los maya itzáes.* Introduction by George E. Stuart. Collección Divulgación. Mexico: National Geographic Society and Instituto Nacional de Antropología e Historia.

———. 1992. "The Can Ek Manuscript in Ethnohistorical Perspective." *Ancient Mesoamerica* 3: 243–68.

———. 1994. "El Manuscrito Can Ek." *Revista de la Universidad del Valle de Guatemala* 4: 10–33.

Jones, Grant D., Robert R. Kautz, and Elizabeth Graham. 1986. "Tipu: A Maya Town on the Spanish Colonial Frontier." *Archaeology* 39: 40–47.

Joyce, Rosemary A. 1981. "Classic Maya Kinship and Descent: An Alternative Suggestion." *Journal of the Steward Anthropological Society* 13(1): 45–57.

Karttunen, Frances. 1983. *An Analytical Dictionary of Nahuatl.* Austin: University of Texas Press.

Kaufman, Terrence. 1976. "Archaeological and Linguistic Correlations in Mayaland and Associated Areas of Meso-America." *World Archaeology* 8(1): 101–18.

Kemp, Peter, ed. 1976. *The Oxford Companion to Ships and the Sea.* London: Oxford University Press.

Landa, Diego de. 1941. *Landa's Relación de las cosas de Yucatán.* Ed. and trans. Alfred M. Tozzer. Cambridge: Peabody Museum of American Archaeology and Ethnology, Harvard University.

———. 1973. *Relación de las cosas de Yucatán.* 10th ed., with introduction by Angel María Garibay K. México, D.F.: Editorial Porrúa.

León Pinelo, Antonio de. 1960. *Relación que en el Consejo Real de las Indias hizo el Licenciado Antonio de León Pinelo, Relator de su Alteza, sobre la pacificación, y población de las provincias del Manché, y Lacandón, que pretende*

531

hacer don Diego de Vera Ordóñez de Villaquirán, Caballero de la Orden de Calatrava, &c. In France V. Scholes and Eleanor B. Adams, eds., *Relaciones histórico-descriptivas de las provincias de la Verapaz, el Manché y Lacandón, en Guatemala*, pp. 251–72. Guatemala: Editorial Universitaria.

———. 1986. *Report Made in the Royal Council of the Indies on the Pacification and Population of the Provinces of the Manche and Lacandon, which Don Diego de Vera Ordóñez de Villaquiran, Cavalier of the Order of Calatrava, etc., Wishes to Undertake.* Ed. Frank E. Comparato; trans. Doris Zemurray Stone. Culver City, Calif.: Labyrinthos.

Lizana, Bernardo de. 1893. *Historia de Yucatán: Devocionario de Nuestra Señora de Izamal y conquista espiritual* (1633). 2d ed. México: Museo Nacional.

Lockhart, James. 1992. *The Nahuas after the Conquest: A Social and Cultural History of the Indians of Central Mexico, Sixteenth through Eighteenth Centuries.* Stanford: Stanford University Press.

López de Cogolludo, Diego. 1688. *Historia de Yucatán.* Madrid: J. García Infanzón.

———. 1971. *Los tres siglos de la dominación española en Yucatan, o sea historia de esta provincia.* 2 vols. Graz, Austria: Akademische Druck- u. Verlagsanstalt.

Love, Bruce. 1994. *The Paris Codex: Handbook for a Maya Priest.* Austin: University of Texas Press.

Lovell, W. George. 1992. *Conquest and Survival in Colonial Guatemala: A Historical Geography of the Cuchumatán Highlands, 1500–1821.* Montreal and Kingston: McGill-Queen's University Press.

Lutz, Christopher H. 1994. *Santiago de Guatemala, 1541–1773.* Norman: University of Oklahoma Press.

MacLeod, Barbara, and Andrea J. Stone. 1995. "The Hieroglyphic Inscriptions of Naj Tunich." In Andrea J. Stone, *Naj Tunich and the Tradition of Maya Cave Painting*, pp. 155–84. Austin: University of Texas Press.

MacLeod, Murdo J. 1973. *Spanish Central America: A Socioeconomic History, 1520–1720.* Berkeley: University of California Press.

Magdaleno, Ricardo, ed. 1954. *Títulos de Indias.* Catálogo XX del Archivo General de Simancas. Valladolid: Patronato Nacional de Archivos Históricos.

Maler, Teoberto. 1910. *Explorations in the Department of Peten, Guatemala, and Adjacent Regions: Motul de San José, Peten-Itza.* Memoirs of the Peabody Museum of Archaeology and Ethnology, Harvard University 4(3): 131–70. Cambridge, Mass.

Marcus, Joyce. 1973. "Territorial Organization of the Lowland Classic Maya." *Science* 180: 911–16.

———. 1976. *Emblem and State in the Classic Maya Lowlands: An Epigraphic Approach to Territorial Organization.* Washington, D.C.: Dumbarton Oaks.

———. 1983. "Lowland Maya Archaeology at the Crossroads." *American Antiquity* 48: 454–88.

———. 1993. "Ancient Maya Political Organization." In Jeremy A. Sabloff and

John S. Henderson, eds., *Lowland Maya Civilization in the Eighth Century A.D.: A Symposium at Dumbarton Oaks*, pp. 185–217. Washington, D.C.: Dumbarton Oaks.

Martínez, José Luis. 1990. *Hernán Cortés*. México, D.F.: Universidad National Autónoma de México, Fondo de Cultura Económica.

Means, Phillip. A. 1917. *History of the Spanish Conquest of Yucatan and of the Itzas*. Peabody Museum Papers, 7. Cambridge, Mass.: Peabody Museum, Harvard University.

Molina, Antonio de. 1943. *Antigua Guatemala: Memorias de Fray Antonio de Molina*. Guatemala: Unión Tipográfica.

Morales Padrón, Francisco. 1979. *Teoría y leyes de la conquista*. Madrid: Ediciones Cultura Hispánica del Centro Iberoamericano de Cooperación.

Okoshi Harada, Tsubasa. 1995. "Gobierno y pueblos entre los mayas yucatecos postclásicos." *Revista de la Universidad Nacional Autónoma de México* 534–35: 22–27.

Ortiguera, Toribio de. 1968. *Jornada del Río Marañón*. Biblioteca de Autores Españoles, vol. 216, pp. 218–358. Madrid: Ediciones Atlas.

Patch, Robert W. 1993. *Maya and Spaniard in Yucatan, 1648–1812*. Stanford: Stanford University Press.

Pendergast, David M., and Grant D. Jones. 1992. "Poor Beds of Sticks and Rings of Pure Gold: Material Culture in the Canek Manuscript." *Ancient Mesoamerica* 3: 281–90.

Piña Chan, Román. 1977. *Campeche durante el período colonial*. México, D.F.: Instituto Nacional de Antropología e Historia.

Piña Chan, Román, and Raúl Pavón Abreu. 1959. "¿Fueron las ruinas de El Tigre, Itzamkanac?" *México Antiguo* 9: 473–91.

Pincemin, Sophia. 1987. "El Tigre, Candelaria, Campeche: Estudio preliminar." *Cuadernos de Arquitectura Mesoamericana* 10: 4–9.

"Plano de la Provincia de Yucathan, su Capital la Ciu.d de Merida con las Villas de Valladolid, Campeche, y Vacalar, con los demas Pueblos sujetos a su Cap.nia Gen.l y a su Obispado: Tavasco, Laguna de Terminos y Peten Ytzá." C. 1734. In *Cartografía de ultramar*, 1955, vol. 2 (*Atlas*), no. 119. Madrid: Imprenta del Servicio Geográfico del Ejército.

Prem, Hanns J., Berthold Riese, and Anje Gunsenheimer. 1996. "¿Apareció un nuevo Gonzalo Guerrero?" *Arqueología Méxicana* 18: 3.

Proskouriakoff, Tatiana. 1962. "Civic and Religious Structures of Mayapan." In H.E.D. Pollock, R. L. Roys, T. Proskouriakoff, and A. Ledyard Smith, *Mayapan, Yucatan, Mexico*, pp. 87–163. Carnegie Institution of Washington, Publication 619. Washington, D.C.: Carnegie Institution of Washington. **533**

Quezada, Sergio. 1993. *Pueblos y caciques yucatecos, 1550–1580*. México: El Colegio de México.

Reina, Ruben E. 1966. "A Peninsula That May Have Been an Island." *Expedition* 9: 16–29.

Remesal, Antonio de. 1932. *Historia general de las Indias occidentales y particular de la governación de Chiapa y Guatemala.* . . . 2 vols. Biblioteca "Goathemala" de la Sociedad de Geografía e Historia, vols. 4–5. Guatemala: Tipografía Nacional.

Rice, Don S. 1986. "The Peten Postclassic: A Settlement Perspective." In Jeremy A. Sabloff and E. Wyllys Andrews V, eds., *Late Lowland Maya Civilization: Classic to Postclassic,* pp. 301–44. Albuquerque: University of New Mexico Press.

Rice, Don S., Prudence M. Rice, and Grant D. Jones. 1993. "Geografía política del Petén central, Guatemala, en el siglo XVII: La arqueología de las capitales mayas." *Mesoamérica* 14(26): 281–318.

Rice, Don S., Prudence M. Rice, Rómulo Sánchez Polo, and Grant D. Jones. 1995. "El Proyecto Geografía Política del Siglo XVII en el Centro del Petén, Guatemala: Informe al Instituto de Antropología e Historia de Guatemala sobre la primera temporada del trabajo de campo." Unpublished report on file in Department of Anthropology, Southern Illinois University, Carbondale.

———. 1996. "Proyecto Maya-Colonial, geografía política del siglo XVII en el centro del Petén, Guatemala: Informe Preliminar al Instituto de Antropología e Historia de Guatemala sobre investigaciones del campo en los años 1994 y 1995." Unpublished report on file in Department of Anthropology, Southern Illinois University, Carbondale.

Ringle, William M. 1990. "Who Was Who in Ninth-Century Chichen Itza." *Ancient Mesoamerica* 1: 233–43.

Ringle, William M., and George Bey. 1992. "The Center and Segmentary State Dynamics: African Models in the Maya Lowlands." Paper presented at the conference "Segmentary State Dynamics," Cleveland State University, Cleveland, October 1992.

Ringle, William M., George Bey, and Carlos Peraza L. 1991. "An Itza Empire in Northern Yucatan? A Neighboring View." Paper presented at the forty-seventh International Congress of Americanists, New Orleans.

Robicsek, Francis, and Donald Hales. 1984. "Maya Heart Sacrifice: Cultural Perspective and Surgical Technique." In Elizabeth P. Benson, org., and Elizabeth H. Boone, ed., *Ritual Human Sacrifice in Mesoamerica,* pp. 49–90. Washington, D.C.: Dumbarton Oaks.

Roys, Ralph L. 1931. *The Ethno-Botany of the Maya.* Middle American Research Series, Publication 2. New Orleans: Department of Middle American Research, Tulane University.

———. 1940. *Personal Names of the Maya of Yucatan.* Carnegie Institution of Washington, Publication 523, Contribution 31. Washington, D.C.: Carnegie Institution of Washington.

———. 1943. *The Indian Background of Colonial Yucatan.* Carnegie Institution of Washington, Publication 548. Washington, D.C.: Carnegie Institution of Washington.

——. 1957. *The Political Geography of the Yucatan Maya.* Carnegie Institution of Washington, Publication 613. Washington, D.C.: Carnegie Institution of Washington.

——. 1962. "Literary Sources for the History of Mayapan." In H.E.D. Pollock, R. L. Roys, T. Proskouriakoff, and A. Ledyard Smith, *Mayapan, Yucatan, Mexico,* pp. 25–86. Carnegie Institution of Washington, Publication 619. Washington, D.C.: Carnegie Institution of Washington.

——. 1965a. "Lowland Maya Native Society at Spanish Contact." In Gordon R. Willey, ed., *Handbook of Middle American Indians,* vol. 3, part 2, pp. 659–78. Austin: University of Texas Press.

——. 1965b. *Ritual of the Bacabs: A Maya Book of Incantations.* Norman: University of Oklahoma Press.

——. 1967. *The Book of Chilam Balam of Chumayel.* 2d ed. Norman: University of Oklahoma Press.

——. 1972. *The Indian Background of Colonial Yucatan.* New ed. Norman: University of Oklahoma Press.

Ruggiero, Daniel A. 1997. "Ethnic Formation Processes in San Luis, Petén, Guatemala." Unpublished paper written for Seminar on Anthropology and History, Davidson College, Davidson, N.C.

Sahlins, Marshall. 1981. *Historical Metaphors and Mythical Realities: Structure in the Early History of the Sandwich Islands Kingdom.* Ann Arbor: University of Michigan Press.

San Buenaventura, Fray Joseph de. 1994. *Historias de la conquista del Mayab, 1511–1697.* Eds. Gabriela Solís Robleda and Pedro Bracamonte y Sosa. Mérida: Universidad Autónoma de Yucatán.

Sánchez Polo, Rómulo, Don S. Rice, Prudence M. Rice, Anna McNair, Timothy Pugh, and Grant D. Jones. 1995. "La investigación de la geografía política del siglo xvii en Petén central: La primera temporada." In Juan Pedro Laporte and Héctor L. Escobedo, eds., *VIII Simposio de investigaciones arqueológicas en Guatemala, 1994,* pp. 707–20. Guatemala: Ministerio de Cultura y Deportes, Instituto de Antropología e Historia, and Asociación Tikal.

Schele, Linda. 1984. "Human Sacrifice among the Classic Maya." In Elizabeth P. Benson, org., and Elizabeth H. Boone, ed., *Ritual Human Sacrifice in Mesoamerica,* pp. 7–48. Washington, D.C.: Dumbarton Oaks.

Schele, Linda, and David Friedel. 1990. *A Forest of Kings: The Untold Story of the Ancient Maya.* New York: William Morrow.

Schele, Linda, Nokolai Grube, and Erik Boot. 1995. "Some Suggestions on the K'atun Prophecies in the Books of Chilam Balam in Light of Classic-Period History." *Texas Notes on Precolumbian Art, Writing, and Culture 72.* **535** Austin.

Scholes, France V., and Eleanor B. Adams. 1936–37. "Documents Relating to the Mirones Expedition to the Interior of Yucatan, 1621–24." *Maya Research* 3: 153–57, 251–76.

——, eds. 1938. *Don Diego Quijada, alcalde mayor de Yucatan, 1561–1565: Documentos sacados de los archivos de España.* 2 vols. Bibliografía Histórica Mexicana de Obras Inéditas, vols. 14–15. México.

——, eds. 1960. *Relaciones histórico-descriptivas de las provincias de la Verapaz, el Manché y Lacandón, en Guatemala.* Guatemala: Editorial Universitaria.

——. 1991. *Documents Relating to the Mirones Expedition to the Interior of Yucatan, 1621–24.* Ed. Frank E. Comparato; trans. Robert D. Wood. Culver City, Calif.: Labyrinthos.

Scholes, France V., and Ralph L. Roys. 1948. *The Maya Chontal Indians of Acalan-Tixchel: A Contribution to the History and Ethnography of the Yucatan Peninsula.* Carnegie Institution of Washington, Publication 560. Washington, D.C.: Carnegie Institution of Washington.

——. 1968. *The Maya Chontal Indians of Acalan-Tixchel: A Contribution to the History and Ethnography of the Yucatan Peninsula.* 2d ed. Norman: University of Oklahoma Press.

Scholes, France V., and J. Eric S. Thompson. 1977. "The Francisco Pérez *Probanza* and the *Matrícula* of Tipu." In Grant D. Jones, ed., *Anthropology and History in Yucatán,* pp. 43–68. Austin: University of Texas Press.

Schumann, Otto. 1971. *Descripción estructural del maya itzá del Petén, Guatemala, C.A.* México: Universidad Nacional Autónoma de México.

Schwartz, Norman B. 1990. *Forest Society: A Social History of Petén, Guatemala.* Philadelphia: University of Pennsylvania Press.

Sharer, Robert J. 1993. "The Social Organization of the Late Classic Maya: Problems of Definition and Approaches." In Jeremy A. Sabloff and John S. Henderson, eds., *Lowland Maya Civilization in the Eighth Century A.D.: A Symposium at Dumbarton Oaks,* pp. 91–109. Washington, D.C.: Dumbarton Oaks.

——. 1994. *The Ancient Maya.* 5th ed. Stanford: Stanford University Press.

Solís Robleda, Gabriela. 1996. "Respuesta a los comentarios del Dr. Prem y sus colegas." *Arqueología Mexicana* 18: 4.

Soza, José María. 1970. *Monografía del Departamento de El Petén.* 2 vols., 2d ed. Guatemala City: Pineda Ibarra.

Stone, Doris Zemurray. 1932. *Some Spanish Entradas, 1524–1695.* Middle American Research Institute, Tulane University, Publication 4. New Orleans: Tulane University.

Tedlock, Dennis. 1985. *Popul Vuh: The Definitive Edition of the Mayan Book of the Dawn of Life and the Glories of God and Kings.* New York: Simon and Schuster.

Thomas, Hugh. 1993. *Conquest: Montezuma, Cortés, and the Fall of Old Mexico.* New York: Simon and Schuster.

Thompson, J. Eric S. 1930. *Ethnology of the Mayas of Southern and Central British Honduras.* Field Museum of Natural History, Publication 274. New Orleans.

———. 1938. "Sixteenth and Seventeenth Century Reports on the Chol Mayas." *American Anthropologist* 40: 584–604.

———. 1951. "The Itza of Tayasal, Petén." In *Homenaje a Alfonso Caso*, pp. 389–400. México.

———. 1954. *The Rise and Fall of Maya Civilization*. Norman: University of Oklahoma Press.

———. 1970. *Maya History and Religion*. Norman: University of Oklahoma Press.

———. 1972. *The Maya of Belize*. Belize City: Benex Press.

———. 1977. "A Proposal for Constituting a Maya Subgroup, Cultural and Linguistic, in the Petén and Adjacent Regions," in Grant D. Jones, ed., *Anthropology and History in Yucatán*, pp. 3–42. Austin: University of Texas Press.

Thompson, Philip C. 1978. *Tekanto in the Eighteenth Century*. Ann Arbor: University Microfilms (79–10255).

———. n.d. *Tekanto: A Case Study of a Mayan Town in Colonial Yucatan*. Forthcoming.

Thurston, Herbert S. J., and Donald Attwater. 1963. *Butler's Lives of the Saints*. 4 vols. New York: P. J. Kennedy and Sons.

Tovilla, Martín Alfonso. 1960. "Relación histórica descriptiva de la provincias de la Verapaz y de la del Manché del reino de Guatemala y de las costas, mares, y puertos principales de la dilatada América, escrita por el Capitán don Martín Alfonso Tovilla, año de 1635." In France V. Scholes and Eleanor B. Adams, eds., *Relaciones histórico-descriptivas de las provincias de la Verapaz, el Manché y Lacandón, en Guatemala*, pp. 21–250. Guatemala: Editorial Universitaria.

Traven, B. 1966. "A New God Was Born." In B. Traven, *The Night Visitor and Other Stories*, pp. 161–69. New York: Hill and Wang.

Vayhinger-Scheer, Temis, ed. 1996. *Fray Andrés de Avendaño y Loyola: "Relación de las dos entradas que hice a la conversion de los gentiles ytzáex, y cehaches."* Mexican Occasional Publications 3. Möchmühl: Sauerwein.

———. 1997. *Fray Andrés de Avendaño y Loyola: "Relación de las dos entradas que hice a la conversion de los gentiles ytzáex, y cehaches."* Fuentes Mesoamericanas, vol. 1. Möchmühl: Sauerwein.

Villagutierre Soto-Mayor, Juan de. 1701. *Historia de la conquista de la provincia de el Itza, reduccion, y progressos de la de el Lacandon y otras naciones de indios barbaros, de la mediacion de el reyno de Guatimala, a las provincias de Yucatan, en la America septentrional*. Madrid.

———. 1933. *Historia de la conquista de la provincia de el Itzá, reducción y progresos de la de el Lacandón*. Biblioteca "Goathemala" de la Sociedad de Geografía e Historia, vol 9. Guatemala: Tipografía Nacional.

———. 1983. *History of the Conquest of the Province of the Itza*. Ed. Frank E. Comparato; trans. Robert D. Wood. Culver City, Calif.: Labyrinthos.

———. 1985. *Historia de la conquista de Itzá*. Ed. Jesús María García Añoveros. Crónicas de América, no. 13. Madrid: Historia 16.

Vos, Jan de. 1980. *La paz de Dios y del rey: La conquista de la selva lacandona, 1525–1821.* Mexico: Colección Ceiba del Gobierno del Estado de Chiapas.

Weeks, John M. 1988. "Residential and Local Group Organization in the Maya Lowlands of Southwestern Campeche, Mexico: The Early Seventeenth Century." In Richard Wilk and Wendy Ashmore, eds., *Household and Community in the Mesoamerican Past,* pp. 73–96. Albuquerque: University of New Mexico Press.

Ximénez, Francisco. 1929–31. *Historia de la provincia de San Vicente de Chiapa y Guatemala.* 3 vols. Biblioteca "Goathemala" de la Sociedad de Geografía e Historia, vols. 1–3. Guatemala: Tipografía Nacional.

———. 1971–77. *Historia de la provincia de San Vicente de Chiapa y Guatemala.* 4 vols. Biblioteca "Goathemala" de la Sociedad de Geografía e Historia, vols. 28–29, 24–25. Guatemala: Tipografía Nacional.

Zantwijk, Rudolph van. 1985. *The Aztec Arrangement: The Social History of Pre-Spanish Mexico.* Norman: University of Oklahoma Press.

Index

For ease of reference, in this index words are alphabetized without regard to glottal stops. An "f" after a number indicates a separate reference on the next page, and an "ff" indicates separate references on the next two pages. *Passim* is used for a cluster of references in close but not consecutive sequence.

Abad, Juan Jerónimo, 486n75

Abalos y Fuentes, Marcos de, 58, 365ff, 373, 375, 403, 430n24

Acevedo, Tomás de, 237

Acha, 31, 38

Achcauhtli (Aztec title), 87–88, 101

Ach Kat (Itza title), 60, 71, 73, 85–86, 87ff, 94, 101–6 *passim*, 451nn, 461n35

Ach Kat, Jalach Winik (Itza title), 85–86. *See also* Jalach Winik

Ach Kat Kit Kan, 89

Acté, 8, 17, 471n15

Acuña, Diego de, 51

Adams, Eleanor B., 51, 440n71

Adelantado, 39, 411, 455n17, 519n88

Agriculture, 151f, 160. *See also* Itzas, agriculture of

Aguada Kantixal, 488n5

Aguada Yawilain, *xx*, 130

Aguardiente, 226, 287

Aguilar, Jerónimo de, 498–99n42

Aguilar y Galeano, José de, 388–98 *passim*, 404–11 *passim*, 513n17, 514n39, 515nn, 516n71, 517n76

Aikales, 21

Ain (estancia), 416

Ain (town), 469n16

Aizuani Ursúa, Bernardo de, 260, 489n15

Ajaw (Itza title), 81, 92, 308, 318, 383f

Ajaw (Yucatec title), 449n66, 452nn

Ajaw B'atab' (Itza title), 92–95, 104, 384

Ajaw B'atab' K'in Kante, *see* Kante, Ajaw B'atab' K'in

Ajaw Che (town), 62

AjB'ojom (town), 325, 371. *See also* B'oj; Tib'oj

AjChak May, 507n53

AjChak Tun (town), 461n35

AjChan, 55f, 168, 239, 270–73, 295–99 *passim*, 306, 315f, 327f, 335, 348, 389, 468n4, 492n7, 506n49; baptism of, 184, 186, 224; as cacique, 391, 402, 418, 420; deserts Spaniards, 230–32, 250, 275, 302, 323, 343–45, 356, 388, 391, 418, 475n96; in hiding, 343f, 356, 367–70, 388, 396; as Itza emissary, xxv–xxvi, 138, 162f, 167–86 *passim*, 187f, 213, 217, 219, 223, 231, 240f, 246–50 *passim*, 256, 271–77 *passim* 284f, 291, 308–11, 324, 326, 384, 418, 426n1, 468n11; as post-conquest ruler, xxvii, 231, 368, 384f, 388, 418–21; relatives of, 11, 56, 167–73 *passim*, 271–74, 297, 304, 328, 343, 367f, 467n2, 468nn; testimony of, 89, 93f, 180–84, 226, 273–82, 290, 308, 502n86. *See also* Chan, Martín Francisco

AjChant'an, 170, 468n10. *See also* Chan, Nikte; Chan, Pedro Miguel; Nikte, Pedro

539

AjChata, Noj, 87, 90, 96, 96, 277. *See also* Chata; Tesukan, Reyezuelo
AjCh'ata, Noj, 85
AjCh'atan Ek', 85, 90, 96. *See also* Kan Ek', Cacique
AjChata P'ol, 43, 45, 49, 452n92, *see* P'ol, AjChata. *See also* AjK'in P'ol; P'ol, Nakom
AjItza, 50. *See also* Itzas
AjItzk'in, 507n53
AjKan, 90, 191
AjKan Chi, 76–77
AjKan Kanek', 62
AjKan Kante, 95. *See also* Kan, Cacique; Kante, Ajaw Batab' K'in; Kante, Reyezuelo K'in
AjKawil Itza, 62. *See also* Kawil Itza
AjKawil K'in, 438n36
AjK'in Kan Ek', *see* Kan Ek', AjK'in
AjK'in Okte, 272, *see*, Okte, AjK'in
AjK'in P'ol, 48–49. *See also* AjChata P'ol; P'ol, Nakom
AjK'in, Reyezuelo, 90, 182
AjKit Kan, Reyezuelo, *see* AjK'in P'ol; Kit Kan
AjK'ixaw, 89, 140f, 172, 233–37, 318f, 369, 382, 391, 396, 402, 404, 461nn, 462n44, 510n104
AjKokaj Mut, 71, 197, 444n26. *See also* Yax Kokaj Mut
AjKowoj, 197, 206ff, 227, 273f, 280, 311, 324–28 *passim*, 335–37, 348f, 385, 497n12. *See also* Kowoj, Cacique; Kowoj, Captain
AjK'u, 170, 468nn
AjK'u, B'atab', 461n35
AjKuch Kab' (title), 97
AjKukulin (province), 438n36
AjLalaich (town), 63, 65
AjMatzin, 62
AjMay (town), 240
AjMojan, 37f, 437n33
AjMuan Pana, 62. *See also* Moan Pana
AjPana, 278, 282
AjTek, 170f, 186, 468n10. *See also* Tek, Juan Francisco
AjTut, 92, 95, 96, 312, 384, 396, 402,

451n91, 491n40, 510n110. *See also* Tut, B'atab', 92; Tut, Cacique; Tut, Captain
AjTzam, 63
AjTz'ik Tzin, B'atab', 85, 87, 90, 91f, 96, 244. *See also* AjTz'ik Tzin; Tzin, Ajaw; Tzin Ajaw, Reyezuelo; Tzin, Cacique; AjTz'ik Tzin
AjTzuntekum, 62
Akalan (province), 31, 435n10, 452n98. *See also* Chontals
Akalan Chontals, *see* Chontals
Ak'alche, 151
Ak'e, Juan, 150
Akjok (town), 62
Akte (site, town), 8, 17, 471n15
Alarcón, Juan de, 500n58
Alcaraz de la Mancha (town), 50
Alcoser, Fray Tomás de, 148, 160f, 227
Alliances, Maya, xxiv, 58f, 101, 344, 381; Chak'an Itza-Kowoj, 95, 167, 223, 326, 402–3
Altars, Maya, 50
Alta Verapaz, *see* Verapaz
Alzayaga, Jacobo de, 233, 243
Amésqueta, Bartolomé de, 233–45 *passim*, 500n58
Ammunition, 252f, 268f, 327, 347, 359, 366, 486n78, 490n25
Anahtes, 470n33
Analtes, 183
Anatto, 184, 433n48
Ancona, Eligio, 124f
Andino y Arze, Antonio de, 376, 508–9n92
Antigua Guatemala, *see* Santiago de Guatemala
Archaeological evidence, 66, 266, 489n13. *See also* Ruins, archaeological
Archers, 43, 48, 134–39 *passim*, 229, 239, 266, 280, 297f, 382, 391, 400, 408. *See also* Weapons, Maya
Archivo General de Centro América, xxiii
Archivo General de Indias, xxiii
Armor, cotton, 139
Arriaga, Fray Antonio de (bishop), 246, 252, 328f, 497n24
Arroyo Cantetul, 6, 8, 17, 471n15
Artiga, Fray Gabriel de, 333f, 366

Artillery, 228f, 251, 253, 265–72 *passim*, 298, 327, 363, 365, 400ff, 486n78, 490n27
Atran, Scott, 429n9, 522n127
Augustinians, 328. *See also* Arriaga, Fray Antonio de
Avendaño, Juan de, 240
Avendaño y Loyola, Fray Andrés de, 10, 67, 71ff, 84, *85–86*, 88–95 *passim*, 101, 143, 148–64 *passim*, 170f, 175ff, 182, 187–219 *passim*, 200, 223–30 *passim*, 255, 262, 271, 275, 281, 283, 300, 309–13 *passim*, 321–26 *passim*, 334, 426n5, 427n1, 432n42, 444n26, 464nn, 469n21, 471nn, 479n, 485n70
Avila, Francisco de, 178
Avila Pacheco, Diego de, 291, 306, 321, 326, 489n15
Axes, 135–39 *passim*, 144, 205, 208, 212, 267, 283, 288, 309, 315, 324, 348, 354, 365ff, 390, 503n1. *See also* Tools, metal
Aya, Nicolás de la, 291, 332, 489n15
Ayikal (Itza title), 21, 138, 460n32
Ayikal Chan, 138, 460n32
Ayikal Puk, 138, 277, 460n32
Aztecs, 88, 209, 441–42n2, 451n88. *See also* Mexicas

Bacalar, Salamanca de, *xx*, 4, 39–46 *passim*, 52–55, 75, 95, *130*, 168, 175, 230
Bacalar-at-Chunjujub' (villa), 168, 171, 176, 188, 477n31, 485n68, 488n6
Bahía de Amatique, *xx*, 31, 38, 130
Bahía de Campeche, *xx*
Bahía de Chetumal, *xx*, 130
Bahía de Espíritu Santo, *xx*, 130
Bahía de la Ascención, *xx*, 130
Baizabal, Juan de, 230
B'aka (town), 88, 103, 450n82
B'aka, Ach Kat, *85*
B'ak'jalal, 438n40. *See also* Bacalar, Salamanca de
B'akpeten Laguna (town), *63*
B'ak Tun, 62
B'ak'tun (calendrical period), 14, 431n33
B'alam (lineage name), 24. *See also* B'alam, Te; IxKan B'alam

B'alamna (lineage name), 24
B'alamtun (town), 6, 8, 63, 65, 384f, 511n115
B'alche, 217
Baltonado, Lic. Manuel de, 500n58
Baptisms, 232, 309, 365, 379; of Itzas and Kowojs, 168, 177, 182–86 *passim*, 203–7 *passim*, 214, 224, 230, 328, 336f, 344, 373ff, 411, 419; of Kejaches, 184f, 248; of Musuls, 169
Barajoan (Navarra), 113
Baraona, Juan, 339
Barcena, Juan José de, 124
Barrera Vásquez, Alfredo, 428n8, 453n115
Barrios Leal, Jacinto de, 57, 120, 124–28, 132–35, 141f, 146, 150, 162, 232ff, 426n1, 469n21
Barter goods, 364–67, 503n1. *See also* Trade, Maya-Spanish
Bastán, Valle de (Navarra), 114f
B'atab' (Itza title), 65, 87, 91–95, 101, 140
B'atab' (lineage name), 24
B'atab' (Yucatec title), 144, 449n66
B'atab' Ajaw (town), 461n35
B'atab' AjK'u (town), 461n35
B'atab' Sima (town), 461n35
B'atkab' (town), *xx*, 23, 157–62 *passim*, 189, 226, 254f, 466n44, 467n60, 484n53, 484nn, 485n62
Batons, *see* Staffs of office
B'atun (lineage name), 24
B'atun, Ach Kat, *85*
B'atun, Alonso, 484n59
Beads, 192, 267, 283, 287, 315, 324, 359, 367, 398
Beans, 202, 207, 346, 369, 473n46, 503n1
Beef jerky, 235, 346
Beeswax, 47, 117, 380, 458n55
Beheadings, 48, 228f, 291, 400, 472n22, 476n23
B'elaik (town), 461–62n41
Belén (town), 242f
Belize, *xx*, 3, 20, 22, 39f, 120, 218, 385, 388, 408, 417–20, 517n72. *See also* Toledo District, Belize
Belize River, *xx*, 3, 12, 22, 40, 53–56 *pas-*

sim, 75, 76–77, *130*, 168, 171, 218, 412, 418, 433–34n48

Bells, 158, 161, 180, 421

Beltrán, 137

Belts, 283, 287, 324

B'en, Tus, 433n45, 459n19

Benches, 72f, 197, 302, 444n36

Beneficios Altos (partido), 250, 256f, 263f, 485n66

Beneficios Bajos (partido), 250, 256f, 263f, 485n66

B'e Ob'on, AjKali, *63*

Bey, George, 9, 450n68

Bilateral descent, 446n44

Bilingualism, 5

Blacksmiths, 262, 347

Blood letting, 204

B'ob'at (Yucatec title), 47, 452n98

B'ochan, *6*

Body decoration, *see* Scarification; Tattooing; *under* Itzas

B'oj (town), 8, *17*, 325, 371, 469n16. *See also* AjB'ojom; Tib'oj

Bolio, Manuel, 119, 186

Bolio y Ojeda, Juana, 119, 121

B'olon (lineage name), 435nn, 461n41

B'olonch'en (partido), 484n57

B'olonch'en Kawich (town), *xx*, *130*, 144–50 *passim*, 464n13. *See also* Kawich

B'olonch'en Tikul (town), 258, 263

Bones: horse, 301; human, 230, 303f, 337

Bonxajan (town), 488n5

Books, Maya, 101, 183f, 206. *See also* Chilam B'alam, books of

Boot, Eric, 9, 430n18

Bóvedas, 333, 337, 498n38

Bows and arrows, *see* Archers; Weapons, Itza and Kowoj

Bravo, Feliciano, 41f, 438n45

Bricker, Victoria Reifler, 425n

British Honduras, *see* Belize

Bucareli y Ursúa, Antonio María (viceroy), 455n12

Buenavista (town), *6*, 384

Bugles, 185, 229, 235, 237. *See also* Trumpets

B'uk'te (town), *xx*, *130*, 152–56 *passim*

Burgos, Fray Francisco, 480n81

Cabecera, 32, 93

Cacao, 35, 39f, 151, 207, 433n48, 437n32

Cacicazgo, 44, 93

Cacique (title), 65, 91f, 140. *See also* B'atab'

Cacique principal (title), 84

Cádiz, Spain, 124

Cahabón (town), *xx*, 7, *130*, 133, 135, 142, 305, 337f, 345f, 358f, 375–380 *passim*, 502n89, 518n79

Cakchiquel language, 429n8

Calendar, Mayapan, 97, 431n34

Calendar, Tik'al, 431n34

Calendrical prophecies, *see* K'atuns; Prophecies

Calendrical rituals, *see* New Year rituals; Wayeb' rituals

Calpolli, 87

Camino real, *6*, 111–15 *passim*, 119, 125f, *130*, 232, 339, 343, 455n16, 500n59; northern section of, xxiv–xxv, 120–32 *passim*, 144–64 *passim*, 170, 185–90 *passim*, 218f, 224–29 *passim*, 245–64, 265f, 281, 388, 398, 410, 483nn, 518n79; salaries and payments for, 247, 252, 257–64, 467n61, 482n23, 485–87n74; southern section of, 133–41 *passim*, 144, 244, 252, 280–84 *passim*, 288, 290, 304, 338, 341, 345f, 365, 401, 410, 413, 420, 517n72, 518n79, 521n124; supply trains on, 40, 245–64 *passim*, 482n23, 486nn, 487n78; working conditions on, 245, 256–64 *passim*

Camino real (partido), 256

Campeche (villa), *xx*, xxv, 42, 47, 117–20 *passim*, 125–29 *passim*, *130*, 142, 150, 152, 162, 230, 241, 245–53 *passim*, 260–68 *passim*, 286, 319, 327–33 *passim*, 337–41 *passim*, 345, 347, 374, 388, 414, 454n7, 483n37, 486n74; merchants of, 116, 119, 143, 261f, 458n55, 487n79

Campo, Fray Andrés de, 258, 484n57

Campos, Francisco de, 229, 476n23

Canek Manuscript, 426nf

Canizan (town), *xx* 57–58

Cannibalism, claims of, 51, 57, 133, 138f, 191, 214, 276, 304, 313, 318–21, 330–34, 372, 495n55, 498n42, 498nn, 516n52

Cano, Fray Agustín, 22, 113, 134ff, 141, 234, 237f, 242, 303, 478nn, 500n58

Canoes, 33f, 41, 43, 57, 64, 95, 194f, 215, 228f, 236f, 242f, 266–71 *passim*, 280f, 286, 288, 296f, 314, 332, 348, 351, 359, 365, 398, 400, 436nn, 472n24, 478nn, 479n

Cano y Sandoval, Juan (bishop), 124, 126, 163, 169, 246

Cantores, *see* Maestros

Capitals, indigeous, *see* Tik'al, Chetumal; Chich'en Itza; Itzam K'anak; Mayapan; Nojpeten; Tenochtitlan; Tipuj

Captain (Itza-Kowoj title), 92

Cárdenas, Diego de, 46, 48

Cardenia, Nicolás, 144, 180

Caribbean Sea, 7

Carlos II, King of Spain, 123, 177, 181, 199ff, 206, 224, 283, 310, 335

Carlos V, King of Spain, 188

Carmack, Robert M., 425n

Carpenters, 260, 265–68 *passim*, 347

Carrillo, Dr. Gregorio, 375

Carrillo y Ancona, Crescencio, 113–16 *passim*, 455n16

Cartagena (city), 114

Carvajal, Antonio de, 345

Casanova, Juan Bernardo, 48

Castas, 144

Caste War of Yucatán, 444n20

Castillo (title), 411

Castillo Cetina, Gaspar del, 270f, 489n15

Castillo y Arrúe, Juan del, 143f, 147, 150, 263

Castillo y Toledo, Juan del, 120, 123, 143, 263f, 456n31, 484n62

Cattle, 244, 359, 398

Cattle ranches, *see* estancias

Caves, 304, 461n41, 479n

Cédulas, 112f, 119–24 *passim*, 181, 188, 248–51 *passim*, 342, 357f, 404, 412f, 417

Censers, 47, 301

Censuses, 509n92; of Petén, 360–61, 360f, 377–78, 387, 394, 394–95, 404–11 *passim*, 407, 410, 415–17, 416, 517n76, 518n79, 521nn; of Tixchel, 449n63. *See also* Matrículas; Population estimates

Chab'in (lineage name), 24, 62, 63, 393

Chab'in, AjB'en, 62

Chab'in, AjNoj, 62

Chab'in, Chamach, 507n53

Chab'in, Juan, 419

Chab'le (lineage name), 24. *See also* IxKib' Chab'le

Chacha (town, Belize), 385

Chacha (town, Petén), 62, 381f, 442n4

Chachach'ulte (town), 62. *See also* Chach'ulte

Chachaklum (estancia), 416

Chachaklun, 443n15

Chach'ulte (town), 384. *See also* Chachach'ulte

Chakak'ot (town), *17*

Chakal (town), *130*, 234, 238ff, 438n34

Chak'an (town), *xx*, 6, 8, *17*, *130*, 325. *See also* San Andrés, 33

Chak'an Itza (province), 6, 8, 19, 67, 92, 95, 402, 430n18, 443n14, 483n39, 488n6

Chak'an Itza (territory), 96–100 *passim*, 157, 167, 188–94 *passim*, 208, 213ff. *See also* Rulers of the north; *under* Alliances, Maya

Chak'an Itzas, 96, 157, 167, 188–94 *passim*, 213, 226f, 253, 281

Chak'an Peten, 430n18

Chak'an Putun, 430n18

Chak'an Putun (town), 15–16

Chaklol (town), 55

Chakok'ot (town), 8

Chaktemal, *see* Chetumal

Chaktis (town), 62

Chakujal (town), 435n10

Chaltunja (town), 6, *17*, 43, 65, 325, 439n55

Chamach (Itza title), 63

Chamach Xulu, *see* Xulu, Chamach

543

Chamay Zulu, *see* Xulu, Chamach
Champoton (town), *xx*, *130*, 430n18
Chamuxub' (town), 230
Chan (AjChan's father), 56, 167, 273
Chan (Itza prisoner), 137–39
Chan (lineage name), 23, 24, 76–77, 138, 140, 434n53, 441n95, 448n55, 460n32. *See also* AjChan; IxChan Pana; IxKan Chan; Kan Chan; K'eyan Chan; NaChan Ch'el; NaChan Kanche
Chan (province), 384
Chan, Ach Kat, 461n35
Chan, Ayikal, 138, 460n32
Chanchanja, Santa Clara de (town), *xx*, *120*, *130*, 161, 218, 380, 385–91 *passim*, 511n121. *See also* Santa Rosa de la Pimienta
Chan, IxMuluk, 76–77
Chan, K'in, 138, 460n32, 467n2. *See also* K'in Chan, Ach Kat
Chan, Martín Francisco, 168, 186, 274, 315, 327f, 346, 384f, 402, 418–19. *See also* AjChan
Chan, Nikte, 170. *See also* AjChant'an; Chan, Pedro Miguel; Nikte, Pedro
Chan, Pedro Miguel, 170f, 186, 328, 369f. *See also* AjChant'an; Chan, Nikte; Nikte, Pedro
Chan, Tab'in, 468n16
Chan, Taxim, 21, 134–35, 459nn
Chan, Tz'ib'it, 369
Chaneb' (lineage name), 24, 448n57
Chan Pana, *see* Chan Pana, K'in; IxChan Pana
Chan Pana, K'in, 318.
Chans, 160, 384, 466n60, 476n10, 484n53, 510n110. *See also* Pak'ek'em
Chata, 276f, 280f, 312. *See also* AjChata, Noj; Tesukan, Reyezuelo
Chata (lineage name), 24, 62, 461–62n41
Chata, Bernardo, 414, 520n107
Ch'atan (Itza title), 87
Chatas, 318ff
Chatoko (town), 384
Chávez Figueroa, Nuño de, 42
Chay (lineage name), 24
Chayax (lineage name), 24, 63, 272

Chayax, Juan, 368
Chayax, Manuel Joseph, 171, 272, 297, 302, 306, 313, 328, 367ff, 468n11, 491n31
Che (lineage name), *see* Noj Che, Cacique
Che, Cacique Noj, 91. *See also* Ajaw Che (town); AjTut; Tut, B'atab'; Tut, Cacique
Chekan (town), 37
Chek'ub'ul (town), *130*, 458n56
Chel (lineage name), *see* K'awil Chel
Ch'el, *see* NaChan Ch'el
Ch'em (lineage name), 21, 24, 433n46
Chen (lineage name), 24
Chenak (town), 62f
Chetumal, *xx*
Chetumal (province), 3, 39f, 242
Chetumal (town), 39
Chetumal Bay, 3
Cheusij (town), 458n56
Chi (lineage name), 24. *See also* AjKan Chi
Chiapas, *xx*, 30, 42, 112, 125ff, 339, 341, 358
Ch'ib'al, 80, 447n51
Ch'ich' (town), 6, *8*, *17*, 95, 192, 228–31 *passim*, 296f, 302, 306–9 *passim*, 313f, 367, 463n66, 486n74, 488n5, 488n6, 489n13; as Spanish encampment, 253, 265–70, 274, 286–89. *See also* Nich; Nixtun
Chich'en Itza, xix, *xx*, 9–18 *passim*, 74, 83, 105, 273f, 308, 429n11, 430nn, 431n28, 454n116
Chikb'ul (town), 58
Chiken, Chamach, 507n53
Chikuy (lineage name), 21, 24, 433n48
Chilam B'alam, books of, 9–15 *passim*; Chumayel, 15, 104–5, 190, 428n8, 429n9, 431n30, 432n39, 453n115; Mani, 104, 453n115; Tisimin, 104, 429n9, 432n39, 453n115
Chilonche (estancia), 416
China (town), *130*, 458n56
Chinaco (town), 518n79
Chinamitas, 19–22, 43, 101, 432n43, 433–34n48. *See also* Mopans
Chinoja (town), 6, *18*, 63, 65f, 368ff, 378,

496n73, 511n116. *See also* Nuestra
Señora de los Dolores de Chinoja
Chirimías, 194, 272, 282, 470n36
Chiwoja (town), *130*, 458n56
Cho, Gaspar, 380
Chok Ajaw (town), 240, 480n67,
509n82
Cholan language family, 5
Chol Lakandons, 41, 58, 112f, 119–22 *pas-
sim*, 132f, 142–47 *passim*, 232, 235,
241, 243, 339, 379, 384, 427n4, 429n10,
509nn. *See also* Nuestra Señora de los
Dolores del Lacandón; Sakb'ajlan; San
Román Nonato
Cholo (estancia), *416*
Chols, 38, 83. *See also* Manche Chols
Chomach Ajaw (Itza title), 208
Chontal language, 30, 140, 435nn
Chontals, 5, 9f, 23, 30f, 449n63, 452n98,
458n56
Chronicles, Maya, *see* Chilam Balam,
books of
Chuk, María, 150
Ch'ulte (town), 8, 366, 506n36
Chultuns, 151
Chulul (town), 62
Chumayel, *see* Chilam Balam, books of
Chun Ajaw (town), 383, 511nn. *See also*
Chun Mejen
Chunjujub' (town), *xx, 130*, 175, 179, 230.
See also Bacalar-at-Chunjujub'
Chun Mejen (town), 383f, 511nn. *See also*
Chun Ajaw; Mejen
Chunpich (town), *130*, 131, 154–57 *pas-
sim*, 465nn, 485n62
Chuntuki (town), *xx, 130*, 145, 147, 156–
63 *passim*, 189, 213, 219, 225ff, 251ff,
256–63 *passim*, 463n66, 469n21,
481n11, 486n74
Chunuk'um (town), *xx*, 54–55, 75, 76f, 84,
130, 440nn, 441n95, 445n43
Churches, mission, 47f, 52, 72, 160, 348,
390, 513n24, 518n79
Church ornaments, 48, 52, 148, 158, 191,
320, 329, 396
Cihuacoatl (Aztec title), 91, 451n88
Ciuatan River, 30

Ciuatecpan (town), 31
Ciudad Real, *xx*, 127, 248, 339. *See also*
San Cristóbal de las Casas
Ciudad Vieja, 67, 443n15. *See also* Ciudad
Real
Clareda, Fray Gregorio, 258f
Classic period, 3, 9, 78, 105, 445–46n44,
452n93
Clergy, *see* Dominicans; Franciscans; Mer-
cederians; Secular clergy, Yucatán
Cloth, *see* Cotton cloth
Cloth, European, 188, 201
Clothing: Itza, 47, 50, 169, 188, 194f, 205,
236, 239, 334, 480n63; Spanish, 188,
191, 208–14 *passim*
Cobán (town), *xx*, 49, *130*, 338, 345, 371
Cochineal, 46, 184, 207, 473n64
Coe, Michael D., 96
Coello Gaytán, Br. Luis, 412
Coins, silver, 366
Colegio de Cristo Crucificado (Santiago de
Guatemala), 376
Collins, Anne C., 464n11
Comitán (town), *xx*, 132
Communion, Christian, 185
Companies, *see* Militias
Company of Jesus, *see* Jesuits
Comparato, Frank E., 463n10, 474n80
Concepción (stream), 153
Concepción (town), 410, 518n79
Concepción, Fray Pedro de la, 132
Conversion, religious, *see* Baptisms
Cooks, 245, 267, 379, 406
Copal, 47, 301
Copán, *see* Kopan
Corozal Bay, 3
Cortés, Hernán, xxiii, 5, 23, 29–39, 99,
200, 284, 301, 429n9, 435nn, 436n23,
437n29, 438nn, 440n88, 499n42,
511n20
Cortés, Juan Francisco, 297, 327, 345ff,
373, 381–92 *passim*, 397, 400, 489n15,
512n123
Cosio, Toribio de, 411ff
Cosmology, spatial, 60, 93–104, 96, 98,
206, 441n2, 452n98. *See also* New Year
rituals; Wayeb' rituals

Cotton, 37, 117, 184, 437n32

Cotton armor, 139

Cotton cloth, 40, 44, 117f, 207, 405f, 458n55

Cotton thread, 117f, 405f

Council of the Indies, xxii, xxiv, 42, 46, 111–23 *passim*, 143, 147, 153, 238, 245–55 *passim*, 342, 357, 412f, 455n16, 519nn, 520n100

Cozumel, *xx*, *130*, 241, 499n42

Crossbows, 35, 437n27

Crosses, 47, 151, 259, 291, 325, 464n19; among Itzas and Kowojs, 34, 36, 44, 348, 369f, 378, 511n122

Crowns, Itza, 175, 206, 240, 301, 308

Crucifixes, 53, 194f, 213

Crucifixion, 303, 479n, 498n33

Cuauhpipiltin, 88

Cuauhtemoc, 435n12

Cuba, 38

Dancing, Itza, 73, 97, 191, 203, 453n112

Dávila, Alonso, 39

Decapitation, 47f, 194, 213, 215, 515–16n52

Deer, 36f, 135, 139

Deerskins, 50

Deities, 428n8, 431n28, 461n41; Itza, 74, 102f, 197, 317. *See also* AjKokaj Mut; Itzas, ritual objects of; Itzimna K'awil; Job'on; Joxchuncham; K'in Chil Kob'a; Pak'ok; Talking "idols"; Yaxcheel Kab'

Delgado, Fray Diego de, 46ff, 134, 230, 433n48, 459n15

Descent systems, *see* Double descent; Lineages; Matrilineal descent; Patrilineal descent

Diarrhea, 373

Díaz del Castillo, Bernal, 5, 29–37 *passim*, 69, 429n9, 435n13, 436nn

Díaz de Velasco, Juan, 83f, 132–42, 232–43 *passim*, 318, 332, 339, 382, 479n

Díaz, Ramón, 236

Díez de Armendáriz, Miguel, 114

Dogs, 135

Dolores (estancia), 416

Dolores (town), 408–19 *passim*, 410, 416, 517n72, 518n79, 521n124, 522n127

Dolores del Lacandón, *see* Nuestra Señora de los Dolores del Lacandón; Sakb'alan

Dominicans, xxiv, 41, 49, 83, 112f, 134, 140f, 161, 232f, 242, 244, 303, 337f, 412, 459n18, 479n, 519n95, 520n100

Double descent, 447n51

Drums, 185, 229, 237, 453n112. *See also* Tunkul

Dual rulership, 60, 73, 92–97, 308, 441n2, 451n88, 452n101. *See also* Itzas, political organization of; Ranking, senior-junior

Duardo, Juan Jerónimo, 500n58

Durán, Bartolomé, 298

Dyes, 207, 405, 473n64

Ear plugs, 50, 138

Earrings: Itza, 211, 236; Spanish, 173, 267, 287

Echevarría, Fray Diego de, 158, 160, 189, 310

Edmonson, Munro S., 429n9, 430n17, 431nn, 471n15, 102, 428n8, 432n39

Eguaroz Fernández de Ijar, Pedro de, 375

Egües y Beaumont, Diego, 114

Ek' (lineage name), 24, 76–77, 78, 81, 167, 447n51. *See also* AjCh'atan Ek'

Ek', AjCh'atan, 87

Ek' B'alam, *xx*

Ek', Bernardino, 48, 236

Ek'ixil (town), 8, *17*, 344–51 *passim*, 469n16

Ek' Mas, 76–77

El Guacamayo (town), 511n115. *See also* Gwakamay

El Naranjo, 438n45

Elorza y Rada, Francisco, 113ff

El Salvador, 88

El Tigre, 435n10

Encomiendas, 3, 23, 30, 39–43 *passim*, 49, 117, 127, 129, 143, 155f, 458n56

Engineer-surveyor, 245, 251. *See also* Sesere, Manuel Jorge

English, *see* Slave raiding, English

Enríquez de Guzmán, Enrique, 112, 122, 455n16

Ensenada de San Jerónimo, 33, 42, 99f, 140, 266, 436n20

Ensenada San Pedro, 234

Epidemics, xxvii, 337, 360–61, 370, 376–80, 387, 397, 408, 507n52, 517n77. *See also* Diarrhea; Illness; Influenza; Measles; Pneumonia; Smallpox; Yellow fever

Escals, José de, 134, 140, 233, 238, 480n75, 500n58

Escobar, Br. Francisco de, 57

Escribano mayor, 178

Espíritu Santo (villa), 29f

Estancia del Rey, 416, 515n44, 516n55. *See also* San Felipe (estancia del rey)

Estancias, 127, 129, 398, 416

Estoraque, 301, 493n23

Estrada y Azpeitia, José Agustín de, 500n58

Executions, 336, 348, 435n12. *See also* Beheadings; Hangings

Families, extended, *see* Households, Itza

Farriss, Nancy M., 426n1

Feldman, Lawrence, 429n10, 521n112

Felipe III, King of Spain, 114

Felipe IV, King of Spain, 114

Felipe V, King of Spain, 409

Fernández, Antonio, 487n79

Fernández de Estenos, José, 143f, 152–55 *passim*, 185, 260, 291, 327f, 336, 346–52 *passim*, 372f, 380, 465n32, 489n15

Fernando, King of Castile, 199

Ferrer, Miguel, 316, 331

Figueroa, Antonio de, 44, 200

Flight, Maya, 46–52 *passim*, 253–259 *passim*, 455n18, 517n72. *See also* Itzas, abandon towns; Kowojs, abandon towns

Flores (city), 69, 390f, 417

Flores Mogollón, Marcelo, 358, 370f, 507n61

Flutes, 453n112

Food, Itza, 50, 136, 139, 196f, 202, 204, 211, 214, 218, 235f, 368, 399, 472n36

Forest products, 40. *See also* Beeswax; Logging; Logwood

Fortifications: Maya, 23, 31f, 66, 147, 152, 278, 297, 314, 348, 385f, 435–36n14,

489n13, 511n116; Spanish, 133, 232, 240, 253, 267f, 272, 343, 347, 350, 463n66, 483nn. *See also* Petén Itzá (presidio), fort of; Stockades

Fox, James A., 445–46n44

Franciscans, xix, xxv, 12f, 34, 42, 54, 57, 120–25 *passim*, 146–64, 171–82 *passim*, 186–220 *passim*, 244, 248f, 303, 380, 412; on camino real, 156–64, 225, 253–57, 469n21, 476n10; conflict with secular clergy, 157, 163f, 176, 180, 220, 225–30, 245f, 300

Freidel, David, 105, 428n8, 446n44, 452n93

Fresno de la Fuente, Conde de, 114

Frías Salazar, Juan de, 487n79

Fuensalida, Fray Bartolomé de, 11f, 19f, 43–49 *passim*, 53f, 69, 71, 78, 81, 197–202 *passim*, 300f, 426n1, 439nn, 451n92, 453n112, 493n20

Fugitive Mayas, 55. *See also* Flight, Maya; La Pimienta

Galeota, xxvi, 192, 271f, 281–85 *passim*, 289, 295–302 *passim*, 315, 324–27 *passim*, 346–50 *passim*, 363, 373, 399–403 *passim*, 483nn, 492n8; construction of, 252f, 260–72 *passim*, 463n66, 486n78, 492n8, 515n52

Galindo, Fray Simon, 363

Gallegos, Fray Francisco, 134

Galve, Conde de (viceroy), 124. *See also* Sandoval, Gaspar de, Conde de Galve

García de Bustamante, Manuel, 455n16

García de Colmenares, Fray, 338

García de Monsabal, Francisco, 414

García de Palomares, Fray, 337

García de Paredes, Alonso, 57, 125–34 *passim*, 142–63 *passim*, 176, 187ff, 213–17 *passim*, 223–30 *passim*, 244, 251f, 260, 262, 267, 270, 285–91 *passim*, 304f, 328, 337–40, 458nn, 476n17, 479n, 483n39, 484n62, 487n79, 489n15, 500n58

Garma Alcedo y Salazar, Bartolomé de, 162f, 229, 251, 258, 271, 291, 321, 476n25, 489n15

Garrastegui y Oleado, Pedro de, 118, 186, 249, 257. *See also* Miraflores, Conde de

Garza, Diego de la, 400, 515n52

Garzón, Juan, 40

Gifts: Itza, 35, 44, 169, 285, 368, 386, 436n23; Kowoj, 324f; Spanish, 34, 172–75 *passim*, 188–94 *passim*, 201, 216, 230, 235, 240, 243, 254, 266f, 272, 275, 282–89 *passim*, 296, 315, 324, 351f, 359, 390, 398, 469n21, 485n62. *See also* Barter goods

Gil de Azamar, Pablo, 171–75 *passim*, 188, 250, 475n96

Gillespie, Susan, 451n88

Gold, 35f, 184, 211

Golfo Dulce, *xx*, 31, *130*. *See also* Lago de Izabal

Gómez, Br. Francisco, 477n31

González, Juan, 298, 489n15

González Ricardo, Francisco, 127

Gracias a Dios Falls, 38

Granaries, 366–69 *passim*

Gregorian calendar, 14

Gronca, Domingo de, 502n86

Grube, Nicolai, 9, 430n18

Guatemala, Audiencia of, 120–24 *passim*, 330, 338–42, 356, 375f, 394, 397, 411, 500n59; presidents of, *see* Barrios Leal, Jacinto de; Cosio, Toribio de; Enríquez de Guzmán, Enrique; Escals, José de; Sánchez de Berrospe, Gabriel

Güemes, Br. Gaspar de, 230f, 477n31

Guerra, Fray Joseph, 459n15

Guerrero, Gonzalo, 39, 241f, 499n42

Guerrero, Juan, 507n57

Guillén, Francisco, 487n79

Gulf of Honduras, *xxiii*, 30

Gunflints, 489n13, 490n25

Gunpowder, 252f, 268f, 366, 486n78, 490n25

Gutiérrez, Roque, 255

Gutiérrez de la Peña, 500n58

Guzmán, Antonio ("Guatemala"), 324

Gwakamay (town), 8, 62, 511n115. *See also* El Guacamayo

Gwakut (estancia), 416

Hacienda Papactún, 471n15

Hamlets, 64ff, 131, 154, 157, 335, 367, 396, 443n10

Hangings, 48f, 435n12

Hanks, William F., 426n5

Hariza, Juan de, 506n45

Hariza y Arruyo, Francisco, 168–75 *passim*, 216, 219, 224f, 230f, 282, 475n96, 506n45

Hawaii, 288

Heart excision, 47f, 303, 316, 320, 330–34, 479n, 498n31, 516n52. *See also* Sacrifice, human

Hellmuth, Nicholas, xxiii

Heredía, José de, 489n15

Herrera, Br. Bernabé de, 401, 409, 411, 514n39

Hidalgo, Mateo, 162f, 255, 259

Hieroglyphic writing, 9–13 *passim*, 195, 307, 333, 445–46n44, 452n93, 470n33. *See also* Books, Maya

History, Maya theory of, *see* K'atuns; Prophecy

Hofling, Charles Andrew, 429n9, 432n35, 437n33

Holy Virgin Mary of Cortés, 50

Homosexuality, *see* Sexuality, Itza

Honduras, 30, 112, 290

Honey, 35, 184

Horse, Cortes's, xxiii, 36f

Horse bone, 198

Horse image: legends of, 36–37, 44, 53, 72, 197, 301, 437nn. *See also* Tzimin Chak

Horses, 228, 235, 252, 256f, 261, 341, 347, 359, 398, 485n67

Households, Itza, 81f, 394ff, 406, *406*, 449n63

Hoxchuncham, 102

Huehuetenango (province), 384

Huehuetenango (town), *xx*, 112, 125, *130*, 132, 232, 248, 314, 342, 384

Hunak' Keel, 15

Hunting and hunters, 65, 135, 139, 160, 227

Hurricanes, 240, 317

Ichek (town), 62

Ichmul (town), *xx*, *130*

Ichmuxan, 471n15, 483n39
Ichtun (town), 468n16
Ich Tutz (town), 385
Idols, *see* Itzas, ritual objects of; Ritual objects
Illness, 141, 154, 233, 238ff, 254, 259, 328, 369–73 *passim. See also* Epidemics
Indigo, 207
Indios del monte, 54f
Influenza, 381
Inheritance of kingship, *see under* Itzas
Interpreters, 5, 83, 135, 137, 141, 144, 178ff, 232ff, 238–42 *passim*, 268f, 307, 426n1, 435n7, 480n81, 489n17
Isabel, Queen of Castile, 199
Isla Pedregal, 503n101
Islote Grande, 234, 279. *See also* Motzkal
Islote Lepete, 297
Isthmus of Tehuantepec, 29
Itza (defined), 428n8
Itza (lineage name), 24, 318f, 507n53. *See also* AjKawil Itza; Kawil Itza
Itza, Ach Kat, 85
Itza, Chak, 507n53
Itza, Pascual, 144
Itza language, *see* Itzas, language of
Itzaj language, 429n9
Itzam (defined), 428–29n8
Itzam K'anak (town), *xx*, 31, 38, 435nn, 452n98
Itzamna, 428n8
Itzas, xxv, 21, 43, 190, 204, 239; abandon towns, 335, 345, 350, 356f, 365–68, 379, 387, 390, 401, 409, 411, 417, 443n10; agriculture of, 7, 33, 37, 57, 65f, 184, 207, 229, 244, 315, 429n10, 437n32, 443n10; ancestry of, xix, 8, 11, 172, 183f, 274, 308, 430n24; attack neighbors, 22f, 49–52, 56ff, 331, 440n71, 441n101, 484n62, 498n27; body decoration of, 53, 137–40 *passim*, 191, 205, 210f, 226, 319ff, 478n49; burn their towns, 357, 366, 370, 379; inheritance of kingship among, 83–84, 94–95, 136, 167, 308, 383f, 393, 439n58, 447n51; language of, 3, 137, 195, 201f, 208, 244, 426–27n1, 434n50, 479n; mil-

itary organization and practices of, xxiv, 32, 43, 54–61, 83, 87ff, 101ff, 440n71, 451n85, 453n112; nobility of, 60f, 82–104, 106ff, 167f, 404; political organization of, xxiv, 31, 43, 45, 60f, 64ff, 71, 82–107, 136–40 *passim*, 207, 278f, 295, 307–11 *passim*, 425n, 454n116; post-conquest kingdoms of, xxvii, 383ff, 388, 403; precontact history of, 3, 7–13; priests of, 44, 183, 194, 203–7 *passim*, 277ff, 291f, 308, 334, 384; prophecies cited by, xxiv, 44f, 202–8 *passim*; religion and rituals of, 102, 191, 203f, 217, 291f, 313–38 *passim*, 453nn; reputation of, xxi, 39, 41, 133, 139f, 230, 244, 290f, 329–35, 510n110; ritual objects of, xxvi, 34–37 *passim*, 41, 44, 50, 53, 73, 102, 194, 197, 277f, 300–303, 333, 418, 440n71, 453n112, 461n41, 493nn, 494n28; ruling council of, 64, 84, 89, 92, 103–4; territorial expansion of, 7f, 54, 83; territory of, 5, 6, 7, 41, 67, 133, 366, 429n10, 434n52. *See also* Cosmology, spatial; Deities; Horse image; Milpas; Milperías; Quadripartite governance; Quarters; Ranking, senior-junior; Warfare
Itzimna K'awil, 197
Itzk'in Tzakwan, 434n49
Itzunte (town), 62
Ix, yearbearer, 97, 98
IxB'akab' (town), 254, 484n53. *See also* Yajb'akab'
IxB'am (town), 130, 157
IxB'en Kan, 76–77
IxB'ol (town), 234, 240, 478n43
IxChan Pana, 79, 214–18 *passim*, 282, 308, 313, 367, 448n55, 474n80, 495n51
IxKab' Us, 76–77
IxKan B'alam, 76–77
IxKan Chan, 76–77
IxKan Jaw, 76–77
IxKante, 167, 273f, 311, 467n1
IxKib' Chab'le, 76–77
IxKi May, 76–77
IxKojech (town), 62
IxKotyol (town), 62

IxKoxol (estancia), *416*
Ixlu (site), *17*, 66, 439n55, 510n99
IxMen Kan, *76–77*
IxMukuy (town), *384*
IxMuluk Muk'ul, *76–77*
IxMutnaj (town), 62
IxPapaktun (town), 62, 512n123
IxPetzeja (town), *8, 17*, 62
IxPimienta (town), *xx*, 46–47, 452n98
IxPop (town), 450n81. *See also* Pop
IxPuk, 138, 460n32
Ixtatán, San Miguel de (town), *xx, 130,
    132, 358*
IxTinal, 76f
IxTus (town), *18, 63, 66*, 368ff, *378, 385,
    511*n116. *See also* Ich Tutz; San José de
    IxTus
IxTutz Pix, *76–77*
Izamal (town), *15*
Izot, 312

Jalach Winik (Itza title), *85*, 89, *94, 101*
Jalach Winik (Yucatec title), 104, 449n66,
    452n93
Jamaica, *412*
Jaw (lineage name), *24. See also* IxKan Jaw;
    Mas Jaw, K'in
Jaw, Gabriel, 484n59
Jekelchak'an (town), 47, *130*, 341, 345,
    356
Jerena, Conde de, *114*, 455n10
Jesmoj (town), 62
Jesuits, 178–79, *412*f, 419, 519n94,
    520n100
Jesús María (town), *390, 409, 410*, 518n79
Jesús María, Fray Joseph de, 148–52 *pas-
    sim*, 157f, 189, 213, 310, 466n50
Jewelry, 184, 211, 288. *See also* Beads; Ear-
    rings; Necklaces
Jews, 199
Jicaques, 237
Job'on, 453n112
Job'onmo (town), 65, 464n16
Jocotenango (town), 67
Joil (lineage name), 24
Jokab'a (town), 41, 485n68
Joktun (town), 485n68

Jola (lineage name), 24, 421
Jolail (town), *130*
Jolalil (town), 62
Jolkaj (town), 62
Jolpat (town), 62
Jol Pop (Yucatec title), 89, 97, 451n86
Jomun (town), 485n68
Jones, Grant D., 426n5
Jop'elch'en (town), *xx*, 46f, 55, *130, 150,
    155*f, 161, 254, 263, 484n62
Joxchuncham, 102
Joya, Francisco Antonio de la, 331
Joyop (town), *8*, 62, 65, 366f, 384,
    511n115
Juez de grana, 46
Julian calendar, *14*
Junak Keel, *12*
Juntecholol, 478n43
Justeson, John S., 445–46n44

Kaan (lineage name), 75, *76–77*, 80, 84
Kaan, Chuen, *76–77*
Kaan, IxMen, *76–77*
Kab' (lineage name), 24, *76–77*
Kab'an (day name), 81
Kab'an Kawil, 449n59. *See also* Kawil,
    Kab'an
Kab'an Kawil (town), 461n35
Kaj Jol (Nojpeten quarter), 84, 98, 99,
    450n70
Kalk'ini (town), *130, 150*
Kamal (lineage name), 21, 24, 319ff, 321,
    330f
Kamal, Ach Kat, *85*
Kamal, B'atab', 431n28
Kamal, Chamach, 496n73, 507n53
Kamal, Chamay, *see* Kamal, Chamach
Kampin River, *xx*
Kan (lineage name), 24, 62, 447n51. *See
    also* K'ix Kan
K'an (yearbearer), 97, *98*
Kan, Cacique, 95, 476n12. *See also* Kante,
    Ajaw Batab' K'in; Kante, Reyezuelo K'in
Kanchan (lineage name), 24, 62, 81,
    448n57
Kan Chan, 80f, 320, 449n58
Kanchan, Koti, 62

Kanche (lineage name), 24, 421. *See also* NaChan Kanche; NaMay Kanche

Kan, Chuen, 76–77

Kanch'ulte (town), 63

Kan Ek', *see* Kanek'

Kan Ek' (cousin of Ajaw Kan Ek', of 1695–99), 324f, 349; exile of, 372–76; as political prisoner, 312, 318ff, 344, 351f, 372–76, 508n72; Kit Kan

Kan Ek' (defined), 80

Kanek' (lineage name), 24, 62, 366f, 448n57, 514n37

Kan Ek' (Nojpeten quarter), 84, 98, 99, 298

Kan Ek', Ajaw, of 1525, xxiii, xxv, 34–36, 44

Kan Ek', Ajaw, of 1616–19, 44f, 200

Kan Ek', Ajaw, of 1695–99, xxvi, 11, 19, 20, 29, 38, 55, 60, 84, 89–96 *passim*, 90, 95, 98, 106, 138, 159, 171, 187–220 *passim*, 226, 231, 241, 253, 265, 272–91 *passim*, 298, 302–6 *passim*, 315–28 *passim*, 367, 384f, 448n55, 449n64, 451nn, 461n35, 468n4, 472n22, 488n6, 491n33, 492n7, 508n76, 514n38; baptism of, 344; exile of, xxvii, 95, 357, 372–76; family of, 56, 79, 167, 214–18, 295, 305–10 *passim*, 315, 467n1, 474n80, 495n51; palace of, 69, 71, 99, 363, 444n26; as political prisoner, 305–28 *passim*, 332, 344, 349–52 *passim*, 357, 372–76, 508n72; spoke Spanish, 375f; and submission to Spaniards, xxv, 17, 162–64, 168–77 *passim*, 181, 186, 208–13 *passim*, 219–24 *passim*, 230, 240, 308, 474n77; temple of, 73; testimony of, 61, 67, 92, 306–15, 325, 495n56, 502n86. *See also* Kan Ek', Joseph Pablo

Kan Ek', Ajaw, penultimate, 83, 87, 91, 104

Kanek', AjBak', 63

Kanek', AjKan, 62

Kan Ek', AjK'in, 60, 73, 94, 98, 186ff, 272, 278ff, 331, 363, 479n, 491n33; baptism of, 344; exile of, 357, 372–76; as political prisoner, 303, 308, 312, 315, 320–30 *passim*, 344, 349–52 *passim*, 357, 372–

76, 474n89, 508n72; testimony of, 283ff, 316–19, 330, 332, 502n86; Kan Ek', Francisco Nicolás

Kanek', AjTzazko, 63

Kan Ek', B'atab', 98

Kan Ek', Cacique, 90, 91. *See also* AjCh'atan Ek'

Kan Ek' dynasty, 55, 80, 84, 274, 281, 308, 439n59

Kan Ek', Francisco Antonio, 373f. *See also* Kan Ek', cousin of Ajaw Kan Ek'

Kan Ek', Francisco IxK'in, 374f. *See also* Kan Ek', IxK'in

Kan Ek', Francisco Nicolás, 344, 373. *See also* Kan Ek', AjK'in

Kan Ek', Ixk'in, xxvii, 357, 372–76, 373, 449n64, 508n79. *See also* Kan Ek', Francisco IxK'in

Kanek', Jacinto, 414, 520n105

Kan Ek', Joseph Pablo, 344, 373–76. *See also* Kan Ek', Ajaw, of 1695–99

Kan Ek', Kali, 369f, 396, 514n38

Kan Ek', Tz'ib'it, 396

Kan Itzam (town), *xx*, 57–58

Kan, IxB'en, *see* IxB'en Kan

Kan, IxMen, *see* IxMen Kan

Kan Kante, AjK'in, 96. *See also* Kante, Ajaw Batab' K'in

Kan matrilineage, xxiii, 54f, 75, 80f, 94f, 103–6 *passim*, 140, 167, 414, 447n51. *See also* Ach Kat Kit Kan; Kit Kan (Itza title); Kuch Pop Kit Kan; Noj Tz'o Kan Noj; Noj Tz'o Kan Punab'; Tz'o Kan Tz'ik

Kan Noj, Noj Tz'o, 85, 96

Kan Panak (town), 508n82

Kan Punab', Noj Tz'o, 90, 96. *See also* Noj Tz'o Kan Punab'

Kante, *see* IxKante

Kante (lineage name), 24, 421, 448n57

Kante, Ajaw B'atab' K'in, 95ff, 98, 106, 140, 167, 191, 205, 213f, 253, 274, 310f, 326, 385, 451n87. *See also* AjKan Kante; Kan, Cacique; Kan Kante, AjK'in; Kante, Reyezuelo K'in

Kante, Domingo, 243

Kante, IxMen, 76–77

Kante, Reyezuelo K'in, *90. See also* AjKan Kante; Kan, Cacique; Kante, Ajaw Batab' K'in

Kantemo (town), 254

Kantetul (town), *6, 8, 17*, 190, 469n16, 471n17

Kan Tz'ik, Tz'o, *see* Tz'o Kan Tz'ik

Kan, Tz'o, 87, 91f, 384

Kanul (lineage name), 24

Kanul, Marcos, 150

Kanyokte (lineage name), 24, 448n57

Kastamay, Hacienda de, *xx, 130*, 251

K'atun 1 Ajaw, 103

K'atun 2 Ajaw, 284

K'atun 3 Ajaw, 43ff, 428n8

K'atun 4 Ajaw, 10, 190

K'atun 8 Ajaw, 10–16 *passim*, 44f, 104f, 174, 190, 404, 430n17, 432n36, 453n115

K'atun cycle, 14f, 101–6 *passim*, 190, 206, 430n17, 431n34

K'atun prophecies, 102f, 172. *See also* Prophecy, *under* individual k'atun periods

K'atuns, 10, 14, 60, 101ff

Kaufman, Terrence, 426n1

Kawak (yearbearer), 97, *98*

Kawich (lineage name), 24

Kawich (town), *xx*, 129, *130*, 144–50 *passim*, 155, 224, 342, 464nn. *See also* B'olonch'en Kawich

Kawich, Ventura, 484n59

Kawij (lineage name), 24

Kawij, IxEtz'nab', 76–77

Kawij, IxKawak, 76–77

Kawil, *see* Kab'an Kawil

Kawil (lineage name), 13, 24, 81, 140

K'awil Chel, 431n30

Kawil Itza, 81, 449n59. *See also* AjKawil Itza

Kawil, Kab'an, 81, 461n35

K'ayom, 451n83

K'ayom, Ach Kat, *85*

K'eb', Andrés, 171–75 *passim*, 324

K'eb', Catalina, 468n15

K'eb', Pedro, 468n15

Kech (lineage name), 24

Kech, IxKaw, 76–77

Keel, *see* Junak Keel

Kej, Juan, 240, 480n67

Kejach (defined), 435n13

Kejaches, xxv, 3, 19, 31–34, 42, 52, 58, 100, 120, 132, 145, 154–60 *passim*, 184f, 189–94 *passim*, 213f, 262, 385, 466n60, 468n11, 476n10, 484n53, 484n62; abandon missions, 249, 253–56, 363; Franciscans among, 42, 154–61, 245, 249, 255ff; territory of, xxiv, 5, 22f, 31f, 99, 131, 150, 175, 285, 465n30

K'ek, Juana, 378

K'ek'chis, 421, 433n46, 522n127

Keliz (lineage name), 24

Ken (lineage name), 63

Ken, Diego, 150

Ketz (lineage name), 24

Ketz (town), 6, 17, 63, 66, 325, 347, 350, 382, 442n4, 443nn, 496n8

K'eyan Chan (town), 461n35

Ki (lineage name), 25, 76–77

Ki, Luis, 150

Kib' (lineage name), 25, 76–77

Kib', Ik, 76–77

K'iche Mayas, 87

K'in (lineage name), 21, 25, 433nn. *See also* AjKawil K'in

K'in, Mas, 469n16

K'in Chan, Ach Kat, *85*, 467n2. *See also* Chan, K'in

K'inchil (lineage name), 25

K'inchil (town), 88, 103

K'in Chil, Ach Kat, *85*

K'in Chil Kob'a, 88, 197, 451n83

King's milpa, 364–65, 398–403 *passim*, 516n55

Kinship, *see* Double descent; Households, Itza; Lineages; Matrilineal descent; Patrilineal descent

K'inyokte (lineage name), 25, 448n57

Kischan (lineage name), 25, 433n46

Kisteil (town), 414

Kisteil rebellion, 414

Kitis (Kowoj leader), 516n60

Kitis (lineage name), 25 62, 402

Kitis (town), 391, 513n17

K'itis, AjChikan, *62*
Kitkaan (Itza title), 208
Kit Kan (Itza title), 89–95 *passim, 98, 103,*
272, 283, 288f, 312, 384, 393, 451n88,
508n76. See also Ach Kat Kit Kan; Kan
Ek' (cousin of Ajaw Kan Ek'); Kuch Pop
Kit Kan
Kitkan (lineage name), *25*
Kit Kan, Ach Kat, *85*
Kit Kan, Ajaw B'atab', 98, 138
Kit Kan, AjUs, *62*
Kit Kan, B'atab', *98*
Kitkan, Cacique, *90, 91*
Kitkan, José, *413f*
Kit Kan, Kuch Pop, 89, 90, 97, 138,
460n32
Kit Kan, Reyezuelo, *90, 92,* 182, 451n90,
461n41
Kit Kan, Tesak, *62*
K'ix (lineage name), *62*
K'ixab'on (cacique), 402
K'ixab'on (lineage name), *25, 62, 392f,*
433n46, 448n57, 513n24, 513nn
K'ixab'on, Ach Kat, 89, *90, 91, 96,* 101
K'ixan, *see* AjK'ixaw; K'ixaw
K'ixaw, *185. See also* AjK'ixaw
K'ixaw (lineage name), *23, 25,* 140,
470n36, 484n53
K'ixaw, Bartolomé, *185,* 468n11
K'ixaw, Juan, 484n59
K'ixchan (lineage name), *25*
Kixchan (lineage name), *21*
K'ix Kan, *62*
Knives, 188–92 *passim, 201, 205, 229,*
235, 267, 324, 352, 366. See also Tools,
metal
Kob' (lineage name), *25*
Kob', IxMen, 76–77
Kob'a (town), *17, 18,* 451n83
Kokom (lineage name), 10, 13, 18, *25,*
430n20, 454n116
Kol (lineage name), *25*
Kontal (town), *6, 62, 382, 391*
Kopan (site), *xx*
Kowoj (lineage name), 19, *25, 62, 63, 413f*
Kowoj (wife of AjChan), *167, 273, 304*
Kowoj, AjK'itan, *63*

Kowoj, Cacique, *92, 213. See also*
AjKowoj; Kowoj, Captain
Kowoj, Captain, 66, *92, 95, 325, 348,*
371, 443n14. *See also* AjKowoj; Kowoj,
Cacique
Kowoj, Captain (son), *371. See also* Kowoj,
Kulut
Kowoj, Kitam, 402
Kowoj, Kulut, 66, 371ff, 391–402 *passim,*
443n10, 452n101, 496n8, 502n86,
513n17. *See also* Kowoj, Captain (son)
Kowoj, Lax, 280
Kowojs, 3, 17–18, 27, 56, 106, 167, 173,
192, 214, 220, 226–27, 280, 289, 315,
323, 334, 344–50 *passim,* 385, 387, 392,
403, 443n10, 446n45, 496n1, 497n10,
510n110, 511nn, 516n60; abandon
towns, *323,* 348–49, *401, 409, 411, 417,*
443n10; capital town of, *66, 325, 348;*
history of, xix, 3, 11, 16–19 *passim,*
430n24; political organization of, 66,
452n101; territory of, 5, 6, 17, *17, 66–*
68, 99f, *315, 324f, 346, 365,* 370ff, *381–*
84 *passim, 391,* 402; Alliances, Maya
K'u (lineage name), *25,* 140, 470n35
K'u, B'atab', *65*
K'u, Cacique, *185. See also* Joseph K'u
Kuch Kab'al, 93–94
Kuch Pop Kit Kan, *see* Kit Kan, Kuch Pop
K'u, Francisco, *150*
K'u, Joseph, *185,* 468n11. *See also* K'u,
Cacique
Kuk (lineage name), 507n53
Kuk, Martín, *51*
K'uk'ulkan, temple of, 74
Kulut Kowoj, *see* Kowoj, Kulut
Kuman, *236,* 478n55
Kumux, Francisco, 43
K'unil (lineage name), *25*
Kupul (lineage name), *see* NaOb'on Kupul;
O'bon Kupul; Tzuk Kupul
K'u, Xok, 76–77
Kwa (lineage name), *25. See also* Matan
Kwa

Labranzas, 33
La Costa (partido), *256, 345*

Lago de Izabal, *xx*, 31, 38, *130*. *See also* Golfo Dulce

Lago Petén Itzá, *xx*, xxiv, xxvi, 5, 7, *8*, 10, 17, 21f, 38, 64, 66, 67, 111, 127, 129, *130*, 133, 141–45 *passim*, 156, 187, 190, 200, 207, 210, 215, 226–44 *passim*, 248–53 *passim*, 260, 265–72 *passim*, 278–87 *passim*, 306, 324, 342, 344, 356, 358, 363, 371, 375–417 *passim*, 390, 417, 421, 443n10, 486n74, 518n79, 521n124

Laguna Chunpich, 465n33

Laguna de Bacalar, *xx*, *130*

Laguna del Civalón, 465n35

Laguna Ijá, 6, 64, 281

Laguna la Amapola, 465n35

Laguna Mangüito, 465n35

Laguna Oquevix, 6, 64, 138, 281, 382

Laguna Perdida, 100

Laguna Petenxil, 100

Laguna Quexil, 6, 7, *8*, 17, 100, 351, 496n1, 503n101

Laguna Sacnab, 6, 17, *18*, 22, 56, 66, 100, 280, 368, 496n73

Laguna Sacpuy, 6, 7, *8*, 68, 95, 99f, 145, 306, 326, 348, 365ff, 382, 384, 393, 442n4, 496n1, 506n36, 514n38

Laguna Siviltuc, 464n21

Laguna Yaxhá, 6, 7, 17, *18*, 22, 56, 66, 100, 280, 348, 368

Laguneta El Sos, 6, 7, *8*, 506n36, 514n38

Laguneta Macanché, 6, 7, *17*, *18*, 56, 64–66, 100–101, 278

Laguneta Picú, 6, *8*, 65

Laguneta Salpetén, 6, *17*, *18*, 65f, 100f

Laines, José, 152, 260, 271, 325, 489n15

Lakandon Mayas (Chol), *see* Chol Lakandons

Lamanai, *xx*

Lamanay (town), 53

La Mejorada, Convent of, 178, 180, 259

La Natividad de Nuestra Señora (villa), 38

Lances, 43, 205, 207

Landa, Fray Diego de (bishop), 79, 97, 105, 446n49

Lan García, Juan de, 500n58

Languages, *see* Cholan language family; Chontal language; Nahuatl language; Yucatecan language family

La Palotada, 190

La Pimienta (province), 3, 46, 120, 143. *See also* Santa Rosa de la Pimienta

Lara, Br. Joseph de, 359

Lara, Fray Pedro de, 258

Lard, 346

Las Casas, Guillen de, 41

Layseca Alvarado, Antonio de, 55

Lineages, 54–55, 60, 65. *See also* Double descent; Kan matrilineage; Matrilineal descent; Patrilineal descent

Lizárraga, Conde de, 113, 115, 409, 454n1. *See also* Ursúa y Arizmendi, Martín de

Lizarraga, Nicolás de, 333, 360–61, 374, 377, 380, 384, 397, 418f, 429n10, 505n23, 515n44

Lizarraga, Nicolás de (son), 400

Loaysa, Fray Miguel de, 480n81

Logging, 127, 143, 458n55

Logwood, 42, 127, 458n55

López de Cogolludo, Fray Diego de, 11, 19, 53, 69, 78f, 102, 301, 437n29, 439n53, 451n92

López, Fray Domingo, 244

Lorenzo, Fray Pedro, 41f

Los Remedios (presidio), *see* Petén Itzá (presidio)

Los Zinzontles (town), 517n72

Lovell, W. George, 437n29

Lucas de San Francisco, 148, 159–61, 189

Macal River, *xx*, 5, *130*, 218

Machetes, 135–39 *passim*, 144, 173, 188, 194, 201, 205, 208, 212, 228, 235f, 283, 288, 303, 309, 315, 324, 351, 354, 365–67, 390, 400. *See also* Tools, metal

Machich (town), 58, *130*, 254

Machuca, Antonio, 135–41 *passim*

MacLeod, Barbara, 433n47

Madrid, Juan Bernardo de, 186

Madrid, Spain, 112, 115

Maestros: cantores, 150, 189, 192, 204, 215, 226, 464n11; de capilla, 150, 464n11; de escuela, 464n11

Maize, *see* Granaries; Itzas, agriculture of;
　Milpas; Milperías
Makanche (town), *see* Tajmakanche
Makocheb' (Nojpeten quarter), 84, *98*, 99,
　450n70
Maktum (site), 438n45
Maler, Teoberto, 471n17
Malinali, *see* Marina, doña
Malnutrition, 377
Mama (town), 485ff
Mamantel (town), *130*, 458n56
Manche (town), *xx*, 5, 49–50, *130*, 240,
　433n48
Manche Chols, 5, 7, 49–52, 65, 99, 111,
　120, 122, 133–34, 134, 240–43 *passim*,
　384f, 417–20, 433n48, 438n36, 459n18,
　479n, 502n89, 522n127. *See also* Chols
Mani (province), 18f
Mani (town), *xx*, 48, *130*, 219, 263,
　452n93. *See also* Chilam B'alam, books
　of
Manila, Philippines, 114
Mantas, 33. *See also* Cotton cloth
Mantilla, Pedro de, 230
Maps, 512n12, 513nn
Marcus, Joyce, 82, 449n66
Margil de Jesús, Fray Antonio, 243, 379,
　509n92
Marina, doña, 30–35 *passim*, 435n7
Marriage, 75–81 *passim*, 354, 382, 445–
　46n44, 446n45. *See also* Polygyny;
　Polygyny, sororal
Martín, Br. Manuel, 477n31
Martín, Fray Nicolás, 254–55
Martínez de Mora, Br. José Francisco, 268,
　270, 286, 296, 328–29, 333, 338, 345,
　348–51, 502n86
Mas (lineage name), 25. *See also* Ek' Mas
Mas, Nicolás, 150
Masa, Tzutz, 396, 514n38
Mas Jaw, K'in, 63
Mas K'in (town), 469n16
Mas K'in, Ach Kat, *85*
Mass, Christian, 34, 179, 185, 203, 296,
　303f, 413
Massacres, 47–52 *passim*, 134, 228ff, 244,
　272, 277, 281, 285, 291, 296–303 *pas-*

sim, 312f, 318f, 327–32 *passim*, 339,
　396–401, 474n89, 479n
Matab' (lineage name), 25
Matan, Ajaw, *90*
Matan, Ajaw, Reyezuelo, 92, 182
Matan Kwa, *85*
Matrículas, 27, 458n56, 467n60, 484nn; of
　Chunuk'um, 54, 75, 76–77, 440nn,
　441n95, 445n43, 468nn. *See also* Cen-
　suses
Matrilineal descent, xxiii, 78–81, 445–
　46n44, 447n51, 449n63. *See also*
　Tzakab'
Matrilocal residence, 449n63
Matronyms, 75, 80–81, 445n43, 448n55
Mats, bark, 50
Matza, AjJe, 62
Matzin (lineage name), *see* AjMatzin
Matzkalek' (town), 491n38. *See also*
　Motzkalek'
Maxkanu (town), 150
May (calendrical period), 14, 430n17
May (lineage name), 25. *See also* AjChak
　May; IxKi May; NaMay Kanche
May, Nicolás, 150
Mayaktun (defined), 71
Maya Mountains, *xx*, 38
Mayapan, *xx*, xxi, 10–12, 16–19 *passim*,
　74, 79, 104–5, 199, 429n11, 453n115,
　454n116
Mayapan calendar, 174
Mazatecas (province), 435n13. *See also*
　Mazatlan
Mazatlan (province), 31, 511n20. *See also*
　Kejaches; Mazatecas
Measles, 517n77
Media anata, 252
Medina, Juan de, 324
Medrano y Solorzano, Estévan, 358, 363,
　373, 500n58
Mejen (title), 447n51, 511n112. *See also*
　Chun Ajaw; Chun Mejen
Mejía Céspedes, Juan Jerónimo, 500n58
Men (lineage name), *see* IxMen Kob'
Mencos y Coronado, Juan Bernardo de,
　358, 366, 505n23
Mencos y Medrano, Melchor de, xxvii,

332, 335f, 356–77 *passim*, 377, 389, 409, 419, 504n8

Méndez, Br. Manuel, 477n31

Méndez de Canzo, Antonio, 48

Mendía y Sologastoa, Cristóbal de, 358, 367–70

Mendoza, Juan de, 112–13, 119, 122, 378

Mendoza y Galindo, Fray Simon de, 370

Meneses, Br. Pedro, 414

Meneses Bravo de Sarabia, Fernando, 517n73

Mercederians, 68, 112f, 132, 243f, 299, 333, 338, 366, 370, 372, 376, 499n58

Merchants, Maya, 31

Mérida (city), *xx*, *xxv*, 39, 89, 111, 118ff, 127, 130, 138, 149f, 156, 161, 163, 168–80 *passim*, 184–201 *passim*, 216–20 *passim*, 225, 231, 245–56 *passim*, 274f, 282, 286, 308f, 324, 326, 339, 397, 412, 487n89, 520n105; cathedral of, 177–78, 185–86. *See also* Tihoo

Mesoamerica, 60

Mestizoization, 354

Mestizos, 144, 267

Metates, 366

Mexicas, 29f, 37, 39. *See also* Aztecs

Mexico, Audiencia of, 124–26, 245ff, 252, 260

Mexico City, 37f, 117f, 122, 126, 246–50 *passim*, 343

Migrations, xix, 3, 8–13 *passim*, 56, 520n108, 522n127

Militias: Maya, 142–44, 153–54, 162–63, 260, 263, 297, 462n49, 465n33; Spanish and mixed-caste, 142, 144, 151f, 162f, 229, 260, 267, 467n61, 489n15

Milpas, 348–54 *passim*, 366–69, 390, 398, 406, 478n43, 506n34; and Spanish barter, 345, 357, 363, 372, 381f; Spanish pillaging of, 229, 323, 347f, 357, 359, 367, 371f, 381, 476n17, 503n1. *See also* Itzas, agriculture of; King's milpa

Milperías, 65, 216, 346, 366, 371

Miraflores, Conde de, 118, 186, 249. *See also* Garrastegui y Oleado, Pedro de

Mirones y Lescano, Francisco de, 45–51 *passim*

Mis (lineage name), 25

Miskitos, 408, 412, 419f

Missionaries, *see* Dominicans; Franciscans; Jesuits; Mercederians; Secular clergy, Yucatán

Missions, Petén, xxvii, 344, 349, 357, 387–421 *passim*, 390, 395, 407, 518–21nn

Mixe, 29

Mo (lineage name), 25

Mo, Diego, 150

Mo, IxKab'an, 76–77

Moan (lineage name), 25, 81, 437n33

Moan Pana, 81. *See also* AjMuan Pana; Mompana

Moho River, 385

Mojo River, *xx*

Mompana (province), 6, 95, 382–85 *passim*. *See also* Moan Pana

Monkey River, *xx*

Montejo, Francisco de (Adelantado), 39, 242

Montejo, Francisco de (son), 13

Montezuma, 200, 209

Montezuma, Conde de (viceroy), 251

Monzabal, José, 417

Moors, 118, 199

Mopan (town), *xx*, 7, 19, 22, 49, 51, 130, 134, 233, 240, 243, 304f, 338, 358, 419, 433nn, 461n41, 480n75, 517n72, 521n124. *See also* San Luis

Mopan (town, Yalain area), 468n16

Mopans, 3, 19, 49, 51, 56, 65, 67, 83, 133–37, 169, 175, 183, 236, 242, 408, 418–21, 433n47, 434nn, 438n34, 439n54, 446n45, 459nn, 522n127; Itza influence over, 99, 135, 239, 434n52; language of, 19, 137, 234, 240, 419, 421, 426–27n1, 434n50; lineage names of, 21, 27–28, 34f, 459; territory of, 5, 19–22, 101, 232, 341, 384, 433nn, 517n72; Chinamitas; Musuls

Morales y Vela, Br. Pedro de, 328, 333–50 *passim*, 354, 366, 388, 502n86

Morán, Fray Francisco, 49–52 *passim*

Moreno, Juan Antonio, 520n102

Motul de San José, 6, 8, 17

Motzkal (island), 8, 17, 278f, 282, 491n38

Motzkalek' (town), 469n16. *See also*
Matzkalek'
Muk'ixil (town), 385
Muknal (estancia), 416
Muk'ul (lineage name), 25. *See also*
IxMuluk Muk'ul
Mulattos, 144
Mules, 235, 239, 252, 256f, 261–64 *pas-
sim*, 341, 347, 479n, 487n89
Muleteers, 129–37 *passim*, 142f, 162, 245,
249, 252, 257–63 *passim*, 267, 341,
345f, 358f, 364, 487n89, 501nn
Mul Kaj (town), 88, 103
Mul Kaj, Ach Kat, 85
Multepal, 104–5, 453–54n115
Muluk, yearbearer, 97, 98
Mumunt'i (town), 6, 63, 382f, 385
Musical instruments, 185, 194, 229, 237,
239, 272, 282f, 286, 453n112, 470n36.
See also Bugles; Chirimías; Drums;
Flutes; Recorders; Trumpets; Tunkul;
Turtle shells
Musul (lineage name), 21, 25, 433nn,
434n48
Mutinies, 230, 251, 258
Muwan (lineage name), 25. *See also* Moan
Muzuls, 175, 179, 183, 185, 224, 275, 408

Na, Cristóbal, 47
Naa (lineage name), 25
Naal names, *see* Names, naal
Nab'a (town), 65, 510n110
NaChan Ch'el, 79
NaChan Kanche, 79–80
Nahuatl language, 30, 87–91 *passim*,
435n7, 450n75, 451n90
Naj Tunich, 433n47
NaKajun Noj, 431n28
Nakom (title), 45, 92, 453n112
Nakom P'ol, *see* P'ol, Nakom
NaMay Kanche, 79
Names, 54, 420, 448nn; baptismal, 54; boy,
445n43; compound, 54f, 75–81,
431n28; day, 75, 445nn; given, 75,
445nn; lineage, 21f, 22–27, 54f, 75–81,
393; naal, 79ff, 432n28, 448n53. *See also*
Matronyms; Patronyms

NaOb'on Kupul, 13, 448n53. *See also*
Ob'on Kupul
Navarra, 113ff, 409
Navarrete, Pedro de, 385f, 511n121
Navas y Quevedo, Fray Andrés de las
(bishop), 499n58
Necklaces, 35, 188, 191, 267, 287, 437n26
Negrón, Br. Pedro Martín, 477n31
Nek'nojche (town), 63, 65, 511n115
New River, *xx*, 3, 12, 130
New Spain, 291; viceroys of, 122, 124,
232, 342, 409, 411, 455n12. *See also*
Bucareli y Ursúa, Antonio María; Mon-
tezuma, Conde de; Ortega Montáñez,
Juan de; Sandoval, Gaspar de, Conde de
Galve
New Vizcaya, 291
New Year rituals, 97ff
Nich (town), 6, 8, 92, 95, 192, 197, 266,
488n6. *See also* Ch'ich'; Nixtun
Nikte, Pedro, 271, 284, 304, 490n30. *See
also* AjChant'an; Chan, Nikte; Chan,
Pedro Miguel
Nisam (estancia), 416
Nito (town), *xx*, 31, 38
Nixtun (town), 6, 8, 95, 192, 266, 489n13.
See also Ch'ch'; Nich; Punta Nijtún
Nobility, *see* Itzas, political organization of;
Ranking, senior-junior; Ruling council,
Itza; Titles
Nochija (town), *see* Chinoja
Nojb'ekan (town), 130, 388
Noj Che, Cacique, 85, 87, 90, 96
Noj-jem, ravine, 190, 471n11
Nojk'u, 130, 151
Nojk'ute (lineage name), 26, 448n57
Nojpek', 130, 151
Nojpeten, *xx*, 6, 7, 8, 12, 17, 19–22 *pas-
sim*, 29–38 *passim*, 46ff, 54, 60–74 *pas-
sim*, 78, 84, 92f, 105, 130, 138, 141,
147, 149, 156f, 161f, 167–77 *passim*,
182, 189, 194–217 *passim*, 223–40 *pas-
sim*, 265–92 *passim*, 297ff, 310, 323,
346, 348, 367, 387, 403, 436nn, 449n64,
460nn, 469n21, 479n; burned by
Kowojs, 72, 197, 205, 326, 385, 444n33,
497n12; descriptions of, 42, 68–74,

196–97, 234, 300–302, 333, 363, 436n19, 461n41; palaces of, 69, 99, 197f; quarters of, 84, 99–100, 450n70; Spanish occupation of, xxvi, 57, 116, 197, 249, 253, 295–304, 328, 337, 367, 380, 392, 494n28; temples of, 69–74 *passim*, 99, 197f, 203, 278, 291, 300ff, 320f, 436n19, 437n29, 445nn, 499n45; Nuestra Señora de los Remedios y San Pablo, Laguna del Itza (presidio); TajItza

Nojpeten (Nojpeten quarter), 84, 98, 100, 450n70

Nojpolol (town), 468n16

Nojt'ub' (town), xx, *130*, 152, 465n24

NojTut, 507n53

Noj Tz'o, 87, 92

Noj Tz'o Kan Noj, *85*, 87, 96

Noj Tz'o Kan Punab', *85*, 87, *90*, 96

Nojuk'um, *see* Río Nojuk'um

Nuestra Señora de Carmen, 419

Nuestra Señora de Guadalupe (town), 390, *390*, 393, 394, 513n29

Nuestra Señora de la Candelaria (town), 390, *390*, 394, 394. *See also* Punta Candelaria

Nuestra Señora de la Merced (town), 389, 391, 394

Nuestra Señora de los Dolores de Chinoja, 370. *See also* Chinoja

Nuestra Señora de los Dolores del Lacandón (town), xx, *130*, 133, 142–47 *passim*, 232f, 243, 248, 250, 297, 346, 350, 358, 363, 379f, 509nn. *See also* Sakb'alan

Nuestra Señora de los Remedios (saint), 297, 328

Nuestra Señora de los Remedios y San Pablo, Laguna del Itza, xxvii, 295, 300, 304, 343, 390. *See also* Petén Itzá (presidio), 304

Nueva Granada, 114

Ob'on (lineage name), 26, 453n112. *See also* B'e Ob'on, AjKali; NaOb'on Kupul

Ob'on, Chuen, 63

Ob'on, Matz, 63

Ob'on Kupul, 431n28

Ocaña, Nueva Granada, 114

Ocosingo (town), xx, *132*

O'Kelly, Teodoro, 372

Okte, AjK'in, 272

Olid, Cristóbal de, 30

Oloriz, Navarra (town), 113

Orbita, Fray Juan de, 20, 43–49 *passim*, 58, 200, 202, 300f, 439nn

Ordóñez de Avilez, Sancho, 500n58

Orozco, Pedro de, 500n58

Ortega Montáñez, Juan de (bishop, viceroy), 248

Ortiguera, Toribio de, 114

Ossuaries, *see* Bones, human

Oxk'utzkab' (town), 48, 143f, 258, 263, 501n84

Ozaeta, Pedro de, 500n58

Pacha (lineage name), 461–62n41

Pachayil (estancia), 416

Pacheco, Alejandro, 364, 505n27

Pacheco, Alonso, 39

Pacheco, Diego, 346, 502n89

Pacheco, Melchor, 39

Pacheco de Sopuerta, Br. Juan, 178, 267–71 *passim*, 286, 296f, 304, 325, 328

Pak'ek'em (town), 23, *130*, 159–61, 185, 253–56, 344, 363, 434n53, 466n60, 468n11, 470n40, 484n53, 484n62, 485n62

PakLan, 140, 461n35

PakNek, 140

Pakoc, *see* Pak'ok

Pak'ok, 102, 461n35

Palenque (town), xx, 41, 339

Paliak (town), 385

Paliak River, xx

Palomino, Alonso, 487n79

Pamplona (Navarra), 113f

Pamplona (Nueva Granada), 114

Pana (lineage name), 26, 63, 81, 218, 278, 313, 368, 393, 433n47, 461–62n41, 474n80, 474n89. *See also* AjMuan Pana; AjPana; Chan Pana, K'in; IxChan Pana; Moan Pana; Punab', Chamach

Pana, Tanche, 390

Panama, 114

Panub', 368
Parcialidades, 84, 92, 93
Pardos, 229, 259, 267, 467n61
Parker, Joy, 428n8
Patch, Robert W., 55, 117f
Patrilineal descent, xxiii, 75–81 *passim*,
   396, 439n58, 447n51. *See also* Ch'ib'al
Patronyms, 54, 75–81 *passim*, 433nn,
   446nn, 448n57
PaxB'olon, Pablo, 458n56
PaxB'olon Acha, 31, 38
PaxB'olon Acha (Pablo PaxB'olon),
   435n9
Peccary, 473n46
Pecoc, *see* Pak'ok
Pendergast, David M., 426n5
Penis incision, 204
Peraza L., Carlos, 9
Pérez, Br. Thomas, 477n31
Pérez, Francisco, 54
Pérez, Rodolfo, 235, 241
Pérez de Güémes, Lorenzo, 477n31
Pérez de San Román, Fray Antonio, 148f,
   189
Peruvian Amazon, 114
Peten (defined), 93, 452n96
Petén, Department of, xix
Petenekte (town), xx, 130, 339
Petenil (estancia), 416
Petén Itzá (presidio), 304–420 *passim*, 410,
   416, 518n79; barracks of, 307, 327, 363;
   Campeche Mayas at, 364, 379; church
   of, 304, 332, 363, 365, 398, 405; food
   shortages at, 323, 345, 347, 356, 359,
   365, 372, 380; fort of, 347, 350, 365;
   garrison of, 327f, 345, 347, 353ff, 359,
   364f, 372f, 387, 398, 403, 411, 486n77;
   general conditions at, 323, 347f, 356;
   governance of, 327, 357, 381, 389, 408–
   412, 417, 505n23; Guatemalan settlers
   of, 334, 357–63, 360–61, 377f, 397; Itza
   and Kowoj workers at, 353ff, 398f,
   404ff; supplies and support for, 338–41,
   345ff, 356, 359, 363f, 500n59, 501n68,
   502n89, 505n23, 507n61. *See also*
   Nuestra Señora de los Remedios y San
   Pablo, Laguna del Itza (presidio)

Petenja (town), 65, 237
Petmas (town), 63, 510n104
Peto (town), xx, 130, 263f, 341, 477n31,
   485n68
Philippines, xxii, 113, 115, 408, 411
Physicians, 245, 359, 372
P'ich (town), 17, 469n16
Piedras Negras (site), 445n44
Pimienta, *see* La Pimienta; Santa Rosa de la
   Pimienta
Pintado, José, 487n79
Pipils, 88
Piracy, xxiv
Piragua (menor), 226, 252, 260, 265, 327,
   347, 354, 367
Piste, Manuel, 150
Pix (lineage name), 26. *See also* IxTutz Pix
Pix, IxEtz, 76–77
Plantains, 136, 325, 399
Playa Blanca, 371
Pneumonia, 381
Pochutla (town), 41
Polain (town), 65
Political geography, *see* Cosmology, spa-
   tial; Quadripartite governance; Quarters;
   Rulers of the East; Rulers of the North;
   Rulers of the South; Rulers of the West
Political organization, Maya, 82, 449n66,
   450n68. *See also under* Itzas
P'ol (lineage name), 26. *See also* AjChata
   P'ol; AjK'in P'ol
P'ol, Diego, 150
P'ol, IxKab'an, 76–77
P'ol, Nakom, 45, 49, 452n92. *See also*
   AjChata P'ol; AjK'in P'ol
Polol (town), 62
Polygyny, 81, 405. *See also* Marriage
Polygyny, sororal, 405, 516n69
Poot (lineage name), 26
Pop (defined), 89
Pop (Poop) (town), 17, 88, 103, 325, 350,
   382. *See also* IxPop
Pop, Ach Kat, 85
Pope, 199, 201
Popola (town), 458n56
Popolna, 71, 451n86
Popol Vuj, 87

Poptun (town), 433n48
Population decline, *see* Censuses; Epidemics; Population estimates
Population estimates, 346, 416, 458n56; of Chol Lakandons, 379f; of Itzas, 183, 442n4, 443n15; of Ixtus, 370; of Kejach missions, 254f; of Kowojs, 325, 442n4; of Petén, 66ff, 395, 395f, 406–9, 407, 415ff, 444n20, 521nn; Censuses. *See also* Epidemics; Matrículas
Porras, Antonio de, 55
Postclassic period, 14, 443n15, 445–46n44, 452n93
Pot, Marcos, 144
Pottery, 368, 418
Prada, Fray Cristóbal de, 233–37 *passim*, 303, 479n
Preclassic period, 452n93
Prem, Hanns J., 426n5
Presidios, *see* Mopan (town); Nuestra Señora de los Remedios y San Pablo, Laguna del Itza (presidio); San Pedro Mártir (presidio)
Pretil (defined), 445n40
Priests, Maya, 14, 40, 47
Principal pairs, *see* Ranking, senior-junior
Prophecy: Franciscan interpretations of, 12, 156–59, 176, 197, 206–10; of Itzas, xxiv–xxv, 11–14, 44–45, 61, 106f, 172, 174, 181–84 *passim*; at Tipuj, 52; K'atun prophecies
Proyecto Maya Colonial, xxiii, 426n4, 442n2, 489n13
Puk (lineage name), 23, 26, 63, 276f, 484n53
Puk, Ajaw, 43, 452n92
Puk, AjUs, 63
Puk, Ayikal, 138, 277, 460n32. *See also* Puk, Cacique
Puk, B'atab', 62, 65
Puk, Cacique, 280f. *See also* Puk, Ayikal
Puk, Felipe, 370
Puk, Lucas, 484n59
Puk, Marcos, 470n40
Puk, Sal, 76–77
Puks, 138, 319
Punab', Chamach, 218

Punta Candelaria, 514n32. *See also* Punta Nijtún
Punta Gorda (town), 421
Punta Nijtún, 33, 266, 271, 297, 349, 394, 436n22, 514n32. *See also* Punta Candelaria
Putuns, 430n12. *See also* Chontals
Pyrenees Mountains, 113

Quadripartite governance, 60, 83, 91–101 *passim*, 441nn
Quarters, 97, 441n2, 452n98; of Itza territory, xxiii, 60, 96–100; of Nojpeten, xxiii, 69, 71, 84, 96–99, 98. *See also* Rulers of the east; Rulers of the north; Rulers of the south; Rulers of the west

Rabinal (town), 7, 242
Rajón, Br. Diego, 477n31
Ranchería, 65
Rancho, 65
Ranking, senior-junior, 93–96 *passim*, 104, 441n2. *See also* Dual rulership
Rape, 51
Rattlesnakes, 239
Rebellions: of Itzas and Kowojs, 405; of Kowojs, 335f; of Manche Chols, 51; of Petén missions, xxi, xxvii, 357, 387, 397–405, 413–17 *passim*, 512n12, 514n39; rumors of, Petén, 323–24, 349–52, 365, 386, 512n123; in Tz'ul Winikob', 40, 49, 52, 56, 58
Recopilación de las Indias, 238
Recorders (instruments), 185
Redhead, mysterious, 235, 241, 478n48
Reductions, "de paz y de paso", 121, 153, 283, 286, 291, 343
Regidores, 127, 150
Remesal, Antonio de, 237
Rendón, Sylvia, 428n8
Rentero, Julio, 258
Repartimientos, 40, 47, 117, 121, 129, 186, 380, 455n18
Repúblicas de indios, *see* Town councils
Requerimiento, 198, 473n40
Residencia, 126
Resistance, passive, 260–64 *passim*

Rey (Itza title), 82
Reyezuelo (Itza title), 22, 82, 89–95 *passim*, 182, 308
Rhetoric, Spanish, 329–35, 372, 510n110
Riachuelo Pixoyal, 33
Rice, Don S., xxiii
Rice, Prudence M., xxiii
Ringle, William M., 9, 450n68
Río, Diego Bernardo del, 133f, 145, 271, 297, 303f, 336f, 341, 377, 489n15
Río Acté, 6, 8, 190, 472n21, 483n39
Río Cancuen, 137
Río Candelaria, 31, *130*, 153, 435n10
Río Caribe, 153
Río Chakal, 233. *See also* Chakal
Río Chilapa, *xx*
Río Chixoy, *130*
Río Coatzacoalcos, 29
Río de los Dolores, 373
Río de Tachis, 41. *See also* Río San Pedro Mártir
Río Dulce, *xx*, 38
Río El Subín, 6
Río Grande, *xx*, 385
Río Grijalva, 30
Río Hondo, *xx*, 39, *130*
Río Ixkonob, 472n21
Río Lacantún, *xx*, *130*
Río Machaquila, *130*
Río Mamantel, 155
Río Mopán, *xx*, 6, *18*, 22, *130*, 218, 411
Río Motagua, *xx*, *130*
Río Nojuk'um, *xx*, *130*, 190, 226. *See also* Río San Pedro Mártir
Río Pasión, *xx*, 7, 99, *130*, 243, 314, 346, 350, 363, 371, 384, 429n10
Río Polochic, *xx*
Río Saklemakal, 472n21
Río Sanicte, 137
Río San Juan, 6, 137
Río San Martín, 6, 137
Río San Pedro Mártir, *xx*, 6, 31, 42, *130*, 163, 190, 224, 226, 251, 438n45, 483n39. *See also* Río de Tachis; Río Nojuk'um
Río Subin, 429n10
Río Tacotalpa, 30

Río Uk'um, 157
Río Usumacinta, *xx*, 31, 41, 112, *130*, 339, 371, 417
Río Xocmo, *xx*, *130*, 137
Río Xoyte, 385
Río Yaxal, 385. *See also* Waxal
Ripalda Ongay, Blas Felipe de, 489n15
Ripalda Ongay, José de, 304, 337–40, 500n58, 508n72
Ritual objects, 40, 47, 53, 151, 190. *See also* Crosses; Horse image; *under* Itzas; Saints (images); Tzimin Chak
Rivas, Fray Bernardo de, 300
Rivas, Fray Diego de, 68, 113, 132, 232, 243, 299, 333, 358, 363, 376, 379, 383, 388, 394–97 *passim*, 429n10, 449n64, 500n58, 504n6, 515n39
River of the Toads, 136
Road blockades, 42, 366, 385f
Roads, Itza, 366f
Rodríguez, Francisco, 487n79
Rodríguez, Fray Lorenzo, 459n15
Rodríguez, Melchor, 132
Rome, 199
Rosaries, 213
Royal Council of Castile, 114
Royal milpa, *see* King's milpa
Roys, Ralph L., 11f, 79f, 104f, 435nn, 438nn, 449n66, 451n83, 452n93, 453n115, 458n56
Ruggiero, Daniel, 522n127
Ruins, archaeological, 151, 333, 337. *See also* Bovedas
Ruíz de Bustamante, Juan Antonio, 412, 517n76, 520n97
Rulership, *see* Dual rulership; Itzas, political organization of
Rulers of the east, 98, 100, 392
Rulers of the north, 94–99, 98, 140, 223, 226, 253, 281, 326, 402–4
Rulers of the south, 98, 99
Rulers of the west, 98, 99, 104
Ruling council, *see* Itzas, ruling council of

Sab'ak (lineage name), 26
Sacalum, 51
Sacrifice: animal, 97; human, 47f, 57–58,

71, 191, 197, 303, 313, 316, 321, 330–34, 372, 453nn, 479n, 498nn; Heart excision

Sacristanes, 150

Sáenz, Gregorio Carlos, 330

Sagüés y Sabalsa, Sebastián, 261f, 487n79

Sahagún, Fray Bernardino de, 88

Sahlins, Marshall, 288

Sailors, 267, 483nn

Saints (images), 53, 300f, 391, 419, 421

Sajkab'ch'en (partido), 254, 458n56

Sajkab'ch'en (town), *xx*, 42, 58, 129, *130*, 131, 144, 153–56, 227, 255, 262, 339, 458n57, 462n49, 465n33, 466n41

Sakalaka (town), 485n68

Sakalum (town), *xx*, 42–52 *passim*

Sakatan (town), *xx*, *130*

Sakb'ajlan (town), *xx*, 5, *130*, 132–33, 142–46 *passim*, 232, 248, 427n4. *See also* Nuestra Señora de los Dolores del Lacandón

Sakche (town), 468n16

Saki (Sakiwal), 13, 431n28

Saklemakal (Chak'an Itza town), 443n14

Saklemakal (town), 6, *17*, 63, 65f, 216, 325, 370f, 382, 385, 496n1, 507n61, 510n99, 510n110. *See also* San Antonio del Itza, Puerto Nuevo de

Sakluk (estancia), *416*

Sakpeten (town), 6, *17*, *18*, 468n16

Sakpuy (town), 6, 8, 366, 384, 442n4, 469n16, 511n115

Sakpuy, Santa María de (town), 366

Saksel (town), 62, 511n115

Saksuus (town), *xx*, 168, 468n6, 468n15

Sakwan (lineage name), 26

Sakyaxche (town), *xx*, *130*, 429n10. *See also* Sayaxche

Salama (town), *xx*, *130*, 135f, 502n89; carriers from, 233ff

Salamanca, Spain, 114

Salamanca de Bacalar, *see* Bacalar, Salamanca de

Salas, Fray Diego de, 158, 160, 254

Salazar, Fray Gabriel de, 52

Salazar, Nicolás de, 185

Salazar y Córdoba, Francisco de, 263f

Salt, 267, 288, 346, 366, 398, 458n55

Salted meat, *see* Beef jerky

Sambos, 408. *See also* Miskitos

San Agustín (town), 345, 371, 507n58

San Andrés (apostle), 393

San Andrés (town), 27, 33, 81, 389, *390*, 392f, *394*, 402, 409, *410*, 414f, *416*, 446n45, 448n57, 471n17, 496n73, 513nn, 520nn. *See also* Chak'an

San Antonio (town, Belize), 22, *420f*, 433n48

San Antonio (town, camino real), 518n79

San Antonio (town, Lago Petén Itzá), 389, *390*, 393–95, *394*, 399–403, *410*, 514n35

San Antonio del Itza, Puerto Nuevo de, 371. *See also* Saklemakal

San Antonio de Padua, 190

San Antonio Viejo (town, Belize), 22

San Benito (town), 391f, 503n101

San Bernabé (saint), 493n20

San Bernabé (town), *390*, *410*, 413, *416*, 520n103

San Buenaventura, Fray Francisco de (bishop), 417

San Buenaventura Chávez, Fray Juan de, 148, 153–62 *passim*, 227f, 303, 312, 341, 469n21

Sánchez, Br. Juan Francisco del Canto, 477n31

Sánchez, Fray Cristóbal, 153

Sánchez de Berrospe, Gabriel, 240–44 *passim*, 321, 337–40, 347–58 *passim*, 364, 372, 379f, 499n58

Sánchez Polo, Rómulo, xxiii

San Cristóbal de las Casas (city), 339. *See also* Ciudad Real

San Cristóbal Extramuros (Mérida), 150

Sandoval, Gaspar de, Conde de Galve (viceroy), 124, 246–51

Sandoval, Gonzalo de, 29

San Felipe (estancia del rey), *416*, 518n79

San Francisco (saint), 212

San Francisco (town), *390*, *390*, 393, *394*, 399, 513n24

San Francisco, Fray Lucas de, 469n21

San Francisco de Sales (saint), 393

San Francisco Xavier (saint), 419
San Francisco Xavier (town), 408f, *410*,
 413, 419, 517n72, 518n79, 521n124
San Ignacio del Cayo (town), 218
San Ildefonso, Fray Jacinto, 51
San Jerónimo (saint), 392
San Jerónimo (town), *390*, 390–94 *passim*,
 394, 401f, *410*, 415, *416*, 513n17,
 518n79, 520n102
San Joaquin de Chakal, *see* Chakal
San José (saint), 391
San José (town), 27, 81, 389, *390*, 391,
 394, 396, 402, 406, *410*, 413, *416*, 417,
 446n45, 448n57, 513nn, 520n102
San José de Ixtus (town), 370. *See also* Ixtus
San José Nuevo (town), 392, 421
San Juan (town), *410*. *See also* San Juan
 Baptista
San Juan, Bernardo de, 297
San Juan Baptista (town), *390*, *390*, 393,
 394, 399, 401, 513n29, 518n79
San Juan de Dios (estancia), *416*
San Juan del Obispo (town), 67f
San Luis (town), *xx*, 7, 19, 21, *130*, 134,
 408, *410*, 413, *416*, 419ff, 433n46,
 517n72, 518n79, 521nn, 522n127. *See
 also* Mopan
San Martín (town), 389, *390*, 392–95, *394*,
 399–403, 409, *410*, 417, 513n24,
 514n35, 518n79, 520n103
San Martín Obispo (saint), 392, 513n22
San Miguel (town), *see* San Miguel,
 Arcángel
San Miguel, Arcángel (saint), 513n13
San Miguel, Arcángel (town), 389–91, *390*,
 394, 396, 402, *410*, 518n79
San Miguel, Br. Francisco de, 389–98 *pas-
 sim*
San Miguel, Br. Marcos de, 388
San Miguel Ixtatan (town), *see* Ixtatan, San
 Miguel de
San Miguel y Figueroa, Br. Francisco de,
 334, 383, 477n31
San Pablo (apostle), 212, 300f, 493nn
San Pablo (estancia), *416*
San Pedro (town), *390*, *390*, 393, *394*, *410*,
 513n29

San Pedro (apostle), 199
San Pedro de las Huertas (town), 67
San Pedro Inocente (pope), 199
San Pedro Mártir (presidio), 233, 238–43
 passim, 363f, 372f, 480n75
San Pedro Mártir, Savannah of, *see* San
 Pedro Mártir (presidio)
San Reymundo (town), 140
San Román, Fray Antonio de, 226
San Román Nonato (town), 379f, 509nn
Santa Ana Vieja (town), 37, 414, *416*,
 518n79, 521n110
Santa Cruzada, 118, 186, 249
Santa Elena (town), 365
Santa Isabel (town), 518n79
Santa María de Nojk'u, *see* NojK'u
Santander, Colombia, 114
Santa Rita (town), 518n79
Santa Rosa (estancia), *416*
Santa Rosa de la Pimienta (town), 380. *See
 also* Chanchanja, Santa Clara de
Santiago, Order of, 113, 115, 124, 409,
 455nn
Santiago de Guatemala (city), *xx*, xxvii, 49,
 61, 67, 132f, 140, 144, 172, 233, 248,
 299, 305, 337ff, 345, 357f, 359, 374ff,
 388, 419, 479n, 502n86, 515nn, 517n77
Santillán, Diego de, 41
Santos, Manuel de los, 487n79
Santo Tomás (fort), 290
Santo Toribio (town), 21, *130*, 408, *410*,
 413, 415, *416*, 433nn, 434–35nn,
 438n34, 446n45, 513n29, 517n72,
 518n79
Sapos (rancho), *461n35*
Sapote (estancia), *416*
Saraús, Estévan de, *129*, 458n1
Saraza, Francisco de, *126*, 457n50
Sarmiento, Juan Ramos, 487n79
Sarstoon River, *xx*, 7, 38
Sarteneja, *151*, 465n24
Sawyers, 260, 267, 347
Saxkumil (town), 62
Sayaxche (town), 7. *See also* Sakyaxche
Scarification, 140, 319ff, 478n49
Schele, Linda, 9, 105, 334, 428n8, 430n18,
 446n44, 452n93

Scholes, France V., 51, 435nn, 438n45, 440n71, 458n56

Schwartz, Norman B., 512n1, 521n111

Secular clergy, Yucatán, xxvii, 118, 122, 129, 148, 161, 163, 175–82 *passim*, 230f, 249, 257f, 267f, 401; conflict with Franciscans, 157, 163f, 176, 180, 187, 220, 225f, 230, 245f, 300; in Petén, 323, 328–37 *passim*, 349–55 *passim*, 359, 366, 372, 388–98 *passim*, 405, 409–13 *passim*, 411–418 *passim*, 492n1; at Tipuj, 40, 43, 230f, 249–52 *passim*, 477n31

Segmentary states, 450n68

Sermons, 34, 44, 48, 153, 195f, 204, 479n

Servicio personal, 129, 143, 353, 405

Sesere, Manuel Jorge, 142, 158, 163, 189, 251, 483n37

Sexuality, Itza, 211, 267, 287ff, 331–35, 352ff, 499n45

Shackles, 316, 325f, 373, 404

Shamanism, 316ff

Sharer, Robert J., 9, 429n11

Shrimp, 202

Sib'alch'en (town), 518n79

Sibun River, *xx*

Sierra (partido), 46–49 *passim*, 143, 249f, 256ff, 263, 484n57, 501n71

Silva, Fray Juan Antonio, 148f, 158–61 *passim*, 167, 177, 187, 198, 225

Silver, 184, 211. *See also* Coins, silver

Sima (lineage name), 26, 140

Sima, B'atab' and Cacique, 65, 231

Sima, IxMen, 76–77

Singers, *see* Maestros: Cantores

Singing, Itza, 191, 203, 453n112

Sinib'akan (Zinibacan) (town), 12

Sinoja (town), 385

Sintla, José de, 487n79

Sisal (town), 431n28

Sittee River, *xx*, 385

Slave raiding, English, 408–12 *passim*

Slaves, black, 185, 412

Slaves, Maya, 408–12 *passim*

Smallpox, 376, 387, 408, 408f, 517n77

Soberanis y Centeno, Roque de, 111–15 *passim*, 119, 123–26, 177, 223, 263f, 305, 339–45, 356f, 374, 409, 454n7, 469nn, 484n57; excommunicated, 111, 124, 126, 246; opposes Ursúa, 245–51, 256f, 323, 329f, 341, 497n24

Social organization, Maya, *see* Bilateral descent; Double descent; Lineages; Matrilineal descent; Patrilineal descent

Sojkol (town), 325

Solis, Br. Salvador de, 477n31

Solis, Jerónimo de, 487n79

Sosa, Agustín de (s), 228

Sotuta (province), 18f

Sotuta (town), 263

Sousa, Br. José Estanislao, 520n105

Soyte River, *xx*

Spears, 31

Spies, Itza, 139, 228, 436n23

Spondylus shell, 35, 437n26

Squashes, 50, 202

Staffs of office, 43, 188, 209–13 *passim*

State, archaic, 82

Stockades, 48, 66, 236f, 478n55, 511n116. *See also* Fortifications, Maya

Stone, Andrea J., 433n47

Sub'elnaj (town), 62

Sumb'ob' (estancia), 416

Sumkal, Francisco, 420

Sumpan (town), 63

Surnames, *see* Names, lineage

Suyuja Peten Itza, 7, 92, 427–28n8. *See also* Zuyua

Tabasco, *xx*, 9, 30, 35, 41f, 88, 341, 417, 449n63

Tab'in Chan (town), 468n16

Taiza, 429n9

Taj (defined), 429n9

TajItza, 7, 29. *See also* Nojpeten

TajItza (town, Sarstoon River), 38

TajMakanche (town), 6, 17, 18, 63, 429n9

TajWital, 438n35

Talking "idols", 102f, 277f, 461n41

Tamaxu (town), 502n89

Tamay, Pedro, 468n15

Tankaj, 430–31n24. *See also* Mayapan

Tanxulukmul (site), 6, 8, 10, 17, 130, 190, 430n17, 471n15, 483n39

Tapia, Manuel de, 373
Tattooing, 138, 211
Taxim Chan, *see* Chan, Taxim
Taxim Chan (town), 21, 459nn
Tayasal, 429n9, 434n2. *See also* Nojpeten, 33
Tayasal peninsula, 520n103
Teab'o (town), 258
Te B'alam, 65, 366
Tek (lineage name), 26, 421
Tek, Chamach, 507n53
Tek, Juan Francisco, 171, 186, 328. *See also* AjTek
Tek'ax (town), 48, 143f, 228–29, 263, 297, 501n84
Tek'it (town), 257, 485n66
Tekoj (town), 485n68
Telchak (town), 150, 463n10
Telchaquillo (town), 463n10
Tello, Br. Juan, 259
Tello y Guzmán, Bruno, 120
Temchay (town), *130*, 151f, 464n20
Temples, Maya, 41, 88, 333. *See also* Nojpeten, temples of
Tenab'o (town), *130*
Tenkis (town), 38
Tenochtitlan, 29, 37, 88, 441n2
Tenosique (town), *xx*, 41f, 57, *130*
Teotihuacan, 10
Tepakam (town), 150
Tequío, 404
Tesukan, Reyezuelo, *90, 96, 96*, 277. *See also* AjChata, Noj; Chata
Tesukun (lineage name), 21, 26, 62, 433n46. *See also* Tesukan
Tesukun, Cacique, 459n19
Tetlepanquetzatzin, 435n12
Thompson, J. Eric S., 20, 420f, 425n, 430n12, 432n43, 434n53, 494n34, 478n48
Thompson, Philip C., 446n44
Tiak (town), 32
Tib'ayal (town), 140, 461n35
Tib'oj (town), 371. *See also* AjB'ojom; B'oj
Tib'olon (town), 461–62n41
Tichak (town), 463n10
Tihoo (Tijoo), 201. *See also* Mérida

Tik'al (site), *xx*, 6, 17, 105, *130*, 219, 350
Tik'al (town), 350
Tik'intunpa-Mamantel (town), 458n56
Tik'uch (town), 431n28
Tikul (town), 62
Tilaj (town), 63
Timul (town), 63
Tinal (lineage name), 26
Tipuj (town), *xx*, 4f, 22f, 39–47 *passim*, 56f, 65, 100f, *130*, 134, 138, 156–61 *passim*, 168–77 *passim*, 183f, 201, 210, 214–18 *passim*, 225–231 *passim*, 242, 273–78 *passim*, 282, 284, 302, 320, 324, 326, 384, 388, 408, 433–34n48, 439n54, 441n95, 468n6, 468n15, 475n96, 477n30, 485n67, 506n42; 1696 entrada to, 230f, 249–52 *passim*, 256f; Itza influence over, 8, 20, 52–55, 103; people of in Petén, 324, 368, 369
Tisimin (town), *xx*, *130*. *See also* Chilam B'alam, books of
Titles, Aztec, *see* Achcauhtli; Cihuacoatl; Tlatoani
Titles, Itza, *see* Ach Kat; Ajaw; Ajaw B'atab'; Ayikal; B'atab'; Cacique; Cacique principal; Chamach; Ch'atan; Jalach Winik; Kuch Pop Kit Kan; Nakom; Noj Tz'o; Rey; Reyezuelo; Tz'o; Tz'o Kan; Tz'o Kan Tz'ik
Titles, Kowoj, *see* Captain
Titles, Yucatec, *see* B'ob'at; Jalach Winik; Jol Pop; Nakom
Tixb'ol Pululja (town), 138, 460n32
Tixchel (town), *xx*, *130*, 449n63, 458n56
Tixkakal (town), *130*, 263, 485n68
Tixonte (town), 433n48
Tlatoani (Nahuatl title), 451n88
Toledo District, Belize, 419–20, 433n48, 521n124
Tools, metal, 40, 159, 184, 194, 201, 208, 212, 288, 364; trade in, 40, 192, 205. *See also* Axes; Knives; Machetes
Topoxte (site), 6, *18*
Toro de Acuña (town), 50–53
Torture, 48, 50, 306, 316–19, 332
Tovilla, Martín Alfonso, 49–51
Town councils, 43f, 150, 263, 414

Towns, Itza, 61–66, 442nn, 443n10
Towns, Kowoj, 66
Tozzer, Alfred M., 499n42
Trade: Maya, 31, 37–40 *passim*, 47, 49,
    99–101, 150, 192, 205, 212, 309, 314,
    333, 427n6; Maya-Spanish, 135–39 *pas-
    sim*, 174, 181, 184, 348. *See also* Barter
    goods
Traven, B., 437n29
Tree, cosmic or world, 444n26. *See also*
    Yaxcheel Kab'
Tribute: Itza, 44; Spanish, 13, 65, 117, 129,
    143, 155, 404, 411, 455n17, 519n88
Triple Alliance, 91
Troops, *see* Militias
Trujillo (villa), 38
Trumpets, 185, 194, 239. *See also* Bugles
Tulumki (town), 19f
Tulumkis, 67, 432n42, 433–34n48
Tun (calendrical period), 14
Tun (lineage name), 26, 140
Tun, AjChak, 461n35
Tun, AjSoy, 62
Tun, Jerónimo, 255
Tunkul, 185. *See also* Drums
Turtle shells, 185
Tut (lineage name), 26, 62, 429n10,
    507n53
Tut (province), 384
Tut, 63. *See also* NojTut
Tut, AjChak, 62
Tut, B'atab', 95–99 *passim*, 98, 140,
    192, 228, 281, 318, 382, 386, 391, 402.
    See also AjTut; Noj Che, Cacique; Tut,
    Cacique
Tut, Cacique, 90, 92. *See also* AjTut; Noj
    Che, Cacique; Tut, B'atab'
Tut, Captain, *see* Tut, Cacique
Tut, YumKuk, 507n53
Tuts, 314, 318–20, 510–11n110
Tutul Xiws, 18f, 432n39, 452n93
Tutz (lineage name), 26, 76–77
Tz'akab' (defined), 80, 447n51, 450n73
Tzak (lineage name), 21, 26, 320, 433n46,
    433nn
Tzak, Cacique, 459n19
Tzakal (lineage name), 21, 26

Tzakwam (lineage name), 26. *See also*
    Tzakwan
Tzakwan (lineage name), 21. *See also*
    Itzk'in Tzakwan; Tzakwam
Tzam (lineage name), 26
Tzawi (lineage name), 26
Tzel (lineage name), 26
Tzib' (lineage name), 63, 421
Tz'ib' (lineage name), 26, 393
Tz'ib', B'ak, 390
Tz'ib', Nikte, 390
Tzimin Chak, 44, 53, 58, 437n29. *See also*
    Horse image
Tzin (lineage name), 26, 62, 392, *see*
    AjTz'ik Tzin
Tzin, Ajaw, 89ff, 90, 96. *See also* Tzin
    Ajaw, Reyezuelo; Tzin, B'atab'; Tzin,
    Cacique; AjTz'ik Tzin
Tzin, Ajaw, Reyezuelo, 182. *See also* Tzin,
    Ajaw; Tzin, B'atab'; Tzin, Cacique;
    AjTz'ik Tzin
Tzin, AjTz'ik, *see* AjTz'ik Tzin
Tzin, B'atab', 98, 100, 392. *See also* Tzin,
    Ajaw; Tzin Ajaw, Reyezuelo; Tzin,
    Cacique; AjTz'ik Tzin, B'atab'
Tzin, Cacique, 90, 91. *See also* Tzin, Ajaw;
    Tzin Ajaw, Reyezuelo; Tzin, B'atab';
    AjTz'ik Tzin, B'atab'
Tzin, Pedro, 401f
Tz'o (Itza title), 92
Tzok (town), 468n16
Tz'o Kan (Itza title), 87f, 91f, 384
Tz'o Kan Tz'ik (Itza title), 85, 90, 96
Tz'ola (town), 325
Tzol k'in (calendrical period), 14, 445n42
Tzotz (town), 8, 62
Tzuk (lineage name), 26
Tzuk Kupul, 431n28
Tzukte (town), *130*
Tzuktok' (town), *xx*, 42, 129–32, *130*,
    145, 152–62 *passim*, 189, 224, 230,
    248–59 *passim*, 363, 465n30, 466n41,
    481n11, 484nn
Tz'ul, Agustín, 484n59
Tz'ulub', Diego, 254
Tz'ul Winikob'(defined), 427n2
Tz'ul Winikob' (province), 3, 5, 39f, 52–65

Tzun Kal (town), 509n82
Tzunpana (province), 510n110
Tzunpana (town), 381
Tzuntekum (lineage name), 26, 62. *See also* AjTzuntekum
Tz'ununchan (lineage name), 433n48
Tz'ununwitz (town), 8, 62, 65

Uk, Diego, 144
Uk, Pedro, 41, 438n45
Urrán Valley, 7
Ursúa, Francisco de, 126, 250, 456n26, 481n9
Ursúa, Pedro de (16th century), 114, 454n7
Ursúa, Pedro de (17th century), 114
Ursúa y Arizmendi de Egues y Beaumont, Pedro de, 114
Ursúa y Arizmendi, Martín de, xix–xvi *passim*, 73, 92, 94, 111–33 *passim*, 142–56 *passim*, 162f, 168–89 *passim*, 198–201, 206, 219–33 *passim*, 239, 243–346 *passim*, 352, 356–73 *passim*, 384–89 *passim*, 404, 412, 454n1, 455nn, 456nn, 469nn, 482n23, 484n62, 492nn, 494n28, 495n56, 500n59, 519n88; as future governor of Philippines, xxii, 113, 115, 408, 411; opposed by Soberanis, 245–51, 256f, 323, 329f, 341, 497n24; titles of, xxii, 113, 115, 409, 411. *See also* Lizárraga, Conde de
Ursúa y Arizmendi, Pedro de, 114
Us (lineage name), 27. *See also* IxKab' Us
Us, Bonifacio, 144
Uspeten (town), 8, 17, 325
Ustariz, Juan Andrés de, 454n7
Usulab'an (town), 458n56
Usumacinta (partido), 42

Vacant see, 246
Valencia, Br. Manuel, 477n31
Valladolid (villa), *xx*, 5, 11, 13, *130*, 485n66
Valtierra, Antonio, S.J., 413, 419
Vanilla, 184, 207
Varaya, Gaspar Reymundo, 395, 399–402, 514n39
Vargas, Alonso de, 148f

Vargas, Fray Jacinto de, 233, 237, 303, 463n66
Vargas, Juan de, 259
Vargas Dorantes, Br. Marcos de, 388–98 *passim*, 405f, 479n, 513nn, 516n71
Velasco, Captain, 150
Velásquez y Valdéz, Pedro, 338ff
Verapaz, *xx*, 5, 7, 42, 49, 99f, 112, 125, 132–35, 142, 232f, 238, 242, 252, 333f, 342–46 *passim*, 356ff, 371–77 *passim*, 384, 418–21 *passim*, 427n6, 502n89, 507n61
Verganza, Agustín de, 330
Veytia, Juan José de, 454n7
Villagutierre Soto-Mayor, Juan de, xxii, 57, 73, 116, 131, 303, 342, 358, 364, 374, 425n, 455n16, 468n4, 485n62, 495n56
Villahermosa (city), 30
Villa Real, 39
Villatoro, Diego de, 454n7
Visitas, 40

War captains, 117, 129
War councils, 243, 286–92 *passim*
Wards, *see* Quarters
Warfare, 7–10, 88, 106; deities of, 74, 102, 440n71, 453n112; Itza-Chinamita, 20, 43, 101f; Itza-Itza, 66, 68, 95, 100, 167, 192, 223, 274, 289, 381–87, 402, 510n110; Itza-Kejach, 31f, 253, 484n62, 498n27; Itza-Kowoj, 56, 95, 101, 167, 197, 213, 220, 223, 274, 289, 325f, 381–87, 402, 444n33; Itza-Manche Chol, 49–52, 440n71; Itza-Mopan, 441n101; Itza-Spanish, xxv, 139ff, 171f, 223–32 *passim*, 248, 277, 281, 288–94
Wax, *see* Beeswax
Waxal (town), 385. *See also* Río Yaxal
Wayeb' rituals, 69, 95–99, 444n26, 452n106
Waymil (province), 39f
Weapons: Itza and Kowoj, 43, 50, 135–41 *passim*, 194, 205, 228f, 365, 382, 400, 479n, 510n100; Kejach, 31, 131; Spanish, 35, 139, 144, 150, 229, 235, 252f, 265–69 *passim*, 359, 403, 437n27, 479n,

486n78, 489n13; Ammunition; Artillery; Bows and arrows; Crossbows; Gunpowder; Lances; Spears
Weaving, 405f
Whipping, 405
Wikab' (town), 468n16
Wikab', Juan, 468n6
Wikab', María, 469n15
Wikab', Mateo, 169–75 *passim*, 181, 183, 188, 324, 468n6, 469n15
Wine, 226
Women, Itza, 55, 76f, 79, 214f, 267, 287ff, 296, 352ff, 366f, 379, 382, 405, 440n88, 489n11; captured by Spaniards, 352ff, 367f

Xalal (province), 510n110
Xewlila (town), 63
Xicalango (province), 30
Xiken (lineage name), 27
Xiken, Kuk, 507n53
Xililchi (town), 8, 17, 325
Ximénez, Fray Francisco, 51, 303
Xiws, *see* Tutul Xiws
Xokmo (town), 240
Xoyte, *see* Río Xoyte
Xulu (lineage name), 27
Xulu, Chamach, 63, 65, 170, 216f, 270f, 280–84 *passim*, 306, 313, 367–70 *passim*, 507n53

Yaj, Lorenzo, 150
Yajb'akab' (town), 254, 484n53
Yajkab' (lineage name), 21, 433nn
Yajkab', Cacique, 83–87 *passim*, 91, 99, 135–38 *passim*, 450n69, 459n19
Yalain (province), 6, 7, 18, 23, 55f, 93, 95, 99, 138, 167, 310, 365–70 *passim*, 385, 389, 451n83; Christian conversion of, 306, 323, 348, 369, 371
Yalain (town), 6, 7, 17, 18, 55f, 65f, 130, 167, 171, 173, 216, 227, 231, 271–84 *passim*, 295, 302, 304–9 *passim*, 344–50 *passim*, 365, 381, 385, 391, 443n10, 496n1, 511n116; abandoned, 348ff, 367–70

Yalak (town), 62
Yalkanix (estancia), 416
Yalxut (estancia), 416
Yasuncabil (town), 32
Yawilain, aguada, 190
Yaxb'ete (town), 62
Yaxche (town), 62, 63, 429n10
Yaxcheel Kab', 69, 197, 444n26
Yaxchilan, 105
Yaxja (town), 63
Yaxja River, *xx*
Yaxkab'a (town), 263, 485n68
Yax Kokaj Mut, 444n26. *See also* AjKokaj Mut
Yaxle (town), 63
Yaxtenay (town), 17, 325
Yearbearers, 97, 98
Yellow fever, 508n74
Yochjalek' (town), *see* Yoxjalek'
Yol (town), 49
Yoxjalek' (town), 464n19
Yucatán: bishops of, *see* Arriaga, Fray Antonio de; Cano y Sandoval, Juan; Landa, Fray Diego de; San Buenaventura, Fray Francisco de; governors of, *see* Barcena, Juan José de; Figueroa, Antonio de; Méndez de Canzo, Antonio; Meneses Bravo de Sarabia, Fernando; Soberanis y Centeno, Roque; Tello y Guzmán, Bruno; Ursúa y Arizmendi, Martín de
Yucatec language, 3, 5, 426–27n1, 435n7, 520n101
Yucatecan language family, 3, 426–27n1. *See also* Itzas, language of; Mopans, language of; Yucatec language, 3
YumKuk Tut, 507n53

Zacpeten, 66
Zantwijk, Rudolph von, 87
Zavaleta, Manuel de, 478n55
Zubiaur, Bernardino de, 116, 142f, 455n16
Zubiaur Isasi, Pedro de, 152, 189, 213, 227ff, 244, 259f, 265–69 *passim*, 291, 303, 325f, 344–50 *passim*, 354, 484n62, 487n79, 489n15, 502n89
Zuyua, 7, 428n8. *See also* Suyuja Peten Itza

Library of Congress Cataloging-in-Publication Data
Jones, Grant D.
    The conquest of the last Maya kingdom / Grant D. Jones.
        p.   cm.
    Includes bibliographical references (p.   ) and index.
    ISBN 0-8047-3317-1 (cloth : alk. paper) —
ISBN 0-8047-3522-0 (pbk. : alk. paper)
        1. Itza Indians — History — Sources.   2. Itza Indians — Politics
and government.   3. Itza Indians — Government relations.
4. Petén (Guatemala : Dept.) — History — Sources.   5. Mexico —
History — Conquest, 1519–1540.   6. Spain — Colonies —
America — Administration.   I. Title.
F1465.2.I87J65   1998
972.81'2004974 — dc21   98-16556

Original printing 1998

Last figure below indicates year of this printing:
06   05   04   03   02   01   00   99   98